The Wall Is Strong:
Corrections in Louisiana

3rd edition

The Wall Is Strong:
Corrections in Louisiana

3rd edition

Edited by Burk Foster, Wilbert Rideau,
and Douglas Dennis

Published by The Center for Louisiana Studies
University of Southwestern Louisiana
Lafayette, Louisiana

Front cover illustration and frontispiece:
The north wall of the Baton Rouge Penitentiary, "The Walls," ca. 1901. Photo courtesy of the Andrew D. Lytle Collection, Louisiana and Lower Mississippi Valley Collection, Louisiana State University Libraries.

Library of Congress Catalog Number: 95-71535
ISBN Number: 0-940984-99-7

Published by The Center for Louisiana Studies
P.O. Box 40831
University of Southwestern Louisiana
Lafayette, LA   70504-0831

"I know not whether laws be right,
Or whether laws be wrong;
All that we know who lie in jail
Is that the wall is strong;
And that each day is like a year,
A year whose days are long."

Oscar Wilde.
The Ballad of Reading Gaol (1898)

Dedication

To C. Paul Phelps and Ron Wikberg:

Two men whose lives show that changes
in corrections must come from both
sides of the wall.

C. Paul Phelps
(Photo courtesy of *The Angolite*)

C. PAUL PHELPS*

by Wilbert Rideau

The year of 1975 was in its final death throes, soon to pass away and give birth to a new year, when the small blue twin-engine plane winged out of the wintry clouds to land on the small Angola airstrip. A neat, well-dressed man scrambled out of the pilot's seat and got into a waiting car. He was C. Paul Phelps, deputy director of the Louisiana corrections department, here to assume temporary management of Louisiana State Penitentiary until a new warden could be found. Traditionally, an official in the prison hierarchy had always moved up to assume such duties. But not this time. The number-two man in the department was taking over the reins, a bold departure from tradition. It was an omen of things to come.

At that time Angola steered a course independent from the rest of the penal system. Historically ruled by vested local interests, Angola obeyed and listened to Headquarters in Baton Rouge, its official parent, only if it desired to. When it chose not to, Angola rulers had usually been powerful enough to resist the will of their nominal supervisors.

The prison had grown into a monster, with a potential as dangerous as the quality of life in its bowels. It was jammed. There was no end to the flood of new inmates, some forced to sleep on floors for lack of beds. Nerves stretched tight and tension ran through Angola like unharnessed electricity, exploding here and there in sparks of violence. It was a brutal time: the preceding three years had seen 40 prisoners stabbed to death and over 350 seriously injured from knife wounds. It was a dog-eat-dog jungle, and having a knife was almost a prerequisite to survival. The prison's small employee force was disenchanted and divided into vying factions preoccupied only with their special interests and the struggle for power.

Within that context inmate cliques reigned supreme, governing human existence and much of prison operations. The strong ruled, and the weak either served or perished. Slavery was widespread. The only law was that of the knife. It was the bloodiest prison in the nation.

It was an ultramasculine, macho world, and Phelps, a social worker by profession and correctional bureaucrat by trade, was a most unlikely man to assume Angola's reins of power. After serving in the Air Force from 1953 to 1954, he earned an undergraduate degree from LSU in 1957 (later attaining a masters degree in social work). Interested in trying to help juveniles in trouble, a passion he never lost, Phelps began as a probation officer in 1957 with the Baton Rouge Family Court. Ten years later Corrections Director David Wade hired him to head the state's juvenile corrections system. In 1975, he was promoted to deputy corrections director.

A man taking over as warden generally does so with an announcement of grandiose plans. Phelps didn't. He knew little about running a penitentiary and next to nothing about Angola, something he admitted with unheard of candidness.

"I don't have any plans," Phelps told surprised inmates soon after arriving. "I don't know enough about Angola and what it takes to run it. First, I'm going to educate myself about this place. After I learn what's going on, then I'll start thinking about what I'm going to do."

And that's what he set about doing.

*Appeared in *The Angolite,* March/April 1993, 19-24. Reprinted with permission.

He'd be seen roaming the prison's 18,000 acres, acquainting himself with the place. He was rarely in his office. A casual, unpretentious man, he strolled all over Angola, unexpectedly dropping in on prisoners and employees to chat with them, always asking questions about what they were doing, how, and for what purpose.

Phelps was not a physical person, but he paid little heed to physical dangers. Soon after his arrival there was a disturbance in the Main Prison. As he was leaving the Administration Building to find out what was going on, a prison official stopped him, warning: "You can't go down there. There's too much danger. You're the warden." He quietly thanked the man for his advice and said, "I'm not going to learn anything sitting on my ass in an office." At the Main Prison he walked unhesitatingly into the midst of the angry prisoners and politely asked, "What's your problem?"

He was most unconventional, nothing at all like the smooth executive types running the nation's prisons. Given a choice, he preferred to encourage someone to do something rather than order him to do it. He'd just as soon spend his time chatting with a lowly inmate field worker as he would a sleek politician. He often ate with the prisoners, something that had never been done by prison officials. It was unthinkable in the prison's race and caste system of 1975, like a black going to a KKK luncheon. At a time when blood flowed freely on Angola walkways, Phelps took his teenage daughter around with him. Some called him naive; others said he was crazy. He was neither. His behavior reflected his abiding faith in the human animal's basic potential for good.

He hadn't been in the Warden's Office long when Corrections Director Elayn Hunt was hospitalized with terminal cancer, dying shortly afterwards. Phelps found himself both warden of the tinderbox maximum security prison and head of the state's entire penal system. He would spend a half day at corrections headquarters in the state capitol, then fly to Angola to spend the rest of the day serving as warden. It was a tall order, one that would have intimidated many, but he kept the entire penal system on a course of "business as usual." While there were touchy moments at the huge state prison during his three-month tenure as acting warden, Phelps kept the lid on. In late March 1976, Governor Edwin Edwards appointed him director of corrections.

Phelps had utilized his stint as acting warden to educate himself, studying the state penitentiary and its workings. He made few waves because his official power was, at the time, tenuous. Consequently, most inmates and employees wrote him off as just another laid-back, easy-going bureaucrat keeping the seat warm for the next warden.

Phelps surprised everyone by becoming the most demanding corrections chief Louisiana ever had, one who refused to accept "can't" as a response or excuse for not taking action. He initiated unprecedented and sweeping changes. The violence and problems that had traditionally defeated corrections administrators, he conquered. He rose to the occasion, growing into his role and responsibilities and becoming the most successful correctional administrator in the nation.

Two years after he put on the mantle of authority, the country's most violent prison had been converted into the safest maximum security prison in the nation. Angola had for the first time also been brought under the authority of the

Department of Corrections. Headquarters was running the show, and there was no question about it.

A penal management philosophy was introduced based upon what Phelps fondly described as "just plain common sense," which brought about massive improvements in conditions affecting Angola prisoners. Food and medical services were upgraded. Education, classification, record-keeping, legal services and numerous other operations were improved. Scores of professionals were hired. Minorities gained, moving into top supervisory positions. The most liberal disciplinary process in terms of procedural safeguards in the country was fully implemented (it no longer exists in that form). An Internal Affairs division was created to investigate the complaints and abuses of inmates, and a work ethic was introduced at every level at Angola and eventually throughout the state's prison system. An administrative philosophy took root that made everyone accountable for his/her actions. Every letter or complaint got an administrative response, whether from inmate or employee.

His greatest asset, and perhaps the key to his effectiveness in managing the state penal system, was that he was not glued to tradition or to any particular penal philosophy. He was always open to new ideas, rejecting nothing until its possible applications had been considered. When in doubt, he was willing to experiment to learn.

That was the way he approached the idea of a free prisoner press. At a time when Angola officials, as well as the nation's top penal administrators, religiously believed in censorship, Phelps wanted to create a credible vehicle of information in a place historically ruled by rumor. His idea was revolutionary: free *The Angolite* from censorship and equip it with the freedom to investigate, photograph and publish whatever it desired so long as it told the truth and adhered to basic journalistic guidelines. In the face of strident opposition, he simply shrugged his shoulders and said, "Let's try it, and see what happens."

What happened is now publishing history. Winning wide acclaim, *The Angolite* received prestigious journalism awards, and became recommended or required reading for criminal justice students at some colleges and universities.

Frank, bold, different. That was his way . . . and accessible. He was perhaps the most accessible corrections head in the nation, thinking nothing of hopping into his plane and flying to any point in the state to see what was wrong, to settle disputes, or just to see what someone wanted. Unlike his colleagues around the nation, Phelps rejected traditional administrative secrecy, welcoming the press into Louisiana prisons, and encouraging free exchange and open communication between keepers and kept as the key to peace and stability in prisons. He advocated that officials be accessible to inmates, preventing the need for them to resort to desperate measures to get attention to their problems as in other penal systems.

Even as director he continued to prowl the various prisons around the state, alone or with his youngest daughter in tow, checking operations, chatting with inmates and employees, and always on the lookout for a dirty mop. "Discipline begins with a clean mop," he often said. Guards and wardens alike caught hell if he found a dirty mop in their institution.

He enjoyed what he was doing, something he readily admitted: "It's certainly the most challenging and exciting job I've ever had." Through it all he kept his sense of humor, and remained basically the same man who scrambled out of a plane on a cold December day to baby-sit the nation's toughest prison.

Unlike most administrators, Phelps kept a running personal interest in everything he touched, always checking back to see how it was doing. That extended also to the people whose lives he touched—from watching how one inmate descended through the system to Camp-J lockdown, to how an aspiring inmate artist fared in his artistic pursuits while in prison and even after he was freed. Phelps was always ready with advice and assistance for those who pursued constructive and meaningful endeavors.

His basic decency and sense of fair play even when dealing with the cutthroat world of bureaucratic politics sometimes drove his supporters up the wall. Asked once why he did not move on his enemies like anyone else would have done, he replied: "I'm not made that way. I don't care how the rest play the game. I play fair, and if I can't play fair, I won't play at all." While his practice of being fair with his enemies anguished his supporters, it was the reason for the respect and loyalty he commanded from those who knew him.

While Phelps became the corrections system's most effective and successful manager, the flipside is that he also was its most vocal critic. His criticisms persisted long after penal reform groups had folded in Louisiana, crunched by the demoguery of the law-and-order crowd.

He had barely taken office when he pointed out to state lawmakers that the basic fault underlying the system was that Louisiana had no philosophy governing its criminal justice system. "We talk about the criminal justice system, but it isn't a system," he stated. "It's a series of unconnected programs and agencies operating autonomously." Because of public and political pressure, he said, corrections is forced to "take people we know to be the worst risks and set them free. People we know are good risks we have to keep under the gun." Louisiana's prison overcrowding problem, Phelps often explained, reflected "the system's inability to differentiate among people, to distinguish who's dangerous and needs to be locked up from who's not dangerous and doesn't need to be locked up."

He opposed the popular political notion of increasing severity of punishment for juvenile offenders: "What's going to be accomplished by giving kids 99 years for armed robbery? Adolescents can't handle time. They have no concept of time except the immediate, and they have difficulties enough coping with that. Aging is the only thing that is going to cure many juvenile problems. Many, many juvenile problems resolve themselves at age 17, because in Louisiana you become an adult then and can act like an adult. You don't lock up a 17-year-old because he ran away from home."

It was inevitable that Phelps' outspoken commitment to truth and a meaningful corrections system would land him in political trouble. On September 17, 1981, Phelps, who had been publicly expressing dissatisfaction and concern at the course of corrections under David Treen, Louisiana's first Republican governor since Reconstruction Days, was fired for what the governor termed "philosophical differences."

Shortly afterwards, U. S. District Judge Frank Polozola, who oversees all jails and prisons in Louisiana, appointed Phelps to be the official court "expert" in setting standards for all 64 parish jails in the state.

In 1984, Phelps was re-appointed as corrections chief by newly-reelected Governor Edwards. His second administration was devoted to fighting for realistic solutions, for incarceration alternatives that would solve overcrowding, and for addressing the hopelessness that long sentences were creating within Angola.

He instituted a grievance procedure, which became the first in the nation to be approved by federal courts. Phelps standardized operations among the state's prisons and implemented a sensible, major revision of visiting regulations.

He continued to oppose increasing penalties and building more prisons as a solution to crime. His was the loudest voice decrying punitive excesses, warning that if continued they would bankrupt the state. He called instead for revision of sentencing laws, increased probation and parole, incarceration alternatives, and for the state to face the problem of increasing numbers of long-termers, pointing out that many could be freed with no risk to the public. His was often the lone voice crying for reason, an unpopular position. But that mattered not.

In 1988, Phelps retired after incoming Governor Buddy Roemer failed to reappoint him. Roemer claimed he wanted someone with law enforcement experience to head corrections, but he replaced Phelps with Bruce Lynn, a man experienced only in banking and ranching. Lynn, however, was a close personal friend and staunch supporter of the new governor.

Retirement did not translate into a rocking chair on a porch from which to watch life go by. That was not his

lifestyle. Phelps taught a juvenile delinquency course at LSU's School of Social Welfare, served as president of that school's alumni association, and co-founded and managed Criminal Justice Services (a firm offering incarceration alternatives, hands-on supervision and rehabilitative services to help criminal defendants change their lives and avoid the waste of imprisonment—putting into practice what he had always preached).

On the afternoon of March 10, 1993, C. Paul Phelps died unexpectedly at age 60, reportedly from a heart attack. He was married and the father of two daughters.

"I'm pleased with the cooperation I've gotten from both sides of the fence," reminisced Phelps at his retirement party. "Inmate input into policies that affect them has been good. I value their opinions, their judgment and their recommendations." He had an abiding faith that people were basically decent and good. The trick, he often said, was to encourage the good to grow.

"If you're going to be in the keeper business, then you should do it the very best that you can," Phelps said. "Today is the only day that makes any difference. Tomorrow is what you look forward to, and yesterday is history. If I had the chance to do things over, I might do them a little bit different. On the other hand, I'm hardheaded enough not to change a single thing. When I look at the quality of life that exists in Louisiana's system as compared with the quality of life that exists in prisons in other parts of the country, I don't have any regrets about what I've done."

C. Paul Phelps will forever stand as proof that, contrary to public perception, one person can make a world of difference.

Ron Wikberg and Kay Smith on their wedding day, August 8, 1992.
(Photo courtesy of Kay Smith)

RON WIKBERG*

by Francis X. Clines

Having forfeited the heart of his life to prison as a convicted murderer, Ron Wikberg was dying the other day and hoping he might be remembered as "a bad guy who did good."

Fair enough: He shot down a grocery store clerk during a holdup 25 years ago and then, within what he called the "niche" of life left to him, he became a prison journalist.

He developed into a muckraker with enough creativity and compassion that some people on the outside actually considered him an exemplar of the now largely quaint, once seriously debated theory that a prison can be a place for rehabilitation, not just punishment.

"This wasn't what I started off to be," Mr. Wikberg said as he lay dying. He mixed regret and pride in a review of his 51 years of life, quitting his terminal morphine medication to focus on his past during a two-day interview with a friend, Dave Isay of National Public Radio. "I never thought I'd be in prison, or would be doing bad things and have to work so hard doing good things to try and make up for it."

He finished among us on the outside, an ex-con who managed two years of freedom before dying of cancer last weekend. He was a foolish and dangerous young man when he went to prison, but managed to age on the inside in complex, human ways. He often spoke of "the harm I've done" through murder as he sought a life of expiation, carefully investigating prison life and detailing how it was part of the problem, not the hard-edged solution the public might prefer.

Across 23 years inside the notorious Louisiana State Prison at Angola, Mr. Wikberg grew to become nothing less than a thoughtful prison expert. He was even occasionally consulted, though eventually ignored, in the nation's ever-escalating political debate over precisely how much more of a crackdown on criminals each new political season's voters are craving.

This season's candidate commercials have compressed the issue to hot-button tag lines like "And, of course, the death penalty." Or, for the moderates, "Three strikes and you're out."

Readers who prefer journalism about criminal justice to be as simplistic as the candidates' commercials have little to learn from Ron Wikberg. He was taught jailhouse reporting by another convicted murderer, Wilbert Rideau, an illiterate teen-ager who was self-educated and became the gifted, fiery editor of *The Angolite*, the nation's leading prison magazine, honored with a dozen professional awards.

Ron Wikberg joined an inmate staff whose level of work perversely earned them the freedom to roam the prison at will with tape recorders and confidentiality guarantees. They produced pioneer exposes on a score of subjects, from the prison rape culture to the nation's looming glut of superannuated felons consigned under modern parole-proof sentences.

"You got to approach life objectively," Ron Wikberg said, "like writing a story." His stories offer some enlightenment to all sides in the prison debate at a time when the United States has come to lead the industrialized world in incarceration now that the Soviet Union and South African police states have fallen.

The Angolite stories of Ron Wikberg can be as easily read for their "taxpayers'

*Appeared in the *New York Times,* October 9, 1994, A45. Copyright © 1994 by the New York Times Company. Reprinted by permission.

waste" spin as for their "prison crackdown" insights.

He was a lanky and sad-eyed prisoner, a friendly romantic whose wife, Kay, was courted in three years of letter writing and married as soon as he was free. "We had a good marriage," she said after helping him die. "I don't mind people knowing we were happy."

His friend and editor, Mr. Rideau, carries on the work with stories that resist the prison simplicities of the campaign commercials. He is perennially rejected as a candidate for clemency; state officials candidly admit the editor is a hostage to his own rehabilitation and celebrity, as the family of his murder victim continues to urge no mercy for him after 33 years inside.

"Have enough fun for me," the editor told Ron Wikberg two years ago when he walked out from Angola into freedom itself. Ron smiled at the gate and said he would wait out here for the day when they could meet free as "two bad guys who did good."

Law-abiding people of all sorts—those who opt for crackdown and those who hold out for rehabilitation—are left the comfort of Ron Wikberg's final cold-eyed summary of his convict's life. "Do I think the good that I've done overshadows the bad that I've done? No. I don't have that feeling. I think there's a lot more I could do. And it's that that I regret, 'cause I want to do some more. I'm just not going to get a chance to."

Contents

C. Paul Phelps
  by Wilbert Rideau ....*ix*

Ron Wikberg
  by Francis X. Clines...*xv*

Preface to the Third Edition ....*xix*

Preface to the Second Edition...*xxi*

Preface to the First Edition..*xxiii*

Introduction..*xxv*

1. Plantation Days at Angola
   by Burk Foster... 1

2. Major James and Convict Leasing
   by Mark T. Carleton..6

3. Women in the Walls: The Imprisonment of Women at the
   Baton Rouge Penitentiary, 1835-1862
   by Marianne Fisher-Giorlando............................... 16

4. Changes in the Convict System.. 26

5. Blood Took Penitentiary "Out of Red"
   by R. L. Krebs 33

6. America's Worst Prison
   by Edward W. Stagg and John Lear.................................... 46

7. Angola in the Seventies
   by Burk Foster.. 54

8. In Search of Alternatives
   by Burk Foster.. 70

9. What Is the Meaning of Life?
   by Burk Foster.. 80

10. Pen State: A Year in the Life of Angola
    by Jason Berry.. 90

11. In the Field
    by Wilbert Rideau 102

12. The Clubs
    by Wilbert Rideau 107

13. Prison Medical Care
    by Ron Wikberg and Wilbert Rideau.......................................111

14. The City of Angola
    by Michael Glover...137

15. Prison: The Sexual Jungle
    by Wilbert Rideau 142

16. The Shirley Coody Story
    by Tommy Mason..167

17. Protective Custody
    by Ron Wikberg and Wilbert Rideau.......................................174

18. Educating the Educated
    by Lane Nelson...193

19. Ages
    by Douglas Dennis..200

20. The Planted
    by Lane Nelson...206

21. The Living Dead
    by Douglas Dennis..231

22. When Mercy Seasons Justice
    by Burk Foster..269

23. The Hanging Game
    by Douglas Dennis..285

24. Death of the Big Yard
    by Douglas Dennis..301

25. Big John
    by Douglas Dennis..307

26. A Man and a Prison
    by Michael Glover..321

27. Staying Out: The Reality
    by Douglas Dennis..336

PREFACE TO THE THIRD EDITION

Much has changed since publication of the second edition of *The Wall Is Strong* five years ago. You will notice that this edition is dedicated to two men: C. Paul Phelps and Ron Wikberg.

C. Paul, a former social worker, headed Louisiana's Corrections Department for many years during the 1970s and 1980s. He was the guiding force behind correctional reform in Louisiana for two decades. Recognizing both the value and limits of imprisonment, he sought to create more humane prisons and to implement effective alternatives to long-term incarceration. C. Paul died on March 10, 1993.

Ron Wikberg, our co-editor on the first two editions, was paroled from Angola in June 1992, and moved to Maryland later in the summer with his new bride Kay and her two sons. He returned to Louisiana only once more, to promote the publication of *Life Sentences* (Times Books, 1992), before he was diagnosed with cancer. Surgery and chemotherapy inspired hope of long-term remission, but the cancer returned in the summer of 1994. Ron died at home with his loved ones the morning of Sunday, October 2, 1994. It was the first Sunday of the annual Angola rodeo, an event Ron loved, not because he was a cowboy, but because it raised money to benefit inmate needs and gave convicts and free people the chance to work together.

Ron was glad to die a free man, forgiven by the family of the man he killed 25 years before. During his all-too-brief opportunity at normal life, he had demonstrated that convicts are capable of decency, love, responsibility and charity. Ron embodied the rehabilitative potential that is the foundation of C. Paul's penal philosophy.

Douglas Dennis replaces Ron as co-editor on this third edition. "Swede," as everyone calls him, is a staff writer on *The Angolite*. He began serving his life term in 1957, nearly 40 years ago, and considers himself an Angola convict "dinosaur." So, the balance among editors remains constant—two convicts serving life sentences and one ex-cop college professor, trying to collect the most revealing, current writing about Louisiana corrections.

Our editorial focus covers two major areas: how corrections evolved in Louisiana and the nature of prison life. We continue to use the Louisiana State Penitentiary at Angola and the writings of *Angolite* staffers as the backbone of this book. No other American prison publication has so consistently for so long produced high-quality feature journalism. More than two decades have elapsed since *The Angolite* changed from a folksy newsletter into an award-winning newsmagazine with a national and international readership.

In expressing our thanks to those who guided this edition, first on the list are present and former *Angolite* staffers. Without their cumulative efforts, this would be just another collection of articles by "outsiders" about the "inside." The insight and perspective of those who really know the prison world—prisoners—would be missing. Thanks, too, to *The Angolite* for many of the photographs that appear within.

We would like to thank others who have helped:

Billie Ault, the secretary of the USL criminal justice department, who helped mightily with the computer work and was most diligent in proofreading successive drafts.

Kelly Reed Stringfield, who helped search out potential articles.

Sally McKissack and Marianne Fisher-Giorlando, criminal justice professors and careful observers.

Carl Brasseaux, Regina LaBiche and Rebecca Batiste of the Center for Louisiana Studies, for their continuing editorial and computer expertise.

For the use of their photographs, assistant district attorney Clifford Strider and investigator Ray Delcomyn, of the Rapides Parish District Attorney's Office.

Finally, we want to individually thank the Angola wardens of the past 25 years—C. Murray Henderson, Ross Maggio, Frank Blackburn, Hilton Butler, Larry Smith, John P. Whitley and Burl Cain—who have dared to be unique in their profession and reject prevailing penal policies of secrecy. These stalwarts have consistently supported a "no-censorship" doctrine regarding *The Angolite*, making its accomplishments possible. They also maintained an "open-door" policy for news media and the public that allowed scrutiny of what went on inside the prison. Angola is a testament that allowing people to see the reality of prison life does not compromise safety or security.

Current Warden Burl Cain, upon assuming the job in February 1995, announced he would continue the "hands-off" policy for *The Angolite* and would respect the freedom of all prisoners to openly express their views without fear of censorship or retaliation. He has also promised to encourage more outsiders to come into Angola to work with inmate organizations, and to allow inmate organizations to venture more often into the outside world.

The strong walls of our dedication verse still stand, but at Angola the spirit of redemption remains alive.

PREFACE TO THE SECOND EDITION

It was only a little more than a year ago that the first edition of *The Wall Is Strong* came out in paperback. This edition is shorter than the first; a few selections have been dropped, and a smaller number of more current replacements have been added. A center section of photos, mostly from the files of *The Angolite,* is new, and what were the two middle sections of the first edition have been combined into one. The intent is still to combine readability with purpose in presenting up-to-date views of Louisiana's state corrections system.

Several people were especially helpful in the transition from the first to the second edition:

The editorial stalwart of the second edition is Kim Barrilleaux, who spent several months doing the computer and editorial work needed to trim the "fat" first edition into shape.

Leonard Pourciau's cover design and interior art work are filled with his usual (and most uncommon) insight into prison life.

Julie Leday assisted with computer translations.

Carl A. Brasseaux and the staff of the Center for Louisiana Studies continue to lend expert guidance and support.

Finally, we would like to thank John Whitley, the new warden of Angola and publisher of *The Angolite,* for his interest and spirit of cooperation.

To these and others who have helped and offered suggestions, we say thanks. We hope the "new, improved" model stands up to their informed scrutiny and that it will continue to play a part in increasing public understanding of corrections in our state.

PREFACE TO THE FIRST EDITION

Each book is different, writers say. But this book is more different than most, and we found working to get it done a uniquely challenging experience.

To begin with, one of the editors is a professor of criminal justice at the University of Southwestern Louisiana in Lafayette. The other two are convicts serving life sentences for murder at the Louisiana State Penitentiary at Angola. All three share a common interest in corrections—in providing a decent environment for people living in confinement and in improving correctional programs, particularly those offering alternatives to imprisonment. They also share a common belief that a better informed public can make a difference in the future of corrections.

Finding points of agreement (and occasionally of disagreement) is one thing; putting together a readable, useful book is another thing altogether. This one took most of a year to do. Editorial conferences are no easy matter when 150 miles, the Tunica Hills and seven locked gates separate two of the editors from the third. Much of the conferring that went into the choice of articles for the book was done through the mail. Toward the end, weekly telephone discussions speeded up the final cuts and the preparation of the table of contents. Relations throughout were marked by a cordial, cooperative spirit we can't help thinking would apply equally well to other enterprises shared between the two worlds—prison and free.

The actual preparation of the book was done at the University of Southwestern Louisiana. The "nuts and bolts" of editing, copying, laserprinting and assembly was done by Jeannine LeBlanc, our editorial assistant, who has become so good at this work she can now go and do her own books without our hindrance. After Jeannine, there are several other people whose contributions we wish to acknowledge:

The present and former staff of *The Angolite*, the prison newsmagazine at Angola. It is their work which is the source of most of the articles included here.

Warden Hilton Butler of Angola, who along with his immediate predecessors Frank Blackburn and Ross Maggio has demonstrated continuing support for the vital role a free press can play in prison life.

Assistant Warden Roger Thomas, whose own historical work on Angola will one day make a good book or two.

Leonard Pourciau, *The Angolite* artist whose sketches are used in this book.

Regina R. Migues, whose computer work and usual good spirits were a last minute godsend.

Aaron Martin, the editor of *The Vermilion* at U.S.L., for his technical assistance.

Kathy Lynn Cook, whose review of articles and assistance with preparing proof pages is much appreciated.

Lt. Col. Larry P. Cornwell and his wife, Mrs. Leanne Cornwell (blisters and all), for their work in the Library of Congress.

Joseph Norwood, editor of the *Chainlink Chronicle* at Washington Correctional Institute, for his contribution of articles.

Dr. Tom Carleton, of the L.S.U. history faculty, whose earlier work in the history of Louisiana corrections made it easier to follow along.

To all who have helped, our thanks. We hope they have no cause to be dissatisfied with this book. For ourselves, we have no regrets, other than having to delete many good selections to keep the book down to a reasonable length. But these may yet burst into print in future publications. We have some good ideas left over.

The Wall Is Strong has been a hard labor, but we consider our involvement to have been a reward and not a punishment. We hope that its publication will above all contribute to greater public understanding of the complexities of a modern state corrections system, and to greater public participation in shaping the future of corrections in Louisiana. Much remains to be learned; much remains to be done.

INTRODUCTION

Louisiana's first penitentiary opened in Baton Rouge in 1834. Called "The Walls," it was based on the Auburn model then popular in American corrections— tiny, one-man cells stacked in tiers, a high-walled urban prison where inmates would do factory and craft work in silence. Imagine how surprised its creators would have been to return at the end of the century and see what had happened to their dream of an efficient, reform-minded prison. Their ideal institution had somehow been replaced by a huge prison farm—Angola—where a thousand convicts, 85% of them black, labored in the fields and along the levees under the most brutal, primitive conditions. The dream penitentiary in Baton Rouge had become a nightmare.

This odd twist is typical of the Louisiana corrections system, where results have historically been determined more by misadventure than design. It is a system where certain recurring themes— neglect, stinginess, isolation, hard labor, racism—have mingled with pressures of the moment—political opportunism, natural disasters, scandal, occasional bursts of outrage followed by short-lived attempts at reform—to chart an indecisive, meandering course. It is a system in which personality has been more important than policy, and in which public opinion, the ultimate arbiter of political action, has been mostly silent.

Louisiana has never been certain what to do with convicted offenders. For most of the 1800s, it found a way to avoid the problem altogether: the state leased its convicts to private businessmen, who reaped huge profits from their sweat and blood. This is how the penitentiary came to be located at a private plantation named Angola.

For the first half of the 1900s,

Angola was the only state prison in Louisiana. Prison referred to a place, not a program. No one expected men and women to leave Angola better for the experience. The prayer of the convict was to survive the cane fields and brutal camps and return home in one piece.

Mark T. Carleton describes this period in *Politics and Punishment: The History of the Louisiana State Penal System*, a book as important to the study of American correctional history as T. Harry Williams' *Huey Long* is to the study of political history. Carleton documents important penal events, describes public and political attitudes toward Angola, discusses the problems and abuses of prison administrators and depicts the malevolent atmosphere that hung over the penitentiary for a hundred years. His book ends in 1968, the year the creation of the Department of Corrections officially marked the start of the "modern era" in Louisiana corrections.

The quarter-century since 1968 has been the most eventful in Louisiana corrections history. Unprecedented turmoil, growth and change have marked the corrections system. Its atmosphere has been one of continuing crisis, and it has struggled to balance pressures applied from many directions at once.

The people of Louisiana and the political officials who represent their views have taken a much harder attitude toward crime during this period. Harsh criminal laws have sent more men and women to prison and made it more difficult for them to get out. "Lock 'em up and throw away the key," the people have said. Politicians, who may have sold them on the idea in the first place, have fervently done their bidding.

The prison population has increased five-fold. The three state prisons of 25 years ago have grown to eleven, the new institutions mostly medium-security prisons for men.

The cost of corrections has skyrocketed. Vast sums, more than the state can easily afford, have been spent to built new prisons and add onto old ones. New correctional officers have been hired, prison services expanded and a professional corrections bureaucracy established.

Intervention by the federal court in 1975 brought dramatic change to Angola and the state's penal system. Under federal pressure, legislators appropriated millions to beef up Angola's security staff, physical plant, and health care and services for prisoners. In the two decades since, the federal court has expanded its supervisory role to include parish jails and all state and adult juvenile prisons.

Despite vast increases in spending and prison capacity, parish jails have played an increasingly important role in housing state inmates. They now confine fully one-third of Louisiana's 27,000 state prisoners. With only a minimal increase in the number of state prison beds projected for the next few years, the prison of the future in Louisiana is not a prison: it is a parish jail, which is often very different from a prison operated by the state.

This "double standard" of custodial care—in housing, security, staffing, services and programs—has advantages and disadvantages. Paying sheriffs to house state prisoners is somewhat cheaper for the state, and many sheriffs enthusiastically embrace the economic boon. Indeed, many have become utterly dependent on the income from "renting" jail cells. Nevertheless, the inferior conditions and lack of self-improvement programs disadvantage inmates in many parish jails. Jails were, after all, not built to confine long-term prisoners, only those awaiting trial or serving short sentences.

State officials and politicians have long chafed under federal rule of "their" prisons. In the early nineties, they attempted to substitute "accreditation" by the American Correctional Association (a non-governmental professional corrections organization) for federal supervision. Initially receptive, the federal court released most state prisons from its supervision. But recently, dissatisfied with the maneuvering of sheriffs and state corrections officials, the court reimposed federal supervision over both state and parish facilities.

As we approach the end of the 20th century, Louisiana corrections remains a muddle. Powerful forces compete to rule the state's penal system: sheriffs and district attorneys allied with certain lawmakers and other public officials; aggressive, self-appointed victims-rights advocates riding a wave of public support; the federal court; and the corrections bureaucracy. Powerless on the sidelines, prisoners and their friends and families, along with those interested in penal reform, fearfully await the outcome of this clash. It will determine the direction Louisiana's corrections system will follow into the next century.

The title of this volume, *The Wall Is Strong,* has two important meanings. First, as in Oscar Wilde's poem, it suggests the seriousness and importance of imprisonment—the most severe sanction, short of execution, civilized men can impose on one another, and how it affects those "who lie in jail." Second, in the context of Louisiana corrections history, it suggests the extent to which the public has physically and spiritually isolated convicts behind a wall. A prison wall, to be strong, need not be made of stone, six feet thick and thirty feet tall. In Louisiana, fear and hatred of criminals, public and political fixation on punishment, and the broad sweep of the Mississippi River have built a wall around Angola and its prisoners that is stronger today than the stout walls of the Baton Rouge penitentiary built two centuries ago.

The Editors:
Burk Foster
Wilbert Rideau
Douglas Dennis

The Wall Is Strong:
Corrections in Louisiana

3rd edition

1

PLANTATION DAYS AT ANGOLA:
MAJOR JAMES AND THE ORIGINS OF
MODERN CORRECTIONS IN LOUISIANA*

by Burk Foster

If you wanted to trace the development of corrections in Louisiana, from its origins to the present, there are four possible starting points for your search. You could go back to the New Orleans City Jail of the late 1700s and early 1800s. Accounts of the time describe this jail as a nasty place—a dirty, insect-ridden dumping place for men, women and children, who were mixed together for a variety of criminal and non-criminal offenses. Like other colonial jails, its function was primarily that of detention, until disposition was made or debts paid. Its principal attribute was that most of its occupants did not stay there very long. This was in a time when most sheriffs charged their clients "fees" for daily necessities, and inmates were not released until they or their families paid or worked out all outstanding bills. While this model was important at the parish level, it had little lasting effect on corrections as it would develop at the state level in Louisiana.

In your search you could move forward to the penal reformers who were active in Louisiana after statehood in 1815. Many of them, like Edward Livingston, were familiar with progressive ideas from "up North." They argued for the creation of a penitentiary based on the Auburn model that had recently been built in New York.

This penitentiary, Louisiana's first, opened in Baton Rouge in 1835. The prison fit the style that later came to be called "fortress"—made of stone and iron,

single-man cells, with high walls around the perimeter, and inmates doing factory and craft work together in silence. It was a real prison, the prison that eventually became the model for most nineteenth-century American penitentiaries, but for Louisiana this prison proved to be a temporary side step rather than a lasting model.

The real origin of Louisiana's modern corrections system came later, after the Civil War, and it followed two important changes that took the penitentiary down a different road from what its founders had intended. The first development was the lease system, through which convict labor was leased to private contractors. Convict leasing began in Louisiana in 1844, in direct response to complaints about the cost of operating the Baton Rouge penitentiary.

Dr. Mark T. Carleton, the LSU history professor who wrote *Politics and Punishment: The History of the Louisiana State Penal System*, has pointed out that penal reform in Louisiana has often been frustrated by forces of "habit, hostility, fiscal conservatism and official inertia." Such was the case with the dream penitentiary, which was simply too expensive to last.

The second development was the Civil War itself, which turned the prison system upside down. Before the Civil War, the great majority of Louisiana's convicts were white men who labored at the craft and industrial jobs common to other walled prisons. The Civil War freed

---

*Appeared in *The Angolite,* November/December 1993, 19-24. Reprinted with permission.

the slaves and granted them the rights of citizenship, but it also imposed on them one of the liabilities of citizenship: imprisonment at hard labor for convicted felons.

Overnight, in Louisiana and the other Southern prisons, the prison population became predominantly black (in even greater percentages in several states, including Louisiana, than it is today), and the prisons were populated by young men who were mostly accustomed to agricultural labor. Dr. Carleton has suggested this is how agriculture came to be so important to Southern prisons in the post-Civil War years. In Louisiana and in the other states that established large prison farming operations, "convict," "slave," "Negro," and "farm work" became synonymous terms in the public and political mind.

The real origin of modern Louisiana corrections was the purchase of the convict lease by Major Samuel L. James in 1869, followed the next year by the relocation of the great bulk of Louisiana's convicts from Baton Rouge to a large plantation on the Mississippi River in the northwest corner of West Feliciana Parish. The year was 1870, and the plantation was called Angola.

Angola, or Angora, as it was sometimes called in the early days, was established as a plantation in the 1840s. It was part of the property acquired by Isaac Franklin, the Southern slave trader and planter, from Francis Routh in the 1830s. Angola first operated primarily as a woodyard and sawmill. Wendell Holmes Stephenson, in his 1938 biography of Isaac Franklin, writes:

"Fronting the Mississippi River opposite the mouth of Red River, it was advantageously situated to profit from wood-burning river craft."

Isaac Franklin died in West Feliciana Parish in 1846. His widow, Adelicia Hayes Franklin, married Colonel Joseph A.S. Acklen in 1849. The well-known "Norman's Chart of the Lower Mississippi River," printed in New Orleans in 1858, shows Col. Acklen as the owner of four plantations—Panola, Belle View, Killarney and Angola—at the present site of Angola.

Col. Acklen died in 1863, in the middle of the Civil War. By this time Major Samuel Lawrence James had served briefly in the Confederate Army and resigned to pursue business interests in Louisiana and abroad. Like Captain Rhett Butler, he appears to have found commerce much more to his liking than war: by 1869 he had accumulated enough capital to buy the re-instituted convict lease from John M. Huger and Colonel Charles Jones.

Major James leased Angola, then about 8,500 acres in size, from Col. Acklen's widow and moved the convicts there by steamboat. According to court records, Adelicia Hayes finally sold Angola to Major James on December 22, 1880, for $100,000, payable in a series of notes.

Until he died in 1894 (the lease survived him, not expiring until 1901), Major James ran what Dr. Carleton has called "the most cynical, profit-oriented and brutal prison regime in Louisiana history." Convicts worked on private property—both Major James's and that of other plantation owners who sub-contracted their labor—for the profit of the lessee, Major James. They worked the land, farming and cutting timber, they performed as household servants, they travelled not only "up the river" but "down the river" as well, on Major James's steamboat, repairing and building levees in the never-ending struggle to contain the Mississippi and protect the rich farmland.

The convicts lived in camps, which were merely open wooden buildings with bunk beds (much like the Florida road camps of the 1940s depicted in "Cool Hand Luke"), built along the river and around the plantation. Angola covered about 13 square miles of area, and the convicts shared the land with black share-croppers, several hundred families of free blacks who paid rent for their land and house, bought their supplies at the two plantation stores, and settled up at the end of the year when their crops came in.

Major James's granddaughter, Cecile James Shilstone, who lived on Angola until she turned 13 in 1900, wrote reminiscingly of these days in her memoirs, titled "My Plantation Days." By the time Cecile was born, her grandfather was one of the richest men, perhaps the richest, in Louisiana. (Although Cecile insisted that her grandfather was deep in debt and Angola heavily mortgaged at the time of his death.) She described Samuel James as a very popular, internationally-traveled, well-known man, as much at home in Europe or New Orleans as on his plantation. He was President of the Pickwick Club, New Orleans's leading men's club, for years up to his death.

When he died suddenly, at the "Big House" at Angola on July 26, 1894, Cecile described the scene at Angola: "There were a few hundred of our Negro 'croppers' in the yard. Some were crying softly, others wailing, 'De Co'nel is done gone! Oh, lan' sakes, de Co'nel done gone!'"

If Major James's loyal croppers and the business and civic elite of New Orleans were saddened at the news of his death, the convicts whose labor had made

him a rich man might have wanted to give a cheer instead. Those who were still in custody soon made a very unpleasant discovery: it didn't matter whether Major James or his descendants owned the lease; convicts' lives were just as worthless with one owner as another. Indeed, the *Annual Report of the Louisiana State Penitentiary*, from 1901, suggests that the last seven years of the lease, from 1894 to 1900, were likely the most brutal of its entire history: about 732 convicts, averaging over 100 a year, died during this period.

I indicated earlier that there was a fourth possible starting point in your search for the beginning of modern corrections in Louisiana. This would be the expiration of the lease and the resumption of state control over its convicts on January 1, 1901. If the state had set out to do things very differently, to change the location and the very style of imprisonment to get away from the legacy of the James era, 1901 might have marked a new direction, a time for starting over.

But what you see, when you look at the state penal system of the early 1900s, was more of the same. The state resumed control of the convict lease not to abolish its evils but to exploit its financial possibilities. Profit, not reform, was the prime mover in ending the lease. The penal system would no longer be privately-operated; it would be a state-operated business enterprise. Most officials and employees of the James era were retained, and in the most basic decision of all—where the penitentiary was to be located—the state purchased Angola from the James family, removed the remaining free sharecroppers, and over the next two decades purchased surrounding properties to expand the penitentiary to its present area of 18,000 acres. The original Baton Rouge Penitentiary continued in use for several more years, as a receiving station for new convicts and to manufacture shoes and clothing for prisoner use, but the great majority of the working convicts were shipped to Angola to serve their sentences.

Aside from an apparent decline in the death rate (accompanied by an even sharper decline in the profit rate) after the state resumed control, it is doubtful that a Louisiana convict of 1884 or 1894 could have told a whole lot of difference in the Angola of 1904, and even in the Angola of 1914 the only major differences were in sugar cane replacing cotton as the main crop and in the introduction of formal parole as a possibility for early release.

Major Samuel James owned Louisiana's convicts for three decades, and it was his ideas about convicts and imprisonment that have guided Louisiana corrections in the century since the end of the lease. If Major James had returned for a walk around Angola in 1969, a hundred years after he bought the lease, he would have found that conditions had not changed greatly since his time. He would have observed these enduring traditional features of Angola— the plantation and the prison:

1. agricultural work. Angola was first and foremost a farm, and its convicts have always done farm work.

2. isolation. The location of the prison, in a remote part of the state away from urban areas, made it hard to visit and easy to keep out those who might have been critical of prison practices. Outsiders were never welcome at the old Angola.

3. plantation mentality. By this I mean a "master/servant" relationship which was more than strong discipline. Convicts were subservient to their keepers, who exercised absolute authority, either directly or through armed inmate guards, over them.

4. mostly black inmates. The population of Angola has been 75% or more black for over a hundred years.

5. worthlessness of convicts. The value of a convict's life was nil. If a convict died, no one was held accountable, and you just got another one to replace him.

6. neglect of rehabilitation. As forces to get work done, convicts were not educated, trained, counseled or otherwise improved. They worked, they did their time, they went home: prison administration at its simplest.

7. emphasis on economy. The best prison was the cheapest prison. Many of the political decisions that have had the most negative impact on Angola were rooted in the desire to save every dollar possible in maintaining convicts at a subsistence level.

8. the "Angola attitude." Until the 1950s, every adult felon sentenced to hard labor went to Angola to serve time. Its capacity to confine inmates was limited only by its ability to hire employees to guard and care for them. Thus the nature of prison administration at Angola tended to define the entire corrections philosophy of the state of Louisiana. Most other states at least had alternative places of confinement; in Louisiana everything was centralized at Angola until the adult reformatory opened at DeQuincy in 1957.

Take these principal features, and nurture them within the environment described by Dr. Mark T. Carleton in the conclusion of *Politics and Punishment* in 1971:

1. lack of public interest in corrections.

2. the absence of modern corrections practices and policies and professional corrections staff.

3. a penal system whose policies were based entirely on the mutually-beneficial relationship of a few key prison officials and a few key politicians.

The result was a prison system that was always in the running for the dubious honor of being called the "worst prison in the United States." Not until Judge Gordon West's federal court order of 1975 would the state prison system seriously and continuously seek to follow a course different from that set by Major Samuel James in the aftermath of the Civil War.

Major James stands today as the one person who did the most to shape the idea of the prison, the convict and the nature of punishment in the minds of the people of Louisiana. The modern Louisiana corrections system is the lasting legacy of this enterprising, manipulative businessman who acted, before anyone else could beat him to it, to corner the market on convicts. Angola thrives today as a lasting memorial to his vision.

2

MAJOR JAMES AND CONVICT LEASING*

by Mark T. Carleton

The most decisive event in the history of southern penology was the Civil War. The conflict itself, of course, had no direct bearing upon penal law or practices, but the war changed the status of half of the population—the slaves—who were most liable to penal action, and it thus created a wholly new situation for the penal system to deal with. Negro slaves became free Negroes and, subsequently, citizens. From this sizable component in the population came a correspondingly large group of Negro criminals. Insofar as such persons had previously committed offenses defined as crimes, they had, as slaves, been punished largely on the plantations; but after 1865 they were jammed into overcrowded and dilapidated penal facilities constructed in antebellum days primarily "for whites only." Even if nothing was done to alleviate these conditions—and nothing was—the added expense of feeding, clothing, and guarding so many more prisoners, white as well as colored, was an undertaking that southern state and county governments viewed with concern. Faced with these real and immediate problems at a time when their economies were prostrate, southern legislatures considered the lease system an attractive proposition, particularly when it seemed possible to avoid the financial embarrassment of supporting convicts and, in addition, to derive a revenue from the transaction as well.

Southern penal systems were affected on two levels, therefore, by the sudden influx of Negroes into the prison population after 1865. The sheer numbers of convicts to be maintained within inadequate facilities and on meager budgets strongly recommended the lease system as both an economical and potentially profitable alternative to state maintenance and responsibility. And as Negroes were experienced agricultural workers, most of them were eventually employed by the lessees as cotton and fruit pickers, sugar cane cutters, and vegetable gardeners. From these circumstances arose the penal farm, an institution uniquely southern, which in Louisiana still serves as the sacrosanct nucleus of penal operations.

While prison reform made headway elsewhere in the nation during the latter nineteenth century, in the South no comparable progress would be evident for decades to come. Private contractors, eager to obtain cheap labor for a variety of projects ranging from levee and railroad construction to plantation work, found southern legislatures equally eager to accommodate them. By 1870 most arrangements had been made. For more than a generation in some states the convict lease system would remain the dominant feature of southern penology.

Louisiana was briefly in charge of her penitentiary during the period immediately following the Civil War. In January, 1868, penitentiary officials submitted a detailed report on conditions within the institution, the last such detailed report, in fact, for almost thirty years.

There had been 228 convicts within the penitentiary on January 1, 1867.

Admitted during the ensuing year were 229 more. Within this same year 167 convicts were released, 11 were pardoned, 41 escaped, and 16 died. Half of the deaths resulted from scurvy, which authorities ascribed to lack of fruit in the prison diet. No data were provided on the number of white and black prisoners, but a subsequent report, issued several months later, listed 85 white males, 203 black males, 9 black females (but no white females) in the penitentiary as of June 14, 1868.

Crimes for which 229 prisoners admitted during 1867 had been convicted included: 198 against property, (of which larceny alone counted for 131); and 31 against the person, of which three were for murder, three for rape, five for manslaughter, and the rest for various forms and degrees of assault. By occupation, most of those admitted, 191, were "laborers."

While no correlation was given of race-to-crime-to-occupation, it can be seen that a majority were laborers, a majority were Negroes, and a majority had committed no crime more serious than larceny, for which the average sentence was four months to one year. Prison officials asked, indeed, if the legislature would not "inquire into the reason why so many are sent to this institution for the term of three, four, and six months, upon the most trivial charges? Does there not lurk beneath, the low, mean motive of depriving them of the right[s] of citizenship?"

Of the 222 convicts in the penitentiary on January 1, 1868, 116 were under the age of twenty-five, 73 having been in the twenty-to-twenty-five-year age group, 40 between the ages of fifteen and twenty, and 3 between ten and fifteen years of age. The penitentiary had cost the state

of Louisiana $61,838.88 to operate during 1867. An appropriation of $210,000 was requested for the following year. On March 18, 1868, Governor Joshua Baker signed a contract leasing the penitentiary to John M. Huger and Colonel Charles Jones. The contract would, however, have to be ratified by the legislature.

In the meantime, Louisiana had been placed under military supervision, as provided for by the Reconstruction Acts of 1867. A new state constitution had been written, adult male suffrage established, and elections set for state executive offices and seats in the legislature, henceforth (until 1921) to be called the General Assembly. The elections were held in 1868, and when the lease came up for ratification the following year it faced an assembly in which there was a majority of white and Negro Republicans. Louisiana's new chief executive was a handsome, twenty-six-year-old "carpet-bagger," Henry Clay Warmoth, who had been inaugurated on July 13, 1868.

The lease of the penitentiary to Huger and Jones was ratified by the assembly in January, 1869, but was vetoed by Governor Warmoth, who issued this morally outraged message: "There is too much power given to the lessees over the institution, and the Board of Control is ignored. The health, comfort, food, religious training and discipline of the prisoners should be under the charge of disinterested officers of the Government . . . Where the lessees have absolute power over the prisoners the tendency is to work them too much and feed them too little and give no attention to their comforts and instruction."

The Board of Control, a legacy from antebellum days, consisted of five gubernatorial appointees who were supposed to ensure that humane standards of convict welfare were maintained by the lessees. Before the war the board had not been too successful: "humane standards" conflicted with the objective of the lessees, which was to make money. The lessees, moreover, rather than the board, possessed the authority to manage the penitentiary. Between 1865 and 1868 the state Board of Control had actually managed the penitentiary; but now, in 1869, Huger and Jones appeared determined to relegate this agency to limbo in order that the convicts might be worked at the lessees' pleasure. The governor found this attempt distressing. Later in the session, however, a modified bill, which became Act 55 of 1869, legalized the arrangements made previously between Baker and the new lessees. The Board of Control was given the "direction and control of the health and religious regulations of the convicts," although final authority remained with the lessees. Warmoth signed the bill granting a lease to Huger and Jones for five years (from 1868). Annual net profits would be divided evenly between the state and the lessees. Finally, in order to get the penitentiary into operating condition again following wartime damage, $500,000 worth of state bonds were authorized for the purpose of buying new manufacturing machinery.

Act 55 was signed by Governor Warmoth on March 5, 1869. Hardly before the ink had dried, Huger and Jones were packing their bags. Were they disappointed? Were they not making money? They had just made a great deal of money—probably in excess of $100,000—by having sold out to a firm calling itself James, Buckner and Company. For the next eleven months James, Buckner and Company managed the penitentiary and worked the convicts

without legal authorization, either from Warmoth or the General Assembly. When the assembly convened in January, 1870, James and his associates were in New Orleans to do business.

House member O. H. Brewster of Ouachita Parish sponsored a bill proposing that "Samuel L. James, C. B. Buckner and T. Bynum, having purchased from Messrs. Huger and Jones, the lease [of the penitentiary] . . . be and the same are hereby substituted and placed instead of [Huger and Jones] as lessees of the Louisiana State Penitentiary. The measure further proposed to award a twenty-one year lease to S. L. James and Company. On January 28 the bill was reported favorably (6-1) by the House Penitentiary Committee. The dissenting member, however, expressed dissatisfaction with the length of the contract, believing that it should be reduced to ten or even five years and "be given to the highest responsible bidder." The vote on final passage three days later revealed a crossing of party lines as some Democrats and some Republicans supported, while others opposed, the bill. Of the twenty-five Negroes who were present and voting, however, all but one were in favor. Forty-seven white members supported the bill, while thirteen opposed it. In the upper house, Senator John Lynch sought first to amend the bill by providing for an annual rental of $35,000. When this was voted down, he suggested $20,000. This, too, failed. The bill as passed on February 24 retained the twenty-one-year contract and provided for a graduated scale of annual rentals, $5,000 being due the first year, $6,000 the second, and so on, until by 1891 the lessees would have paid the state $25,000 for the final year of their lease. All four Negro senators favored the bill, which became Act 56 of 1870 when signed by Governor Warmoth a week later. One motive behind passage of this measure was to obtain a revenue for the state from the labor of her convicts. But other "inducements" seem to have been applied as well.

A financial victim of the clandestine "switch" from one set of lessees to the other charged that, while the James bill was being debated, the bonds issued a year earlier had in fact been obtained and used by James as a colossal bribe: $100,000 worth had gone to Huger and Jones to sell their equity in the lease, and part of the remainder to members of the General Assembly, with the understanding that all necessary transactions and endorsements should be legalized. The documented performance of latter-nineteenth century Louisiana politicians, during and after Reconstruction, lends substantial credibility to these charges. Insofar as Louisiana was concerned, the leasing of convicts originated in antebellum days and was readopted following the Civil War. Reconstructionists, therefore, were not to blame for instituting the system in Louisiana, as was the case elsewhere in the South. But within the assembly of 1870, white Democrats had joined white and black Republicans in adding the nasty odor of corruption to the traditional motives of fiscal conservatism and indifference to humanitarian considerations.

Samuel Lawrence James, who by 1870 had become Louisiana's dominant postbellum lessee, was born in Clarksville, Tennessee, in 1834. A competent civil engineer at twenty, James, in 1854, moved to New Orleans where he became associated with P.G.T. Beauregard and helped construct the United States Custom House, a hospital, and the city's first streetcar lines. When the Civil War

broke out, James assisted in raising an Irish brigade from New Orleans and was commissioned a captain in the Sixth Louisiana Infantry Regiment, with which he fought at First Manassas. Promoted soon thereafter to major, James was believed in later years to have served "valiantly" throughout the remainder of the conflict in the Trans-Mississippi Department. (The official records disclose, however, that James resigned from the Confederate army in December 1861.)

The major's activities for the next few years are vaguely documented. He traveled abroad after the war and managed somehow during the late sixties to accumulate a considerable amount of money, which he used in part to purchase Angola, an extensive cotton plantation in West Feliciana Parish, and to purchase the convict lease in 1869 from Huger and Jones. That he may also have "purchased" members of the General Assembly the following year was not acknowledged.

Physically, the major was an impressive specimen of the Gilded Age: with the features and sideburns of a beefy Chester A. Arthur, from the neck down James could double equally well for Grover Cleveland. But the major's affinities with the time were not merely symbolic. A man of property and influence in 1870, James continued to demonstrate that he possessed the means to secure for himself an abundance of good things in this life. When he died in 1894 newspaper obituaries described James as having been a "singularly sagacious man of business," "gifted with indomitable will," "eminently successful in all that he undertook," and "endowed with a nature that knew no defeat." Rendered by friend and enemy alike, these post-mortem tributes to Samuel L. James rather fairly portray the man who initiated and personally maintained for twenty-five years the most cynical, profit-oriented, and brutal prison regime in Louisiana history.

With the penitentiary comfortably out of its hands, and with twenty-one years of revenue anticipated, the Louisiana General Assembly returned to the "normal" business of Reconstruction politics in the early 1870s. Amidst party and factional squabbling, few persons bothered to keep an eye on the lessees or concern themselves with the matter of convict welfare.   In 1873, however, a joint committee of senators and representatives inspected the penitentiary in Baton Rouge and submitted the following report: "Bucking, gagging, and [the] shower-bath had been abandoned . . . Whipping was still used, also the dark cell . . . in extreme cases . . . . The guards generally were competent men, and not malicious or cruel . . . . White as well as colored convicts were whipped; they made no discriminations as to race in the punishments inflicted."   None of the lessees was at the penitentiary; the clerk of the institution, one Matta, "did not know who the owners of the lease now were, except Major Samuel James." The warden was not on hand either, but his deputy, Captain F. Guidry, informed the committee that "the warden . . . had authority to punish convicts for misconduct without special directions from the board."   Guidry further "suppose[d] that the board of control knows the character of punishments used by the warden and his deputies; they ought to know if they did not." Action taken on this report by the assembly consisted of having it printed in the journal. Perhaps Major James still had a number of legislators in his pocket.

Where was Major James? Where was the warden? Where, for that matter, were most of the convicts? The committee had found the penitentiary nearly deserted. A year later, in 1874, Senator Thomas Cage, a Negro from Terrebonne Parish and chairman of the senate Committee on Parks and Public Buildings, submitted his report on the status of the penitentiary:

> The penitentiary building was found in much better repair [than was supposed].   It is true the building is going to wreck [sic] in many particulars, and looks much forsaken and weather-beaten, mouldy and dilapidated, but still it is more than amply sufficient for all that is going on within its walls or inclosures [sic].   Almost all the convicts are now constantly farmed out—sent promiscuously, it seems, to different portions of the State to work in competition with free labor—so that there would seem scarcely any use any more for any Penitentiary building at all, and if matters go on for a few more years as they have been going on . . . we shall have none, except as a den or hiding place for owls, bats, and reptiles.

In 1875 the president of the Board of Control disclosed that "the walls and buildings . . . have been but very little used since the last report [of the Board, submitted in 1872], most of the prisoners being outside the walls working on the levees, railroads, plantations, etc."

Convict leasing in the nineteenth century conformed to one or the other of two basically different patterns.   The contract system, strictly applied, left state officials directly responsible for feeding, clothing, and guarding the convicts, who remained (and were worked by the lessees) within the prison structure.   Under this type of arrangement, lessees hired only convict labor, and not the convicts themselves.   South Carolina, Texas, and Virginia had adopted this system by the

1880s. The lease system required that lessees maintain the convicts but empowered them to work convicts outside the prison structure. All other southern states, plus Nebraska and the New Mexico Territory, were using the lease system by the 1880s. Louisiana's antebellum arrangements had combined features of both systems, for while the lessees had been responsible for convict maintenance, they had also worked the prisoners "within the walls" at Baton Rouge. And in the early 1870s state authorities had assumed, or had pretended to assume, that James also would work the convicts within the penitentiary in the customary manner as "manufacturers," utilizing the machinery therein. Although some of this machinery was antiquated, all of it was not. According to the president of the board, $300,000 worth of new textile machinery was available and in excellent condition. But aside from a few elderly convicts who were assigned the job of oiling and polishing, no one came near this equipment.

James had been working the prisoners at more lucrative employment from the very beginning. Between March and November, 1869—even before his lease had been legally ratified—James had made almost $100,000 from working his convicts on the state's Mississippi River levees. "Experienced" Negro convicts could be worked almost as profitably on farms or plantations, while any able-bodied convict could be subcontracted for railroad construction. James and his associates worked the prisoners under their control on all three of these projects from the moment prisoners were "bought" from Huger and Jones until they were returned to the state in 1901. The system that prevailed in Louisiana from 1869 to 1901 was, therefore, the pure lease system, and

not the hybrid system of prewar years. And anyone wishing to locate the major, by the way, might have inquired either at Angola or at Lagona plantations, the latter a sugar estate in St. Mary Parish also owned by the enterprising lessee and worked, not surprisingly, by convicts.

In general, it made no difference to white legislators how James worked the convicts or where, so long as the penitentiary was not the state's responsibility. But to many of the Negro senators and representatives, this matter was of genuine concern, for low-priced convict labor at work throughout the state frequently deprived their constituents of jobs. It was one thing to establish a convict lease by which the state might avoid expense or even derive revenue, but it was highly undesirable to see convicts at work "in competition with free labor," as Senator Cage had expressed it in 1874. The apparent logic of this argument convinced enough legislators, white as well as Negro, to result in the passage of Act 22 of 1875 which prohibited the lessees from employing or permitting employment of the convicts outside the penitentiary itself. Penalties for violation could include a $5,000 fine and abrogation of the lease.

Major James found himself harassed from two directions during the spring of 1875. Act 22, which could be invoked to put him out of business, was actually the less formidable of the two obstacles placed in his path. On March 20 the district attorney for East Baton Rouge Parish filed a lawsuit against James demanding that he pay immediately two years' delinquent rentals for his use of the convicts and that he forfeit the lease. Thus, James could lose the convicts if he continued to work them profitably outside the penitentiary. At the same time, he stood to lose them anyway.

On January 3, 1876, Governor William Pitt Kellogg submitted his annual message to the General Assembly. Part of his address was devoted to Act 22 and its effect on the status of the penitentiary. After recommending that the convicts be authorized to work on the levees, as if they had not already been engaged in this work for several years, Kellogg got down to the dilemmas occasioned by the passage of Act 22:

> An attempt to enforce the law developed the fact that there was no appropriation for the support of the convicts within the walls of the penitentiary, and that the machinery and other appliances for manufacturers previously provided . . . could not be made available in their existing condition without a large outlay of money for which there was no authority of law, and even with such an outlay, would in all probability fail to render the institution self-sustaining for some years to come . . . . The convicts are now nearly all working on the line of the New Orleans Pacific railroad [sic], a work of great importance to the State. I believe that they are as well provided for and as humanely treated as is practicable under the circumstances. Unless the State should make some arrangements otherwise to utilize their labor and ma[k]e it self-sustaining, I am convinced . . . that it is better to permit the present lessees to continue working the convicts under their existing lease.

Thinking perhaps of the lawsuit pending against James, Kellogg concluded his discussion by suggesting that "some provision should be made . . . to meet an exigency that might be presented in the future by reason of the convicts being thrown upon the State." Whatever virtues the governor's analysis may have possessed, certainly frankness and honesty were not among them. Kellogg failed to explain why he himself had signed Act 22 one year earlier. Surely, if he had read the bill, he would have noticed that it contained no appropriation. As for the condition of machinery in the penitentiary, Kellogg had either been misinformed or was telling a lie. Unless James had deliberately sabotaged the machinery (a distinct possibility under the circumstances), it is most unlikely that $300,000 worth of new equipment would have deteriorated to uselessness within one year. How could Kellogg possibly know, moreover, that James would not prosper by working the convicts within the walls? Finally, to whose advantage would violation of Act 22 really accrue—to the state's, to the railroad's, or to Major James's?

The house of representatives, in which there were a number of Negro members, briefly defied the governor. On February 7, William Murrell, a Negro representative from Madison Parish, proposed a resolution which ordered the penitentiary committee to investigate the matter and to determine if legal grounds existed for canceling the lease. The resolution passed but no further action on it was reported. Nor was there any attempt made in either chamber to provide for the "exigency," alluded to by Governor Kellogg, of the convicts "being thrown upon the State."

The "Home Rule" administration of Governor Francis T. Nicholls had no more intention of interfering with the lessee than its predecessor. Nicholls spoke frankly and to the point in his message of 1878: "As matters now stand [that is, with the lease still in financial arrears and most of the prisoners still working on the New Orleans Pacific Railroad] though the State gains nothing in money from her convicts she is at no expense for their support, and . . . I think that the present arrangement should continue." In case there might be legislators so unrealistic as to desire an abrogation of the lease, Nicholls concluded with a remark calculated to render the situation crystal clear: "I am not aware of a desire on the part of any one to lease the Penitentiary should the present lease be set aside."

During an extra session, convened two months later, a bill to resolve the dilemma was rushed through the senate and arrived in the house on March 15. It provided that the amount due the state from S. L. James and Company be set by arbitration and, in addition, that the convicts continue to work on the New Orleans and Pacific Railroad. Once again, as in the Kellogg episode, the house—in which there were more Negroes than in the senate—rebelled. Immediately following introduction, the bill was tabled by a vote of 49-24, without being read. For one reason or another, the members were in a more receptive mood three days later. To quote the House Journal's description of what took place, the bill "was taken up on its first reading, passed to a second reading, and under a suspension of the rules the bill was read a third time and passed." No votes are given for any of these august deliberations. The following year Governor Nicholls reported that an arbitration committee had fixed the sum owed by the lessees at $44,833, and that S.L. James and Company had begun to settle accounts. Not until 1881, however, did the major actually make a payment.

What of the legal proceedings filed against James in 1875? During the assembly session of 1878 a senate committee disclosed that Governor Kellogg, followed by Governor Nicholls, had urged officials in Baton Rouge "not to press the suit." Two administrations, one Radical Republican, the other Home Rule Democrat, had considered it less prudent to evict the lessee than to settle with him out of court. Between 1873 and 1878 Major James violated one law six times and another at least once. (He failed to pay his rent for six consecutive years and continued to employ convicts outside the penitentiary between the passage of Act 22 and its repeal three years later.) The state of Louisiana, therefore, possessed legal grounds on at least seven counts for canceling the James contract. State officials, however, whether Republican or Democratic, found it easy to abandon their sworn obligation to enforce the law as they had earlier abandoned their official responsibility to support the penitentiary. Both the institution and its inmates remained securely in the control of Major James during the transition from one state regime to another, so anxious were both to avoid that dreaded "exigency" of having the convicts "thrown upon them."

There is the additional possibility that James, in order to ensure absolutely his continued tenure in Baton Rouge, might have seen that various sums of money reached appropriate individuals at critical times. It is always difficult to prove that public officials have been bribed. Neither the source nor the recipient of such a transaction is likely to disclose his guilt or to leave written evidence thereof lying about. There is considerable evidence, however, to substantiate the general charge that bribery in late nineteenth century Louisiana was as popular a sport as football has become in the twentieth, with almost as many participants. Traditionally, the most corrupt, and corrupting, agency in the state at that time was the notorious Louisiana State Lottery Company, an organization which "with its gigantic 'slush' fund . . . debauched legislators, muzzled the press, [and] made and unmade public officials."

The lease, like the lottery, was a vested interest, and relations between the heads of these unsavory organizations remained as close after 1877 as beforehand. Charles T. Howard and John A. Morris, chiefs of lottery, were both personal friends of Major James. All three of these gentlemen, moreover, were boon companions of Edward A. Burke, the state treasurer from 1878 to 1887. Burke, who also carried the title of "Major," had played an important role in the negotiations which sent Rutherford B. Hayes to the White House. In Louisiana, where he soon had "his fingers in scores of pies," Burke acquired the *New Orleans Times-Democrat,* which he converted into a stanch pro-lottery organ. With the possible exceptions of the *New Orleans Daily States* and the *Shreveport Weekly Caucasian,* Burke's newspaper was the most reactionary sheet in postbellum Louisiana. Rounding out this coterie were two other men, Louis A. Wiltz, governor of Louisiana from 1880 to 1881, and his successor, upon his death, Samuel Douglas McEnery, the state's chief executive between 1881 and 1888.

The lessee had, indeed, made friends in high places. But they were not his only supporters. Within the General Assembly those members who voted for the lottery also stood by Major James, with very few exceptions, when both enterprises renewed in 1890.

It has been shown that James also might well have "debauched legislators" in the process of ratifying his lease in 1870. His ability to continue the practice would depend, in large measure, upon his being able to afford it. An examination of the major's financial condition—to the extent that he let it be known—sheds considerable light on this question.

The annual report of the Board of Control for 1870 contains a long and lavish "General Balance Sheet of the Books of the Louisiana Penitentiary, under the Lease of James, Buckner and Co., on the first day of November, 1869" (three months before the major's lease was officially confirmed). Within eight months James and his associates had worked up a debit-credit balance of $478,456.75. Among the more revealing individual entries are the following:

	Debit	Credit
Company account	$90,141.99	$133,311.50
S. L. James	10,931.67	7,463.80
Lessees' cash account	36,931.59	36,762.46
Levee account	50,900.01	147,449.30
Expense account	57,806.05	4,298.15
Provision account	21,481.33	7,894.71

James had received almost $150,000 for working convicts on levees; their labor had cost him a third of that amount, leaving a net profit for levee work alone of a tenth of a million dollars. Personally, the major himself had already drawn more than $10,000 from his new enterprise, while both the "Expense account" and the "Lessees' cash account" seem to have been actively employed, although for what purposes was not indicated.

It was officially known, therefore, by members of the General Assembly of 1870 that Major James had already done a half million dollars worth of business in less than a year. No wonder it was suggested in the house that the lease be cut to five years and sold to the highest bidder. No wonder Senator John Lynch recommended, for openers, that James be charged an annual rental of $35,000. But, as it developed, James emerged with a twenty-one-year contract, obliging him to pay, as his initial rental, a sum equal to approximately one-one-hundredth of the magnitude of business he was known to have carried on. How the major had been able to secure official endorsement of a contract so advantageous to himself can be easily imagined.

Once established in the penitentiary, James closed his books to both public and official scrutiny. No other report of the Board of Control during the subsequent thirty-one years of the major's regime contains any financial information relative to the lessees whatsoever. No reports of any sort, in fact, emerged from the penitentiary in 1873, 1874, 1876, 1877, or during the inclusive period from 1879 to 1889.

However, some idea of what was going on, financially and otherwise, within the major's domain may be gained from scattered available figures taken from official sources:

Year	Number of Convict Deaths Reported	Rental Paid the State	Debit-Credit Balance
1870	19	$5,000.00	$478,456.75
1871	21	6,000.00	Unknown
1872	9	7,000.00	Unknown
1875	53	None	Unknown
1878	31	None	Unknown
1888	99	5.00	Unknown
1889	68	17,181.49	Unknown
1896	216	48,553.70	Unknown

As we have seen, before the Civil War, leasing of convicts in Louisiana was undertaken for reasons of economy. If the state could acquire a share of lessee profits, this, too, was desirable but not really necessary, because the principal objective in contracting with lessees was to spare the taxpayers the "expensive luxury" of maintaining the penitentiary.

However, by 1870, fiscal conservatism had begun to serve as a mask for official avarice and personal greed, both of which sought through convict labor a most reprehensible form of monetary enrichment. In such an atmosphere, rehabilitation of convicts became an utterly dead letter—as dead in fact, as an increasing number of convicts themselves.

Samuel Lawrence James acquired control of the penitentiary from a state administration dominated by Radical Republicans of both races. But white Democrats had also supported the major at the outset. They continued to do so, in greater numbers and with sustained effect, following their self-proclaimed redemption of Louisiana in 1877 from the other "evils" of Reconstruction. The Louisiana State Penitentiary was not redeemed until 1901, and even then only partially. In the meantime, and with James still in command, punishment for profit continued to be Louisiana's objective in penal policy.

3

WOMEN IN THE WALLS:
THE IMPRISONMENT OF WOMEN AT THE
BATON ROUGE PENITENTIARY, 1835-1862*

by Marianne Fisher-Giorlando

The Board would bring to your notice the case of a negro woman named Celeste, sent to the Penitentiary, from the parish of St. Landry, she was convicted of the crime of striking a white person named Eloise Lavergne. The said slave Celeste was the property of the estate of Louis Charhere [sic], of said parish, and was sentenced for life by a Court composed of W. Boutte and B. Martel, Justices of the Peace, and ten slave owners, the papers doubtless in proper form. But it appears to this Board, as a thing almost past belief, that the said slave Celeste could be a proper subject for judicial action or for imprisonment in the Penitentiary, she appears to be at least one hundred years of age, scarcely able to sit or stand, and must have been a charge upon the Estate for many years; she of course, can be of no value, and under the circumstances, the Board recommend the pardon of said slave, and that she be returned to the owners, and that, if the State has paid the owners of said slave, Celeste, that they be required to return it, and if they have not yet received anything from the State, that the Auditor be instructed not to audit any claim for the said slave. All of which is respectfully submitted.

The story of Celeste, the 100-year-old slave sentenced to life in prison for striking a white woman, is the story of the forgotten inmates of Louisiana's prison history—"the women in the walls." "The Walls" was the popular term for the old Baton Rouge Penitentiary, opened in 1835 and finally shut down in the early 1900s when the last of its convicts were transferred to the Angola prison farm.

Before the Civil War, it housed in one high-walled prison all the men and women sentenced to state custody in Louisiana.

Little has been written about the women who were sent to the Baton Rouge penitentiary. This is not particularly surprising, given that references to the women inmates tend to be scant, scattered and often lost among the yearly reports and other official documents that relate mostly to the men inmates. The reference to Celeste, cited above in a 1853 Board of Directors report, is the longest single passage devoted to incarcerated women found in any state document relevant to the pre-Civil War penitentiary. We know more about Celeste from official records than we know of any other woman inmate.

The discovery of this old slave woman and her convict sisters in the Baton Rouge penitentiary challenges commonly-held beliefs about Southern imprisonment and raises important questions about imprisoned women. Where did these women come from? What crimes had they committed? In what ways were they alike, and how were they different?

Historical studies of women in Southern prisons of the 1800s have tended to follow three lines of thought:

1. Very few women were imprisoned; certainly fewer than current rates of 5% to 6% of the total prison population.

2. Slaves were not imprisoned, because their punishments, generally whippings, were handled privately by their owners under the Black Codes.

*A revised version of this article was read before the annual meeting of the Louisiana Historical Association, March 17, 1995. Printed here with the author's permission.

3. Women who went to prison did not stay there long because of the shorter sentences and more abundant use of clemency during this era.

My review of Baton Rouge penitentiary records suggests that the first assumption is clearly in error, at least in Louisiana. The records I have found so far indicate that sixty-one women were admitted to the penitentiary between 1835 and 1862. The most women in prison at any one time was 19, in 1854, and 20, in 1856.

Of the 14 pre-war years for which information is available, the percentage of women in the total prison population ranged from a low of 3.4% in 1844 to a high of 7.5% in 1847 (See Table 1). Women averaged right at 5% of the total prison population throughout the decade before the Civil War.

More recently, the Bureau of Justice Statistics reported: "On June 30, 1989, 5.4% of all prison inmates were women, the highest percent since record keeping began in 1926." Even during the decade of the 1980s, when women's incarceration rate reached its all-time national peak, the percentage of female prisoners in the U. S. prison population was no greater than it had been in the 1850s in Louisiana.

This comparison remains true for Louisiana as well. Of 23,000 inmates serving state sentences in 1994, about 1,100, or just under 5%, were women, a percentage remarkably similar to the rate of a century-and-a-half earlier. So much for chivalry in the old days.

What about the second assumption, that only whites or free blacks were imprisoned? This may have been the practice in other states, but in Louisiana a majority of the women in the Baton Rouge penitentiary were slaves. Before the Civil War, of the 61 women admitted

to the penitentiary, 33 were slaves, five free women of color, and 23 white. In every year for which records are available, slaves outnumbered free women in the prison population.

In Louisiana, the Code Noir (Black Code), prescribed "the rules and conduct to be observed with respect to Negroes and other slaves of this territory." And although slaves were generally considered property in the eyes of Southern law, when they committed a criminal act in Louisiana, they were then considered human beings, fully responsible and punishable for such behavior. Under the code, slaves were held even more responsible, since they could be convicted of more crimes than whites or free people of color, and the punishments prescribed for slaves were often harsher, as exemplified in the case of Celeste, who was sentenced to life imprisonment for striking a white woman.

For her time, some would say Celeste got off lightly. If Eloise Lavergne was her mistress, Celeste's crime would have originally carried an automatic death sentence.

The original 1806 territorial code included a long list of offenses punishable by death such as "maliciously burning or destroying stacks of rice, corn . . . other grain, or produce, raw or manufactured [burning] any building or house. . . wilfully or maliciously poison[ing] or wilfully or maliciously administer[ing] poison to any free man, woman, child, servant or slave. . . ." Additionally the "killing of any person, causing an insurrection, and willfully striking his master, mistress, or his child, or children so as to cause a contusion, or effusion or shedding of blood shall be punished with death." Finally, "the third offense of striking a white person and grievously and

Table I
Prison Population by Race and Gender

	Men		Black		Women		Women		Total
Year	Black	White	No.	%	Black	White	#	%	
1834	–	–	–		–	–	–		91
1835	–	–	–		–	–	–		–
1836	–	–	–		–	–	–		–
1837	–	–	–		–	–	–		–
1838	–	–	–		–	–	–		–
1839	–	–	–		–	–	–		182
1840	25	141	32	18.4	7	1	8	4.6	174
1841	–	–	–		–	–	–		195
1842	–	–	–		–	–	–		206
1843	0	182	6	3.1	6	1	7	3.7	189
1844	0	170	6	3.4	6	0	6	3.4	176
1845	–	–	–		–	–	–		–
1846	–	–	–		–	–	–		183
1847	–	–	–		13	–	13	7.5	172
1848	–	–	–		–	–	–		152
1849	–	–	–		–	–	–		194
1850	62	173	74	29.7	12	2	14	5.6	249
1851	65	219	78	26.1	13	3	16	5.3	298
1852	72	186	87	31.2	15	0	15	5.4	273
1853	82	186	97	34.3	15	0	15	5.3	283
1854	85	191	100	33.8	15	4	19	6.4	295
1855	–	–	–		–	–	–		347
1856	99	237	116	32.6	17	3	20	5.6	356
1857	89	232	101	30.0	12	4	16	4.7	337
1858	88	221	103	32.0	15	2	17	5.2	326
1859	93	219	109	33.0	16	2	18	5.4	330
1860	92	233	107	31.2	15	3	18	5.2	343
1861	–	–	–		–	–	–		–
1862	–	–	–		–	–	–		–
1863	–	–	–		–	–	–		–
1864	–	–	–		2	1	–		46
1865	22	26	26	49.1	4	1	5	9.4	53

willfully wound[ing] or mutilat[ing] any white person although first offense" shall suffer death.

By 1823 Louisiana had passed an act which allowed the substitution of life imprisonment at hard labor for the death penalty. According to the first section of the act, the governor could commute the death sentence to life imprisonment when the jury/judge recommended it and circumstances allowed. The available evidence suggests that Louisiana was the only Southern state to use the life imprisonment substitution in place of execution for slave capital offenses. Evidently, this substitution was used for the women. Although probably underreported, the execution files of Watt Espy, the Alabama archivist, include only 6 women known to have been executed in Louisiana from 1835-1862, while at least 26 slave women are known to have been sentenced to life imprisonment during the same period.

Celeste's crime of assaulting and wounding Eloise Lavergne was classified as a capital offense and punishable by death. Apparently, the justices of the peace and the jury had pity on the old woman and recommended that the governor commute her sentence to life imprisonment.

The Board of Directors was concerned about the state's payment to Celeste's owners. Even though slaves may have been perceived as human beings when they committed a criminal offense, Louisiana's slave code statues maintained simultaneous perceptions of slaves as property. As property, when a slave was either executed or imprisoned for life, the state recognized the slave's value and compensated the owners' for their losses. The amount of reimbursement varied through the years. Celeste's owners were not entitled to more than $300 compensation.

Celeste and the 32 other slave women in the Walls—the greatest number of slave women found in any antebellum Southern prison—were all tried and convicted under some version of the Black Code. They were property converted to humanity for

punishment, but still considered primarily for the economic compensation due their owners. How much was a 100-year-old slave worth?

In considering the third assumption about women in Southern prisons of the 1800s—that their stays were brief—a more in-depth profile of the women who came to the Walls is in order. This profile considers the women's age, nativity, sentencing parish, criminal offenses, sentences and finally, their release status.

We know already that a majority of women in prison at any given time were slaves. In 1852, the year Celeste was admitted, the 15 women in prison were all slaves. Celeste was the oldest, and Phoebe, who had entered the prison at age 12 in 1847 from Plaquemines Parish, was the youngest at 17.

As the Civil War approached, the average age of the women's population increased, partly from the number of slave women growing older as they served life sentences but more, it appears, from the admittance of several slave women past age 40 when they came into prison. But no one else was as old as Celeste or as young as Phoebe when they entered the Walls.

Where did the women in the Walls come from? Although it is not known where Celeste was born, surprisingly few of the women in the penitentiary with her were from Louisiana. In 1852, seven were born in Virginia, and only four in Louisiana. The majority were from Southern slave-holding states, a pattern generally reflective of all the imprisoned slave women.

Information on nativity is known for 40 of the 61 incarcerated women. The majority of them (mostly slaves) were from Louisiana and Virginia, with 12 from each state. Seven white women emigrated from Europe, three from Ireland, and two each from Scotland and Germany. An additional five women with nativity information not available have last names such as Murphy, Fea, Fitzpatrick, Gillooly, and Moore, indicating that they also could be Irish immigrants.

Their birth places reveal an interesting nativity pattern. If Maryland is defined as a Southern state, all but one of the imprisoned slave women was born in a Southern slave-holding state, which suggests the 15 slave women born out-of-state either moved to Louisiana with their owners or were sold to new owners in Louisiana.

As for the imprisoned white women we know about, all of them came from Northern states or from Europe. Although their fugitive status is not known, Robert Reinders's observation, in his 1964 book *End of an Era*, that the high crime rate in New Orleans was due to a "professional criminal class who were usually fugitives from eastern states or foreign countries" is consistent with the nativity patterns of the white women found in the penitentiary.

In summary, the slave women were born in slave-holding states but none of the white women were born in Louisiana or any other slave-holding states. While all the Louisiana-born women were slaves, all the white women were from outside the state and predominately from outside the country. The penitentiary women were "not from around here," as they say in south Louisiana, which probably made them ideal candidates for incarceration.

Of the 61 women in the Walls, records show that 52 were sentenced from 14 different parishes, and here some interesting patterns emerge. Thirty of the women were sentenced from urban New Orleans. Twenty of these were white, five free women of color, and only five slave

women. Of the 22 women sentenced from rural parishes, all were slaves. Four slaves known as the "Williams' negroes" were sentenced in Virginia. Three white women and two slave women do not have any parish designation. So as far as imprisonment of women was practiced in pre-Civil War Louisiana, the white women came from New Orleans, and the black women came from rural parishes.

The women from New Orleans and the river parishes probably traveled to Baton Rouge by boat. But for the other women, mostly slaves, from parishes like Rapides, St. Landry, Lafayette, St. Mary, St. Martin and Lafourche, one can imagine the difficult overland trips they must have made, accompanied by deputy sheriffs, traveling to the penitentiary—probably on foot, as slaves were expected to walk, or perhaps following dirt roads in wagons— looking around at the countryside as they passed, wondering if this would be the last time they saw the outside world.

The great majority of the slave women in prison had been convicted of capital offenses; when they did not get the death penalty, life imprisonment was intended to be the only sentencing option. The crimes they had committed included arson, murder, poisoning, attempt to poison, assault and wounding, and wounding a white mistress, all theoretically punishable by execution when committed by slaves.

Table 2 indicates, however, that the types of crimes for which antebellum women were imprisoned differ categorically by race and status. Consistent with Celeste's 1852 group, 33 slave women were convicted and imprisoned for the same types of offenses. One hundred per cent of the slave women's crimes were designated as violent offenses. Judging by their offenses, it appears that

Table II

Offenses by Race

Types of Crimes	Slaves #	%	FWC #	%	White #	%
Violent Crime						
Murder	4	12.1			2	8.7
Arson	10	30.3			1	4.3
Manslaughter	2	6.1			2	8.7
Poisoning	4	12.1			–	–
Attempted poisoning	6	18.2			–	–
Assault to kill	2	6.1			–	–
Assault to wound	1	3.0			–	–
Wounding white mistress	1	3.0			–	–
Striking white	1	3.0			–	–
Assault white	2	6.1			–	–
Mayhem	–	–			1	4.3
Attempt to set fire	–	–			1	4.3
Subtotals	33	100	---		7	30.4
Property Crime						
Larceny			1	20	9	39.1
Entering dwelling house (daytime)					1	4.3
Receiving stolen goods					3	13.0
Counterfeiting/forged coin					3	13.0
Subtotal			1	20	16	69.4
Other Crime						
Perjury			1	20	---	
Emigrant/Contravention to law			3	60		–
Subtotal			4	80	23	99.8
TOTAL	33	100	5	100	23	99.8

Totals do not add to 100 percent because of rounding.

most of the slave women had escaped death sentences. Only the two slave women convicted of manslaughter would not have been at risk of execution, as manslaughter was technically not an offense under the Black Code. Because slaves were perceived as human beings once they committed any criminal act, the courts held that they could be charged with any criminal offense. Not limited to the Slave Code charges only, the two slave women could therefore be convicted of manslaughter.

Although only five free women of color were found in the penitentiary, most of them were there because of problems regarding their marginal legal status. Even though Louisiana's free people of color constituted one of the largest populations in the antebellum South, various attempts were made through the years to restrict their numbers. White inhabitants often feared that free people of color would join with the slaves and revolt. Consequently, extensive legal restrictions regulated the entry of free blacks into the state.

These statutes were selectively enforced in practice. Three free women of color had been convicted of being in the state "in contravention of the law" or as "emigrant." Each of these offenders previously had been given an official bond notice stating they had 60 days to leave the state. If found in the state past that time they would automatically have to serve one year in the penitentiary.

The three free women of color were thus imprisoned because they were illegal immigrants. The other two were convicted of perjury and larceny. Liza Discon, charged with perjury, denied her son's identity in order to help him establish his right as a legitimate heir and administrator of an estate. In this case Discon was attempting to help her son "passant en blanc." The court did not believe her and sentenced her to five years. By contrast the larceny case was similar to white women's patterns of offenses, the only case not relevant to the marginal status of free woman of color.

Finally, although seven of the 23 white women were found guilty of violent crimes, the remaining 16 were convicted of property crimes such as larceny, receiving stolen goods, and various activities related to counterfeiting. Consistent with women's offending patterns into this century, white women were convicted for larceny more often than any other offense. The types of crimes they committed suggest that they were

women with few material resources, who in some cases had to negotiate both room and board in exchange for work. Antebellum offenders shoplifted from stores and stole from families who had employed them. The most common items stolen were articles of clothing and pieces of cloth.

For example, when Catherine Miller was caught shoplifting a piece of merino cloth worth $6 at V. Menville's Dry Goods Store, also recovered were two alpaca pallots from John Hahn's clothing store, worth $3 each. In addition to the cloth and pallets, Miller had two worsted shirts and two remnants of calico which could not be identified. Charged with two counts of larceny for the stolen goods, Catherine Miller was imprisoned a year for shoplifting goods worth a total of $12.

Mary McDonald also spent a year in the penitentiary, for taking goods worth $13. McDonald had stolen a number of articles from Eliza Hartwell, including one cloak worth $10, one lace cap worth $1, and two pieces of calico worth $1 each. In the complaint recorded on November 21, 1847, Hartwell claimed that McDonald "had been living [with her] on charity for a few days past."

Three white women were imprisoned for various counterfeiting activities. The two for which information is known, Mary Grogan and Sabrina Moore, were each charged with counterfeiting and were given disparate sentences—Grogan a year and Moore only three months. Moore was charged with "uttering forged coin" (she attempted to pass a forged half-dollar piece to buy some cooked food in the market); Grogan was found in possession of 216 counterfeit half-dollar pieces, and also the plaster of paris molds used to make the counterfeit coins. Although it was not known at the time of Moore's arrest, she had been living at the same house with Grogan. A woman who initially looked like a poor hungry soul, Moore may well have been part of the famous New Orleans "Irish girls" counterfeiting ring. If she was, she was fortunate to get off with only three months in prison.

The majority of the apparently poor white women in the penitentiary were serving short sentences for relatively minor property offenses. The slave women appear to be a much more violent group than the white women. But counting only those crimes in which someone died—murder, manslaughter and poisoning—only 10, or less than one-third of slave crimes, are serious violent offenses. About 20% of the white women's crimes can be similarly classified.

The most heinous offense we have record of was a murder committed by a white woman. Ann Jane Doyle was well known for "butchering the German along with two accomplices." Intending to rob a guest in her boarding house, Mrs. Doyle and her male companions accidently killed the man with a drug overdose. For reasons unknown, they then cut him up in pieces and hid the body parts under the floor in the boarding house. This bloody crime was the media sensation of 1838 New Orleans.

The third assumption, that women served short sentences, describes the free women but not the slaves. Of the three white women who had life sentences— Ann Jane Doyle, Catherine Rohfritch and Bridget Fury—all were released early. None spent more than five years in the penitentiary. Although Doyle committed the most heinous offense of all the incarcerated women, she served only five years before her release.

Catherine Rohfritch had been convicted with her husband of arson, apparently burning their coffee shop for the insurance. Rohfritch was pardoned March 13, 1860, after serving only three years of a life sentence. Her husband John remained in the penitentiary.

Finally, Bridget Fury was convicted of murder in 1860 and should have been transferred to New Orleans with the other prisoners for the duration of the war. She does not appear in the next available report which lists the state convicts remaining in the New Orleans Parish Prison on August 16, 1864. Apparently, Fury served at most four years of her life sentence for stabbing a man to death, allegedly because he offended her with a casual remark.

In contrast, the 13 slave lifers confined with Celeste served from nine to 24 years of their sentences, spending an average of 15.7 years in the penitentiary. Of the 33 slave women admitted to the penitentiary, only three were pardoned. Letie, property of E. Jackson from East Feliciana Parish, received a death sentence for attempting to poison her master. Her death sentence was commuted to life, and she was pardoned in March 1857 after serving only three years, the shortest term of any of the slave lifers. Phoebe, at age 12 the youngest woman ever admitted to the penitentiary, was convicted of wounding her white mistress with an axe. Also commuted to life, she was released in March 1857 after serving 10 years. Rhoda, convicted of arson in New Orleans in 1839, was finally pardoned in March 1860 after serving 21 years.

Seven women died in the penitentiary. Only one of these women was a white woman. Catherine Walsh, convicted of larceny from New Orleans, died in October 1856, just two months short of serving her full two years. The story is much different for the slave women, six of whom, almost one-fifth, died in the penitentiary.

In fact, four of the first five women sent to the penitentiary died there. Eliza, sentenced in 1833 for attempting to poison, died at age 42 of inflammation of the brain after serving 24 years. Also convicted for attempting to poison, Nancy, aged 48, died of influenza in 1843 after serving eight years of a life sentence. Mary, who was sentenced in 1831 for attempting to poison, died in 1840 after serving nine years. The younger Celeste, serving life for murder, never returned to St. Mary Parish as she died in 1854 after serving 18 years in the penitentiary. Sophy, convicted of arson in Lafayette Parish, and admitted to the penitentiary June 14, 1859, served less than a year. Even though the state paid Jane Timms, midwife, $10 "for attendance of convict woman Sophie [sic]" on January 2, 1860, Sophy was dead of tetanus by April 25, 1860.

And what of Celeste, the "old woman" of the Walls? The legislature apparently never responded to the 1852 Board's recommendation for "old" Celeste's pardon. She died in the penitentiary on September 27, 1853, less than one year after the Board discovered her. Both state auditor and parish conveyance records reveal that no one ever requested compensation for Celeste.

Only pardons and death gained the women early release from the penitentiary. No evidence of "good time" releases appears in this data. An examination of the sentencing, pardon and release patterns clearly illustrates the different treatment of slave women compared to the other incarcerated women. In almost all cases, slave women not only received the longest sentences, but actually spent the longest time in prison of all three groups. Even

in cases where slave women somehow got out of prison alive and early, they had served a considerably longer period of time than the free women.

The sentencing and release patterns of Louisiana's antebellum penitentiary were a precursor of Southern incarceration patterns after the Civil War and into the present day for African-American women. From before Emancipation, African-American women have constituted the majority of Louisiana's imprisoned women.

CONCLUSIONS

My research into antebellum Louisiana's imprisoned women counters many traditional ideas about Southern pre-Civil War imprisonment. Contrary to the established belief that slaves were not found in Southern penitentiaries, Louisiana continuously imprisoned men and women slaves (who represented a third of the total prison population during the 1850s). Even though Southern historians agree that women could seldom be found in any antebellum Southern penitentiary, Louisiana was again the exception.

For all the years for which the information is available, never were there fewer than five women in the Baton Rouge penitentiary. During the decade of the 1850s there were always at least 12 imprisoned women, constituting at least 5% of the imprisoned population. The proportion of female prisoners in Louisiana's antebellum penitentiary is comparable to the 1980s in both state and national figures, when female imprisonment was supposed to be at an all time high.

Other studies have tended to emphasize the impact of Emancipation in changing Southern prison populations from almost exclusively white to predominantly black. But in the Louisiana State Penitentiary prior to Emancipation, African-American women were already in the majority.

Louisiana's Black Code, which allowed for the substitution of life imprisonment for execution, did spare these slave women's lives, but it also resulted in a unique Southern incarceration pattern: in Louisiana's antebellum penitentiary, white women came and went, while black women came to stay.

4

CHANGES IN THE CONVICT SYSTEM*

Soon will the extensive but dilapidated buildings known as the Louisiana state penitentiary pass into a memory. To many it will be a most unpleasant one, and few will have occasion to regret that it has passed away. For sixty-seven years it existed and was used for the purpose originally intended, but while progress was the watchword in every other public institution, the Louisiana state penitentiary retained the features of the prisons of half a century ago, and for the past thirty years at least there has been no change, no legislation looking to the improvement or betterment of the condition of the people who, defying the laws, had felt the power of its wrath.

A great many people like to look upon the misery or wretchedness of others, and to such the Louisiana state penitentiary was an attraction; and societies giving excursions to Baton Rouge during the summer were wont to advertise the fact that excursionists would be allowed to visit the institution as an additional attraction. Then crowds of people, most of them friends—perhaps relatives—of some of the unfortunate inmates, would flock into the confines of the state prison and look upon the convicts with various emotions. The convicts themselves rather enjoyed these weekly visits, for it was a variation of the dreadful monotony of their existence. Some, however, still retained sufficient pride to seek concealment to hide their shame from the outer world.

Now all this will be changed. The penitentiary will be such only in name, and every convict consigned to the state penitentiary who is able will be sent away, and only those will remain who are physically incapacitated from doing manual labor. The old, the weak, the sick and the cripples will be kept within the walls, provided there can be found no employment of kind suitable to them elsewhere in the property which the state has recently acquired with a view to employing them to better advantage than heretofore. Instead of sending all the prisoners (males) to the levee camps to toil in the swamps, subject to exposure from the weather, and to work of such a nature that only the very strongest and most robust men could endure, a distinction will be made, and the CONVICTS WILL RECEIVE BETTER CARE AND TREATMENT, while it is hoped that the advantages accruing to the state will be much greater than under the old rules and regulations.

The Louisiana state penitentiary was erected in 1834. It was modeled after the famous "Tombs" in New York, which was at that time considered the model prison of this continent. It is only necessary to look at the arrangements of the interior of the old building to see why the institution from which it was copied was called the Tombs. Four tiers of cells, placed one above the other, for all the world like the crypts in the tombs in the cemeteries of ancient date, no doubt gave it the name in New York, and the only reason perhaps that the Louisiana state penitentiary did not also receive the name was that the authorities did not want to be tautological. The cells or crypts are about 4 feet wide by 7 feet long, and into these holes the prisoners were thrust every night, and the iron faced doors, with openings not much larger than 12 inches square, guarded by

*Appeared in the *New Orleans Daily Picayune,* January 9, 1901, 6. Reprinted with permission.

heavy iron bars were closed upon them. There was no ventilation, and the tiers of cells being inclosed in high walls roofed over, and with but few openings, they were damp, warm and unhealthy in summer, and cold, damp and unhealthy in winter. To warm the prison was impossible, and it was equally an impossible task to cool the place in summer, so the prisoners sweltered in summer and froze in winter, without any chance for alleviating their sufferings, even had the authorities been ever so well disposed.

After the first building was erected, as the number of convicts increased, it was found necessary to add to it. Then additions were built just like the original, and in consequence there are now two buildings containing in the aggregate 850 cells, one just like the other as far as discomfort was concerned. One of the buildings, which contained about half the number of cells, say 425, has not been in use for a long time, and the bats and an immense number of pigeons have quartered themselves within, and there they lay their eggs and hatch young birds in security, for rarely does any one visit either of the unused buildings.

Other additions were made from time to time. An infirmary was built, but one day a cyclone came along and struck it and killed twelve prisoners and wounded thirty. The wall fell in on July 6, 1891, but was rebuilt almost immediately after the cyclone.

Among other additions was a three-story brick cotton factory, a building about 300 feet long and about 50 feet wide, and an immense quantity of cotton spinning machinery was placed therein. The cotton mill ran for a time, one of the partners in the enterprise being the state of Louisiana, and the other the penitentiary

lessees. It was a losing venture and never could be made to pay, so it was finally abandoned. There lies the machinery yet, a pile of old junk, which will one day be sold for perhaps a hundred dollars, and that is ALL THAT REMAINS TO SHOW FOR THE EXPENDITURE of hundreds of thousands of dollars. Looms, spindles, carding machines, bolts, rods, bars, pieces of shafting, belting and various pieces of machinery are piled up on the damp floor in a heterogeneous mass, unfit for any use except to melt the metal over again and manufacture modern machinery out of it. The only portion of the old cotton mill machinery that can ever be put to any use in its present shape is the shafting, which is intact, the one part of the establishment which still remains in the position it was put originally.

After failing to make cotton spinners of the convicts, they tried to make shoemakers of them, but this was also unsuccessful. They then tried to make carpenters and tinkers of them and built a factory for the building of refrigerators. This, too, fell through, and then they tried to make tailors of the prisoners. A hundred sewing machines were laid in, and the third floor of the old cotton mill was cleared of the machinery, which was thrown into piles on the lower floor. The sewing machines were run by steam power, and cutting tables as there are in a regular pants factory in town, were placed in position. Clothing was manufactured, but the outside manufacturers objected and the product of the state penitentiary was boycotted and they had to quit this also. Other industries were attempted, but all failed and at length nothing remained but to send the convicts out to work on the levees, for this was work that did not enter into competition with honest labor to any appreciable extent. But it was hard work, and not every convict could endure the exposure and toil, and the result was that many sickened, some died, and some became invalids for life.

The penitentiary property is about 1,000 feet long, by about 300 feet in width, and on this ground stands buildings which would shelter an army. They are, it is true, in bad repair, but the walls are solid and firm, the roofs of slate, water tight, and the flooring in the upper stories in fairly good condition. The buildings, which are all of brick, could be placed in repair, but there is no more need for them as a prison. Only two of the buildings are in use, the cells where the prisoners are confined at night, and the hospital, but when the plans of the present board of control are carried out, not even this much of the buildings will be necessary.

There are at present within the walls 123 inmates and 5 female prisoners, and these are nearly all recent arrivals. Several batches which have arrived within the past three or four months still remain within the walls, the lessees, whose lease expired on the 1st of January, 1901, not deeming it necessary to send them to the works or the various convict camps established throughout the state.

When the property was transferred to the board on the 1st of January, 1,014 prisoners were among the property, and these were scattered throughout the state. The main object of the board of control will be first TO MAKE THE CONVICTS SELF-SUSTAINING, and, if possible, profitable to the state, instead of a burden.

It was also intended to improve the condition of the prisoners, and to keep a strict watch and ward over them, and at the same time keep an accurate record of all their movements and their condition. This is, in brief, an outline of the work which the board has before it.

Since the penitentiary was first leased out the world has progressed. The treatment of convicts and prisoners has been a subject which has enlisted the attention of the humane and charitable people, and no longer are they looked upon in well-regulated communities as being beyond the pale of humanity. They are no longer treated as animals, but as human beings, in whom there yet remains some good which might be developed, and the convict or prisoner yet become a good and useful citizen. There are many kinds of work which convicts can do that will not clash or enter into competition with honest labor, and this is the kind of work the board intends to put them to.

The penitentiary was first leased in 1868, while Joshua Baker was governor of the state of Louisiana. The lease was first given to Messrs. Jones and Huger, on March 31, 1868, for a term of five years, the conditions being that the state was to derive one-half the profits which should accrue from the work of the convicts. The lease was approved by Major General Hancock, who was then commander of the fifth military district. The lessees were to advance all the moneys necessary to carry out the project, and for the support and management of the convicts. The employment of the convicts was stipulated in the lease. They might be employed in all manufacturing or mechanical work, and such active labor as the lessees might deem proper, including the right to employ them in brickyards and tanneries outside of the walls, or in hauling wood or other useful labor in the vicinity of Baton Rouge, which might be advantageous. They were also allowed to work a portion of the able-bodied convicts on levees and on railroads for the joint account of the state and lessees. It was also stipulated that the lessees should establish, as soon as practical, cotton and woolen cloth factories, the state to furnish the necessary funds, which were, however, subsequently to be reimbursed by the lessees to the amount of one-half the original cost.

There were numerous other stipulations, all properly safeguarded by bonds furnished by the lessees. It was also obligatory on the part of the lessees to furnish each discharged convict with $10 in money and a suit of rough clothing, and $100 was to be applied annually to purchase books for the convicts. The cotton factory was to have 200 looms for the manufacture of cotton cloth, and as many as might be deemed necessary to make woolen cloth within the walls.

In 1870 the lease was bought from Messrs. Jones and Huger by Messrs. S.L. James, C.B. Buckner and T. Bynum, and a new lease from 1870 to 1891 was signed, H. C. Warmoth being then the governor. This was signed April 8, 1870, and was for twenty-one years, but the state dissolved the partnership with the lessees in this lease, the new lessees being expected to pay $5,000 for the first year, $6,000 for the second year, $7,000 for the third, increasing $1,000 each year, until the expiration of the lease so that at the twenty-first year the lessees would be expected to pay $25,000.

In 1891 the lease was renewed for ten years, and this is the lease which expired on the 1st of January last. In 1875 the legislature made an amendment to the law which made it unlawful to employ convicts on any public or contract work outside of the walls, and if sentenced by the courts to hard labor, the convicts were expected to perform this labor inside the walls. This was, in fact, the only legislation with regard to the state penitentiary that had been taken since the contract system went into effect. Of late

years the convicts were used almost exclusively on levee work, and being in the camps nearly all the time, the buildings were not utilized, and, therefore ALLOWED TO FALL INTO DECAY but still it was thought that the buildings might become useful in cases of emergency when it might be necessary to withdraw all the convicts outside the walls and bring them in.

During the lessee system 15,032 convicts were admitted into the penitentiary, one of the first prisoners admitted being John Angelo, who was received in 1866, and was sentenced for life for murder, his name appearing first in the books and numbered 5. The No. 1 of the present system is Mary Davis, of Orleans parish, convicted of robbery.

The present board is constituted as follows: C. Harrison Parker, president; Ed P. White and G.A. Kilgore, treasurer and secretary. Upon assuming charge the board appointed Mr. L.B. Duncan captain of the penitentiary, George Fisher, bull pen guard; Charles Hariat, James Jamison and John Murchy, yard guards, and Dr. Sterling, physician. One of the first orders issued to Captain Duncan was to inspect the prisoners and find out how many of them were able-bodied men, and how many would be incapacitated from heavy work by reason of delicate health. The board also desired to ascertain how many of the prisoners within the walls could operate sewing machines or were cutters, the idea being to commence as soon as possible to manufacture clothing, such as was required by the convicts. The captain found seventy able-bodied men in the walls who would be able to endure the work on the levees. One cutter and about ten or twelve machine operators were found, and as soon as everything is arranged, these will be placed at work in the clothing factory. From 6,000 to 8,000 suits of clothing will be required annually for the convicts, and from 5,000 to 6,000 pairs of shoes, and all these will, in the course of time, be manufactured in the penitentiary, within the walls. Should the force of clothing manufacturers be able to make more clothing than the convicts will require they will be set to work manufacturing clothing for the inmates of the state insane asylum or other public institutions. No clothing or shoes will be made for sale or to enter into competition with honest labor.

Up to the present time all the convicts who became ill were sent to the hospital in the walls, there being no accommodations provided for the sick in the various camps.   The board will establish hospitals outside in the camps, and thus the penitentiary hospital will be relieved. At the present time there are only a few chronic cases in the hospital in the walls, and all of these are doing well.

Yesterday a communication was sent to Governor Heard, stating that the necessity for quarters and hospitals on the Hope and Angola plantations were very necessary, and plans had been asked for and submitted. The governor was requested to examine the plans at his earliest convenience, and they will probably be examined this week, when work will be commenced forthwith. The board has not sufficient funds on hand to erect brick buildings, and, therefore, have decided to build frame structures, which will be completed rapidly.

A thorough and complete system has been inaugurated in the office of the board, and the three members are devoting all their time, energy and talents to bringing about the reforms they intend to institute. A stenographer, a bookkeeper and a clerk is all the force they have employed, and

these are worked all day and far into the night.

THE   STATUS   OF   EVERY PRISONER turned over to the board has been examined and new numbers commencing at No. 1 have been given them. A record of time, their condition, where they are at work and how employed, their state of health, how long they have to serve, etc., has all been arranged, and all business is conducted on the voucher system. Reports have to be made by all the officers at frequent intervals, and in cases of sickness special reports are required at once.

President Parker visited Captain Hurst's camp, on bayou Lafourche, immediately after taking charge, and upon his arrival there he found that illness prevailed in the camp.   The camp is located about three miles from Labadieville, on bayou Lafourche, and upon his arrival there he found that the regular physician of the camp, Dr. Truxillo, was ill, and that Dr. Landry was acting in his stead. He sent Dr. Landry, as he thought that there was something suspicious about the illness which had been reported to him as prevailing among the men. Dr. Landry investigated, and reported that smallpox was prevalent. Colonel Parker at once instructed the physician to vaccinate all the convicts who had not yet been attacked, and sent for disinfectants and supplies to Donaldsonville, which was the nearest accessible and convenient point. The camp was thoroughly fumigated and disinfected, and the sick people isolated as far as possible. This caused a change in the plans of the board, who had intended to distribute the prisoners, it being impossible to remove the men from Hurst's camp, as they might carry the infection into other camps. The doctor was to cooperate with Captain Hurst, and to make every effort to stamp out the disease. The main office of the board of health was notified of the state of affairs existing in Hurst's camp, and the board of health sent a physician out there, and yesterday word was received that three cases had proven fatal, and that nineteen cases were under treatment. Colonel Parker also notified the office of the board in Baton Rouge, and Secretary Kilgore at once acquainted the governor with the facts in the case. A special agent was dispatched from Baton Rouge to investigate and report, and yesterday another agent was sent to the camp with instructions to purchase all the necessary supplies, to contract for the supply of fresh meat every day to the sick, and thrice a week for the men who were well. He also instructed the agent to provide for a daily supply of fresh water, and under no circumstances would the convicts or keepers be allowed to drink the bayou water. He was also authorized to contract for a supply of fresh milk daily for the sick, as well as for any food or supplies which the surgeon might think proper to order for the sick. Colonel Parker held that it was a heavy expense on the state to treat the sick, and the quicker the patients or convalescents regained their strength and got well the better for all concerned. Everything possible has been done by the board to stay the spread of the disease and to cure those attacked. Among those who died was Dr. Truxillo. How the disease came into the camp, except that the physician himself introduced it, the captain of the camp was unable to say. He stated that not far from the camp a man was sick with smallpox, and he had placed a guard to prevent any of the convicts from going near the place. Dr. Truxillo, however, was attending the patient, and also visited the camp professionally, and it may be that the disease was thus introduced.

The new board is in no wise to blame for the state of affairs existing in Hurst's camp, and are ready and willing, and have done all in their power, to keep the disease from spreading. All the other camps visited were found in excellent condition as regarded the health of the prisoners. In one camp not one man was on the sick list, and in another only one was sick, but the disease was not of a contagious character.

THE FOLLOWING DISTRIBUTION of men has been decided upon:

Three hundred convicts will be placed on the Angola plantation to cultivate cotton. The plantation consists of 9,000 acres, of which 2,300 will be cultivated in cotton and 100 acres in corn, cowpeas, vegetables, etc.

Two hundred convicts will be put to work on the Hope plantation to raise sugar. One hundred will be used to cultivate sugar on the 1,000 acres of cleared land, and it is expected that by spring 400 or 500 acres will be ready for planting, in which corn will be planted. Next year this new land will be planted in cane. There is a sugar mill on the place, with a capacity to dispose of the crop of all the lands, some 2,800 acres, as well as the crop of the 200 adjoining, known as the Rosedale plantation, the lease of which was conveyed to the state in the title to the Hope plantation. The Hope plantation only cost the state $78,000, while the mill alone on the place is appraised at $115,000.

This will leave two levee camps of 200 men each, and these will be recruited from time to time from the convicts sent to the penitentiary. Only first-class, healthy and strong, able-bodied men will be selected for these camps. Great care is to be exercised in selecting the class of work for the convicts.

With regard to the penitentiary buildings and the grounds, they are the property of the state and cannot be disposed of. Under the present system not one-tenth of the grounds or buildings would be necessary, and they could be put to other uses. The board has not gotten fully to work as yet, as the undertaking is a colossal one, but the members of the board are energetic, active and tireless, and are working hard to make the penitentiary system of the state of Louisiana a model one.

5

BLOOD TOOK PENITENTIARY
"OUT OF RED"*

by R. L. Krebs

They made money out of the state penitentiary while Huey P. Long, O. K. Allen, Richard W. Leche and others with briefer official terms were governors of Louisiana. It was one of the proudest boasts of the old administration that the penitentiary had been put "on a paying basis."

The Angola and St. Gabriel prison farms had lost money for years before the machine took over the state in 1928. The machine politicians promised the taxpayers they would take the penitentiary "out of the red"—and they did.

But they didn't tell the people of Louisiana that money they were making at the penitentiary—and stealing 20 times as fast from other departments and institutions—was coming from blood and sweat and agony of 10,000 officially recorded floggings.

There was nothing said about the more than 30 convicts, beaten in cane, rice and vegetable fields with five-foot clubs, redoubled grass ropes, blacksnake whips and in later years with the lashes of the captains, who dropped dead of "sunstroke" (one of them in the month of March).

There was little or no publicity about the more than 40 convicts shot dead in officially reported attempts to escape. They were silent about the scores and even hundreds of convicts scourged with as many as 50 and 60 blows of the lash for having dared to escape or attempt to escape from the floggers they had placed in charge of the prison camps.

NO FLOGGING LAW

There had been floggings at Angola and St. Gabriel for years almost without number. There was no law that said the penitentiary authorities had the right to beat a convict's bare flesh into a red jelly for asserted infractions of prison rules. There was no law—and is none today— that said they didn't have the right to do it.

So they went ahead and did it anyway. Most citizens believed, or wished to believe, that it wasn't being done. Others were sure that flogging was being resorted to only in extreme instances.

When the Huey P. Long administration took charge of the penitentiary, flogging at first reached the proportions only of an officially 191 punishments in the second six months of 1928—at the rate of some 400 floggings with a total of 3700 blows of the lash, for a 12-month period.

Five years later, in 1933, according to the official record, floggings totaled 1547, with 23,889 recorded blows of the double lash. Shortly prior to this the machine orators had been able to report proudly to the people of Louisiana that the penitentiary at last was making money.

It was a simple plan that the machine evolved to take the state penitentiary out of the red. Most of the food consumed by the convicts was raised at Angola and St. Gabriel. Clothing—such as it was—other supplies, and the salaries of the officials, captains and overseers, mainly came from

*Appeared in the *New Orleans Times-Picayune,* May 11, 1941, 2:4-5. Reprinted with permission.

the sale of sugar, manufactured from cane grown at Angola and St. Gabriel. If the sugar crop was large enough, the penitentiary would clear money above its expenses.

FORMULA IN COUPLET

A formula was found to ensure the growing of a good crop. It was summarized in an eloquent couplet carpentered from the cynical remark of a high official at Angola:

"Never mind the weather;
We'll buy a car of leather."

Sole leather was what he was talking about. They made the lashes out of it. Strangely enough these lashes—referred to in the prison slang as "the little man in the brown bag"—were made in the shoe shop at Angola itself. Of the hundreds of officials, supporters and favorites of the administration who were turning dishonest dollars to their own personal profit, none seems to have seen the opportunity to make a little out of Angola's flogging tools.

There were two belts of leather in the lash, attached at one end to a wooden handle sufficiently heavy to fell any obstreperous convict who might seek to resist a flogging. The leather belts were loose at the other end. They were thick as the sole of a shoe, three or four inches wide and some five feet long.

Three or four blows vigorously applied to a convict's bare back could and generally did break the skin. Few prisoners failed to start screaming at the fifth or sixth blow. As many as 35 could put a convict in the hospital. Punishments of 50 lashes, however, were not uncommon, the records disclose, in the days when the machine was "making money" at Angola.

BEATEN FOR "LAZINESS"

In 1929, the first full year of the machine administration, the standard punishment at Angola for "laziness" was eight blows of the lash. Frequently it was as few as five or six. Infrequently it might be 10, or in rare cases (with violence reported additionally as justification) 12 or 15 lashes. In 1932, one of the five "flogging captains" installed by the "make money at Angola" administration reported punishments of 43 cases of 12 lashes and 29 of 14 lashes. Another captain reported 15 lashes in 71 cases and as high as 25 lashes in three cases. A third captain gave 10 lashes in 22 instances, 15 in 28 instances and 25 lashes in nine cases.

But other offenses had been evolved at Angola.

In harvesting cane, the last joint of the cane stalk next to the ground had the most sucrose in it, and accordingly yielded the most sugar at the mill. A convict failing to bend low enough with his cane knife to cut off the stalk level with the ground was adjudged guilty of leaving "high stubble" and flogged accordingly. For the pennies that the state lost on each joint the penalty ranged from 10 to 25 blows of the lash. Similarly if the top of the stalk were trimmed too low, with the result that even one joint with a minimum of juice from which sugar might be made was left in the field, a grave offense was adjudged to have been committed, and settlement was made with the prisoner accordingly.

Sinister in the reports were the punishments for "windrowing," "covering cane" and "leaving cane in the field." Not only was the convict required to cut the cane at the ground to avoid leaving high stubble, and to trim it high enough at the top so as not to be charged with "cutting tops low" but additionally to trim it of the cane leaves and throw it out to one side. Lazy workers early discovered that by merely cutting the stalk off at the ground and leaving it buried in its own foliage they might conceivably escape punishment for further evidence of bad work.

FLOG LAST 5 MEN

This also became a desperate expedient to escape a flogging, after the "make money at Angola" administration had evolved a "speeding up" process in the harvesting of cane. A hundred or more convicts in the "long line" would be placed, each at the end of a long row of cane to be harvested. The last five reaching the ends of their rows were forthwith flogged. It worked infallibly, since no matter how diligently the entire crew labored and sweated in the hot sun, five simply had to be last. An unfortunate, lagging behind his companions, might successfully "cover up" an occasional stalk in his effort to keep up with more robust workers—but frequently, as indicated by the records, the pitiful stratagem did not work.

"Bad work" accounted simply for many floggings under the new regimen. "Bad plowing" was a not infrequent entry in the books. "Inferior work" could justify the blows delivered on a prisoner's bare flesh. There were numerous variations of this motif.

Beatings in the field were not a matter of official record.

It was in the sudden dawn, between the harsh cellroom "rapup" that woke the convicts from uneasy sleep and the mustering in ranks in the camp yard that preceded the trip to the field for the long

day's work, that the official floggings generally took place.

They had been locked up in the cellroom the night before, together with a civilian employee and a trusty guard. With faint daylight came breakfast—such as it was—and a lineup for the final checkoff. It was then the captain of the camp received his reports—from the cellroom man if he had any disturbances of which to complain; from the field superintendents and foremen on major offenses in the field sufficiently expiated on the spot with heads bloodied by clubs and doubled ropes, or bodies beribboned by blacksnake whips.

Some shuddering convict in the apprehensive ranks perhaps already was prepared for the summons to step forward. He might be the only one signaled out for chastisement. On occasions there were three or four others, taken in ashen-faced surprise as their names were called. Generally the two men on either side of the selected victim were designated to "throw" him face down on the grass in the yard, or even on the concrete walk.

NO TRIAL, NO APPEAL

"Please, captain, don't do me that way! Please, captain, I won't do it again!" a quaking prisoner might appeal.

"Throw him down," the captain would sternly admonish, as a servile trusty handed him the lash.

There was no appeal here. There was no trial. There had been no orders from the main office. It was not necessary even to advise the unfortunate victims of the charges on which they went under the lash. The captain might not have any definite idea even as to how many times he proposed to flay against the convict's bare skin.

Two of his comrades have him by the wrists as he writhes and twists face down on the ground. Two others have him by the ankles. The captain swings the lash until he feels that perhaps he has administered half the necessary punishment. Lash trailing, he walks around to the other side to complete the flogging.

Unfortunate the man who managed to break loose; to turn on the captain, seize the lash, to threaten the person of the sacred dispenser of "Angola justice." Resisting punishment was an unforgivable crime. Then blows about the head, the unprotected stomach, other parts of the anatomy almost certainly would be rained until abject submission had been enforced.

There was no particular compulsion on other convicts to witness the brutality. They might turn their backs, stroll away even to the limit of the encircling fence. At an extreme distance of a hundred feet their ears—after the falling of the fourth or fifth blow—could not fail to advise them of what was going on.

Angola was different from the concentration camps of the Gestapo in Germany in two respects. It was not considered necessary at Angola—or at St. Gabriel— to place wet cloths on the skin in advance of a flogging to prevent permanent scars. And, except for later years, the yard floggings were officially recorded on the books of the institution.

WRECKED RELEASE HOPE

Not for the information of the public, however. A man officially flogged at Angola not only underwent the pain and humiliation of the beating, but the fact of its being recorded on the books served the further purpose of automatically placing a blackmark against his record which unless

subsequently removed would deprive him of his good time allowance against his maximum sentence. In many of the flogging cases the blackmarks later were removed; in many others, however, the convict served out the last long day of his maximum legal sentence.

It has been four years since Edward Paige, a Negro Pullman porter, died at Angola. The official death report says he was shot "trying to escape." Angola's records are now open to the newspapers. The folder on Paige throws an interesting light on how brutalities went so long unchecked.

He was convicted of murder without capital punishment in New Orleans and sent to the penitentiary for a life term on October 15, 1932. According to official records Captain W. H. Pittman on March 26, 1934, gave him 15 blows of the lash for "insolence." Later he became a trusty waiter in Pittman's camp.

On July 26, 1937, Paige wrote a letter to the then warden, Louie A. Jones. At that time his application for a pardon was pending before the board of pardons, with good prospects. Said his letter:

"Warden Jones—Several months ago I came to your office asking you to transfer me to another camp so I could serve my term in prison . . . You inform me to go back to my camp and try to get along, you would take care of my case. That you did, warden. Until two weeks ago, Captain Pittman [was] in the same mood."

"Warden, I knows that prison is a place of punishment. And I am doing all I can to obey all prison rules. Warden, as my first complaint Captain Pittman had a prison mind toward me. I cannot please him. I knows warden you well experienced in the nature of mankind. Please transfer me to another camp where I can serve my time. Friday past Captain

Pittman strapped two cooks and said I were next. Warden, I would not want to be strapped and blackmarked over hate."

That same day, according to penitentiary records, Paige was transferred to the camp of Captain J. N. Reaux. The next morning, however, he was back in Pittman's camp. The records are silent as to how that happened.

FACE SHOT AWAY

Pittman "broke" him from trusty waiter into the "line" and he was sent out to the field. That evening Pittman sent in a "special death report" to the main office. At 3 o'clock that afternoon Convict Paige's face had been shot away by a trusty guard and he died of the injury. Said the report:

"Prisoner was working with long line and upon reaching the turn row he raised his hoe over his head and advanced toward Guard No. 24,623 (a convict trusty) Davie Curvin, shouting, 'Give me that gun.' Guard Curvin backed away about 20 yards and there he could go no further because of a wide canal. In order to protect his own life and prevent Prisoner Paige obtaining possession of the gun Guard Curvin shot and killed Prisoner Paige."

A coroner's jury empaneled that same afternoon found that Paige had died of wounds "inflicted at the hands of a guard in line of duty while Paige was trying to escape." Members of the jury were J. R. Davidson, H. J. Faucheaux, J. D. Washington, H. B. Wells and John B. Sewell.

An attorney for the Paige family wrote for further details of the affair, indicating their dissatisfaction, especially in view of the fact that Paige had good reason to believe he would be released in the near future by the pardon board. He further expressed surprise that there had been nothing in the newspaper about the occurrence. Said the general manager of the penitentiary in his reply:

"Paige was guilty of gross insubordination and impudence to his captain, for which he was swung to the line, not corporally punished . . ."

"Neither I nor my office have given the press news items of any kind since I have been in charge of the penitentiary. They do carry such items occasionally but secure same from other sources. I have long since learned that a press which too often colors news for one reason or another is best left to its own devices."

LAST ENTRY

Last document in the Paige folder at Angola is a memorandum from Captain Pittman to the general manager, dated August 7, 1937, containing a "list of articles belonging to Paige" which concludes with the following:

"Just prior to the prisoner's demise he gave to Prisoner 18,831, Henry Tolliver, the following:

"One billfold containing $1.13 cash."

"One toothbrush."

"Two and one-half pair of dice."

Official punishment records at Angola in the earlier years of the machine regime closely parallel the rising curve of profits. From a total of 599 floggings in 1929 the punishment record rose swiftly to 766 floggings and a total of 9,597 officially recorded blows of the lash in 1930; to 1219 floggings with a total of 15,897 lashes in 1931; to 1494 floggings and 20,947 blows of the lash in 1932; to 1547 floggings and 23,889 lashes in 1933. These were the punishments reported officially, for the purpose of demeriting the prisoner and threatening him with the loss of good time allowance.

The most severe punishment recorded in 1929 was the 45 lashes given a convict for "impudence and resisting punishment." Second in severity was 40 lashes for fighting and threatening a guard. Third was 35 lashes for laziness, impudence and resisting punishment. All were administered by Captain W. F. Gay. No other captain officially reported a punishment as high as 35 lashes.

MORE LASH, MORE CASH

In 1933 there were 42 officially recorded punishments of 35 lashes or more, of which nearly half were 50 lashes, one was 60 lashes, and one 66 lashes.

Even before this the general manager had been able proudly to report that the remedy for the financial ills of the penitentiary was beginning to take effect. In May, 1932, the official report of the institution declared:

"I would not say that we are making money. I prefer to say that the penitentiary is living within its income. . . . Though denying itself many needed things it can live in a manner becoming to the dignity and humanitarian ideals of our citzens."

The use of clubs on occasion—never officially noted in the punishment records—was admitted by inference. Defending floggings and other forms of corporal punishment, the report of that year went on to say:

"To keep the convict separate from society is partly a physical problem and partly a spiritual problem. As a physical problem it involves iron fences, bars of steel, leather straps, clubs and guns. As a spiritual problem it involves humane treatment, a friendly attitude, tasks suited to strength and talents, trust and loyalties, work and recreation.

"The spiritual factors are the most promising and reliable though the physical factors are a necessary last resort. Therefore we rely on kind and just treatment of the prisoners, using the physical punishment as a last resort after the other fails. . . Some prison keepers and some citizens think the prisoners should be treated rough and their lives made quite miserable. We take the opposite view. His life should be made as happy as possible."

GUNS ALSO BUSY

Among the "happy" inmates of Angola and St. Gabriel 1219 floggings were officially reported. What was being done with the clubs is not of record. Guns were also quite busy. Two convicts fell before the bullets of convict guards seeking to escape. One convict was found beaten to death on the Mississippi river levee. The circumstances were never satisfactorily explained. He was J. W. Stinson, white, a Gretna bank official. One convict "died suddenly" at St. Gabriel, "cause unknown." The penitentiary that year also had its first deaths from sunstroke under the new management.

Captain J. E. Klienpeter gave a convict 12 lashes. The offense was "breaking a new razor." Whose razor was not stated.

Captain Pittman flogged four convicts for "faking illness." If there wasn't anything wrong with them when they reported at the hospital the 20 to 25 lashes they received took care of that. One unfortunate drew 10 lashes for "not cooking good." A convict charged with cutting off his finger to avoid work drew 20 lashes.

Captain T. J. Drewett was bedeviled

with prisoners escaping. It was the invariable rule to flog them if recaptured, no matter how long they had been away. He handled 18 cases of this character, meting out a total of 671 lashes. One of the unfortunates got 45 lashes and two of them 50 lashes each. Another of Drewett's charges received 50 lashes for stealing, one 20 lashes for "staying out at night" and one 15 lashes for "foul language."

MEN VS. MULES

Captain C. F. Jones handed out 10 lashes to each of two convicts for "carelessly injuring" a fellow prisoner. Mules were more valuable than convicts and their bad treatment was punished accordingly. Twenty lashes was the punishment given a prisoner charged with "carelessly injuring a mule's shoulder." The offense of eating sugar cane belonging to the state of Louisiana brought floggings to three of Jones' charges.

Captain J. N. Reaux, who flogged 184 convicts in the period, had some varied punishments to record. They included one flogging of 50 lashes, two of 45 lashes and one of 40 lashes for escaping; 25 lashes for "faking a telegram;" 25 for "refusing to work," 15 for "sleeping after rapup."

One wonders from what dreams a man could have been so rudely awakened. Dreams, perhaps of the Baton Rouge hotel, where a governor was then telling the people of the state he might as well be boarding the Angola convicts; so magnificently were they being fed, housed and clothed. The governor must have been reading the reports of his penitentiary managers; the convicts could have told him differently—the man, for instance, who was given 20 lashes for "agitating

against the food."

Captain J. H. Leggett gave a prisoner 20 lashes for "leaving camp and rambling in the woods."

R. L. Himes was general manager of the penitentiary and Wade Long was warden in those early years. Long and Himes didn't agree, according to reports, and Long had little to say about the conduct of affairs. Himes had been business manager at LSU prior to his appointment to the penitentiary. He put Angola on a paying basis, and as long as the deficits of former years did not recur, his authority was unquestioned.

He aided many convicts, shortened prison terms, instituted the system of "reprieves" that after many years was declared to be illegal. But he could not be persuaded that flogging in itself was harmful and brutalizing. Like many persons who defend corporal punishment in the abstract, it is doubtful if he ever witnessed a flogging. He accepted the word of his captains. If unusually severe punishments for apparently trivial offenses showed up in the daily reports he either didn't see them or he failed to realize their significance.

PUNISHMENTS DECLINE

His feud with Warden Long ended with the latter's retirement in 1934. Warden W. L. Whitman, who succeeded Long, got along no better with the general manager. Punishments declined in number while Whitman was at the penitentiary—although the 1935 total of 963 floggings, for a total of 16,258 lashes, certainly was hugely in excess of anything imagined by the people of Louisiana. Louie Jones became warden in 1938. That year the floggings jumped again to 1107. But in his biennial report in the spring of 1936, General Manager Himes was able to say:

"Huey P. Long did what he said he was going to do—make the penitentiary pay its own way. For five years the penitentiary has operated on its own income and has added an average of over $50,000 each year to its capital investment."

"From time to time one reads opinions directed against use of the strap. . . We use the strap where corporal punishment is needed. It works. The real question is whether the punishment is reasonable and just. In handling these convicts we are kind without being sentimental; firm without being brutal."

A few months before this was written General Manager Himes' cherished waterless cooker came loose from the back of his car and fell onto the highway, where a convict driving a cane cart ran over it. It is doubtful if the convict thought the 20 lashes he received for this mischance was a "reasonable and just" punishment. The flogging was officially reported by Captain Kleinpeter. Says the record:

"Twenty lashes—for running over Mr. Himes' waterless cooker."

LAZINESS, 25 LASHES

Some punishments taken at random from the books of that year show:

Cutting down cane, 15 lashes; attempting to escape, 35 lashes; hiding to escape work, 20 lashes; cursing trusty guard, 25 lashes; refusing to bathe, 15 lashes; destroying state property (generally cutting off the toes of shoes too small to wear), 15 lashes; cutting another prisoner, 25 lashes; laziness, 25 lashes; inferior work, 15 lashes; playing sick, 15 lashes; carelessly allowing team to run away, 15

lashes; escaping, 50 lashes; wasting peas, 15 lashes; high stubble, 15 lashes; accidentally cutting mule, 12 lashes; inferior work in cane field, 25 lashes; making beer, 30 lashes; giving away food from kitchen, 25 lashes; sleeping on guard post, 35 lashes; breaking tools, 15 lashes; destroying onion plants, 15 lashes; beating mule, 15 lashes; stealing bread, 12 lashes.

After 1936 there was a change in policy as to the reporting of punishments. Apparently either it was deemed inadvisable to have so many listed on the books, or someone in authority had raised objections. The number officially recorded dropped sharply; but the same old crowd was in charge and floggings actually reported showed no lessening of severity.

Actually the captains went into the fields with their lash. While several hundred punishments were reported in succeeding years, most of the yard floggings had been ruled out. Where the captain wanted to do flogging in the camp, the kitchen was the preferred punishment ground.

Characteristic of the new order was what took place at the women's camp. Here Captain J. M. Willis, in charge since 1929, had flogged a total of 16 Negro women up to the end of 1935—only one of them in the last two years of the period. In 1936 the officially reported floggings of women jumped to 19, there after dropped to a nominal figure.

"I was away from the camp most of 1936," declares Captain Willis. "The floggings that year were on orders of Warden Jones. I have occasionally whipped an obstreperous Negro woman because that was always the policy and I had to do it occasionally to be able even to stay at the camp. But I have never broken the skin or drawn blood with a flogging.

WOMEN LASHED

"Warden Jones had his spies and informants everywhere. After my return to duty he would come up to the camp, sometimes with a couple of assistants, direct me to call out as many as half a dozen women without even telling me what they were charged with. He would sometimes flog two or three of them himself or have his assistants do it. He would order me to flog others. Then he would tell me to report the punishments."

"How many women were flogged after you returned; a hundred?" he was asked.

"I wouldn't want to name any figure offhand, but there were plenty of them."

The official records show eight floggings from 1937 through the first half of 1940. However Captain Willis says he always wrote on his report "flogged on orders of the warden," and in only one instance does this appear on the books, indicating that most of the reports disappeared after they left his camp.

In the first five months of 1940 only 33 floggings at Angola and St. Gabriel were entered on the penitentiary books. And most of those reported were suspiciously mild. Captains who formerly thought nothing of inflicting 20 and 25 lashes for "laziness" and "bad work" were solemnly writing down "five lashes" for the same offenses.

But Warden D. D. Bazar, who took charge of the penitentiary from the Sam Jones administration in May, 1940, says he was shocked to discover in going through the institution that at some of the larger camps as many as 25 convicts would be "laying up" in the yard; too weak from hunger, from floggings or from both, to work in the fields.

BEATINGS CHECKED

Orders were immediately issued that no corporal punishment should be administered by a captain without permission of the warden. This was further amended by the administration to require the presence of the warden at punishments. The beatings in the field with doubled up ropes, clubs, blacksnake whips and lashes were forbidden. At first, say the convicts, some of the foremen merely would conceal their ropes when they saw the warden coming. He was bound to catch one of them sooner or later, however, and did. After a foreman was immediately fired when caught flogging a prisoner in the field with a doubled up rope, the "die hard" element among employees took the hint and discarded their weapons.

Quantity and quality of the food was bettered by Warden Bazar and by General Manager Henry W. Frity, a Jones administration appointee. Orders were that all convicts get as much to eat as they wished. A tuberculosis hospital was built on the hillside, living quarters were improved, and a start made on introducing some recreation. Flogging, in a greatly diminished amount, has remained. The Jones administration apparently believes that a Louisiana penal institute can't be run without corporal punishment; that the present restricted and regulated punishment can be indefinitely controlled, although it never has been in the past.

"What do the convicts think of Warden Bazar?" said one of them, repeating a question. "Why he can go anywhere in the penitentiary. Anybody that would raise a hand against him would be torn to pieces by the other convicts.

When they had the fire in the power plant he was right in there with prisoners fighting it, instead of standing on the outside flogging them on."

"As for the Negro convicts—after he stopped the daily floggings and beatings they would fall on their knees and dust off the walk with their caps when he showed up."

Curtis Ogden, Negro, probably would have felt that way about the new warden, if the change had been made during his days at Angola. He was sent there on July 20, 1928, from Orleans parish, for assault and robbery. He was released May 1, 1940. His stay coincided almost exactly with the regime of the machine administration. Its employees officially flogged him 38 times, for a total of 579 blows of the lash.

LASHED FOR LAZINESS

Seven penitentiary captains saw his flesh quiver and bleed under their hissing lash. Twenty-four days after he arrived at the penal institution Captain A. M. Anderson gave him 20 lashes for fighting, and six days later another 10 lashes for the same offense. Captain C. J. Doherty took him over in September, 1928, and lashed him twice with eight blows each time for laziness (this was before the "make money" campaign was launched, with its higher penalties).

In 1929 he was flogged officially nine times for a total of 100 lashes. Doherty punished him four times for laziness, with six to eight blows on each occasion. Captain J. H. Leggett then got hold of him and gave him 15 lashes for fighting and 20 lashes for laziness. Captain M. Hood, into whose hands he fell, gave him three floggings. Leggett got him back in 1930 and flogged him four times,

including one punishment of 20 lashes for laziness. Captain Reaux took him over briefly near the end of the year and gave him 20 lashes for "laziness." He then went back to Leggett, who in 1931 and 1932 flogged him officially six times. Captain Pittman had a couple of "go-arounds" with him in 1933. Then Captain Drewett took him over, and between the latter part of 1933 and February 18, 1936, flogged him 12 times for a total of 224 lashes. His punishments included one of 29 lashes for laziness, one of 20 lashes for destroying cane, another of 31 for laziness, one of 10 for talking in the dining room, and 14 lashes for "changing clothes under the shed." Whether he was finally "flogged out" early in 1936, or whether subsequent beating went unreported under the policy inaugurated by Warden Jones the records do not disclose.

There was no age limit floggings at Angola and St. Gabriel—in either direction. They would beat them as young as a careless judge and district attorney might illegally send them to the penitentiary; as old as they were able to be sent tottering out to the cane field to make a little money for the state of Louisiana.

Seventeen years was the legal age at which to send prisoners to the penitentiary—except for offenses where capital punishment could have been imposed by the jury but a life sentence was voted instead. Kervis Jackson, Negro, at the age of 15 was sent to Angola from St. Landry for 10 years for burglary. If the age and the crime were both correctly stated, the sentence was illegal. This made no difference to the penitentiary authorities. A month after he was received there he was lashed by Captain F. L. Rhodes for "laziness and indifferent work." He died a couple of years later from "a brain lesion caused by an old injury." It could have been one of those clubs with which they were so handy in the field. J. D. Rodgers, Negro, 15, was sent from Washington parish for having stolen goods in his possession. The sentence was illegal. He was flogged by Captain Kleinpeter for fighting in the dining room.

Joseph Preston Fulgence, 15, Negro, sent from Lafayette parish for lying in wait, was flogged within two months; receiving 15 lashes for "losing his slicker." He was one of a large group flogged by Captain Reaux for that offense. Presumably they took their slickers off in the field, wound up their day's work some distance away, and were whisked away to camp without the chance to recover them. Presumably also the slickers were there the next morning when they returned.

Convicts sent to Angola at the age of 17 were supposed to be classified for light work. Nobody paid any attention to that. Records are frequent of 17-year old youths being flogged in the fields where the heaviest work was done.

Another polite fiction of the "make money" years was that prisoners unaccustomed to hard labor were "broken in" gradually for field work. Records tell a different story.

J. Randolph Foote, white, New Orleans stock salesman, was received on March 22, 1936, to serve a three-to-nine-year term for embezzlement. Three days later he was dead in the field from "sunstroke." The penitentiary records carry the following summarized version of the incident, as telephoned to the Baton Rouge office by Captain Pittman:

On the morning of that day Foote told the foreman, Cliff Leake, that he felt bad and did not believe he could work much. Leake advised him to stay at the camp but Foote said, "No, I'd rather go out and follow the gang and get some exercise. I believe it would do me good." The foreman told him to take a hoe and follow the gang and "do what he felt like doing." About 11:30 a.m. Foote said he didn't feel good. A companion told him to sit down, that "the boss won't care." Foote said, "No, I'd better keep moving." Pretty soon after that he fell over and died in 10 minutes or so en route to camp.

DIED IN YARD

A sunstroke death of the summer of 1939 was that of O. Myers, Jennings cattle buyer, who had been sent up from Cameron parish on confidence game charges. He was 51 years old, weighed over 200 pounds when received on June 29, 1939. He died in the yard hospital on July 14, two hours after being brought into the cannery with a temperature of 105 degrees. Captain C. T. Carmichael reported the facts substantially as follows:

Myers complained of feeling badly on July 8 and was placed in the yard hospital for three days and spent another day in the yard. He worked in the cannery July 13. On the morning of the 14th he complained of feeling badly and "was assigned to a light task pasting labels, where he could sit down." He ate his dinner normally, but fell out soon after returning to work.

Later that month the general manager wrote as follows to Sheriff Gus Broussard of Jefferson Davis regarding Myers:

"The penitentiary has no funds to compensate the family of a deceased prisoner and no authority under the law to do so."

"On account of the destitute condition of subject's children I regret that this must be my answer. I can make no suggestion, except that they apply to the usual relief sources."

Myers was the last of 33 convicts to

die at Angola of sunstroke in the "make money" years from 1931 through 1939. The worst years were 1934 and 1935, with a total of 16 deaths; however the 1936 report of the penitentiary, issued in May, asserted:

"Sunstroke is rare. Any prisoner who feels oppressed by the heat is rested."

Three convicts died that summer after the report was published; five others in the ensuing three years.

FLOGGING DECLINES

From the time the new administration took charge of the penitentiary in May, 1940, up to the end of March, 1941, a period of about 10 months, there have been 23 officially recorded floggings at Angola. Four of these were for 10 lashes each, and two (the highest) for 25 lashes each; one of them for peddling dope and one for attempting to strike a foreman and refusing to obey orders. A cellroom fight involving three convicts who obtained 15 lashes each accounted for three of the punishments; a "kangaroo court" by prisoners over another prisoner brought five under the lash.

Morale at Angola is higher than it has been in more than a decade, despite the gloomy predictions of the "old-timers" among the captains and foremen there. Authorities, however, still contend that flogging must be retained as a "last resort;" as it was similarly contended in the 1936 report of the old regime, after 5,000 floggings had been administered in four years.

Said the *Angola Argus*—the paper published weekly by inmates—in a recent issue:

"We hold that farming plus humane treatment and kindness comes as near to solving the prison problem as we can

expect in this day and age. Former Angola administrations were guilty of fostering the soul-canker which came to a head in the riot of September, 1933 . . ."

"What former administrations did not have the courage to tell was this: That the most abject forms of brutality, administered by as craven a bunch of sadists possible to get together in one spot, were practiced. A comparison of Angola of those years with an escapee's narrative of Devil's Island, would have put that infamous French penal colony to shame."

FUNDS DIVERTED

"A high public official of Louisiana, now deceased . . . led many citizens of Louisiana to believe that Louisiana convicts were living high and waxing fat. What they did not know but what was brought to light later was that funds supposed to be used for feeding, clothing and housing prisoners were mysteriously diverted; that the per capita cost of convict care in those days was actually but a fraction of the 'mark-up' cost published by the officials."

"Today there is no 'coddling.' Farm work is not easy . . . But the unnecessary farcical travesty of management which perpetuated a scheme of incessant labor simply in the interest of punishment is gone—God granting, forever. No more does heat-prostration; a polite form of saying 'worked to death in the hot sun' exist on Angola. Gone are the dietary deficiencies of a daily table fare of grits, greens, sweet potatoes and black-strap . . ."

"No man is so wholly bad that there is not a spark of good in him. It is the appeal to each and every one of us to use and exercise this spark of good that has accomplished this present-day wonder of a prison without walls. It redounds to the credit of those who have us in their charge that this latent spark has been recognized. It is a refutation of the disciples of Lombardo [Lombroso], who hold that criminals are a class separate and apart. It is a step closer to the teachings of our Master, whose foremost thought and act was kindness."

6

AMERICA'S WORST PRISON*

by Edward W. Stagg with John Lear

All the prisoners were assigned to hard labor. Often the work was nothing more useful than cutting wild grass by hand. But it always began at "can see" and ended at "can't see," at times a twelve-hour stretch.

A man was expected to keep up strength for this grinding toil on 28 cents' worth of food a day.

His normal clothing ration was two suits of black-and-white-striped cloth a year. No underwear.

He was frequently permitted to leave the camp whenever the convenience of a politician outside demanded, undertake whatever job the politician had at hand and then return to his old work gang.

If he failed to follow orders, he often was flogged. Or fed a massive dose of salts or castor oil. Or thrown into a blank-walled dungeon on bread and water for weeks. Regulations forbidding such punishment were consistently ignored.

Did this happen on The Steppes of Soviet Russia? No. Right here in our own United States not long ago, in the prison called Angola.

Angola, the state penitentiary of Louisiana, is hidden in a big, looping bend of the Mississippi River just south of the line where the state of Mississippi ends. Shaped like an animal trap, with one side barricaded by a ten-mile arc of levees rimmed with quicksands, and the other cut off by the brush-tangled jaws of the Tunica Hills, it held within its gates in February, 1951, 2,640 humans—1,760 Negroes, 880 whites—and treated them as beasts.

"I have seen almost seven thousand men discharged from this institution," cried the first woman nurse who ever ventured into the place, "and I have never seen a man discharged . . . who was as qualified (for a place) in society as he was the day he was admitted . . ."

By day, each prisoner lived in constant dread of his guards, some of whom were fellow convicts serving time for murder and other crimes of aggression. Despite their guns and authority, these guards ignored the existence of "harems" for all-male prostitution.

At night, he slept little better than a dog, lying in a tight-bedded pack with hundreds of his fellows snapping and snarling, under the steady glare of unshaded, never-dark light bulbs, keeping one eye open the night long against surprise sex assault by another male animal.

This ugly fester on the face of democracy stood untouched right up to last spring, a standing indictment of neglect and forgetfulness on the part of Louisiana citizens over more than half a century. Although the system is not yet destroyed, Angola's inmates have been freed from their former state of peonage. The dungeons have been dismantled. What remains of its terror has been thoroughly exposed, and is now in the course of what I believe will be total reformation. (I rely here on the conviction that my fellow citizens of Louisiana are too dedicated to humanity to consent to less.)

The story of how the exposure of Angola was brought about has meaning for you, wherever you live. Angola is a telling example of man's habit of trying to get rid of problems by forgetting them. Angola was established in 1901. Origin-

*Appeared in *Collier's Magazine*, November 22, 1952, 13-16.

46

ally it was a family plantation, with a mansion on a bluff overlooking a rich half circle of delta land.

River boats were its only connection with civilization. In 1928, Louisiana's political Kingfish, the late Huey P. Long, told the taxpayers Angola was costing them $1,000,000 a year when it should be self-supporting. As governor he ordered the prisoners dressed in wide-striped uniforms of black and white—a debasement that had been abandoned long before—and rigidly disciplined. But the penitentiary still was "losing money" when Huey's brother, Earl, was elected governor twenty years later. And Earl applied a remedy as unavailing as brother Huey's had been: he abolished the state Department of Institutions, under whose jurisdiction the prison had operated, and continued the Angola superintendent's post as a political plum to be dangled from his own fingers.

The first recipient of the plum was a distant relative of Long's, a kindly gentleman named Rollo C. Lawrence. Long was dissatisfied with Lawrence before two years passed, but was unwilling to fire him. Instead, in 1950 the governor sponsored a law. It allowed him to appoint Rudolph Easterly, vice-chairman of the penitentiary committee of the state Senate, to run Angola as warden under Superintendent Lawrence. The only nonpolitical change of any consequence that either of the two Longs brought about at Angola was a road. It gave the prison access to the outer world by faster route than the Mississippi River.

It was a dead-end road, rough and rutted, meandering 22 miles from a paved highway. Its intersection with the pavement was 40 miles from the nearest large city: Louisiana's capital, Baton Rouge. The route was long and dreary. But it could be traveled by news reporters.

I am capital correspondent for the *New Orleans Item* and United Press Associations. I drove up the dead-end road to Angola's gate on Monday, February 26, 1951, to learn, if I could, why 31 inmates of the prison had crippled themselves by severing their left heel tendons with razor blades.

The *Shreveport Journal* had broken the story on Saturday. Reporters for the *New Orleans Times-Picayune* and the Associated Press had visited the prison by invitation on Sunday. I went without an invitation and was stopped outside the gate by order of Warden Easterly.

PRESSURING THE GOVERNOR FOR A PASS

The Angola gatekeeper, in transmitting the warden's ban, said cryptically, "If you'd ask Superintendent Lawrence, I'm sure he'd let you in." Lawrence couldn't be reached, but the hint that he and Easterly were at odds gave me an opening. I telephoned the *Item*, the *Item* telephoned a protest to Long, and the governor phoned the warden to let me pass.

The delay was a lucky break for me. It put me in the prison hospital just in time to see the last of a limping procession of ten men who had, only a few minutes before, cut their right heel tendons now that their left heels were mending.

"Why did you do it?" I asked them. Most of them gave an identical reply: "I had to get out from under that stick." But a few said, "I was forced." I couldn't tell who was lying.

Since that day I have come to believe that if people really want to get to the bottom of a suspicious situation, and if they keep trying, something unexpected will happen to help them. Certainly one unexpected thing after another happened to help expose the truth about Angola.

The first surprise came from Governor Long. He always had made a policy of ridiculing press criticism. Now he abruptly chose to accept a *Times-Picayune* editorial writer's proposal for an inquiry into the reasons behind the heel slashings. Summoning reporters to his anteroom, he pulled a rumpled scrap of paper from a pocket and said, "I'm appointing this committee to investigate Angola." We looked at the names. The proposed list for the investigating committee included judges, peace officers, public-spirited women, Negro leaders. But predominantly the names were ours, and those of radio and newspaper executives in the state. As reporters, we sensed a political trap. We could not see how to escape it. We agreed to investigate.

"I thought the committee would have to vindicate me," Long admitted a long time afterward. "But it hanged me instead."

That last sentence simply isn't correct. Long hanged himself. If he had instructed his political coattail riders at Angola to mitigate the most obvious outrages at the prison and do everything they could to make us feel we were getting the real low-down on the place, I don't think we ever would have got anywhere. There were too many of us to start with— 28 active members altogether, holding strong and often different opinions. We were well matched for a debating society, perhaps, but as investigators some of us had to learn—and learn fast.

We conducted "hearings" at Angola in March of 1951 in an almost dreamlike atmosphere of first come first served. For two days we listened to men who were sent before us we know not whence, nor

how, nor why. We were in a state of complete confusion until, just before going home, we turned wearily to listen to one more employee—a dark-eyed, gentle-voiced woman who had been waiting patiently to be heard.

She was Mrs. Mary Margaret Daughtry, Angola's first woman nurse. She had served the prison for seven years. It was clear from what she said that she blamed Warden Easterly for wrecking small humanitarianisms she had attempted among the prisoners when Lawrence had been the institution's only boss.

Her information consisted of a typewritten statement, which she presented without reading: two match-folder-size wax-paper decks of heroin she reported buying from a narcotics ring within the prison camp; the number of a five-dollar bill (H77490278A) she said she had paid for the dope through an intermediary, and a corner she had snipped from the bill before making the payment.

So quiet was her appearance that none of us realized she was making headlines until we got back to the Capitol pressroom in Baton Rouge that night and read her statement.

DAYS OF THE
"RED HATS" RECALLED

"No one has ever asked me if I have seen evidence of brutality," it declared. "But I have seen plenty." Referring explicitly to the heel slashings, she revealed that the first men to mutilate themselves included inmates then in solitary-confinement cells known as Red Hats in memory of the time when dangerous prisoners had to wear red hats to make their whereabouts constantly evident. Some of the heel slashers had been sentenced to sixty days in Red Hats but had been kept there for as long as eight months.

"Angola is still in the Dark Ages," the nurse's statement went on. "Degenerates of every type, . . . psychopaths and neurotics, are huddled in bedside companionship with the new arrivals, in huge dormitories that, as one inmate described to me, '. . . stink like the hold of a slave ship.'"

"There is . . . no trade school, no handicrafts or arts—not even a library. A man sentenced here who cannot read or write leaves here the same way. . . . No effort . . . is made to help him stay out of the penitentiary once he obtains his release . . . . Their only choice is to steal or beg."

"Governor Long said the penitentiary has been a cancer on the state treasury— and I say that the penitentiary is a cancer on the soul of every citizen in the state of Louisiana who knows of conditions at Angola and has made no effort to remedy them."

That hit front pages all over Louisiana on a Friday morning. By the following Monday, Mrs. Daughtry was being threatened with arrest "for illegal possession of narcotics." The dope, however, was in the hands of our vice-chairman, Mrs. Margaret (Maggie) Dixon, managing editor of the *Baton Rouge Morning Advocate*, who refused to surrender it. Her grounds were that the committee held the stuff as custodian for the governor. Sheriff Teddy Martin of West Feliciana Parish, where Angola is located, had sat as our committee secretary by Long's appointment. He now resigned in a huff and went to court to demand the drug. "If it's really heroin," he announced, "I'm going to prosecute her (Mrs. Daughtry) and whoever sold it to her."

Our chairman, editor Dolph Frantz of the *Shreveport Journal*, stepped in at that point with a loud protest. The sheriff's action, he charged, "violates every sacred confidence. We promised immunity to all who appeared before the committee." He summoned our full membership to discuss the issue. But on March 14th, one day before the meeting, a local judge issued an order, and Maggie handed over the heroin.

This maneuver put Sheriff Martin in a position to complicate our efforts. On the insistence that "a murder plot" would be revealed, an attempt was made to turn the meeting into a secret session. I objected, taking the position that the one unquestioned accomplishment of our inquiry had been to let the people see everything we did just as we did it, good or bad. A committee majority backed me up.

At the open meeting, a former prison captain (overseer) who was called admitted that he himself had flogged a prisoner until his arms were tired; and then given the whip to a younger relative, who had flogged until he was tired; and the younger man had returned the whip to the captain, who meanwhile had regained strength to finish the punishment. The victim of this outburst was a Negro. His offense, as stated by the captain: he "brushed against my daughter."

POLITICAL HACKS
ON PRISON PAYROLL

A few of us slipped out of the hearing after that to pay a surprise visit to Angola. At the prison, we checked the records. They openly identified paid jobs as rewards for political hacks. They disclosed an accounting system so contrived that wholesale graft was possible without detection. There wasn't even an inventory. We couldn't determine what form of favoritism was used to choose the convict-guards, except that it clearly didn't reward good behavior.   Punishment was medieval, one of the most pathetic victims being a sixty-one-year-old man who had been lashed with a leather strap 15 or 20 times until he lost consciousness.

Prisoners who welcomed our prying didn't dare to betray it openly. But crude notes had a way of appearing in our hands as men brushed past us. The information set us stumbling blindly around the seven camps that are scattered over the prison farm's 18,000 acres, hunting this and that.

One of the peculiarities we came upon appeared to be a solid block of concrete. Three iron pipes stuck up from the top of it like periscopes.

On closer examination, we discovered three steel doors on one side of the block. Each was of solid metal, except for a small louvered rectangle near the bottom, similar to the draft vent beneath the grate of a furnace.

We banged on one door with our fists. A man's voice answered from within! We saw that the door was locked, and that there was no one around who could open it. We asked the man inside if he was all right, and he said he was. We saw that the second door was locked, and we assumed there was a man behind it, too. When we came to the third door, we found it unlocked and swung it open.

The walls and ceiling were painted black. There were no windows. The only sources of light or air were seven inch-wide, down tilted slits in the bottom of the door and a two-inch hole in the ceiling. The hole led into a pipe on the roof that was bent in the opposite direction from the prevailing wind.

A bed stood along the wall. In an opposite corner was a concrete box for a toilet. The entire cubicle was the size of a small clothes closet.   Into this stifling space as many as seven men were jammed at a time. At least one man had been removed in a state just short of roasting.

Back at the committee hearing in Baton Rouge that afternoon, Warden Easterly still insisted there was no justification for the heel slashings. He continued to insist there was nothing amiss at Angola even after this succession of events:

One of the heel slashers, William Richardson, twenty-two, summoned a lawyer to his hospital bed in New Orleans (he had been sent there from the prison to have his appendix removed; a simple operation Angola was powerless to cope with for lack of a surgeon). He sought a court injunction preventing his convict-guards and their "free people" bosses from carrying out threats to kill him.   His application was denied on grounds that he had failed to establish a case. But—

A prisoner named Clifford Lacoste, thirty-seven, hanged himself in a Red Hats cell. And —

A West Feliciana Parish grand jury indicted Angola's machine-shop chief, J. D. Pearson, who had pleaded not guilty to a charge of soliciting $250 from a prisoner's family to "obtain a pardon" for the prisoner. The case is still pending at this writing.

Our committee didn't need those three events to be convinced that Angola really was, as Mrs. Daughtry had said, "a sewer of degradation."

WHY A CAPABLE NURSE
QUIT IN DISGUST

I personally shall always regret that we didn't get our backs up in time to prevent the resignation of Mrs. Daughtry. She quit her nurse's post in disgust early in April when it became apparent that Governor Long would transfer his kinsman, Superintendent Lawrence, who had been sympathetic to her efforts.

As we fitted together the terrible picture of Angola which Mrs. Daughtry had exposed, the thing that amazed us was not that there had been disturbances among the prisoners. What we couldn't understand was why the whole place hadn't either blown up or burned down.

Guns and ammunition were in the hands of trusties, some of whom were the very toughest inmates. Matches were strewn around the dilapidated old wooden shacks in which the men nested two and three tiers high—as many as 294 of them in a single room, locked behind steel doors to which a single guard had the keys. A half-dozen kitchen-size water faucets were the only means of fighting flame in barnlike shanties with wooden floors, crumbling plaster walls, and roofs whose corrugated iron shingles creaked loosely in the slightest breeze.

Motives for arson and murder were everywhere: favors peddled in return for cash . . . furloughs to work for pay outside the prison—for as much as six months to a year—granted in response to political pull . . . sexual perversion forced by assault . . . whisky making and dope peddling through connivance with the "free people" . . . open gambling, at crap tables patterned on those of fancy casinos . . . eight toilets for 300 men in the best dormitory, and often no toilet paper . . . government by buckshot, leather strap and rubber hose . . . many deaths by violence.

Our committee reported to Governor Long, recommending an end to corporal punishment, appointment of a trained prison man as warden, new and modern housing, and a positive program of rehabilitation of prisoners.

"You want us to teach those convicts . . . ping-pong, baseball, elocution, and gee-tar playin'?" he chortled. "Those fellows aren't up there for ringin' church bells."

Long did name a member of our committee, Angola's former warden, D. D. Bazer, to be deputy warden under Senator Easterly. The advantage of this maneuver was that Bazer was politically opposed to Long and had never been in trouble with the press when he ran Angola before. The disadvantage, which Long ignored, was that some of our committee didn't approve of Bazer because he had admitted building the dungeons we saw.

By the summer of 1951, Long thought he had the Angola scandal nicely under control. Just then, his attorney general, Bolivar Kemp, Jr., broke with him politically and undertook a second inquiry into the prison. It ended with recommendations that whoever was guilty of the floggings on the Angola farm should be prosecuted in the local courts on charges of assault. Although Easterly was not cited in this connection, directly or indirectly—in fact, the records showed many improvements under his administration—he resigned as warden shortly thereafter, leaving Governor Long in a curious dilemma.

Long now had to find a warden to fit the law. Bazer wouldn't do because he was over sixty years of age, the maximum provided by the law. So Long appointed L. H. Mulina, a competent former sheriff and parole officer, discovering too late that Mulina, too, was over sixty. One more shuffle made Bazer the superintendent and Mulina a deputy warden. There was no warden. But Mulina made the "mistake" of acting like a warden. Bazer fired him.

The endless acts of this tragedy of errors kept Angola on the front pages of all Louisiana newspapers from the heel slashings of February, 1951, to the gubernatorial primary elections of February, 1952. A vigorous campaign for reform of Angola was carried on by the press of Louisiana, with my paper, the *Item*, in the vanguard. Throughout that time, Long consistently refused to acknowledge that a modern prison must be run on a humanitarian philosophy. He would not consider the fact that 95 to 97 per cent of the men who go to Angola return to society one way or another, and that it is sound economy to return them as healthy, as happy and as useful as possible.

The people of Louisiana vigorously disagreed with Long's anachronistic thinking. They defeated his candidate for governor by electing Robert F. Kennon, who was first on the ballot to declare for penal reform. Recognizing publicly that "Angola was one of the big reasons why I was elected," Kennon stated his firm intent "to change Angola from one of the worst prisons in the country to one of the best."

PROGRESSIVE WARDEN SOUGHT FOR ANGOLA

Even before his inauguration on May 13, 1952, Kennon was making overtures to borrow the United States Prisons Bureau's noted humanitarian—Reed Cozart, progressive warden of the model penitentiary at Seagoville, Texas, where the prisoners live in unlocked cottages—to move Angola from the world of beasts to the world of men.

Although he had only two years left before he would reach voluntary retirement age, and was under a doctor's orders to cut down on exertion in order to control his high blood pressure, Cozart saw a chance that extended far beyond Louisiana.

Beginning last June 16th, he agreed to take a leave of absence from the easy life of Seagoville, to undertake the backbreaking reform of Angola because, he said:

"I am a Southerner (Texan) and I feel that if a Southern state could show the way in prison reform, it would be worth while. The states are always discounting the good example of federal prisons by saying, 'But you have lots of money.' I believe Louisiana has the money to provide the kind of prison we want."

To prove that Cozart was right, Governor Kennon went to the 1952 legislature and got $4,000,000 for new buildings. That's probably a third of what the whole job will cost. But, according to plans that are now being drawn, that third will build decent housing for about 2,000 prisoners whose abilities and attitudes make them good prospects for return to decent citizenship. The buildings will be put up largely by the prisoners themselves, thus providing training for jobs outside. Actual work should be well under way by 1953.

Already Cozart and Sam A. Anderson, a Mississippi-born associate in the federal service whom he has brought in as the new warden, have prohibited private deals for use of prison labor outside the Angola farm. It is definitely understood by all that prisoners are no longer slaves. Stern orders have been posted against corporal punishment of any kind. A disciplinary board has been set up to take legitimate punishment out of the hands of convict-guards and brutal overseers. An assignment committee has been organized to classify the men according to their skills and give them work suited to their abilities. Blue denim cloth for suits has been ordered to replace the black and white stripes, which will go instead into mattress covers. A former Navy steward has been placed in charge of planning the farm's food production to meet the dietary needs of the prisoners, and of seeing to it that all prisoners get the same healthy food instead of whatever the individual overseers happen to throw together on any given day. Segregation of prisoners according to their behavior has been started. A man trained in vocational education has been hired to start a program. And the first corps of paid guards has passed its strenuous physical examination preparatory to taking the guns out of the hands of the convicts. We can take it for granted that Angola never will be allowed to revert to its former state of bestiality.

7

ANGOLA IN THE SEVENTIES*

by Burk Foster

The picture is of four young men in prison garb crowded together—doing nothing—sitting in a small, bare cell at the Louisiana State Penitentiary at Angola. The caption underneath describes the scene as an isolation cell, where an inmate would normally be kept separate from his fellow prisoners. This photo, from a 1975 issue of *Corrections Magazine*, ironically but accurately describes conditions in Louisiana's prison system in the early 1970s and lends further credence to the ancient Chinese proverb: "One picture is worth more than ten thousand words." It graphically portrayed the problem that would be the subject of considerably more than ten thousand words of litigation, journalism and public debate over the next ten years—prison overcrowding and its effects on the state's correctional system.

The many problems of prison overcrowding were not Louisiana's alone during the seventies. Several states were already under court orders to deal with prison overpopulation and deteriorating conditions of prison life, and several more would join the list before the decade was out. But because of a persistent inattention to prison needs in Louisiana, a "blind eye" going back to the post-Civil War convict leasing period, Louisiana would have much more to make up for with its reforms. It would find the road to reform slower to travel and would find, ten years after starting out, that rather than the problems being resolved, they were actually intensifying.

LSU history professor Tom Carleton, writing in *Politics and Punishment: The History of the Louisiana State Penal System* in 1971, described the environment that would challenge the prison reform efforts of the seventies: "Underlying and sustaining deficiencies of Louisiana's system have been three interrelated and historically pervasive factors (1) public opinion, the ultimate arbiter of policy formulation in a democracy, has in Louisiana generally ignored the penal system and has been disinclined to bestow upon it the kind of support readily bestowed upon other state agencies; (2) political control of the penal system has easily occupied the near-vacuum caused by public apathy, with the result that penal policy on all levels in Louisiana has been formulated exclusively by politicians, who have been able until recently to subordinate completely penological objectives to political considerations of cost, race and patronage; (3) modern penology, with its necessarily higher costs, professional personnel and popularly exaggerated overtones of convict-coddling, has had a difficult time supplanting the old ways in Louisiana, where public officials have preferred to utilize the penal system as a patronage mill, where public opinion has been satisfied when it could be assured that convicts were being punished, and where both officials and public opinion have long agreed that the least expensive penal system is the most desirable one."

Louisiana had passed through the

---

*Appeared in *The Angolite*, March/April 1988, 19-39. Reprinted with permission.

tumultuous decade of the sixties with its old-fashioned prison system relatively intact. The racial antagonisms and political rebellions, the arguments about rehabilitation and reintegration, the deep questioning of the basic role of the prison that occurred in more progressive states never caught on here. In Louisiana prison meant Angola, and Angola was simply a big old prison farm in the Mississippi River where most inmates did agricultural labor.

The only other men's prison in the state, the medium security reformatory officially titled the Louisiana Correctional and Industrial School (LCIS), had opened at DeQuincy in 1957. Most Louisianans did not know it existed.

The state had made a brief feint at modernizing its prison system in the 1950s, when a rash of inmate Achilles tendon-slashings focused attention on Angola and encouraged reform efforts. Professional penologists were imported from the federal system and state politicians pledged to keep their hands off the prison to give new rehabilitation programs a chance to succeed.

In 1962, in the administration of Governor Jimmie Davis, the budget of Angola was cut by about 30%. Employees were laid off (inmate guards returning to take their places), programs abandoned and the professional administrators gradually squeezed out. Angola had nine wardens between 1964 and 1968, the year the state Department of Corrections was created. In Louisiana's prisons, it was back to business—and politics—as usual.

The inmate population of Angola held fairly constant during this period, from an average of 3,523 in fiscal year 1962 to 3,463 in fiscal year 1966 to 3,390 in fiscal year 1972. The average cost per day

to house inmates remained steady in the $2.50 per day range during the first part of this period and then increased sharply toward the end ($4.86 in fiscal year 1972) as free people were hired to replace the inmate guards.

The prison population's stability or slight decline was not unlike what was going on across the rest of the country, and the trend came to an end in Louisiana at the same time as it did elsewhere—in 1972.

If you were an Angola inmate, 1972 seemed to promise a new period of enlightened prison administration in Louisiana. The populist Edwin Edwards was inaugurated governor and Elayn Hunt, recognized as a progressive in prison reform, was appointed director of corrections. Back-breaking labor in the fields was ended, the use of inmates as guards was stopped, the notorious Red Hat Cell block (where escape artist Charlie Frazier had once been welded inside his seven-by-three-and-a-half foot cell for seven years) was closed, radical revision of the disciplinary procedures occurred and unnecessary restrictions were removed, giving the inmates a little more freedom of choice. In short, life at Angola became less harsh, a little more humane.

Those who anticipated change soon saw it, but in a form different from what they expected. Tougher sentencing practices drove the inmate population up steadily, an average increase of twenty to thirty inmates per month. The legislature failed to appropriate funds to hire new staff or make improvements to the prison's physical plant. And the relaxation of discipline, though more humane in one sense, broke down the old forms of social control: the prisoners ran wild.

From 1972 to 1975, Angola was a full-blown monster, with potential as dangerous as the quality of life in its bowels. It was a particularly vicious period. Forty prisoners were stabbed to death and more than 350 treated with serious knife wounds. It was a dog-eat-dog jungle and having a knife was almost a prerequisite to survival.

Gang wars and clique power struggles kept the stretchers rolling, to the point where "One on the stretcher!" became a morbid call that was soon ignored, generally accepted as a routine risk factor of doing time. One senior correctional officer, who was a rookie guard during this violent era, tells of working the late night shift—often the only guard on duty in a 200-man dormitory. It was a rare day indeed, he says, when he came to work without finding fresh blood on the floor somewhere in the dormitory.

Half the prisoner population wasn't working, dope traffic was rampant, pilferage and exploitation were the rule. The strong ruled, and the weak either served or perished. Sexual abuse and homosexual slavery were widespread, with inmates auctioned, sold and traded like cattle by other inmates. By mid-1975, Angola was the number one prison in America on two counts: with 4,300 inmates, it was the largest, and with one or two inmate stabbing deaths each month, it was also the bloodiest.

State district court Judge Frank Marullo, taking a tour of Angola during this period, described the prison as "essentially unmanageable." He said: "Everyone knows that the mammoth prison must be broken up into several smaller institutions in the future but (they) are unwilling to do anything about Angola today." "Part of the problem," he said, "is educating the general public that improving prisons is not coddling criminals."

Although state officials, including the prison Warden Murray Henderson and corrections director Hunt, were working diligently to correct Angola's problems, the simple fact was that they lacked the resources to undertake substantial lasting reforms. As would be the case in so many other states, it would take federal court intervention to finally bring the prison out of its "dark ages."

A lawsuit filed by prisoner Hayes Williams and other Angola inmates protesting the prison's poor living conditions had been kicking around the federal courts since 1971. United States magistrate Frank Polozola had been designated by federal district judge Gordon West to look into the complaints, and in late April 1975 he issued his 55-page report. Despite "good faith" efforts by state officials, prison conditions were terrible. Polozola found a lack of adequate physical protection of inmates, including the failure to detect and remove weapons, dormitories beyond capacity, and safety and health hazards in abundance. To clean up these conditions amounting to "cruel and unusual punishment," the report made several recommendations. To the 585 guards then employed, another 365 should be added. More medical personnel, especially physicians, were needed. The physical plant needed to be modernized. And the prison had to work to end the segregation of its predominantly black inmate population.

The state vigorously objected to the report's recommendations, some of which it was already putting into effect and others is said simply could not be done— such as hiring 385 new guards immediately. Mrs. Hunt said there was not enough money available to bring about real prison reform. Even if there was, she said, "The legislature could give me a blank check, and we still couldn't clean up Angola . . . because of where and what it is." She said she wouldn't mind if it was closed down altogether. Her prime hope for prison reform was decentralization, breaking up Angola into smaller prisons closer to cities.

Officials of the Department of Corrections almost seemed to be anticipating Judge West's decision to sign the magistrate's report, thereby giving it the effect of a court order. The judge's action was expected to give them the leverage they needed to get funds from the state legislature.

Judge West did in fact sign the order, on June 10, 1975, and Louisiana's corrections system has not been the same since. In signing the order, Judge West observed that conditions at the prison "not only shock the conscience," but also fragrantly violate basic constitutional requirements. The order touched upon practically every aspect of prison life: security, health and medical care, food service, religion, fire safety, overpopulation, mail service, prison disciplinary procedures and the physical facilities. Some changes were to be made immediately, and state officials were to file long-term improvement plans in his court within 180 days.

Douglas Murphy, writing in the *Times-Picayune* on June 12, gave this summary of Judge West's 20-page "Judgment and Order:"

—that the penitentiary within six months hire about 400 more corrections officers (guards), to bring the staff up to a minimum of 950;

—that at least two guards be placed in each cellblock or dormitory at Angola on a 24-hour a day basis, equipped with walkie-talkies and telephones, to prevent homosexual rapes, fights and gambling in

the living areas;

—that the warden immediately remove overt and aggressive homosexuals from the general prison population;

—that inmates known to engage in or constantly cause fights and violence be separated;

—that temporary housing be erected to eliminate as much as possible overcrowding at Angola, which is bulging with some 4,000-plus inmates;

—that Angola immediately hire more and more competent medical personnel, and that doctors at the New General Hospital at the prison be fully licensed by the state of Louisiana;

—that each newly-arrived inmate be examined by a physician within seven days of arrival;

—that all inmates presently held in the so-called "Psychiatric Unit" at Angola be placed in a "therapeutic environment" and cared for. The "PU," as it is known, has often been described as a "hellhole."

The court judgment also ordered that the prison buildings and facilities be brought up to state fire, safety and health standards, something that has so far never been done, according to the inmates and some prison officials.

Perhaps Judge West expected the state to get right to work on prison improvements. If he did, he should have paid close attention to a remark Governor Edwards made on being told the order had been signed. "We didn't take the magistrate's recommendations that seriously," the governor said. "Now that it's been elevated to the status of a formal court order, we'll have to treat it with more deference." How much deference was "more deference?" Not enough to satisfy Judge West apparently. A July newspaper article, titled "Judge Unhappy Over Angola," contains his criticisms of the state legislature, which had just ended its 1975 session without dealing in a substantive way with prison reform.

Judge West was most irritated by the legislature's decision to appropriate funds for expansion of the LSU football stadium while failing to approve additional operating revenues for Angola. State officials told the judge that the prison monies had gotten lost in the maze of bureaucratic procedures through which budget requests had to travel, and consequently no funds were available for the 1975-76 fiscal year. Judge West commented, "I find it's always so easy for people to say what can't be done rather than what can be done." The legislature's only real prison-action—and a portent of things to come—was to appropriate $15 million for prison construction, five million for additions to Angola and ten million for two new first-offender prisons in other parts of the state.

State officials were not so sure they wanted to go ahead with Judge West's reforms—at least according to his time-table. They did what all red-blooded Southerners would do in the face of a federal court order: screamed that the federal courts were interfering in state business and appealed to the Fifth Circuit. They would eventually lose their argument, and in September Judge West turned up the heat. He placed a population limit of 2,640 prisoners on Angola, at a time when the prison had 3,751 inmates officially confined in its cellblocks and dormitories and another 200 in-processing. Prison officials reported a net population increase of 64 a month, 200 coming in and only 136 going out. There could be no new admissions, the judge said, until the population was brought down. The only reply from the legislature, which was not then in session, was silence.

Meanwhile state corrections officials were pursuing their answer to the Angola problem—decentralization. Their idea was to build new prisons across the state, gradually decreasing the reliance on Angola and eventually phasing it out. Let it be a farm again, Mrs. Hunt had said.

Faced with increasing political pressure from Judge West, no proposal to reduce the inmate population was too bizarre to consider. In late September, Mrs. Hunt was reported to be exploring the use of a mothballed U.S. Military Transport Ship for use as a work release center. She had already been to the Norfolk navy yard shopping.

The prison ship idea soon sank without a trace (someone probably ran across the tales of the horrors of the British prison hulks), and so did other hopes for early reforms. Prison reformers and the inmates themselves would later admit that they had been naive—to think that a mere federal court order could overturn a century of prison neglect and bring about quick improvements.

At the end of the crisis year 1975, Angola's population had declined to about 3,500 (causing a backlog to begin building in parish jails). The violence toll for the year: 18 men murdered, 173 verified stabbings with injury. Was the prison any different after the order? One inmate said, "The food got a little better for awhile and nothing really got worse."

As it turned out, 1976 would be the year the prison reform ball really got going. There has never been another year quite like it in the history of Louisiana corrections. The year got off to a bad start when Mrs. Hunt died of pancreatic cancer in early February. The assistant director, Paul Phelps, was appointed to succeed her in March. He continued to move the DOC in the same direction it had been headed under Mrs. Hunt, toward decentralization.

In July 1976 Governor Edwards announced his ten year plan for Louisiana corrections. He called it a decentralization plan, but the original idea had been modified by now, as he found little political support for locating prisons anywhere near urban areas, so a better description would be to call the plan a hybrid—part concentration, part decentralization.

Angola was to house long-term offenders, including violent and sex offenders. Three new outcamps would be built there, to bring the population back up to 4,000 or so. "Only the bad guys would be left," one inmate said.

The "not-so-bad guys" would presumably be dispersed among other facilities, mostly in rural areas: the reformatory at DeQuincy, a medium security prison already under construction at Jackson, a new prison at St. Gabriel to house 500 permanent inmates and another 500 for in-and-out processing, a 500-man prison in Bossier Parish in north Louisiana, and a 250-man work release center at Camp Beauregard in central Louisiana. This was an ambitious plan, made necessary by the DOC's projection that the state prison population would increase by 700 to 800 inmates each year for the foreseeable future.

The state legislature, meeting in regular session in 1976, ignored the governor's plans, the judge's orders and virtually everything else having to do with prison reform. What everyone was talking about was an incident—almost trivial in itself—that illustrated how totally opposed to putting prisoners in the cities the public and the legislature were.

A nursing home in New Orleans, the Ponchartrain Lodge, was sold to the state which announced plans to begin housing a number of elderly prisoners there, as one of the schemes to reduce Angola's population. The uproar was so great—the viciousness of the response likened to a hurricane's fury—that the state backed off and promised to lease the facility to a church group instead. And the businessman who had sold the property to the state soon came under indictment for allegedly selling and reselling the home to inflate its value. "Don't call us about decentralization," the public seemed to be saying, "we'll call you."

Meanwhile, back on the farm, a new prison warden had brought a new style to Angola. Ross Maggio, who had been in the DOC's agri-business office, had been brought in, it was said, because he had the right attitude to whip the prison into shape—tough, disciplined, no nonsense. An April newspaper article, titled "Prison Warden Forges Ahead, Then Slips Back," pointed out that Maggio was about to get the population down to the court-ordered 2,641. That was some accomplishment, even with 1,200 inmates waiting in the parish prisons. He had hired 200 more guards and was just 150 shy of what the court had ordered. But the turnover rate among guards was 50%, and there were few prospective employees left in the remote rural area around Angola. It was truly a "three step forward, two steps back" approach to prison reform.

Problems with prison personnel would continue through the summer as Warden Maggio moved to end corruption and tighten security. The number of guards actually began to decline, and prison officials recognized they could not hire more guards from the surrounding area. Part of Governor Edwards' plan was to eventually increase the population of Angola to 4,000. Warden Maggio, estimating that 2,000 staff members would be needed by then, said that the state would need to spend ten million dollars to build housing for these new employees on the grounds.

Prison critics observed that Maggio was beginning to take control of the giant institution. Only two men were murdered in the first half of 1976. Very few knives were being found in the periodic shakedown searches, down from the "two bushel baskets a day" of a few months earlier.

Inmate Ken Plaisance, who had been at Angola fifteen years, agreed that the level of violence had been drastically reduced. "It is working," he said, "thanks to Judge West's order." The prison was being cleaned up, better medical care provided and safety hazards—human and physical—reduced.

It all made good sense, the warden said. "There was nothing in the court order . . . nothing we are now doing to comply with the court order, that wasn't just common sense in running a prison," Maggio said. He conceded it took the order to bring "common sense" into play as an institutional policy.

The state legislature, urged on by the governor and the federal judge, was finally ready to do its part. Meeting in special session beginning on August 15, 1976, in two days it approved $90.6 million in prison bonds: $30.8 million for expansion of Angola, $24 million for the prison and reception center to be built at St. Gabriel, $19.8 million for new highways around Angola, and smaller amounts for improvements at other prisons. The dam had finally been broken; the trickle of prison funds had suddenly become a torrent.

By the latter part of 1976, then, Louisiana had yielded to the irresistible force and begun to modernize its antiquated prison system.   The state's initial approach to prison reform could not have been more conventionally simple; as outlined in Governor Edwards' plan, it would add enough new prison beds to relieve overcrowding and keep up with expected population increases.

Over the next seven years, from 1976 to 1983, Louisiana would open four medium security prisons and greatly expand two minimum security work training facilities, increasing the capacity of the system by about 4,500 inmates. The first of the new prisons, the Margaret Dixon Correctional Institute, opened on April 1, 1976, at Jackson, halfway between Baton Rouge and the Mississippi line. The prison grounds had once been part of a mental hospital, the East Louisiana State Hospital, and had been quickly renovated after the court order was imposed.

The prison opened with a maximum intended population of 750, men moved over from Angola. Most of them were quite happy to be moving from the "big farm" to the "funny farm" and so was Warden Hayden Dees, also out of Angola, who said this was the kind of prison that could be used all around the state for 90% of the prisoners in Louisiana. Warden Dees even managed to keep the big oaks that provided shade for the yard within Dixon's fences—something that would never have been allowed at Angola.

The next medium security prison to open was the Hunt prison at St. Gabriel, built on land adjoining the women's prison that had opened in 1973. Named for the recently deceased corrections director, the Hunt prison was always identified as a model facility and often contrasted with Angola.   Hunt was designed by former Angola Warden Ross

Maggio, who had moved over to build the new prison and open it on January 31, 1979. Its anticipated population was about a thousand men made up of permanent residents and those new inmates just entering the system for classification.

The third new prison, Wade Correctional Institute, located near Haynesville in Claiborne Parish, opened a year-and-a-half later, on December 15, 1980. It was the first prison in north Louisiana. The fourth, called the Washington Parish Prison, was dedicated at Varnado, near the Pearl River in east Louisiana, on May 28, 1983. Its 1600 acre complex was expected to house 1,120 inmates by the end of that year.

The two work training centers, at Camp Beauregard near Alexandria and at Jackson Barracks in New Orleans, were already in use as small work release facilities (along with the State Police Barracks in Baton Rouge and a small section of LCIS at DeQuincy) before 1975. Both were on state-owned property used by the National Guard. The expansion of Camp Beauregard aroused no controversy, but the Jackson Barracks location was bitterly contested: it was the first state prison (to be called a prison, anyway) in an urban area since before the Civil War. New Orleans legislators fought it tooth and nail when the conversion from military to prison use was proposed late in 1976. Three years later, the same legislators were still arguing that it should be shut down and prisoners transferred to the new Hunt Prison.

But prisons, once opened, tend to be impossible to close. Just look at Angola. The old farm, which in 1974 and 1975 everyone wanted to shut down as a blighted anachronism, was suddenly more popular than ever. It was cleaned up, had

a new warden, Frank Blackburn replacing Ross Maggio in 1978, new dormitories under construction, hundreds of new employees and a new reputation for safety and security: in 1977 not a single inmate was murdered.

The transformation had come about with almost miraculous speed, and corrections officials had every right to be pleased with their successes. In an interview at the end of 1978, Paul Phelps was optimistic about changes within the system. The state might be released from the federal court orders by 1980, he said, and theoretically should be able to house all state prisoners in local jails by then. The state was even planning to begin the American Correctional Association's accreditation process.

In a speech a few months later, Phelps said of the changes, "I'm of the opinion that we're doing as good a job as anyone in the country. We've come out of the dark past and into the modern-day world in one great big three-year leap."

Change of this magnitude, occurring this quickly, did not come cheap. The Louisiana legislature, once it decided to go along with the program, spent money hand over fist. By 1980, over $300 million had been spent on capital improvements alone—three new outcamps, new dormitories and other renovations at Angola, highway improvements, two new medium security prisons open by that time and another underway, the work training centers—a prison boom unlike anything the state had ever seen.

The DOC's operating budget had skyrocketed, too. In 1971 the state spent seven million dollars to confine 4,000 inmates. By 1975 the budget had increased to $25 million for close to 5,000 inmates, and by 1981 over $100 million for 8,000 inmates. In that one decade, prison expenditures had increased more than tenfold, and corrections officials were coming to be thought of as panhandlers—always going around, hands out, asking for still more money.

Small wonder that the public and the legislature were beginning to protest the high cost of prison operations. If they had been listening carefully, they would have known the day was coming. Paul Phelps had predicted as early as 1976, his first year on the job, that the state would go bankrupt in ten years if it didn't reevaluate its approach to corrections. He suggested the corrections department was in a "futile foot race with the judicial system," which was sentencing 50 more people a month to prison than the state released.

In 1979, speaking before committees in the legislature, Phelps said, "If the state of Louisiana does not change its policies, we are firmly dedicated to building a new prison every other year. Our policy right now is to put everybody in prison."

Legislators were displeased with the huge budget increases Phelps asked for. "Something's got to be done," said Sen. Foster Campbell Jr. of Bossier City. "Pretty soon prisons will be more expensive than schools in this state."

"That's a distinct possibility," Phelps agreed. He argued for more probation officers—three times the 168 then employed—to increase the strictness of probation supervision. But Sen. Campbell said he did not believe the voters were ready to broaden probation programs. "I don't think the people of Louisiana are willing to lessen penalties," he said.

Overuse of imprisonment and underuse of probation were themes Phelps would come back to with increasing frequency. "We have to change the concept that the only way you can punish someone is by putting them in jail," he said in 1981. The state had to ask "how much money the public is willing to spend to guarantee that people will be locked up and remain unproductive." He cited figures of $60,000 a bed to build new prisons and $20 a day (which would be up to $30 a day by 1984) to keep men in them once they opened. The public, he said, needs to change its "mental concept of punishment. For a lot of people the worst thing you could do them is to make them get up every morning and go to work."

Although he clearly believed that alternatives to prison were being ignored, Phelps was firmly committed to taking good care of all inmates in state custody. He insisted that the state continue to build and adequately staff the new prisons needed to house the hundreds of new inmates coming in each year.

His position would cause him serious problems as he tried to work in the administration of Dave Treen, the Republican governor who replaced Edwin Edwards in March 1980. Phelps hung on as head of the DOC for eighteen months, then was replaced on September 17, 1981. Was he fired or did he resign, and for what reasons? Phelps would say only that he had been removed, and Treen would never give specific reasons why, speaking only of a "difference in philosophy," mainly over the issue of putting more inmates into existing facilities.

The nature of those differences became more apparent the next month, October 1981, when Phelps' successor, John King, announced a two-year halt in prison construction. The state would hire more guards, reduce the ratio of guards to inmates—from one guard per 3.1 inmates to one per 3.5 in maximum security and 1 to 5.5 in medium security—and use existing facilities more intensively. By reducing the living space allowed dormitory inmates—"double bunking"— King proposed to add more than 4,000 new prison beds.

This was rather an abrupt reversal, for the public to be told after years of publicity about prison overcrowding that Louisiana's prisons weren't really overcrowded after all: it was just that space had not been managed properly.

Louisiana's prisons not overcrowded? That was surely news to the federal courts. Middle District Judge Frank Polozola, the former magistrate who had taken over the court order on his elevation to the bench after Judge West's retirement, took a dim view of the Treen administration's proposal. He asked for more information on how double-bunking would be carried out, reports shuttled back and forth from the DOC to his office for several months, and finally, on December 3, 1982, the judge lowered the boom.

Polozola gave Louisiana officials a four-hour dressing down about failing to come to grips with overcrowding. He wanted concrete data on prison plans; what officials had submitted to him was "garbage." Officials were beginning to get the idea that Polozola was not enthusiastic about double-bunking. Having an alternative plan ready, he told them. And furthermore, they should stop blaming him for the state's prison problems, when it was their own lethargy that was at fault. Warning them that "the credibility of the DOC is at an all-time low with me," Polozola sent the officials away to get down to work.

The announcement that state prisons were not overcrowded had been received with skepticism by another of the DOC's critical audiences, the parish sheriffs, who must have ranked the statement's credibility somewhere up there with Richard Nixon's "peace with honor" Vietnam proclamation. The sheriffs were in the midst of serious jail overcrowding problems of their own, most of them caused by a backlog of state prisoners being held in local jails there since 1975. The state's excuses had been first, no room, and second, not enough guards, to move the prisoners into state custody.

The larger jails had it the worst. Sheriff Charles Foti of Orleans Parish was having lawsuit problems even before Angola was closed to new admissions late in 1975, and those problems would get much worse in the next few years. They would spread across the state as well, as Angola pursued its population-control target by releasing inmates and simply refusing to accept transfers in from local jails. By May 1977, there were 1,867 state prisoners in local jails. State corrections officials were hopeful, however, that nearly all of them would be in state custody by later that summer (when the new dormitory beds at Angola came open).

It never happened. New prison construction would dent the backlog but never completely eliminate it. Sheriffs became accustomed to the cycle: a new prison would open, most of the state prisoners would be taken from the jails and then, inexorably, like flood waters rising toward the top of the levee, the numbers, would begin to inch upward again, each time reaching higher than the time before. The new prisons were like emergency spillways, temporarily relieving the pressure, but the flood of inmates rushing into the system was like the massive deluge engineers say will one day reroute the Mississippi down the center of the state—beyond the means of the system to contain.

Local jail overcrowding would worsen during the Treen administration, which only completed building the prisons begun under Edwards and added no new facilities of its own. Sheriff Foti dramatized the plight of the local authorities in April 1980 by taking 147 state inmates to St. Gabriel and abandoning them in the Hunt Prison parking lot. A grand gesture it was, though Paul Phelps criticized Foti for "blaming the state" instead of trying to solve his problems locally. Phelps pointed out that even though the state might have a few empty bed spaces, it did not have the manpower to guard the prisoners that would fill those spaces.

Several propositions were forthcoming. A New Orleans area legislator proposed that a regional prison be built in the city (or somewhere around it) to hold just those convicted felons on appeal, who by Louisiana law are still the local sheriff's responsibility. Governor Treen, by his count down to 495 state prisoners in local jails by May 14, 1981, promised that all state inmates would be in state facilities by September 1. Had his double-bunking proposal been accepted, sheriffs would have been granted immediate, lasting relief from the problem.

But none of these things happened, and finally, on September 21, 1982, the sheriffs' turn in federal court came: Louisiana became the first state in the nation in which every sheriff was under court order specifying how many prisoners he could house in his jails. Judge Polozola, under authority granted by the Fifth U.S. Circuit Court of Appeals, signed the last of the consent decrees stipulating to the number of prisoners to be confined and the number of guards to be employed in every parish prison in Louisiana.

By the end of the next year, Polozola would reach consent decrees with the rest of the DOC's adult prisons, the 105 city jails and the five juvenile training schools. As of December 7, 1983, one federal judge had supervisory authority over the state's entire correctional apparatus, with the exception of local juvenile detention homes.

It should be noted that while the DOC was arousing the ire of some sheriffs by keeping inmates in their jails, it was also contributing to their enrichment by paying them a daily maintenance fee. This fee, which began at $4.50 a day per inmate in the mid-1970s and would eventually increase to $18.25, was a source of considerable income to some sheriffs who had space available. Some of them even enlarged their jails or juggled bed arrangements to house more state prisoners, though any steps causing overcrowding had to cease after the consent decrees were signed.

It was in February 1983, at the beginning of the last year of the Treen Administration, that Judge Polozola approved the comprehensive plan state officials had reworked to submit to him. The plan, as approved on February 11, called for the state to spend $34.1 million to provide pre-fab modular housing additions at several prisons. In return Polozola was to allow limited use of double-bunking at three smaller prisons. The effect of these changes, coupled with the opening of the new Washington Parish Prison, would be to increase the state's prison population from 9,500 to 12,000 by the end of 1983. Governor Treen in announcing the plan said, "At the end of this calendar year, it should give us total relief from our problem." Corrections Secretary King predicted that only 600 to

700 state prisoners would be left in local jails at year's end (of the 1,600 waiting there in February).

It was a good plan; the only thing wrong with it was that the Treen administration forgot to carry it out. Early in 1984, as Dave Treen was preparing to leave office and Edwin Edwards preparing to return as governor, the legislative fiscal office issued a report highly critical of the corrections department as managed by Treen's appointee John King. "The department has not managed its prison construction program in an efficient manner and has failed to adequately plan for future growth." The pre-fab cells authorized in 1983 were never built. The backlog of state inmates in local jails was greater than ever; the jails were very near their stipulated capacity of 9,215.

The fiscal office projected cost figures that were truly staggering: three new prisons needed immediately, at a cost of $170 million; the DOC budget, which stood at $160 million in 1984, projected at $322.5 million in 1989; $240 million, some of it state funds, needed for parish jail expansion.

Running for governor in 1979, Dave Treen had promised to be tough on criminals, and where convicts were concerned he had kept his word: he ignored the problems of prisons, especially after the departure of Paul Phelps, took no action to increase the capacity of the system (other than the double-bunking scheme the federal courts found ludicrous) and then walked away, leaving the chaos to his successor. State Representative Kevin Reilly summed up the mess the DOC created under Treen: "It shows what happens when you have a bunch of amateurs running a department that needs professionals."

When Edwin Edwards was inaugurated to start his third term as governor of Louisiana in March 1984, he reappointed Paul Phelps secretary of corrections. Phelps' mission—sounding like an assignment from the old "Mission: Impossible" television series—was to bring rampaging prison population and cost figures under control.

Phelps hit the trail, sounding in his public statements even more certain than he had been three years before that Louisiana could not continue to send more and more people to prison. It was a straight-forward, repetitious message: the state's oil money was gone, they would have to borrow money, mortgaging their children's future to build new prisons, prison construction and operating costs were continuing to rise, there were 2,500 state inmates in local jails. "How long can we afford it?" Phelps asked. "My concern is that if we don't get away from this lock 'em up business, we're going to go bankrupt."

Hawking intensive probation on the Georgia model, Phelps toured the state. Doomsday headlines—"Corrections Could Bankrupt State," "Louisiana Facing Key Penal Crisis," "Jail Terms Too Costly, Says Phelps"—marked his trail as he tried to sober up a public drunk on locking people up.

This time around Phelps had more help from the governor's mansion. Edwin Edwards himself was more personally involved in publicizing the need for change. Early in his term Edwards said, "You can look forward to an emphasis on prison alternatives, bearing in mind an emphasis on protecting society. Off the top of my head, I'd say there are a significant number of people who could be let go with no danger to society."

The governor appointed two executive

committees to consider different aspects of imprisonment. The 80-member Forgotten Man Committee held its first meeting on April 25, 1984. This committee, the reincarnation of a similar committee appointed by Governor Earl Long in the 1950s, was to look into the plight of the "practical lifer," the inmate sentenced to an exceptionally long period of confinement. Angola had 2,500 to 3,000 of these inmates, men ineligible for parole and serving either life sentences or terms so long they could expect to be geriatric cases before they got out.

In the late summer of 1984 Edwards appointed the Governor's Prison Overcrowding Policy Task Force. This group's purpose was pretty much self-explanatory—to investigate possible measures to reduce prison population and make policy recommendations to the governor) and undoubtedly through its hearings to help focus public attention on the crisis). It began meeting in the fall.

Between the start-up dates of these two committees, the 1984 legislative session had come and gone. It had rejected Phelps' package of probation and parole reform bills, reflecting the view that people would prefer to spend money building new jails rather than putting criminals back on the street.

The Overcrowding Task Force encountered similar opinions as it held public meetings around the state in the fall. "We have to develop a rationale to convince the people of this state that there are better, cheaper ways to punish people than to put them in jail," Paul Phelps said.

Persistence at putting people in jail had created an unprecedented prison overcrowding problem in Louisiana. The state prison system was operating at 99.9% of capacity (11,118 beds) and there

was a backlog of state prisoners (3,161) that consumed one-third of parish jail space—the largest backlog in the U.S. Louisiana's overall incarceration rate—counting all state and local prisoners—was 502 per 100,000, the highest in the nation and nearly twice the national average of 286 (The same year the state ranked only 19th in population and 19th in reported crime).

But Phelps and other members of the task force acknowledged that popular opinion was opposed to alternatives to prison. "In South Louisiana, whenever a crime is committed, the people want to see them in jail," said Minos Hardy, chief of police in Abbeville. "Our legislature is doing what they think the public wants them to do" when lawmakers take a tough line on mandatory sentences, added Frank Serpas, an assistant to the mayor of New Orleans.

In early 1985, as the two committees were preparing interim reports and the legislature was gearing up for another session, Phelps continued emphasizing the economic impact of the continuing high rate of imprisonment. The get-tough on crime policy was all right, he said, long as the oil money was rolling in. But that money was dwindling and there were still 115 more admissions to prison than releases each month. More money needed to be spent on halfway houses, probation and parole. The trouble was, Phelps said, "People think probation and parole is soft on crime." The state legislators have only "reflected the attitudes of their constituencies . . . that the only way to punish people is to lock them up."

It was to the point, he said, that corrections would be taking money from education, highways and other functions of state government. He issued a clear warning: "In 1986, the financial crisis will be so great that the legislature will not have many alternatives."

In their interim reports, submitted in March 1985 before the legislature began meeting on April 15, the two committees said basically the same thing. "Louisiana now faces a set of circumstances that it literally cannot build itself out of—cannot because the numbers are too large, the projected growth too fast and the cost too great," the Forgotten Man Committee wrote in its report. Among this committee's recommendations, and sure to excite controversy, was the proposal to make all prison inmates, including murderers, eligible for release after 20 years in prison.

The Overcrowding Task Force, a group more dominated by professionals in criminal justice, recommended a more conventional approach: more prison and jail construction to alleviate overcrowding until other measures could be developed to correct the problem. The 1985 legislature accepted this recommendation and created a Louisiana Corrections Facility Corporation to sell bonds to finance five more new prisons. The legislature also began a five-year plan of increasing probation and parole supervision by adding the first installment of 100 new field agents. Other major reform measures were either defeated outright or postponed until the 1986 session.

As 1985 came to a close, the Corrections Facility Corporation exercised its bond-selling authority. On December 27 it sold prison bonds in the amount of $156 million, sufficient to build three new prisons and plan two more. These five prisons, all medium security facilities holding 500 beds each, were planned for Avoyelles, Allen, Winn, East Carroll and Union-Ouachita Parishes, all rural parishes where jobs were badly needed.

Thus Louisiana closed out ten years of prison reform preparing for still another round of prison-building. From the date of Judge West's initial court order on Angola, June 10, 1975, through the end of the 1985 fiscal year on June 30, the corrections department's prisoner population had grown by 150 percent, from 5,300 to 13,300. The department's operating budget had grown by nearly 600 percent (from $29 million to $200 million)—a growth rate three times faster than state government overall.

The economists had been mistaken: it wasn't oil that was the state's growth industry, it was prisons. If prison stock had been for sale to the public in 1970, and you had been smart enough to buy, a thousand dollar investment would have been worth $25,000 fifteen years later.

Louisiana remains bullish on prisons. Jim Morris, the head of adult services for the DOC, said late in 1985 that he expected the prison population to continue to increase for the next several years as children of the baby boomers reach young adulthood. Paul Phelps had estimated that the state would need space for 5,300 more prisoners by 1990, when its budget would approach $400 million a year.

How had this ruinous situation come about? How had the state run itself into this predicament? The specific actions are easy to identify: the simplest explanation is to say the state legislature changed the laws to get tougher on criminals. Between 1975 and 1985 it passed at least 47 statutes increasing criminal penalties. Most violent felonies now carry mandatory prison terms. Stricter laws were enacted punishing DWI offenders. The 1977 legislature passed a law reducing goodtime credit from 25 days a month to 15, obviously an important determinant of how long people remain in prison.

The criminal justice system has made its contribution to the problem. Prosecutors, especially in the New Orleans area, stand on their hard-line approach, judges impose longer sentences, repeat felons are legally forbidden from being placed on probation, even one arm of the DOC helps out. The Parole Board in 1985 was paroling inmates at less than half the rate it had ten years earlier (2,400 parolees to 5,300 inmates in 1975; 2,600 parolees to 13,300 inmates in 1985). Part of the parole situation is due, of course, to legal changes that make an increasing number of inmates ineligible for parole. For many of Louisiana's practical lifers, the only hope of getting out of prison before they are old men lies in executive clemency, the power to commute sentences, which, following Dave Treen's parsimonious example, is also being used much less frequently today than it was in the past.

Is it fair to pin the responsibility on state legislators and criminal justice officials, then? Not really. Officials could act, by changing laws and policies, to reduce the prison population, but they are unlikely to do so in the face of strong public opposition to deinstitutionalization. Public opinion in Louisiana is not apathetic to prison reform (apathy at least allows public officials to do what they think best without interference), it is downright hostile.

In early 1985, after Louisiana's citizens had been exposed to prison problems for a full decade, a public opinion poll commissioned by the *Baton Rouge Morning Advocate* showed that almost 69% of the voters preferred increasing taxes to lock up more prisoners. Only 4.2% said more prisoners should be let out on parole to alleviate crowding in state prisons. The other 27%

gave other responses, including "neither," "other," "depends," and "don't know."

A critic of the poll's structure might argue that the question could be reworded to include probation, supervised half-way houses and other options that sound less threatening than parole, but the fact remains that in every section of Louisiana, among male or female, young or old, rich or poor—the ratio is at least 10 to 1 favoring higher taxes over turning prisoners loose on parole. The only exception to this ratio was among blacks, with 61% favoring more taxes and 8% more parole.

Those seeking to promote prison reforms are well aware of the public's hard-headedness. John Vodicka, who was the director of the Louisiana Coalition on Jails and Prisons during the turbulent period of the late 1970s, said the public's fear, anger and misconceptions about prisons and inmates were blocking meaningful progress in corrections. In Vodicka's view, society needs maturity and self-confidence to develop a rational corrections program. The present prison system, he said, is irrational, an answer to fear and an expression of society's fear and anger.

In a later interview, commenting on the changes Judge West's order had brought about in the DOC, Vodicka said, "It's nice to see the department operating prisons which aren't as brutal as they were in the past. But when you make nice prisons, you just make more of them." Vodicka argued that Judge West's order had trapped the state into spending more and more money only to incarcerate more and more prisoners.

What Louisiana was left with, then, ten years after, was a nicer, safer prison system, one that Paul Phelps could call the best in the South at providing secure custody of inmates, but a system still emphasizing long-term confinement as the appropriate response to crime. Attempts to win acceptance for non-custodial alternatives continue to encounter a stone wall of public opposition which only the most persistent efforts will eventually demolish.

Ask Paul Phelps. He's been trying to knock some holes in the wall for ten years without a whole lot of visible success. A 1985 *New Orleans Times-Picayune* editorial called him "a voice crying in the wilderness." If Phelps has put himself in the position of a prophet trying to prepare the way for real change in Louisiana's approach to corrections, he has yet to receive much of a response from the people he has been preaching to. As he said on the occasion of his removal from office by Governor Treen in 1981, "My basic failure was that I was unable to convince people that locking people up was not the best way to deal with the problem."

Mr. Phelps should not feel so bad: so far no one else has been able to convince the citizens of Louisiana of that, either. His remark stands as the epigraph to a decade of prison building.

8

IN SEARCH OF ALTERNATIVES*

by Burk Foster

When Edwin Edwards returned to begin his third term as governor of Louisiana in March 1984, he found a state in far different circumstances than the one he had passed on to his Republican successor, Dave Treen, only four years earlier. Edwards might have felt a bit like the owner of a prosperous estate who goes on an extended vacation, only to return and find that his caretaker has allowed the place to fall into near-ruin.

The oil boom had gone bust, the golden days of the seventies were a fading memory. The state was beset with problems—economic, environmental, educational, ethical—that the Treen administration (aptly described as "government in slow motion") had been able to do little about. Coming into office, Edwards already faced a budget deficit of $100 million (or maybe as much as $400 million), a deficit that would steadily worsen during his term and eventually play a big part in denying him his matched set of gubernatorial terms; his quest for a fourth term would end in defeat in the 1987 primary.

The question at this point was: which division of state government was in the worst shape? Many were hurting, none more evidently so than the Department of Corrections. When Dave Treen was campaigning for governor in 1979, he promised to be tough on criminals. Seldom has a Louisiana politician kept a promise so well. Treen refused to confront the problems of prison overcrowding directly, declined to build new prisons and dismissed Edwards' holdover head of the DOC, Paul Phelps, when

Phelps refused to support Treen's "double-bunking" plan to cram more inmates into existing spaces. Treen compiled the stingiest record on executive clemency (pardons and commutations) of any governor in modern Louisiana history, and it was toward the end of his term that capital punishment was resumed in Louisiana after a 22-year layoff. Finally Treen walked away and left the whole mess for Edwards to deal with.

Early in 1984, shortly before Treen left, the legislative fiscal office issued a report highly critical of the DOC. "The department has not managed its prison construction program in an efficient manner and has failed to adequately plan for future growth." Pre-fabricated prison cells, authorized in 1983 to house some of the thousand additional inmates by which the DOC's population was growing every year were never built. The backlog of state inmates in parish jails was greater than ever, bringing jails dangerously close to capacity.

The fiscal office projected cost figures that were truly staggering: three new prisons needed immediately, at a cost of $170 million; the DOC budget, which stood at $160 million in 1984, projected at $322.5 million in 1989; $240 million, much of it in state funds, needed for parish jail expansion.

The first thing Edwards did, to deal with this hand-me-down disorder (much of it, in all fairness to the Treen administration, readily apparent in legislative and judicial trends clearly established while Edwards was still governor in the 1970s),

*Appeared in *The Angolite*, July/August 1988, 37-51. Reprinted with permission.

was to reappoint Paul Phelps to his old job. The first thing Phelps did was to start talking about alternatives to imprisonment, a recurring subject that would carry him through to the end of Edwards' term in 1988 and into his next career, as the once again former director of the DOC.

This time he would have four years (plus a bit of warm-up time, to follow up on his almost six years in office the first time) to sell Louisiana's people, its criminal justice officials and its lawmakers on the advantages of not locking up criminals. Like another Phelps on a once-popular television series (now defunct), his would prove to be a "Mission Impossible." Or at least a "mission unpopular," with Phelps and his allies fighting an uphill battle for every inch of new ground.

Phelps said, when Edwards announced his reappointment as secretary of the DOC on October 26, 1983, that he had "some very good ideas and a plan in mind." He said there was an absolute requirement for new prisons to be built. "There is no way around it that I can see."

But building more prisons was not the only answer Phelps had in mind; it never had been. Property criminals did not need to be locked up at huge taxpayer's expense, he said. "The basic solution has to be in the probation and parole area," though with a lot more supervision than exists today if it is to work.

Though Edwin Edwards had not been known as a prison reformer his first two terms, this time around he seemed more inclined to support Phelps' efforts to reduce the state's overemphasis on imprisonment. "You can look forward to an emphasis on prison alternatives, bearing in mind an emphasis on protecting society," Governor Edwards said, early in his term. "Off the top of my head, I'd say

there are a significant number of people who could be let go with no danger to society."

While Phelps was promoting intensive probation on the Georgia model, Edwards was appointing the first of two study committees he wanted to look into ways of reducing prison overpopulation. The Forgotten Man Committee held its first meeting on April 25, 1984. This 80-member committee was the resurrection of a 1958 committee, appointed by Governor Earl Long, that had urged major penal reforms in a 1960 report. The new committee was intended specifically to consider the problems caused by the accumulation of a large number of "practical lifers" within the system; in a broader sense, it was to present the governor with a package of suggestions for safely reducing the prison population.

The committee set to work and Phelps did, too—trying to convince the 1984 legislature of the merits of intensive probation. Testifying before a legislative committee on the budget, Phelps said he could save the state $21 million a year by putting 3,000 convicts on intensive probation. He calculated the cost of the program at $10 a day, versus $31 a day it cost to keep a man in prison.

Phelps wanted to hire more regular probation and parole officers as well, citing full prisons and parish jails nearing their court-set capacity of 9,126 inmates (2,700 of whom were state prisoners). Phelps pointed out the facts: "If we don't do something very shortly, every cell in this state will be full."

It made sense to Phelps, but not to the public or the legislature. Rep. Ed Scogin, R-Slidell, said, "The public is still insisting that those who violate the law be taken off the streets." Orleans Parish District Attorney Harry Connick was even more plain: "The purpose of having a penitentiary is to provide for the safety of the public, not to cut corners and save some money."

The Edwards administration received a strong indication of how its reform legislation would fare in two House votes on May 22. Legislators overwhelmingly rejected, by votes of 71-22 and 68-21, bills that would have increased the rate of "good time" from 15 days to 25 days a month for some less dangerous offenders and would have allowed second time felony probation for non-violent offenders. One legislator, deriding the second bill as "three strikes before you go to jail," summed up the mood of this first "reform" session: "People would prefer to spend money building new jails rather than putting criminals back on the streets."

In the off season Edwards went on to appoint his second committee, the awkwardly-named Governor's Prison Overcrowding Policy Task Force. The Task Force, which began meeting in September 1984, would have plenty to study. The state's prison population was increasing by an average of 124 inmates a month, and the legislature had made clear its preference for new prisons over substantive reforms (except that many of the anti-reform legislators were also anti-taxes, making it difficult to raise new funds for any purpose).

The Task Force was intended to follow a separate path from that of the Forgotten Man Committee. The Task Force was a much smaller group, a kind of insiders' club made up mostly of influential political leaders and criminal justice officials. It was supposed to come up with practical, immediate, politically acceptable measures to relieve overcrowding. The Forgotten Man Committee, on the other hand, was the broadly-based citizens'

group, valued as much for public relations as for any specific proposals it might make. The Forgotten Man Committee was to dream, and to try to popularize its dream among the public; the Task Force had to face reality.

Paul Phelps was hard up against reality, too, as he prepared for the next legislative session in 1985. In speeches around the state, Phelps described Louisiana's overflowing prisons as the product of oil money and a get tough on crime policy. But with oil revenues dwindling, the state would have to borrow money to build new prisons. He urged that more money be spent on halfway houses and on probation and parole. The trouble was, he recognized, that "people think parole and probation is soft on crime." State legislators have "reflected the attitudes of their constituencies . . . that the only way to punish people is to lock them up."

The Prison Overcrowding Task Force, meeting early in 1985, was told by Pete Adams, the executive director of the Louisiana District Attorneys Association, that the public was not going to buy any task force recommendations based on cost alone. "If you have ever been victimized, your priorities changed very quickly," he said.

An editorial in the *Lafayette Daily Advertiser* a few days later made the same point. "We do not like prison overcrowding and we do not like the millions upon millions that it costs to maintain penal facilities. But more important than the expense is the protection of the public. Expense absolutely cannot become the sole justification for avoiding justice and thus increasing risks to the public."

Somewhere along the line, it seemed, justice in Louisiana had become equated with imprisonment: justice was locking people up, injustice was any lesser punishment. Paul Phelps would have been the first to admit that, conditions being what they were, there was considerable merit in the public's skeptical view of probation and parole. In November 1984, DOC figures showed 249 probation and parole officers trying to supervise 29,522 probationers and parolees. This was an average caseload of 119. Probation and parole services needed to be expanded, Phelps said, and the state ought to go ahead with intensive probation, which he had over-optimistically hoped would be ready to try in a pilot program by January 1, 1985.

A *New Orleans Times-Picayune* editorial on the prison crisis suggested that "the two publicly acceptable alternatives would seem to be to increase the number of parole and probation officers to realistic levels and to plan now for some more prisons. It is irresponsible to insist on tough law enforcement and sentences and then disregard the consequences faced by state and local correctional authorities."

Before the legislative session began, the Forgotten Man Committee submitted its first report to the governor. The introduction sounded an ominous warning:

"Discussions with decision-makers, top administrators and professional staff who work within the state's corrections system indicate clearly a developing crisis. Louisiana has outgrown its ability to incarcerate all those who commit felonies but has not defined or even generally agreed on the necessity of developing a range of alternative approaches to punishing felony offenders. In fact, legislators have traditionally shied away from serious discussion of any approach other than incarceration.

"Louisiana now faces a set of circumstances that it literally cannot build itself

out of—cannot because the numbers are too large, the projected growth too fast and the costs too great. Over 11,000 offenders are now in the physical custody of the Department of Public Safety and Corrections (DPS&C). About 3,000 more have been sentenced to the legal custody of DPS&C but remain in the parish prisons. The pool of all those sentenced to state custody is increasing by about 1,400 annually. At the same time, costs of construction average $35,000-$50,000 per bed. That means a 1,000 bed prison (which would accommodate 70% of next year's increase in total population, or 33% of the 3,000 presently backlogged in the parishes) would cost millions more to operate and would, after a year, leave the state in the same place it was before the new 1,000 bed prison was built—i.e., with over 4,000 inmates it has no space to house."

In its 31-page report, the committee offered 20 major recommendations concerning prison operations. Of these, several would directly affect alternatives to confinement, including: 1) increased use of work release centers; 2) an intensive probation supervision program; 3) second felony probation; 4) more probation and parole officers; 5) the use of shock probation (split sentences), with a prison term of up to two years; 6) to make all inmates eligible for parole consideration after 20 years.

With encouragement from these quarters, the legislature did finally get around to serious corrections legislation. In summary, the legislation adopted included: 1) planning funds for five new medium security prisons, 2) approval to hire 100 new probation and parole officers, 3) limiting probation and parole caseloads to 50, 4) reestablishing a program to have the state pay 70% of new parish jail construction costs, 5) expanding three existing prisons.

This approach, heavy on additional confinement and light on alternatives, did not set well with Paul Phelps. He warned, "In 1986, the financial crisis will be so great that the legislature will not have many alternatives."

Phelps had tried to get legislative approval of an early parole program. He described his proposal—in which offenders would serve six months in prison and then go home to house arrest—to a legislative panel and said a pilot program could begin soon in the New Iberia area. But the outcry from New Iberia political officials was so immediate and so strongly negative that the proposal was abandoned. The legislature killed the bill the next week.

Parole was not a popular choice in Louisiana at the time. A January 1985 opinion survey by the *Baton Rouge Morning Advocate* showed that even in economic hard times, 69% of registered voters preferred increasing taxes to lock up more prisoners. Only 4.2% preferred releasing more inmates on parole to relieve overcrowding.

A House committee showed the public where its heart was, late in the session, voting to require inmates to return to the good old days of wearing striped uniforms. The debate, heated at times, actually lasted longer than the discussion on some of the reform legislation. And three months later, another legislative committee voted to take back the 100 new probation and parole positions just created, then impose a further 3% budget cut on the probation and parole divisions.

Probation might be cut back, but prisons were popular as ever. At the end of 1985, bonds were sold to begin construction of five new medium security prisons with a capacity of 2,500 inmates,

in five rural parishes. Politicians were perfectly willing to spend state money to help out the ailing economies of these rural areas, even as they ignored cheaper alternatives for supervising Louisiana's mostly urban offender population.

The Prison Overcrowding Task Force continued its work throughout 1985. At a November hearing, witnesses said that only legislators could solve Louisiana's costly prison crowding problems. Some of the state's mandatory sentencing laws should be repealed, they said. DA Paul Carmouche of Shreveport said, "I don't believe in minimum mandatory sentencing except in rare instances." District Judge Frank Marullo of New Orleans said, "We're putting people in jail who don't belong in jail. The public wants everybody who's convicted to be locked up in jail, but we're going to have to educate the public that this isn't always the best solution."

The Task Force would continue meeting through the winter and issue its second report on March 1, 1986, before the next legislative session. In this report, the Task Force made several major recommendations to reduce the use of imprisonment: 1) Hire 100 new probation and parole officers each year for the next five years (1986 to 1990), until the workload was 50 per officer. Probationers would help pay the cost of their supervision according to a sliding fee scale. 2) Set up an intensive probation supervision program. 3) Allow probation upon a second felony conviction. 4) Noting the declining use of parole (from 11% of all DOC offenders in 1975 to 6% in 1985), develop a parole risk assessment model. 5) Establish an intensive incarceration program: three to six months of participation in para-military "boot camp" training, as an option with first and second offenders serving terms of seven years or less.

Although these alternatives would help reduce Louisiana's prison population, the Task Force noted that the state would need another 6,400 prison beds by 1990, at a construction cost of $320 million. Parish jails, holding the backlog of state prisoners, would also need attention. Replacement and expansion of jail facilities was estimated at $300 million, with state and local governments sharing the cost on a 70/30 grant program. The Task Force recommended against the private management of state prisons and local jails and warned that with the children of "baby boomers" growing up, we could expect another crime wave in the early 1990s. That was the bad news. The good news was: deinstitutionalization was finding a larger measure of political acceptance.

In support of one of the Task Force's recommendations, Attorney General William Guste sent every member of the legislature a letter outlining his support for an "intensive supervision" probation plan. It would provide a "viable punishment" while requiring offenders to support themselves. Violent criminals would be excluded. Even so, Guste pointed out that over 1,500 first-time offenders serving sentences of five years or less remained as prime candidates for the program.

When the 1986 legislature met to consider the now-perennial question of what to do about prison overcrowding, the *New Orleans Times-Picayune* pointed out that legislators seemed to recognize the need for alternative programs but did not want to spend the money. "Think of what will happen if we don't do it," John Baiamonte, the chairman of the Prison Overcrowding Task Force, told the subcommittee on prisons, alluding to the thousands of additional prison beds that would be needed.

With the bells of doomsday faintly audible, the legislature did approve, by a vote of 96-2 on May 27, the use of a boot camp "intensive incarceration" program for first offenders. They would serve three to six months, then be recommended for parole. Only volunteers serving a sentence of seven years or less would be eligible. The bill, sponsored by Rep. Raymond Jetson, D-Baton Rouge, was estimated to save the state $25 million to $40 million a year.

By now the state needed every dollar it could save. On July 8, 1986, the DOC stopped accepting new inmates for three months, because of budget cuts that forced guard layoffs and reduced operating expenses. Staff cuts were estimated at about 500. Paul Phelps admitted that space was available to house more inmates, but he refused to lower the quality of care by reducing the ratio of staff to inmates (which would have required the approval of federal Judge Frank Polozola anyway, under the existing consent decree). One state legislator reacted by demanding that Phelps be fired, because one of the economies Phelps was considering was shutting down the girls' training school at Ball, in the legislator's district.

At least Phelps knew he had their attention now, and 1986 turned out not to be such a bad year after all. Funds were appropriated to hire 100 new probation and parole officers, just as in the previous year. Intensive probation trial projects were finally begun in Lafayette and St. Martin Parishes in March.

In the Fall, Governor Edwards spoke up for other alternatives. He recommended use of house arrest for first-time non-violent offenders. And he spoke out against mandatory sentencing. "The legislature may wish to look at some 38 to 40 laws that now require a mandatory jail sentence and hopefully modify some of them to give the judge more discretion in some areas where he thinks the mandatory jail terms may not necessarily be required," the governor said.

Jack Wardlaw, in one of his *Times-Picayune* columns, pointed out the continuing incentive for prison alternatives: between 1975 and 1985 the number of state prison inmates rose from 5,325 to 13,386, or 151%. During the same period, the crime rate increased by only 28%.

On February 9, 1987, one of the new alternatives, the military boot camp, opened at Hunt Correctional Center near St. Gabriel. About 30 inmates had been selected for the first class. For three months they would be subject to strict discipline and physical training; if they passed, it was on to the Parole Board.

Three months later, on May 19, the first 18 graduates were handed their parole papers. Of the ones who did not graduate, three dropped out and were sent back to prison, eight were held back to finish later and one died of a lung hemorrhage during physical training a month into the program.

The inmate graduates had good things to say about the experience. "It taught me a whole lot more than I knew," said inmate Timothy Jackson. "Self-respect. Discipline. The value of life. I've learned to deal with things in a positive way." They were nevertheless relieved to give their places to the 100 other inmates, including four women, making their way through earlier phases of the program.

The 1987 legislature, which would be the last to work with the Edwards administration, must have been encouraged to see one of the new alternative programs off to such a good start, and a well-publicized start at that. Many of the same reform

measures legislators had debated the past three years would come up again this session. The pace of corrections legislation was definitely picking up.

HB 533, labelled a bill for geriatric offenders, could just as easily have been called a "prison retirement" plan. It made inmates serving sentences of 30 years or more eligible for parole consideration after serving 20 years and reaching age 60. Lest the public think they were getting too soft on the elderly, legislators retained a clause excluding lifers, unless their sentence had been commuted to a fixed term.

HB 12 was the 1987 reincarnation of a bill that had been around awhile, including earlier the same session under a different number. This bill made certain offenders eligible for second felony probation, provided at least five years had passed between offenses. A committee had earlier killed an amendment which would have required the DOC to reduce probation and parole caseloads to 50, but the main bill did pass.

HB 537, dubbed the "flagship" of 1987's prison overcrowding package, established the Louisiana Sentencing Commission. This 22-member permanent commission was instructed to develop a uniform policy on criminal sentencing for the state and to prepare advisory guidelines for judges. Its creation reflected a consensus that had developed among members of the Prison Overcrowding Task Force and others urging reform, that bringing criminal penalties under control was the first step in reducing the state's prison population. The 18 voting members of the Sentencing Commission would consist of legislators, judges, attorneys and sheriffs—not a group likely to run rampant through the fields of reform but one capable of making meaningful, responsive changes over time. The commission was given a start-up budget of $100,000 to begin its review of Louisiana's criminal sentencing statutes.

One bill which did not get past the legislature this time was HB 531, which would have given judges ex post facto power to reduce felony sentences—after the offender had served six months in prison. This bill was vehemently opposed by the Louisiana District Attorneys Association. "The principle and concept is repugnant to us," spokesman Pete Adams said. He pointed out that there were already numerous ways to cut short jail time. "Do you want to provide another mechanism, where a person is actually convicted, to go get out?" he asked.

The legislature apparently did not. But it did approve with less controversy the companion bill, HB 532, which allows the same practice—sentence reduction—in non-hard labor felonies (called relative felonies in Louisiana) and in misdemeanors, after the person has begun serving his sentence. The offender is allowed to make one request, like one phone call, to the court that sentenced him.

Several of the measures the 1987 legislature approved seemed more in the line of "safety valves" than truly sweeping reforms. As safety valves, these options would give legal authorities power to "vent off" small segments of the criminal population passing through the courts and on into the prison system. If prison overcrowding reached crisis proportions, the vents could be opened; when the crisis was over, they could be shut again.

If indeed these alternatives were adopted according to plan (whether Edwin Edwards' or Paul Phelps' or the Prison Overcrowding Task Force's or someone else's), the legislature deserved praise for its provident thinking. As 1987 went along, the twin crises—budget and correc-

tional—continued locked in an irreconcilable confrontation. The state was deeply in debt, with no immediate prospect of getting out. Budget cuts were the order of the day, across all departments of state government. And yet, inexorably, the number of people locked up—in state prisons and local jails—continued to increase. Once again the prison system was caught between the rock of increasing numbers and the hard place of the federal courts—Judge Frank Polozola in Baton Rouge monitoring head counts, inmate to staff ratios, violence and escapes to insure that living conditions did not begin to deteriorate.

The DOC limped through the rest of the year, cutting back wherever it could. Edwin Edwards turned his attention from administration to reelection. He was one of six major candidates running for governor. None of them had much to say about prisons, though the rest all had plenty to say about Edwards' mismanagement of state government in general and budget woes in particular.

When he ran a weak second to Democratic Congressman Buddy Roemer in the September open gubernatorial primary, Edward capitulated the office to Roemer and then virtually dropped from sight, spending a good part of his last six months in office on his ranch outside Junction, Texas. Now it was his turn to play caretaker, and he demonstrated that he was not well-suited to the role. When Roemer's transition government wanted to start early with deep budget cuts to reduce deficits, Edwards made some cuts, refused more, and hinted that he would be available in four years to save the state from calamities of the "Roemer Revolution."

On March 14, 1988, Edwards went out of office; this time Paul Phelps resigned and went out with him. As Buddy

Roemer was inaugurated governor on a cool, blustery Monday in Baton Rouge, he had not yet named a new Secretary of the Department of Public Safety and Corrections to take Phelps' place. It was the only cabinet-level post remaining unfilled, surely not a promising indicator of the DOC's standing in the new administration.

So in the end, in uneasy retirement, what did Paul Phelps and Edwin Edwards have to show for four more years together? How much success could they claim in their efforts to develop correctional alternatives at the state level? The answer is, objectively, not much. Try as they might, they had not been able to reverse the trends of the 1970s and begin de-emphasizing the state's reliance on confinement as a means of punishing criminals.

Phelps was right, undoubtedly, when he said that Louisiana's prison overcrowding problems were the product of oil riches and a punitive public mood. For a few years in the late seventies, Louisiana could easily afford to construct and staff new prisons. This period happened to coincide with hardening public attitudes on what should be done with criminals, and the result was an unprecedented growth in the number of persons in confinement. From the standpoint of the people trying to run the DOC from 1984 to 1988, the economic prosperity could not have come at a worse time. It encouraged the state to take the easy way out—locking everyone up—instead of diversifying its options. As an excessive dependence on oil revenues would devastate the state's economy when oil prices began to fall, so an excessive dependence on imprisonment would eventually devastate the corrections system, when the extra money needed to support the huge prison system was no longer available.

Probably the most curious aspect of the hard-headed public mood is how quickly it developed and then how firmly it took hold. Before the 1970s, Louisiana was not a particularly punitive state. It ranked 13th nationally in 1965, with a rate of 109.1 prisoners per 100,000 population. Like most Southern states, it sent a lot of people to prison, but with the executive's generous use of good time, commutations and parole, people who went to prison, even for very long sentences, were usually out again quickly. Until 1972, the standard was: any inmate who behaved himself in prison would be let go after ten-and-a-half years—the so-called "10-6 rule."

What happened in the seventies was that the state stopped letting people go. People who had once convicted offenders and sent them off to be managed by correctional and political authorities without public interference began to put their foot down. "Just say no!" we would be told later, in the war on drugs. In the 1970s the people of Louisiana had already discovered the phrase: they addressed it to convicted felons, who they did not want back in their communities, and to the authorities they did not trust to protect them.

Existing alternatives were de-emphasized. The 10-6 rule was disallowed, good time was cut back, parole and sentence commutations became less frequent. At the same time, the state jumped heavily into mandatory sentencing for violent crimes and drug offenses and judges began to apply longer sentences to repeat property offenders. This was not exactly a case of the right hand not knowing what the left hand was doing, more like the right hand of imprisonment taking every opportunity to slap down the left hand of alternatives. Thus in the early

1980s, when the public, the media, and the legislature were confronted with evidence that lack of prison space was indeed a serious problem, it was as if they no longer remembered the old days of leniency. That part of corrections history had been erased from the collective memory. People did not want to hear about old alternatives, new alternatives, any alternatives at all, until finally they were left with no other choices.

That time is now at hand. Since U.S. District Judge Gordon West imposed his "cruel and unusual punishment" court order on the state penitentiary at Angola in 1975, Louisiana has opened six new prisons for men. Three more are now under construction and two others are authorized. The number of state prisoners has tripled, from 5,300 in June 1975 to 15,329 at the end of June 1987 (This is close to the same prison population as Louisiana's mother country, France, a nation of 55 million people). The state had custody of 11,758 of that total; 3,571 were in parish jails.

Set against these numbers, the alternatives adopted under the last Edwards administration seem puny; in practice they are probably even weaker than they look on paper. From following the course of legislation, for instance, it might appear that the state has invested heavily in the expansion of probation and parole in the last few years. Not so. The DOC budget has been cut back in two successive years, many of the cuts coming in non-institutional programs. The legislature giveth with the one hand and taketh away with the other; at the end of 1987 Louisiana had 320 probation and parole

officers supervising 37,198 cases. This is about 70 more officers than four years earlier, but the caseloads have remained virtually constant during this time, averaging between 110 and 120 cases per officer. Intensive probation remains an interesting experiment, used selectively in a few parishes; it has not yet been adopted statewide.

Other alternatives have fared no better. The use of second felony probation is no more common in most state courts, now that it is legal, than it used to be when it was illegal and judges simply ignored previous convictions to put offenders on probation regardless. The high-powered Sentencing Commission has been put on hold, its operating funds withheld for now as one of the Roemer administration's economy moves. Boot camp continues to operate with only about 100 offenders in processing at any given time. Few people—on either side of the law—are even aware that judges can grant sentence reduction for non-hard labor offenses. And the new governor, Buddy Roemer, has indicated that he will look at the parole and pardon options "most severely," whatever that may mean.

That is one of the traditional problems of correctional administration in the states: just when you get organized, governors change, and off corrections goes in a different direction. Edwin Edwards and Paul Phelps may have planted the seeds of correctional diversification in Louisiana, but now the orchard belongs to Buddy Roemer; we will have to meet again in four years to see what the harvest will bring.

9

WHAT IS THE MEANING OF LIFE:
THE EVOLUTION AND IMPACT OF
NATURAL LIFE SENTENCES IN LOUISIANA, 1973-1994*

by Burk Foster

When philosophy professors ask, "What is the meaning of life," they are usually trying to get their students to reflect deeply on the nature and purpose of human existence. When corrections officials ask, "What is the meaning of life," they usually have pencils and calculators in hand, seeking a practical answer in finite temporal units—ten years, fifteen years, twenty years, some minimum time period after which a life-sentenced criminal offender becomes eligible for release consideration.

Philosophy professors are probably most happy if their question generates many answers—existential argument is enhanced by contradictory, wide-ranging responses. Corrections officials are probably less than thrilled when their question generates the same multiplicity of answers, and when those answers vary widely not only from jurisdiction-to-jurisdiction but also from time-to-time within the same jurisdiction. They would much prefer the simple, enduring answer that the philosophy professors would abhor.

The best recent guide to the many-forked path among life sentences in America is the January 1993 issue of *Corrections COMPENDIUM*. Referring to their survey conducted September 30, 1992, Su Perk Davis reports that 8.2% of the American prison population is serving life sentences. The results of this survey are summarized in my Table 1, which combines several tables from the January 1993 *Corrections COMPENDIUM* into

one. It compares with a similar table, lacking statistical detail, prepared by the Pennsylvania Prison Society for their article, "The Need for Parole Options for Life-Sentenced Prisoners" (see "Parole for Lifers," *The Angolite*, November/December 1994, pp. 14-21); it also compares with Table 6.63, "Prison inmates serving life sentences," in the *Sourcebook of Criminal Justice Statistics 1993*.

Table 1 summarizes information on life sentences by states, listing each state, its prison population, numbers of men and women lifers, whether it has a no-parole life sentence, and if so, the numbers of men and women serving no-parole life.

According to the state reports in the survey, in 1992 a total of 65,281 men and 2,482 women were serving life sentences, more than 44,000 for first or second degree murder and another 20,500 for other offenses—kidnapping, drug offenses, sexual assault, robbery or habitual offender.

The number of lifers continues to increase, of course, as the prison population grows. In 1974, in a prison population of 187,500, there were 21,900 lifers, or about 12% of the total. Twenty years later, as the prison population surpassed one million, the number of lifers approaches 82,000, if the percentages from Su Perk Davis's article hold. So on the whole, one can argue that life sentences are being imposed less frequently now than they were 20 years ago.

*Printed with permission.

On the other hand, the trend that is in many respects more ominous for those who project the consequences of long-term imprisonment is toward a dramatic increase in the number of lifers serving no-parole sentences. Thirty-three states, the District of Columbia and the Federal Bureau of Prisons have a specific sentence of "life without parole" or a statutory provision of parole ineligibility for certain offenses, as of 1992.

Twenty-five years ago there were perhaps a handful of true no-parole life sentences (and Kentucky, one of few states with no-parole life in the early 1970s, abolished the sentence in 1975). Now more than 10,000 men and women know the reality of true natural-life sentences. Their numbers remain small for now. Only California, Florida, Louisiana, Michigan and Pennsylvania have more than a thousand no-parole lifers in their state prisons at present. But the prospects for increasing their numbers appear good in many states.

As America continues its search for new ways to get tougher on criminals, no-parole life sentences have an undeniable appeal. Remember "three strikes and you're out?" The habitual felons sentenced under these statutes are parole ineligible. Their numbers are just beginning to show up in current prison population statistics. And it takes very little imagination (no more than most state legislatures display, at any rate) to convert more of the 75,000+ life with parole sentences to life without parole.

Of all the states that have jumped on the life without parole bandwagon, Louisiana has ridden it most enthusiastically for the longest time. No-parole life sentences took effect in Louisiana in 1973; over the next 20 years, through September 30, 1992, Louisiana accumulated 2,230 lifers, over 90% of whom were no-parole natural lifers. The only parole-eligible lifers in Louisiana at present are a group of fewer than 200 second-degree murders who entered the system between 1973 and 1979 (The number reflects updated statistics prepared by Corrections Services after the *Corrections COMPENDIUM* 1992 survey). All other lifers in Louisiana are serving natural life: 2,154 according to *Corrections COMPENDIUM's* 1992 survey, right at 2,400 according to the Louisiana Department of Public Safety and Corrections's year-end 1994 figures. What is most striking about this number of no-parole lifers is how methodically it has come about, and how quickly and deliberately the policy effecting it was accomplished.

Before 1973 in Louisiana, there was no such thing as a natural life sentence. The best legal history of life sentences in Louisiana up to 1979 is Ron Wikberg's "A Graphic & Illustrative History, 1879 to 1979, Life Sentences in Louisiana." Written long before Wikberg became associate editor of *The Angolite* and published author, this unpublished mimeographed pamphlet bears the imprint of the Lifers' Association of the Louisiana State Penitentiary. In 15 pages Wikberg outlines the legislative and judicial history of life sentences in Louisiana.

Wikberg's fundamental observation is that for most of the 100 years a life sentence meant much less than life. In the 1890s, the penitentiary's Board of Control, the Pardon Board and the Governor were authorized to release a lifer after 15 years. In 1902, this fifteen-year period was reiterated. In 1914, the legislature adopted a new parole provision under which life-termers became parole eligible after serving one-third of this fifteen year period, or five years. In 1916, the Board of Control was abolished and the Board of Parole created, with the same authority to parole lifers after a minimum of five years in prison.

In 1926, the legislature established the procedure that would prevail for almost half a century:

That whenever a prisoner who has been convicted of a crime and sentenced to imprisonment for life, so conducts himself as to merit the approval of the General Manager of the State Penitentiary, he may apply for commutation of his sentence and upon the approval of the said General Manager, the same shall be forwarded to the Board of Pardons, and upon their approval, the same shall be forwarded to the Governor; provided, that no commutation under the provisions of this section shall reduce the term of service (to) less than 10 years and six months.

This was the "10-6" rule, so-called in that it established the normal length of a life sentence as ten-and-a-half years. Both statute and case law for the next half century make reference to the general expectation that a convict on good behavior would serve ten years and six months; he could then expect a favorable recommendation from the head of the penitentiary—the General Manager became the Superintendent and later the Warden— which would be forwarded along to the Pardon Board and the Governor for approval, leading to the convict's outright discharge from prison. He would have used up his life sentence.

In the 1970s this procedure was done away with. Wikberg maintains in his research that the 10-6 rule was not officially repealed until July 13, 1979, when Act 490 of the 1979 legislature abolished the recommendation process. It is clear from the record, however, that the

10-6 rule died in practice several years earlier. By 1973 the Warden of the penitentiary stopped making recommendations to the Pardon Board; without this starting impetus, the release process ceased.

The men who had come into the prison system serving life sentences when the 10-6 rule was in effect came to be known as the "forgotten men" (one of several occasions this term has been applied to a group of Louisiana convicts): "forgotten" because the rule change had been applied to them retroactively. When they applied for release from prison on the grounds that the release procedure in effect when they entered prison ought still to apply to them, they were told that this was an administrative process and not a legal requirement: if the Warden quit making recommendations for the release of lifers after ten-and-a-half years in prison, the courts could not require him to start again, nor could they release any of the forgotten men who had served longer than ten-and-a-half years.

The only route open to the forgotten men was the traditional commutation process. According to statutes enacted in 1914 and 1916 and filled-in with more detail later, a lifer could petition the Pardon Board for a reduction of his life sentence to a fixed term of years. If this petition were granted and then approved by the Governor, the term would be commuted (what the convicts still call a "time cut") and parole eligibility would occur after one-third of the term. In this way, a pre-1970s convict might get a life sentence reduced to 15 years, become parole eligible after five, or reach his good-time release date in a little over eight years, if he did not make parole.

Many convicts did try this route successfully, in an era when it was much easier to obtain a pardon than it is today. Plenty of lifers were released on parole or good-time long before they ever reached their 10-6 release date. The old-time convicts say only the nobodies, which in Louisiana translates into those without political pull, stayed for ten-and-a-years; the advantaged went home early.

Lifers today still follow the same century-old steps—Pardon Board for a time cut, Governor's signature, then to the Parole Board after one-third—but their chances of success are much reduced, and when they do successfully run the political gauntlet, their fixed terms are more likely to be in the 60- to 90-year range, meaning they must serve at least 20 to 30 years before becoming parole eligible. This process turns young men into old men.

In the 1970s, while the Department of Corrections was finding clever ways not to release the old 10-6 lifers from the penitentiary, the Louisiana legislature was finding new ways of insuring that these men would have plenty of company growing old.

Act 111 of the 1973 legislature provided that second-degree murderers would not be eligible for parole for 20 years. Two years later, Act 380 of the 1975 legislature raised this minimum period to 40 years. Act 74 of the 1979 legislature went all the way: it made second-degree murder punishable by a natural life sentence.

It took the Louisiana legislature most of the decade to get its penalties straight for first-degree murder and aggravated rape. In the aftermath of *Furman v. Georgia*, Louisiana had first tried to make the death penalty mandatory for first-degree murder, and had continued to allow the death penalty for rape. After the U.S. Supreme Court struck down mandatory death penalty laws and then said in *Coker v.*

Georgia there could be no death penalty for a rape in which the victim did not die, the legislature reluctantly rewrote its statutes in conformity with the court's rulings (in Act 657 of 1976 and Act 239 of 1978). First-degree murder was left with penalties of death or natural life, and aggravated rape was left with natural life only.

The legislature also set natural life sentences for three other crimes; for aggravated kidnapping and distribution of Schedule I narcotics, natural life was mandatory, for third and fourth felony convictions, natural life was either mandatory or optional, depending on exactly what crimes the prior convictions were for.

Thus within less than a decade Louisiana went from turning all lifers loose in ten-and-a-half years or less to keeping virtually all of them in prison for their natural lives. The amazing aspect of this change, according to Paul Phelps, who was Secretary of Corrections in Louisiana during most of the 1970s and again in the 1980s, after a political break, was how directly it was done, and without controversy or substantial disagreement. Phelps said that it was all "black-and-white;" the legislature decided natural life sentences were a simple, straightforward solution to the problem of violent crime. There was no transition or period of legal evolution; one day the law was this way, the next day it was vastly different.

Phelps was also fond of pointing out that these changes were made during a time when Louisiana was oil rich. Phelps would blame oil money for supporting the "lock 'em up" mindset that developed in his state in the 1970s. He often said, before his death at age 60 from a heart attack on March 10, 1993, that the money could not have come at a worse time, because it discouraged shorter sentences and non-institutional alternatives.

Revenues from oil and gas production enabled Louisiana to embark on a vigorous campaign of prison building from 1976 on, to hold more lifers and more non-lifers as well (which by the early 1980s would start Louisiana's 15-year run as one of the top three states in per capita imprisonment rates). Louisiana could afford to lock lifers up for life; for a time in the 70s when new mandatory sentencing bills were introduced in every legislative session, its legislators seemed determined to lock up every violent felon, every drug dealer, everyone using a weapon to commit a crime, every repeat burglar, every repeat offender. For a time we didn't really notice how many lifers there were, because there were so many other convicted felons in state prisons and parish jails the numbers were almost overwhelming.

The Department of Corrections's operating budget increased from seven million dollars, for 4,000 inmates in 1971, to over $100 million for 8,000 prisoners in 1981. This spending did not include over $300 million appropriated between 1976 and 1980 for prison-related capital improvements—three new outcamps, new dormitories and other renovations at the Angola penitentiary, improvements in the state highway from St. Francisville to the penitentiary, two new medium security prison already opened and a third ready to open by the end of the year, expansion of two work training centers.

Paul Phelps was already suggesting in his speeches that the corrections department was in a "futile foot race with the judicial system," which with the legislature's new mandatory sentencing laws was sending 50 more people to prison each month than prisons were

releasing. Phelps, speaking before a legislative committee in 1979, said, "If the state of Louisiana does not change its policies, we are firmly dedicated to building a new prison every other year. Our policy right now is to put everybody in prison."

State Senator Foster Campbell Jr. of Bossier City agreed, saying, "Pretty soon prisons will be more expensive than schools in this state." But when Phelps proposed expanded use of probation as an alternative to imprisonment, Campbell said he did not believe voters were ready to broaden probation programs. "I don't think the people of Louisiana are willing to lessen penalties," he said.

Sen. Campbell's observation remains as valid in 1995 as it was in 1979. The state of Louisiana has still not lessened any of the natural life sentences adopted during the "punishment decade" of the 1970s. The percentage of lifers in the state prison population has not changed dramatically over the 20-year period, remaining at a fairly constant level of between 11% and 12%. Figures on the numbers of lifers in the Louisiana prison population are shown in Table 2.

We can see from this table how steadily the number of lifers—over 90% of whom are natural lifers—has increased. Before the mid-1970s, the Louisiana prison system never accumulated more than a couple of hundred lifers at any given time; the outgo—from the 10-6 rule, parole and good-time—and the influx of new inmates were roughly in balance.

By the late 70s, the balance had been destroyed: lifers were still coming in, but they weren't leaving. They were no longer eligible for parole, and the commutation process slowed to a virtual trickle.

Out of over 600 first-degree murderers sentenced to death or life imprisonment since the new statute was adopted in 1973, only 11—nine men and two women—have received a commutation of sentence, and only eight of these have been released from prison. So 98% of the first-degree murderers who are still alive are still serving the no-parole natural life sentences they came in with, and the percentage of natural lifers for other offenses—second-degree murder, aggravated rape, aggravated kidnapping, distribution of narcotics and habitual felons—remains nearly as high.

Table 3 lists the number of natural lifers incarcerated for the six life imprisonment offenses in Louisiana. Of the total 2,595 lifers in the system as of March 1, 1995, 181 entered prior to the change of practice and law in 1973—the end of the 10-6 era. The balance, 2,414, have entered the system since.

Louisiana's lifers still go through the clemency application process. "What else is there to do?" they might ask. But the hard truth is that clemency is no longer an avenue open to the masses. It has become very individual and selective, with over 90% of lifers either being denied by the Pardon Board, rejected by the Governor, or never even bothering to apply for clemency in the first place. Their numbers increase by more than 100 each year now, and the most common way for them to leave prison now is death.

The rate of increase in the number of lifers has tended to keep pace with the increased number of new admissions, as indicated earlier. 1980 was the first year in which the increase went above 100, and the increase continued at this pace through the rest of the 1980s and into the early 1990s, as shown in Table 2. It is interesting to note that by 1993 and 1994, the annual increase had jumped to 159 and 153, indicating, if anything, a renewed commitment by the system to putting

lifers away. Only Florida and Pennsylvania today reportedly have a slightly larger number of natural lifers than Louisiana's total of 2,400.

You can tour the Louisiana corrections system today, looking at the 16,500 men and women in state prisons and the 7,000 additional state inmates serving their sentences in parish jails, and not be struck with how many lifers there are—until you visit the Louisiana State Penitentiary at Angola. The oldest, the largest, the most remote and the most secure of Louisiana's prisons, Angola has become the repository for the largest number of Louisiana's lifers. Table 4 indicates where life inmates are housed.

About 88% of Louisiana's life-term inmates are confined at Angola; almost half of the prison's 4,600 inmates are lifers, and half of the rest are what Louisiana calls "practical lifers," whose fixed terms for armed robbery, forcible rape and other crimes extend beyond their normal life expectancy.

Becoming a "lifers' prison" has had a big impact on Angola. The average age of the inmate population in 1990 was 36, and by 1994 it had climbed to 37, which is probably the oldest of any large, general purpose prison in the United States. As of March 15, 1994, Angola held only 34 prisoners under age 20, but 2,429 age 35 or older. Douglas Dennis, in his article "The Living Dead" in the September/October 1994 *Angolite*, points out that Louisiana held 344 inmates confined 20 years or longer, of a total prison population of 23,502. The great majority of these long-term inmates are serving their time at Angola.

What lies ahead for these men? As long as 20 years ago, Paul Phelps and other corrections officials were predicting that Angola would eventually become the nation's largest "old folks home," as more and more lifers came there to live the rest of their natural lives in this most unnatural place.

The Pennsylvania Prison Society discusses the problems of aging offenders in its recent report, "The Need for Parole Options for Life-Sentenced Prisoners." The report points out, among other concerns, the high cost of medical care for older inmates—estimated at two to three times that of younger inmates—greater vulnerability to injury, the increased likelihood of victimization by predatory younger inmates, and resources wasted guarding older inmates who are no longer a real threat to society.

Richard Stalder, the current Secretary of Public Safety and Corrections in Louisiana, has appealed to the state legislature the past two sessions for more authority to turn older lifers loose, so that he can make more room in his prisons for more active younger criminals. So far the legislature has not granted his request. Legislators have directed Stalder to proceed with plans to open a geriatric satellite prison in North Louisiana, at the site of the old Caddo Parish Prison. When the natural lifers said they didn't want to die at Angola, being sent to Shreveport to die instead was not the alternative they had in mind.

"What is the meaning of life?" Inmates at the Louisiana State Penitentiary are not philosophy professors, but they probably yearn for the same variety of responses the professors hope for. After 20 years of living with the reality of "life means life," any variation on the theme would have to be cause for hope.

It probably gives no sense of satisfaction to Louisiana's lifers to know that their numbers are being supplemented by thousands more no-parole lifers in many other states. Most of them would cheerfully trade their place on the cutting edge of punishment for a realistic chance to go home, even after 20 or 25 or 30 years in prison, while they still have a few good years left.

It is a puzzle to them that after so many, many years in prison, growing gray and tired, and in some cases wise and benevolent as well, they are likely never to get the chance to show the free world what they have learned, or how they have changed. From the point of view of Louisiana's lifers, if the question is, "What is the true meaning of our lives, to the outside world," the answer, quick in coming, is, "Nil."

Table 1
Life Sentences in the States, 1992

State	Prison Population	Number of Lifers Male	Number of Lifers Female	Life w/o Parole	No-Parole Lifers Male	No-Parole Lifers Female
Alabama	17,221	2,548	58	Yes	685	11
Alaska	No response	—	—	Yes	NA	NA
Arizona	16,021	739	24	Yes	196	11
Arkansas	8,165	467	27	No	—	—
Arkansas	8,165	467	27	No	995	42
California	108,183	11,275	492	Yes	995	42
Colorado	8,961	500	12	Yes	22	1
Connecticut	11,086	149	3	Yes	NA	NA
Delaware	4,027	397	6	Yes	95	5
D.C.	11,122	774	10	Yes	10	0
Florida	47,619	4,767	145	Yes	2,332	44
Georgia	24,829	3,236	145	No	—	—
Hawaii	1,473	3	0	Yes	28	3
Idaho	2,265	189	6	Yes	174	6
Illinois	31,018	551	14	Yes	532	14
Indiana	No response	—	—	No	—	—
Iowa	4,512	374	17	Yes	374	17
Kansas	6,139	488	19	No	—	—
Kentucky	10,362	562	24	No*	8	—
Louisiana	21,165	2,158	72	Yes	2,083	71
Maine	1,574	44	0	Yes	11	0
Maryland	No response	—	—	Yes	?	?
Massachusetts	9,409	925	24	Yes	389	10
Michigan	38,513	3,096	107	Yes	1,729	66
Minnesota	3,582	153	7	Yes	1	0
Mississippi	9,058	49	0	Yes	151	0
Missouri	16,051	1,166	52	Yes	318	24
Montana	1,300	27	0	Yes	8	0
Nebraska	2,639	79	5	No	—	—
Nevada	6,191	903	31	Yes	214	9
New Hampshire	1,850	26	2	Yes	26	2
New Jersey	22,047	890	20	No	—	—
New Mexico	3,325	156	9	No	—	—
New York	61,373	9,033	444	No	—	—
North Carolina	19,868	2,171	66	No	—	—
North Dakota	561	12	1	No	—	—
Ohio	37,131	2,935	143	No	—	—
Oklahoma	14,780	929	62	Yes	87	8
Oregon	6,480	439	23	Yes	17	2

| | Prison | Number of Lifers | | Life w/o | No-Parole Lifers | |
State	Population	Male	Female	Parole	Male	Female
Pennsylvania	24,670	2,324	93	Yes	?	?
Rhode Island	2,858	83	0	Yes	10	0
South Carolina	18,697	1,290	67	No	—	—
South Dakota	1,498	99	3	Yes	99	3
Tennessee	14,500	1,246	44	No	—	—
Texas	51,887	4,152	85	No	—	—
Utah	2,691	41	0	Yes	?	?
Vermont	1,206	14	0	Yes	?	?
Virginia	16,939	1,248	25	No	—	—
Washington	10,039	588	20	Yes	125	7
West Virginia	1,808	254	6	Yes	124	1
Wisconsin	7,825	498	25	No	—	—
Wyoming	1,075	108	3	Yes	0	0
Federal BOP	81,822	1,177	41	Yes	?	?

*Abolished life without parole in 1975.
Source: *Corrections COMPENDIUM*, January 1993.

Table 2
Life-Sentenced Inmates in Louisiana Prisons

Year	Number of Natural Lifers	Increase from Previous Year
1970	143	28
1971	164	21
1972	193	29
1973	257	64
1974	323	66
1975	382	59
1976	454	72
1977	528	74
1978	601	73
1979	699	98
1980	802	103
1981	935	133
1982	1,084	149
1983	1,219	135
1984	1,330	111
1985	1,445	115
1986	1,573	128

Year	Number of Natural Lifers	Increase from Previous Year
1987	1,698	125
1988	1,807	109
1989	1,933	126
1990	2,039	106
1991	2,155	116
1992	2,280	125
1993	2,439	159
1994	2,592	153

Source: Office of Information Services, Louisiana Department of Public Safety and Corrections.

Table 3
Louisiana Lifers by Offense

	Offense Committed Prior to 1973	Offense Committed 1973 to Present	No Date	Total
1st Degree Murder	75	575	4	654
2nd Degree Murder	33 *	1,073 **	92	1,198
Agg. Rape	69	513	0	582
Agg. Kidnapping	4	54	0	58
Dist. Sch. I Narc.	0	101	0	101
Habitual Offenders	0	2	0	2

*Second degree murder was created as an offense in 1973. These are resentencings, re-convictions or data entry errors.

**Includes 193 lifers who are 20-year or 40-year parole eligible.

Source: Office of Information Services, Louisiana Department of Public Safety and Corrections, March 1, 1995.

Table 4
Louisiana Lifers: Place of Confinement

Louisiana State Penitentiary (Angola)	2,275
Louisiana Correctional Institute for Women	66
Other State Prisons for Men	130
Parish Jails (State Inmates)	53
State Police Barracks (Trusties)	35
Adult Services/Other	36

Source: Office of Information Services, Louisiana Department of Public Safety and Corrections, March 1, 1995.

10

PEN STATE: A YEAR IN THE LIFE OF ANGOLA*

by Jason Berry

The day after Easter 1990, John Whitley became warden of the Louisiana State Penitentiary. The job pays $70,000. Whitley, 46, has a thick mustache and a penchant for cowboy hats, a worthy symbol for the challenge of managing the largest state penitentiary in America. The place has a tortured history, and is reeling from a scandal that is pure Southern Gothic.

The prison occupies a region called Angola, tucked away in a remote wedge of the state, cradled by the Mississippi River. Angola has 5,179 inmates, about three-quarters of whom are black. It covers 18,000 fertile acres, with approximately 1,200 head of full-grown cattle, 900 calves, 90 horses, and dozens of chickens and dogs. In spring and summer, 1,300 inmates earn an average of five cents an hour working cotton and soybean fields under fierce heat broken by semitropical rains. Guards with shotguns ride horseback while men toil the land much as slaves did over a century ago.

For decades Angola was a huge anachronism, making headlines when cruelties got out of hand. Today, a financially-strapped state is paying for that past. Armed with a court decree to halt overcrowding, Federal Judge Frank J. Polozola of Baton Rouge sets inmate population levels at all state and local facilities, dictating how many guards and medical staff the prisons must hire.

Angola has forced Polozola to go beyond traditional legal mechanisms and use micro-management techniques.

In July of 1989, after a rash of inmate suicides and escapes, Polozola hauled Angola officials into a civil hearing. "I am tired of these band-aids," the judge stormed. "If the state can't do it, I will do it. That's not a threat—that's a promise."

Polozola declared a state of emergency at Angola and got Gov. Buddy Roemer to fire warden Hilton Butler. State officials searched seven months for a new man, raising the salary by $20,000. Whitley, with a pension from two decades' work in Louisiana corrections, was running a privately-owned medium security prison in Bridgeport, Texas, when he agreed to return to Angola, where he started out as a low-level officer in the early 1970s.

Whitley told one inmate that compared to Angola, the Texas prison "was a piece of cake." I asked Whitley why he took the job. "It may be hard to understand," he drawled, "but in Louisiana, Angola is the prison. It's somewhat at the end of the world, but it's here, and we're gonna deal with it."

Staring in December of 1989, I made several trips to Angola, trying to gauge the challenges it poses. Seasons changed, and I saw images of the prison culture shift like colors in a kaleidoscope.

Angola is a worst-case study in the national crisis of overcrowded prisons. Nearly 2,000 inmates are serving life without parole, while another thousand have terms so long they're called "practical life." Scores of prisoners, some in wheelchairs, others infirmed geriatric cases, take up valuable space while younger criminals—the "narco-boomers"—often pass through revolving

*Appeared in *New Orleans Magazine,* March 1991, 40-9, 98-101. Reprinted with permission.

doors of a clogged criminal justice system.

Some 600 employee families live in an all-white village on prison grounds. Many workers grew up at Angola. To them, the warden is both boss and effectively their mayor.

As inmate numbers swelled, criminal activity hit a new threshold. In 1986, a pardon-selling scandal stained the Edwin Edwards administration. Since October 1989, 17 people—including prisoners, guards, attorneys and inmates' wives or girlfriends—have been indicted for a drug-running and sexual blackmail scam that allegedly netted $5 million and allegedly led to the contract murder of a Mississippi judge and his wife.

Whitley inherits a new team of prison managers struggling to repair systemic damage, which the most successful prison journal in the country chronicles as the editors try to get out.

America's prison industry costs $13 billion each year. As crime rates escalate, many states are building new prisons to cope with bulging facilities. The U.S. prison population now exceeds 627,000, and if current rates hold, one million people will be incarcerated by the year 2000.

Penal experts agree that overcrowding does not stem from escalating crime alone; rather, a confluence of long sentences, a cutback in paroles, and the recent surge of crimes linked to the drug epidemic created the space crunch.

In the 1970s, before crack became an issue, many state legislatures scorned penal rehabilitation and churned out laws mandating long sentences with little or no chance of parole. Harsh sentences curried favor with voters. But inmates who a decade earlier would have been paroled on good behavior simply stayed put. The

strain of human warehousing precipitated legal actions, alleging cruel and unusual punishment in living conditions. Those suits triggered a unique transfer of power from politicians to the courts. Forty-two states now operate under mandatory release orders issued by state or federal judges.

Louisiana is spending $3 million a week to incarcerate approximately 13,000 criminals. Orleans Parish Prison is so jammed that a tent city houses men behind the police complex. During 1987, under Polozola's orders, Sheriff Charles Foti, because of overcrowding, had to release 12,000 prisoners, of whom 44 percent reoffended. One such man was convicted of killing a North Carolina tourist as he walked to dinner in the French Quarter on November 6, 1989.

November 6 was a day like any other for 67-year-old Quentin Brown, who has an I.Q. of 51, as he passed time quietly in the Angola infirmary. With a collapsed esophagus and bleeding ulcer, Brown, who had suffered prior convictions, was in the 16th year of a 30-year, no parole term for stealing a pie and $117. He was hiding under a house near the store he robbed in Monroe when police arrested him in 1973.

In 1988, the state Pardon Board recommended Brown's release. Governor Roemer refused to sign it. After diplomatic lobbying by then-Tulane University law professor Jonathan Turley with Roemer's staff, the governor signed Brown's release, and on April 22, 1990, he left for a halfway house in Florida.

When Turley began researching parole procedures, he was struck by how many old men had been swallowed by the system. Long-term prisoners, 55 or older, have a five percent recidivism rate. Turley considers 400 men at Angola "good candidates for release."

"Louisiana's prison system did not develop by accident," explains Turley. "The South is infatuated with life sentences. Terms run three to four times longer than in most regions on a range of crimes. Louisiana probably has the worst asymmetrical sentencing. The national average for a first offense in drug trafficking is 51 months, with actual time served at 17 months. In Louisiana, it's not uncommon for such offenders to receive life without parole. It's hard to get attorneys here to do pro-bono work in criminal justice. Much of the appellate research finds poor work by original defense counsels. When you have a system with so many constitutional failures, the state bar association bears a heavy responsibility."

Turley, a graduate of Northwestern Law School, was attracted to Tulane by its requirement that each student perform 20 hours of public service legal work in order to graduate. In 1988, he launched "Project on Older Prisoners," a nationwide database to strengthen parole appeals for inmates who might otherwise die behind bars. George Washington University Law School hired Turley to launch a similar project. With the Tulane program established, he moved to Washington in August.

When Turley addressed Tulane students, explaining that Pardon Board appeals require in-depth research, 250 future attorneys volunteered. Many later donated books to the prison law library. Turley and students visited Angola on Fridays.

RAZOR-RIBBON WIRE

To get there you drive northwest from Baton Rouge for 60 miles, following highway 61 into West Feliciana Parish, where restored plantations offer tourist lodgings. The last leg snakes up 20 treacherous miles of a scarred single lane through red bluffs of the hill country settled by Tunica Indians. Then the land flattens out, a seemingly endless expanse beyond the gate house and fence topped by razor-ribbon wire. A communications tower looms over the landscape. Prison dorms, miles apart, flanked by towers and surrounded by fences, dot the distant landscape. Angola has no back fence; it just ends at the Mississippi River.

On a cold December noon in 1989, law students Sherri Evans and Thomas Pierce passed through a security gate. Prisoners on benches stared at the blonde in a stylish blue dress and young man in a business suit. She worked in a Dallas bank before entering Tulane; he was a reporter in Syracuse. They entered a drab conference room as Robert Rasberry, 70, frail and limping, sat down.

"We're preparing for your parole hearing, Mr. Rasberry."

"Yes, ma'am," he smiles, looking down.

They ask about his childhood. "My mother left us," he begins. "I had two sisters. My father had to get someone look after us. Then she came back. I'm not positive, but think my daddy died in '26. . . . In school, I was promoted to the fourth grade. . . . My mother died in a fire in a bus station."

"What happened to your sisters, Mr. Rasberry?" asks Evans.

"To my understanding, after my mother died, they dropped out of school. Oldest girl is somewheres in California. The baby is in Opelousas. She can't speak English. She speaks French."

"Have you been in touch with them?" asks Pierce.

"No, sir. I was aimin' to."

And if parole is granted? "I could get by without huntin' for trouble. I don't fool with no drugs, no alcohol."

"Would it scare you," asks Evans, "to be on the outside?"

"No, ma'am. Be on my own . . . It learned me a lesson."

They ask where he would live. "My mother's sister needs someone to look after her," he replies, with no hint of irony. In Angola since 1961, he is a shell of a man. Who will care for him?

They ask about the crime that put him here. "Rape," he mumbles. "But I did not do it. After they brought me out the cell, she asked was I guilty. I was upset, afraid. I never had it in my mind to rape nobody." What was he doing before prison? "I was doin' good, runnin' a milk dairy. This fella jumped me. Boss had told me to help him look for a cow. He got kinda salty about it, speakin' such words before his wife." His minds drifts through fragments of a past. Then he says: "I didn't mean to kill him."

"Kill who?" they ask.

"My sister's husband."

That explains why he has not contacted his sisters. When the session is done, they realize that the case needs much work. Mr. Rasberry poses no physical threat to society. He appears to be senile. But if he is released, where will he go?

On December 22, 1989, four months before Whitley became warden, arctic winds were whipping Louisiana as Bishop Stanley Ott of Baton Rouge, wearing a black hat and dark overcoat that swallowed his diminutive frame, went to Angola for a Christmas pastoral visit. Several years ago, when Ott officiated at the funeral of a prisoner who died in the electric chair, angry letters crackled in the press. People were incensed that a Catholic bishop had buried a murderer in a cemetery of departed nuns. But there was no family to cover burial. Ott remarked: "If we believe in redemption, then we must practice forgiveness."

Louisiana has executed 20 men since the death penalty was restored—more executions per capita than the USSR and South Africa. Only Texas and Florida, much bigger states, have executed more men. Thirty-five men are presently on Death Row at Angola.

Bishop Ott and Father Gary Engles, the prison's Catholic chaplain, drove down the road through B-line, Angola's residential community where, at the time, 600 white staffers and their families lived, well removed from prison dorms. In the car ahead was Larry Smith, the 39-year-old acting warden, a black man with a neatly trimmed beard. Smith, an assistant secretary in the Department of Public Safety and Corrections, has a master's in social science.

Smith stared at the frame houses of B-Line. "This is a segregated town," I marveled. "You bet," said Smith.

At least 100 employees grew up on B-Line—guards administrators, clerks, farm overseers. Some are third-generation Angola dwellers. That free people raised inside prison walls stay on is one intimation of Angola's bizarre hold on the imagination. The legendary blues singer Leadbelly did time here; so did Carl Smith, a Depression-era Louisiana State University president, for embezzling college funds. The late Governor Earl K. Long once said, "You don't fool with Angola or LSU if you've got good sense."

Now, for the first time, a black man was running Angola. He got the opportunity because inmate scams had fooled men in high places. Indictments had come down after the previous warden,

Hilton Butler, was sacked. Larry Smith insisted he was not a candidate for the job; he was going back to Baton Rouge once a new warden was hired.

MICROSCOPE OF INVESTIGATION

News had just come that a grand jury 40 miles away in St. Francisville, with three Angola employees and the wife of a fourth among its members, returned a "no true bill" on the cigar-chomping Butler, who raised 1,500 fighting gamecocks on prison grounds, tended by inmate labor, with feed bought on state funds.

"Butler took his chickens and moved to Mississippi," bristled Smith, pulling into the carport of the warden's handsome brick residence. "You think that failure to indict him makes my job easier? I just promoted four men to majors, and two of them were black. Black majors are a rarity at Angola."

Inside, prisoners had prepared a buffet of vegetables and fried catfish. Several assistant wardens and officers had come to lunch with the bishop—Smith's gesture of appreciation to new colleagues working under the microscope of a state police investigation of Butler's regime. After lunch, Bishop Ott celebrated Mass for 50 men in a prison chapel.

The Roemer Administration had just boosted Angola's $40 million budget by $7 million to meet standards set by Judge Polozola. "My concern," said Smith, "is that we're spending only about $2 million for juvenile corrections. If we're going to combat the problem, it has to be at that level—or we pay heavier at the back end, here at Angola. We fail to give (juveniles) not just vocational skills, but life skills— reading, math, etiquette—so that one can function as a full citizen."

In a recent study by the Center for the Study of Social Policy in Washington, D.C., which analyzed high school dropout rates, juvenile arrests and social services by the states, Louisiana ranked last, with 30 percent of its youths locked in poverty. Angola's population hovers at 5,100, just about 400 less than the number of Louisiana children in foster homes. The New Orleans ACLU filed suit against the state Department of Health and Human Resources for widespread incompetence. Dr. Stephen Hales, a New Orleans pediatrician, joined the suit, saying "the system crumbles" once children enter it.

In the prison chapel, Mass is over. Prisoners in blue jeans, tennis shoes, sweat shirts, and heavy coats line up to chat with Ott, who gives each man a private blessing. A prisoner eyes my notebook: "Do you know we got some women guards at Angola?"

"Yes, I've seen some."

"People outside think of us as savages locked away.

But in our dorm they got longtimers in for rape—and women guards."

"Are you in for rape?"

"No, armed robbery."

"Do women guards bother you?"

"No. I think they kinda humanize the place."

DEATH ROW

Ott and Father Engles drive to the new wing housing "death row." A room off the tier is marked "Law Library." Inmates can order books from it to research appeals—three books at a time, three days at a time—but cannot keep copies of cases in their cells. "No meaningful legal research can occur within the constraint of this system," the ACLU National Prison Project charged in a 1989 class-action suit. Each man spends 23 hours a day in his cell, with an hour to shower and walk. Outside exercise rotates three days weekly. But all can see the row of television sets, droning morning till midnight—movies, sitcoms, news—a nation's noisy dream life on pedestals none can touch.

Each cell has a cot, toilet and wash stand. Prisoners are shackled hand and foot when their lawyers visit. The lawsuit reads:

> It is impossible to review important papers between lawyer and client . . . A corrections officer must be summoned and requested to take the papers from one side of the room around the outside of the room to the person on the other side. This procedure invites breaches of confidence between lawyer and client.

Bishop Ott stops at a cell, draping his arms through the bars, greeting a white man wired to his Walkman. The man stares back coldly. The bishop moves on. The next prisoner, a full head taller than the bishop, clasps his hands and together they pray.

In a nearby cell, Dobie Gillis Williams, a 29-year-old black, has a copy of "American History: A Survey, Volume II." Reading helps pass the time, he says. "Waking up every day to the same thing, you get bored. I put on headphones and try to drown the noise." On television, Michael Jackson is dancing.

"Are you familiar with the author Toni Morrison?" he asks. "Certainly," I respond. Says he: "I wanted to get one by her I saw. It was called 'Nimba,' or something like that."

"I believe she wrote a book called 'Sula.'"

"Maybe. But it was a hardback. I know that."

In another cell, a man tells the bishop: "I'll read most anything but a sex novel or a mystery."

"I been here since May '85," continues Williams. "Before that I was at (prison) Camp Beauregard. I was on a five-day furlough when the murder happened. I was railroaded. I'm a victim of circumstance."

In a prison many men claim innocence. It goes with the psychological territory. But a check on Williams' case proved interesting. In May 1989, an assistant district attorney in the parish where Gillis was convicted was chatting with the officer who took his confession the night of the murder. "So what if I told Dobie he wouldn't go to the chair if he confessed?" the policeman said. "I do what I have to do to make a case."

Realizing that the statement was new evidence, the prosecutor informed Williams' attorneys, who subsequently filed an appeal after taking a statement from the arresting officer. The officer testified that he could not recall the conversation "but never denied the possibility of having made the statement," the appeal states. Officers made Williams take off his shirt and pants when they interrogated him. The confession tape turned up blank. The appeal argues that the confession was coerced, and Williams deserves a retrial. There is no witness to the murder for which he is to die. The appeal is pending.

Bishop Ott pauses at the cell of a young white man with eyes like poached eggs — Michael Perry, who murdered his mother, father, a nephew, and two cousins one night in 1983.

"Pope! Pope! Pope!" yells Michael Perry.

Ott winces, "No, I'm just a bishop."

"Get me to see the Pope?"

"No, I'm afraid not. God bless you, son." Ott moves on.

Word has spread of a reporter on the tier. Michael Perry, shaking, grips the bars and yells: "Ask me a question!"

"Why did you kill them?" I say.

"The voices told me! A voice said: 'Your bone broke nine commandments. The tenth says kill!' I said no! They said yeah!"

Michael Perry has been diagnosed a schizo-affective psychotic. Perry's attorneys are fighting the trial court's order that Perry be forcibly medicated with a drug called Haldol until the point where he might become mentally competent, so that the state can then execute him.

"The overreaching question," according to Perry's attorney, Keith B. Nordyke of Baton Rouge, "is whether physicians are breaching ethics by taking a step in causing the death of their patient."

In the next cell lived Dalton Prejean, 31, a black man who suffered organic brain damage from beatings as a child. At 14, he committed a murder and was released after two years in a juvenile center without rehabilitative follow up. At 17, he murdered a state trooper in Lafayette who was arresting his brother. Passions ran high in favor of his execution. In November 1989, Prejean came within six hours of electrocution when the Supreme Court issued a stay to review his appeal. On May 18, 1990, he was electrocuted.

That day in December, I had asked what it was like living next to Michael Perry. "What gets me," said Prejean softly, "is they have a hospital for mental patients but won't put him in it. He wouldn't take a shower if they didn't make him. When he drinks coffee, he be up all night. Once he start, he carry on real bad."

Night had fallen as reporter and clergy made for the parking lot. Icy winds assaulted the land. Gate guards checked my car for contraband. Then I drove down the serpentine trail, heading home on the coldest day of the century. On the radio a black woman sang: "Jesus is a battle-axe. You can depend on him. "

Last April, the rains came and I went back. Down in a pen behind the cemetery, dogs were wailing—bloodhounds, beagles, Catahoulas—waiting for the feed truck. The cemetery, Point Lookout, lies on a knoll overlooking horses, lush fields, and a cluster of decaying wooden sheds that convey the permanent authority of time. Sandbags, stacked on the road, waited for convicts to pack them along the levee as Mississippi waters rose.

Three hundred white crosses serve as headstones at Point Lookout. Some bear names; many more are etched only with the serial numbers of men who died here, with no one to claim their remains. Ron Wikberg, associate editor of *The Angolite,* the inmate news magazine, walked among the furrows, calling names of men he remembered. He won a Silver Gavel award from the American Bar Association for coverage of the aging inmate phenomenon.

Wikberg was convicted in 1969 for killing a store owner in a robbery. In 1980, he was first recommended for parole by the state Pardon Board. Two governors denied him clemency. The dead man's family has publicly forgiven Wikberg. With a fiancee and job waiting in New Orleans, he had a third Pardon Board appeal in mid-June. His sentence was reduced to 60 years, making him eligible for parole; Roemer has yet to sign the order. Roemer, who campaigned for penal reform, has signed only 25 percent of the sentence commutations recommended by the board.

A curtain of rain hovered over the levee, giving the graveyard an eerie emerald glow. A guard waited in a truck.

"What does Point Lookout mean to you?" I asked Wikberg.

"Nobody wants to be buried in a prison. Hope is the only thing a prisoner has to live for—the hope of one day being free. People never visit this cemetery."

ONCE A PLANTATION

No one knows how many people have died at Angola.

In 1869, when it was a plantation, named for the nation whence many of its slaves had come, the landowner began leasing convicts from the state. An 1886 newspaper wrote of "those poor devils almost to their waists, delving in the black and noxious mud . . . a thousand times more grievous (lot) than the law even contemplated they should endure in expiation of their sins." In 1885 and 1886, 42 convicts were reported buried in one camp, killed "by overwork, exposure and brutality." In 1896, prison officials recorded 216 deaths. No records show where the bodies were buried. Historian Mark T. Carleton of LSU has estimated 3,000 deaths between 1870 and 1902, when the state bought Angola and surrounding plantations to found the penitentiary.

"Penal reform in the state has had to combat an apathetic, vengeful, and sometimes a hostile public," Carleton has written, calling it "a thoroughly politicized" system. In 1902, the prison earned $120,000 profit from cotton. At first juvenile inmates were thrown in with adults, a policy soon changed. The plantation psychology did not. Between 1928 and 1940, guards are estimated to have inflicted 10,000 floggings on prisoners, "as many as 50 lashes each."

Two governors outlawed flogging, but reports persisted until 1944. In 1952, after 37 convicts made national news by slashing their heel tendons to avoid harsh field work, *Collier's Magazine* called Angola "America's Worst Prison."

It also became a patronage hive. Guards and farm workers lived cheaply in houses on the grounds, raising families with trustees for servants. Legislators came to hunt and fish. Today, house rentals average $70 per month; guard pay starts at $1,100.

Connie Oliveaux, 28, a purchasing agent at Angola, lives in B-line with her husband (a Security officer) and their four children, who attend school in the town of Tunica. Her mother, two brothers and a sister also work at Angola. "Growing up here was like in any country town," she reflected. "Daddy never locked the doors. There was a swimming pool and a recreation center where we went skating. The (road) paving came in the early '70s; we got street lights in the mid-'70s. The chief disadvantage was isolation. Kids in Baton Rouge and St. Francisville could go to the movies; it took us an hour or more driving."

A world away from B-Line, inmates created cultural passageways to ease the suffering. Bluesman Robert Pete Williams and country singer Freddie Fender recorded albums while serving time. New Orleans saxophonist Charles Neville, who went to Angola in 1965, once said in a television interview that he went to Angola "for possession of two skinny little marijuana cigarettes. My whole life was divided by Angola. I remember the fields, chopping that sugar cane, the sun was hot, and I didn't want that man on the horse to crack me in the head with his axe handle. We'd be singing, 'Oh, lawd, have mercy, Oh,

Lawd have mercy on my soul, now,' and chops would come on the downbeat."

Cotton supplanted sugarcane, but in the 1970s, Angola roiled with homosexual rapes and awesome fights as men wielded double-bladed hatchets, makeshift swords and gladiatorial shields. "Prisoners practically ran the place," one inmate recalls.

MOST REHABILITATED PRISONER

In 1975, new expressions emerged with *The Angolite,* under editor Wilbert Rideau. It won a prestigious George Polk Award for stories on prison sexual abuse and capital punishment, and in 1989 became the first prison journal to receive a National Magazine Award.

Rideau has been called "the most rehabilitated prisoner in America" by Angola officials. The Pardon Board has three times recommended his parole. Bishop Ott and the *New Orleans Times-Picayune* support his appeal; he has a newspaper job waiting out of state. Former Governor Edwards balked because of a campaign promise he made to the victim's family. "If I acted solely on my beliefs," Edwards later said, "I'd sign the pardon."

In 1961, Rideau killed one hostage and wounded two after a bank robbery. When the Supreme Court barred the death penalty in 1972, he became a lifer. A prosecutor protested his parole: "This man committed the most heinous crime Calcasieu Parish has ever seen." But the state corrections chief said: "(By) whatever standard of rehabilitation you pick, Wilbert Rideau exceeds it."

"In the old days, if you did right, and stayed out of trouble, you could get out of prison," Rideau says. "That doesn't work today. The system changed on us. I've

been in 29 years. I spent 11 years on old death row in a six-by-eight cell. I educated myself. Since I came in here, 70,000 men have gone through. Where are they now? Police didn't kill them. Other state systems respect individual initiative. Here, the key to getting out is anonymity—which I don't have."

If Rideau was victim of his own celebrity, Roemer was trapped in the Willie Horton syndrome, sensitive to media fallout. Last April, the Pardon Board again recommended Rideau's release, but Roemer refused.

Calcasieu Parish has seen more heinous crimes. One man murdered his two infants; another drew multiple life sentences for killing a couple and their child. But those men were white, and Rideau is black.

Linda LaBranche, a Loyola University scholar writing a book on Rideau, has researched Calcasieu homicides dating to 1891. She found a 100 percent death sentencing rate, when it was available, for black males convicted of killing a white. The rate for white-on-white homicides was 23.5 percent and for black-on-black homicides, 10.4 percent.

No black convicted of killing a white from Calcasieu has been paroled. George Kendall of the NAACP Legal Defense Fund calls LaBranche's findings "a shocking indictment of law enforcement resources in that county. In a lot of communities, it's only the white-victim cases that draw attention."

ALLEGED MASTERMIND

Judge Polozola is a Republican known for tough sentences and for encouraging attorneys in civil cases to compromise in order to avert long trials. The role of de facto lord and prison master has not come easily to the judge, who declined to be interviewed.

Troubles began in 1985 when the Department of Corrections (DOC) began receiving complaints from people in scattered states who offered to help inmates they thought were being released, and got milked out of money. The alleged mastermind, murderer Kirksey McCord Nix, is accused of bribing guards for phone privileges. Nix has been linked to the Dixie Mafia, an alleged syndicate of drug dealers and common criminals. DOC officials pressed Warden Butler to take action, but the scam widened.

In 1986, state police began tailing Pardon Board Chairman Howard Marsellus, who supposedly rode his motorcycle up to Angola's gates with pardons to sell. Marsellus took gold jewelry from one inmate, $30,000 from another. That Labor Day, troopers videotaped him giving $20,000 to Joe Delpit, the then Speaker of the state House.

Marsellus quickly accepted a plea bargain that sent him to a Federal penitentiary, rather than Angola, where money was in the pipeline for aborted pardons. Speaker Delpit was tried in state court (with Gov. Edwards as a character witness), sobbed on the stand, and was acquitted. Edwards' DOC secretary then killed the state police probe, which reportedly infuriated Polozola.

Prisoners, meanwhile, were scouring gay magazines for ads seeking sexual encounters. Letters went forth, with helpers outside providing phony addresses and patching phone calls through to inmates. A civil suit filed in New Orleans by a *San Jose Mercury News* reporter accuses Kirksey Nix of passing himself off as a lonely youth, seeking a friend. The reporter, Jim Dickey, eventually sent

$17,200 before realizing that the youth was not coming his way. The scam also affected Puerto Ricans in New York, who thought relatives were arrested in far-off places and needed money quickly.

Nix made frequent calls to attorney Pete Halat of Biloxi, Mississippi. On September 17, 1987, Halat's former law partner, a Biloxi circuit judge, Vincent Sherry, and his wife were murdered in their home. Halat found the Sherry's bodies. Halat's link to Nix was unknown when he was elected mayor of Biloxi in spring 1989.

That is how things stood in June 1989 when an Angola prisoner found hung in his cell was classified as a suicide. Mortuary embalmers discovered that his back was broken, but no charges were filed. Roemer sent state police back to Angola. Judge Polozola ordered his own probe by Ross Maggio, a respected former warden. Maggio was tough. During his tenure as warden in the early '80s, two inmates broke into the warden's house, captured him and his visiting mother, and packed them into a vehicle at knifepoint. Maggio crashed the truck into the front gate, grabbed a gun from a guard and shot the two men, killing one. Not for nothing was Maggio called Boss Ross.

Boss Ross' report to Polozola cited collapsed security standards—rusting metal detectors, visitors who were not being frisked, prisoners making endless phone calls. One inmate toting garbage simply walked out of Angola; he was soon captured. Polozola prevailed on Roemer to sack Warden Butler.

On July 20, 1989, Angola's long dirty finger reached into Mississippi, when an inmate told a Jackson television reporter that he was present when attorney Pete Halat visited Kirksey Nix at Angola, and planned the contract murder of Biloxi's

Judge Sherry, who supposedly was hoarding $400,000 in scam money. Halat, who had just become mayor, heatedly denied the prisoner's story.

Authorities in the neighboring states agreed to a Federal investigation in Mississippi of the murders. As this article went to press, Halat is the subject of an ongoing grand jury now hearing testimony in Jackson.

On October 2, 1989, a St. Francisville, Louisiana, grand jury indicted Nix and his wife for drug-peddling and wire fraud. The 15 others indicted include a New Orleans attorney, Joseph Rome, accused of helping Nix. Several have pleaded guilty. Nix's trial is scheduled to begin later this year. "There are so many victims I can't begin to keep up," says St. Francisville prosecutor Hal Ware. "One individual bilked out of $80,000 won't testify. Many people are reluctant to testify because they're ashamed."

THE REAL PROBLEM

"The real problem is independent of criminality," states U.S. Attorney Ray Lamonica of Baton Rouge, who drafted the consent decree giving Polozola his powers. "When Kirksey Nix gets 273 phone messages returned, you ask how prison management got so incredibly bad. It was law unto itself. Hilton Butler raised thousands of fighting roosters. In pictures it looks like a Southern calvary embanked on Tunica Hills. Prisoners built cages with materials brought in on 18-wheelers. They baked cornbread to feed those roosters. He (Butler) was lord of the manor."

"I'm certainly not a fan of Hilton Butler," Kirksey Nix told the *Baton Rouge Morning Advocate* on December 13, 1989, "but he was a better warden than Ross

Maggio . . . All they really have on him, in the end, is chickens and cornbread."

That afternoon I found Butler puffing a cigar in the St. Francisville courthouse, waiting to give grand jury testimony. A rough-hewn man who spent 38 years at Angola, working up from guard, Butler was building a house across the river in Mississippi (where gamecock fighting is illegal). I asked what caused all the ruckus. "Maggio wants everyone to look up at him," grumbled Butler, "and I don't look up to nobody. Maggio thinks he's God. "

Why was Butler not indicted? "I'm not going to second-guess a hardworking grand jury," said prosecutor Ware. They did indict Butler's cousin, an assistant security warden, for failure to search the food manager's office through which marijuana was smuggled to inmates, and he copped a plea. Inmate scammers went to Angola's "lockdown" tier. Guards limited inmate-attorney letters to one per week and monitored conversations with attorneys. Civil rights lawyers challenged those strictures, but Polozola maintained legal control over the scam tier.

Angola gives the judge many fish to fry. When interim Warden Larry Smith demoted a security colonel, an angry state legislator, John Travis, demanded that his brother be reinstated. Smith wrote Polozola, complaining of "interference" in a scatalogical term associated with bulls. Polozola asked if Angola could be run without judicial weight behind it. Smith said no.

One of these years that may change. Roemer has promised a streamlined parole system to help meet the crisis. But with anti-tax passions at a pitch, Louisiana has no agenda to keep the Dalton Prejeans of tomorrow from becoming violent offenders. Meanwhile, the penal farm that turned a modest profit in 1902 now drains the state of nearly $50 million annually.

"If the people of Louisiana feel like locking up more prisoners," said Warden John Whitley, "then building new prisons is the way to go. When money gets tight and it hurts to build those prisons, then we start listening to alternatives. Personally, I think we've reached that point."

Jason Berry is a New Orleans-based writer whose work appears in many publications. He has received several awards for investigative reporting and an Alicia Patterson Fellowship in Journalism. His recent books include Lead Us Not Into Temptation: Catholic Priests and the Sexual Abuse of Children *(Doubleday, 1992) and* The Spirit of Black Hawk: A Mystery of Africans and Indians *(University Press of Mississippi, 1995).*

11

IN THE FIELD*

by Wilbert Rideau

The Louisiana State Penitentiary is the nation's biggest prison. 18,000 acres big, it is situated in the middle of the most rugged and desolate region of the state, surrounded by the Mississippi River on three sides and the steep Tunica Hills on the fourth—but inside that bowl-shaped perimeter lies some of the most fertile land in the state, river bottom rescued from the muddy Mississippi long ago.

While there are numerous and varied jobs and endeavors to engage the labor of the prisoners here, the major occupation is the farming operations. Angola farms 3,200 acres of soybeans, 850 acres of cotton, 300 acres of assorted vegetables, and 400 acres of corn. These crops keep approximately 1,200 inmate field workers and 68 supervising employees busy each day—except when it rains. Unlike other prisoners, those assigned to the field don't work when it rains. They used to a long time ago, oldtimers will tell you, but that was before the penitentiary became security-conscious, during the era when Angola was regarded and managed as just a large plantation-business worked by inmate slaves. However, that attitude has undergone considerable change with the passage of time and the little enlightenment that has managed to creep into this place. So now, while inmate field workers pray for rain so they'll be returned to their dormitories and not have to work, field personnel pray for the opposite because, if it does rain, they will be re-assigned to work somewhere else within the prison for that day . . . and the gods are caught in the middle.

Unless an incoming prisoner is classified as being medically or physically unable to engage in that type of labor, the first job of the new inmate is in the field, regardless of personal talent, skill, or abilities (official rhetoric states differently, but this is the reality). Prison rules require that a prisoner remain in the field for 90 days without a disciplinary infraction before he can qualify for transfer to a "job" out of the field. Many prisoners say that the rule is a sham, that even if they do 90 days without a write-up, they still stay in the field. Others charge that prison farm security personnel deliberately write them up for petty reasons as part of a large conspiracy to keep them in the field. And there could be some truth to what they say since there must be field workers and there is the naked reality that there simply aren't enough jobs out-of-the-field to go around to all the inmates even if all conducted themselves in an exemplary manner. Prison officials, on the other hand, counter that there is no need for a deliberate effort on the part of the prison to keep prisoners in the field because prisoners, because of their peculiar nature, can be expected to inevitably, if not constantly, get in trouble and thus keep the prison provided with an adequate labor force for the field.

Many, if not most, prisoners regard assignment to field work as punishment. Officials, on the other hand, say that's not so, that it's good therapy for prisoners and a meaningful attempt on the part of the administration to teach the inmates good work habits. Yet, the Disciplinary Board,

*Appeared in *The Angolite,* September/October 1979, 51-56. Reprinted with permission.

and even individual administrators, will transfer guys to the field, without the slightest hesitancy, as punishment. So the inmates aren't altogether wrong in their assessment and view of field work— that is, Main Prison inmates. But neither are they altogether right because the majority of Angola's 4,000 prisoners live in outcamps where, except for a small number of jobs in the camp itself, the only jobs available are in the field, thus making field work the normal endeavor for them. Now if this is beginning to sound like a contradictory and somewhat confused affair, it's because it is . . . but that's prison. Logic doesn't apply—never has and probably never will. If it ever did, it wouldn't be prison anymore.

Recently, *The Angolite* toured the fields to see what was going on in what everyone refers to as "the desert." Originally, our plan was to actually join the field workers for a day, working right along with them in order to really get the "feel" of the story. However, our request to work in the fields for a day somehow got misconstrued somewhere down the bureaucratic line and was taken to mean that we were requesting transportation around the field for a day (apparently, the administrative secretaries and/or officials couldn't believe that we were actually volunteering for field work for a day— which kind of reinforces the prisoners' claim that field work is punishment). But, by the time Major Bert Dixon showed up in his pickup to drive us around the field, second thoughts about the hot sun and the omnipresent dust that we'd have to put up with in the field had considerably diminished our original desire to spend a day working out there, so we weren't about to argue the point or bring the mistake to anybody's attention.

We took off, cruising around on the concrete roads that sections off the field and when we ran out of those good roads, we hit the dirt roads, bouncing up and down over bumps and holes with thick clouds of dust billowing around and behind us. The heat devils dancing feverishly in front of the vehicle made us appreciate the air-conditioned comfort in the cab of the truck.

Major Dixon is a 25-year veteran employee at Angola and oversees the security aspect of the farm lines. He is also a member of the prison's chase team and had just returned from chasing two escapees the night before. "We found out that they had stole a truck," he told us, "so we went on and called off the chase. They could be anywhere by now." He was now back at his regular prison duties, seeing to it that each of his 17 field lines had something to do. "The primary task," he said, "is to keep the men busy. If there are periods when there is little to do in the field, we'll put them to work in the ditches, cutting grass, and working the roads."

Inmates assigned to the field work almost eight hours a day, sometimes less because any of a number of things can hang up the start of the work day—the prison count being messed up, fog in the morning, an escape, slow roll call, etc. But they try to make them do eight hours. Farther back in time, field workers used to work from "kin see to can't see," from dawn to dusk. But that kind of driving of the prisoners in the field no longer goes on. This is 1979, not the 1950s.

Those inmates working in Lines 5 and 6 ride to work each morning in "hootenannies"—a string of wagons pulled by a tractor. The other lines are made to walk to and from work (which still beats Texas where they must run to and from work). "That helps keep them in good physical shape also," Major Dixon commented. "Most of the inmates we have working in the lines do a good job," he added. "They do what they have to do. It's not a job they like but it's one they know they must do. So most of them just do it."

And since they don't like it, there will be that natural tendency to avoid it if at all possible. One of the more common ploys in the past was to become ill on the job, in which case the inmate had to be taken to the hospital to be examined. But now there is a roving technician who travels around the farm, examining inmates on the spot in the field when they complain of being ill. If the technician determines that nothing's wrong with the inmate, he is written up for disciplinary action. "But we don't have that many write-ups," the major says. "In fact, by the time the technician does get to the man, he's usually working and really doesn't want to see him. This has really helped us with the previous problem we had of having to deal with those who faked at being sick, trying to get a lay-in." With that write-up awaiting him at the other end of that technician's decision, it's easily understandable that even the genuinely ill might think twice about requesting medical attention. After all, that technician is human and is certainly capable of making a wrong determination, in which you pay for his mistake.

While field work is no longer the man-killer that it used to be, it's still a long way from being the most desirable work in the prison. From the prisoner's perspective, the working conditions must be classified as lousy. The major punishers are the elements, the biting winds of winter and the furnace-like days of summer. Under that hot sun, tempers can flare and fights break out. It's no big

deal if the field workers are pulling grass with their hands, but if they're cutting grass with those long ditch-bank blades, the fight can get nasty and a guy suddenly find himself minus an arm or his decapitated head lying in the dirt with his bewildered eyes staring upwards at the sky. And, of course, there are the snakes; the place is infested with them. "They kill them all the time," Major Dixon tells us, "but surprisingly, only a few hands have been bitten by them, and they weren't bitten by poisonous ones." Then, while most of the field foremen are pretty decent supervisors, asking only that the inmates do their job, sometimes you can draw a bad one, and he can give you the blues out there. And there are the work stoppages that a majority of the inmates in the line might decide to stage in protest of something or another, catching you in the middle even if you don't want any part of it. Earlier this year, the Main Prison cellblock line reportedly stopped work often, in which case they were locked down and disciplined later, with some of the workers being sent to Camp J. And for a short period recently, there was a rash of escapes from the farm lines, but that has quietened down now. The only problem experienced lately in terms of guys running have been workers throwing down their tools and taking off in hot pursuit of rabbits. "But in terms of problems, I'd say that most of the trouble we've been experiencing lately," the major says, "has been with Camp C cellblock."

Camp C was harvesting the corn crops when we went through. It's hot, sticky work, made more irritating by the dust and tassels from the corn which finds its way all over your body. We stopped for pictures. "Man, don't forget to tell 'em about us!" one inmate hollered. We yelled back, surprising him by asking his name.

"The name is 'Big Daddy' Compton," he said. "I've been here for 12 years and spent the past four in the field. It's hard, it's hot, but we can do it, baby, 'cause that's the price we pay for it all." Apparently, there's some type of underlying competitiveness between the lines and the inmates in them, at least, outside the Main Prison, because as we passed by the cellblock line cutting grass alongside the road, some of the inmates disputed Compton's claim about being the hardest-working line. "About time we get some attention!" Joe Asher yelled. "We do more work than any other line out here!"

While few inmates would voluntarily work in the field (and there are some), there is no problem getting prison employees for field work. "There's not a man out there who didn't ask to be out there," Major Dixon told us of his field foremen. One of Camp D's field foremen, Carolo Roy, has been pushing field lines for eight years now. Wondering about this, we caught a group of foremen during their lunchbreak beneath a guard tower on the outside of the Main Prison cellblock.

"The best job there is," Foreman Joe Kelly told us. And, "we don't have to worry about turning keys and opening doors in the dormitory every five minutes," Steve Dauzat added. There are no problems with the inmates, whom all the foremen agreed give them 90 percent cooperation.

"If there is a problem," Charles Barkin stated, "it's getting the inmates to work. But that's really not a problem. Most of them get down and do their job. It's our job to make sure they do their job. But they're no problem."

The field foremen also like the job because they're off Saturdays and Sundays and all holidays; and when they work the extra-duty line, they're paid overtime. "Some people think it's bad out there, but that's not really true . . . Summer is our worst working season," Richard McGovern said. "It's hot and dusty. Cotton is our best season, and we're fixing to get into that now."

But Jerry Courvelle probably described their attitude about their work best: "We ain't nothing but good coon-asses and country boys," he said. "We've been raised around field work and horses all our lives. It's sorta in our blood. So, while most people would think of all this as bad work, we take it as bread and butter. There's nothing to it."

On this particular day, Camp D field workers were cutting okra and another group hoeing grass. "Say, man—take a picture of this bitch here!" one of them yelled. "She ain't got no business being out here in this hot sun—not as fine as she is!" We looked, and the young effeminate homosexual blushed under our gaze. The heat and the work doesn't keep the men's mind off sex—Major Dixon stated they often have problems with sex and sometimes rape when they work the okra. "You just can't see nothin' in there." The okra stands taller than the workers, like trees, obscuring view of what's going on in them. Perhaps the problem is compounded by the fact that Camp D, whose inmates work the okra, has more "pretty boys" housed there than any other facility in the penitentiary. Apparently, guys learning that they're going to be working in the okra patch on a given day, make it a point to perhaps bring their little "sally cans" with them.

We passed by a number of other lines at work, but they weren't doing anything particularly interesting. Except for the Camp C line harvesting the corn, the rest were more or less engaged in make-work, biding their time until officials decided to put them to picking cotton the "next week," the major speculated. We wondered idly about the difficulty involved in picking cotton that was grown on rows so close together until the cotton stalks embraced each other, making the rows seem impassable. It looked like the kind of jungle brush that even Tarzan would have to cut through with a machete—and, of course, there was the thought of those snakes you're liable to pull up when you reach down to pick what you believe to be cotton . . . and, on that chilling thought, having seen enough, we decided to return to the office. True, we didn't have the indepth story that we originally wanted to get, but the thought of that sun beaming down on the earth with a vengeance and that inescapable dust that finds its way into every opening of your body, making you gasp for breath, we concluded that we felt basically the same way about the field as does the bulk of the convicts here. If you've got to be in the desert, that's one thing. But if you don't have to be there, you try like hell to avoid it. So, shelving our journalistic zeal, we did like any other convict given the opportunity—we split. To hell with it!

12

THE CLUBS*

by Wilbert Rideau

It was a chilly night. The October wind whistled outside the window. The convicts wished they had remained in the dorms. They were in Angola's Education Department patiently awaiting a tabulation of the votes. It was club election night. The convicts had a great deal to gain from the election. For the past year, this handful of men had painstakingly mapped out their political comeback. They still licked their wounds from being ousted from power last year. But the past year gave them time to plan. They eased new members into the club to build a solid voting block. The new members were instructed to take an active role in various club committees, to work closely with club members identified as neutral. It was a deliberate and methodical strategy. Free world politicians would envy its Machievillian character. And it paid off. The old group won the election. The new group had failed to do its job during the year of control. Back in power, the old group will run things as they see fit.

The first club was formed in Angola in 1953. It was the Sober Group of Alcoholics Anonymous. Clubs have since played a major role in the prison's social life. Like any other society, prison also has its own social life. Angola's social life has traditionally evolved around inmate organizations, referred to by prisoners as "clubs." The clubs provide prisoners avenues in which to work constructively; to take their minds off the daily loneliness, boredom, and depression so rooted in prison life. Clubs offer a means of development, growth, and rehabilitation in a compressed and stifled world, a world whose dog-eat-dog violence sometimes ends all hope for life.

But clubs offer more than a mere escape from the unpleasant aspects of prison. They provide a man with the opportunity to become a dynamic speaker, an organizer, or a leader. For the politically ambitious, clubs offer an opportunity for leaders to exercise political maneuvers, rising through the ranks of the club structure. For those who possess an itch for tyranny, clubs provide an opportunity to engage in ruthless power struggles. For the criminally corrupt, clubs offer a means to steal and rip-off the profits made by the club's concession. For the believer in God, clubs offer an opportunity for him to preach and spread God's Word. For the teacher, clubs offer classes in a variety of subjects. For the homosexual, clubs provide an opportunity to meet a lover. Regardless of the motive, clubs provide an invaluable way for convicts to cope with their caged life.

While clubs do open positive doors for most prisoners, they also reflect the nature of political organizations through the nation. The intrigues and exploits which have occurred in the clubs over the years is comparable to the national election psychology or the disappointing failure of Watergate. The face of any organization is shaped by its leaders. Each administration creates its own personality of leadership. It has its own hopes and ideas about success and maintaining control. The eventual strengths and weaknesses of the organization will show

*Appeared in the *Angola Prison Rodeo Program,* 1980, 62-68. Reprinted with permission.

in the track record set by the club. Like free world organizations, prison clubs strive for power, wealth and influence as the means to accomplish their goals.

Each club at Angola must have an internal sponsor. The sponsor must be a free person. Clubs will generally seek out a strong sponsor from the prison's powerful security force. Someone who will lend influence and prestige to the club. Other clubs get saddled with a do-nothing sponsor who is sponsor in name only. These clubs accomplish little and fare no better in the amount of influence they wield.

The name of each club conjures up different meanings in the minds of people at Angola. For example, the Angola Jaycees represent power, success, and independence. The Angola Amateur Boxing Association represents elite power and has a reputation for vicious in-fighting. Vets Incarcerated represents efficiency in performing its functions. The Pardon Board Finance Committee represents wealth. The World Community of Al Islam and the Church of God in Christ represent different expressions of a universal God. On the other hand, the former Narcotics Anonymous Club represented corruption and swindles which led to its downfall.

Since the early '50s, clubs have gradually increased in number and range of activities they participate in. When C. Murray Henderson became warden in 1968, clubs began to flourish and have substantial impact on the prisoners' daily life. The clubs also began to reach outside the prison, primarily with trusted prisoners being able to speak at local schools on drugs, delinquency and crime. They also addressed colleges, anti-poverty programs, participated in fund raising charitable projects, and helped communities establish various crime prevention programs. These outside trips brought favorable exposure to prisoners as well as the prison administration. The inmates often benefitted by people wanting to help get them out of prison. While there were a few negative incidents (like drinking, escaping, and narcotic involvement), they were extremely rare occurrences.

When Ross Maggio became Angola's Warden, he also saw the rehabilitative value and need for clubs. It was during his tenure that the Angola Jaycees started their rodeo steer raffle; that the Angola Amateur Boxing Association traveled around the state participating in boxing tournaments; and when Vets Incarcerated, Inc. was allowed to get a Discharge Review Board in the prison to review veteran cases.

Angola's present warden, Frank C. Blackburn, followed the club tradition, placing administrative emphasis on the clubs being permitted to grow and expand. Blackburn does not believe in forced treatment, but he is one of the nation's most respected penologists and he stands unreservedly behind the philosophy that rehabilitation is possible in the prison setting. One of his favorite rehabilitative avenues is the positive projects many of the clubs are involved in. Blackburn is a bold and innovative man—and that's why he is the only warden in the nation who can boast of having pulled off the nation's first Cop/Con Walk; a charitable fund-raising project that matched teams of convicts and state troopers who walked across the entire state in 1978 to raise nearly $20,000 for the Cystic Fibrosis Foundation. It took guts to back that kind of project. Blackburn is one of the few wardens who would have done it.

But Blackburn's tenure hasn't always been easy when it came to clubs. The law 'n order attitude so prevalent in the free world reaches behind prison walls as well. One of the effects of that attitude came when the legislature curtailed outside travel by prisoners. That curtailment had a devastating effect on the clubs. Incentive to get involved in the clubs dried up, hopes for gaining some benefit from being involved in the clubs vanished and dreams of what could be done with the clubs collapsed.

The legislative restriction on travel and subsequent lack of inmate interest didn't deter Blackburn's objective to keep the clubs open as viable rehabilitative avenues. His administration began encouraging outside groups to attend the prison. Since the inmates couldn't travel to the various groups to speak, Blackburn created an "open door" philosophy inviting outside groups to come into the prison, tour it, and understand its workings. This past year the legislature repealed its band on inmate travel—and interest in clubs is once again mounting. Blackburn must be credited with having pulled the clubs through that two year "dry period" when all life seemed drained from Angola's social life. Blackburn personally created interest in drama, hobbycraft exhibits, and legal seminars. It wasn't easy for him to accomplish these things when, on one hand, he had to deal with hard legislative restrictions, and, on the other hand, lamenting prisoners constantly complaining to him about how stifled their efforts seem to be.

The "dry period" also gave rise to new problems. Since the positive incentives were taken from the clubs, more corrupt inmates began jockeying for positions in them. They didn't give a damn about rehabilitation or helping others. They wanted to help themselves, primarily to the club's concession funds. Each

established club is permitted to maintain a concession in the prison's visiting room which generates revenues that pay for the club's sports programs, banquets, and charitable events. But the corrupt inmates want to steal and embezzle the funds. Blackburn's administration maintains a constant vigilance for this type of illegal conduct and shut down several clubs because of it. He delivered a stern message to all the club heads that he would not tolerate any illegal and unethical conduct.

That administrative attitude helped some of the more responsible inmates ease the corruptive influences out of the club's key positions. In effect, they cleaned up their own backyard—and while there will always be incidents of wrongdoing, most of the clubs have responsible leaders who will not tolerate that kind of conduct by the club members or officers.

It's not easy being the leader of a prison club. He must possess a keen awareness of the convict personality and have a remarkable ability to walk through mud without getting his shoes dirty. To maintain control, he maintains a survival paranoia. It's necessary because set-ups by enemies or the undermining of his control by opposing factions is a daily reality he must deal with. Through all of the intrigues and plots, he must keep the club functioning, assigning his most trusted aides to key positions and delegating work responsibilities to the individuals he knows will get the job done. He makes the club what it is.

Racism has also played a significant role in the history of Angola's clubs. In the beginning the clubs had all-white memberships—but as the racial balance of the prison's population began to shift, so did the membership of the clubs. Blacks assumed control of previously all-white clubs or created clubs of their own. On both sides, groups re-wrote bylaws and altered constitutions to accommodate the new movement yet still protect as much as possible the vested interest of each side. In some instances dictatorial policy became the best way to protect those interests—and today there are still a couple all-white and all-black clubs. It's not a matter of force but a matter of mutual acceptance and understanding. It adds to the peace and security of the institution by balancing the prison's subcultural power structure.

One important advantage of the clubs is that they provide a vehicle for religious expression. There are seven religious clubs in the Main Prison complex alone. Namely, Church of God in Christ, headed by Allen Brown, Jr., Full Gospel Businessmen Fellowship International, headed by Robert L. Guy; Jehovah's Witnesses, headed by Cy Parker; Pentecostal Fellowship, headed by Robert L. Guy; United Methodist Men, headed by Maurice Bickham; World Community of Islam in the West, headed by William Muhammad Bila; and St. John Institutional Baptist Brotherhood headed by Emmanuel Smith.

Other clubs offer an opportunity for sport and recreation. For example, the Angola Amateur Boxing Association, headed by Charles Daniel, offers an extensive boxing program, featuring weekly boxing matches in the prison's A-Building which are open to prisoners and public as well. The AABA has also established scholarships in law enforcement for outstanding students across the state.

The Alcoholics Anonymous groups, the New Hope Group and Sober Group, offer programs of assistance like Big Brother and Elderly Assistance projects. The Lifers' Association sponsors numerous projects that promote the political and legal interests of the prison's nearly 800 lifers. Other clubs, such as Angola Jaycees, Dale Carnegie, and Human Relations, primarily focus their efforts on self-development projects.

There are other clubs at Angola and they serve the same vital purpose outlined in the mention of the other clubs in this article. They provide a positive and stable influence over the overall prison population. The remaining prison clubs are: Angola Amateur Judge & Referee Association; Camp A Hardhitters Boxing Club; Camp C Wings Social Relation Club; Camp D Wings Social Orientation Club; Camp H Lifers' Association; Camp I Social Advancement Club; Camp J Boxing Club; Camp A & D Christian Fellowship; Drama Club; Gladiator Boxing Team; Gospel Melodies Group; R.C. Social Orientation Club; Social, Education, and Athletic Club; Weight Lifting and Body Building Club; and Wonders of Joy Gospel Group.

13

PRISON MEDICAL CARE*

by Ron Wikberg and Wilbert Rideau

The world hates change, yet it is the only thing that has brought about progress.
—CHARLES F. KETTERING

Medical services for Louisiana prisoners have only been a matter of importance in recent times. In the 1800s, there was little, if any, medical treatment. At the end of the nineteenth century, the prisoner death rate was 216 per year. The *East Feliciana Patriot-Democrat* said at the time that to be prisoners of the lessee system "is a grievous lot a thousand times more grievous than the law ever contemplated they should endure in expiation of their sins." The *New Orleans Daily Picayune* was also critical of the prison conditions, saying it would be more humane to impose a death sentence immediately upon anyone sentenced to a term in excess of six years because the average convict lived no longer than that anyway.

When Angola was officially constructed in 1901, the prisoner death rate plummeted to an average of 35 per year, an accomplishment credited to the efforts of one man, Warden W. M. Reynaud, who was also a medical physician. But, it wouldn't be until the 1940s that Angola would have its first general hospital, located at Camp-H, where it remained until moved to the newly constructed Reception Center in 1951. With only one doctor who visited the prison three times a week, one nurse and a medical technician, medical health services were delivered to a prisoner population of nearly three thousand. In 1965, the current prison hospital, adjacent to the Main Prison, was constructed to accommodate an inmate population that had grown to four thousand. With a then modern and equipped facility, state budget cuts not only prevented the hiring of professional medical employees to staff it, the cuts also eliminated other prisoner services, including a reduction in prison security personnel.

It wasn't long before the level of violence increased. Mortality rates began to soar; five homicides in 1965 to ten in 1970. Six 1965 deaths by natural causes rose to fourteen in 1970. Severe overcrowding, an almost non-existent medical program, an open sewage system, and poor food services prompted inmates to file a lawsuit in 1971 protesting unhealthful living conditions. It would not be until 1975 that U.S. District Judge E. Gordon West, of the U.S. Middle District in Baton Rouge, issued a sweeping order to clean up and improve conditions at the Louisiana State Penitentiary, placing emphasis on the delivery of proper medical care to inmates.

What followed was the first determined effort by the State to improve the delivery of medical care to Angola inmates. A massive advertising campaign to hire professionals, a boost in salaries, and a dramatic increase in the medical budget followed. Later, the hospital facility would be expanded slightly to create office and treatment areas for the growing medical staff.

Judge West's declaration of sub-human and unconstitutional conditions would include how many doctors, nurses and other medical personnel he wanted at the prison hospital.

*Appeared in *The Angolite,* November/December 1991, 29-56. Reprinted with permission.

111

* * *

Occasionally, some horrific medical stories zip through the prisoner rumor-mill. At other times, inmates with serious illness or injury express praise and gratitude for the medical attention that preserved life or limb.

Given that the initial court-ordered improvements were now in their sixteenth year, *The Angolite* embarked on a fact-finding mission to determine how much progress had been made in prison health care. Word of our project went out to the prisoner population. It wasn't long before stories began filing in.

Leslie Sheridan resided and was employed in St. Tammany Parish when a gunfight broke out in a barroom in Pearl River, Louisiana. A bystander, Sheridan was shot in the abdomen and taken to Slidell Memorial Hospital during surgery, it was necessary to install a colostomy bag until his colon healed, a process that generally takes about eight weeks. He was released from the hospital and shortly thereafter was involved in an auto accident resulting not only in the death of another person, but also kept Sheridan unconscious for nearly a month. When he regained consciousness, he was arrested and charged with vehicular homicide and deputies removed him to the St. Tammany Jail. Later convicted of the offense, he was sentenced to six and-one-half years in prison.

"I was taken to St. Tammany Jail and stayed there for the next 18 months with the colostomy on me," stated Sheridan. "They never made a real effort to have it removed. I had appointments for surgery made at New Orleans Charity Hospital, but the deputies never took me for the surgery." The need for the colostomy operation was only part of his concern.

The auto accident had also resulted in the loss of his left eye and the loss of hearing in his left ear.

After a year and a half in St. Tammany Parish confinement, Sheridan was transferred to the reception center at Hunt Correctional Center for processing into the state prison system. "I was then sent to Allen Correctional Center, that private prison run by Wackenhut Company. I was there one week and they made a surgery appointment for the following Monday at the Huey P. Long Hospital in Alexandria. Finally I was going to have this colostomy bag removed," Sheridan exclaimed. "But, when Monday came, instead of taking me to the surgery appointment, they brought me here to Angola. I've been here ever since."

When interviewed in October 1991, Sheridan told *The Angolite* he had been seen several times by doctors from Earl K. Long Hospital and New Orleans Charity Hospital. "They told me they would schedule me for surgery, but nothing ever happens," he said. "I saw a doctor here the other day, and he looked in my medical file and said I'm not scheduled to see anyone until January 1992. I'm supposed to be out by January 27, 1992, so it looks like I'll have to leave prison still wearing this colostomy. I've been wearing it two-and-a-half years now."

There is legitimate cause for Sheridan, now 35, to be seriously concerned. "The longer the colostomy bag is on me, the less chance my colon has to stay healthy because nothing is passing through it," he explained. "One doctor told me here that I had a 60/40 chance against it being successful. So, if they don't do it soon, I may have to wear this bag the rest of my life."

Sometimes injuries or illnesses occur during a prisoner's confinement, and not unlike the Sheridan case, medical treatment is slow in coming.

Thirty-six-year-old Albert Landry arrived at Angola following a 1976 murder conviction in Orleans Parish. The then-20-year-old first offender had been a student at Dillard Junior College, majoring in biophysics. Just after his arrival at the Louisiana State Penitentiary, he joined a prisoner football team, The Broncos. During a practice game on the prison Big Yard in 1978, he was tackled from the side, below the waist. His knee bent and collapsed.

"I was brought to the infirmary and they placed an ice bag and ace bandage on it and issued me a single crutch," he described. "They sent me back to my dorm and it's given me trouble ever since." Over the years since the injury, corrective surgery for Landry has been recommended by a plethora of physicians. "One of the oriental doctors back then said I had torn and hyperextension of ligaments. All of the doctors I've seen in the past 13 years recommended surgery, but I haven't had it yet," he added.

Landry has been on one type of medical duty status or another ever since, performing menial chores here and there. Interviewed inside the prison hospital ward where he was recuperating from a second-surgical procedure to his left shoulder from an unrelated injury, Landry said he showed his knee to the surgeons performing his recent surgery at New Orleans Charity Hospital. "They said they would schedule me for surgery as soon as my shoulder heals," he said, smiling. "Do I believe that? No," he chuckled. "It's hard for me to believe anyone about medical things. I've been lied to so many times."

Landry's injury is one that requires caution each and every step he takes. "I can't walk very far, and I can't walk very fast. If I make any lateral movement at all, the knee buckles and I fall flat on my face. The knee becomes disengaged from the rest of my leg. It wobbles on its own. I have no control over it. It bends any way it wants to, sometimes hanging there like a string, swinging back and forth," Landry described.

Sitting on the hospital bed next to Landry was Archie McDaniel, who has gone blind in prison. Serving a 12-year sentence for a 1987 attempted murder in Caddo Parish, McDaniel said that even though he's eligible for release in December 1992, that he is being recommended for early release. "The doctors and other officials are making efforts to have me released on medical furlough. I am a first offender and they say I could be released from prison by Christmas," McDaniel said.

* * *

Sometimes a prison injury does result in immediate surgery, but when it comes to the delivery of care following the surgery, the system experiences a breakdown.

Paul Ramos, arrested in Ascension Parish as a parole violator, was returned to prison in 1986 to complete a previously imposed 6-year burglary sentence. The 23-year-old native of Puerto Rico was returned to the Ascension Parish jail in March 1991 as a witness in a civil court proceeding. Following an altercation with several inmates in the jail, he suffered cuts on his back and stab wound to his right knee. Ramos told *The Angolite* the deputies wrapped some bandages around the wounds and returned him to Angola.

"I could hardly walk," he stated. "I went to the prison hospital and they scheduled me for surgery at New Orleans

Charity Hospital. After surgery on September 9, 1991, I was released back to Angola four days later. When I got back to Angola, they sent me back to my dormitory (Hickory 4) in a wheelchair pushed by an inmate orderly. I was dropped off in my bed. I was left no wheelchair, crutch or anything to help me walk. There was 57 staples and stitches in my knee. I couldn't even defend myself. There was no way I could walk to the dining room or pill call room. The guys in the dorm had to help me get to the bathroom. All I could do is lay there in pain," Ramos explained.

The scenario described by Ramos is a frequent complaint by inmates either diagnosed with, or recuperating from illness, injury or surgery. The Louisiana State Penitentiary is a sprawling megalopolis of buildings comprising the Main Prison, and an assortment of outcamps that stretch across 18,000 acres of prison grounds. The walkway from one end of the Main Prison to the other is three-quarters of a mile in length. The location of the dining room at one end of that walkway means any of 960 inmates assigned to the Medium Yard-East must walk a half mile, one-way, in order to eat a meal. This poses a significant burden to those inmates with medical problems.

That same evening Ramos returned from surgery, he explained his situation to security Major Charles Labored and Captain Darren Bordelon as they made routine rounds of prison dormitories. "They called for an ambulance and I was taken back to the prison hospital, but the person on duty read a report in my record that said I was very capable of walking on my own without assistance," said Ramos.

Major Charles Labored recalled the incident well: "I could see the man was laying there in pain. Beads of sweat were rolling off him. I had the same surgery he had, and so did my son. It's very painful. That's why I ordered him transported back to the hospital by ambulance," Labored said.

Though prison security officialdom acted with Ramos' best interest in mind, it wasn't quite enough. Ramos was issued a disciplinary report by the hospital staff and ordered locked up in administrative lockdown pending hearings. "I was taken to CBD in a wheelchair and an EMT (Emergency Medical Technician) carried me up the stairs. I stayed in the Hole until September 17th. When I went to court, they found me guilty, but they sent me back to my dorm in a wheelchair." [Ed. When informed of Ramos' situation, *The Angolite* contacted Warden John P. Whitley, who said he would look into the matter. Shortly afterwards, Ramos was admitted to the hospital ward where he remained under care for the next two weeks].

A diagnosis by a prison physician is generally accompanied by a "duty status" declaration by the doctor that informs prison security officers of the limitations and restriction of activity in individual cases. In the world of prison, a medical opinion is binding. It supersedes any other regulation or directive governing the activities of prisoners. A duty status differs in each case, ranging from "No Duty" to "Limited Duty", each accompanied by a special instruction, e.g., an inmate with a broken left arm is generally placed on Limited Duty with instruction not to use the left arm. This instruction implies, however, that the inmate is able to work with his right arm and security officers generally require the inmate to perform some menial chore involving use of his right arm. Sometimes, especially following some surgical procedures, inmates are placed an "No Duty with Bedrest" which allows him to be exempt from any of the menial chores he otherwise would be compelled to perform. It is the interpretation of these duty statuses by non-medical prison employees, especially security officers, that occasionally causes confusion for the prison staff, and grief to the inmate patient. When the doctors at New Orleans Charity Hospital discharged Paul Ramos back to the prison, they ordered "Bed Rest" and "No Duty" until he was seen at his next post-surgical appointment. However, when he was released from his 2-week stay in the prison hospital, Ramos was issued a pair of crutches and required to perform some work. "Because of the Light/Limited Duty status issued by the prison doctor, I was ordered to wash windows," Ramos stated. "While washing them, the crutches slipped on the wet, soapy floor and down I went." Records show that Ramos was transported to Charity Hospital on October 1st where doctors checked his knee, ordered he not perform any duties and ordered his return to Angola. But, when Ramos showed *The Angolite* the duty status issued by the prison doctor, it said: "L/D, crutch walking only for one month; minor duty; no mopping or sweeping."

Inmates assigned to "L/D" are required by security officers to report every morning and afternoon to a Light Duty "check-out" area. Failing to report invariably results in a disciplinary report, usually charging the inmate with a Work Offense violation. In Ramos' case, it could mean another trip to disciplinary court, perhaps even another stint in administrative lockdown or isolation.

On October 10th, while Ramos was using the stairs leading to the yard, he fell and again twisted his knee. He was rushed to the prison hospital where he was placed

in another ambulance and transported to New Orleans Charity Hospital. "The doctors there said the knee was too swollen to do anything, so they released me back to Angola and told me not to use it at all," said Ramos. The duty status issued by the prison doctors upon his return, in a copy viewed by *The Angolite*, provided: "No Duty 2 days; then Limited Duty; no climbing stairs, no mopping and avoiding prolonged walking for 1 month."

A part of the post-operative treatment regimen for Ramos were appointments for physical therapy at Charity Hospital. At one of these appointments just four days following his fall down the stairs, the therapist noted a small lump on the knee. Ramos said, "It was one of the screws pushing through the skin, so they ordered me returned to New Orleans the following day to see my surgeon." When he was taken to New Orleans the following day, Ramos said the surgeon was livid because of the trauma to the delicate surgical procedure performed on the knee. Ramos told the surgeon to give him a copy of any orders so that he could be able to show others to make sure the Angola doctors wouldn't make any changes. The doctor wrote, on a medicine prescription form: "Patient is to be avoiding activities—per upper level surgeon who did surgery. No Duty. 10-15-91. s/Kathy Robertson, M.D." This time the Angola medical authorities issued a duty status simply saying "No Duty for 3 weeks."

* * *

Some inmates simultaneously fall through prison classification and medical cracks, finding themselves assigned to prison duties they're unable to perform because of some physical/medical infirmity. Robert Roy Randle, 28, lost all the fingers of his right hand in an accident at the age of four. An injury to his head at the same time has caused him to experience epileptic seizures ever since. Following a Calcasieu Parish conviction for armed robbery and battery in 1989, Randle was sentenced to serve 45 years. He arrived at Angola in the Spring of 1991.

"I've been working in the fields for about three months now," said Randle. "Right now I'm assigned to Line 5-A. I can't do too much. When I was at Camp-D, they made me use a hoe. I tried to for a couple of days, but couldn't do the work, so I went to the hole. Here at the Main Prison they gave me a rake to use, but I couldn't do that with one hand, so I went to the hole again," he explained.

The medical duty status viewed by *The Angolite*, dated August 29, 1991, said: "PERMANENT DUTY STATUS, LD/RS, A-SQUAD WITH SEIZURE PRECAUTIONS." Under the Scars and Marks section of his Master Prison Record, it was noted: "Missing fingers, right hand." When *The Angolite* checked Randle's prison assignment on November 24th, he was still assigned to the prison farmline.

The policies and standards governing prisoner health care in the Louisiana Department of Corrections is regulated by Departmental Regulation Number 30-6B, a 13-page document that not only outlines particular medical requirements, but also places responsibility for ensuring implementation and adherence upon "the Assistant Secretaries for Adult and Juvenile Services, and all wardens, superintendents, medical directors and hospital administrators."

DOC Regulation No. 30-6B(b): "Each warden and superintendent is responsible to provide inmates in their charge with a complete annual health evaluation for each inmate over (40) years of age and, in the case of females, an annual pap smear/pelvic exam for those over thirty (30) years of age. A medical evaluation is to be conducted on all inmates at least yearly."

DOC Regulation No. 30-6B(c): "A health evaluation consists of a medical evaluation conducted by a medical doctor, a dental evaluation conducted by a dentist, a mental health evaluation conducted by a psychologist or psychiatrist, and a vision evaluation conducted by an optometrist or ophthalmologist when visual acuity is less than 20-20."

Though annual medical examinations are a matter of departmental regulations and on paper signify the existence of an effective medical program for inmates, the reality is that very few, if any inmates ever receive an annual physical. Some inmates have never had such an examination.

Not to be confused with routine annual examinations, the "intake examination" is generally performed upon state prisoners when they are received at the Adult Reception Diagnostic Center (ARDC) at Hunt Correctional Center. It is there that most state prisoners are first taken before being assigned to any one of the state's twelve adult prisons. While an intake medical examination is the responsibility of ARDC, any subsequent medical examination is the responsibility of prison officials in charge of the facility where the inmate is designated to serve his prison sentence.

Albert Landry, who has been waiting 13 of his sixteen years in prison for surgery on his knee, hasn't had an annual checkup in 13 years. "The only one I ever had was the initial exam. I never had a regular, annual or any physical examination. I've never had a chest x-ray besides the one they did at Charity Hospital before my recent surgery. I've never had any blood or urine analysis at Angola," Landry stated.

A random sampling of other inmates also indicates annual or regular medical examinations are not being routinely performed at the prison hospital. Terrance Marks, now in his 26th year of a life sentence from Calcasieu Parish for an aggravated rape conviction, said his last physical examination was performed about 1983. Joseph Woods, 58, said his last examination was in 1984 or 1985. Woods, serving a 20-year sentence for a 1979 habitual offender conviction from Orleans Parish, said: "In addition to the exam in the mid-80s, I was given a complete physical at ARDC in 1980. Right now I take medicine for high blood pressure and arthritis, but never has any lab work to see what effect long use of the medicine is having on me."

* * *

DOC Regulation No. 30-6B(e): "An adequate dental evaluation is one which will identify all acute problems (toothaches, pain, mouth infection, inability to eat a regular diet, etc.) and provide a dental treatment plan (for correction of defects, improving dental attitudes and habits, etc.) for each inmate and student. All intake and annual dental evaluations are to be recorded on DOC Medical Form No. 2-05. . . ."

Robert McCuin, 32, began experiencing problems with his teeth following his arrest in 1984. Following his conviction and sentence to mandatory life imprisonment for murder in Ouachita Parish in 1986, Angola dental officials began extracting his teeth in 1988. On June 14, 1990, the last of his teeth were pulled. For the next year he waited for impressions to be taken, being forced to eat the regular meals served in the prison dining room. "I ate till my gums became raw, sore and sometimes they'd bleed," McCuin said. "I'd break the meat apart with my fingers and swallow the whole pieces. I asked for a softer diet, but am told there's no special diets at Angola for dental patients."

On June 14, 1991, exactly a year after his teeth were pulled, the dental office took his impressions. Four months later he was called back to the dental office to have impressions re-taken. "I overheard them discussing that the other impression had been lost," McCuin told *The Angolite*. "For a year and a half now I've been trying to eat food with my gums, and they are shrinking and being flattened all the time. I get little cuts in them all the time from trying to chew my food. When the teeth do come in, they won't fit because the gums will no longer be there for the teeth to fit to."

Initially losing weight, the strapping 6'5" McCuin eventually regained the weight by supplementing his prison diet by goods purchased from the inmate canteen. "I spend about $12.50 of my own money each week buying peanut butter, bread, cookies and instant soups. I dunk the cookies in coffee to make them soft. I eat about five pounds of peanut butter every week," he explained. The money spent had been slated for the purchase of shoes and personal clothes. "I learned to budget my money to buy certain foods to help get me by," McCuin added.

Written inquiries, including an Administrative Remedy Procedure (ARP) were filed to prison authorities. Hospital Administrator Ella Fletcher, in one written response, explained to McCuin of a six-month wait for work to be returned from the dental lab at each phase of the dental process. Referring to it as "turn around" time that medical officials were working hard to reduce, the time element doesn't make McCuin happy. Given the six-month waiting period at each step of the dental process, McCuin said he will not receive his dentures until June 1993, three years after his teeth being extracted. "All the guys I know who've had teeth pulled are in the same position, or worse," McCuin stated. Asked if he could continue his dietary habits and difficulty eating without teeth until 1993, he responded: "I have no choice in the matter. I have to do it. You must find a way to survive."

Some patients who are assigned to and are actually housed on the prison hospital wards have difficulty receiving dental care. In addition to efforts to have his colostomy bag removed, Leslie Sheridan has actively sought dental attention. "Before my father died, he got a letter from one of the Angola authorities telling him all they could do here is take care of my teeth. I only have 12 teeth left and they're all rotting out. It's real painful. I've been living here in the hospital for six months now, just a few feet away from the dental office, and they haven't done anything yet," stated Sheridan.

"I talked to the hospital administrator and she told me she went and checked and they had me scheduled for an appointment to come back and have x-rays and teeth worked on, but still nothing has happened. That was two months ago," added Sheridan.

* * *

The Louisiana State is also home to 2,280 inmates serving life sentences, and 1,600 inmates serving such otherwise long prison terms (30 to 300 years, and in some cases, more), sentences that in a practical sense relegate them to remain there until they die. Over two hundred of these inmates have been confined over 20 years. According to Department of Corrections statistics, the average age of the over 18,000-state prisoner population is 35.

While the greying of prisons is becoming a national phenomena, Louisiana now has about 500 inmates imprisoned who are over fifty years of age. By 1995, that number is expected to increase to eight hundred. In 1984 when the Forgotten Man Committee made its report to the governor, they said: "There are 299 persons over the age of 55 incarcerated in the Department of Public Safety & Corrections. This is just the beginning of an upward trend. . . ."

Inmates who came to prison young or middle-aged, have now grown old. Hundreds of them. They've traded in shovels and hoes for eye-glasses and dentures. Men who toiled for decades in the fields and industries of the penitentiary are shuffling from place to place with the aid of crutches, canes and wheelchairs. No longer able to perform any meaningful work, they may clean doorknobs, windows, plant flowers or just sit staring off into space. Some are now so old they're not able to verbalize exactly what aspects of life they may have missed; the world outside prison long lost in memory.

An official effort by state senator Larry Bankston, D-Baton Rouge, to have elderly prisoners integrated into nursing homes outside prison, never materialized. The cost-saving measure that placed responsibility for more costs upon the federal government was brought to Governor Buddy Roemer's Special Budget Task Force in 1988. In that year, state correctional officials identified forty elderly and/or severely disabled inmates who were unable to care for themselves. Bankston was informed by the corrections officials that the placement of these 40 inmates into nursing homes would bring an annual minimum savings of $388,200 to tax payers.

The senator's noble effort failed. In order for the plan to work, the cooperation of three administrative functions were necessary: (1) the prison medical staff needed to review each case; (2) the state board of pardons needed to . . . recommend the elderly/ill inmate for release; and (3) the governor needed to approve the recommendation. Steps #1 and #2 were not a problem. Both of those agencies proceeded to identify and process each individual case. However, as time would reveal, the conservative clemency policy of Governor Roemer made the measure ineffective. The elderly and ill inmates were left to die in prison. Some did.

The costs have been high. In 1982, the corrections budget for prisoner health care was $5.6 million. For fiscal year1986 it jumped to $9.1 million, and shot up to $10.3 million in 1989. When *The Angolite* asked for the 1990 medical budget, Ron Granier, chief fiscal officer for the corrections department said: "I must inform you that the information you requested is not readily available . . . therefore, I am unable to accommodate your request at the present time . . . "

Sixty-five-year-old Leonard Griffin, still on appeal since his conviction for murder in Concordia Parish, arrived at the prison in 1985. Though unable to read or write, Griffin worked hard all his life, raising a family and putting four children through school. His wife died since his imprisonment. "I ain't never been no trouble. I worked the saw mill and hauled pulpwood all my life," said the elderly first offender. Now assigned to Oak dormitory of Angola's Main Prison, Griffin isn't required to do much in the way of work. "All I do is clean the window and little things they tell me to do. I do what they say for me to do," he said.

It was shortly after his prison arrival that Griffin began having pains in his leg that made walking any distance a painful burden. The relatively long treks to the dining room became not only a physical chore, but additionally strained relationships with prison security officers charged with keeping an orderly, single-file movement of prisoners on the walk. "My leg aches all the time. Sometimes I have to stop two and three times before I get to the kitchen, my leg be hurting real bad. I can't go no further, then. The officer always be hollering 'move on!' I tell 'em I can't, but I have to go ahead on, you know. It takes me a long time to walk to the kitchen. Sometimes when I get there they be done feeding already," Griffin said.

His difficulty in walking is aggravated by an increasing inability to breathe. Griffin has smoked all of his life, and during the interview with *The Angolite*, he hand-rolled a cigarette of pipe tobacco. "I can't get my air sometimes. I have to stop, lean against the fence and catch my wind and wait for my leg pain to ease before going on. So, now I sometimes go to the kitchen once a week."

Griffin has exchanged his three daily trips to the dining hall for a single weekly or bi-weekly walk to the prison canteen. He said, I send to home for my people to send me money so I can buy a little stuff out of the store. If I could walk with no trouble, I'd eat three meals a day. I likes to eat, but I have to pass them up. I get me little cans of tuna fish, vienna sausages, sardines, bags of chips and bread. I spend $30 or $40 every two weeks. I went there yesterday and had $103 in my account and I spent it down to $56," he explained.

Griffin readily admits that life in prison hasn't been easy for him. He's losing his hearing in one ear and, with only one tooth in his mouth, he said no one over the years asked if he wanted any dentures. If fact, Griffin said no one has told him what is wrong with his legs or lungs. If they did ask him about dentures, he would tell them he doesn't want any: "I can eat anything you eat! I can bust ice with my gums, real good!" he exclaimed.

Asked to what he attributed his survival in prison the past five years, the kind-spoken Griffin admitted: "If it wasn't for the money, I wouldn't be able to make it in here. This is a hard place to try and survive. If you ain't got no money, you in bad shape, especially when you're old."

A general fear among inmates, dying inside prison, becomes more pervasive as inmate death by natural causes continues to rise. As Angola's population becomes "grayer" and acquires the medical problems and illnesses of the elderly, that fear turns to reality. In 1982 and 1984 there were six deaths due to natural causes, a number that jumped to fifteen in 1985. In 1989 twelve inmates died of natural reasons and according to prison records, six inmates expired of natural causes in the first three months of 1991 .

Professor Jonathan Turley, a law professor at George Washington University, is an expert on the elderly in the nation's prisons. While teaching law at New Orleans' Tulane University in the mid 1980s, Turley founded the Program for Older Prisoners (POPS) because, he said, the South has more older prisoners than most other states in the last 10 years. "This is particularly so in Louisiana," he

said, citing a recent study showing 343 inmates that are 55-years old or older, and another 1,231 inmates (of the state's 18,000 prisoners) 45 years-old or older.

A major concern of this growing population is experiencing a heart attack or other coronary problem. Dr. Ronald Shansky, director of prison health services in Illinois, told *America* magazine [Feb 10, 1990] that not only do prisoners have a higher rate of heart attacks than those outside prison, but also that "prisoners are subject to them at a much earlier age: 50 percent of heart attacks among the incarcerated occur among inmates under 35 years of age.

While the Angola hospital provides a fully-staffed and trained crew of Emergency Medical Technicians (EMT) and vehicles, there is no cardiologist assigned. In fact, there is no medical position authorized on the hospital staff, in spite of the rapidly aging prisoner population. Now generally accepted that unless immediate profession medical intervention is provided, surviving a heart attack becomes quite uncertain. The Louisiana State Penitentiary is a large megalopolis comprising eight individual prison units incarcerating over 5,000 inmates. It sometimes takes as long as seven to ten minutes for emergency vehicles and staff to reach such victims. A majority of the prison's most serious heart patients are found housed in one of the three crowded hospital wards.

Wilfred James Freeman, 45, is assigned to a private room of Ward II. The first offender has been serving a life sentence for a Lafayette Parish second degree murder in 1983. Freeman had two heart attacks in 1981 and underwent open-heart surgery. While in prison he had another heart attack in 1988, and underwent another open-heart surgery at the LSU-Medical Center in Shreveport. In

1990, while assigned duties at the Avoyelles Parish Jail, he experienced further cardiac problems and was flown to St. Francis Cabrini Hospital in Alexandria where he underwent an angioplasty procedure and learned that four of his main heart arteries were 90 to 100 percent clogged.

"Last week they say I had another light heart attack," Freeman told *The Angolite* when interviewed October 15. "They say there is nothing they can do for me unless it's a heart transplant. They tell me I can go at anytime, and told me to call my people and let them prepare, because nothing can be done for me any more," he stated.

Freeman said that he has asked prison officials for a heart transplant. "They told me definitely that would not happen. When I asked them why not, they told me 'I was lucky I had open-heart surgery.' I'm suffering and in pain every day. It's so hard," he said.

Corrections Sergeant Charles Alford, assigned as security for Ward II, said: "I see no reason why he shouldn't have the heart transplant." Alford's parents were both correctional employees at the prison. His mother worked in the hospital medical records office for years. "I feel like even though he is incarcerated, he's a human being. A transplant is saving a life, and the Lord looks at that as another life saved. I believe if somebody needs a part of me after I'm gone, I'm going to give it up because that will be saving a life. Even though Charles has committed a crime and is in prison, I'll do what I can to save a life or help preserve a life," Alford added.

Freeman said he has three daughters in Milwaukee making efforts to have him released. "My children told me that after I get home, they would make arrangements for getting me on the list for a transplant

at the hospital in Houston, Texas," said Freeman.

* * *

Complaints or examples of prison medical-care delivery notwithstanding, there is a respectably large portion of the prisoner population believing they have received decent medical treatment when it was needed. Only a relatively small portion of the prisoners actually have chronic illness, disease or injury requiring frequent attention or monitoring. But, some prisoners do not hesitate to vocally praise the medical department.

"I cannot complain about the medical treatment," stated George Brumfield, who is in his 18th year of a fifty-year sentence for a 1973 armed robbery in Tangipahoa Parish. "These medical people at Angola are definitely slow about getting things done, I'm not going to lie about it. They're real slow, just like in the military. But, I could never complain about it because I almost died here, twice. If it wasn't for these people, I wouldn't be talking to you today," he said.

A Vietnam vet, Brumfield, 46, was wounded by shrapnel that entered his chest, nicking a portion of his heart. The U.S. Army gave him a purple heart, bronze star and a disability discharge. The performance of any activity thus restricted, he was told his heart might give him trouble in the future. In his sixth year of Angola imprisonment, it did.

"I was 36-years-old when I had my first heart attack in 1981," Brumfield stated. "In 1985 I had another one. Each time I was given emergency treatment and transported to outside hospitals. I stayed at one hospital for four months. So far, my heart isn't giving me more trouble." Then, in the Spring of this year, Brumfield began losing his voice and had difficulty swallowing his food. He complained several times to the sick call technician at Camp-C and was eventually seen by the prison physicians. "They didn't see anything right away, but gave me antibiotics, thinking I had some infection. After a few months, I couldn't swallow any food at all, so the doctors referred me to an ENT specialist. He didn't know what was wrong, either, so he sent me to New Orleans Charity Hospital. There they found some polyps growing on my vocal cords. The Angola hospital didn't have the right instruments to find them. They operated right away and, because I was a heart patient, they kept me there a couple of days to be sure I was okay." explained Brumfield.

When interviewed two weeks following his surgery, Brumfield was able to speak with a slight rasp in his voice. "I'm getting better and better every day," he said, adding: "If I had to point my finger at any real medical problems here, they would be the mis-communication between the outside hospitals and the doctors here. The doctors outside order one thing, like medicines, and the doctors here change it the moment you return to some other type of medicine or treatment. The second problem I see is there is not enough doctors here at the prison to treat all these people. They are spread too damn thin. But, I'll never complain about them. They saved my life twice, and I can talk and eat again."

* * *

Louisiana's prisoner population has quadrupled since the prison hospital opened in 1965, and so has the number of security officers hired to watch over them. The Angola inmate population has doubled since then, increasing from 3,000 to the present 5,200. To determine whether there has been concomitant increase in medical staff to accommodate inmate health care needs, *The Angolite* dropped in at the hospital. There were also questions needing answers about the medical care complaints raised by the inmates.

Dr. Kenneth L. Perego has been a physician at the prison hospital since March 1989, serving as its medical director for the past two years. A native of Leesville, Perego attended McNeese State College and graduated from LSU (New Orleans) Medical School. Perego readily acknowledged there were serious problems and needs confronting the medical staff.

"Being short of staff doesn't help us a bit," Perego said. "We need more doctors, and how we're going to get them I don't know for sure. Of course, at this time we're short of nurses also."

Though there have been improvements in the increase of professional medical staff, the required number of staffers has been set by a series of Consent Decrees filed in federal court. The court has declared the need for nine full-time physicians at the prison, however, there are only five. Perego said: "If we had a full complement of doctors and nurses, we could start having specialty clinics. We could also start doing the annual physicals and other needed functions."

The director of nursing corroborated staffing woes. Barbara Edmisten, R.N., is in her tenth year as a nurse at the hospital, its nursing director for the past three years. "We are supposed to have a total of twelve registered nurses, we only have six. The authorized number of LPNs [Licensed Practical Nurses] is 24, and we have twenty. We do have a full quota of NACs

(Nurse's Assistant-Corrections]," Edmisten stated, adding that the shortage will become even more critical by the end of the year. "When we only have fifty-percent staffing of nurses, it becomes very difficult. We're soon going to be in worse shape. I have two pending retirements of RNs, one in late December and the other in March of 1992. This will reduce the RN staff to four. It requires four RNs to maintain minimal staffing levels, one for each shift. There must be an RN on duty at all times."

The recruitment of doctors and nurses has traditionally been a problem, according to Perego and Edmisten. Both attribute non-competitive salaries, remoteness of the prison and conditions of the only road leading to the prison as the major setbacks in attracting medical workers. In 1989, the inability to hire prison medical employees was so critical that DPS&C Secretary Bruce Lynn seriously considered handing the prison medical program over to a private company, or as an alternative, moving the state's medical prison closer to Baton Rouge.

Perego and Edmisten also admit to an irony attached to the aggressive recruitment efforts. "We'd need more space in the hospital to put them. This building is not sufficient for the staff and medical responsibilities that we have now," Perego stated. Edmisten added: "I'd have no offices or equipment for them to use. We outgrew this structure more than ten years ago. Right now, we have no office space for supervisors to maintain any confidential files, or to hold private discussions." Edmisten said just to accommodate a "full" nursing staff, the hospital would have to be expanded by one third. When asked how much space would be needed for a full physician's staff, Perego said: "We'd have to add at least half as much space just

to have room to put them. If we give them sufficient work space, then this facility would have to be doubled."

Delivering health care to a community of five thousand people with a medical staff operating at 50-percent capability, is the major underlying reason prompting inmate complaints of poor medical treatment. The small number of doctors and nurses are finding themselves struggling to serve an overwhelming number of inmates. Consequently, some fall through the cracks, turning what would usually be considered "preventive" medicine into a program where the staff finds itself busy putting out brush fires.

"What we do now is address medical complaints," Perego explained. "If that requires looking into all the body systems, we do that. But, as far as annual physical examinations being given as a preventive medicine regimen, it cannot be done. We just do not have the staff." When queried of the possibility some inmates haven't had a physical exam in ten years, he responded: "It's possible." In comparing costs between "preventive" and "brush fire" methods, Perego said it was definitely cheaper to have annual physical examinations. "With today's cost of surgery and pharmaceuticals, it would save taxpayers lots of money if we could detect and treat a problem that could have been prevented."

No major surgeries are performed at the prison hospital. Such procedures are usually done at two of the state's charity hospitals, Earl K. Long Memorial Hospital (ERL-Baton Rouge) and Charity Hospital (CHNO-New Orleans), where special wards and appropriate security arrangements are available. However, in the past couple of years, a backlog of these recommended surgical procedures has grown. Dr. Perego said the surgeries are generally grouped into those considered major—needing general anesthesia—and minor surgery, which can be performed at the prison hospital. How large was the backlog for major surgery? "Probably a hundred and fifty, or so," Perego said. Asked whether this included the colostomy surgery for Leslie Sheridan, he acknowledged it was probably one of those on backlog.

There is some light at the end of the tunnel for those awaiting surgery, said Perego, explaining that corrections headquarters had recently hired Cal Bankston as facilitator in coordinating surgery arrangements at area hospitals. As former hospital administrator at EKL, the Feliciana Hospital in St. Francisville and Lallie Kemp Hospital in Independence, Bankston is working to reduce the surgery backlog. "I was called in reference to having some of our surgery also done at Lallie Kemp," said Perego. "I've now written a letter to the warden seeking his approval for us to go ahead and start scheduling some of these surgeries there."

When confronted with the case of Wilfred Freeman who is in need of a heart transplant, Perego assured *The Angolite* he was being scheduled for re-evaluation at the Shreveport Medical Center. "I've asked the specialists to be specific and I will consider another recommendation for medical furlough when that is done," he said. Asked to consider Freeman's situation from a worst-case scenario, Perego said: "I think he will eventually have a massive heart attack and die."

In his sixth year at the prison hospital, James Priddy, D.D.S., is head of the dental department. Assisting him are two fulltime dentists and dental assistants, and one contract oral surgeon who comes to the prison for 16 to 20 hours each week. Priddy says he could use one more

dentist and three dental assistants. "Each dentist should have an assistant," he stated. "In the years I've been here, we've yet to catch up on the dental work the inmates need. We spend most of our time fighting fires, instead of preventing the fires from starting."

According to the National Correction Health Association (NCHA), there's a standard ratio of dentists to the number of inmates. "The NCHA says they could get by with one-thousand inmates per dentist. The Texas Department of Corrections base their inmate-to-dentist ratio on 850 inmates to each dentist," explained Priddy. "Using the NCHA ratio, we should have five dentists, and given the Texas ratio, we should have six dentists. We only have three. Our ratio right now is about 1,700 inmates to each dentist. It's way out of proportion," he added. With enough dentists, Priddy said they could get the patient to the point where his dental health could be more easily maintained. "We're not able to give annual dental checkups like we should."

The extraordinary high ratio is not responsible, Priddy says, for the growing backlog of inmates needing dentures. "We have a denture backlog of about nine months. That is way too much. A nine month backlog translates into about three or four hundred inmates waiting for their dentures. We have no control over it."

Priddy fingers the dental laboratory services, a private firm under contract to provide dentures, as the culprit. "About a year and a half ago the lab virtually stopped sending dentures and partials back to us. We had so many cases backlogged, we had to stop taking impressions. But, the situation is getting better." He said that recent pressure applied by the new hospital administrator has improved the volume of completed dentures being returned. "In the six years I've been here, this is the second or third time that we've had a major problem with contract dental laboratory services virtually shutting down," Priddy recalled.

Until the contract lab is able to catch up, inmates will have to contend with the backlog. Priddy says, "It's the only fair way to do it, put a man's name at the bottom and let it work its way to the top. We have nothing else we can do."

The equipment used by the dentists is not new. "Our equipment is horrible. Only three units are operable. The units we use are over ten years old. But, we were recently informed that the new units I've requested for six consecutive years are expected to arrive any day," Priddy stated.

Expressing sentiments similar to medical director Kenneth Perego, Priddy said if they could save a tooth, it wouldn't have to be pulled and replaced with a denture. "The way we do business right now costs a lot more money than if we could prevent dental problems. If we invested a dime today, we'd save a dollar tomorrow. If we had more equipment and just a little more help, we could do a lot more."

* * *

The efforts of prison officials to find and retain a hospital administrator is nearly synonymous to their ability to hire enough doctors and nurses. Differing from the medical director, who is accountable for the delivery of medical care to patients, a hospital administrator is responsible for the support and coordination of all other services that ensure the delivery of health care by the medical team.

For years the prison hospital functioned without one, with a long string of medical directors serving in both capacities, thereby reducing their ability to deliver medical care. For a time, non-medical persons were hired to fill the important function of administrator. Dr. Perego, the current medical director, maintained that duo responsibility until mid-1990 when 30-year Navy medical officer, Lt. Commander Michael E. Teague (retired), assumed the position. After several months on the job, Teague left for greener pastures, again requiring Perego to fulfill both positions.

In the Spring of this year, retired U. S. Army Colonel Ella L. Fletcher, armed with a Bachelor of Science Degree in Nursing, a Masters Degree in Hospital Administration and thirty years of military hospital experience, assumed the reins as prison hospital administrator.

In no-nonsense terms, Fletcher candidly expressed the abilities, the inabilities and other shortcomings which impact the delivery of health care to Angola's large and peculiarly situated inmate population. Among the top of her assessment list was the hospital structure itself.

"This building is outdated and needs to be replaced," stated Fletcher. "We don't have any built-in oxygen and suction capability and we don't have enough electrical outlets to support patient care in all the areas. There are no 'call bells' built into this hospital. In most hospitals you have what is called 'Nurse Call Systems' that basically are used in patient bed areas to communicate with the nurses station. We need a telephone-access intercom system which most hospitals do have, where you pick up a phone, dial a certain number and have instant access to the paging system. This is especially important when a doctor or nurse is needed right away. Right now we have to yell out into the hallway for a security officer to go find that person, having to leave his assigned security area to do so. The doctor in the emergency room has to leave his patient to yell his need down the hallway. Security officers should not have to leave their functions and perform another one that is not security related. Also, this building is not a totally sprinklered facility that certain fire codes require that hospitals be," Fletcher explained.

The busiest area of the hospital, the emergency and trauma rooms, is where much of the medical care is delivered on an around-the-clock basis. And, as the inmate population rises, with a growing segment becoming older, this area of beehive activity is becoming too small to meet medical needs. Fletcher joins Perego and Edmisten, saying more space is required. "The emergency room needs a holding area in addition to the trauma and treatment space for patients you have to keep for a few hours after you do treatment," Fletcher said. "All emergency rooms have these types of areas, the coronary room, trauma room, exam rooms and holding areas. Patients that drugs and medications are given to need to be observed for response afterwards for a short period of time."

Fletcher said if there was a single need that she would consider greater than any other, it would be the need for computers so information could be automated and available for instant access. "A great deal of the health provider's time is consumed by answering telephone requests by any one of several hundred prison employees wanting to know some relatively minor information about an inmate. It is a terrible waste of resources having a doctor, RN, LPN, or EMT have to leave his medical duties to respond to such phone queries. This is one example of the benefit of computers," she explained.

With a mainframe computer and local area network at each inmate housing area, Fletcher said this minor, but important information would be available to those authorized by punching in the prisoner's number. Prison employees would be able to determine an inmate's duty status, what medication he is on, and even if a special diet has been ordered so the culinary department would know what foods needed to be provided each meal.

At any given time, a large number of inmates have been prescribed medications, and because of transfers and housing assignment changes, it takes days for the inmate to receive it. Fletcher said this was one of the major problems for the pharmacy, and a major complaint by inmates. She described: "An inmate comes in today, is seen by the doctor and he orders five prescriptions. Those prescriptions may be filled today, or first thing in the morning. Once the prescriptions are filled, they are placed in the box for the inmate's housing area, which is picked up at 5:00 p.m. each day. If the inmate is transferred for some reason, the medicine goes to his old housing area and will remain there for seventy-two hours. When the pill-call officer realizes the inmate doesn't show up in that period, he returns the medicine to the pharmacy. The inmate patient, meanwhile, is somewhere in the prison not getting the medication. This problem is information oriented." If this information was computerized, the transfer of medicine would almost be instantaneous.

Head nurse Edmisten said the acquisition of computers would substantially improve the delivery of medical care. "We definitely need computers to start up an Infection Control Program, something that is desperately needed here. We've asked for these things, but we never get them."

* * *

Dipping deeply into medical resources the last several years, the advent of AIDS (Acquired Immune Deficiency Syndrome) and HIV-related treatments is having an impact on prison health care delivery. Corrections officials estimate 600 of the state's prisoners carry the virus, a number considered to be deflated because AIDS testing is not mandatory in Louisiana. "AIDS is taking up a larger portion of the budget every year," said Edmisten. "Special tests are required to follow the progression of the disease. The pharmaceuticals are very expensive, and these things are needed in order to support the therapy."

The HIV-infected inmates and medical staff pretty much agree that the Angola AIDS program is better than programs in other places. Medical director Perego acknowledged: "We're doing a good job presently of addressing HIV patients. It's costing a lot of money right now, and the costs are rising. A person can be HIV-positive and not show any signs of decomposition for a period of years, maybe as long as seven to ten years. When they do begin to deteriorate, we have to start all this expensive medication and care, including AZT and other prophylactic medicines."

Perego's prognosis of the prison AIDS menace indicated some very real needs within the next two years. "The life expectancy of an AIDS patient, once he begins experiencing one of the spin-off opportunistic illnesses, averages about 700 days. So within two years we're going to need more hospital beds for AIDS patients," he estimated. Edmisten said that need is not so much for acute care

at first, but as a place where they can receive support. "It would be like a hospice care," she said. "They will not be well enough to be in population, but not bad enough for acute care. They will be unable to walk the long distances required for pill call and meals." She also pointed out that the current shortage of nurses in two of three existing hospital wards contributes to their inability to provide that care.

In general, the staff gives high marks to the team of EMTs. "I think we have a top-notch emergency medical service," Perego stated. "We do real well in trauma situations."

But, some of the services that are sorely needed, Perego said, reverts to our staff shortages. "We need to hold hypertension clinics, diabetic clinics, arthritis clinics and coronary clinics, those things we need for the chronically ill. These are needed. These are the things the inmates would really benefit from," he explained.

The prison hospital at Angola serves not only as the only medical care center for inmates, it also functions as a geriatric home and hospice for the terminally and chronically ill. If he had them, Perego said he could easily fill another one-hundred beds. "I know there are inmates out there in population that would probably fare better in the long run being on a hospital ward," he said.

Perego was also pleased with progress in other areas . "We've improved our X-ray facilities and are now able to perform fluoroscopies, upper GI's, gall bladders and barium enemas. We've received several good pieces of laboratory equipment and a staff very capable of doing much of the chemistry work," he said .

"Other things we're working on are coming up to standards so far as the

American Correctional Association is concerned. There's an awful lot of work being done, but there's also an awful lot that needs to be done," Perego concluded .

* * *

Looking back nearly two decades to the original lawsuit and subsequent federal court order, it's difficult to prove that any real progress has been made in the prison medical scene. The inmate population has increased, the quality and quantity of health care has improved, yet the same complaints and problems that existed in 1971 still exist in 1991. The only difference, perhaps, is that many of the inmates are now twenty years older, the same aging process as the hospital facility and a few veteran health care providers. For the most part, the hospital is staffed by relatively new professionals, working with insufficient tools and space, having to perform double duties to make up for the understaffing, and working inside an old structure that is filled with old problems. Under those circumstances, from a professional medical perspective, the hospital staffers deserve a lot of credit.

But, from the prisoner perspective, those who are not getting the care they need, or should receive, the picture somehow doesn't look the same. Those in pain must live with it a little longer. Those who cannot walk very well will continue to do without some meals, or depend on financial support from others. Most hope, some pray, their good health continues, considering themselves more fortunate than the guy in the next bed.

Chief nurse Edmisten summed it up best: "Just because we treat an inmate population, there's no reason why they should receive any less care than on the outside."

The United states Justice Department agreed. In a letter to Gov. Buddy Roemer, dated May 13, 1991, the Civil Rights Division of the Justice Department reported its findings of a two-year investigation into the state of medical services at Angola. The probe was initiated at the instruction of U. S. District Court Judge Frank J. Polozola, following his June 1989 declaration of a "state of emergency" following a rash of escapes, suicides and murders at the prison. *The Angolite* obtained a copy of the report, which has never before been made public.

When queried about the report, Warden Whitley said: "We were asked to respond to the findings. When it came to the medical part, we basically agreed they were true."

Whitley said some of the findings were matters he could address administratively on the prison level. In August 1991, after studying the sick-call procedures, he ordered that inmates requesting medical evaluation could do so during daytime hours, from noon to 5 p.m. "Previously, inmates would be awakened from midnight to 3:00 a.m. That seemed unreasonable, especially since pill call was held at 4:00 a.m. It made getting a decent night's rest a little difficult," Whitley explained. He said there was some opposition. "Some security and medical employees said it wouldn't work. But, how are you going to know until you try it? It's worked out pretty well so far," he added.

Numerous other changes have occurred. Especially noted is the ability of sick-call technicians to issue over-the-counter type medications instead of having the inmate scheduled to be seen at the hospital, a process that often took several days. Cough syrup, cold tablets, and a variety of other medicines being dispensed immediately, has reduced the logjam of inmates at the hospital. "This allows the health care providers to use their time to address the more serious inmate medical problems," Whitley said.

The nurse shortage is being addressed immediately. At a meeting scheduled at Angola in the near future, the warden will be presenting a workable package designed to raise nurses' salaries within the framework of the existing prison budget. "We're going to be very competitive with other institutions and the private sector," he said, adding: "Following that, we're going to present a similar package to raise the salaries of the doctors."

Where's the money coming from?" We're going to have to let go a few of our maintenance and clerical personnel who are on restricted appointments. We're going to have to tighten our belts a little and realize it's a matter of prioritizing our resources," Whitley said.

Budget increase requests for the purpose of equipment acquisition have been rejected in the past, the warden said. "For fiscal year 1992-93, we've asked for an additional $1.5 million. Angola has been left alone for so long, it has been here for so long, that the new facilities around the state start out with all these things in place, the staff and equipment. Angola has never had it. We're constantly playing 'catchup', but we never quite make it," he described.

As to the NACs performing routine triage functions during sick-call, the warden said the answer lay with having EMTs fulfill such tasks. But, this would first require the hiring of security officers before they could be trained. This, and the current equipment needs, again pointed to the original problem: funding.

"Under the present circumstances, our

understaffed medical department is putting out a Herculean performance under very adverse conditions," Whitley said.

The other non-medical aspects of the critical U. S. Justice Department report have already been addressed, some even before the report was issued. However, as Whitley said: "Frankly, I'd like to be able to do everything that's requested in the report. But, we cannot. We either do not have the money, or the staff, to implement all of them. "

* * *

FEDERAL COURT-ORDERED MEDICAL IMPROVEMENTS AT ANGOLA - 1975

2. Medical Care

(a) Provide immediately for the upgrading of medical services available to inmates at the Louisiana State Penitentiary and in connection therewith:

(1) Immediately employ and continue to employ such additional medical personnel as is required to make the fulltime medical staff at the Penitentiary consist of at least four (4) physicians; one (1) psychiatrist; eleven (11) trained physician assistants; one (1) dental assistant; three (3) nurses certified as RN; one (1) x-ray and physiotherapy technician; one (1) pharmacist; one (1) laboratory technician; and two (2) medical records technicians. Each professional medical employee shall meet the requirements for licensure in the State of Louisiana. Persons who fill the positions of physician assistants, which are not subject to licensure in the State of Louisiana, shall be qualified by their education and training to perform the type of medical services which are assigned to physician assistants by the U. S. Bureau

of Prisons or shall meet the standards required of licensed practical nurses in the State of Louisiana. All medical treatment furnished to inmates shall be administered by licensed physicians or by the trained personnel here provided for, and no medical treatment shall be administered by untrained inmates. This does not prevent the supervised use of inmate personnel to supplement the civilian medical staff where such is necessary for adequate health care.

(2) Take whatever steps are necessary to ensure that every inmate in need of medical attention, either for diagnostic or treatment purposes, is seen by a qualified medical attendant when required, and by a physician when necessary.

(3) Maintain at all times an adequate supply of drugs and medical supplies. No prescriptions for medication shall be made except on a case by case basis and then only upon authorization of a physician. No prescription shall be filled, prepared or dispensed except under the authority of and under the personal supervision of a qualified pharmacist, and no inmate shall be used or permitted to deliver drugs of any type to any person at the Penitentiary. A complete record of all drugs administered to each inmate shall be kept and a copy thereof placed in the inmate-patient's medical record. No inmate shall have access to another inmate's medical records.

(5) No inmate shall be harassed, punished or in any way discriminated against because he seeks medical diagnosis or treatment.

(6) Provide, within a reasonable time, to those inmates found to require eye glasses, dentures, and other prosthetics prescribed by a physician.

(8) Immediately implement a plan whereby each newly arrived inmate shall

be examined by a physician within seven (7) days after arrival at the Penitentiary. Promulgate the necessary regulation to ensure that no inmate is required at any time to sign a document entitled "Consent to Operation and Other Medical Treatment" whereon the surgical procedure and the name of the person to perform the procedure is left blank.

(9) Within sixty (60) days from date hereof, acquire by lease or purchase, or acquire the use on a contract basis, of a sufficient number of adequately equipped ambulances to provide transportation for inmate patients within the prison area and to other institutions when necessary.

(10) Take whatever steps may be necessary to remove, within one hundred and twenty (120) days from date hereof, all persons confined to the psychiatric unit or units at the prison and replace them in a therapeutic environment under the direct care and supervision of a qualified physician. These inmates shall, subject to the doctor's orders, be accorded all rights given other inmates at the prison.

* * *

JUSTICE DEPARTMENT ISSUES
SCATHING REPORT

U. S . DEPARTMENT OF JUSTICE
CIVIL RIGHTS DIVISION
OFFICE OF ASSISTANT ATTORNEY
GENERAL
WASHINGTON, D. C. 20530

May 13, 1991

Honorable Buddy Roemer
Office of the Governor
State Capitol Building
4th Floor

Capitol Access Road
Baton Rouge, LA 70804

Re: Notice of Findings of Investigation of
Louisiana State Penitentiary at Angola

Dear Governor Roemer:

By letter dated August 8, 1989, we notified you that, pursuant to the Civil Rights of Institutionalized Persons Act, 42 U. S.C. 1997 et seq., the Civil Rights Division of the United States Department of Justice was commencing an investigation into conditions at the Louisiana State Penitentiary (LSP), located in Angola, Louisiana. As specified by the statute, we are now writing to inform you of the conditions at LSP that we have found are depriving inmates of their constitutional rights, the facts supporting our conclusions, and the minimum measures we believe may remedy those conditions.

Our investigation consisted, first, of several comprehensive tours of LSP with independent experts, most recently in October 1990. We observed conditions in the cellblocks, dormitories, infirmary and mental health unit at various times of the day, interviewed administrators, staff and inmates, and examined a variety of records. Further, we gathered and analyzed documentation relating to the policies and practices of the prison. Throughout the investigation, we received complete cooperation from the administrators and staff at LSP. We look forward to continued cooperation. Based upon our extensive investigation, we have concluded that conditions at LSP deprive inmates of their constitutional rights. These conditions include:

1. Failure to provide adequate medical and psychiatric care.

2. Failure to provide a safe environment.

3. Segregation of inmates by race in cell assignments.

4. Arbitrary and excessive use of extended lockdown.

The state's failure to provide prisoners with the core requirements of adequate medical and psychiatric care, and a safe environment violates the Eighth Amendment. *West v. Atkins,* 487 U. S. 42 (1988); *Rhodes v. Chapman,* 452 U. S. 337 (1981); *Estelle v. Gamble,* 429 U. S. 97 (1976) . Additionally, the state's intentional segregation of cells is a violation of the Equal Protection Clause of the Fourteenth Amendment, *Lee v. Washington,* 390 U. S. 333 (1968), and Title III of the Civil Rights Act of 1964, 42 U. S.C. & 2000b. Set forth below are our findings and recommendations .

A. *INADEQUATE MEDICAL CARE*

Our medical consultant identified serious flaws in the provisions of medical care at LSP. These deficiencies begin at the intake point in the system, sick call, and permeate the entire process. Sick call takes place in the middle of the night, between 12 A.M. and 3 A.M., and is conducted by untrained uncertified nurse assistants who spend less than a minute with each inmate. The nurse assistant does not take vital signs or perform an examination. A sick inmate who does not wake when the nurse assistant makes the rounds will not be seen nor will his complaint be referred to physicians. Moreover, our medical consultant concluded that because the nurse assistants are not formally trained or certified they are simply not qualified to conduct sick call and assess which inmates should be seen by physicians. As a result of the deficiencies cited above, our consultant determined that because sick call is not appropriately conducted, inmates who need medical care and attention are not receiving it.

If the nurse assistant determines that inmate's illness warrants medical attention, a clinic appointment is scheduled. Due to shortages of both physicians and nurses, an inmate may wait three to five days to see a physician. Because there are so few full-time physicians at LSP, inmates are sometimes seen by registered nurses. Our medical consultant found that nurses are not competent to make some of the diagnostic and treatment decisions which they are required to do at LSP.

Our consultant additionally found that the care provided to inmates with chronic illnesses is grossly inadequate. LSP's infirmary maintains two wards with 60 chronic care beds; however, no nurses or medically trained personnel are assigned to provide care to patients in these wards. They are examined by physicians only after going through the inadequate sick call procedures described above. Our medical consultant additionally found that there is a lack of long range planning for treating inmates with chronic medical conditions. Inmates with diabetes are not provided special diets and appropriate glucose levels are not performed. Inmates needing physical therapy services often do not receive them due, in part, to the fact that equipment is unavailable, obsolete, or beyond repair. Acceptable procedures for monitoring the course of chronic diseases, such as high blood pressure, are practically nonexistent. During our investigation, inmates reported receiving blood pressure medications for years without appropriate blood work done or seeing a physician to review progress or adjust medication. Our review of inmates' records and LSP's

practices confirms those reports. Such failure to monitor and treat chronic illness can jeopardize inmates' health.

Although medical attention is afforded in emergency situations, the aftercare provided is deficient. There is inadequate follow-up when diagnostic tests are ordered or emergency care provided. For example, our investigation revealed that months after inmates were sent to nearby hospitals for radiologic procedures, LSP had not received the results. Inmates may not be referred to the clinic for removal of stitches. The failure to provide such follow-up when tests are ordered or when emergency care is provided is not consistent with professional standards of care, jeopardizes inmates' health, and subjects them to unreasonable risks of harm.

Our consultant additionally found that both the storage and distribution of medication are inadequate. Medication orders may take more than two weeks to fill. Minimally trained security guards dispense medications. There is no adequate procedure for assuring that inmates receive the correct medications nor are there safeguards in place to be sure inmates ingest medication. Additionally, our consultant found that LSP does not adequately monitor the effectiveness of medications prescribed. As a result, inmates may not be treated for side effects or may continue to receive medications that are not effective and do not resolve their medical conditions.

Generally, our consultant found that documentation of medical evaluations and treatment is inadequate, especially for inmates with more serious and chronic diseases. There are also unacceptable delays in placing hospital communications, *e.g.,* results of radiological procedures and emergency room reports, in inmates' charts. Because current and complete medical information is not maintained in the chart, professional staff lack important information on which to base their judgements and services. This deficiency subjects LSP inmates to unnecessary risk of harm from questionable treatment decisions.

Our consultant found that LSP lacks adequately trained and sufficient numbers of staff, both professional, *e.g.*, physicians and nurses, and security. Due to such shortages, untrained personnel are sometimes required to make health related decisions. As a consequence, inmates do not receive appropriate medical care.

LSP has not formulated sufficient or current policy manuals relating to its health care delivery system. Our consultant concluded that such manuals are crucial in order to provide all inmates with consistent and adequate care. The result of all the deficiencies cited above is that LSP inmates are being denied access to diagnosis and treatment by qualified health care professionals. As a result, their health is jeopardized and they are subject to undue risk of harm.

B. *INADEQUATE PSYCHIATRIC CARE*

Inmates placed in LSP's Mental Health Unit (MHU) are those assessed as chronically or acutely mentally ill, mentally retarded, and/or lacking behavioral controls. The MHU houses both treatment and extended care units. Both areas are staffed by correctional guards who are not trained in mental health and visited by the mental health team. Our psychiatric consultant found that the extended care unit—the unit that houses inmates with the most severe ental disorders—is essentially an extended

lockdown area. Inmates housed in this unit are treated in the same fashion as inmates housed in extended lockdown throughout the institution—e. g., they are locked within cells up to 24 hours a day, are shackled in leg irons, cuffs and chains when transported or let out of their cells— even though they have not necessarily been determined to be violent, only mentally ill. Further they do not receive any active psychiatric or psychological treatment. Our investigation revealed that a number of chronically and acutely mentally ill inmates are housed in extended lockdown throughout LSP, particularly in Camp J, the punishment camp, where they also receive inadequate psychiatric care. Our psychiatric consultant found that LSP's treatment of mentally ill inmates significantly contributes to deterioration of their mental condition and does not approach accepted standards of care.

Our consultant found there is no place to treat LSP's acutely psychotic inmates. They are sometimes placed in locked rooms in the infirmary, sometimes in locked cells on the MHU. In either case, they receive no psychiatric treatment. Our consultant found that the failure to provide adequate psychiatric treatment to these and other mentally ill inmates results in excessive chemical and physical restraint and jeopardizes their mental and physical health. During our investigation, LSP informed us that Camp A is being renovated to provide additional mental health care. LSP will house some of its mentally ill inmates in dormitories in Camp A and anticipates that additional space for programming will be available there. However, the deficiencies cited above will continue to exist for a large number of chronically and acutely mentally ill inmates.

Our expert additionally concluded that the lack of treatment and the manner of dispensing psychotropic medications leads to an excessive use of high dosages of long acting psychotropic medications. These medications can have dangerous side effects and need close monitoring, which is not available at LSP. As a consequence, the inmates taking such drugs are being subjected to unnecessary risk of harm.

In October 1990, the mental health staff reported a caseload of almost 1500, 300 of whom receive psychotropic medication. The current staff of two psychiatric consultants who spend a total of 20 hours a week at LSP is totally inadequate to monitor drug side effects, review charts, examine inmates and provide necessary oversight. Additionally, there are no staff to provide coverage for staff attending in service or other training; security staff assigned to the mental health unit must volunteer for specialized training on their own time. As a result of staff shortages and untrained staff, there is a failure to monitor and treat mentally ill inmates. Our psychiatric consultant found that a number of suicides that took place on this unit may well have been prevented if there were adequate numbers of trained staff available. Our consultant concluded that this level of staffing translates into the inadequate psychiatric treatment and consequent harm described above.

The deficiencies cited above endanger the physical and mental health of the inmates and subject them to unreasonable risks of bodily harm.

C. *UNSAFE ENVIRONMENT*

The temperature in the majority of cells and dormitories at LSP was well over 90 degrees when we toured the prison in early September 1990. Fans were scarce; ventilation was inadequate. Bars were hot to the touch and inmates were observed lying nude on the concrete floor, ostensibly to stay cool. For those in extended lockdown, there is no way to seek escape from these unhealthy conditions. Such conditions put the inmates at risk for any number of heat-related maladies. In particular, excessive heat poses a danger to those LSP inmates on psychotropic medications whose high body temperatures can cause serious and life threatening side effects. This is especially true for inmates on such drugs because, as has been noted above, there is inadequate oversight by qualified staff of inmates with chronic conditions.

Our fire safety consultant found several fire safety violations. One major deficiency cited is that no cells or cellblocks are sprinklered. Our investigation revealed in addition, that smoke detectors are not consistently placed and not many of those tested did work. Fire alarm pulls were not readily accessible and correction staff were not properly trained in their operation. The alarms are not wired into the fire station. Notification of a fire requires radio or telephone contact and creates unacceptable delays.

Safe evacuation in the event of a fire is quite problematic. Our consultant determined that in some buildings, egress cannot be accomplished without passing through spaces more hazardous than those from which an inmate is exiting. Corridors are not sufficiently protected from areas of potential hazard. Doors do not meet accepted standards, and are made less effective by undercutting and the use of transoms. Our consultant concluded that all cell doors should be able to be released at a single control (gang release) in order to effectuate a safe evacuation of the tiers.

However, on several tiers, it was necessary to manually unlock individual cells. When asked to open these, guards often failed to do so or took minutes to complete the task. We found that many electrical and manual gang releases were inoperative and that some tiers had none. Our consultant concluded that there is a significant danger that inmates would not be able to be safely evacuated from many tiers, dormitories, and other buildings at LSP in the case of fire.

Our consultant also found that the structure of Camp A and Camp H endangers inmates confined there. The roofs in both camps are made of combustible material and are not reinforced. He recommended that the second floors of the buildings in both camps not be used to house inmates.

D. *SEGREGATION OF INMATES BY RACE IN CELL ASSIGNMENTS*

Most inmates who are confined to cells at LSP live in single cells. However *all* cells that house more than one inmate are segregated on the basis of race. We were informed that it is LSP's policy and practice to assign inmates to cells on the basis of their race, *i.e.,* black inmates with black inmates, white inmates with white inmates. This state implemented intentional segregation violates the Equal Protection Clause of the Fourteenth Amendment to the Constitution and Title III of the Civil Rights Act of 1964.

E. *ARBITRARY AND EXCESSIVE USE OF EXTENDED LOCKDOWN*

Our investigation reveals that a significant minority of LSP inmates are assigned to extended lockdown for months and years at a time. The conditions in

extended lockdown are quite severe. Time out of cells is limited to one hour per day, three or four days per week. Inmates are limited to one outside visit a week; some are limited to one a month. Their telephone privileges are severely circumscribed. Many receive no reading material. When inmates are taken from cells, restraints, in various combinations, are used. During our tours, we observed inmates wearing leg manacles, handcuffs, and waist chains whenever they were transported from their cells. Absent a finding that a particular inmate has a propensity for violence or that security concerns justify them, the imposition of such restrictive and punitive conditions is arbitrary and without penological justification. LSP has not demonstrated that its decision to treat all lockdown inmates in this fashion is based on such findings or concerns.

Moreover, even as to those who are placed in extended lockdown or administrative segregation because of rule infractions or a demonstrated propensity for violence and for whom penological justification for some of the above cited restrictions may be appropriate, our penological consultant found that a minimum of one hour per day of out-of-cell exercise is necessary to prevent physical and mental deterioration.

Finally, some of the inmates assigned to extended lockdown are inmates who are in protective custody because they need protection, e g., they are vulnerable to assaults by other inmates, are former law enforcement officers, etc. Our consultant found the placement of such protective custody inmates in extended lockdown where they are subjected to the restrictive conditions of confinement reserved for the most violent inmates or others who are being disciplined for rule infractions to be without penological justification.

MINIMALLY   NECESSARY REMEDIES

Based upon the circumstances discussed above, we have concluded that LSP inmates are being subjected to conditions that deprive them of their constitutional rights. In order to eliminate the conditions that result in these deprivations, at a minimum, LSP must implement the following remedies:

1) The state must provide adequate medical care to LSP inmates, including identification, treatment, and management of their acute and chronic medical conditions. Among other things, the state must ensure that appropriately trained health care personnel conduct triage for sick call, that there is adequate oversight by qualified personnel of inmates with chronic conditions or on psychotropic medications, and that procedures are instituted to ensure appropriate administration of medications.

2) The state must provide adequate psychiatric care to LSP inmates, including identification, treatment, and management of their acute and chronic mental illnesses.

3) The state must ensure that there are a sufficient number of trained, competent and qualified professional and security staff to provide LSP inmates with adequate medical treatment and psychiatric treatment and to adequately supervise and protect them from harm.

4) The state must remove fire hazards and make appropriate renovations to protect LSP inmates from undue risk of harm due to fire.

5) The state must ensure that adequate ventilation is provided in areas where inmates are housed.

6) The state must immediately cease assigning inmates to cells on the basis of race and must assign inmates to cells based upon neutral classification criteria.

7) The state may only subject an inmate to extended lockdown based upon a finding that a particular inmate has a propensity for violence, has violated LSP rules, or that security concerns justify the assignment. All inmates, including those assigned to extended lockdown, must receive at least one hour out-of-cell time per day.

To rectify the deficiencies at LSP and to ensure that constitutionally adequate conditions are maintained thereafter, we propose to negotiate an agreement with the state of Louisiana, to be entered as an order of a federal court, which shall provide, at a minimum, that the above referenced remedies will be implemented at LSP.

Our attorneys will be contacting the State's Attorney General's Office to discuss this matter in greater detail. In the meantime, should you or your staff have any questions regarding this matter, please feel free to call Arthur E. Peabody Jr., Chief, Special Litigation Section, at (202) 514-6255. To date, we have been able to conduct this investigation in the spirit of cooperation intended by the Civil Rights of Institutionalized Persons Act, and look forward to continuing to work in the same manner with State officials toward an amicable resolution of this matter.

Sincerely,

s /John R. Dunne

JOHN R. DUNNE

ASSISTANT ATTORNEY GENERAL

CIVIL RIGHTS DIVISION

14

THE CITY OF ANGOLA*

by Michael Glover

When most people envision a prison, they picture the walled structure dished up by Hollywood in countless prison movies. The more realistic envision a tight cluster of buildings with many wings and long lines of cells. Angola is not like either of these visions. Angola is the largest plantation penitentiary in the nation.

Counting inmates and staff, Angola's population exceeds 7,000, and it is spread across 28 square miles. The complex includes 522 buildings with a total of two million square feet. There is a complicated electrical distribution network containing 60 miles of overhead and underground high voltage transmission lines, 500 transformers, 12 transformer stations, and 11 emergency generators. There is a water distribution system using a one-million gallon tank, a 250,000 gallon tank, three ground wells, and a huge water treatment facility which handles 1.2 million gallons daily. The waste-water system contains 25 miles of water and sewage mains and 11 sewer lift stations. There are thirty miles of gas mains, 10 large boilers, a water softener system, 540 roof-top heaters, 35 institutional-size freezers and coolers, 89 central air and heating systems, and 2,000 security fence and street lights.

Angola is larger than 259 cities and towns in Louisiana. It is comparable to places like Covington, Gonzales, or New Roads. But unlike them, there is no listing of contractors in the town yellow pages. No electric company fixes downed power lines, no gas company repairs broken mains. Angola's own maintenance department is responsible for the upkeep of the entire physical plant.

The man in charge of the Angola Maintenance Department is "Bud" Honeycutt. *The Angolite* recently interviewed him at his office.

Honeycutt sat at his desk. The phone rang constantly as his 28 subordinates reported and requested instructions. He has a ready remark for all of them; his 23 years experience with Angola's physical plant and constant monitoring of day-to-day problems enable him to pin-point and anticipate most areas of trouble.

"It's going to be cool tonight," he tells one supervisor. "Better get over to Camp D and check the roof heaters on Falcon-3. They're going to try to turn them on tonight, and they haven't been tested since the storm.

Another supervisor calls and asks about a part that's been on order for months. Putting him on hold, Honeycutt sends his inmate clerk, Paul Howard, on a record search. "The only thing that's come in like that is a reversing starter for the Training Academy lift station," Honeycutt says after a few seconds. "Check your paperwork and see if that's what you ordered."

Still another call. A foreman's wife is trying urgently to contact her husband, but he's off somewhere fixing something in the 18,000-acre prison complex, down some pipe chase or in a manhole out of radio contact. Honeycutt spends precious minutes calling every point where the supervisor might surface, leaving the urgent message to be relayed.

In addition to the phone, a high-tech calculator, a radio, and reams of maintenance reports, a three-tray basket

*Appeared in *The Angolite*, September/October 1992, 15-20. Reprinted with permission.

sits on the desk. Instead of the usual "In," "Out," and "Pending" labels, these are "Emergency," "Rush," and "Stock." More than anything else, these trays symbolize the problems the department must deal with.

"We have to manage a permanent crisis," says Honeycutt. "The 'Emergency' tray is for life and death situations. A transformer down that serves the hospital, or cell doors jammed at the Camp-C Tiger Unit, these are emergencies. If the stove goes out in the Camp F kitchen, that's a 'Rush.' Broken fans and missing light bulbs are just stock problems."

Woefully understaffed, Honeycutt has asked for 34 additional maintenance positions. Compared to other institutions, his present staff of 28 supervisors and 58 inmates would seem to be sufficient for the 5,200-man prison. But Angola is more than a prison. It's a city. "We can't just call the utility company when the electricity goes out, or when the gas lines go out, or when the water starts acting up," says Honeycutt. "Service from utility companies stops at the front gate. Anything that goes wrong from that point on we have to fix ourselves."

Over the years the eighty-six man department has handled it all, but as equipment ages and is not replaced, it becomes increasingly more difficult. The job is too big and the crew is too small to fix things before they break. The crew is in a constant crisis mode, dashing to fix one broken piece of equipment after another.

Preventive maintenance would greatly reduce the cost. "We have a preventive maintenance program set up," says Doug Durrett of Angola's Business Office. "The problem is that everything is either an emergency or a rush. We don't have the men, the supplies, or the time to do many of the things that would keep equipment from breaking down in the first place."

The age of the physical plant greatly complicates the problem. "The heaters we installed in 1976 were manufactured in 1957," says Honeycutt. "They were obsolete when we put them in. That doesn't mean they are not functional working systems, but you can't find parts for them, and they take a lot of maintenance attention." In comparison, other Louisiana prisons have heating and ventilation systems that are basically new. Angola's system is much older and in need of constant repair.

The system of gas lines is another example. Durrett points out that four-inch lines were installed in Angola in 1953. Ten years later a six-inch gas line was added, but it didn't run throughout the system before it was tied into the old four-inch line. Then in the '80s they "upgraded" to an eight-inch system. But there are places where it ties into the old six-inch system, and even to the four-inch system. "You can say the system was upgraded," says Durrett, "but it's not a complete job. There are places where even the newest system is tied into a system that's 40 years old."

Budgeting plays a major role in prison maintenance work. "Look at it this way," says Honeycutt. "Say a 15-year-old air conditioner in the administration building goes down. It needs a new compressor which costs $1,000. A new unit doesn't cost but $2,000, and I know I'm going to have to replace that compressor more than once in the next two years. I know it's also going to need a new fan and new points. It's going to cost more than $2,000 to keep the old air conditioner going—but I can't buy a new one. There is no money for new equipment."

"Equipment comes out of the equipment fund," explains Durrett. "That has to be approved by DOC Headquarters and the Division of Administration a year or more in advance. Angola has been asking for a large chunk of money to replace aged and worn-out equipment because of the age of this place. We don't get it. So what we have to do is fix what we've got, and sometimes we spend more money fixing obsolete equipment than new equipment would cost."

Thirty of the thirty-four additional maintenance positions requested are needed just to hold the line against the aging physical plant. The other positions are needed to staff the prison's water treatment facility to bring it into compliance with state law.

Both Honeycutt and Durrett readily admit the law is being violated, but insist the population is in no danger from the water supply. "The Health Department checks our water," says Durrett. "The system is good. We put the proper chemicals in and operate the system according to mandated standards."

"We are only in violation because the law changed," says Honeycutt. "Before we only had to have one licensed water treatment man there. We have that. But now we have to have a man there 24 hours a day." That means Angola now needs four employees where one was sufficient. When the legislature changed the law they did not increase funding to hire the additional men.

Prisoners often complain about the water. "If anything, the water is over-chlorinated," Durrett explains. "That doesn't mean the water is bad. Chlorine does not hurt you. The water could even be brown and still be good water if it meets all the other standards and the brown is just a certain percentage of iron. You might not like the way it looks, but it's not bad water. That's a confusing thing with water. People say 'Well, I see it's clear, and it doesn't smell so it's good.' But it could still be bad water. You can't judge water just by what you can see and taste and smell."

Honeycutt added, "Maybe once or twice a year our water samples don't fall within optimal parameters. When that happens the Health Department comes out here and checks it out. We find out what caused the problem and we fix it. Our water has never fallen into the dangerous category, where we would have to shut the place down."

Honeycutt understands the special problems associated with water inside the prison. "On the street if the water is bad they make an announcement. They tell people the water is bad and they should boil it before using it. They've complied with the law. But I can't do that. Inmates can't boil water. It has got to be safe when it comes out of the pipe."

The aging plant, the lack of money, and the personnel shortage are the daily realities maintenance must live with. "We're taking care of the minor and major problems now as best we can," says Durrett. "But one day it's all going to catch up with us. When that happens there's going to be a whole bunch of major problems here at Angola that, if you had the maintenance staff we're asking for, could have been headed off. Those problems are going to be very expensive."

Despite it all, Honeycutt loves his work and concentrates on the positive aspects. "I wouldn't swap this job for anything," he says. He knows his department is essential and likes the feeling of being needed. Holding it all together is a source of pride for him and the entire crew.

"One problem we recently fixed was the pay for our inmates," says Honeycutt. "They're the hardest working crews on Angola, but they weren't making as much as a 40-hour-a-week inmate clerk in an air conditioned office. We just got them a raise to top wage, 20 cents an hour.

"One other thing I'd like to say," Honeycutt adds. "Maintenance is like a family. Supervisors, foremen and inmates, we all play our part. When we are out on the job we are all maintenance. We all eat out of the same pot."

ANDREW SWATS ANGOLA

Hurricane Andrew hit land late Tuesday night August 25, and raged across Louisiana like a giant bowling ball, spinning and rumbling, and hooking slightly to the right as it headed north. Angola stood like the king pin at the end of the alley and suffered a direct hit.

Days before the storm, forewarned crews were out placing loose objects in secure buildings, tying down equipment, taping windows, storing water, and doing everything they could think of to prepare for possible disaster. Evacuation was out of the question. There is no place to safely transfer over 5,200 maximum security inmates on short notice. Though Andrew had been down-rated to a tropical storm by the time it hit the prison, it was still packing sustained winds of 60 miles an hour, gusting to 85 and 90.

On Wednesday, August 26, the prisoner population was locked down in their cells and dormitories, waiting anxiously with security officers, listening to the howling wind outside. The heart of the storm arrived at lunch time, around 11:30. An hour later, though no one was sure at the time, the worst of it was over. Prisoners remained locked down without

food until after 2:30 when security was certain the storm had passed. "We weren't hungry," said prisoner Gary Gremillion, "but when you are used to eating at a routine time, and that routine changes, your stomach can make you think you're hungry." Within an hour prisoners were fed twice, a hot tray for lunch and bagged sandwiches and fruit for supper.

During the following days, prison routine was shattered. Flooded fields idled farm workers, and loss of electrical power idled everyone else. The inmate canteen was closed, the hobbyshop was closed, the TV was out. "There was nothing at all to do," said prisoner Henry Miller. Inmate Charles Daniels adds, "I felt sorry for the 65% of the population that can't read. Complete idleness can be very severe punishment for them."

During the hour of Andrew, the prison suffered $750,000 in damage. The Main Prison's old kitchen, once condemned and then renovated to serve as a gymnasium, was hardest hit. The high wind peeled away roofing layers causing an estimated $350,000 worth of damage. Many other roofs were battered, trees and power lines were knocked down, and the prison was left without power for four days.

"The hurricane was nothing but a big storm," said modest Angola Maintenance Supervisor "Bud" Honeycutt. "It was nothing that we don't go through every time the power goes out." But this storm was bigger than any before, and the work needed to maintain safety and restore essential services was commensurately greater.

"The real heroes were Al Chenoweth, Johnny Young, Hank Gentile and Dale Bouffanie," said Honeycutt. "These are the guys who were actually out there in the storm."

Chenoweth, 46, a native of Alexandria, is Angola's Electric Shop Supervisor and has worked in maintenance for 14 years. After the storm struck Wednesday morning, he worked 46 straight hours. He slept for three hours, then worked an additional 18 hours. "Me, Johnny, Hank and Dale are the high wire crew," said Chenoweth. "When work has to be done on the overhead lines, we're the ones who have to do it. When there's an emergency, we just stay with it until it's over."

Johnny Young and Dale Bouffanie are inmates. "It's easy to forget that," said Chenoweth. The work is hard and long and we spend a lot of time together. I'm proud to work with them, they're the best crew a man could ask for and it's sad, because when the work is done I drive out the front gate, they walk back to their prison dormitories."

Bouffanie, lean, well-muscled, and good with his hands, is camera shy and doesn't talk much. Young, the more outgoing, is happiest when on the job. "When something needs to be done me and Dale just get in there and do it," he said. "It doesn't matter what the conditions are. If it has to be done we find a way to handle it."

Hank Gentile, electrical foreman, put in 7 hours of overtime between the time the storm hit and Sunday afternoon. "We had too many poles down and too many transformers out. Still, we had essential service ready to go back on line in about 25 hours. Insuring the overall integrity of the network took a little longer, but we had the essential system up and ready."

It was not the fault of Angola's maintenance department that the power outage lasted so long. "We were ready to go in one day," said Honeycutt. "Gulf States Utility Company took four days bringing the power to the front gate. I'm proud of the job my men did."

15

PRISON: THE SEXUAL JUNGLE*

by Wilbert Rideau

Leaving the bullpen, he strolled toward the cell area. Stepping into the darkened cell, he was swept into a whirlwind of violent movement which flung him hard against the wall, knocking the wind from him. A rough, calloused hand encircled his throat, cutting off the scream rushing to his lips, the fingers digging painfully into his neck. "Holler, whore, and you die," a hoarse voice warned, the threat emphasized by the knife point at his throat. He nodded weakly as a rag was stuffed in his mouth. The hand left his neck. Thoughts of death moved sluggishly through his terror-strickened mind as his legs, weak with fear, and his facial muscles twitched uncontrollably. He was thrown on the floor, his pants pulled off him. As a hand profanely squeezed his buttocks, he felt a flush of embarrassment and anger, more because of his basic weakness which prevented his doing anything to stop what was happening than what was actually going on. His throat grunted painful noises, an awful pleading whine that went ignored as he felt his buttocks spread roughly apart. A searing pain raced through his body as the hardness of one of his attackers tore roughly into his rectum. "Shake back, Bitch!" a voice urged. "Give him a wiggle!" His rapist expressed delight as his body flinched and quivered from the burning cigarettes being applied to his side by other inmates gleefully watching. A sense of helplessness overwhelmed him and he began to cry, and even after the last of his attackers had pulled his penis out of his abused and bleeding body, he still

cried, overwhelmed by the knowledge that it was not over, that this was only the beginning of a nightmare that would only end with violence, death or release from prison.

Rape . . . one of the most terrifying words in the English language for women. It haunts their footsteps like a vengeful ghost and creeps into their dreams like a silent thief in the night, stealing their peace and security, gripping their souls with icy fingers of fear. Rape and the possibility of becoming victim to sexual violence is a part of every woman's consciousness but, while many women live in fear of it, the odds of it happening to the average woman are nothing like the odds facing the typical man walking into the average jail or prison in the nation, where rape and sexual violence is as much a part of their pained existence as are the walls holding them prisoner.

Penal administrators rarely talk about the sexual violence that plague their institutions, turning them into literal jungles. Prisoners are too involved to ever want to do anything more than forget it once they regain their freedom. On the rare occasions the subject is discussed, it is mildly referred to as "the homosexual problem," as if it's a matter of individual sexual preference or perversion, something done only by homosexual "perverts," sickos slobbering at the mouth for an attractive young boy. And it's often the butt of jokes. But rape and sexual violence in prison has little to do with "heterosexuality" or "homosexuality" and is not the work of sexually-crazed perverts.

*Appeared in *The Angolite*, November/December 1979, 51-78. Reprinted with permission.

And, despite the humorous references to it, it is a deadly serious affair in the pained world behind bars, almost always a matter of power and control and often, of life and death.

Man's greatest pain, whether in life or prison, is the sense of personal insignificance, of being helpless and of no real value as a person, an individual—a Man. Imprisoned and rendered powerless and without any voice or control in the things that affect him, his personal desires and feelings regarded with gracious indifference, and treated as a child at best and an animal at worst by those having control of his life, the existence of a prisoner is one of acute deprivation and insignificance. The psychological pain involved in such an existence creates an urgent and terrible need for reinforcement of his sense of manhood and personal worth. Unfortunately, prison deprives those locked within the normal avenues of pursuing gratification of their needs, leaving them nothing but the instruments of sex, violence and conquest to validate their sense of manhood and individual worth. And they do, channeling all of their frustrated drives into the pursuit of power, finding gratification in the conquest and defeat, the domination and subjugation of each other—the only avenue left them. Thus, the world of the prisoner is one ruled by force, violence and passions. Since the prison population consists of men whose sexuality, sense of masculinity and whose sexual frame of reference is structured around women, weaker inmates are made to assume the role of "women," serving the strong, reinforcing their sense of manhood and personal importance, and providing them the gratification of their needs that would, in the normal world, be provided by women. Within that peculiar societal

context, an exaggerated emphasis is attached to the status of "man" and the pursuit of power becomes a thing of overriding importance because power translates into security, prestige, physical and emotional gratification, wealth—survival.

Rape in prison is rarely a sexual act, but one of violence, politics and an acting out of power roles. "Most of your homosexual rapes is a macho thing," says Col. Walter Pence, the Chief of Security here at the Louisiana State Penitentiary at Angola. "It's basically one guy saying to another: 'I'm a better man than you and I'm gonna turn you out to prove it.' I've investigated about a hundred cases personally, and I've not seen one that's just an act of passion. It's definitely a macho/power thing among the inmates. And it's the basically insecure prisoners who do it."

The act of rape in the ultramasculine world of prison constitutes the ultimate humiliation visited upon a male, the forcing of him to assume the role of a woman. It is not sexual and not really regarded as "rape" in the same sexual sense that society regards it. It is and means something entirely different in the world behind bars. In fact, it isn't even referred to as "rape." In the Louisiana penal system, both prisoners and personnel generally refer to the act as "turning out," a non-sexual description that reveals the non-sexual nature of what is really an act of conquest and demasculation, stripping the male-victim of his status of "man." The act redefines him as a "female" in this perverse subculture and he must assume that role as the "property" of his conqueror or whoever claimed him and arranged his demasculation. He becomes a slave, in the fullest sense of the term.

"Sex and power go hand in hand in

prison," C. Paul Phelps, Secretary of the Louisiana Department of Corrections, explains. "Deprived of the normal avenues, there are very few ways in prison for a man to show how powerful he is— and the best way to do so is for one to have a slave, another who is in total submission to him."

The pursuit of power via sexual violence and the enslavement of weaker prisoners is not peculiar to the Louisiana penal system. It is an integral feature of imprisonment throughout the United States, in both jails and prisons, and even in juvenile institutions—yes, the children do it too. Dr. Anthony M. Scacco, Jr., a criminologist formerly with Connecticut's Department of Corrections, publishing the results of a study in his book, *Rape in Prison*, reported that rape and violence was rampant in the juvenile and young adult institutions in Connecticut. Michigan's Wayne County Jail once candidly admitted that "guards are unable to prevent cases of robbery, assault, and homosexual rape among inmates." An exhaustive 1968 study of the Philadelphia prison system by the Police Department and the District Attorney's Office concluded that sexual violence, in the words of Chief Assistant District Attorney Alan Davis, was "epidemic." Illinois' Cook County Jail officials, in 1968, reported mass rapes to be "routine occurrences at Cook County Jail."

And while few prisoner-victims ever want to talk about their experiences, every now and then, one will. In 1977, during hearings in federal district court in Cincinnati, inmate Johnny Anders told Judge Timothy Hogan that he had been raped shortly after his arrival at Ohio's Lucasville State Prison. "The guys that raped me put a straight razor to my throat and held me down," he testified, adding

that he had to become a "wife" to one prisoner in order to protect himself from random sexual attacks by others. "I had no choice, so I got a man," he said. "I didn't want to be killed." He testified that he had been "sold" for sexual purposes by one prisoner to another. "I was sold four times to different guys," he told the court, once for $400.

Dr. Frank L. Rundle served as Chief Psychiatrist of the 2200-man California Training Facility at Soledad, also as Director of Psychiatry of Prison Health Services for all of the correctional institutions, both juvenile and adult, in New York City. His observations have led him to conclude that rape and sexual violence is universal in the nation's prisons. "I think that that same picture is true of any prison," he states. "It's not just Angola or San Quentin or Soledad. It is a feature of prison life everywhere."

"This whole macho/power, master/slave thing certainly does go on, and it goes on in several different categories," he explains. "There certainly are weak men who become forced into the position of being a slave or the whore and accept it unwillingly—but accept it. They have no alternative—they're either going to be hurt or killed if they don't. On the other hand, there are a lot of younger, weaker guys who are unwilling to get into the struggle of establishing themselves as strong macho men and who will seek out a strong man to protect them—and in that case become a voluntary sort of slave, knowing that that is the only way they're going to survive. The alternative would be to be forced into it by someone else that they don't really want, or become sort of gang property . . . and that's much less acceptable to a lot of them." And, he points out that "generally, those who are turned out and made into slaves remain slaves and never can get out of that."

James Dunn was one of the exceptions; he freed himself from his enslaved state, but at a terrible price. Dunn first came to Angola in March 1960 at the tender age of 19, toting a three-year sentence for burglary. A month after his arrival, he received a call to go to the Library, where an inmate "shoved me into a dark room where his partner was waiting. They beat me up and raped me. That was to claim me," Dunn explains. "When they finished, they told me that I was for them, then went out and told everyone else that they had claimed me." He recalls his reaction as being "one of fear, of wanting to survive. Once it happened, that was it—unless you killed one of them, and I was short and wanted to go home. So I decided I'd try to make the best of it." He cites as an influencing factor in his decision: "During my first week here, I saw 14 guys rape one youngster cause he refused to submit. They snatched him up, took him into the TV Room and, Man, they did everything to him—I mean, EVERYTHING, and they wouldn't even use no grease. When they finished with him, he had to be taken to the hospital where they had to sew him back up, then they had to take him to the nuthouse at Jackson cause he cracked up." Shaking his head at the memory, he says: "Man, I didn't want none of that kind of action, and my only protection was in sticking with my old man, the guy who raped me."

Few female rape victims in society must repay their rapist for the violence he inflicted upon them by devoting their existence to servicing his every need for years after—but rape victims in the world of prison must. And, Dunn, like the others, became his "old lady," his "wife." And, as his wife, he did "whatever the hell

he wanted me to do." The alternative, Dunn points out was: "Back then, they'd throw acid in a kid's face, beat 'em up, and everything else you can think of." But Dunn was fortunate, in that all his owner required of him was for him to be a good housewife. And he was. He'd wash and take care of his old man's clothing, fix the beds, prepare meals, bust pimples in his face and give him massages, and generally do all of the menial things needed doing. As with all other wives around the world, he'd also take care of his man's sexual needs, with the only difference being that he could never say "no." His old man had a dope habit and once, while not having enough money to get a "fix," he sold Dunn in exchange for two bags of heroin and the settlement of a hundred dollar debt. As a slave, his market value at the time was $150. "Two weeks later," Dunn recounts, "he bought me back because he was loving me." Two months later, Dunn was paroled.

At the age of 21, Dunn returned to Angola for parole violation and a five-year sentence for burglary. His former owner was still here and "He let me know in no uncertain terms that things hadn't changed, that I still belonged to him, that I was still his old lady," he says. "And he had a clique to back him up if I had any questions about it. Back then, cliques were running everything and that was how you survived."

Dunn did not rebel. He was eligible for parole again in two years and he didn't want to do anything that would mess up his chances of perhaps making it. But he had changed somewhat. While he went on and accepted the role of slave again, he was already thinking of ways to free himself of that state. "I waited on the parole, playing it cool, so that I wouldn't jeopardize it," he recalls, "but I made up my mind that if I missed the parole, I'd do something to stop this and become a man again, the kind of man I could respect . . . I was being used. I was a slave. There was nothing I could do on my own. I had to have permission from my old man for everything I wanted to do, even to just step out of the dormitory, to go anywhere or do anything. Hell, my life wasn't mine—it was his, and I just lived for his pleasure. I didn't want to live like that. I was tired of it."

The Parole Board denied his request for a parole. "And I decided that I wasn't going to live that kind of life no longer," he says. "And when my old man went home, I had made up my mind that I wasn't gonna be for nobody else." He knew it wouldn't be easy and that he could be killed. "You know how it was back then, the attitude and all—once a whore, always a whore," he explains. "Everything and everybody in here worked to keep you a whore once you became one—even the prison. If a whore went to the authorities, all they'd do is tell you that since you already a whore, they couldn't do nothing for you, and for you to call the whore's old man up and tell him to take you back down and keep you quiet. Now, if you wasn't a whore and you went to them, that was different—they'd take some action. But if you was already a whore, their attitude was more or less that you just go on and be one, and the most you'd get out of complaining is some marriage counseling, with them talking to you and your old man to iron out your difficulties. As for the courts, they didn't give a damn about prisoners back then and they wouldn't interfere in what happened up here. So, when I decided to quit being a whore, I knew that I would be bucking everything—prisoners, personnel, the whole damn system."

He told his old man how he felt and expressed the desire to be a man again. When his old man was freed from prison, probably because he cared for Dunn, instead of selling him or transferring his ownership of him to a friend, he left Dunn on his own. Without an old man, other inmates moved in on Dunn in attempts to claim him as their property. It wasn't difficult for him to find the determination to stick to his resolution to be a man. "After literally being screwed in and screwed over, misused and treated like an animal for so long, I had learned how to hate," he explains. So he fought. There were between fifteen to twenty fights during the next two months. But the strain and pressure he had to live under soon wore his nerves to a frazzle. "I was tired of this dumb shit. They wouldn't let me be a man, and I was tired of having to fight off everybody." His last fight was with Coyle Bell, an inmate serving time for kidnapping and rape. "He threatened me," Dunn says. "I did the only thing I could do. I killed him." That cost him an 18-months stay in a cell, but the killing made a difference. "Nobody tried to claim me anymore," he recounts. "I was finally free—but it cost like hell." That killing added a life sentence to his original time, and, after 17 years here, he's still paying the price of his freedom from sexual enslavement.

For the next four years, his life was relatively peaceful, and he was his own man, belonging to no one. But this peaceful state of affairs only lasted until 1968 when he had to fight once more, an incident in which he stabbed another inmate. That added six more years to his sentence and got him a 13-month stay in a cell, a period that proved beneficial to him. "Man, I got to thinking that this was all so futile," he recalls. "I wanted to get out of prison, but I was just getting deeper and deeper into it. And it was there that I decided that, no matter what happened, I would do everything in my power to try to prevent what happened to me from happening to other kids." That became his personal mission in life, one he's pursued since. Upon his return to the Big Yard, Dunn went to work, waiting for the weekly new arrivals to the prison and pulling the youngsters over to the side and educating them on the various games of con and violence that other inmates would play on them in attempts to turn them out. If they needed money or items from the store, he would personally take them to the canteen and buy whatever they needed so as to prevent their borrowing things from guys who would later insist upon collecting their debt by turning them out. A substantial number of youngsters have been helped over the years by Dunn, taking them by the hand and personally leading them throught the thicket of games and intrigues played by inmates to snare the unlearned and unwary into a cobweb of violence and slavery. Doing something to help and protect the young and the weak has been a constant theme of his in the various inmate organizations he's been a member of. When he learned that the Lafayette Juvenile & Young Adult Program, which houses area juvenile offenders, was in need of money, he conducted Green Stamps fund drives to raise money for it and, with a group of other inmates, created the L.J.Y.A. Club of Angola which operates a pizza concession at the prison with all proceeds going to help support the juvenile home. When prison authorities approved him for outside travel a couple years ago, Dunn took his tragic tale to Louisiana school kids as part of an Angola Jaycees juvenile crime prevention program, telling them

about his experience as a slave, the violence he had been involved in, and pleading with them to obey the law and stay out of prison.

It is a truism that men will attempt to function as "normally" as possible given the situation they are forced to contend with. A world of deprivation is marked by the pursuit of substitutes—the law of supply and demand prevails. So, while homosexual rape in prison is initially a macho/power thing, slaves are created because a need exists for slaves—a need for a woman-substitute, for the expression and reinforcement of one's masculinity, for a sexual outlet, for income and/or service, for the sense of self-worth and importance, etc. Slaves are "property" and, as such, are gambled, sold, traded and auctioned off like common cattle. What results is a widespread system of slavery and exploitation created and maintained via the instrument of fear and violence, a system that involves all either by choice or by force, a system that also serves as the foundation for the maintenance of the peculiar macho/homosexual culture that exists in the nation's jails and prisons.

The deprivation of basic human needs existent in the state of imprisonment and the need to find substitute gratification are the forces that shape the world of prison, its culture, its lifeway, its values and the roles of those trapped within it. Class lines are drawn, making a sharp social division between the prisoners who are men ("studs," "wolves," "jock," etc.) and those who are slaves ("whores," "turn-outs," "galboys," "prisoners," "kids," "bitches," "punks," "old ladies," etc.). The identification is always on the continuum of passive and dominant, weak and strong, with the weak and passive viewed and related to as being "female." As those investigating sexual violence in the Philadelphia prison system observed, the "stud" in a homosexual relationship "does not consider himself to be a homosexual, or even to have engaged in homosexual acts." The peculiar belief system found in jails and prisons across the nation defines the strong and aggressive partner in any homosexual relationship as being a "man," a "stud," with the weaker and passive partner defined as being a "homosexual," a "whore." (The prison sexual terms "pitching" and "catching" exemplifies the basing of their definition upon aggressive and passive sexual roles.) An elaborate subcultural code exists with respect to the treatment and behavior of the enslaved. As Dr. Rundle points out: "There are rules which every inmate is expected to follow in dealing with a man's boy or whore—that they're off-limits and they know if past those limits, they're in trouble from the old man . . . even to the point of risk of death. On the other hand, all those who are identified as whores or punks are required to show respect to all those identifed as old men or studs. I think that's part of the prison culture everywhere."

While the first sexual act of the prisoner, the rape of him, was non-sexual and a re-defining of his role, the ensuing sexual activity he will be made to engage in as a "female" while in prison will be sexual in nature. Jails and prisons are crammed full of men at the peak of their sexual potential and they need sexual outlets. He will serve that need for his man and perhaps for his friends. But since the majority of the prisoners don't own slaves, their need for a sexual outlet creates a large market for potential profit. In an economic sense, a slave is capital stock, property that can be made to produce income, and prison pimps don't

hesitate to put their whores to work hustling the profit to be made. How many tricks a whore will turn depends upon how much administrative heat there is. If there's none, he handles as many as possible. As for physical limitations, one Angola homosexual explained: "Well, a man who has forced another into this life—do you really believe that he cares? The boy handles as much as he can, all day, everyday, until he gets hemorrhoids, and then his old man might feel something for him and give him a break." But most of the turn-outs don't hustle because their relationship with their old man is mostly a man-wife thing, in which case all they have to worry about is satisfying their old man.

"—and don't come back in my face, Bitch, unless you got the money!" a lean, sturdy young black was telling another prisoner at the railing of The Walk as I passed the Bandroom on the Big Yard. "Do you understand me, Whore?" he asked the other prisoner, who nodded his head nervously and left quickly. "Having trouble with one of your whores, Silky?" I asked smoothly with a smile. "Man, you know how them bitches is," he answered, looking bored. "Ah tell the bitch to make me twenty dollars, and the bitch come back with fifteen. So ah had to send her back out—got to make her know ah mean business."

It was 1974 and Angola was wide-open; it was a time of cliques, violence, lawlessness and everything was possible, including owning as many boys as you were strong enough to claim and hold. Silky had two and he kept them hustling. They produced around $600 income per month for him. After extracting what was needed to provide for their personal needs, the remainder was loaned out to other inmates at high interest rates or invested in illegal or blackmarket enterprises that would turn a quick profit. Each month he was able to send four to five hundred dollars out of the prison to meet the expenses involved in his effort to secure his freedom. Ruining the lives of the two youngsters by making them prostitutes was immaterial. "Ah wish ah didn't have to do this," he once explained to me, "but ah ain't got no choice. I'm fighting for my freedom and ah can't support myself and pay my lawyer on the two cents an hour the state gives me. So it's either ah stay here with them, or ah use them to get myself out of here." He did, and he got out of prison.

In some prisons, "prostitution of an organized sort does go on," Rundle points out. "There are young guys who are taken over by mobs, by the prison version of the mafia, and who become the whore for this group of pimps, who set up their schedule every day and night. They tell him you go to this cell, and after that to that cell—they take either the money or the cigarettes or whatever the medium of exchange is." While organized, clique-controlled prostitution no longer exists in Angola, it is definitely a feature of prison life at California's Soledad Prison, according to Dr. Rundle. "A young kid who was in for the first time had been forced into it and was really upset about it and came to see me because of it. But he couldn't say anything about it to the administration because if he did, he's ratting, and he's setting himself up to be either killed or hurt badly or having to accept protective custody for the rest of his prison stay, and he was unwilling to do that."

One of the perverse mores of the world of prison is that the victims of sexual violence are rarely regarded as "victims." One of the key elements of the

prisoners belief system is that a "man" cannot be forced to do anything that he does not want to—a "real man" cannot be exploited. Those unable to meet the stringent demands of that standard are regarded as not being "men," as being weak and unworthy of respect from those who are "men." Their weakness both invites and justifies exploitation. Many prisoners, upon learning that someone has been turned out, commonly state of the victim: "That's his issue—if he didn't want it, he wouldn't have let the dude do it to him." The attitude reflected in that comment isn't that much different from that of the inmate's rapist, who often feels that he was not only "justified" in turning out the inmate but also had a "right" to do it because of the inmate's weakness. "He can't protect himself," one guy explained to this writer a couple years ago after having claimed and turned out an inmate. "Hell— I just proved that. He can't make it in here, and you know it. As his old man, I'll take care of him. He give me sex and I give him protection. That ain't no bad deal if you look at it right. Hell—it's more to his benefit than mine." Neither do the prisoners who patronize the services of galboys forced to prostitute regard them as "victims" or see any wrong in having sex with them. "Ah ain't got him prostituting—his old man got him doing that," is the typical attitude. "Ah'm not making him a whore. He's already one. And ah ain't misusing him in any kind of way. All ah'm doing is buying what he's selling. And fair exchange ain't no robbery." The victimization and continuing exploitation of the inmate is regarded as part of the natural order of things.

And, with one of the major concerns of prisoners being sex, studs will "get down" with an available whore . . . during the day, at night, hidden behind doors or bushes or in the middle of a crowd of on-lookers, in buildings or under them, just anywhere circumstances will permit. The form of sex engaged in is dictated by opportunity which, in turn, is determined by the degree of administrative "heat" or supervision. Where opportunity exists, anal intercourse will be the normal form of sexual expression. On the other hand, where tight security supervision is imposed on the inmate population, oral sex (fellatio) will be switched to since it is quicker and easier to conceal from authorities as it does not involve the removal of clothing, which requires time. Given this situation, administrative action does not halt sexual relations; it only effects a change in form. The bitter reality for weak inmates is that what kind of sex they will have to perform for their exploiters—anal or oral—is, in the final analysis, determined by the jail or prison administrator's action or lack of action. (It is doubtful if any administrator would ever bother to ask the weaker inmates which type of sexual act they might prefer to perform since they have to regardless of what the administration does.) "There is nothing that prison authorities can do to stop two consenting prisoners from entering into homosexual relationships," Phelps admits. It's a crazy world, though, because, while the initial rape-demasculation might have been effected by physical force, the ensuing sexual acts are generally done with the galboy's "consent" and "cooperation." Given his basic weakness, his no-win situation, and the psychological pressure of an entire world which dictates that, once demasculated, he must accept the role of a female, he generally resigns himself to that manner of existence and cooperates. Feeling that being a "good woman" is the path to good treatment and protection against abuse

during his confinement, he pursues that goal, sometimes playing his female role as well as a real woman.

How extensive is homosexual activity in the nation's penal system? Rundle believes that it's almost universal. "That doesn't mean that everyone who is in prison is regularly into homosexual behavior," he states, "but almost everybody at least sometime." Colonel Pence's estimate of its extent here at Angola: "Roughly, I'd say about seven out of ten inmates here either is now participating or have participated in homosexual activities at one time or another during their confinement." But Phelps points out that "They're not medically or clinically homosexual. Many resume normal heterosexual relationships when they're released from the institution." He adds: "Homosexual sex in prison is a natural phenomena of all one-sexed institutions and environments."

Penal administrators generally claim that much of the violence between prisoners in their institutions results from the homosexual state of affairs, a claim that Rundle feels is somewhat exaggerated because it ignores the racial conflicts in many institutions. Phelps, on the other hand, admits that there is no way for him to know how much of the violence is attributed to the homosexual state of affairs but "I do know that in the ten years preceding 1976, statistics show that the Louisiana State Penitentiary was the most violent prison in the nation."

It was. The fabric of life in Angola was woven by the thread of violence. The only law was that of the knife, and the only protection available to you was what you could acquire through sheer force of character and the ability to impose your will upon others. Slavery was widespread and human life, the cheapest commodity on the market. It was a jungle that only the strong survived and ruled. The pursuit of survival fueled a heated arms race among the prisoners for the superior weapon—a sword over a knife, a broadaxe over a sword, and a gun over everything. Individual disputes, gang wars and factional feuding kept the blood flowing incessantly, keeping the concrete floors stained despite daily moppings. Locked in the violent fishbowl of that period, men fought, killed and died with little thought. The knife claimed the lives of forty prisoners between 1972 and 1975 and left 350 more seriously injured.

"The formation of inmate power groups or cliques is symptomatic of a high level of homosexual activity and enslavement," Phelps states, pointing out that "During the ten years preceding 1976, the inmate power structure at Angola was very, very powerful. And anytime that happens and a high level of homosexual rapes and enslavement is taking place, there has to be a tacit trade-off between the inmate power structure and the administration." Most of the trade-off, he says, generally takes place on the lower level of the administration. "When it gets down to the lower level, it's usually an agreement between the inmates and security officers, and the agreement doesn't have to be verbal. Much of the communication between inmates and between staff and inmates is on the non-verbal level. They have their own peculiar method of communicating what they want to say without really saying it and each understands exactly what the other is saying. It's probably the most sophisticated non-verbal system of communication ever invented in the world."

He explains the typical minor trade-off: "Take the cellblocks for example.

You put two men in a cell together, then suddenly you're getting complaints—one of them can't get along with his cell partner, then he tells you that there's another inmate farther on down the line who he can get along with, and would you put them in the same cell? We know what's happening there. But officers would prefer to have two people in a cell who get along rather than fight, spit and yell at each other—so they put them together." The officers, playing dumb, grant the request, giving the two inmates the opportunity to engage in homosexual relations, in exchange for peace in the cellblock.

But the practice of "trade-offs," as Phelps calls it, is not peculiar to Angola. The generally unrecognized reality in the prison business is that smooth prison operations can only be achieved by penal administrators through the implied consent of the prisoner population. While prison administrations possess the power of Force, the prisoner population, on the other hand, possess the power of Rebellion. So, as it is with all governments, all penal institutions afford some form of accommodation in its functioning, conscious or unconscious compromises made between the keepers and the kept to prevent or minimize conflicts and to ensure control and peace. Thus, the only differences in penal administrations and institutions lies in the degree of accommodation practiced and those peculiar factors in an institution that especially favor the accommodation process. The less harsh and less oppressive institution that has a high degree of informal relationships between staff and inmates, automatically allowing for things to be accomplished without having to go through the chain of command particularly favors the process of accommodation.   On the other hand, institutions burdened with a sluggish chain of command and/or a top-heavy bureaucracy which prevent the needs of prisoners and personnel from being met quickly and effectively automatically create a demand for short-cuts, thus fueling the accommodation process.   Staffers at the bottom must then meet the needs of their operations and those of the inmates and solve the problems that the bureaucratic red tape doesn't, and they can do so only through "trade-off."   The process of accommodation flourishes in institutions plagued by insufficient personnel and supervision because, crippled by lack of manpower, staffers are forced to resort to trade-offs with the inmates to a large degree in order to maintain control and peace. Numerous other factors influence the degree of accommodation practiced in penal institutions, a major one being the degree of deprivation imposed on the inmates, a condition that varies from institution to institution.

Accommodation takes the form of a corruption of authority, a pattern of relations through which administrators and staffers pursue the maintenance of control and the minimization of their personal trouble through personal relationships and trade-offs with the prisoners they supervise. This is especially true in the operations of jails but also true of large prisons where emphasis is upon security and uniformity with little incentive provided to induce prisoner compliance. In the absence of meaningful incentives to make compliance desirable and when there is little difference between reward and punishment, staffers are forced to sacrifice a degree of their authority through trade-off to secure compliance. Physical coercion and the threat of punishment are ineffective instruments to achieve long-

term compliance because its power to intimidate is limited. The more it is used, the less intimidating it becomes, and once prisoners are existing close to the tolerable limits of punishment/deprivation, its continued use will elicit rebellion. Within that context, staffers tend to adopt accommodation over the use of force. Recognizing their inability to achieve their ends through the enforcement of impersonal rules and the continued threat of force, they pursue it through friendship, ignoring infractions that do not threaten the overall security of the institution, making deals, and doing favors—all consciously or unconsciously designed to bring both sides to a mutually tolerable, if not agreeable, working relationship within the framework of the administration's goals. What a strict administrator at the top might regard as irresponsible and unethical performance of the line-staffer's duties is not that at all but, instead, a realistic response to an undesirable working situation that allows him control, maintenance of order and self-protection only through the sacrifice of a degree of his authority via "trade-off."

While it is the accommodation process that determines the kind of sexual behavior that will or will not be tolerated within an institution (with administrations generally drawing the line at actual rape), it is fueled by the almost natural inclination of the institutional security force to be tolerant of any type of situation that divides the prisoner population into predators and prey, with one group of prisoners oppressing another, a situation which prevents the formation of the kind of unity among prisoners that could tear down the very walls of the institution.   A homosexual jungle-like state of affairs is perfect for that purpose. It's another means of control, perhaps the most effective, and prison security forces will utilize any and every means available in their pursuit of control, security and peace. This readiness to utilize any means to secure a division among inmates is confirmed by Rundle, who points out that inmate gang divisions along racial lines are utilized in California prisons. "The whole system is set up in such a way as to, if not overtly, at least covertly encourage racial war," he says. "They (the staff) even encourage it."

There is a certain amount of staff involvement in maintenance of the homosexual status quo in penal institutions either via encouragement, active involvement, tolerance, or silence. In his report of sexual violence among the kids in Connecticut's juvenile institutions, Dr. Scacco charged that "Administration knows who the victims and aggressors are, and in many instances, the guards are directly responsible for fostering sexual aggression within the institution themselves." On the other hand, Davis' study of the Pennsylvania jail system revealed that many security guards discouraged complaints of sexual assaults by indicating that they didn't want to be bothered or pressuring victims to not complain by asking the victim if he wanted his wife, parents or friends learning of his humiliation. An indictment of guard exploitation of homosexual situations in institutions was leveled by Simon Dinitz, Stuart J. Miller and Clemens Bartollas who, reporting the results of their study of the situation to the First International Symposium On Victimology at Hebrew University in Jerusalem, Israel, charged that "some guards will barter their weaker and younger charges to favored inmates in return for inmate cooperation in keeping the prison under control." The reality is that penal

security forces operate much the same as any police force in the world, pursuing control and peace in penal institutions in the same manner that police pursue the maintenance of law and order in any city; and one of the traditional instruments employed has been the utilization of prostitutes, gamblers, pushers, street characters and minor criminals as agents and informants, unofficially "rewarding" them by permitting them the freedom to practice their vice in return for their cooperation. The matter of acquiring control and access to information in prison "is a game played by both sides," Phelps acknowledges, pointing out that information is power in prison, another form of currency. Penal security staffs will also, if not encourage, definitely tolerate involvement in a homosexual relationship by a potentially dangerous or troublesome prisoner, banking on the reality that a prisoner who is getting some degree of emotional and sexual gratification from his prison wife is less likely to cause trouble than the prisoner who is not because he's comfortable and, once emotionally attached, will not want to lose his "wife." This tactic is also often employed against a partner in a homosexual relationship to elicit information and/or induce cooperation with the administration in pursuit of its ends.

Much of this kind of tolerance and acceptance of the homosexual state of affairs in penal institutions is produced by the conditioning effect of the prison's macho-homosexual culture upon staffers working in its atmosphere for lengthy periods of time. While they might initially be shocked and concerned about it on their first day of employment, one cannot realistically expect them to retain that same shock and revulsion after years of daily exposure to it. After a while they become influenced by it to some degree, some developing a certain tolerance of it, others perhaps even coming to accept it as being a part of the natural order of things if not actually being Right.   They eventually come to adopt the prison homosexual jargon and games and even some of its belief system, an effect evident in the playing and joking that takes place between bottom-line staffers, with jokes about turning each other out, of playfully referring to each other as "whores," "galboys," and "bitches," in very much the same manner as the inmates they work around daily (though this is not to imply that they go all the way with it as inmates do). But the peculiar prison homosexual culture does have an effect. Rundle points out the preoccupation among them: "When I first went to Soledad, like for two weeks, ALL that the staff asked me questions about or talked to me about was homosexuality."   While Phelps admits that he had no idea to what extent the continuous exposure to the prison's macho/homosexual culture affects the attitudes and behavior of Angola correctional employees, he does admit: "I know situations where staff got involved in overt homosexual relationships with 'boys' and even owned them."

But all of this is nothing new. On the contrary, it's been a traditional feature of prison life almost everywhere. In 1937, over forty years ago, Haywood Patterson, chief defendant in the famous Scottsboro rape case, came face to face with that reality when he arrived at Alabama's Atmore State Prison and had to fight to prevent other inmates from making him into a "galboy." In his autobiography *Scottsboro Boy*, published in 1950, he told that homosexual rape was not only tolerated but actually encouraged by prison authorities, primarily because "it helped them control the men. Especially the tough ones they called devils. They believed that if a devil had a galboy he would be quiet. He would be a good worker and he wouldn't kill guards and prisoners and try to escape. He would be like a settled married man." He stated that the most valued material for making a galboy out of was a young teenager. "A fifteen-year-old stood no chance at Atmore," he wrote. "Prisoner and warden were against him and he was quickly made into a woman"—a process that was both methodical and brutal. "I've seen young boys stand up and fight for hours for their rights. Some wouldn't give up." He reported in his book that both prisoners and security guards would watch the assaults with impassive interest. "They knew a young woman was being born," he said. "Some just looked forward to using her a little later themselves," Once made into a galboy, "Some carried on like real prostitutes," he reported. "They sold themselves around on the weekends just like whore women of the streets . . . Usually you could hunk up with a galboy for two or three dollars. Galboys got sold to different men. If a guy had a galboy but didn't get along with him any more, he could put him up for sale. He could sell him for twenty-five dollars. News of a sale went through the prison pretty fast and bids came in every time." He described the extent of sexual enslavement of Atmore prisoners: "I once heard Deputy Warden Lige Lambert tell some state patrolmen that fifty percent of the Negro prisoners in Atmore were galboys—and seventy percent of the white."

That was more than four decades ago, and there is no reason to believe that Louisiana's penal system was any different from Alabama's. According to Louisiana State University Professor Mark Carleton, who gives a historical account of the development of Louisiana's penal system in his book, *Politics and Punishment*, homosexuality was unrestrained in Angola's best. And oldtimers here at the prison still tell of how, not too long ago, staffers instead used to perform prison marriages in which the convict and his galboy-wife would leap over the broomstick together in a mock ceremony. But a lot of changes have been brought by the passage of time: that could not happen today in Angola, where sexual violence elicits swift administrative reprisal and prosecution.

Ironically, most of the sexual violence occurring not only in Louisiana but across the nation takes place in the parish/county jails, which act as a sort of sieve, filtering the strong from the weak and producing the sexual slaves long before they reach the penitentiaries. A number of factors make this situation possible, the major one being the fact that the typical jail is grossly understaffed and constructed in a manner that makes adequate policing of inmate activity within it extremely difficult if not impossible. Given that situation, jailers can only maintain some degree of control and order through the process of accommodation, generally in the form of unofficially designating a strong inmate or group of inmates to maintain control and peace in exchange for favors and the privilege to practice their own vices (usually homosexuality and profitable rackets). But it's a Catch-22 situation for the jailers because, regardless of their efforts at securing control in this manner, the strongest inmate or gang will, via the process of natural selection, rise and do it anyway. So, often the jailers' efforts are

merely an attempt at exerting some degree of control and/or influence upon the strongest by obligating them through "trade-off." Tragically, while they'll never admit it, given the typical jail situation, what little control and order they are able to maintain is had only by an unholy degree of "trade-offs" and sacrifice of authority.

With the exception of the few prisoners serving small jail sentences, the jail population generally consists of people who are simply sitting there "waiting," some for months or even a couple years—the majority waiting to go to court; the others, having already gone to court, waiting out an appeal or transfer to penitentiary. Their existence is one of prolonged idleness and profound boredom, which is accompanied by an urgent need to "find something to do." The stronger quickly discover that the weaker prisoners are good for passing time by playing games of violence and abuse with them. On the other hand, the macho homosexual culture of penitentiaries are transmitted, though in grossly exaggerated form, to the jail population by former convicts, and it has its effect. The real and imagined tales about prison instill a certain amount of fear and create an imagined need among those expecting to go to prison to secure reputations as tough, macho men in the hope that the reputations will precede their transfer to prison and have an intimidating effect upon convicts who might have designs upon them once they reach prison. It's a futile effort, but some pursue it anyway. Prisoners with minor charges waiting to go to court and weak and old men are the most vulnerable for exploitation.

The jungle in jail is vicious. In his book, *Rape in Prison*, Dr. Scacco wrote the following account:

"Many cases could be cited of actual rape of an individual in jail, but one in particular is chosen to let the reader hear the events from an ordinary citizen. He is married with a family, no previous criminal record, and a former Georgia legislator and businessman who found himself the victim of a jail situation. William Laite was indicted and convicted in Texas of perjury relating to a contract he had with the Federal Administration Housing Authority. He was sentenced to the Tarrant County Jail in Fort Worth, Texas. The moment he entered the tank or day room, he was approached by five men. The first comment from one of them was, 'I wonder if he has any guts. We'll find out tonight, won't we? Reckon what her name is; she looks ready for about six or eight inches. You figure she will make us fight for it, or is she going to give up to us nice and sweet like a good little girl? Naw, we'll have to work her over first, but hell, that's half the fun, isn't it?' 'I couldn't move,' said Laite. 'I was terrified. This couldn't be real. This couldn't be happening to me.' Laite was saved from sexual assault when a seventeen-year-old youth was admitted to the day room as he was about to become the victim of the five men in the tank. The men saw the boy and turned on him, knocked him out, and then, 'they were on him at once like jackals, ripping the coveralls off his limp body. Then as I watched in frozen fascination and horror, they sexually assaulted him, savagely and brutally like starving animals after a raw piece of meat. Then I knew what they meant about giving me six or eight inches.'"

"The attack did not end there according to Laite, for while the boy was still unconscious, the attackers jabbed his arms, neck and body with the burning tips of erasers of pencils, so that the boy's body twitched making it more sexually exciting for the aggressors. Then one of the attackers, 'in a final sadistic gesture ... shoved his fingers deep into the boy's rectum and ripped out a mass of bloody hemorrhoids.' Laite was shocked by the unconcern shown by the guards. He stated that the 'guards were protected from the violent prisoners, but I, an inmate myself, was not. The guards never made an attempt to discipline the prisoners. In fact I suspected that they might pass the time of day watching the fights and sexual activities from some secluded location.'"

No, Laite's experience is not the exception, selected because of its horror and ability to shock and offend. The Louisiana State Penitentiary and other prisons around the nation are crammed full of men who can attest to this kind of thing being fairly common in jails (it is worth noting that incidents that brutal and senseless are rare in penitentiaries where there are established cultures and inmate power structures influencing inmate behavior). The study by Davis and his team of investigators concluded that over 2,000 sexual assaults had occurred in the Philadelphia jail system during the two year period they investigated, many of them matching the horror of the Laite experience in the Fort Worth jail. According to Davis, "virtually every slightly built young man committed by the courts is sexually approached within a day or two after his admission to prison. Many of these young men are repeatedly raped by gangs of inmates. Others, because of the threat of gang rape, seek protection by entering into a homosexual relationship with an individual tormentor ... Only the tougher and more hardened young men," he stated, "and those few so obviously frail that they are immediately locked up for their own protection, escape homosexual rape." The district attorney attributed the sexual violence to the violent subculture's definition of masculinity through conquest and subjugation.

Davis' study also revealed the involvement of a racial factor in sexual violence in the Philadelphia jails or, as he put it, "a disproportionate number of Negro aggressors and white victims." 56 percent of the rapes were black-on-white rapes; only 29 percent were black-on-black and only 15 percent were white-on-white. This corresponds with Dr. Scacco's conclusion in his study of Connecticut's reformatories that the homosexual rapes occurring there were usually blacks raping white boys for power and revenge, citing that blacks saw more social prestige in having sex with whites rather than black sissies. Rundle confirms the racial factor: "It does happen that blacks often have a preference for white slaves, and that gets into the whole business of racial subjugation and revenge—the same way it does in society. There are a lot of blacks who prefer white women and it has to do sometimes with a conscious kind of revenge and also has to do with a conscious status which it confers upon them in the eyes of other blacks. I don't think it works that way with whites for blacks. I think in that instance it would be more of an individual matter and preference." However, he points out that the racial factor "really depends on the atmosphere of the prison. For example, in Soledad, blacks and whites stayed strictly apart and a struggle was always going on for the power within the institution. And if any white associated with or consorted with a black in any way, he was in trouble with the white group." Interracial rape under those circumstances, he states, would "precipitate racial clashes."

"Every inmate must somehow establish his role," Dr. Rundle says, explaining every inmate's situation. "Either that he's a strong man or a weak one, either that he's willing to fight, even to the death, to protect himself and maintain his status, or he can be dominated by the threat of violence—and that may include as part of establishing oneself as a strong and dominant person, enslaving others, either generally or sexually or both." He admits that "this factor contributes most to making prisons into the whole domination-submission kind of jungle" they presently are, but "I would stress that it's not always on a sexual basis . . . and, in fact, I think initially it's much more a matter of survival—in that, one establishes himself as one you don't mess with because if you do, you might get killed. And that means don't mess with him in any way, not just in terms of whether he's available sexually or not."

The sexual violence found in large jails is far more vicious and senseless than that found in prisons, where, if nothing else, the religion of private property prevails, affording a certain protection from abuse to weaker inmates belonging to stronger ones. Prison, with its unwritten understandings with respect to the treatment and behavior of sexual slaves, is sometimes a welcome relief after months or years of abuse in the jail jungle, with the inmate sometimes being grateful to belong to an old man, to be a housewife, and have to worry about nothing other than satisfying his man—a far cry from what he faced in jail. But prison only rescues him from the jail-type abuse, not his status as a female. Having been turned-out in the jail, he must continue his role as a woman in prison.

Davis discovered that reality in his Philadelphia study: "After a young man has been raped, he is marked as a victim for the duration of his confinement. This mark follows him from institution to institution. Many of these young men return to their communities ashamed and full of hatred."

The classroom-bred "experts" generally attribute homosexual activity in the world behind bars to "the failure of prison authorities to properly identify and segregate overt and latent homosexuals from the general population." And it sounds practical. But, as Rundle points out: "One of the unavoidable facts is that, considering the organization of the inmate society, the hands of the administration are often tied." One of the strengths of the society and the exploiters is the refusal of the inmate-victim to admit that he was raped or is being used as a "female" for fear of his family and friends ultimately learning of his humiliation. Given that situation, who will distinguish who's a "girl" and who isn't—in a world in which everyone looks the same? If the administration makes an official determination of who is homosexual and who isn't, it would inevitably touch off a flood of lawsuits requiring the authorities to prove their allegation and demanding civil damages if they can't. However, the whole effort would prove fruitless because when someone talks about the homosexual activity in penal institutions, they automatically think of the obvious homosexuals, the gays, the passive homosexuals. If they were responsible for the horrendous situation in these institutions, the problem would be easier to deal with since they are often easily identifiable. But the reality is that the passive, gay homosexuals are not responsible for the sexual violence. On the contrary, they are often also

victims of it, though generally treated better by their exploiters than non-gays. The truth of the matter is that the sexual violence, the turning out of youngsters and the enslavement and abuse of weaker prisoners is primarily the product of criminally-corrupt "heterosexual" males, the "studs." Trying to identify them before they commit their first homosexual rape is almost impossible, much the same as trying to identify the potential-rapist in a city before he assaults a woman. So, given that reality, the mere removal of the "girls" (usually "gays") from a prisoner population solves nothing and is impractical as it automatically creates a demand for a new batch of "girls" to be found or made to replace those removed. And, as Angola Warden Frank Blackburn points out, "The studs will just turn out some more"—the law of supply and demand.

That doesn't mean that the situation is hopeless because it isn't. While little can be done to stop homosexuality, given the pragmatic approach to the psychological and sexual needs of heterosexuals confined in one-sexed institutions for long periods of time, forced homosexual rapes can be reduced to a tolerable level. Where forced homosexual rape used to be a regular feature of life here at the Louisiana State Penitentiary, it is now a rare occurrence. Homosexuality still thrives, but the former violence and forced slavery has been removed from that activity. This resulted from a massive crackdown on overall violence at the prison ordered by former Federal District Court Judge E. Gordon West, an order which paved the way for the provision of money, manpower and sophisticated electronic equipment needed by correctional authorities to do the job. Since 1976, when the crackdown began, ANY kind of violence at all between inmates elicits swift administrative reprisal and certain prosecution. It has been this, more than anything else, that has made Angola safe for the average youngster coming into the prison today. No longer does he have to worry about being raped. Of course, if he lets himself be "conned" into giving up his manhood, that's his business—the institution is only concerned about the possible use of violence.

Every prison in the nation has a section which it refers to as "protective custody." While always defined as nonpunitive, Dr. Rundle points out the reality that "protective custody is punitive, as well as punitive segregation, as its usually in the same place with the same kinds of restrictions." This is where authorities keep prisoners who request protection from the possibility of being killed or exploited by other prisoners. Generally, persons confined in protective custody are there for their own request. It's usually a locked-down situation, a condition of existence which forces the weaker inmate to eventually reach a point where he decides that it's better to permit himself to be sexually exploited and enjoy a certain amount of freedom rather than the mental and physical anguish of solitary confinement where he stands a good chance of losing his sanity. The punitive and painful nature of "protection" is one of the major influencing factors in the decision of victims of sexual violence to go on and accept the role of a female rather than report the victimization to the authorities and request protection. In many respects, the "protection" offered by the authorites is seen as being worse than the exploitation by the inmates. However, perhaps not wanting to get into the dangerous area of making official determinations of who are "whores" and who aren't, authorities here at Angola

generally lock up whores only when they request it or they are involved in a security or disciplinary incident. Asked for an estimate of the number of whores of Angola, Col. Pence replied that he "couldn't say how many are socially-classified as 'whores' because there are a lot of 'undercover' whores. I think it's impossible to guess how many because a lot are never brought to our attention . . . and that's the only ones we know of— those who are brought to our attention."

In the prison's pursuit of protecting weaker inmates from sexual exploitation, the authorities also arbitrarily lock some up who do not wish for this simply because of what they are—homosexuals. For the most part, they are transvestites, the "queens" and "ladies" (as opposed to turn-outs and galboys). Of the 4,000 prisoner population at Angola, "I'd roughly estimate that there are between 60 to 80, but not over a hundred," Col. Pence states. Unlike the turnouts, the gays want the role of a female, as they regard that as their natural role. They don't want to be protected from the men. Despite what they want, the authorities lock many, if not most of them up, in places designated as protection locations—Camp D, Camp H, and the Main Prison's Cellblock "B".

Gary "Sheila" Keylon is a 25-year-old gay from Oklahoma serving five years for receiving stolen property. He's been here two years. "I've been in lockdown ever since I been here . . . When I came to Angola and arrived at AU (Admissions Unit), they looked at me and my record and just bluntly told me that I was a whore and that I go to Camp H lockdown, giving me no choice in the matter." He asked to be permitted to live and work with the other prisoners, but the authorities refused. In an attempt to be transferred someplace else, he deliberately cursed the camp supervisor. He was immediately transferred—to Camp J, the prison's punishment unit. Brought before the Disciplinary Court, he explained that he had violated the rules in the hope of achieving any type of transfer that would remove him from his lockdown situation, that he didn't want to be locked up, that he wanted to live and work with the rest of the prisoner population. Sheila was lucky—Col. Pence was acting as Chairman of the court on that day and, instead of imposing a punishment, he tried to help Sheila by transferring him to the Main Prison's Cellblock, where he could at least work in the field in the special work detail made up of "protection" cases. And that's where he is now, a little freer, but still segregated from the rest of the prisoner population.

"Security shouldn't put as many bonds on us as they do because if we feel that we can't live on The Walk, we'd be the first ones to know it," Sheila says. "I'm not afraid to go anywhere in this penitentiary. Many of us are perfectly capable of taking care of ourselves, but they won't let us go down The Walk. They're more afraid than we are—and we're the ones involved. I don't need no protection. I want OUT, to get myself an old man of my choice and to live as normal an existence as is possible for me here."

Thirty-four-year-old Calvin "Carol" Clark from New Orleans also lives in Cellblock "B" and, like Sheila, does not want to be protected. "Hell, what are they supposed to be protecting me from—sex? I do it in here anyway. So I don't see why I can't do it in the population. You see, you have to understand—I'm a homosexual and doing it is a natural thing with me." He points out that he's been doing it since the age of 12. "I feel that if

we need protection we can ask for it. We don't need it forced on us. Boy-gals are comfortable with this lock-up situation cause they can lay up here and do their thing together—they related to each other. I don't and can't relate to a turn-out. I feel like I'm caught in a mental cobweb, having to live with them all the time. I don't want to be locked up like this. I've got time to serve and it's hard doing time like this. I even signed papers saying that I don't want protection, but they still locked me up. I want to go down The Walk, choose an old man, and do my time peacefully and constructively."

As Carol points out, doing time in protective custody is hard. "Protection cases" are always segregated from the rest of the prisoners, denied the kind of freedom and wide range of activities afforded ordinary prisoners. They are also denied access to the prison's education and vocational programs and, so long as they are confined in protective custody, they carry the social stigma that goes with that particular custody—being a "catch-out," a "rat," a "coward," etc. The regulations and restrictions governing their existence are the same as that governing those prisoners locked in Cellblock "A" across the hall from them for "punishment." While authorities state that protective custody is nonpunitive, the reality is that there is absolutely no difference in the manner of treatment accorded the protection cases and the punishment cases—same rules, same restrictions, same everything. They live right across the hall from each other separated only by a fence. So when an inmate is transferred to protective custody, he moves to the same treatment reserved for the punishing of those who have committed serious violations of prison regulations. "You're caught between two extremes," Sheila states. "Sure, you may be mistreated by some inmates in population, but then, security turns right around and mistreats you in the name of protecting you from it." Then too, the "girls" say that there is a jungle and abuse among those confined in protective custody, with the gays sometimes being exploited and abused by the non-gays confined with them—a case of the stronger among them becoming the top-dogs, the rulers in the house of the weak. (Following our interview, we received reports that Sheila received a black-eye from a non-gay in protective custody for refusing to have sexual relations with him.)

"It's not so much that they're being protected, as it is for the rest of the population because of the confusion and trouble that follow them wherever they go," Col. Pence explained when asked about the logic of "protecting" the gays when they do not want protection.

"They keep saying that homosexuals start arguments and fights in this penitentiary no matter where they go," Sheila says, "when actually it's not the homosexuals at all—they're just the excuse used by the authorities for a lack of security."

Phelps points out that prison administrators are generally convinced that homosexuals and kids with violent backgrounds are more likely to cause trouble than anyone else. For example, Col. Pence cites the problems at Camp D, an outcamp that houses the more sexually attractive and younger inmates. "Now, here's a camp with about 530 prisoners," he points out, "and you have damn near as many disciplinary actions and problems in that camp as you have in the entire Main Prison where you have in excess of 1800 men. Of course, not all of the problems are sexual, but that serves to demonstrate

that there are problems with whores." He adds: "Everytime you put a whore in population, you're re-establishing the pecking order—which is a particularly dangerous thing to do in a prison. You got to worry about more than just their own protection. You've got to worry about all of the mess you're going to kick off among the other inmates by putting them in there."

Gwen White is a 25-year-old Morgan City native serving time for prescription forgery. An admitted gay ("I've never made it with a woman and have never had a desire to be with a woman."), he is also confined to B-Block. He recognizes Pence's concern about putting a gay in population because of the definite power and influence they can wield over other prisoners, the feminine charm and grace they can utilize as a weapon to pit prisoners against each other, to foment jealousies and rivals. But, he points out, "It depends upon the individual—she can be a lady or a whore. She can conduct herself where she don't create chaos, confusion or conflict, or she can constantly keep trouble stirred up." But he feels that "most of your problem in this area comes from the prison turn-outs—they don't really know how to handle themselves as real homosexuals do. We've lived this life all our lives, not just our prison lives and that gives us more experience at it . . . I don't like playing the field," he points out. "I get me one man and stay married. If I see anything else developing with someone, I let them know quick that it can't go like that." Sheila points out that he's also not promiscuous: "When I'm with a man, I stay with that man." Col. Pence, acknowledging that all of that may be true, stated that "there's always the possibility that no one will permit them to settle down." And that's where the problem enters the picture.

"I feel like I'm being punished simply because I'm a homosexual," Carol complains. "And I'm not the only one. The rest of the girls—the real ones—will tell you the same thing. We all feel as though they've singled us out and locked us up."

"We do the same thing with young people coming in with long sentences for acts of violence," Phelps states. "We lock them up until we, the administrators, are satisfied that he can do his time without bothering anyone. So homosexuals are not the only ones locked up."

"They're a source of violence and as long as that's the case, we have to separate them," Warden Blackburn says of the present practice of arbitrary lockup of gays upon arrival. "They should go to some type of lockdown until we can judge them." However, he states that he does feel that they should be given a chance to work their way out of the cell and into the normal prison population like all other prisoners on the basis of merit.

Mark Dwayne Smith ("Melody"), a 21-year-old homosexual, worked his way out of his former lockdown status and into the prisoner population. Serving a life sentence for murder, he was initially confined to Camp H, where he participated in that camp's incentive program, then transferred to Camp D, and a few weeks ago to the Main Prison where he now lives in a dormitory on the Big Yard. "I haven't had any problems since I've come here," he says. "Free folks (personnel) say that girls cause trouble—well, some do and some don't. It all depends upon how you carry yourself and what you do. If you're into criss-crossing and all that, eventually it'll come back on you. I don't engage in that kind of thing." He went

down The Walk, got an old man, settled down, and is now doing his time peacefully. "The only trouble I'll get, if I get any, will come from the free folks," he states. "With me being the only out-front white gay on The Walk, any kind of trouble that might come up on The Walk, I'll probably get the rap for, even if it has nothing to do with me. They have a lotta out-front black whores on The Walk and, while I've only been here three weeks, I don't see where they have any problems. But with me, free folks are always kind of watching me and all. I have to be extra careful." Toward that end, he points out that while he "tricked" at Camp D, he no longer does so because, in addition to now having an old man, "I know that if I started doing that here in the Main Prison, pretty soon I would be gone, and I don't want to go back to no cell." He's perfectly content as a "housewife." His dread of being sent back to "protective custody" says a lot about that state of confinement and his preference. "Definitely, The Walk," he says quickly without reservation. "The freedom—when I came from Camp D and hit The Walk, it was just like letting me out of the Front Gate. It's so big! And there's so much to do! You do good time here on The Walk." Based on his experiences in protective custody and his experiences now in the Main Prison population, he says: "From what I saw at Camp D and what I've seen since I've been on The Walk, a youngster could make it better on The Walk than at Camp D. 'D' is supposed to be for the protection of check-outs, rats, homosexuals, and people who couldn't make it anywhere else. But a youngster's chances of getting turned out is 75 percent better at Camp D than here on The Walk. He could make it better here in the Main Prison." Melody adds that "prisoners who are doing a lot of time and carry themselves properly should be allowed to go and live wherever they want to."

Gay prisoners are the only prisoners in Angola who are locked up because of what they are rather than what they do, and the practice of arbitrarily locking them up raises the question of "discrimination." "Homosexuals are being discriminated against here because of the fact that they are homosexuals," Sheila states. "They should be allowed the same choices and privileges as other inmates—the freedom to make right decisions and to make bad ones, and even to fall on your face if that's the case. But classification officers, and especially security officers, tell us no to almost everything . . . because we're homosexuals. They aren't supposed to treat us this way—we have rights too."

Just what "rights" gays have as prisoners, other than the right to protection, is still unclear at this point. A couple of inmate counsels, asked to research the matter for this article, reported back that they could find nothing on the books in the prison's law library pertaining to the treatment to be accorded gays in prison other than that they have a right to protection from sexual abuse. "Apparently, it's still pretty much left up to the authorities," one of them said. While the United States Bureau of Prisons appears to have no firm policy on the treatment of gays in federal institutions, it does advocate that "the feminine appearing, sometime 'pretty' prisoner, must never be classified as a suspected homosexual . . . nor be issued identification that differentiates him from other prisoners" (*The Jail, Its Operation and Management*; U.S. Bureau of Prisons and University of Wisconsin). However, it urges personnel to be careful in the selection of housing for him (for his own

protection), placing them in single cells whenever possible.

Phelps points out that the federal court order by Judge West requires the segregation of overt, aggressive homosexuals from the rest of the prisoner population. But some prison jailhouse lawyers contend that the order does not apply to gays, as they are "passive" homosexuals, not "aggressive." "They don't rape anyone," one pointed out, "if anything, they might get raped."

Phelps agrees with the gays in principle, stating that "Nobody should be discriminated against just because of who and what they are. But if who or what they are presents a security or control problem, then it is our responsibility to see to it that they don't cause a security or control problem—and in that context, they are not being discriminated against. We're not dealing with classes of people. We deal with individuals, and they haven't proven discrimination as a class."

Still, they claim that they are discriminated against as a class of people merely because of what they are. "There is a built-in discrimination against homosexuals," Gwen says. "That's part of the society within the prison. Most people, free people and inmates alike, think that we have some kind of mental problem because we're homosexuals. That traditional attitude has a lot of discrimination built into it." Gwen, who is a first-offender and who intends to return to college to continue his education in medicine, was a registered nurse prior to coming to Angola. According to him, Prison Hospital Administrator Dianne Peabody and Medical Director Thomas Beamon refused to let him work in the prison hospital because of his being a homosexual. "I was denied a job assignment there," he states, "simply because I am a homosexual. There are other homosexuals working over there, inmates and one free person I know for sure. But I am quite obviously a homosexual and that's why they would not let me work there. That's part of the discrimination thing we constantly have to put up with."

"I'm a first-offender with five years," Sheila adds, "not a violent person. I wrote the officials at the State Police Barracks, told them I was a high school graduate with two years of training in air conditioning and refrigeration. I've never heard from them, though they've responded to other inmates who wrote them at the same time I wrote and even afterwards. Instead of denying me, they just ignore me which puts me in a situation where I can't do nothing. I can't even appeal because they have not actually denied me." He doesn't really think that they would seriously consider him "simply because I'm a homosexual. They'll let your old man go to the Police Barracks but not you because you're homosexual. Hell—what he's doing to you doesn't make him that different. He's homosexual too."

"Discrimination? . . . That's the system," Warden Blackburn acknowledged after being apprised of the gays' complaints and their overall situation by us. However, he states that he will look into the matter of their being given no choice and their charges of being discriminated against "and, hopefully, see what can be done to remedy the situation, to make it fairer for them." Colonel Pence is also studying the matter.

"Sexual deprivation is apparently a part of the system, an unwritten rule or part of the punishment," Phelps states. But it doesn't have to be.

"While it wouldn't end it, I feel that a lot of the homosexual activities could be

reduced through a conjugal visiting program tied into the disciplinary system or some type of honor system," Colonel Pence, the prison's chief of security, says, adding that it would have to be restricted to only medium and minimum security prisoners, not maximum security inmates. "It would be controversial, but it wouldn't be the first controversial thing to come up in this business." He feels that most of the prison's security force would accept it if it's adopted as a policy. "There will always be some disagreement," he states, "but we will stand with policy and enforce it. Naturally, there would be problems, but I feel that the overall good would offset the problems."

Pence is not alone in his desire to see conjugal visiting in prison. Professor Columbus B. Hopper of the University of Mississippi spent ten years making a comprehensive study of the evolution and effects of the practice of conjugal visits at the Mississippi State Penitentiary at Parchman in an attempt to determine the total impact of the program. His study concluded that conjugal visiting is at least a partial solution to the sexual problems plaguing the nation's penal institutions. While admitting its inadequacies, he states in his book, *Sex in Prison*, that "conjugal visiting deserves serious consideration by those who wish to develop normal sexual adjustment among the inmates of American penal institutions." He concedes, "As its critics argue, conjugal visiting may have relatively little effect on the biological needs of prisoners. Under current visiting regulations in most prisons, the conjugal visit could not occur often enough to significantly reduce the sexual needs of those participating in such a program. What it would influence, however, is the image of a man. It would allow a man to keep his masculine image and reduce the need to establish it through homosexual conquests."

Unfortunately, too many people, including penal administrators, see conjugal visiting as strictly a physical thing. However, as Professor Hopper discovered, and the inmates in his study indicated: "Physical satisfaction is not the most important aspect of conjugal visits. The most important element is emotional satisfaction. It's influence on his self esteem and emotional needs keeps a man who has conjugal visits from resorting to homosexuality." And that is also a factor in many prison homosexual relationships. Dr. Rundle points out that, despite the jungle-like state of affairs, "A lot of inmates form very close emotional and affectional relationships which many times include the sexual. And that's purely voluntary—that doesn't get into this whole power and domination and what we consider a normal emotional relationship. And as far as I'm concerned, for that to happen in prison is healthy. It can in some way ameliorate the really desocializing process which goes on in a prison."

While Warden Blackburn states that he does not see conjugal visiting as THE answer to homosexuality, he would like to see it instituted, "but sort of at the end of the prison process—a family-type affair with emphasis more on family than just sex."

There are no state or federal laws that demand that sexual deprivation be imposed upon Louisiana prisoners, but it has been as a matter of tradition . . . and politics. And, while both Angola's warden and chief of security would like to see some form of conjugal visiting instituted here at the prison, Colonel Pence doesn't really expect to see it happen anytime soon at Angola. "I wish it would," he says, but

acknowledges that the political atmosphere in the state will prevent it from happening, much the same as it has virtually killed the furlough program that the Louisiana Department of Corrections had promoted as a better solution than the conjugal visits.

So, while politicians play politics, the "experts" theorize, and penal authorities censor *Penthouse* and *Hustler* to prevent a possible "obscene" influence upon the inmates, the nightmarish situation in the nation's jails and prisons continue as does the violence, the abuse, the murders, the suicides and the warped psyches.

The effect of it all upon those subjected to it has to be regarded as a contributing factor, if not a major one, to the recidivism rate among ex-convicts and the institution's failure to rehabilitate them. Rehabilitate? With one segment of an institution's prisoner population enslaved and the other part in constant struggle among themselves to escape deprivation, abuse, and exploitation, a prisoner too often has a tough enough time just keeping his head together, staying alive and safe. The effect of it all upon the victims of sexual violence? "It's got to be bad," Corrections Secretary Phelps states. "If you're a sexual slave or in a homosexual relationship for an extended period of time, it will have a great effect upon you. While most return to normal heterosexual relationships, there is the strong possibility that, having become comfortable in a homosexual relationship, you'll choose to stay with it, rejecting heterosexual relationships."

That's what happened to Melody. "I got turned out in St. John the Baptist Parish Jail and discovered that I liked it," he admits. "So I just stayed with it . . . I enjoy it. The attention turns me on.

When I was young, I didn't get much attention. This way, I get plenty attention and I like it."

"It does happen that sometimes although the relationship may be established against the will of another, it may become a relationship which becomes positive, desirable, and the person who is forced will then continue in it voluntarily," Dr. Rundle states. "But to say that if that happens, the role is accepted as a natural role in life, has to be taken in the context of the prison, where I would see it as a healthy kind of compensatory or coping behavior. It could certainly mean for someone who had been in prison for a long time, that that would become established as the kind of relationship most desirable and would continue after release. For instance, I knew people in Soledad who had gone into the Youth Authority institutions when they were like 12 to 13 or 14, stayed there til they were 18, transferred to the Adult Authority, which meant going to adult prison, and had been there for ten years, so maybe had never had any kind of normal social sexual relation with women, and who would say 'I don't know if I'm homosexual or not—never had the chance to see what it would be like with a woman. All I know is that I've been for 14 years in prison and that I only know what it's like to be with a man, both emotionally and sexually.'"

Melody states that he never had a normal social sexual relation with a woman and only had one nervous sexual experience with a woman in his life. He feels that the lack of a healthy relationship with a woman "definitely had some bearing on my willingness to accept homosexuality."

Unlike Melody, however, most sexual slaves forced to play the role of a woman during their confinement do return to heterosexual relationships upon release. But the experience is not without its effect. Dr. Rundle states that "if this was all against his will, he has to deal with all the fear and anger and resentment and frustration that goes along with that. It would really mess up his head." And it does. To what extent, nobody knows.

The deprivation of basic human needs imposed upon prisoners and the violence resulting from it has created a horrible situation in the nation's jails and prisons, one that adds an extra dimension to the punishment of an offender, one that it can be reasonably assumed that no sentencing judge intended. It would be easy for one to blame the whole affair on the prisoners, using the violent situation as proof that they're criminals or animals and justification for the present penal practices. But the prisoners didn't create the situation. Their behavior merely reflects the response of desperate men, locked in a cruel and abnormal situation, exercising the only avenues left them to cling to the very normal need to feel strong, masculine and worthwhile, to "normality," trying desperately to not lose touch with the "real" world by creating an artificial one patterned after the one they left behind. The violence, the murders, the suicides, and the human debris left in the wake of their effort, is the cost.

* * *

"The degree of civilization in a society can be judged by entering its prisons." Dostoevski—THE HOUSE OF THE DEAD.

The front gate of the Louisiana State Penitentiary: Welcome to Angola!
(Photo courtesy of Cliff Strider and Ray Delcomyn.)

The back of the former Reception Center, which now houses Death Row and CCR.
(Photo courtesy of *The Angolite*.)

Red Hats, Angola's first cellblock, was built in the 1930s. It was closed in 1972. From 1957 to 1961, electrocutions were carried out in the side building, where this replica of the electric chair sets. (Photos courtesy of *The Angolite.*)

The Point Lookout Cemetery is the burial place for inmates whose bodies go unclaimed. It has recently expanded across the road. (Photos courtesy of *The Angolite*.)

This old Angola outcamp, Camp H, was built half a century ago. It is now closed.
(Photo courtesy of *The Angolite*.)

Camp C is one of the newer Angola outcamps.
(Photo courtesy of *The Angolite*.)

A Main Prison guard tower. The horses belong to farm-line guards.
(Photo courtesy of *The Angolite*.)

A tier of cells in the CCR cellblock.
(Photo courtesy of *The Angolite*.)

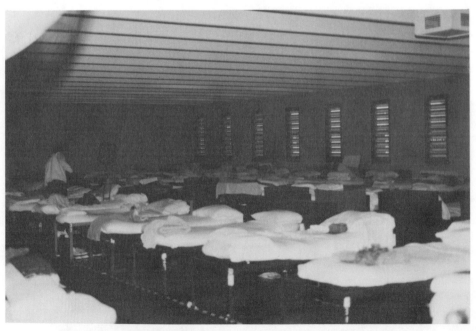

Most inmates live in 60-man medium-security dorms like this one.
(Photo courtesy of Cliff Strider and Ray Delcomyn)

The Main Prison chapel is the center of inmate religious activities.
(Photo above courtesy of *The Angolite;* photo below courtesy of Cliff Strider and Ray Delcomyn)

The Angola Infirmary is the hospital for sick and elderly inmates.
(Photos courtesy of Cliff Strider and Ray Delcomyn)

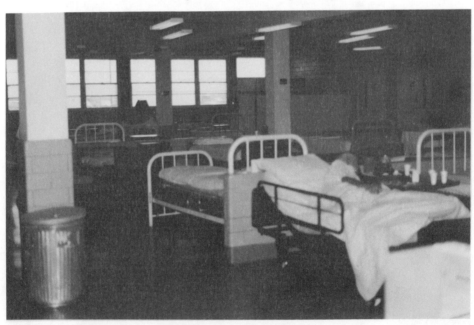

The Industrial Compound houses factory and vocational training buildings,
including the tag plant, where inmates make license plates.
(Photos courtesy of Cliff Strider and Ray Delcomyn)

What most inmates do for work; a farm line goes out to work in the fields.
(Photo courtesy of *The Angolite*.)

Inmates picking cotton at Angola, circa 1975. Inmates still pick cotton
by hand today, just as they did for Major James a century ago.
(Photo courtesy of *The Angolite*.)

Most inmates enter Angola illiterate. Some will have the chance to attend
Adult Basic Education or GED classes, as in these classroom scenes.
(Photo above courtesy of *The Angolite;* photo below courtesy of Cliff Strider and Ray Delcomyn)

A prison prayer meeting, in the Main Prison "A" Building visiting room.
(Photo courtesy of *The Angolite.*)

The yard outside a dormitory.
(Photo courtesy of Cliff Strider and Ray Delcomyn.)

Because most inmates are young men, sports and exercise are
important activities—the weight pile and the gym.
(Photos courtesy of Cliff Strider and Ray Delcomyn)

What else do inmates do for fun? A few take part in the Angola prison rodeo, every
Sunday in October. Many more spend their evenings watching TV in the dormitories.
(Photo above courtesy of Burk Foster; photo below courtesy of Cliff Strider and Ray Delcomyn.)

Visitors to Angola often comment on its wide-open spaces, its natural beauty and its well-tended fields and flowers. They should remember what the inmates, who do all the labor, say: "It's a nice place to visit, but you wouldn't want to live here." (Photos courtesy of Cliff Strider and Ray Delcomyn.)

The prison law library, purchased with inmate funds, is staffed by inmate paralegals.
(Photo courtesy of Cliff Strider and Ray Delcomyn.)

The editors (left to right): Burk Foster, Wilbert Rideau, and Douglas Dennis.
(Photo courtesy of Burk Foster.)

16

THE SHIRLEY COODY STORY*

by Tommy Mason

Shirley Coody made history, at Angola, on June 3, 1987, and she made history twice. She became the first woman promoted to lieutenant at the Louisiana State Prison. Second, she penetrated the aura of machismo surrounding the prison's most notorious section: The Big Yard. She walked to her new assignment alone, and she performed every duty given her as professionally as possible.

The myth of the "Big Yard" has caused many a man, both prisoner and free, to lose their nerve. Male or female— it takes courage to walk into the teeth of the Big Yard the first time.

Women began working in Security at Angola over a decade ago. However, they were removed from the inner prison or constant contact with prisoners. They were assigned to the guard towers, office jobs and to the various visiting areas. A few worked the cages at the various Camp main entrances. However, in each such instance, the women are restricted and not allowed to move outside without male 'protection.' So, the very idea of Coody moving about Angola's inner prison unescorted greatly disturbed certain elements of the male security force.

While there has been a great stir over the promoting of a woman to a supervisory position and her being assigned to the Big Yard, women working in all-male prisons isn't new in other areas of the United States

Women work in the Michigan correctional system. Officer Josephine McCallum became the second woman to

die in the line of duty, recently, there. Her other female co-workers, saw the tragedy as one of the casualties of the job. Since 1982, the women have been working the full range of duties. They asked for the right.

Recent statistics show that Michigan has the third highest number of female correctional officers with 401. California is tops with 600, followed by New York with 540, and Virginia is fourth with 276 women on its staff.

In 1982, some 42 states had women working in custody positions. It has been pointed out by many of the states that women working within the prison has a positive effect on the overall institution. One correctional service pointed out: "The presence of women has a calming effect on the inmates and gives a general feeling of normalcy to the overall situation."

The decision that the time had come to bring some normalcy to the system by providing women with equal opportunity to work and to advance was a decision made by all the corrections heads. When asked who made the decision, Phelps states: "We did."

Why haven't women made rank before now? "There haven't been very many on the promotional registers, until very recently," Phelps said. "They hadn't been here long enough to have seniority and get up there."

"It's a time and space problem," the Secretary points out. "You don't come to work today as a female CO and day after tomorrow show up on the Lieutenants' Register. You've got to have enough

*Appeared in *The Angolite*, July/August 1987, 26-33. Reprinted with permission.

service to get your name up on the list. Women's names are beginning to appear on the list."

As for Coody, Phelps says: "Her name was on the list. She was qualified. She answered all the questions correctly. Her score was higher than some of the male COs and there was absolutely no reason not to hire her."

Phelps sees the matter of women being promoted to supervisory positions quite simple. "In other Departments of Corrections, women are occupying the same jobs that men occupy. Since we took over testing correctional officers, there will be no discrimination on the list between male and female." He adds: "You will appear on the list if you want to be a correctional officer. We are not going to hire females just as tower guards."

Shirley Coody is the first woman lieutenant at Angola, however, two other women turned down the promotion. According to our sources, the two women turned down the position, not out of fear, but because they had no desire to work that closely with prisoners.

The Secretary pointed out, "if you don't want to assume the responsibility of rank, then don't take it. That's fair."

There isn't a time frame as to how long it will be before the change is completed, but in time women are expected to become a routine part of Angola's security force. Louisiana State Prison isn't the first to experience such a change. "This isn't anything new," Phelps told us, "Six or seven years ago, State Police were forced to hire women troopers. After a while they said 'this isn't what I thought it was going to be, I don't want to be a trooper anymore.' They get pregnant, or fall in love, and quit."

In its current posture, the State of Louisiana is no longer vulnerable to discrimination suits regarding its hiring practices. No one was looking for a woman to promote. Coody isn't a special case. She is thirty-four-years old, and she has twelve years of experience. Having worked under at least two colonels, at least that many lieutenant-colonels, and a number of majors as a secretary; she may have a better working knowledge of the rules, regulations, and requirements of rank than the average male security officer.

Making lieutenant at Angola isn't a lightly regarded matter. It's a very competitive place. When Coody earned a promotion to lieutenant, she gained a coveted status, one which many officers have often tried to attain. Phelps put it this way: "Anytime there is a change from the historical way of doing things, somebody is going to get bent out of shape. The problem with promotions is that if you only have one vacancy and five people apply for it, and if all of them are capable of doing the job, you're going to make one person happy and four unhappy."

In this instance, it is primarily the men who are unhappy. Primarily, because there are many women who are disturbed. A few dread the thought of working in Angola's inner prison, and fear that they will be forced to give up their jobs. Others see the ghosts of more traditional Deep South fears, and they blame Coody for opening the door.

Many questions have been asked about the woman who has become the first female lieutenant at the Louisiana State Prison. She first attracted attention when she filed a complaint with the Equal Employment Opportunity Commission in New Orleans. "They were having male-only promotion boards," she said. "And it wasn't right."

She was not the only person to file a complaint about discrimination. When given credit for filing the complaint, she explained, "Not just me specifically, all the women. They are phasing out the female security jobs. They were limiting women as to what they could do."

While the EEOC was treating the complaint, Coody's promotion was not the result of any ruling from them. "I don't really think they have ordered them. Over the last year the EEOC has been submitting questions to the penitentiaries to submit paperwork or documentation, so the institution was aware they were under investigation by the EEOC," Coody told *The Angolite*. Consequently, it is believed the institution acted on its own "to be a step ahead of them."

While she has only recently been promoted to the rank of lieutenant, Coody had taken the required test for the promotion before. "I took the test several years ago," she said, "just to see if I could pass it, because you hear how horrible it is. I just figured why not try. I passed it."

She explains that taking the test was something of a lark. After making a score of "eighty-something," the results just lapsed. In February 1986, Coody took the test again.

"They held half of the Lieutenant's Board on Friday and I was in that half. They started at the top of the register. They completed the register on Monday," she remarked. "Monday afternoon, it is my understanding they had a meeting (those that were on the Board). They decided who they were going to make and Monday afternoon about a quarter after four, I got a copy of the memo showing who was promoted and where they were going."

Coody's first reaction? "Panic."

Although she was frightened at the prospect of working as a supervisor on the Big Yard, she didn't give up her promotion or "bust back" as it is called. "I talked to several people, and they said, "Give it a shot. If you can't do it, fine; if you like it, fine; if you don't like it, you can bust back, but at least give it a shot to prove whether you can do it or not."

"I had never been down the walk," Coody said. "So I had no idea where I was even going."

Having accepted the challenge, she began to discover some things about the prison environment—good things and bad things. Coody is petite, blond, and intelligent. Eighty percent of the inmates at Angola are black. The two present an obvious conflict in the Deep South. Traditionally, the creature with the highest mortality rate in the Deep South is a black perceived as a threat to white females.

Thus, the male officers became very protective—to the point of being ridiculous—of her. She was followed about by groups of two, and on occasion as many as five.

Coody is quick to point out, if she believed her presence would cause someone to be hurt because of her, she would leave.

As a new lieutenant, she has been talked with about the many games that can be played. "There were different situations that were—things that were done in an effort to make me look bad or put me in a situation where I would make a wrong decision," she told us. "But doing that, they were creating problems for the inmates on the yard and I was afraid there would arise a situation where it could endanger them. That's not what I'm here for. I'm not here to create problems for them."

In fact, she points out that the

prisoners have been very respectful. "They have been very polite. They have been very helpful."

There have been the usual games. "You know, let's pull this and see if she'll go for it. There's been several who will come up and ask me, like write me a pass to the law library; I need to go up and take these materials. But they know they have to be on call-out to go to the law library."

Coody's historic assignment occurred during a period when Louisiana was establishing itself as the execution capitol of the United States It also demonstrated something to her about her fellow women in the security force. "Some are very supportive," she pointed out. "You're doing good, we are proud of you. We worry about you because really all you hear about are the terrible things about the yard, how cruel, how vicious it is."

The environment which exists within the prison has opened her eyes to some of the myths about prisoners and she understands the fears of her female counterparts, but she knows better. "They're not like that. I'm down there, I know what it's like," she told *The Angolite*. "There are those who think, 'she's crazy . . . now because of her, we are going to be forced to work on the yards.' There are those who are pleased and those who don't like it at all." Her first weeks haven't been a cake walk.

Many people have asked the question, "Why would a woman want to work with those men?"

"The point being I did not want to go," the lieutenant told *The Angolite*. "Okay, I did not tell the board I want to go on the Big Yard, I want to go down the walk." She emphasized, "That was not my decision. I know in *The Angolite*, the last issue, it was something about 'she wants to go down there.' Something '. . .

how would you feel about your mother, your sister, your daughter or your wife down there?' They wouldn't like it. The statement was made, 'well, she wants to be there.' That's not true. I don't want to be there, but that is where the administration put me. It's their prerogative where they assign supervisors, where they assign anybody, even sergeants."

Because of her assignment to the Big Yard, the line of reasoning emerged that a move existed to force Coody to quit. She admits there were all sorts of games and that a number of cruel insensitive restrictions were placed on her. For example, in the first weeks on the job, she was ordered to 'man' her post for the entire 12 hours. She endured the harassment.

Initially, she worked under a supervisor who was sensitive to her plight and who was fair enough to be concerned with the job being done and not with who was doing it. That supervisor was transferred. His replacement was a man adamantly opposed to women working in the inner prison, according to our sources.

It was under this supervisor that the dam burst, and Coody orally expressed her chagrin at the harassment she received from her immediate supervisor.

"I figured I would be the first for any test, any problems, 'Let's prove women can't do it' would be pulled on me. I expected it. I didn't expect it to go to such an extent. I figured if I made a mistake they would jump on me and say, 'Ha-Ha, we got you. We said women couldn't do it.' I just didn't expect things to be blown so out of proportion."

The first recorded situation came when Coody was written up for failing to respond to a radio transmission. "With a man, I don't think that would have happened," she remarked. "Well, I know it hasn't happened because there have been instances where men had misunderstood radio transmissions. Ambulances go to the wrong place. Nobody gets excited. They laugh about it, but when I made the mistake and they were aware the radio had a problem, and it's no big deal, but they would blow it so out of proportion. 'Let's make an example of her so these other women won't come down here.' And, there's really lots of women leery of going down the walk for the simple fact, 'If I make a mistake, are they going to try and fire me too?'"

The incident is in the past. Coody has been transferred from the Big Yard to the Trusty Yard. There have been no sudden changes in the routines of the prisoners. On occasion, she has been seen observing the softball games, making small talk with this or that inmate. She's even strolled out to game sites to watch a game or two.

Sure, there are problems; so far, she has been up to the task. The pressure is still there.

There are remarks. For example, one security officer observed her talking to *The Angolite* and retorted, "Yeah, they are down there trying to brainwash that woman."

Other incidents have occurred as well. After a number of requests for *The Angolite* to come on the Big Yard and just rap to the prisoners, the staff decided to just walk the yard one evening. It's never been a problem. We always travel to the various yards to do interviews, take pictures, or check out story leads. However, in the wake of an *Angolite* Commentary, "The Lady in Blue," the level of cooperation with the staff took a sudden—though subtle—drop. After checking out at Control Center in the Main Prison, we arrived at the Big Yard

"Snitch Gate" only to be told that Lt. (and Acting Captain) Clarence Lemoine had given orders to keep *The Angolite* staff off the yard. It was a first; never in our history on the magazine staff had we encountered such a situation.

After a walk back to the Main Prison Office, a visit to the Major's Office, and an interrogation by Lt. Lemoine, we gained access to the yard. We began mingling with the prisoners, talking, taking pictures and just, in general, informing the men why we were there. Meanwhile, the irate lieutenant had ordered a number of his officers to follow and watch.

The only difference in this trip to the Big Yard and any of our previous ones was that Shirley Coody was there. We took pictures, and only upon pointing a camera in the direction of Coody did we encounter a problem.

Days later, we were informed that the female lieutenant could not give interviews while on duty. This was a switch because for the past decade or so, we always interview members of the staff and personnel, as they become available.

The trite line of nothing has changed persists, but the truth is a lot of people are demonstrating a greater concern with the gender of the new lieutenant than they are with doing their jobs.

Things have changed. Women working in security at Angola are concerned. Many blame Coody.

Coody admits in examining her situation, that there are a lot of problems. She is quite candid about the role of women in security at Angola. "I see no problem with the women handling the keys on the dormitories, on the gates, in the kitchen, the Property Room, any of the sally port gates, on trips, on patrol, front-gate, ferry-gate or roving security."

However, she does have some reservations about other job assignments. "In all honesty, I do not think a woman should be put inside a dormitory. Not because she can't handle it, because she can," she commented. "Everybody has to have privacy, a place they feel is their own."

"I don't think they (prisoners) want a woman in the dorm," she expressed. "Not because she is a woman, but because everybody needs an area of privacy."

Overall, the new lady lieutenant is handling the pressures, the resentment, the questions with a great deal of skill. "One guy called me on the phone last night," she told us. "He said, 'I mean no disrespect to you, but there are men who have been here longer than you, that deserve lieutenant's rank more than you.' And I told him, 'I understand that.' I know how they feel. Okay, but then Civil Service has rules."

The promotion was not any kind of affirmative action. She qualified by seniority, by test, and by Civil Service Register. In a group of 50, she finished number 8. "There was another lady with a grade point higher than I," Coody pointed out. "She didn't want to go down the walk. She didn't want night shifts, so she declined. Had I declined, they would have gone down to a man, based on the grades, but I know there is a lot of resentment from the men, to have to take orders from a woman."

As a Yard Lieutenant, she supervises ten men. "Once or twice, I have been put into a position, where I had to tell a Sergeant, 'Do this. It's right. It's the way it should be done; I realize you don't agree with it or me, but it has to be done.' And, they've done it." She injected that, "they haven't pitched a fit. Of course, after I've left I'm sure my ears should have turned red from ringing."

Coody is a strong woman and stubborn. She realizes that there are many types of reactions to what she is doing. "Several think she's crazy. She's a trouble-maker. Others say she's got guts," Coody stated. "I think I've proved a point that women are not as weak or as dumb as men like to think. After I made the rank, one guy said, 'I think women belong at home.' That's how a lot of people think, but times are changing. Things cost an arm and a leg. It takes two to work and support a family and give the kids what they want."

Working in the prison rather than on its outskirts has opened her eyes to some things about prisoners. She said of the inner prison, "it's not a bad place. They would like people to believe it is. I'm sure there are going to be situations arise that it's going to be hard for a woman to handle."

Occasionally, in doing a story many of the key players prefer to remain off the record. They have their reasons. That is not to imply that there aren't some who just weren't available for comment; there were.

It is unfortunate that the people opposed to women working in the inner prison chose not to voice their opinions. If they had, we could have presented a total picture. The question of women working in all-male prisons has already been answered. There are some 42 states with a percent of their staffs female. They are willing to do the job and they are able to do the job. "Will they be properly trained? Will they be given a fair chance, or are they going to be scrutinized pen-in-hand, DR-1 ready?" Coody asks.

One issue has been settled. Women will be working in the inner prison at Angola. The resentment, the fears, the questions might stimulate the mind, but the decision has been made. As the Department's Secretary expressed earlier, "It is a time and space problem."

For prisoners, there must be some subtle adjustments. However, the Warden, R. Hilton Butler, has stated quite plainly prisoners are to continue their normal routines. Whatever they have been doing they should keep doing.

Coody sees a benefit to the prisoner population being supervised by women. "It should bring out more of an adjustment in them, rather than hit the streets straight off the walk," she said. "People on the outside don't understand how it is in here. They don't understand the language, the hardness which is a necessity here." Perhaps the presence of women on a daily basis will help prisoners behave more normally.

As far as the dormitories, Coody pointed out that "you have men who can't work in a dormitory. They're not cut out for it, so you have to assign them something that is appropriate or that suits their needs."

Today, she is the first woman lieutenant at the Louisiana State Prison. She has eight years remaining for retirement. "I am taking one day at a time," she expressed. "And trying to stay employed for eight more years, so I can retire."

Before coming to work at Angola, Coody worked as a secretary in a Monroe newspaper office advertising department. Her husband, now retired, is former Security Major Kendall Coody. She is the mother of two children: a boy and a girl, ages nine and four.

There have been problems, but she has a family. She is doing a job, a job which she has invested 12 years. It shouldn't matter what her sex is. It should matter whether or not she can do the job.

The reasoning that some special danger threatens her, because she is a woman, is a joke. The dangers are the same, perhaps less. This is a prison—one termed as the toughest in the state. Prisoners know the best way to survive and do their time is to steer clear of sticky situations with "any" free personnel—female or male.

A woman making lieutenant at Angola is not so special. The prison is changing. Both the kept and the keepers are taking on new appearances, too.

Let's look at it this way, if there aren't enough people to man the positions, what's the alternative? Computers, electronic eyes? There wouldn't be anyone to complain then.

Contrary to popular belief, there are not any ghosts lurking in any corners on the Big Yard or any other yard; they are just in the minds of a few small-minded people. The primary concern of almost all prisoners is how to get out as quickly as possible—not who the lieutenant is going to be.

17

PROTECTIVE CUSTODY*

by Ron Wikberg and Wilbert Rideau

Security is mostly superstition. It does not exist in nature, nor do the children of most men as a whole experience it. Avoiding danger is no safer in the long run than outright exposure. Life is either a daring adventure, or nothing.

—HELEN KELLER

While America was quietly creating its 51st State, comprising nearly three-quarters of a million people locked away in state and federal prisons, the nation's correctional and prison administrations were also busy, silently creating prisons within prisons. Called "Protective Custody" (PC) Units, they house what most prisoners perceive and refer to as snitches, queers, punks, rats, faggots and gal-boys. In reality, PC units are nothing more than sanctuaries used by prisoners and prison administrators, who believe for reasons real or perceived, that the prisoners would be safer in an environment of live-and-let-live.

The need by prison officials to separate some prisoners from others is a real one according to some experts, who attribute the burgeoning problem on overcrowding, violence developing from debts, drugs, a growing number of sex offenders, prison informants, a more youthful and violent offender coming into the prison system and the growth of gangs. An increase of inmate-on-inmate violence is generally acknowledged by the nation's prison officials, and as more prisoners seek protective custody, the more difficult its management becomes.

Critics charge that prisons with large numbers of PC cases is an indication that penal administrators are losing control of their institutions and the existence of PC units themselves is an acknowledgement of less than total control. However, some prison administrators and corrections experts claim that when a prisoner says he's in trouble or danger, there is no way of knowing he is not, thus requiring the inmate to be separated and an investigation conducted.

Thomas G. Christian, a state correctional employee, spent his first seventeen months as a security officer at Dixon Correctional Institute (DCI) in Jackson, Louisiana. For the past nine months, however, the California native has been assigned as a classification officer at the Louisiana State Penitentiary, bringing with him a bachelor's and master's degree in business administration. Christian is quick to point out that a request for protective custody by an inmate receives immediate attention. "It is a 'now' type situation because if he were to return to his unit and have a real enemy, there could be trouble," he says, adding: "You have to go under the assumption the enemy is real and the request legitimate until it is proven otherwise. There is also the consideration of liability and the legalities. One of the main functions incumbent upon prison employees is the protection of the inmate from themselves and from each other, therefore, one must be careful and exercise an abundance of caution in dealing with such cases."

In some instances, victims of crime outside the prison have relatives or friends

*Appeared in *The Angolite,* July/August 1989, 39-60. Reprinted with permission.

inside the prison, setting a scene for personal vendettas and violence. "We have inmates in here who have killed the mothers of other inmates and we have inmates who have raped other inmates' wives or sisters," said Christian. "These are automatically declared enemies and separated. It is pretty much the same thing when an inmate first arrives at Angola. One of the questions asked by the Initial Classification Board is whether the new arrival has any known enemies in the prison. If he does, he will be placed in a protected environment until we do a 'protection review.' Once such a review is done, then we will place the inmate where we can," Christian explained.

Performing protection reviews is the responsibility of the prison classification department and, according to Christian, is not one-hundred percent foolproof. "It sometimes takes an hour to do just one review because there are some inmates with large prison records. A protection review sometimes requires we go through the records all the way back when the inmate was in the parish jail. If he was involved in a fight there, we have to check those names against those currently in the prison. This responsibility is made more difficult by many inmates having the same name, so now we require the name and prison number of the alleged enemy from the inmate requesting protection," he said.

As late as 1980, there were no national statistics on the number of prisoners assigned to protective custody, said *Corrections Magazine*, a bi-monthly publication of Criminal Justice Publications, Incorporated. But, in 1983, the ACA released a report saying that between 1978 and 1982, the Protective Custody population in America's prisons had doubled to almost 23,000. As a search was conducted for other statistics

and information surrounding this peculiar segment of the prison population, *The Angolite* noted an inconsistency in statistical data reported by the nation's state and federal correctional systems.

A survey conducted in 1984 by Thadeus Johnson for the Planning & Research Unit of the Oklahoma Department of Corrections, was published in *Corrections Compendium* [March, 1985], indicating only a little over 10,000 prisoners nationwide, were considered Protective Custody. In that survey, Louisiana was reported having none of their prisoners in PC status, however, it did report a total of 1,845 "restrictive beds" were available for other reasons.

Three years later, *Corrections Today* magazine [July, 1988] released a survey which had been conducted by the Missouri Department of Corrections. Louisiana reported at that time there were 538 prisoners under Protective Custody status, while the nation's PC population amounted to 15,186. For some reason, the 1985 and 1988 surveys reflected smaller PC populations than the 23,000 revealed by ACA in 1983.

The Bureau of Justice Statistics (BJS), the official reporting agency of the United States Department of Justice, has been gathering and reporting national criminal justice and correctional data in the form of bulletins, special reports and source books for the last sixty years. A review of the BJS literature indicates that prison "protective custody" information has not been gathered and reported.

Notwithstanding any of the studies or surveys, Protective Custody has always been an integral part of prison management. There has always been a need to separate some prisoners from others as the prisoner population continues to boom, the community of

Protective Custody continues to expand.

The great majority of the nation's protective custody bedspace is found in individual cells or other small living areas. Some states, however, are unique in providing an open dormitory atmosphere to house protection cases. Louisiana is one of those states. Excluding the newly-constructed medium custody prison in Avoyelles Parish which may be opened when this report is published, there are ten adult penal institutions in Louisiana; 3 are minimum custody; 6 medium custody and one is maximum custody.

At the New Orleans-based Work Training Facility-South (WTF-S) which houses 300 minimum custody inmates, no beds are routinely allotted for protective custody. Most commonly referred to as "Jackson Barracks," it is comprised of inmates who work for the State National Guard on maintenance assignment, work release status and some nearing the end of their prison terms. WTF-S Warden Frank Jobert told *The Angolite*: "I would say we average zero PC cases as a general rule. There are no beds provided for protective custody, but in the event such space is needed, we have a small room containing five beds which can be used for longterm PC status." Jobert described a recent case of an inmate assigned to WTF-South who had killed the father of one of the other inmates assigned there. "All we do in such cases is transfer one of the inmates to another minimum custody facility," Jobert explained, "but these are extremely infrequent."

Another minimum custody state penal facility is Work Training Facility-North (WTF-N) which houses 450 state prisoners in much the same capacity as WTF-S, providing maintenance assignments for the National Guard Training Base at Camp Beauregard, near Pineville,

Louisiana. Larry Jeane, Warden of the facility, said: "Programatically, we have no beds for protective custody cases. However, historically we have housed a few prisoners with PC needs, but I would say this is only 1-to-2 a year. We've had some former correctional officers and ex-policemen do their sentences here." Jeane explained that WTF-N had a small cell-block facility, "but it is for short-term use only, not exceeding ten days. If we have a real serious protective custody situation in which we're unable to meet the needs, we'll arrange a transfer to another facility," he added.

Hunt Correctional Center (HCC), at St. Gabriel, Louisiana, houses 1,850 medium custody prisoners and is also the Receiving and Diagnostic facility for the state department of corrections. Assistant Warden for Treatment, Marianne Leger, said no specific beds were provided for protective custody situations, but in the case of such a need, a cellblock existed for temporary housing. Leger said that HCC averaged from 6-to-8 prisoners in protective custody at any one time.

The adult state prison located at DeQuincy, the Louisiana Correctional and Industrial School (LCIS), holds 850 medium custody inmates. According to Warden Robert Henderson, LCIS also has no specific bedspace allotted for PC cases since it was seldom that such instances arose. However, Henderson said the institution averaged about one PC request each month which generally turns out to be a temporary request only.

Located in rural North Louisiana at Haynesville, the Wade Correctional Center (WCC) now houses 1,181 medium custody inmates since new cellblock additions were completed in 1987. "We have no protective custody beds earmarked as such in the internal operation at the prison," said WCC Warden Richard Stalder. "However, as an external operation, we do have the 47-bed 'N-5 unit' which houses prisoners designated as protective custody by headquarters."

Stalder said while the N-5 unit is located at WCC, only the Office of Adult Services at corrections headquarters can assign inmates to it. "We use PC here in a conservative fashion," he said, "and we have no per se protective custody beds, but use one tier of our extended lockdown space for that purpose if needed, because our disciplinary cases and PC cases are governed by the same policy." Stalder told *The Angolite* that the prison averages between 10 and 12 PC cases at any one time. He also noted that protective custody was subject to abuse by inmates but the problem was not serious at the prison.

In June, 1988, the *Morning Advocate* [Baton Rouge] profiled the correction department's N-5 Unit, which housed specially classified PC inmates such as former police officers, correctional officers, witnesses, juveniles and others, most of which were serving life sentences. The state's prison wardens cannot assign inmates to the N-5 Unit, but can make recommendations to headquarters where a final decision for transfer is made. Gary Gremillion, an official of Adult Services office, said it is difficult to set up separate facilities for every category of prisoner. He said that doing what is best for the inmate while at the same time protecting the state's interests was the primary reason for the unit being opened in 1980.

Louisiana's second largest adult prison, Washington Correctional Institute (WCI) located in Angie, Louisiana, holds 1,022 medium and minimum custody prisoners. "We do not have any specific beds or cells set aside for protective custody cases," said WCI Warden Jack Donnelly. "If an inmate signs a statement saying he needs protection, then we will always find a cell to put him in, the same cells we use for administrative lockdown purposes." A former Angola security officer and assistant business manager, Donnelly said WCI averages 3 to 4 cases at any one time. "If I had to make a ballpark guess, I would say that one of every four cases abuses the protection status. We will afford them all the protection that is necessary. We don't allow any of the PC cases to be moved without an escort, even for inmates who must be moved in restraint gear. Whenever one must be moved, we will shut down the walks," he added.

Kelly Ward is the assistant warden for treatment at Dixon Correctional Institute (DCI) in Jackson, Louisiana. The former classification officer of the state penitentiary told *The Angolite*: "Protective custody is a manageable problem. As long as you have large numbers of people living in close-quarters, it is inevitable that situations will arise where separation is necessary." Ward said that of DCI's population of 1,013, the institution only averages 2 to 3 PC cases at any one time. "We have no special section for such cases," he added. "In a logistical sense DCI has three compounds and our first strategy is to resolve the problem locally and it is effective because 2 of every 3 protection request cases result in short-term separation. When a long-term PC case develops, a transfer to another state facility is made." Ward noted that it had been quite some time for the necessity of transferring a protection case to Angola, saying the state's prison wardens work closely with each other in such situations.

Located at St. Gabriel, the Louisiana

Correctional Institute for Women (LCIW) recently received approval to raise female prisoner capacity limits to 546, according to Nellie Fanguy, deputy warden. "Actually, we have 500 residents now," Fanguy said. "From an administrative standpoint, PC is not a problem. Most of our cases are short-term. We require that residents sign a request for protective custody, but they can also sign a request to be released. LCIW has 16 cells that are available for multi-purpose use, including PC. On an average we have 2 or 3 residents assigned to protective custody status," Fanguy explained.

In her 11th year of a life sentence for a Lafayette Parish murder conviction, Gloria Aucoin told *The Angolite* that protective custody policy at the women's prison differed drastically from the other male facilities. In 1988, she explained, the LCIW policy changed when fifty-five residents requested protective custody at one time in order to get out of work in the heat of summer. "The administration believed that PC was being abused," said Aucoin, "so now when the resident settles down, is no longer considered a danger to self or others, she is released at the end of 30 days. Only rarely are they permitted to stay longer." Aucoin said that the automatic 30-day requirement for persons requesting protective custody discouraged future wholesale requests. "Only the prison director of social services, or the psychiatrist, can decide whether the resident should be retained beyond the 30-day period," she added.

The Avoyelles Correctional Center (ACC) located across the Mississippi River from Angola, in Cottonport, was near opening at the time this report was being researched. Designed to hold 584 medium and minimum security adult prisoners, no protective custody cases can

yet be reported there. Louisiana Governor Buddy Roemer, in April 1989, told the *Morning Advocate* that beds in the soon-to-be-opened prison will be reserved for drug offenders.

The State Police Barracks, another minimum custody adult penal facility, has a 160-man skilled work force which provides maintenance and other services not only for the Department of Public Safety, but also for the domestic chores performed at the governor's mansion. A former capitol area security employee, Fred Kennedy has been warden at the facility since April 1988. "There are no protective custody beds per se," Kennedy told *The Angolite*. "PC has not been a problem, probably in large part due to the minimum-custody atmosphere and working conditions for the inmates. By its very nature, the creature comforts, as compared to other facilities, contribute to the near non-existence of such problems. We do have, however, about 5 cases where probation was requested or recommended by either state or federal authorities."

The great majority of Louisiana's protective custody prisoner population, nearly six-hundred strong, are found at the maximum custody state penitentiary at Angola. Surprisingly, the great majority of the beds allotted for PC cases are found in dormitories, housing from 60 protective cases in the Main Prison's Magnolia dormitory, to 65 cases in Eagle Unit dorms located at Camp D. A cell-block, also at the Main Prison, houses 120 double-bunked PC cases. At the time *The Angolite* was researching and investigating this story, Eagle Unit had 260 inmates, Magnolia had 180 inmates and the cellblock used for protective custody had 120 cases, a total of 560 inmates under some form of protection. While other cellblock facilities located at the 18,000-

acre sprawling complex also held an occasional PC case, a precise count was unavailable.

Why does the Louisiana State Penitentiary have so many PC cases as compared to other adult penal facilities? Classification Officer Christian says one contributing cause is the ease which it takes to get in, but the extreme difficulty in getting out. "Once an inmate is in protective custody, it is not uncommon for them in this situation to be disciplinary problems. They do tend to get write-ups," he said. "If he's in one of the units, he must go 90 days before being considered for a transfer. At the end of that 90 days, a protection review is done on them and a decision made to either move them to another protection unit, require that they remain where they are at, or assign them to the general population," explained Christian.

Other prison officials also acknowledge that protective custody cases at other adult penal institutions are sent to Angola where, from a logistical point of view, numerous camps exist which can be used to further separate prisoners when needed.

Some prisoners find themselves assigned either upon their arrival to Angola or later in their sentence servitude at a classification board hearing, to a PC unit for no reason known to them. Rodney Landry, 30, arrived at the Louisiana State Penitentiary in 1987 from Orleans Parish with a life sentence for second-degree murder committed in June, 1985. "There is no reason that I have come across yet that classifies me as protective custody. I didn't have any enemies. I'm not a homosexual. And I never asked for Protective Custody," said Landry. "I never even knew of Protective Custody when I came here or what it was.

I thought I was just going to another camp, and I didn't know till I arrived that it was called PC and a couple of inmates explained it to me."

Landry said he told the prison Initial Classification Board he was a first-offender, that he had no problems in the parish jail awaiting transfer and that he was not a homosexual, responses to questions routinely asked by the Board. Two years later he is still trying to get out of PC and re-assigned into the general prison population. "I've tried twice to go on the Board to be moved to another unit. One time I was denied because I had a write-up and the other time they told me I haven't been in the penitentiary long enough and because of the seriousness of my charge. I am scheduled soon for another hearing and I hope I make it. I don't participate in none of the homosexual activities, or nothing like that. Most of the time I read me a novel or watch television, or I might go on the yard and walk around, but that is all I do here. I'm not really a part of this community as far as the homosexualism that goes on here—I'm not a part of that," he explained. Landry told *The Angolite* he wanted general population housing so he could benefit himself by getting into school or vocational training.

There are some prisoners who request Protective Custody as a means to avoid committing a violent act against a fellow prisoner. "I opted for PC because I am peaceful. It takes a lot to push me. It takes a lot to make me strike, make me fight, make me do anything," said 24-year-old Bryan Brown. Now serving a life sentence imposed for a Rapides Parish murder conviction, Brown had orginally been sentenced to death before winning a new trial and a lesser sentence. He was assigned to Angola's Camp-D Raven Unit and placed in a cell.

"When I got there, I had the cell to myself, but my first cell partner was a real aggravation at first and then it got to the point where he and others were trying to bulldog me into subjugation by taking and extorting me for the personal items of property I had, typewriter, radios, clothes, jewelry and things I could get sent in from the streets. It went on for about a month," said Brown. "When it would not stop, I was left with two choices, I could either hurt him or I could leave. At one point I definitely contemplated killing him. I stood over him two or three times as he slept to figure out the best way to do it. I could have stabbed him through the eye straight to his brain, or I could cut his throat, or jab him in the heart. But, I had spent a year and 10 months on Death Row."

Brown, who was born in Los Gatos, California, had been on court order pending retrial when Louisiana electrocuted four prisoners. "These people were my friends—I knew them. Death is not funny, death does not play and death is permanent. I killed somebody when I was 18-years-old and I am more sorry that I killed my victim, because she is dead. I know the exact meaning of death, but back then I didn't. To have killed my cellmate would not just put me back on Death Row, it would have turned me into the type of person that wouldn't care any more. So, I stayed for one more month, and then I checked out," he explained. "See, I don't have many friends at all. Most times I could give a f—k less what anyone thinks, it only matters what he does, and when he does something to me, you know, I have to do whatever I have to do. To be persuaded by another person's choice, that is not your own, you're going to get yourself stuck out. I've done it

enough times, so I know."

Occasionally, a prisoner will seek Protective Custody for all the wrong reasons, and once there, finds he can't get out. Thirty-year-old Odell Davis was sentenced to 25 years from Caddo Parish for a 1975 armed robbery committed when he was 16-years-old. When he arrived at Angola in 1979 he was placed into the general population. The Milwaukee, Arkansas-native, married with two children, worked his way up to being a cook at Camp-A where he met and became emotionally involved with a homosexual.

"I requested protective custody in 1988 because I was running behind a whore. I was following a homosexual. It was somebody I met and got to know well. We got close and then he was moved to PC, so I tried to catch up with him. It was a kind of love we had. Things didn't turn out the way I planned, in fact it turned out real bad. We never got together. When I finally caught up with him, he was with somebody else. Now I am over here in PC, by myself, and can't get out," Davis explained.

When advised by *The Angolite* during interview that publishing his circumstance might adversely affect his marital status, Davis became adamant: "I want you to publish this, I don't care. Maybe it will keep other people from doing it and not knowing what they are getting into. I am very sorry I did it. I've tried to do 90 days without a write-up so I can get on the Board to get back in the population, but each time I keep getting one and I have to start all over again."

Davis says what happened in his case should be a warning to others. "Don't come over here in protective custody. It doesn't make any sense. There are all kinds of people here and the majority are here because they want to be here. Me, I was following behind a d—k sucker, a whore. I lived in the regular population for 10 years and I never engaged in such activities in my life till I met this one person at Camp-A. But, it was a sexual release for me. I'd never have done this if they had conjugal visiting here. If we had contact visits, a lot of this 'punkology' stuff would not be happening in Angola," said Davis.

"They have some guys out there [general population] that are just as homosexual as I am," says Wayne "Wendy" Hartman, a 47-year-old native of Los Angeles, California. An admitted homosexual, Hartman is serving a twenty-year sentence from Orleans Parish on a theft conviction, and has been assigned to Protective Custody for the past 10 years.

Hartman says not all homosexuals are put into PC. "If they do not look homosexual, do not carry themselves homosexually, therefore they are not classified homosexual. They have a lot of people that come to Magnolia that show fear, of things they heard about prison while they were in jail or while they were free. Some come here appearing frigid, fragile, weak, scared, timid and that perception at the moment they are classified determines them being sent here. If they are looking like a little mouse, they sure are not going to throw this little mouse into the rattlesnake pit. It is unfortunate, though, as he gets stronger, as he gets accustomed to being in a place like Angola, he is going to want to get out of Protection, and may very well be unable to," he said.

Definitions and normal day-to-day prison jargon of the world of homosexuality take very different meanings in prison. And to understand the macho and somewhat perverse application of those definitions inside the prison, *The Angolite* relied upon the expertise of not only Hartman, but also that of 36-year-old Anthony "Mom" Grubbs, serving four life sentences from Orleans Parish for aggravated kidnapping, aggravated rape and aggravated crime against nature.

"A homosexual," said Grubbs, "is a person that has a physical as well as a mental and emotional attraction of a member of one's own sex. A 'turn out' is a person who engages in homosexual activities because he is either forced or he is, shall we say, talked out his ass; it's a person who really isn't a homosexual, but is doing it because of the situation he's in because he feels threatened in some way. Now, a 'punk' is much the same as a turn-out, I would say."

Other frequently used terms expressing homosexuality in a general sense were also explained by Grubbs. "A 'queer' is someone who has bizarre fetishes, someone who is off into possibly the fringe rim of the gay world, leather, S&M, foot-fetishes—I find these people a bit queer," said Grubbs.

Hartman pointed out the distinction of those meanings within the prison setting which reflects a departure from the clinical and psychological definitions. "Now, there is an Angola or penitentiary definition, and this is if you f—k a man [termed 'pitching'], you're not a homosexual. That is true inside Angola, but if you talk to a Harvard, Yale or Dartmouth psychologist, he's going to let you know that if you f—ked a man in the ass, you're as much homosexual as the man who got f—ked [termed 'catching']," he explained.

With four years of college education, Grubbs is a first-offender who has been a homosexual since age 11. "My first love was one of my friends from school in the sixth grade. His sister was my girlfriend and I used to go see her every day and he'd always be there and I ended [up] getting a crush on him, instead of her," he added.

Hartman, however, recalled his life in the gay world beginning in kindergarten, remembering his family having to pay a child psychiatrist for years because of his behavior: "The school called my parents and recommended I get psychiatric help, which my parents did. I started seeing psychiatrists about my problems of little boys, and from that age till I was thirteen, they tried to cure, which there is no cure for that," Hartman said.

Hartman and Grubbs basically agreed that a majority of Protective Custody is comprised of such inmates. "PC is a weaker environment with the majority of the people homosexuals, whores, turnouts," said Hartman. "The few men that do come here, and they are men, and they are going to stay a man, they usually leave rapidly. If he comes here 'in the closet' or concealing it or hiding it, they'll let their hair down eventually. It may take some a week, it may take two months, it may take others 2 years."

Grubbs believes that the prisoners in PC are discriminated against. "We have no way to pass our time, or to improve or better ourselves. I am put someplace where I don't have access to the same things other prisoners have access to. I do not ask for any more, but I will not accept any less . . . and they say we are in protection and one of the worst murders in the prison took place right here in this dormitory. How are we being protected? We are in dormitories with 60 inmates. There are more fights and more disciplinary reports that come out of the protection unit than anywhere else in this prison . . . apparently I will have to be here the rest of my life—I've been on the

board five times to leave, and have been denied," said Grubbs.

Hartman agreed. "We are discriminated against in the sense if we want to go to a stronger environment, to a different housing assignment. You will try and try and try until you become so exhausted, you give up trying. And you will stay in this protection environment until you get accustomed to it and you adjust to it and finally, you make up your mind, f—k it, I'm not even going to try anymore to get out. I have made many personal attempts, and failed."

Both stated that homosexual activity occurs at all areas of the prison, just not in the protection units. "Not everyone in Protection are whores, and not everyone in the stronger general population are men," says Hartman. Grubbs was more emphatic, "I think there's a lot of homosexuals out there. I also think there's a lot of closet doors that need oiling, too."

Being in the protective custody units causes some resentment among those that have to be there, but it does not stop homosexual activity. "I have a good conduct record. I don't mess with drugs. I don't gamble. I'm not promiscuous, even though I'm homosexual," Grubbs said. Hartman was more succinct: "I do not abide by all the rules here. I have sex and I will have sex and everytime I do have sex, I am violating the rules. But, I do respect the security man in the manner of not letting him see me do it. Therefore I am no trouble to him and he's no trouble to me. But if he catches me, he's going to do his job and I am aware of it. But I have more sense than to do it in his face," he said.

Both Hartman and Grubbs see a need for a protective custody environment in prison. Hartman said, "In Angola, and speaking from many years of experience, PC is something that is essential. It is sometimes abused, by both inmates and security. The screening process today is much better than it used to be, but there is still a need for improvement in allowing some people to be re-assigned into the general population once they establish a desire and ability to live and work there."

Grubbs also saw the benefits of PC for some inmates. "Some are here because their crimes are so heinous that even within a prison population they would not be treated very well. I'm talking about people who have hurt children—if those type people were put into population, they probably wouldn't last very long," he described, adding: "This isn't a good place to be at it's worse and this is its worst. For someone whom is not being punished, I don't know why this situation exists."

Recommendations from parish law enforcement and judicial officials that Protective Custody be considered, sometimes accompany a state prisoner sent to Angola. Such is the case of Raymond Woodall, 58, sentenced from Orleans Parish. In a case involving nearly a dozen co-defendants, Woodall received a seventy-five-year sentence as a first-offender, remaining in parish jail confinement for ten years waiting various appeals. He was placed in a protective custody unit upon his arrival in November, 1986.

"There was a tremendous amount of publicity in the case," said Woodall. "The newspapers, television, radio, and it reached the national news level, also, lasting about two months. I was on protective custody for awhile, until the parish did away with it. When I was transferred here, it was probably the parish authorities that brought my case to the prison officials' attention." Woodall says nine of the twelve defendants received prison terms, three are still confined and all the others have been released for some time.

Woodall does not know if there is anything safer about protective custody. "Since I never lived in some other parts of the institution, I would not know. I don't know how it feels. I think I'd feel much better if I had access to more activities. This is a very structured and restrictive atmosphere," he said. "Most of my time is spent writing letters. I tried to leave on the classification board, but it was denied based upon the board's discretion— whatever that means. It was very frustrating, in fact, I have given up on it."

A prisoner who is extra-ordinarily small may also find himself assigned to Protective Custody by the Initial Classification Board. Physical stature is perceived by authorities as a source of potential problems in the world of prisons. Hue Hoang was seventeen years old when he committed an armed robbery and forcible rape in Vermilion Parish in 1985, and when he arrived at the Louisiana State Penitentiary in 1987 with two 23-year concurrent sentences, he was automatically assigned to PC. He is 5-feet, 1-inch tall. At first, he wanted to be relieved of his "protection" status, but has since changed his mind.

"I feel better here because I don't want to get hurt, or lose goodtime. I don't want to take a chance on that. By being small, it would be hard," Hoang told *The Angolite*. Speaking excellent English which he learned in the parish jail by reading magazines and the tutorship of some good-hearted inmates, Hoang said: "I stayed there two years waiting for court and I learned it. I could see I could speak no English, so I started to learn it."

In 1980, when the Communist authorities attempted to conscript Hoang into military service at age 12, his family and others hid him till arrangements were made for him to leave by boat. While at sea, a North Vietnamese gunboat strafed them, killing his cousin who had to be thrown overboard. Picked up by an American freighter 3 days later, Hoang said he was soon on his way to the United States.

"I've had some problems with write-ups at first. I would refuse to work, but I can work if I want to, you know. But, last year I was feeling bad about me being here in prison. I have a problem with my family who is still back there in my country. My parents, 5 sisters and 2 brothers are still there. I was the only one able to escape," he explained, adding that he does get one letter every 6 to 8 months from his sister in Saigon.

"Really, I don't see any difference in the PC unit and the other units. The only difference is they don't have school, no sports and other things like that. If a person tries to keep a good record, not lose no goodtime, you know, I think he should stay here rather than go to the 'strong line,' because if he lives in a strong unit, he has to be ready to hurt somebody or be ready to stab somebody. Here you don't worry about that."

Being "used up," as referenced by David Clifford and others, is a fairly frequent event in the world of prison protective custody. Jumping on and beating up a younger, weaker or smaller inmate in order to get transferred to a different unit, according to those interviewed, is the quickest means to that end. While those assigned to PC units are already, to a degree, considered victims, being further assaulted by fellow PC inmates would certainly seem to transcend

insult to injury.

Thirty-three-year-old Ray Fruge, serving a nine and ten-year sentence from Acadia and St. Landry parishes for the offense of simple burglary, has been assigned to the prison's protective custody unit since his arrival in 1984. "Since I've been here, inmates have used me up a dozen times, just so they can be moved. The last time was three-and-a-half weeks ago," said Fruge. "They used a butt can and beat me in the head. I was taken to the hospital and I fell twice and they had to carry me. I'm still blowing blood out of my nose, but I have a hospital appointment tomorrow. I am going home in just three days and I hope no one jumps on me anymore."

While Fruge is 5-feet, 8-inches tall, he weighs only 100 pounds, an easy mark for most men in prison. "There are different reasons and ways to use a man up in here. If a guy is sent here and wants to leave to follow a whore, or he has enemies, or he can't turn any tricks to earn some income, they'll walk up to you while you're dead asleep, pick up a butt can or mop wringer and knock people's heads off," Fruge explained. "I am small and very quiet and I stay in my corner and people take my kindness for weakness. You can't be too kind to anyone in here. You can't be too generous. The bigger inmates just see you as more vulnerable and will take advantage of you."

Whenever there is a fight in prison, both the aggressor and victim are separated, locked up in administrative lockdown to await disciplinary court proceedings. Fruge says that is the worst part of being jumped on—being locked in a cell without cigarettes or other comfort till the disciplinary court hears the case. "Most of the time the report on me is dismissed, but I've been to the dungeon at

least 12 times for something I never did—
I was just a victim, but I was still
punished. That part isn't right," he says.
"They will jump on me just so they can
get moved back near their lover, someone
to support their habits and see that they
have nice sexy clothes, cigarettes, and
coffee."

Fruge told *The Angolite* the moment
he is released, he will seek a medical test
for AIDS: "That last inmate who jumped
on me [name omitted] is on the list of
those who are HIV-positive and I want to
be sure I didn't get that disease."

Probably the most despised, by both
keepers and the kept, are the informants.
Informants, whether they be real or
perceived, live a very tenuous and
precarious life behind prison walls.
During interviews and searching
information for this story, it was very
difficult to locate an inmate in protective
custody that would be willing to admit or
discuss the matter.

Informants, rats, snitches, whistle-
blowers, stool pigeons—whatever label
applied—are considered to be the lowest of
the lowest by their prisoner peers. An
excellent description is found in *Walls and
Bars*, by Eugene Victor Debs who, while
serving a sentence in the federal Atlanta,
Georgia penitentiary, would run for United
States President from his cell. He was
noted for his efforts at forming unions and
protecting the rights of employees against
unfair wages and conditions.

In 1927, Debs wrote: "Every prison
is infested with that lowest of mortal
creatures—the stool pigeon. In prison
parlance he is known as the 'Rat.' The
stool pigeon seems to be a necessary part
of a prison under club rule. Human
beings ruled by brute force resist, properly
so, at every opportunity, and they must be
spied upon and watched and betrayed by

their own fellow prisoners in order to be
kept in subjection. The stool pigeon is
the silent ally of the guard. He noses
around to see and hear what he can that he
may report what he considers to be to his
advantage, and what may cause those spied
upon serious trouble. The stool pigeon
finds his reward in immunity from
punishment and in promoting his chances
for favorable consideration of his
application for pardon, or parole, or
commutation. This particular subject was
the source of frequent comment among the
prisoners during my term. The stool
pigeon and his encouragement in the
nefarious part he plays is in itself a
reproach to and an indictment of, prison
management. Not for one moment should
such a perverted creature be permitted to
function in a prison. The service he is
permitted to render betrays a condition
which condemns the prison by the very
means it employs as a low and
demoralizing institution."

Forty-six years later, *Walls and Bars*
was reprinted by the Eugene Victor Debs
Foundation and then-President Patrick E.
Gorman would say: "Today probably
more than ever before, eternal vigilance is
the price of our liberty. Beware, therefore,
of wolves in sheep's clothing, bikinis, hot
pants, tails, blue jeans or evening
gowns—or in whatever shape or form they
might come. The Informers have been
with us always . . ."

Whether an actual informer or one
who is perceived to be one by his fellow
prisoners, he is treated the same, with
disdain, distrust, disrespect and sometimes
with violence. Jarrell Frith is a 39-year-
old 3rd offender, serving a 30-year sentence
imposed in St. Martin Parish for the crime
of attempted aggravated rape. The
Tallulah, Louisiana, native was originally
classified to the general population in

1984, but six months later he was assigned protective custody status because his fellow inmates believed him to be a snitch.

"They call me a rat because I work the walk. My job is to clean the office, come and get this and that for the free man, and most of my time at work is spent around the free man," Frith explained. Weighing 122 pounds, 5-feet, 8-inches tall, Frith said, "I can't fight, I've never done that, so now when a person wants to leave here, they use me up. I've been used up about four or five times already."

Frith said that the security employees have called him into the office and told him that his fellow inmates have told the employees he was a 'rat.' "It is just something you cannot escape from, it is passed on and on, year after year. Once the word goes out, it never goes away," said Frith. "All the people who jumped on me are now at Eagle unit so I can't go there. You know, I've seen inmates tell the officer about another inmate, then turn right around and go tell the inmates that he heard someone else telling the officer the information. Then the other guy gets beat up and he didn't know why. This happens a lot here," Frith described.

Most prison administrators readily admit that the "homosexual" and "snitch" games played in prison are two main sources of management problems. Correctional officers generally encourage prisoners to inform—perhaps the single largest source of information/intelligence for prison security officials. Though informing is encouraged by many, these same correctional employees tend to despise and loathe informants. Probably the best description of the "snitch game" and its use behind prison walls is found in the Report of the Attorney General following the February 1-3, 1980, riot at

the Penitentiary of New Mexico, a finding that was mandated by the state legislature:

"The first detrimental side effect of direct solicitation of information through the snitch game was to diminish the reliability of information," said the report. "Inmates report that writing a 'kite' [a secret note passed to prison staff] became more common.   In fact, it was a convenient way to take revenge on another inmate because the disciplinary committee would use the kite, whether true or not, as 'confidential information' against the targeted inmate.   On other occasions, guards would threaten inmates with harassment or disciplinary actions if the inmates refused to provide information on other inmates' conduct. To avoid these threats, some inmates would say anything, whether true or not. With such a system of information gathering, it was difficult to judge the reliability of information being received by the inmates. Reliable information about potential escapes or disturbances was mixed in with totally unreliable information. With no means to distinguish the two, it became increasingly difficult for administrators to take appropriate action.

"The second detrimental side effect of the snitch game," the Attorney General's Report stated, "was to create suspicion and antagonism among the inmates. 'You can't even trust your old friends,' was a sentiment voiced by several inmates. Inmate opinions of snitches included this often-repeated characterization: 'It's just like in a war. You're all on the same damn side. It's us (the inmates) against them (the guards.)' And it's the same mentality. If you cross to the other side, you're no more, no less than a traitor or a spy."

As the report went on to illustrate, fourteen of the inmates housed in the New

Mexico prison Cell Block-4, the Protective Custody Unit, were brutally murdered as rioters used acetyline torches, crowbars and sledge hammers to enter the security area. Those labelled as snitches were decapitated, had metal bars run through their heads from ear to ear, genitals were burned off before being beaten and stabbed to death, and some were hanged inside the protective cells they believed were secure havens.

The conditions of life within the Protective Custody Units make up the largest consistent complaint expressed by those assigned to it. Because of the more restrictive and isolated environment, prisoners within PC at the Louisiana State Penitentiary have little or no social activities, organized sports and recreation, and they are prohibited from any academic or vocational training despite a great number of them being relegated to protection status for many years.

"The conditions here at Magnolia are sub-standard," said David Clifford, serving a twenty-year sentence for armed robbery from Orleans Parish. "Magnolia is traditionally, ever since Cell Block-B closed in 1981, been shut-off from the mainstream of prison life and isolated. They feel they don't have to do anything for Magnolia. They put all the whores here so they can keep an eye on them and keep them separated from the rest of the population, and they are weak, so what are they going to do?"

Clifford, 32, not only confirmed to the Initial Classification Board in 1985 he had a prior federal prison escape, he also admitted that he was bi-sexual. He was then assigned to a Cell Block (Line 36), one of Angola's protection units, and later transferred to Magnolia. "All I do is run the yard, do some legal work and read. That is all there is to do. There's no intra-

mural sports activities and there is no sports equipment at all, other than one basketball, football or a volleyball for the entire unit. I am familiar with the federal guidelines regarding protection units and the rulings handed down by the courts which say that 'just because a person opts for protection, it does not mean they have to be deprived of the same things that the general population has.' In effect," Clifford continued, "we are being punished for opting for protection. If you are weak and can't live anywhere else, they are going to send you to a place that has sub-standard conditions and you are going to have to stay there."

Efforts to enhance social activities and creature comforts in the world of prison protection units is a self-claimed project Clifford has undertaken. "I have filed numerous ARP's [Administrative Remedy Procedures] regarding conditions here. We also don't have any representative on the Inmate Welfare Fund which we contribute to. I am always told, 'If you don't like it, leave. If you don't like it, get out of protection.' Well, there are only two ways to get out of protection, I guess. I can go on the classification board after doing 90-days without a write-up and tell them I want to go some place 'Strong.' That is one way. Usually, here in Magnolia, if you have never been Strong, like in my case, they're going to give me three more months. Betting on the Board that I will not be able to give them three more months without a write-up, already six months has went by. The second way is that I can start fighting, regularly, punching someone down and use somebody up. Like I can get in a fight tonight, and they send me to Eagle, I get in a fight there and go before the Board and tell them I can't take the 'weak' lines no more—send me someplace Strong. If I cause enough chaos within the weak environment, especially if I have created enemies because of fights, then I will be moved out of protection," he explained.

"But, I chose not to do this and keep out of trouble. The problem here is when I do chose to go someplace Strong, I will be forced into making a showing. The general population knows that I have been in Magnolia a long time and they are going to assume I am a whore and someone is going to try me somewhere down the line. Then, I am going to have to react in an extremely hostile way to show the general population I am, or can be, strong. Hell, I prefer not to be placed in this position. It shouldn't have to be necessary."

The problems created by Protective Custody scenarios are real and they are expensive. In a managerial sense, PC inmates must be kept separated and safe within the limited parameters of overcrowded conditions and the law. The cost of operating these special units is greater than managing routine prisoner housing—it takes an officer to escort every protective custody inmate whenever he is required to go, to eat, to a dental appointment, prison visiting room, or to his work assignment. Unable to participate in routine social activities, self-help organizations, vocational and academic programs, PC inmates have become a peculiar class of prisoner with distinct needs. As every prison bed is filled, the ability to transfer the rising number of cases becomes even more restricted.

"We have situations," says Christian, "where an inmate has been here five years. He's utilized the 'check out' procedure saying that so-and-so was an enemy. He would be moved. Over a period of time he keeps moving. He's been to the main

prison, Camp D, Camp A and Camp C. He soon runs out of places to go. This is very real and it is happening today."

There is a view by some correctional professionals that instead of separating or isolating prisoners who request protection, the aggressor or predatory inmate should be locked up. Robin Moses, program manager at Washington State Penitentiary (Walla Walla), told *Compendium*, "We lock up the victim because we can prove he's the victim. We need just about the same amount of proof (to discipline an assailant in here) as a police officer arresting somebody on the street, except in prison you don't find witnesses very much because they know if they testify, they'll be dead. That limits us in what we can prove."

Christian agreed. "It is easier and it is cheaper to protect the victim than it is to try and chase down everybody and put them somewhere else, because an inmate might have a 3-page protection review showing as many as sixty people's names as enemies. From a fiscal as well as a practical point of view, it's easier to move one inmate than it is to lockup 60 inmates. That would be absolutely unmanageable," he explained.

Other prison experts believe that the protective custody classification should be totally eliminated. When *Compendium* interviewed Warden Gerald Cook of the Utah State Prison in Draper, he said that PC statistics were no longer maintained, instead placing protection cases in administrative lockdown. "We do not have as many inmates gravitating towards a protective unit. Many don't want to live in the rather austere environment," he added. By using the lockdown status, the freedom of inmate movement was significantly reduced and inmates could also be there for disciplinary or classification reasons as well as because they consider themselves in danger. What the Utah warden did was run a single unit, not for protection, but as a single form of security which satisfied several needs.

Cook told *Compendium* that such inmates were allowed out of their cells in compatible groups of ten which, after a time, reduced them from being a distinct category and as easily identified. Eventually, he said, they could be moved back into the mainstream population with little or no stigma attached.

The State of Montana, at one time having the highest protective custody percentage in the nation, reduced its PC population from 200 to 12 in just one year. Previously, Montana prison officials granted protection to inmates upon demand for it. Tom Forsyth, classification officer, told *Compendium* they now interview inmates to find out what the problems are and work out such matters such as gambling debts with both prisoners. "When you interview the people," said Forsyth, "nine out of 10 times they say, 'Sure, he owes me money, but I don't care when he pays me back.' Plus, we put the other inmate on notice, 'nothing better happen to him, or we'll go after you.' He becomes the protector in a weird sense," he added.

The length of stay for prisoners relegated to Protective Custody status differs, depending on the reason for the classification. Time spent in PC also significantly differs according to geographical areas and the diverse correctional philosophies. According to ACA, the typical inmate's stay in protective custody is from two-to-five times longer than his counterpart in administrative segregation or disciplinary detention.

Some Angola prisoners have been in

a protective custody environment as long as seven years—a few as long as nine years—almost fifteen times longer than the national average in both state and federal correctional facilities. A close look at the protection process used at Angola indicates there are numerous ways for an inmate to be assigned/classified to a protection unit, but only two in which he can gain release from it. One is by way of an approved request which is reviewed every 90 days. The other is a disapproved fashion—causing trouble and physically assaulting the weaker inmates already on PC, thus assuring removal through the disciplinary process.

There are some inmates who agree with the system utilized in other Louisiana penal facilities as well as the process in other states where, if a man can sign himself into protection, there should also be a process where he can sign himself out (a waiver or release of liability). Such a process is not used at the Louisiana State Penitentiary.

"I agree such a process could be used here," said Main Prison Assistant Security Supervisor, Lieut. Colonel Fulton Rabalais, "but it's not really necessary because you have boards that meet every 90 days anyway." A seasoned employee with 17 years experience in prison security, Rabalais believes that not all inmates who request protection need actually be placed in a protection unit. "I feel a lot of times that an inmate doesn't have to go to Magnolia, Eagle or to Cellblock C. They could easily be separated by moving them to another medium security area. My point is that an inmate who needs to leave a medium security area at the main prison could be transferred to a medium security area at Camp C, Camp D, Camp A or Camp H and still achieve a goal of protection because the inmate has been separated from the problem which bothered him," Rabalais explained.

Rabalais said this also reduces the probability of a stronger inmate being actually assigned to the weaker environment of a protection unit—where many of the stronger prisoners object being associated with. "Eliminating the harder convicts from those units, in the long run, reduces the number of problems you have there," he said.

Asked why some prisoners can't get out of protective custody when they go ninety days without a disciplinary report, Rabalais stated: "That's not necessarily true. He must live down what he's done. Sometimes his record shows many disciplinary reports and a history of being a behavioral problem and a particular board chairman may want to see if this guy has had a real change of attitude or conduct. With a fair number of cases, it is hard to believe that they existed three months without a report."

Another ranking Angola security official, familiar with the protection "paperwork trail" and the time-consuming efforts required to ensure a safe review of inmate(s') records, said the trek is a long one, touching upon nearly every department in the prison.

Once a prisoner decides to seek protection, he approaches any employee making it known. The matter is then referred to the Yard Supervisor who generally initiates the questions necessary for the Protection Form (why and who is protection needed from). The Shift Supervisor, generally a security major, reviews the form and passes it along to the disciplinary office where the case is logged-in before it is sent to the classification department (charged with screening the record for all possible

enemies). When the record is screened, it is forwarded to the prison control center where updated locations are noted on all potential enemies documented by classification. At this point the paperwork is returned to the disciplinary office for scheduling of a hearing, and the entire case and file handed over to a hearing officer (a security major or above) who will make an assessment of all data gathered and issue a disposition transferring the prisoner to a safe housing area.

"Protective Custody is not going to go away," said Angola's Christian, "and with our cell space being used for the more violent, aggressive and problematic inmates, we must operate within the limitations of the physical plant—mostly dormitories. I think we are doing all that we can right now. I would like to see these cases and information entered on computer so it can be called-up quicker, cutting down the many man hours spent doing protection reviews. It would speed the process from 2-to-3 hours down to just a matter of minutes."

RECOMMENDATIONS FOR ADMINISTRATION OF "PROTECTIVE CUSTODY" UNITS, WHICH HAVE BEEN ISSUED BY THE AMERICAN CORRECTIONAL ASSOCIATION, ARE CAPSULIZED, AS FOLLOWS:

1. MINIMIZE PC USE WHEN POSSIBLE: The use of PC should be minimized or even eliminated if possible. Innovative programs designed to deter potential inmates from that option and to demonstrate

the ability to safely transfer current PC inmates into a less restrictive setting should be encouraged.

2. WHERE USED, PROVIDE AS MUCH SEPARATION AS PRACTICAL: Agencies or institutions that are unable to provide totally separate PC units should provide as much separation as possible and use many of the programmatic suggestions [of ACA].

3. LEGAL ADVICE: A thorough legal analysis should be prepared for each jurisdiction, outlining appropriate safeguards to assist correctional administrators deciding whether or not to use PC.

4. PROGRAM DEVELOPMENT: Program activities available to the general population should be available to PC inmates. Because research has indicated that outdoor recreation and non-orderly work opportunities are available less often than most other programs in PC units, special attention should be directed to these two programs.

5. TRAINING: Specialized staff training programs relating to the problems of the PC inmate and the operation of a PC unit must be designed and implemented.

6. LOCATION: PC units should be separate from Administrative Segregation and Disciplinary Detention.

7. PHYSICAL PLANT STANDARDS: PC unit cells should be modified or constructed so that space and other factors are consistent with ACA standards. This is especially important for PC inmates, due to their typically lengthy commitment to the unit. Because of the recency of the tremendous increase in need for protective custody, most institutions are modifying existing facilities to accomodate PC needs.

8. ACA STANDARDS: ACA policy guidelines distinguishing Administrative Segregation, Disciplinary Detention and Protective Custody status should be strictly followed.

9. RESEARCH AND DATA COLLECTION: Criminal justice data collection agencies should include PC status as a separate item to assist and encourage future studies in this area. Research is especially critical because of the recent nature of PC unit needs and population increases.

10. SEPARATION OF INMATES WITHIN THE UNIT: When establishing a PC unit, consideration should be given to the possible need for dividing PC inmates into appropriate groups (i.e., state witnesses, police officers, assault victims, and institutional informants). In addition, other forms of separation might be considered as PC units of quite different design continue to evolve. One example would be differentiating the level of PC needs. This might be accomplished through a waiver system, with one level of PC having total separation, while the level signing waivers would be permitted some movement without escort, and specified program participation with the general population.

11. VERIFICATION OF INFORMA-
    TION: Criteria for placement in a PC
    unit should be clearly defined. Verifi-
    cation of allegations and statements
    should be thorough and in some
    jurisdictions, the use of a polygraph
    may be authorized within the limits
    allowed by statute.

18

EDUCATING THE EDUCATED

by Lane Nelson

Dressed like a woman, Calvin Clark cruised the streets of New Orleans night after night in search of drugs and a good time. To have either he needed money, for which he often prostituted himself. One evening in 1981 Clark ran across a man scouting the French Quarter for some action. Clark offered himself for a price, but once the man discovered Clark's true identity he refused to pay up. So Clark robbed him. Later, he was arrested, charged and convicted of armed robbery. The sentencing judge was inclined to be lenient because of Clark's part-time role as police informant, but also had to consider his repeat offender status. He sentenced Clark to 60 years at hard labor.

But hard labor was not in Clark's vocabulary. He arrived at Angola in 1982 and continued to masquerade as a woman—wearing bikini underwear, make-up, and as much womanly garb as he could get away with. His feminine demeanor attracted many prisoners who gave him commissary items and drugs in exchange for sex. Clark spent days of leisure in this all-male institution. Now those leisurely days are gone for good. Calvin Clark recently died an AIDS-related death.

Angola prisoners remember Clark as a healthy looking galboy, swishing up and down the Walk with a care-free attitude. On his death bed his appearance was disturbing. Frightening. He was unrecognizable as the same Clark. Those who have never witnessed someone in the latter stages of AIDS have never seen true misery.

It is an excruciating sight that inspires horror.

Clark had no one on the outside who cared enough about him to claim his body, so he received a pauper's burial at the hands of his fellow prisoners and at the expense of the state. He came to prison a healthy energetic young man fully expecting to one day be released. Now his body is entombed in the soil of Angola for eternity. It is anybody's guess how many HIV-infected prisoners he left behind, and how many of them are continuing to spread the disease.

According to information from corrections headquarters, 76 Angola prisoners were HIV-positive as of October 1994. Angola infection control coordinator Shannon Hagar, RN, MPH, admits the count is deceptive. "We don't do mandatory testing at Angola, so we don't really know the full impact of the virus. But my guess is it's much more than 76." Her guess aligns with national findings. The number of HIV-infected prisoners in the nation's penal systems is dramatically increasing. According to Abt Associates, a Cambridge, Massachusetts research firm, the AIDS incidence rate in prisons and jails between 1990 and 1993 was approximately 10 times higher than in the population at large. The firm reported 3,474 inmates died of AIDS during that period. *Corrections Compendium*, a national journal for penal professionals, discovered that during 1989-93, "reported AIDS cases among inmates increased more than 600 percent."

AIDS may be on the verge of solving the problem of prison overcrowding. But as death creeps through the cellblocks, it

*Appeared in *The Angolite*, November/December 1994, 44-53. Reprinted with permission.

casts a shadow beyond the walls. The general public must deal with thousands of HIV-infected prisoners who will be released before they die; and the public must supply tax dollars to federal and state governments to cover medical care for HIV-positive prisoners who are not released.

Community health-care organizations have taken notice. They know they have to coordinate with prison officials or their efforts to slow the spread of the disease among the general public will be in vain. But they find the grip slippery when they join hands with corrections authorities. Reaching into an isolated and unfamiliar world, community based health people are mystified by secretive prison routines. In their world they can distribute condoms, teach safe-sex classes and operate needle-exchange programs. Condoms and needles are contraband in prison, and corrections administrators view safe-sex classes as encouragement for illicit behavior. What's left, then, for the million and a half inmates in the nation's jails and prisons? Education, and education alone.

Hagar, the employees of Angola's medical unit, and the inmate Peer Education Team hosted a symposium to stress the importance of PJDS education within the penal system. Hailed as the first of its kind in the nation, the meeting brought together more than 130 health-care professionals, law enforcement officers, prison officials, inmates and others directly concerned with the AIDS epidemic. Attendees included Louisiana's corrections chief Richard L. Stalder, Angola Warden John Whitley, Dr. Louise McFarland, Megan Foley of the Centers for Disease Control in Atlanta, James Hubbard, an epidemiologist with the Office of Public Health, Anne Jones from Governor Edwin Edward's office, Mike

Rouche, West Baton Rouge Parish Sheriff's Office, David Utter, attorney for the Louisiana Crisis Assistance Center, and Sally McKissack, criminal justice instructor at USL. It was a conference intended to educate the educated about AIDS in prison.

"Education is a first step in what we hope will help the slowing and prevention of this deadly disease," said Warden Whitley, without whose support the symposium could not have occurred. "We hope everyone will come away with a greater understanding of how this disease impacts people incarcerated in our prison system."

The inmate Peer Education Team developed from the efforts of Bill Crawford, an AIDS education activist. "A number of years ago as a college professor," Crawford told the audience, "I realized college students deal better with college students than administrators or their elders do. If we were going to be effective with HIV/AIDS education in the prison setting, prisoners themselves had to carry the message. I needed somebody to translate my message into 'prisonese.' Prisoners talking to prisoners in terminology that will be understood. That's what peer education is all about." The Centers for Disease Control also believe that for counseling to be effective it must be linguistically specific.

Crawford began conducting AIDS seminars at Angola in 1993, attended by more than 40 prisoners—most of them inmate counsel substitutes who have wide access to the prison population. From this group came the four prisoners who comprise Angola's Peer Education Team: Walter Burnette, Theortic Givens, Andrew Joseph and George Witherspoon. Their volunteer work includes talking to groups of new inmates who enter Angola weekly and, occasionally, speaking to health-care gatherings outside the prison.

Because Crawford is not a prison employee, the team needed an "inside sponsor." In stepped Shannon Hagar. Considered the fifth member of the team, she continually advises them and they in turn relay it to the inmate population. "They educate me about prison life as much as I educate them," Hagar said. She also is responsible for TB education, testing and evaluation in Angola, a potentially explosive problem she takes very seriously. "TB and AIDS go hand in hand," Hagar explained, "and any prison system not carefully monitoring these diseases is courting disaster. We already see a near TB epidemic in the New York prison system, where the HIV-infection rate is high.

"Seventy-three percent of inmates nationwide who tested HIV-positive were asymptomatic. They had no symptoms at all," Hagar continued. "That's scary, especially in relation to TB." If a person feels all right, he's not going to the doctor. If that person is HIV-positive and comes in contact with TB, it will latch onto him like a leech, quickly overpower this weakened immune system, and kill him.

Three HIV-positive prisoners spoke at the symposium: David Baptiste and Michael Reedy from Angola, and Patricia Adair from the women's prison near Baton Rouge. "I used to say why me? Why not her, or him, or them," Adair told the audience. "I've stopped saying all that now. I was stripped of my life and I don't think it was my fault, but I've learned to deal with it." Young and beautiful, Adair looks as if she just stepped out of a *Cosmopolitan* perfume ad. She first tested positive while in prison in 1990 and was subjected to a gauntlet of verbal abuse and

ridicule. "It's the ignorance of inmates and security," she explained. "Sometimes I would pass a group of ladies and hear, 'Look at her. Look how pretty she is. Too bad she's dying.' Then they'd start laughing. I'd run to my room and cry." She now finds solace and strength with a small mutual-support group of HIV-infected female inmates.

Robin Noel, a member of that group, spoke up. "There are many ladies in our institution who are HIV-positive and actually participating in homosexual activities and not telling their partner." Noel advocates mandatory testing in prison and wants the results made public. "To know someone has the virus gives them the choice," she said. "But not to know is murder. I understand confidentiality and privacy, but when something like this is happening I think the prisons should do something."

Mandatory testing is controversial. No federal or state law requires an across-the-board mandatory AIDS testing program in or out of prison. "If we had mandatory testing," said corrections head Richard Stalder, "as we do for TB, we would probably identify people who want to start on regimes of medication sooner. But there are legitimate privacy issues at stake. We have many people who do not want to be tested."

Michael Reedy, one of the HIV-positive inmate panel participants, questioned Stalder's concern about inmate privacy. "If they don't want to test everyone because it's too expensive, then they should just say that. Don't tell me it's because they're so worried about my right to privacy."

Routine TB and STD (sexually transmitted disease) screening is done on all new prisoners. Inmates are under constant surveillance, even while showering or defecating, and subject to routine pat-downs, property searches, urine testing and body cavity strip-searches. Privacy in prison is rare.

Testing, medication and treatment of HIV-infected is expensive. Sally McKissack, USL criminal-justice instructor and former head of the state pardon board, is familiar with Louisiana's prison system. She pointed out to the group that, depending on whose study you read, it costs $27 to $31 a day to confine a healthy inmate. That figure triples for the geriatric prisoner housed in a prison clinic. "Can we assume it would be more than $90 a day for an AIDS patient?" she asked.

"We don't have any statistical information right now to determine how much it costs in Angola," replied prison physician Robert Barnes. However, a recent article he read stated it cost $300,000 for an AIDS inmate in New York to be handled from beginning to end.

If the ballpark figure of $300,000 is multiplied by Angola's 76 known HIV-infected prisoners, Louisiana taxpayers would shoulder a total cost of $22,800,000 for the medical care of just these few prisoners until they die. If for no other reason, reducing the spread of AIDS in prison seems a fiscally responsible thing to do. "We've got to get the statistics out there," one health-care worker told the audience. "We've got to be active in getting this information to the legislatures and not shut up. We have to hit people in the pockets for them to listen."

Michael Reedy, an HIV-positive prisoner who favors mandatory prison AIDS testing, related his personal story. Originally condemned to death in 1971 for a violent crime spree committed when he was 17, a sentence later reduced to natural life, Reedy tested positive for HIV in

1991. "They gave me the death sentence again, was my first thought," he said. "I hated everybody and everything. I did what I wanted, when I wanted and how I wanted, and to hell with anybody that didn't like it."

It wasn't until he met Angola social worker Kathryn Broussard that his rage subsided. "She encouraged me to get into different things, like keeping a journal," said Reedy. "That helped. Instead of acting out my anger and frustration, I learned to write it down."

After a bout with the flu in 1992, Reedy's T-cell count fell to 14 and his weight dropped to 118 pounds. Fellow inmates told him he wouldn't live to see 1993. Declining health and negative vibes reignited his anger. "I became worse than before," he said. "Something needed to be done, so I went back to Ms. Kathryn and said I have to be isolated from the rest of the prison population."

With her recommendation, security officials approved Reedy's transfer to a cell in the Angola Clinical Services Unit, where mentally ill inmates are confined. Isolation was exactly what Reedy needed. He used the time to exercise, learn, rest and reflect. "I studied everything I could get about the immune system, T-cells, proper dieting, proper rest, and I started putting everything together," he said. "Nine months later I walked out of there with a T-cell count of 989, which has held steady to this day. I weighed 184 pounds and was in better shape than when they told me I was infected."

In Alabama or Mississippi, Reedy would not have walked out of isolation at his bidding. Those are the only two states that mandatorily segregate all known HIV-positive prisoners. "Louisiana, as with most other states, has a case-by-case review to determine if an HIV-positive prisoner needs to be removed from the general population," said inmate peer educator Walter Burnette. He explained that the decision is determined by the health of the individual—whether he requires extensive medical care that requires placement in a ward in the prison clinic. Burnette, introduced as the best writ writer in Angola, laced technical talk about the legal rights of HIV-positive inmates with a pitch for effective education. "Intensive education is the only method of preventing transmission," he said. "Nothing else works. Jails and prisons are high-risk areas. It is extremely difficult, nearly impossible, for health and correctional officials to effectively present the intensive education needed, without Peer Educators."

Inmate David Baptiste has had a T-cell count of 26 or below since 1991. A panel participant, he told the audience, "My T-cell count has been down to 5. I'm called the 'walking miracle.'" In 1993, Baptiste played in Angola's basketball league and was voted defensive player of the year. Last season, averaging 32 points a game, he was well on his way to another achievement award when the rigors of the court took their toll and he had to stop playing. He continues to fight the virus with the same intensity he displayed on the court. "I refuse to die!" he said. "And I find it strange that those who don't have the disease are scared of me. I don't see why. You are more of a threat to me than I am to you. " Baptiste pointed out that a healthy prisoner cannot catch HIV except through high-risk behavior, while a common cold that might inconvenience a healthy prisoner could be fatal to an HIV patient.

Mental strength and positive attitude are keys to daily survival, Baptiste claims. He and Reedy refuse to take AZT, the medicine commonly prescribed for HIV patients. AZT, according to Angola's Dr. Barnes, prolongs the life of an HIV patient for a year or more. Baptiste and Reedy are not convinced. "I'm a firm believer that the body is made to heal itself," said Reedy, "and if given the opportunity, and with a positive attitude, it will do just that." A positive attitude may also help to combat the discrimination HIV-prisoners face.

Once-rampant discrimination in the free world toward HIV-infected people has slackened due to increasing education and, ironically, the spread of the virus outside the gay and drug-abusing sectors of the population. Not so in prison. "It's lack of education, " said inmate peer educator George Witherspoon. "People fear what they don't understand."

Mike Rouche of the West Baton Rouge Parish Sheriff's Office echoed the results of several regional surveys that show HIV discrimination in the correctional system is across the board. "Inmates don't want to be associated with HIV-prisoners," he said. "And correctional officers are reluctant to handle them because they fear the spread of AIDS."

Witherspoon reiterated the consequences of ignorance. "Because of lack of education, prisoners and staff are fearful. Prisoners admit that their fear leads to acts of rejection, verbal abuse and, in some cases, incidents of violence."

One of the more heated discussions at the conference concerned condoms. "Prevention programs used on the streets—condom distribution, needle exchange programs, safe-sex methods—are not permitted in most prisons, and are certainly not permitted here," Hagar told the group. "Yet, these are the facts folks: you can't lock somebody up and expect their sex drive to die. It doesn't work that way. Communication is absolutely critical among all factions of corrections, health-care providers, community based organization and public health officials. We must begin to build bridges now. We must begin to communicate with each other."

Hagar urged the audience to focus on preventive measures that can be pursued, rather than those which cannot. Some did not swallow the restrictions easily. They had the greatest trouble accepting the notion of condoms as contraband. City jails in New York, Philadelphia, San Francisco and Washington DC, as well as state prisons in Vermont and Mississippi, have condom distribution programs for prisoners. Many activist groups, such as People of Color Against AIDS Network, believe that condom distribution should penetrate prison gates.

"If they can't use condoms, where is the prevention?" asked someone from the audience. Hagar repeated the need to focus on education, that it's nearly all there is in Louisiana to combat AIDS/HIV behind bars.

"What I see is a state of insanity," countered ACLU attorney Joe Cook. "We need to do some things differently. I look back here in the cashier area of this [visiting] room and see you can put cigarettes in an inmate's account. We can buy cigarettes for the inmates, which is a known carcinogen that kills people, but we can't hand out condoms which save people's lives. I wish someone from administration would address that!" He sat down to rousing applause.

"I just want you to think of other things besides the use of condoms in prisons," replied Hunt Correctional Center social worker Carol Gravois. "I heard one of the inmates talking about animalistic desires. We need to consider we're not

animals and that we have ways other than sexual intercourse to relieve our sexual urges, and I encourage that in certain ways."

Inmate peer educator and panel participant Andrew Joseph is a 63-year-old, third-offender with 16 years served on a life sentence. "The first time I was here," he told the audience, "I had to defend myself against all the older prisoners who wanted to make a galboy out of me. The second time around I was the one making galboys out of younger prisoners. This time I've changed my attitude about a lot of things." Joseph is involved with Angola's Christian community, and is a disk jockey at KLSP, the prison's radio station, where he is known as "Reverend A.J."

"A lot of people would prefer to die having their fun," Joseph continued, "rather than lay here knowing they will never get out. With no family, no friends, just prison, they get off into homosexual activity. Some even know their sex partners are HIV-positive. Perhaps in their thinking this may be the best way out for them. In turn, they pass the virus to short-timers coming through, and those short-timers go back into society—where you live—adding to an already devastating problem. There is no program here to suppress sexual desires. Until there is, there will be illicit sex, there will be people getting AIDS, and many of them will be coming out to the streets with it."

Inmate peer educator and panel participant Theortic Givens spoke of the need for an HIV-prisoner pre-release program. "It's in the works," he said. "Once it is approved, we will ask to set up similar programs in other prisons and parish jails. We need the community's help. By networking, we can establish a better quality of life for those persons and close the gap between HIV in the free world and HIV in prison."

The Angola Drama Club closed out the all-day conference with a realistic prison skit, *The Enemy Within,* which illustrated the needless spread of AIDS due to lack of education. Afterwards, Drama Club President Gary Tyler said, "When we took on the project, we quickly found out we were handicapped. We didn't know enough about the subject. We needed to be educated in order to present an effective and dramatic play. Bill Crawford and Shannon Hagar helped us with our education, which can now be used when we perform for other groups."

The future after the conference looks brighter. Hagar expects health-care organizations to enhance education and prevention programs for the state's prisons and jails. "It was an overwhelming success," she said, "more successful than any of us anticipated." Hagar bases this, in part, on the 130 evaluation sheets filled out by attendees.

"A lot of the health-care people had no idea what the AIDS problem is like in prison," she said. "They were shocked to discover condoms can't be passed out and safe-sex classes can't be taught. They didn't realize the expense involved in treating HIV-infected inmates, and most were not aware of the rising infection rate."

In addition to education, Hagar is pushing for an increase in self-help programs. "You build up self-esteem in a person, improve his lot in life, so to speak, and that person will be more apt to pursue positive endeavors and stay away from high-risk activities."

As a result of the conference, Hagar was invited to speak at the Centers for Disease Control. The World Health Organization in Geneva, Switzerland asked for her help in their effort to further AIDS education in the western hemisphere. And the Angola Peer Education Team now has a sixth member, Michael Reedy, due to the attitude and knowledge he displayed at the symposium. The Team was invited to address the 1995 National AIDS Conference in New Orleans.

"People are already contacting me with suggestions for another conference next year," said Hagar. "I'm really amazed at the results." Yet, Hagar and the others know the symposium was but a small step into a closed, dark, restrictive and high-risk environment.

19

AGES

by Douglas Dennis

The Louisiana State Penitentiary at Angola was the only prison in the state not so very long ago. Young, old, healthy, sick, male and female—all felons went to the old plantation to pay their debt to society. Their terms were short and hard. Even murderers seldom stayed more than ten years, then were released and, for the most part, sinned no more.

But in the 1970s the crime rate rose and a punitive fever swept the land. Louisiana reacted by erecting eleven new prisons and filling them with young felons who serve short sentences, then go on for the most part to sin no more. Angola, however, evolved into a maximum-security bastille housing the violent and those committed to criminal careers. They are imprisoned for the duration, until they grow old and die.

Of its 4,600 prisoners, 2,400 are lifers, and hundreds more have sentences so long they are called "practical lifers." 2,429 prisoners are 35 or older. The average age is 37, and rising. As of March 15, 1994, Angola held only 34 prisoners under age 20. Twenty-five are 19 years old, 8 are 18, and one is 17.

Anthony "Knuckles" Jones, at 17, has the current distinction of being the youngest Angolan. He has an extensive juvenile record that includes violence, and a brand-new second-degree murder conviction for killing a woman in a drug deal gone bad. Jones personifies the American nightmare.

On January 30, 1993, a white car slowly cruised the noon-time streets of a blue-collar black Baton Rouge neighborhood called Mall City, according to media reports and court records, until it was flagged down by three young black men. Hiawatha Dewayne Cosby, 20, ran up to the passenger side as the car stopped. Eric "Ugly" Jackson, 17, and Jones, then 16, went to the driver's window. At the wheel sat a 30-year-old white woman, five months pregnant, who wanted $20 worth of cocaine. Someone told Jones not to sell to her because she had previously driven off without paying. He warned that he'd "unload on her" if she tried it again. Cosby saw her wallet was empty and, as she "slowly" pulled away, he picked up an empty beer bottle and shattered the passenger window. Jones, at the same time, reportedly shot her in the left arm and shoulder with a .25 caliber pistol. One bullet pierced her heart. She drove a block or so, pulled into a parking lot, and bled to death behind the wheel.

Concerned Mall City residents quickly volunteered information that resulted in the arrest of all three youths. Jones, a high-school freshman, was taken into custody as he stepped off a school bus. In typical fashion, the district attorney's office cut deals with Cosby and Jackson, rewarding them with less punishment for their testimony against Jones.

Jones, according to evidence introduced during his trial, was a member of a small neighborhood gang called the "Mall City Posse," had been in numerous fights and disturbances in the area and, in short, was apparently regarded by local residents as something of a terror. Cosby testified that Jones was the shooter. Others swore they had seen Jones with a gun and heard him say he had shot the woman.

*Appeared in *The Angolite*, March/April 1994, 22-27. Reprinted with permission.

Jackson was not called to testify. Jones did take the stand to deny, as he had from the moment of arrest, any involvement in the crime. He said he didn't sell dope, and didn't shoot anybody. Despite his denials, it took the jury only two hours to find him guilty. On September 15, 1993, Judge Bonnie Jackson sentenced him to prison for life. By contrast, Cosby and Jackson in December pleaded guilty to manslaughter; each was sentenced to only two years in the local jail and "a lengthy period of probation."

In the not too distant past, a black man who killed a white woman in the South (a pregnant one at that) would have been lucky to make it to the jailhouse. Even in these more enlightened and tolerant times, a person accused of black-on-white murder can still expect a one-way ride to death row on the conviction express. In that context, many would consider Jones fortunate not to have been convicted of first-degree murder, a capital offense. Others, with first-hand knowledge of what serving a lifetime in prison really means, would not be so sure.

On January 31, 1994, a year and a day after the Mall City killing, Jones, 17, arrived at Angola. He was its youngest inmate. Nothing in his past had prepared him for Angola. The Initial Classification Board assigned him to extended lockdown (standard placement for young longtermers who never before have been in prison), where he would live 23 hours a day in a cell and be reviewed in three months for release to a lesser custody status. Prison officials closely observe them to see how they adjust. Or don't.

Tracking Jones for this story, *The Angolite* found him locked in the "dungeon" for an alleged verbal altercation with a guard. Though somewhat upset at his temporary disciplinary predicament—"I

wanta get outta here, man, I don't like this here, man, people acting all funny"—and despite his intimidating size (6'2" tall and 180 pounds), Jones didn't conform to the "terror" image held by his former neighbors. He appeared lost and defensive, with little understanding of the world in which he had been cast to spend the rest of his life.

Every "fresh-fish" longtermer goes through denial, a period of inability or unreadiness to grasp the reality of his situation. Jones's conviction is being appealed, and he believes with a desperate and unquestioning faith that he'll somehow be rescued and return to his neighborhood, the only world he's ever really known. When asked how long he thought he'd stay in prison, he responded, "I don't know. Hard to say. Some of these people been up here all these years and, man, I don't know.... Hope it be tomorrow. Today!"

His upbringing is like that of many at Angola. Jones was reared by his grandmother. "My mama had died when I was eight years old," he explained. "My daddy just like most fathers, man, strike out. Gone. I don't got no father." He spent half his teen years with one foot in school and the other on the streets. Now he's in prison, for life.

Jones has heard his share of Angola horror stories. The farm lines, for instance: he dreads the prospect. "You stay out there in that field a couple years, too," he said, indignation and a trace of fear in his voice. "I ain't suppose to be doin' this work, and all this here. I should be at home. These people ain't tryin' to help me, man, but kill me out there in that farm. You don't supposed to have it good, and all that there, man, but I ain't did nothin'."

Even now, despite the evidence that

convicted him, Jones maintains his innocence. "Everybody thinkin' I killed somebody," he said. "And I ain't killed nobody." Jones, like many in prison, holds a low opinion of his trial defense attorney: "Oh, man, he was weak. He didn't really object to anything. He ain't tried his best."

With aggressive representation, Jones thinks he would not have been convicted of murder. His prosecutor told the jury this case was "about America's great tragedy, its problem in dealing with drugs." And so it was. The dead woman, who had a degree in interior decorating from LSU, was addicted, unmarried, pregnant, and living with her parents. She borrowed her father's car to go "buy some groceries," instead driving to a black neighborhood where she had no legitimate business being in order to again rip-off cocaine from a street dealer (with no regard for the effect the drug might have on her unborn baby). Even after being warned, she pulled away without paying. And was shot.

The cloak of victimhood in this case is threadbare. This troubled woman is a striking example of the extraordinary things people do, the risks they take, that contribute to their victimization. Anyone with walking-around sense knows not to go into a snake pit, or rile them, or "slowly" leave. "They say she was jacking people outta drugs around there," commented Jones. "She jacked the wrong person." A Learjet lawyer might have drawn a lesser punishment by showing that the woman had provoked the situation, that she may have had a death wish and committed suicide with someone else pulling the trigger. But Learjet lawyers seldom represent street criminals.

Jones, like most newcomers, stays to himself because he doesn't know or trust the people around him. He realizes his present status in lockdown is temporary, that eventually he will join the general prisoner population. When that happens, he said, "I'm gonna try to stay cool. You know, try to work my way outta here. I don't wanta get off into no trouble, then I'd be stuck. I gotta try to get outta here. If you don't, there's something wrong with you." And so this youth with no future is trying to find one.

What he's likely to find is perhaps best represented by Walter "Daddy-O" Culbreath, who is at the opposite end of the prison's age spectrum. At 84, he is Angola's oldest inmate.

He lives at Camp-F, one of the prison's smaller outcamps, home to more than its share of ambulatory old-timers who have spent most of their lives in prison. The camp is a harbinger of the future, as Angola prepares to become the largest geriatric institution in the nation. 797 of its prisoners are now over 45, an amount projected to double in five years. And in 16 years, two-thirds to three-quarters of Angola's population will be 45 or older. Culbreath, for now, is the point man.

A slightly built black man, 5'7" tall and 150 pounds, he appears to be in good health and is a spellbinding storyteller. Born in 1909 not far from Angola's front gate, Culbreath had to drop out of school in the fourth grade. "Mama, she taken sick and died," he said, "and I had to go to work. House had holes big as two fingers, creosote walls. It got cold where I grew up at out here in St. Francisville." A child during World War I, he scrabbled for a living during the Depression, and was too old to serve in World War II. He led an uneventful rural/small-town existence, not getting into trouble with the law until he had entered middle age, a time when most criminals have burned out and retired from crime.

Culbreath committed his first offense—aggravated assault—when he was 39 years old. "At Good Hope down there," he recalled, "I workin' on the railroad. Didn't know nobody, started to gambling, and I won 700 and some dollars off of 'em. Broke 'em all with the dice. When I come outside, fella took a bottle and hit me side the head, but it didn't knock me out. Then the rest of 'em grabbed me. Oh, they tore my clothes clean off me, pockets, all that. One tried to hit me with a pole, say, 'Kill him. Kill him!' I had a knife, and I got away from there. Police come for me the next mornin'. I stayed in jail about two months, and the jedge he tried me over here in Arnoudville, give me ten years. Them other people didn't get nothing."

He arrived at Angola in April 1948 and was sent to old Camp-C, where the current Camp-C is now. At that time it was an all-black camp. "They put me to cuttin' cane. Ooooh man, did I cut some cane! I stayed Big Stripe (medium security) one year, and then they made me trusty. After three years and seven months, I made parole. It was a good camp. We didn't have no humbugs, no killin's, no fights, everybody played just like little chilluns going to school."

Although uneducated and said to have an IQ below 70, Culbreath has good common sense. "I never gambled no more, uh-uh, I'm talking about never gamble no more," he said. "But, oh, they gambled all night [at Camp-C], all over the floor. Everybody gambled. Penny, two pennies, on up to nickel and dime, quarter, on up. Shootin' dice, playin' tonk, bourree, all that. There was money here then, you could have money. Now I tell ya, I seen them boys what had money, some had five, six thousand dollars, or more. And

nobody never had no fight."

"Trusty" at that time was a euphemism for inmate guard. For many decades a handful of employees managed thousands of Angola convicts by using hundreds of armed inmates to man guard towers and provide perimeter security in the fields. Culbreath was an "inmate guard carryin' the lines [field crews] out," he said, "checkin' mens out just like these freepeople [employees] do here. . . . I didn't want to be no guard. It wasn't what you wanted to be, it was what they tell you to do. Not to be braggin', I'm the smallest one they had."

Culbreath went home to St. Francisville on parole and lived with a woman in common-law marriage. In May 1957, a year shy of discharging his sentence, he returned to Angola with a new ten-year term for three counts of theft. He had, according to records, been working for a man and "stealing him blind."

"They violated my parole back in '57," he said. "They give me trusty clothes [inmate guards wore khakis], put me at Camp-H [the guard camp]. I'm tellin' you, man, I was back up here a year before [then] Warden [Maurice H.] Sigler knew I was up here. And when he found that out, he went to the governor, told the governor I didn't have no business up here. Stayed another year. Cut me loose." Culbreath discharged in July 1959.

Not welcome in St. Francisville, he headed for New Orleans. "Got me a good job doing a little of everything, cement finishing," he said. "Left my wife behind. Too much naggin' goin' on. I don't go for all that naggin'."

In January 1965, he was arrested for murder, pleaded guilty to manslaughter, and got a new 15-year sentence. He was 55 years old. Information about the killing is not immediately available, and his recollection of the events is confusing. Culbreath said he was escorting two women into a housing project, carrying their groceries, when some shooting broke out and a woman "fell right down on all three a us. It was a dope thing. They put a murder rap on me for that!"

At Angola, "they put me back at the old Camp-F, the Willows," he said, "back trustyin'. They had moved the women [prisoners] who was there to St. Gabriel [near Baton Rouge], and made it a guard camp. Captain Red Norris put me with the cooks, working at nights. I get up at three o'clock, wake 'em up at 3:30 in the morning. Watch over 'em. There wasn't no humbugs, no nothin'. I stayed seven years, all back at Camp-F. Got out on parole, stayed out seven more years, and here I am back in."

On November 5, 1978, according to the police report, Culbreath had words with former live-in lover Annie Sims, 42, near the corner of Washington and South Claiborne avenues in New Orleans, and then stabbed her to death with a butcher knife in front of several witnesses who knew them both. He was 69.

Culbreath was tried, found guilty, and sentenced to death. On appeal, the Louisiana Supreme Court found his punishment excessive and set it aside. He was resentenced to natural life in 1981. Like many prisoners, even when it literally means life or death, he has little grasp of legalities. "I stayed in the parish [jail]," he said, "till they got that [death sentence] turned over or somethin' or another, then they sent me up here."

On his return to Angola in 1982, Culbreath discovered the use of inmate guards had been discontinued. "Trusty" now simply designated a prisoner deemed more trustworthy than most. "They give me trusty at Camp-H," he recalled. "Put

me out there fishin' at Lake Killarney [in the middle of Angola]. Catfish, perch, brim, trout, all kinds. And I had 'em filleted, all in racks, iced down, when [former] Warden [Ross] Maggio and them would come out and pick 'em up. I slept out there on the lake, out there at night by myself. Only thing come by was RS-2 [a 'Roving Security' patrol], check on me every hour see if I'm all right. I fish all night sometimes. I been tryin' to get back out there fishin', but they won't let anybody do it out there now."

Barring a medical excuse, every prisoner must work. That includes 84-year-old trusties, although human decency and compassion have stretched the definition of "work" far beyond what is expected of young prisoners. "What do I do?" he said. "Now, I tell ya, I get up every morning at three o'clock, seven days a week. I done got in the habit of it. I comes up here [to the Camp-F security office] and makes coffee for the free folks. They likes my coffee, so they say. I can go to the hobbyshop, do what I want. Make jewelry boxes, woodwork."

Despite his episodic history of violence, Culbreath wants his freedom. He has outlived most of his relatives, and gained inheritances from them. "Me," he said, "I got to have help to get out. My people just layin' up, ain't nobody doin' nothin' for me. I got money, a house, land, and everything all waiting for me. All I need is out."

Needing out and getting out are two entirely different things. The current mood of the country about crime, violence, and criminals dictates that many people who should get out, won't. Culbreath's understanding of these social forces is nil. He simply can't grasp why he isn't allowed to live out his twilight days on his own patch of earth. "I like the woods," he said. "I like to hunt, like to raise my own self what I want to eat. Raised on a farm, diggin' in the ground all a my life, made a livin' out of it. I ain't got much education. I was an inmate guard three times, carried the lines out, get the work did, bring 'em back, 200 and some mens. Jest like I carry 'em out, bring 'em back, same way. Nobody never left me, nobody never got in a fight, killed one another. They work with all kinda tools, ditchbank blades, hoes, shovels, swing blades, all a that, and there never was a cross word. Everything smooth. On the chases [escapes], I never shot nobody, never wasted a shell. If I was so bad, doing this that and the other, how come they make me trusty all those times?"

No two prisoners could be more unlike than the two who bookend Angola's age spectrum. They also are opposite criminal types. Jones typifies today's statistical profile of a violent street criminal. The young black gangbanger was destined for prison. Culbreath, on the other hand, is an anomaly. His criminal history flies in the face of everything known about felons. Crime and violence is a young man's game; few begin a criminal career at 39 or older. Hardly anyone released at the age he was returns to prison. Yet he came back three times. Except for serial killers, those who kill rarely repeat the act. Culbreath did. Finally, those who recidivate usually do so within the first year. Culbreath stayed out six years after each release, a total of 18 crime-free years in society following his first stint in prison. Jones, who hasn't even been alive 18 years, may never spend another day in society.

Perhaps the ocean of difference separating them is as it should be. One is at the beginning of his journey into a nightmare, the other near the end. Their dubious distinction of being the youngest and oldest Angola prisoners will soon be washed away by the waters of time. Another teenager will displace Jones, and the Grim Reaper will pass Culbreath's torch to another.

20

THE PLANTED*

by Lane Nelson

As he went through Cold-Bath Fields he saw
  A solitary cell;
And the Devil was pleased, for it gave him
  a Hint
For improving his prisons in Hell.
        S.T. Coleridge, The Devil's Thoughts

Herman "Hooks" Wallace lives on the Controlled Cell Restriction unit (CCR), at the end of "A" tier, in cell 15. His life is confined to an area nine feet long and six feet wide. Most of the cherished space is taken by a single metal bunk attached to the side of one wall. There is also a small metal desk top and seat welded into the other wall, and a stainless steel toilet/sink combination secured to the back wall. Two military foot lockers hold his clothes and personal items. Wallace lives in extended lock down. He is enclosed in a one-man cell 23 hours a day, seven days a week, twelve months a year. He has lived this way for the past 22 of the 27 years he's been in prison. Wallace is among a minority of Angola prisoners planted in cells smaller than the average bathroom.

CCR is in a two-story concrete building sitting just inside Angola's front gate. The bottom three tiers of the backside of the building hold death row inmates. Above them on four tiers is CCR—15 one-man cells per tier. Built in 1954, the building originally housed the prison hospital, as well as CCR and death row. Years later the hospital was moved and a receiving dormitory was added. In 1986-87 the entire building was evacuated, remodeled, and reoccupied. During that period of renovation, while CCR and death row were on disciplinary tiers at Camp J,

a heavily guarded outside work-line was instituted for some CCR inmates. Once the building was complete, and the inmates moved back into their own cells, the work-line ceased to exist.

CCR is where you will find the majority of your longest cell confined inmates. Prisoners can be placed in this restrictive extended lockdown unit for several reasons: protection, disciplinary action, threat to the security of the institution, escape risk, or initial classification. CCR inmates hold no jobs, attend no education classes, have no religious services, do not mingle with other prisoners or even among themselves. They leave the tier only after being secured with enough shackles and chains to sink a ship. Some, once they've had a good dose of the cell, will eventually be released into the prison population. Others, like Wallace, are there to stay.

Besides Wallace, four other Angola prisoners have been confined to a cell for over two decades: Lee Lane, Samuel Tropez, Albert Woodfox, and Robert "King" Wilkerson. Their hope to one day be released from CCR, and eventually from prison, carries them through each day. In reality, the chances that any of these five prisoners will ever again enter general population are slim. Each claims time has diminished the reasons for their original lock down, but prison officials disagree and rely on isolation as the safest, surest way of maintaining control.

National popularity for single cell confinement as means for control is a recent phenomena, evidenced by the growing number of state and federal super-

*Appeared in *The Angolite,* January/February 1995, 18-41. Reprinted with permission.

max prisons. First there was Alcatraz, but now there is Marion in Illinois, Pelican Bay in California, and the newly christened state-of-the-art federal facility in Florence, Colorado.

Florence, which cost taxpayers $60 million to construct, will hold 400 high-risk prisoners, including Mafia boss John Gotti and ex-dictator Manuel Noriega. All prisoners will be under constant video monitoring. The worst of the 400 will be kept in soundproof cells 23 hours a day, unable to associate even with each other. Prisoners will no doubt attack these conditions with civil rights lawsuits, but they can only expect a ruling similar to that recently handed down in California.

In that ruling Chief U.S. District Judge Thelton Henderson blasted conditions inside the Pelican Bay State Prison in Northern California: "Dry words on paper cannot adequately capture the senseless suffering and sometimes wretched misery that [state official's] unconstitutional policies leave in their wake," pronounced the 345-page decision. Henderson pointed out that isolated confinement in the Security Housing Unit (SHU), where 1,500 of the 3,700 Pelican Bay prisoners are kept, "may press the outer bounds of what most humans can psychologically tolerate."

Recognizing all that, the Judge said the prison can keep operating, which allowed both the state and attorneys for the prisoners to claim victory. "It is a landmark decision supporting the use of SHU to segregate the most dangerous, predatory inmates who threaten the safety of staff and other inmates at 28 other prisons in the system," said Corrections Director James Gomez. David Steuer, one attorney representing the prisoners, countered Gomez's statement by claiming victory in a decision that found "the entire

way they run the prison there is unconstitutional."

A sign of the times: instead of ordering the unconstitutional procedures halted, Henderson appointed a special negotiator to work with prisoners' attorneys and the state to agree on some changes. This reluctance to shut down the SHU is a reflection of society's perceived need to tolerate super-maximum prisons. Like correctional officials, most courts envision isolation units as a necessary evil.

While short-term solitary confinement has, in some brutal form or another, been an integral part of Angola's long and bloody history, locking prisoners in cells for years on end is a fairly new phenomenon. From the beginning, Angola was never conducive to an individual cell system, such as the cellblock designs conceived in northern states. Angola was a plantation first, housing slaves who cut sugar cane and picked cotton for the master. At the end of the 19th century it evolved into a prisoner lease system, with sentenced prisoners being rented to area companies. In 1901 Angola officially became a state-operated penitentiary, but in name only. It remained a plantation, with prisoners crowded into large wooden buildings and working from sunup to sundown in sugar cane and cotton fields—rain or shine, 12-14 hours a day, seven days a week.

During the plantation era, the prisoner-lease program and six decades of state-run operations, Angola's means of management never changed: ruthless forced labor. The procedure for obtaining work productivity remained the same—whipping, beatings, and death. If the spirit of an unruly prisoner could not be broken he often died. There was no outside law inside Angola. Prison officials made their own.

Obviously, to keep prisoners locked in cells for years on end was counterproductive to Angola's past system of management. Profit was the driving force, and working all able-bodied prisoners was the highest priority.

A most effective way of breaking a prisoner's spirit, and eventually getting some work out of him, was by short-term solitary confinement. In the 30s, 40s, and 50s there was the pisser—a box car type building which was divided into small windowless cells. No bunk, no mattress, no toilet, no ventilation. Rats, heat/cold, and lack of air generally tortured a man into submission. Before the pisser there was the sweat box or hot box—an iron casket buried into the ground. Disruptive prisoners were forced to lie in it for days, with the top clamped shut. It had small holes near the top to let in air. Insects and snakes could also get through those holes. The sweat box went past breaking a man's spirit.

In later years there was the "Red Hats." No account of solitary confinement in Angola is complete without mention of the seven years the notorious Charlie Frazier spent welded in a cell in the Red Hats unit.

Charlie Frazier, a convict who ran with the likes of Pretty Boy Floyd, Bonnie and Clyde and Ray Hamilton was a fearless and criminally-principled man. He came to Angola with a thirty-year sentence for bank robbery, and with an established notorious reputation. He robbed banks, ran illegal whiskey and killed people. In the summer of 1933, Frazier staged the bloodiest escape in Angola's history. It involved ten other prisoners and erupted in a barrage of gunfire in which one inmate guard was killed, two convicts were gunned down and four prison guards shot

to death. Five of the escaped convicts were caught on the run through rural areas surrounding Angola, but Frazier and two other men got away. The three desperados robbed five banks in six days in Arkansas and Oklahoma.

Three weeks after the break Frazier was caught in Texas and sent to Huntsville Prison on a charge of bank robbery. He was eventually returned to Angola, where prison officials were waiting for him with Angola's first extended lockdown unit: The Red Hats—a small brutal cellblock set in the middle of the prison acreage.

Built in 1933 as a direct result of the bloody escape, the Red Hats was a one-story cement structure consisting of thirty cells. Each cell was seven feet long and three-and-a-half feet wide and contained a concrete bunk with no mattress and only a small metal bucket for a toilet. Outside, eight feet of barbed-wire fence surrounded the block of cells, with a guard tower set at each corner. The name Red Hats comes from the red hats prisoners assigned to this block were forced to wear if they worked the fields. Frazier never worked. Legend has it that on Frazier's arrival he was thrown into a cell at the end of the tier, the cell door was welded shut, and he did not come out of that cell for the next seven years. No one did harder time in the Red Hats than Frazier.

In those times of prison violence and unaccountability, why wasn't Frazier killed when brought back to Angola? He had the Huntsville escape to thank. The incident carried national publicity— publicity that spared Frazier's life.

Until the early 70s, Angola officials had free reign to do as they pleased. What pleased them most was a broken-spirited, hard-working prisoner. But then winds of change blew through the nation. The civil rights movement gained momentum, Vietnam war protests were sending tremors of dissension through society, radical American Indians were on the warpath trying to secure a rightful place in their own land, and penal reform swept over the country. Prison literature, prison riots, prisoner litigation and prison reformers prompted federal courts to look into the secretive world of those locked away in our nation's prisons. What they found was not pleasing to their sight. Court rulings came hurling down, providing prisoners their long-denied Constitutional rights. Judges became particularly concerned for the prisoner's Eighth Amendment right to be free from cruel and unusual punishment. Federal courts were scrutinizing prison operations in many states, and Louisiana was no exception. Inmate lawsuits were positioning Angola for a period of unprecedented change.

It was during this time that Elayn Hunt was appointed as Department of Corrections Secretary by then-newly elected Governor Edwin Edwards. A sensible woman dedicated to prison reform, Hunt obediently followed court rulings allowing due process rights for prisoners. She also abolished the Red Hats cell block. In 1973 she eliminated Angola's long-standing use of inmate guards, those specially selected inmates who toted shotguns, hollered orders to other prisoners and were used by prison officials to beat, whip and sometimes kill unmanageable prisoners. The end of the inmate guard system at Angola drastically changed the interior of the penitentiary. Confused prison officials scrambled to find other ways to secure ultimate control. It was during this time that Angola received national notoriety for being the bloodiest prison in the country.

During this change Angola security officer Brent Miller was killed while overseeing a dormitory on the Main Prison Big Yard. Miller, a white security officer, well liked by his peers, was killed in a segregated black dormitory. Four suspected prisoners were locked up. An informant told authorities inmates Herman Wallace and Albert Woodfox, known members of the Black Panther Party, committed the murder. To avoid the very real possibility that they would be lynched, all four suspects were transferred to the protection of CCR, where they awaited their trials. Eventually, Wallace and Woodfox were convicted for killing Miller by an all white judicial system in the country town of St. Francisville. Both received life sentences.

"I'm not surprised that I'm still in a cell as much as I'm surprised me and Hooks are still alive," commented Woodfox, who has been confined to a cell for 23 years. "I thought I'd be dead within a year. It was hell. . . . I use to get all kinds of hate mail, death threats. Ku Klux Klan messages. I could tell the KKK messages were from inside the prison. No postage marks on the envelopes." Nevertheless, Wallace and Woodfox, who have always claimed their innocence in the killing, never imagined they'd be locked down for over 20 years. "I never thought for one minute I'd be in a cell this long," admits Woodfox.

Some say the practice of keeping prisoners locked in cells indefinitely began with the Miller killing and the locking down of Wallace and Woodfox. But extended cell confinement in Louisiana began with men on death row. The capital punishment moratorium of the 60s extended the cell time of many death row prisoners to over a decade. Wallace and Woodfox were placed in CCR in 1972, the year the Furman decision rescued condemned prisoners from their cells.

Prison officials did not confine them to cells after formulating an extended lockdown system to keep them there for decades. What happened just. . . happened. A year passed, five years passed, and somewhere along the line prison officials realized how convenient it was to simply never let some prisoners out of CCR. It played into what they were searching for; a way to secure better control over a potential powder-keg. Convict guards and brutality were out. Extended lockdown was in.

The other long-term prisoners in CCR were simply caught up with Wallace, Woodfox and this newly discovered control device. Under the old rules they would not be treated so gently, but one way or another their treatment would be over by now. Under the new rules the treatment continues indefinitely.

The five CCR long-termers have one thing to be thankful for. They are still alive. The prison reform movement saved their lives, but at what cost? They are plants, shut up in a locked bathroom with no window.

Gloria Dean Williams is the longest cell-confined female prisoner in the state. She has been housed in a cell at the Louisiana Correctional Institute for Women (LCIW) for nearly ten years. Her solitude began on July 4, 1985, after she tried to escape. Williams, carrying a sock filled with pool balls, swung at a guard while attempting to walk through the front lobby of the prison. Guards subdued her before she made it out the front door. Charged with aggravated escape the court tacked 20 years on the life sentence she already had.

The Independence Day escape attempt was not a first for Williams. On two prior occasions she succeeded in escaping from LCIW. The first time, in May of 1973, she simply walked away from guards who escorted her to Charity Hospital in New Orleans. She made it to Los Angeles, California, only to be arrested a month and a half later when, according to Williams, her brother-in-law turned her into authorities for a small reward.

Her second escape was in August of 1973, when she used wire cutters to get through the prison fence. Again she made a clean getaway and returned to L.A. A few months later she traveled to her hometown of Houston where, along with her husband, she was arrested on a robbery charge. Williams served eight years in a Texas prison before she was returned to Louisiana in August of 1982.

After spending time in extended lockdown she was allowed back in the prison population. Not long afterwards she again tried for her freedom. When the Independence Day escape failed, prison officials determined Williams to be an unremitting escape risk and tossed her in a cell, this time for good.

The 49-year-old Williams, mother of five children, tried to escape in the past because she didn't feel she ever deserved a life sentence. "I wasn't the trigger person that killed the man in the store," she claims. "When the store owner pulled the gun, all I wanted to do was get out of there." Court records confirm she tells the truth. Her codefendant, Carolyn Hollingsworth, 16 at the time of the crime, confessed at trial to shooting the grocery store owner. Although Hollingsworth is still in prison (the longest serving female prisoner in Louisiana), she lives in the general population and has never tried to escape. Of the six blacks indicted in St. Landry Parish for this 1971 armed robbery/murder, two, Manuel Hanchett and Nettie Lou Joubert, never went to trial. David Lawrence Killyon, the get-a-way driver, was offered and accepted a plea bargain; 18 years for manslaughter in exchange for his testimony against the other three. He was paroled six years later. Williams, Hollingsworth and Philip Anthony "Pee Wee" Harris were found guilty of murder by an all-white male jury. Each received a life sentence. Williams and Hollingsworth remain in prison. Harris was freed through gubernatorial clemency in May of 1977.

Williams now concedes her escapes were stupid. "Back then I didn't know any other way. I just wanted to be free. Now I know the other way—through the courts. I'm trying to appeal my conviction and sentence. I never did have an appeal and I believe I'm entitled to one."

In some aspects, cell confinement is harder for the women in the extended lockdown unit known as Capricorn than it is for Wallace and the men on CCR. The only TV in Capricorn is in a dayroom at the end of the tier. It is turned on for one hour a week, and only for those who receive no disciplinary reports for a two week period. The only canteen items they can purchase are necessities—paper, pens, stamps, toiletries. They are allowed no food items or soft drinks. They get seven hours yard time per week if the weather is good, and they can socialize during this time because they go out by tiers. Most are allowed to work cleaning the tier, and some, not Williams, do yard work around the institution.

In contrast, CCR prisoners are allowed nearly unrestricted use of the four TVs on each tier and are able to purchase food items and cold drinks through the prison store. But they get only three hours yard time a week, one man at a time. They

are not allowed to work.

Williams refers to her cell life as "a living hell! In the summer time the cells are like ovens, and ventilation is poor. In 1987, I tried to kill myself because of the psychological stress," she admits. Williams is a self-educated and friendly woman who other Capricorn inmates turn to for advice and encouragement. She claims that her faith in Jesus, herself and the support of loved ones in Texas—who visit her twice a year—keeps her going. "The hardest part about my cell confinement is not knowing if I'll die in this cell." Asked if she knew she were going to live in that cell for another 30 years, only to die in it, would she rather be dead now, her reply was an adamant "Yes!"

According to observations and studies of the psychological factors within micro-societies, stress is one of the more serious detriments in an isolated environment. "All contained environments are stressful," explains a chapter in the text *From Antarctica to Outer Space: Life in Isolation and Confinement.* The text focuses primarily on men and women who work in polar ice stations for winter seasons. Like prison cell confinement, solitude in polar ice stations is not a total loss of sensory perceptions. The grouping of individuals along with some types of recreational activities in these stations erodes the completeness of isolation.

Even so, and although less isolated than CCR, stress factors of both microenvironments stem from similar sources: "Social stressors associated with an ICE [isolated controlled environment] include loneliness associated with being separated from one's normal social network, a reduction in privacy, the necessity of forced interaction with the other members of the ICE, dependence on a limited community of individuals for one's social needs with no control over who may be included in that group, and limited ability to help loved ones with problems that may arise."

The text further explains that the "behavioral changes associated with stress include declines in alertness and mental functioning; low motivation; increases in somatic complaints such as sleep disturbances, digestive problems, and symptoms of colds and flu; social withdrawal; self-reports of depression and hostility; group splintering and polarization; feelings of helplessness; and psychotic episodes."

To combat stress in an isolated environment many turn, often unconsciously, to releasing negative energy in an effort for relaxation. Thus, when a heated argument breaks out on CCR, or a physical confrontation between two prisoners in cells side by side where spitting or the throwing of human waste might occur, chances are that the incidents are related to a release mechanism for a high stress level.

Located in the back of this sprawling plantation-like prison, approximately two miles from CCR, sits Camp D. Inside Camp D is Hawk unit, another extended lock down segment of the penitentiary. The primary difference between Hawk and CCR is that in Hawk a prisoner is more likely to be released into the general prison population at some point in time. There are exceptions. Most noted is Lee Lane, the longest cell confined prisoner at Angola and perhaps in the nation. Lane has lived in a cell 23 hours a day for the past 24 years. A longtime CCR resident, Lane was removed from CCR three years ago due to an altercation. He had coaxed another CCR inmate, who was on his way to the shower, up to his cell. With cat-like

movement, Lane lunged a makeshift knife through the small opening in the bars, stabbing the unsuspecting prisoner in the chest. The inmate lived, Lane was issued a disciplinary report for aggravated fighting and sent to Hawk as means of separating the two. Even before this act of violence, Lane's chances of ever being released from a cell were slim to none.

Lane came to Angola in 1956, at the age of 18, for a conviction of simple burglary. He discharged that sentence a few years later but not his life of crime. Another simple burglary landed him back in Angola with another five-year sentence in 1962. In those days of inmate guards, long-suffering work in the cane fields, and warring prison cliques, the name of the game was survival. And survival often depended on who had the biggest knife and the courage to use it. Lane had both. According to prison records, Lane killed two prisoners in 1963 and was convicted on two counts of murder in St. Francisville. He received two consecutive life sentences. It is unclear what happened to Lane between then and the turn of the decade, but in 1971 Lane was placed in CCR for another act of violence, and has been in a cell ever since. Some say he was a predator, others say he was a survivalist. His victims don't say anything.

Lane declined an interview for this article, so only the public record is available to us. The sad irony in that record can't be missed. He came here over 32 years ago with a five-year prison sentence. He now has two life sentences and will probably never be released to the general population, let alone into the free world.

"I did some days in the Red Hats due to a buck in 1961," explained Robert "King" Wilkerson. "At the time they put ten of us in a cell. The last time I was in the Red Hats was in 1970. I did ten days. That place was pure agony."

Wilkerson has been confined to a cell for nearly 23 years. He came to Angola with a 45-year sentence for armed robbery, aggravated escape and resisting arrest. He has discharged his original sentence. Wilkerson is now serving out a life sentence for the conviction of killing fellow CCR inmate Ernest Kelly in 1973. Two other CCR inmates housed on the same tier at the time of the incident testified they saw Wilkerson stab Kelly to death. Those two inmates were later released from Angola, only to return to prison for other crimes. One has again been released.

The 50-year-old Wilkerson appears in excellent physical shape. "I think if a person doesn't make an effort to maintain good physical health, then whether you're here or in (prison) population you'll lose your health." He practices what he preaches by getting up every morning at 4 am to exercise. He spends his three hours a week in the yard pen running. When rain cancels yard call, he runs the length of the tier for most of his shower hour. He appreciates the little yard time that he gets. "It wasn't always this way," remembers Wilkerson.

Before the late 70s CCR inmates didn't have any outside time. What fresh air they got they sucked through heavily screened tier windows. Wilkerson sued in court, complaining that the lack of sunshine and fresh air was detrimental to a prisoner's health. He based his argument on an earlier legal ruling—Sinclair v. Henderson—where the court held that Angola death row prisoners, confined just down the stairs from CCR, should be allowed a certain amount of outside time each week. Wilkerson's suit was denied.

But not long afterwards, as a result of a major prison suit contesting overall prison conditions (Armstead v. Phelps), prison officials provided CCR limited use of the pens originally set up for death row prisoners. Today, CCR prisoners receive the bare minimum of three hours yard time per week. Something is better than nothing, and this was a big step up in their living conditions; a step many inmates took without thought of what the years of inside solitude had done to their bodies.

"I noticed the effect no sunshine and fresh air had," said Wilkerson. "I saw some guys throw a football and break their arms because their bones had gotten so brittle, their muscles so weak. Dudes would run the yard and hit a small hole and their ankle would just snap. Pop! This is the effect that long-term cell confinement has on an individual, who, despite the fact that he may exercise indoors, doesn't come in contact with the outside. It was really devastating to see." Studies concerning life in isolation point to physical exercise as a pertinent means of retaining physical, mental and emotional stability.

"Let's look at it like this," said Wilkerson. "The penitentiary, period, can have a psychological or mental effect on a person's sanity. I think that when you are in a cell the chances are that those factors are greatly aggravated.

"When I came to Angola this time I had, call it intuition, a feeling I'd be put in CCR because of that escape from New Orleans. So what I did, I changed my psychology about myself. I refocused my thoughts on the differences between living in prison population and in a cell. I forced myself to believe that in spite of the major privileges I might be forfeiting from not being in population, prison was still prison. I think this early self-reeducation played a great part in being able to weather the storm. . . . Still, at that time I was looking at six months, maybe two years of cell time. But it didn't happen that way."

All the long-term cell confined prisoners in Angola assumed at the beginning of their solitary journey that they would be released after a year or so. That's just the way it was back then; after a hard dose of the cell, you were released, given another chance. But times changed. These prisoners were caught in the transformation. At some point it became obvious to them all. They had been planted.

Then there was Colonel Nyati Bolt. As prison reform took root in Angola in the early 70s, and as Angola earned a reputation as being the bloodiest prison in the nation, Bolt watched from his cell as the prison took on a new face. Before discharging a 45-year armed robbery sentence in October 1992, Bolt spent 23 years in extended lock down—sometimes more than 23 hours a day in a cell. "I feel like I've been through hell," he told *The Angolite* in a recent interview.

His cell confinement was in contrast to others who have spent over 20 years encased in a cement tomb. Bolt's stay was by choice, not by force. He chose to suffer the torment of cell confinement rather than work in prison. "I refused to work in the fields," Bolt wrote from his home in Oakland, California. At Angola it is mandatory that everyone work; the only exceptions are inmates with serious health problems. For the average, physically fit prisoner, work begins in the fields— hoeing the sides of ditches, picking okra or cutting tall grass with a swing blade. In Bolt's early years of imprisonment that work included picking cotton and cutting sugar cane. "I will not work on a plantation and be a slave for the state," he often told other prisoners who were amazed at his fortitude. While Wallace, Woodfox, Wilkerson and Tropez were filing legal petitions in court, complaining of their long-term cell confinement, Bolt rode out the turbulent years of solitude with stubborn insistence. "A matter of principle," he claimed. Just by saying, I'm ready to go to work, he could have been released at nearly any time during his confinement. He never spoke those magic words.

According to Bolt, his original placement in a cell had to do with his suspected involvement in the Brent Miller killing. He was never charged for that involvement. "The hardest part of living in a one-man cell all those years was the monotony of endless time and blatant solitude," reflected Bolt. "Why didn't I go crazy? I was strong-willed, which allowed me to block out the institutional bullshit by absorbing myself with positive mental feedback." He spent much of his time with "self-constructive endeavors such as reading educational materials, letters from pen-pals/friends, visitations from extended friends and family, and exercising in my cell." Bolt admits positive aspects of his confinement: "I am a stronger man, which allows me to deal with situations I am faced with on this outside world, with helluva patience, and without resorting to stereotypical negative attitudes or behavior such as the use of drugs or resorting to the criminal predatory mentality." Yet, when asked if extended lockdown units are a necessary evil he gave a resounding "No! It is never a necessity. It only increases one's attitudes toward violence. The tension isolation brings with it is incumbent to violent behavior/reaction."

Bolt's choice of a cell did not come without consequences, the worst of which nearly killed him. Just a year before his release Bolt suffered a stroke while reading in his cell. The seriousness of the stroke was not immediately recognized by prison officials. It was only after a security officer noticed Bolt's speech was incoherent and his balance was unstable that the prison medical team was notified. He was whisked to Charity Hospital in New Orleans, where he spent a month under treatment, then two more months in the prison hospital before returning to his CCR cell. Eight months later Bolt regained most of his mental facilities. Today, he says he suffers from lapses of memory and periodic head-jarring headaches. He feels his stroke was brought on by tension and stress that built up over the years of his confinement.

A career criminal when he arrived at Angola in 1970, upon his release he moved to Northern California where he is enjoying his freedom, living a crime-free life.

Samuel Tropez is 47 years old. He would happily work if let out of CCR. Tropez has lived in a cell at Angola for half his life. When he arrived in CCR on August 30, 1971, he expected to be returned to the general prison population within six months. Today, after 23 years of cell confinement, he sees only one way out. "I'm on the pardon board waiting for a hearing. I think I'll get out of prison easier than I'll get out of this cell." He's probably right, and that enhances the likelihood that he will die in that cell.

Tropez was transferred to CCR after a fight with other prisoners. "I got in a knife fight, ya heard me. A knife fight with four dudes for about two hours. I got juked 21 times. You know, you gotta have quick movement, keep the others off balance. You know your life is at stake. I hit one of them under the heart and that

slowed him up," he explained. In fact, it killed him.

Originally sentenced to Angola on a murder and manslaughter charge out of New Orleans, Tropez was young, illiterate and mentally challenged when he entered prison. "I had went to an insanity hearing because I had a lot of murder charges on me. (The prosecution) told me to make a deal to knock out the rest of the murder charges and they'd give me time for two. My lawyer told me to take a life and 21 years. I had to. I had so many murders I was charged with."

Out of the five longest confined prisoners, Tropez is said to be the most unstable. It may be that mental health evaluations are the key factor in preventing him from leaving extended lockdown. Tropez has survived a secluded life in CCR for over two decades. He contributes exercising and TV as ways he's coped with his miserable existence. "The cell. . . the iron takes away your strength; from being around it all the time, sleeping on it, sitting on it, it sucks your strength. That's why I exercise everyday." He is not unlike the rest when it comes to his environment forcing him to study. "I have to do it myself. Struggling with myself to learn, ya heard me."

He admits that his cell confinement has fostered hate. "I have a lot of hate in me. I've been abused like this here. This is what the cell has did to me—made me lose that feeling for a human person." For Tropez and others who were obviously mentally unstable to begin with, cell confinement can agitate the problem. The cell closes them off from the world, their feelings slowly evaporate. They find nothing to focus those dying feelings on. Yet, as they all do, Tropez lives on hopes and dreams. "My hope and dream is to get out and get married and have a nice job, settle down and raise some children. I'm not about too much luxury or too much money, ya heard me. I just want to be free and live. In this cell there is no life."

Tropez doesn't get regular visits. If he is fortunate he will receive a visit a year from his mother. He's okay with that. "They can just send me money. I want my family to live their life and not worry about me."

In Sue Halpern's book, *Migrations to Solitude*, she tells of a 1989 research project in which a thirty-two-year-old French woman voluntarily crawled into a cave to live in isolation for 111 days. She was wired head to toe with electrodes and performed certain visual and mental routines daily. The point of the experiment was to find out what happens when you remove someone from time as we measure it.

Within days, day ceased to exist for the woman. Her sleeping pattern became obscure—up forty hours, sleep thirty hours. She noted a "dull numbness" that took over her senses. But "[t]he true problem is loneliness," she wrote in her journal. "Also you think about your life. . . . You have time to think, you know. You're a thinking machine when you are alone."

One year after completing the experiment the woman killed herself. She parked her van along the side of a street, took a fatal dose of sleeping pills, laid down in the front seat and went to sleep for good. In an interview only two days before her suicide, she told a radio personality, "It was a risk that came with this experiment—to become half crazy, to become schizophrenic. It didn't happen to me. But maybe it's a time bomb—I won't say anything more about it."

Herman Wallace's gentle smile and soft eyes complement the subdued words

he speaks. He is a self-educated man who takes that extra effort to relay a point as clearly as possible. His present demeanor and concentrated communication has not always been a part of him. It is something he acquired through 23 years of cell confinement: "I have been able to elevate myself intellectual-wise. Being in a cell [as opposed from the general prison population] has given me a lot more time to read and has forced me to study. I have to educate myself. If they put me in a cage underneath the ground I'd have to read and study to retain my sanity."

Nevertheless, Wallace admits that the solitude has taken its toll. "Being perfectly honest, I don't think I'm totally sane, per se. There is a lot I'm holding back, a lot I hold within myself to keep what little sanity I have left. In the same token I'm confident I can function within any society, whether that be in a society beyond prison or in general [prison] population. Who doesn't have emotional problems within themselves to deal with these days?"

He also contributes his "togetherness" to the family support he has received through the years. "My parents and my family have always been here for me. I've always gotten visits. . . ." Out of the 55 inmates in CCR, most are like Tropez, who does not receive regular visits. "The reason why they don't is not because their people don't love them or don't want to see them. But because of this setting. People don't want to come here and visit behind a screen they can barely see the face of their loved one behind," said Wallace.

Regular visits in CCR mandate visiting between a heavy mesh wire, which prevents any physical contact. The inmate is kept in handcuffs and leg shackles throughout the two-hour visit.

Through persistent negotiations between CCR inmates and prison officials, approximately three years ago contact visits on a disciplinary report-free basis were instituted. CCR inmates who stay disciplinary-report free for 90 days are allowed to write in for a contact visit once a month. Providing security and available space, they will receive a supervised visit where they can kiss and touch their loved ones. Wallace, a model inmate as far as his disciplinary record is concerned, spends his contact visits with his wife of six years, who he said has been the biggest support in his life. "I can talk to her about anything. I do, and that helps."

For any prisoner, visits and communication with family members and friends is a crucial component to character and intellectual progression. This is especially so for those prisoners locked down in cells. Open lines to the outside world mean more sensory perceptions to keep the mind and soul occupied. Lack of outside communication creates a stagnant reaction. It limits the stimuli on which the mind can draw.

In the July 1993 issue of *Corrections Today*, a magazine for prison officials and employees, the value of human contact is exemplified: "Staff perform inmate [head] counts in the Florida death row unit at least once an hour, compared with six times daily for the general population. The higher number of counts is required for two reasons: to provide greater security against escape attempts and to allow death row inmates a greater opportunity to communicate with staff. Human contact in the unit is considered extremely important because the inmates spend much of the day in isolation." Officers at Angola make more head counts on death row, CCR and other cellblock units than in the general population.

As with all the other long-term CCR inmates, Wallace exercises regularly, trying not to miss any of his three hours a week yard time. He also keeps up a heavy load of correspondence and, depending on the availability of books, studies history and politics, which he also writes about. For those who can afford them, CCR inmates are allowed portable, battery operated or manual typewriters. Wallace has one. "I do a lot of legal work, on my own case and on trying to effect changes in CCR." Wallace has been witness to many changes that have come to CCR over the past two decades. Some good, some bad. "We use to have an hour group hall time, where we could all come in the hall together. Then security, and rightfully so for their own protection, set it up to where only three men could come out at a time. Then that changed, and they started letting only one man come out, about 1981, and that's where we are today." Wallace has discharged the armed robbery sentence that originally placed him in Angola in 1967. He is still under a life sentence for Miller's murder.

Albert Woodfox was convicted along with Wallace for the Brent Miller killing. He has been in CCR since April 18, 1972. The 47-year-old Woodfox originally came to Angola with a 50-year sentence for a 1969 armed robbery conviction out of New Orleans. While in New Orleans jail he escaped and fled to New York for a brief period before being apprehended. Like Wallace, Woodfox is a former member of the Black Panther party. He does not believe his lengthy stay in a cell is a repercussion for once being a Panther. He feels he is being made an example. "I think we're being held in here as an intimidation factor for the other inmates," he said. An intelligent, articulate man, Woodfox has spent his years in a cell educating himself. He says it is how he has managed to keep sane. "I've used the time to educate and reeducate myself in just about everything—economics, politics, history, psychology, sociology—just about anything I can get my hands on." Ironically, he feels that intrusion and not seclusion is the hardest thing for him to deal with. "Not being able to get away from the same people, same conversations, same type of activities going on in the other 14 cells on my tier."

Woodfox is pretty much resigned to his fate in a cell. He sees little hope of ever getting into the prison mainstream. "I don't think I'll ever be placed in population. . . . We have letters from the DOC—myself, Hooks and King—which say as far as conduct was concerned our conduct is exemplary. But that they didn't want to be responsible for letting us back into population. After we filed suit on our confinement and we had a hearing, DOC's position was that they were protecting us. They say they have inmates and security personnel that will want to seek retribution because of the Brent Miller killing. I think that's absurd."

Many who have been locked into a secluded environment seek a religion they can accept to keep hope alive. Just the opposite has happened with Woodfox. "I think I lost a religious faith instead of picking one up. I was raised Catholic. . . . I recall an incident that pretty much caused me to pull away from the Church. I was almost molested by a priest. I never gave the incident any thought until four or five years ago when these things started coming out about these priests molesting all these children. That's when I had this flashback and remembered when I was 12 or 13 the incident with a priest. He didn't do it because of a nun that came in when she did. But if she hadn't came in I think it

would've happened. I really couldn't tell you if remembering that was the beginning of my withdrawal from the Church and religious beliefs, but I can say it wasn't the only factor." Woodfox claims he is spiritual, just not religious.

The flashback Woodfox relates is, according to others who have found themselves in a solitary environment, not unusual. In August 1993, the Associated Press recounted the kidnapping incident of 68-year-old millionaire Harvey Weinstein. Weinstein was held captive for 12 days in a dark 8-foot deep utility shaft. His captors shackled him and covered the shaft with a heavy metal plate. "I begged my captors to take me out and shoot me and leave me on the road where my family could find my body," he told reporters shortly after his rescue by police. He recalled how he combated the solitude in the dark pit that nearly drove him mad. In his mind he wrote "the greatest autobiography never written," and in visualizing his past he found that "it was astounding the memories that would come back," and the clarity of those memories.

Monotony is perhaps the number one foe of a cell confined inmate. For a person planted in a cell, every tomorrow is yesterday. "The only thing that changes is whatever change you can construct on your own," Woodfox said. "I have routines that I follow, but there are times I change up, deliberately change, because I get tired of being so predictable to myself. . . Basically, there's nothing in CCR for an individual to pursue to improve himself. You can hang onto the TV from the time it comes on to the time it goes off. Or you can get involved in the games that make up prison culture. That's what makes it most difficult for me, fighting not to get caught up in these negative pursuits."

In CCR there are four TVs to each tier. The prisoner must view through his cell bars the TV closest to his cell. They can be turned on at 6 am and must be turned off at midnight during the week. They can stay on all night on the weekends. Needless to say, they get a lot of use in this isolation unit.

Woodfox believes those who can control their use of TV can use it to help themselves. "I think the TVs probably fit in more to keep some of these people sane. TV is an escape. It's going to distort their mind unless they have a strong foundation. But you can be objective and always realize that this is fantasy. I really do think these TVs do a lot right now," he said.

There are those who will disagree with Woodfox's opinion of TV watching. Which station to watch, and how loud to set the volume are sources of contention and stress. In addition, most planted inmates have no contact with reality; nothing to balance the endless fantasy marching across the screen. Nonetheless, when the only question is whether or not you will die before you go insane, the demons on the set are more benign than the demons in the mind.

"I think now and in some instances, cell confinement for certain periods of time is a necessary evil," admits Woodfox. "Just not for years and years. It's something like a Jekyll and Hyde situation. Maybe I've developed all the emotions and attitudes society and the DOC wanted me to develop—anger, bitterness, the thirst to see someone suffer the way I'm suffering, the revenge factor and all that. But on the other hand, I've also become what they didn't want me to become. I've become a well-educated, well-disciplined, highly moral man. . . . I've become more focused on what caused me to be in this penitentiary. From the beginning it wasn't just an act on my part but an act on society's part that pretty much decided it. Being an African-American pretty much determined where I'd wind up. It's sad to say that I had to come to prison to find out there were great African-Americans in this country and in this world, and to find role models that probably contribute more now to my moral principles and social values, when I should have had these things available to me in school. So I feel cheated, really cheated. . . . I think what really helps me, I've never considered myself to be a criminal. I've always considered myself a political prisoner. Not in the sense that I'm here for a political crime, but in the sense I'm here because of a political system that has failed me terribly as an individual and citizen in this country."

In the ICE text, a researcher recounts his experiences at a 'winter-over station'. During his stay he clearly noticed a difference between the people who had spent many winters in the Antarctic and knew the ropes of adapting in a micro-society, and technicians on their first or second tour. The researcher found that the novice technicians spent much of their spare time in large groups, engaging in horseplay, drinking, watching TV, and pursuing other passive activities. The veterans, on the other hand, congregated in small groups of two or three close friends; devoted time and effort to personalizing their living quarters; and they were all avidly involved with hobbies, usually things having to do with the Arctic. In comparison with the CCR environment, the researcher's observations are strikingly similar. Longtime CCR prisoners are generally quiet and stay to themselves. Most pursue activities having to do with prison—working on their own cases or litigating to improve the conditions of their confinement.

Due to the highly-charged publicity encompassing his major crime spree, a statewide police task force was assigned to track down and apprehend serial rapist Jon Simonis. Once in custody, Simonis was quickly shuffled from parish to parish to attend court hearings and enter guilty pleas. Not long afterward, he walked through the gates of Angola, and directly into a cell on CCR, where he has remained for the past 13 years. He freely admits that his chance of ever being released to the prison population is dim. He has settled in for the long haul.

Dubbed the "Ski Mask Rapist" by the media, Simonis has been sentenced to serve more time than any other prisoner in the history of Louisiana. He pleaded guilty to an extraordinary number of rapes, aggravated crimes against nature, armed robberies and aggravated burglaries. He received 21 life sentences plus 2,428 years. The 43-year-old first offender takes the dump truck loads of time in stride. "My time has never bothered me, knowing I can't serve it. Just having one life sentence is enough in Louisiana to keep a person from ever getting out. That's just the reality. There are a lot of people in population who have one life sentence. But they are in the same position I am."

The official reason he is in CCR is due to the length of time he has to serve and the nature of the offenses. The unofficial reason is that he is secluded for his own protection. Simonis' rapes occurred primarily in the homes of upper middle class citizens. Family and friends of some victims would like nothing better than to see Simonis dead. Money buys things. Money can buy Simonis' death. He came to Angola under a cloud of well-founded rumors that a price was on his head.

Simonis believes there is another reason for his isolation: "The reason given to me by the state police who had talked with Warden Blackburn," he explained, "is that there wasn't anyone in the DOC who could take the heat if I was ever to run off. The same reason was given to me by someone on the classification review board, that no one wanted to be responsible by signing my release from CCR, in the event I escaped."

Since prison officials have no intention of releasing Simonis into the prison population, his death may well occur in the small cell he lives in—some 30 or 40 years from now. "I have little hope with all the time I got," said Simonis. "I'm sure I'll die in prison." Yet, he is not looking for an easy way out, not looking at death as a relief from his suffering. "Life is important to me. It's not so much where you're at that matters, but how you perceive your situation and circumstances at the time," he explained. "It's mental conditioning. . . . It's either as good as you want it to be or as bad as you want it to be. And I'm determined to make things as good and as pleasant for me as I can if I live to be 90 in prison, in this cell."

A well-spoken and courteous man, he credits a desire to become a proficient writer as the key to keeping his wits. "Writing has held my sanity together. I love to write. I write articles and books. I've sold quite a few articles over the years I've been here. . . . No questions about it, writing is my life-source. Otherwise, I'd been regressing like so many other people. In the 13 years I've been here it's probably been more educational and more productive than all the years I'd been on the street. But it's been a struggle. I've had to do it on my own, self-educate myself, grasping what little I could get a hold of. A text book, a nonfiction book, educationally stimulating correspondence from pen-pals. They don't like you to get college correspondence courses because they don't have anybody that will administer the tests."

Simonis is currently working on a book dealing with the mind and impulsive actions of serial rapists. He hopes it will help in the psychological treatment of what he considers to be a progressive and uncontrollable urge to rape.

"Even though time progresses on the outside, it has a tendency to stand still for us in here. We're just shut up or isolated. Incarceration was designed primarily to separate an individual from society under less than desirable conditions. But it doesn't mean to hold a person down, into a position where he regresses. . . . There are people in CCR who want to be here, and there are people who want to get out into a camp. Some people who they plan on keeping are just here. Some are going to get out one day and if you haven't done anything to improve their minds, society is going to be faced with people who are no better than when they first come here. . . . Any benefits I receive through my isolation, any progression that I go through, is out of a need for survival. I've had to engage in something. I know my situation in prison and what it will probably be like for me in the next 20, 30 years or until the day I die. It's important to me to maintain a positive attitude and to keep doing whatever I can to stay active. To keep my mind active and not let myself deteriorate any quicker than it will on its own."

Simonis brings to light the main factor in the survival or non-survival of long-term cell confinement. "Adaptability. That's all it is. I can do that, adapt. Some

people can't. And some people pay a heavy price because they can't."

Studies conducted at the ice stations revealed that "[o]ne of the most important insights is that living and working for extended periods in hostile, isolated, and physically confined environments requires adaption at many levels." And that "psychological adaptation to an environment characterized by severely reduced sensory input is difficult. With few changes in the physical setting or routine over the course of months, the mind becomes under-stimulated and must seek new inputs." For many, at the ice stations, this meant voracious reading; for others, extended movie watching.

Woodfox has been in a cell ten years longer than Simonis. "I've seen people go crazy, cutting themselves, hanging themselves. I've seen horrors," said Woodfox. "I've seen people do things to themselves and have other inmates do them something because they just couldn't handle being in a cell 23 hours a day." Why some adapt and progress as a person and why some don't is a mystery to proficient researchers that study micro-societies and the effects of isolation. "The reasons for these large individual differences are not fully understood, but it's believed that such factors as the subjects' genetic make-up, personality, attitudes, and perception of the immediate situation may all play some role," according to an entry in the *International Encyclopedia of Social Sciences.*

Monotony, loneliness, the limited stimuli of sensory perception connected with long-term cell confinement causes varying changes in the mental and emotional stability of men and women who live these lives of solitude. They exist in a pool of helplessness and hopelessness. They do not know how to escape their cell confinement, and they do not know if they ever will. It is a stressful life that invites instances of differing degrees of paranoia. In such a condensed world your mind is apt to play tricks on you. As stated in the 1866 report on solitary confinement: "he feels that 'his hand is against every man and every man's hand is against him. . . .'"

There is no doubt that long-term cell confinement in CCR is a punishing existence. Yet, one cannot overlook the positive attitude most of these prisoners exhibit. Yes, they have been planted in cells, but as such they have rooted themselves in self-evaluation, education, spiritual reformation; captured the meaning of self-growth, and capitalized on it. They have done this to preserve their sanity. The solitary existence they live has forced them to take root. Their survival in the face of solitude is astounding.

The American penal system was created on a pretension that solitary confinement is good for the soul. The stark loneliness that struck deep into the criminal was thought to bring his immorality to light, reforming his dastardly ways. It was not long before two obvious repercussions surfaced—mental, physical and emotional imbalance, and economic inefficiency. Thereafter the conditions of solitary confinement took on gradual modification. Today, single cell long-term confinement is used for punishment and control. For that purpose . . . it works.

THE FIRST AMERICAN PRISON

The Walnut Street Jail is known as the first officially recognized prison in America, but this may not be true. There was an abandoned copper mine in Simsbury, Connecticut, which was turned into a prison in 1773. Men, women, and children were housed together and made to work under torturous conditions. Inside the overcrowded tunnels of the mine criminal chaos and perversion prevailed. Escapes were frequent. Just one year after it opened it erupted in the first prison riot in America, which hastened its closure. It never did become an important confinement facility, and, perhaps out of embarrassment, it is not recognized before Walnut Street as the first American prison.

THE BIRD-MAN

Robert Stroud pleaded guilty in 1909 to killing a man in the Alaska territory and received a 12-year sentence. He was sent to Leavenworth prison where, in 1916, he defended himself from a clubbing by stabbing a prison guard. For that killing Stroud received the death sentence.

On April 15, 1920, his mother's unrelenting pleas convinced President Woodrow Wilson to commute the death sentence to life in prison. Upon receiving the order of clemency, Leavenworth warden V.A. Anderson told news reporters: "Stroud will be kept in the segregated ward during his sentence, which is for life. He will never be permitted to associate with other prisoners. He will be allowed only the customary half hour each day for exercise in the court. . . . He will not be permitted to see visitors other than members of his immediate family." So began Stroud's solitary journey. The man later known as the Bird-Man of Alcatraz spent 54 years in prison—42 in solitary confinement. No federal prisoner has ever spent more.

Stroud did not have TV or radio to keep him company, so he turned to birds. By 1931 he became a leading authority on canaries, and in 1942, published *Stroud's Digest of the Diseases of Birds*. Birds kept Stroud from going insane.

Stroud spent most of his time locked in a solitary cell at Leavenworth. He was transferred to Alcatraz in 1942. In 1959 he was again transferred, but this time out of solitary and into the Medical Center for Federal Prisoners at Springfield, Missouri. He was 70 years old. It was the first time since 1916 that he was free from solitary confinement. "I have seen my first TV program, but I've been too interested in people to spend time with it," Stroud wrote to the attorney who helped him get to Springfield. "I probably walk three miles a day and feel like a million. . . the yard is a beautiful park. . . . I've seen more people and spoken more words than I did in forty years. Imagine what a pleasure it was to lie on the grass for the first time since 1914, how it feels to sleep without a door being locked on me. . . . It is amazing to see many of the most controversial things I have advocated for years practiced here as a matter of course. I could live a happy and useful life here, for in this hospital I've seen pitiful cases where an hour's talk at the bedside of a lonely and suffering human being can give a new hope, and where hope is impossible, much less courage." Interestingly, in his early years of isolation Stroud wrote a comprehensive and very critical book of the penal system, *Looking Outward*. Prison authorities confiscated the book. It was never published.

In the fall of 1959, just after his move to the medical unit, Stroud appeared in court for the first time since 1920. He and his lawyer had filed a petition to contest the sentence given some 41 years earlier. Federal Judge Walter Huxman ruled the original order of secluding Stroud to

solitary confinement for life was illegal, then ruled the matter moot. "There are features in the case that challenge the imagination and even shock the court, but what is done is done," wrote Judge Huxman. At the end Stroud tasted bitter victory.

Four years later, on November 21, 1963, his heart gave out. He died while still imprisoned in Springfield at the age of 74. Considering the decades he spent in solitary, Stroud accomplished much during his long life. But some question President Wilson's commutation of Stroud's death sentence. Through hindsight they see it as a curse.

HEADING BACK TO WALNUT STREET

The nation is in an uproar over crime. State and federal legislators are taking away millions and millions of dollars from domestic programs to build more and more prisons. Society doesn't seem to mind, and is willing to pay more for harsher prison conditions. Case in point: H-Unit at the Oklahoma State Prison in McAlester. While state officials call their newly designed state-of-the-art maximum security unit a wizardry in prison control, prisoners confined to the unit see it as a cement tomb. Both sides agree it is a bold step by the state to see just how far they can go in isolating prisoners.

According to a January 15, 1995, article in the *New York Times*, the new unit, which can hold 400 prisoners, is mostly buried in the ground. Air is ventilated through ducts, and no natural lighting exists in the living quarters. Most cells are occupied by two prisoners who share 116.9 square feet—a violation of ACA requirements of 80 square feet per prisoner when confinement exceeds ten hours a day. The double-cell occupancy causes significant psychological stress between the two prisoners who cannot escape one another's presence.

H-Unit inmates are confined to their cells 23 hours a day during the week, and 24 hours a day on weekends. They are allowed a 15 minute shower three times a week. Weather permitting, inmates are allowed one hour a day on the yard during the week. They spend it in individual 23 x 22 foot concrete boxes that have 18-foot concrete walls topped with heavy mesh wire.

Because there are no windows in the living quarters of H-Unit, these prisoners exist in a world of cement—they have only memories of a blade of grass, or a tree, or even the plain dirt ground. Their only contact with guards while locked in their cells is through an intercom system, or at feeding time when a guard opens a slot in the door to deliver the trays. When the intercom is on prisoners can speak to the guards in the control center. When it is off they can speak to one another, or to themselves.

Amnesty International is protesting the living conditions at H-Unit. Will the group's pleas be enough to change the conditions? Probably not. Not at a time when control, not tolerable conditions, is foremost in the minds of prison officials and society. H-Unit is a few steps away from America's first prison, Walnut Street Jail, which spread more insanity than salvation.

DIARY OF A PLANT
(composite diary entries of extended lockdown prisoners)
4/21/74: From my cell I look through the bars and out the iron-framed window across the narrow hallway. I watch a beautiful sunset. The sun is getting tired

after a long day, slowly slipping down for its rest. But its vibrant strength is still magnified through the deep orange bar that stretches across the bottom of the open land far in the distance. My mind wanders. An odor seeps through the window and is powering its way into my cell. The crisp smell of a skunk. It is a long-forgotten fragrance that I associate happier days with. Days of fresh woods, rugged mountains, clear streams, mowing the grass.

4/25/74: I'm scared! What happens if this delightful odor now becomes a nightly routine? Then it will evaporate my thoughts of those carefree times and become a part of the nasty smell of this dark pit I live in. "Hurry skunk, run far and come back only once in a great while. That way your smell will remain a fresh and sweet scent to me."

7/15/76: One, two, three, four, turn. One, two, three, four, turn. One, two, three, four, turn. One, two, three, four, four and a half—yeah!, turn. . . . "No yard today. They say it's too wet. Field lines are out, so it's not too wet to work. That sucks. It always sucks." One, two, three, four, turn. One, two, three, four, turn. . . .

9/3/78: Jacked-off twice on Barbara Walters. Sweet bitch. Wish I could see her do something besides sit behind that desk. Shit fight three cells down. Charlie been savin it in a milk container, soakin it in bleach, for four days. Hit Nub with it comin out the shower. God awful stink.
  Only thing got rid of the smell was the tear gas they put on us.

9/5/78: Barbara didn't show. Jacked-off on the weather girl. Big fine legs.
Charlie tried to hang himself. Didn't try

hard enough.

Goin on the review board next week. Last time, and the time before that, I got denied "based on the nature of my charge."

Haven't been able to change that.

6/17/83: Had a weird dream last night. I dreamed I got shot five times in the stomach. I felt each bullet hit me and sink into my gut. I didn't die, but just laid there in pain as my mom and my sister reached out for me, to help me. We never touched. I woke up holding my stomach and sweating. So real.

12/25/87: One minute past midnight. It's hard for me to believe it's my 15th Christmas in this cell. It just goes on and on. Same thing day after day. I wonder how I've changed? I wonder if I'm crazy? Crazy people don't know that they're crazy, so maybe I am. But who would know? Who would care? Am I gonna make it another year? Do I care if I do or don't? Merry Christmas to me.

3/4/88: I'm sick and tired of this jerk on my tier. His attitude sucks! He prides himself in being a convict, when all he really is is the classic lock down coward. Love to blow hard and heavy because he knows he's protected by his cell. He's a yes-man, a shoo-shoo'er, and believes he's a lawyer. What a piece of trash! A real nuisance to be around, and I can't help but be around him. A small punk that grows ten feet tall once he's locked in the protection of his cell. Someday. . . .

4/27/88: That coward got the best of me today. He said something stupid on his tier hour and I lost it. Grabbed at him through the cell and just missed his hair

and the chance to slam his face in the bars. All I could do was cuss and threaten him. I did. I was out of control. He moved fast from the front of my cell, and I moved to my toilet and spit out the foam coming from my mouth. I'm glad now that my cell wasn't open.

1/28/91: I now have a little mouse that runs about my cell at night. My phobia over rats and mice is no more. I welcome this new friend. A few nights ago I woke up to a rattling noise behind my trash bag. I sat up and there was the furry creature sticking his head out from behind the bag. We both jumped at the sight of one another. After staring each other down for a while, I laid back in my bunk and went to sleep with a smile. Although I've not seen it much the past few nights, I've laid out dinner scrapes and each morning the food is gone. I'm concerned for my new friend's safety. Earlier I heard a guy a few cells down talk of murdering the mouse. Incredible. A man who knows the depth of suffering, knows how it feels to have the hand of authority pressing down on his neck, wants to kill a defenseless creature that is only doing the same as he— surviving. Well tonight my friend feasts! Chicken bits, pieces of a roll and cookie crumbs. Eat and be merry, for tomorrow you may be murdered.

2/17/94: Oh! My back. These cold mornings affect it more than anything. Hmmm. Twenty-years ago I could hop out of this bunk, do 200 push-ups, 100 sit-ups and wait for the breakfast tray. Those days are gone. I'm getting old quick. Too quick. And I haven't even saw the world yet. Hell, I haven't even saw the prison!

10/10/94: Happy Birthday to me, again. Don't ask.

HISTORY OF ISOLATION

Isolating criminals is nothing new. It started when Cain murdered his brother, Abel, and God banished him, isolating him from all that he knew. He wandered the land aimlessly without the comfort of human interaction. Most theologians agree that Cain eventually found another human tribe and began a new life. If so, chances are that his lengthy departure from human companionship drastically altered his personality and perception of reality. On the other hand, if Cain never met up with another human being he probably went insane before he died.

Centuries passed before banishment took a backseat to physical confinement. In 64 B.C., Rome established what scholars suggest is the first formal prison—the Mamertime Prison—where cages confined felons in an underground sewer. This concept of imprisonment in sewers defined the prisoners' value as human waste.

Many ancient places of confinement, such as the Roman sewers, were originally built for reasons other than incarceration. Castles built in the Middle Ages had their basements turned into dungeons to hold chained, blindfolded and caged prisoners who wasted away in isolation. The thick walls of monasteries and abbeys, originally designed for solitude and prayer, were employed to seal away prisoners. Towers like the famous Tower of London, were used to lock away political and influential prisoners from the rest of the world. Even today military bases, barges and other constructions are being turned into prison facilities.

In the 13th century the Roman Catholic Church added a new dimension to the purpose of solitary confinement and imprisonment: Redemption. Besides the punishment of imprisonment to reduce moral contagion, redeeming the sinner's soul became important. Authorities theorized that solitary confinement carried redemptive power; that a prisoner subjected to the solitude of his cell, having nothing other than himself and the error of his ways to reflect upon, would cry out to God for delivery of his evil soul.

Pope Clement XI commissioned Italy's San Michele House of Corrections in 1703. It was the first known cellular prison and confined delinquent and juvenile youths. Inscribed in gold above the main hall for all to see, were Italian words meaning: "It is of little use to restrain the bad by punishment unless you render them good by discipline." Those very words became the motto of Englishman John Howard, the father of prisons and prison reform in America.

In the 1770s, John Howard visited European prisons to learn their operations. He discovered vastly progressive operations in comparison to England's penal system. Prior to 1775, English courts handed down sentences that rarely warranted imprisonment. Felons were generally punished by banishment, the whip, and more often the case, hanging. In London's major criminal court between 1770 and 1776, imprisonment accounted for approximately 2.3 percent of the sentences imposed. And those prison sentences, usually for manslaughter, rioting, and perjury, were considered short by modern standards—generally a year or less.

Howard, a God-fearing man who was disheartened by the English system of punishment, was impressed with the European system of isolation. His knowledge of this system qualified him as the expert in the correctional field. His influence spread to England, Canada and America.

In 1776, the Pennsylvania Quakers played the key role in shifting from corporal and capital punishment—the whip, stocks, hangman's noose—to sincere attempts at rehabilitation. Awed over Howard's prison reform, these Quakers formed the Philadelphia Society for Assisting Distressed Prisoners in 1787. Soon afterwards, during a meeting in the home of Benjamin Franklin, the Society changed its name to the Philadelphia Society of Alleviating the Miseries of Public Prisons (PSAMPP). Today it is known as the Pennsylvania Prison Society.

Outraged at the sight of public humiliation from daily sentences of corporal punishment, the group advocated the use of solitary confinement for hardened felons. Dr. Benjamin Rush, a leading member of the PSAMPP and strong advocate of Howard's theories, took the forefront of prison reform in America. Rush, on behalf of PSAMPP, issued a 1788 memorial endorsing solitary confinement and hard labor as the most effective method of reforming criminals. The group justified the use of solitary confinement by their heartfelt belief that it was a necessity of penitence—confining a prisoner to a cell with only a Bible for company, providing the opportunity for him to reflect upon his misdeeds. It was also felt that solitary confinement protected against moral pollution of offenders who would otherwise group together, conspire and fuel their evil urges.

In 1790, the PSAMPP pushed its prison advocacy into the Pennsylvania legislature. What followed was the first officially recognized prison in the nation. Legislative enactment mandated an additional wing be added to the city jail on Walnut Street in Philadelphia, which would incarcerate the most hardened criminals in single cells. The legislative act ordered: "A suitable number of cells. . . each of which should be separated from the common yard by walls of such height as without unnecessary exclusion of air and light. [Cells that] will prevent all external communication, for the purpose of confining therein the more hardened and atrocious offenders who. . . have been sentenced to a term of years." The only contact the prisoner had with the outside world was the sporadic visits by prison officials and PSAMPP members. Their daily existence amounted to little more than Bible reading and mandatory prayer time.

Soon there were not enough cells available to individually house these hardened and atrocious felons. And despite the good intentions of Quaker reformers, the Walnut Street prison bred more insanity than salvation. Noted author Charles Dickens, after visiting the Walnut Street prison, wrote:

> He is led to the cell from which he never again comes forth, until his whole term of imprisonment has expired. He never hears of wife or children; home or friends; the life or death of any single creature. He sees the prison-officers, but with that exception he never looks upon a human countenance, or hears a human voice. He is a man buried alive; to be dug out in the slow round of years; and in the meantime dead to everything but torturing anxieties and horrible despair.... If his period of confinement has been very long, the prospect of release bewilders and confuses him. His broken heart may flutter for a moment, when he thinks of the world outside, and what it might have been to him in all those lonely years, but that is all. The cell-door has been closed too long on all his hopes and cares. Better to have hanged him in the beginning

than bring him to this pass, and send him forth to mingle with his kind, who are his kind no more.

Still, the concept of isolation was locked into the minds of prison reformists, who were reluctant to release it. They adopted modifications to stop mental and physical deterioration. They tried housing the overflow of prisoners in large congregate rooms and allowing those who remained in single cells to perform some type of labor—mostly shoe repair. Those modifications failed and in 1818 the Walnut Street prison was shut down due to a list of problems: overcrowding, politics, incompetent personnel, lack of financial support. Prisoners' sanity and physical deterioration were at the bottom of the list.

But for ten years Walnut Street Prison did survive. It became the nation's model on which other states would build their own prisons—states such as New York, Kentucky, New Jersey, Virginia, Massachusetts, Maryland, Vermont, New Hampshire, Ohio, and Georgia.

In 1816, New York opened its first prison, but based it on a congregate system in an attempt to eliminate the bouts of insanity caused by total isolation. It was not long before officials became uneasy and announced that immoral contamination was spreading among the prisoner population due to group association. State legislatures took notice and in 1819 passed an act directing prison officials to section off a place of confinement to house the oldest and most heinous prisoners, under what turned out to be even more brutal conditions of solitary than that of Walnut Street. In less than two years the prison, known as Auburn, marred by the prevalence of sickness and insanity, proved a hopeless failure. In 1824, New York Governor Yates pardoned most offenders who remained in solitary.

Local prison authorities at Auburn recognized that both the congregate and solitary system would not work. They created a compromise: the silent system, in which prisoners lived in single cells but were brought out daily to work in groups. They lived under absolute silence. Any prisoner caught even whispering to another prisoner was flogged on the spot.

Despite the failure of Walnut Street, the redemptive theory of isolation pressed on in Pennsylvania. In 1818, the state legislated the construction of a prison on a discarded cherry orchard. Opened in 1829, it was officially named the Eastern Penitentiary. Most called it "Cherry Hill." Here they operated what became known as the "separate system"—a system that required prisoners to be kept completely alone, never speaking or seeing another prisoner. The cells were eleven feet, nine inches long, seven feet, six inches wide, and sixteen feet high. Each cell had two doors, one leading to the main corridor, the other leading to an enclosed high-walled exercise yard. Prisoners were allowed one hour of solitary exercise each day. Prison officials were so serious about solitude they blindfolded every prisoner entering Cherry Hill while escorting him to his cell. For good behavior prisoners were given a Bible, worthless to most of the illiterate population. For extra good behavior they were allowed to do whatever solitary work they could perform. Like Walnut Street prison, some insanity plagued Cherry Hill.

Supporters of the separate system were excited over this new reform, while opponents thought it cruel. Author Charles Dickens wrote: "In its intention I am well convinced that it is kind. . . but very few men are capable of estimating the immense amount of torture and agony which this dreadful punishment, prolonged for years, inflicts upon sufferers."

Battles erupted between reformists of the two systems. Silent system reformers denounced the separate, or Pennsylvania system, for being too cruel. "Its loneliness breeds insanity!" they screamed. Separate system supporters shouted back and proclaimed the silent system as crueler. "Placing prisoners in the same room and not allowing them to speak to one another is tempting them in an unfair way!"

Two French prison reformers visited America and evaluated both systems. De Beaumont and de Tocqueville concluded that at Auburn prisoners were more severely treated. Yet, at Cherry Hill prisoners were more unhappy and emotionally and mentally affected. They also discovered that at Auburn, where whipping was the norm, prisoners died less frequently than at Cherry Hill. The two concluded that the separate system proved less favorable to the health of prisoners than the Auburn system.

Despite all the differences between these two systems, and the strong accusations rallied against one another, supporters for both held similar beliefs on crucial issues. They believed imprisonment, not execution, was often the best way to deal with criminals; and that prisons should rehabilitate more than punish. Thus, these two differing yet similar prison operations were the basis of this country's penal system. One historian described it as the "trinity" of early organized prison operations: separation, obedience and labor. At Cherry Hill and Auburn, prisoners could not speak to one another, they had to obey the rules, and were made to work.

Times changed, not out of heartfelt compassion to eliminate insanity and physical deterioration, but for economic reasons. In the progression of the American penal institution, the Auburn system won out. Northern states, except Pennsylvania, concluded that working in factories was simply more profitable. And due to continued prison overcrowding, across the board isolation dissipated. Along with it went the strict code of silence. Cellblocks in which prisoners shared cells were conceived in the North, while dormitory housing was instituted primarily in the South. Solitary confinement became what it has always been—a punishment tool. The 'dungeon' or 'hole' was created for unruly prisoners: total isolation in a dark, dank cell for a specified amount of time, with diets of bread and water.

In sum, early American prisoners served hard, lonely time at the hands of good-intentioned reformists seeking a viable means of rehabilitation. A few lucky prisoners were released with their sanity and physical stamina intact. The majority either died from such harsh conditions, or were released ill-equipped to start over.

Excerpts from an 1866 report by the Board of inspectors of the Western Penitentiary of Pennsylvania, recommended the separate system be abolished:

> As we have made from time to time our frequent visitations to the convict's cell, and have engaged him in conversation and studied his situation, we have often been oppressed with the feeling of despair that seemed to settle upon his face as he would look forward (sometimes through a quarter of a century) to a hopeless future. In his loneliness he broods over his condition, walking his dreary cell in the quiet hours of the night, and

during the unemployed moments of the day. No human face visible against every man and every man's hand is against him,' and having no save that of the officers and his keepers, he feels that 'his hand is object or interest beyond his own walls to attract his attention or arrest his thoughts, he falls back upon himself and his fancied wrongs, and in sullen anguish preys upon his own vitals!

Man is formed for society. He cannot well live without it. Ostracize him from the world and his fellow men, and he soon loses his own self-respect, because he feels that he has forfeited that of others.

In 1890, the United States Supreme Court ruled that extended solitary confinement was infamous punishment.

ANGOLA'S LONGEST CELL-CONFINED PRISONERS

Living in a single cell 23 hours a day. Depending on the weather they receive a maximum three hours a week yard time.

YRS	NAME	PRESENT LOCATION
24	Lee Lane	Hawk Unit
23	Samuel Tropez	CCR
23	Herman Wallace	CCR
23	Robert Wilkerson	CCR
23	Albert Woodfox	CCR
18	Alvin Dillard	CCR
17	Louis Singleton	Clinical Services
14	Curtis Perkins	Clinical Services
14	Grady Brewer	Camp J
13	James Lee	Hawk Unit
13	George Sharp	Camp J
13	Paul Billiot	CCR
13	Jon Simonis	CCR
12	Dale Albert	CCR

21

THE LIVING DEAD*

by Douglas Dennis

A midmorning sun glowed dimly through glowering South Dakota skies. The year, 1937. Howard Christensen and his friend Norman Westberg, both 17, walked south on the muddy shoulder of a two-lane blacktop called Highway 83. Each wore a suit, hat and tie in the fashion of the day, now rumpled from a nagging drizzle. Westberg grunted under the weight of a large suitcase. A week earlier they had fled their parents' Chicago homes to set out for the promised land— California—where they dreamed of fortunes and fabulous girls, theirs for the taking. Like many dreams, it was not to be.

The world of 1937 staggered under economic chaos and glowed with brush fires that presaged World War II. General Francisco Franco, aided by Nazi Germany and fascist Italy, slowly gained the upper hand in the bloody Spanish Civil War that claimed a million lives. Hideki Tojo readied Japan's military machine to invade China. The Great Depression had impoverished millions in the United States. Life was hard, and cheap. Notorious bandits of the period, John Dillinger, "Baby Face" Nelson, Bonnie and Clyde, "Pretty Boy" Floyd, "Machine Gun" Kelly, Alvin "Creepy" Karpis and Al Capone, were all dead or in prison by 1937. And on May 21, two young hitchhikers on a dreary South Dakota byway planned to steal the car of the first good Samaritan who stopped to pick them up.

Fresh from a visit with friends, Ada Carey, 26, at nine a.m. steered her black Ford sedan out of tiny Gettysburg. She

peered through the rain-freckled windshield at the neatly dressed young men lugging a suitcase. Westberg, the taller of the two, raised a forlorn thumb. She pressed the brake pedal.

Christensen clambered in back with the suitcase, sitting behind the driver. He slid a ball-peen hammer out of his belt. Westberg jumped in front, careful not to bump the .32 caliber Russian revolver in his right coat pocket against the door. "Thanks for the ride, ma'am," he said politely.

"Glad I happened along," said Ada Carey. "Where are you bound?" The heavy car sped down the asphalt ribbon. "California." She smiled. "Imagine that." Westberg wiggled his first and fourth fingers at Christensen in the prearranged signal. The hammer rose like a cobra, and struck. Carey's head rocked; she gasped with shock.

Westberg turned off the ignition, reached for the steering wheel. Christensen hammered her again. Carey's eyes glazed. Dark rivulets ran through her hair and stained the collar of her white blouse. Making long S-tracks, the sedan finally swerved to a stop in a shallow ditch. The acidic odor of fear and panic filled the car. Westberg clawed the .32 from his coat pocket. Carey flung up her right hand as he fired. The bullet tore through the flesh between her thumb and forefinger. She threw open the door, was halfway out, when Westberg's second bullet took her just below the right shoulder blade and plowed diagonally up into her chest. The force of it sprawled her onto the wet pavement. A third shot whistled

*Appeared in *The Angolite,* September/October 1994, 20-57. Reprinted with permission.

harmlessly overhead. The car reeked of cordite. Deafened by gunfire, the boys looked numbly at one another.

"We can't leave her here," shouted Westberg. "Help me put her in the car." They wrestled her bloody body into the backseat. An anguished groan reached their ringing ears. "Shut her up," Westberg said, wide-eyed, "and let's get the hell out of here."

Roaring, the car fishtailed onto the asphalt. Carey moaned again. Christensen kneeled on the front seat and smashed her with the hammer, then pulled a blanket over her crumpled body. Westberg, adrenaline in his blood and alarm in his eye, pushed too hard. At the bottom of a hill, he lost it. The sturdy sedan rolled twice, came to rest in a roadside ditch. A wheel spun slowly in the air. The two banged-up youths tumbled out. Westberg nursed his left wrist. Ada Carey groaned, clinging to life.

A Chevrolet coupe crested the hill. The driver, a salesman, spotted the wreck, slowed down. Frightened, Westberg and Christensen ran fast as their legs would churn, abandoning their belongings and the wounded schoolteacher.

Alerted by the salesman, Sheriff Jack Reedy formed a posse at Onida, the county seat four miles away, while Carey was taken to Heart Hospital. Roads were blockaded. Scores of men with rifles and shotguns searched the rolling prairie. An airplane carrying an armed local sportsman flew over the area. Shortly before noon, Reedy and two posse members found the fugitives hiding in a patch of tumbleweeds, captured them without a struggle.

Reedy rushed the boys back to Onida to face their victim. Though sinking fast, she identified them, pointing out Westberg

as the shooter.

Ada Carey died at 2:50 p.m. Within minutes an angry mob, three-hundred strong, milled around the courthouse, muttering threats. Inside in a cell, Westberg lay on a cot staring vacantly at the ceiling. Christensen paced back and forth. The rolled steel bars he had seen as penning him away from the world, he now saw as a barricade holding the world away from him. Suddenly they seemed flimsy. "Sheriff," he yelled, rattling the cell door. "You have to get us out of here!"

In a display of cold courage reminiscent of legendary Old West lawmen, Sheriff Reedy marched his two prisoners through the angry crowd to his squad car. He then sped to Pierre, the state capital, where he locked the boys safely in jail.

At first, Westberg tried to take all the blame. "I'm guilty and I might as well get it over with," he told Reedy. He spun a tale of how he'd pulled the .32 to "frighten" the schoolteacher, it had accidentally discharged, and he'd hit her afterwards with a "car tool." After questioning both boys far into the night, Sheriff Reedy extracted the truth.

South Dakota did not then have the death penalty. Facing mandatory life terms, Westberg and Christensen pleaded guilty. "Sure, we're sorry we did it," Westberg said, "but there ain't much we can do about it now. We wouldn't do it again." Two weeks after the murder, June 5, 1937, Circuit Judge John F. Hughes imposed sentence and told the youths he would send complete documentation to the warden at the state penitentiary, where it would remain "as a record of the most dastardly crime ever committed in this state." That same day the ubiquitous Sheriff Reedy transported them to the South Dakota State Penitentiary at Sioux Falls.

Six years later, November 2, 1943, Norman Westberg committed suicide. Ironically, he embraced the fate earlier avoided at the hands of the Onida lynch mob; he used a belt to string himself up in his cell. Perhaps he suffered from clinical depression. Perhaps a traumatic event pushed him over the edge. Perhaps an overwhelming weight of guilt became too much to bear. Or perhaps after six years he understood the system well enough to realize his future promised only an existence behind bars, and so chose a quick death rather than one prorated over a lifetime.

Howard Christensen elected to live. He is still in the South Dakota pen, the longest continuously confined prisoner in the United States.

* * *

Every state has prisoners like Christensen, gray and withered by decades of imprisonment. Faded men who plod prison yards with halting steps, nursing a spark of ersatz hope while they wait to die. Their families have forgotten them, and so has society. Called old-timers, longtermers, or simply "Pop," they are usually first-offender lifers like Christensen. Prison is their world. They know nothing else. No longer the dangerous felons they once were, they have come to terms with the system, embrace it. Yet the system has never given them a break, never offered them a second chance. They are a small but growing group of prisoners who have served twenty or more years of continuous confinement. They are the living dead.

No one has ever bothered to determine who they are, how many they are and where, and what they're like. *The Angolite* undertook a nationwide survey to identify those still in prison after serving two consecutive decades or more. Each state was asked to identify its longest continuously confined. Forty-five states responded.

All but Florida (and Michigan for women) know which man and woman in their systems have served the longest, but 24 states refused to release their names. No reason was given, and none is apparent. Names of convicted criminals are public information, along with their charges, sentences, and various other facts. Such widespread reticence can be explained by the traditional secrecy with which prison officials have always tended to enshroud their fiefdoms.

The survey's most striking revelation (see Figure 1) was the difficulty some states had in locating their longest confined. California, with the largest number of prisoners, simply did not know. Neither did Alabama, Rhode Island, Florida and Michigan. Maryland and North Carolina hazarded a guess. This ambiguity compromised the verifiable number of longtimers, particularly in the 20-30 year category, where the total should be much higher.

Even so, the number of longtimers (2,099) compared to the total reported prison population (775,624) is small—but growing fast. This is a modern phenomenon, the product of a law-and-order movement that began with the election of Richard Nixon, who promised to restore law and order to a nation wearied by anti-Vietnam and civil rights protests, college campus revolts, a rising crime rate, and ghetto riots.

Reform and redemption gradually fell out of favor, replaced by a punitive penal philosophy. Public clamor caused traditional incarceration practices to give way to far tougher and longer prison stays.

Avenues of release were fast closing, especially for longtimers.

The movement first began in Louisiana. New Orleans District Attorney Jim Garrison in 1967 took a breather from trying to solve the Kennedy assassination to successfully lobby lawmakers to increase the armed robbery penalty to 99 years. Prior to that, aside from execution, Louisiana's harshest penalties had been a 30-year maximum for armed robbery and a life term for murder, rape or kidnapping. Both provided for release consideration after ten years. Louisiana's abandonment of redemption and rehabilitation proceeded apace from 1967. Each year thereafter state legislators lengthened penalties, invented new crimes, and made it more difficult for people to get out of prison.

If a state's punitiveness is measured by how many of its prisoners are confined for extraordinary periods of time, Louisiana leads the pack. As shown in Figure 1, this state keeps more prisoners locked up longer than any other state. It has 344 longtimers, 288 of them at Angola, who have been continuously confined for 20 years or longer, 2-1/2 times more than any other state. New Mexico has no one who has served more than 20 years. The five states after Louisiana each have only a third as many longtimers. Thirty-nine of Louisiana's lifers have served 30 years or longer, more than twice as many as its nearest rival, Illinois, which has 15.

The dubious distinction of being America's most punitive state is reinforced by Louisiana's other criminal justice achievements. Governor Edwin Edwards, in a recent speech to state lawmakers, stated that Louisiana has more mandatory sentences on its books than any other state, and punishes its convicts with longer penalties on average than any other state. Louisiana, according to the latest figures from the federal Bureau of Justice Statistics (BJS), locks up more of its citizens than any other state except Texas and Oklahoma: 499 per 100,000 people. The national average is 351. Louisiana well deserves its harsh reputation. Ironically, it also enjoys the highest murder rate in the country.

Figure 1 also illustrates the national shift toward permanent imprisonment. The 20-30 year group is more than eleven times larger than the 30-plus group (1,927 to 172). Release cannot account for this disparity. Most longtimers were stuck in place after the public mood changed. Mortality is not the reason. Most 30-plus lifers are in their fifties, some are younger. The sizeable 20-30 year group is, therefore, the fruit from the first planting of "get-tough" laws and policies. These prisoners are the tip of the iceberg.

* * *

Interestingly, war criminals given life terms for atrocities committed during World War II served far less time than America's longtimers. For example, reported the Associated Press, the Netherlands pardoned and freed 109 war criminals between 1950 and 1989, who had originally been sentenced to death, including two Nazi officers who sent Anne Frank to the death camps. For many years, the United States urged the release of Rudolph Hess, the number-two man under Adolph Hitler. Russia wouldn't allow it, and in his 47th year of a life term Hess finally died in Spandau Prison. The former commander of Treblinka, Kurt Franz, according to the New York Times, was freed in 1993 after serving 34 years. He was convicted of complicity in the murder of at least 300,000 people, most of them Jews, and for personally killing 139.

America's longtimers, like Christensen, whose crimes pale to insignificance beside the millions murdered by Nazi butchers, are apparently deemed less worthy of release. This raises troubling questions about the American concept of justice.

The Angolite survey found that the nation has 15 men confined more than 40 years, held by 13 states. Only three states (Fig. 2), South Dakota, Kansas and Pennsylvania have men confined more than half a century. On the other hand, New Mexico's longest longtimer has served only 15 years. North Dakota has only 463 prisoners; its longest confined man has served but 20 years.

South Dakota is a penal puzzle. A rural, agricultural state like its sister, North Dakota, it has a population slightly less than that of San Francisco and a relatively insignificant crime problem. It has the death penalty, but does not impose it. Yet 16 prisoners out of its 1,537 have served more than 20 years. Five of the 16 have served more than 30, and one is America's longest confined: Howard Christensen, imprisoned 57 years.

Christensen, 74, is currently confined in the mental health unit of the South Dakota State Prison. "It's real important," stressed Kris Petersen, the unit manager, "for [*The Angolite* to understand] Howard's placement; he's not mentally ill. He's really classified as a 'special needs' inmate. And at this particular time it's the best housing placement for him."

"Special needs" is a common prison euphemism for "protection." There is that element with Christensen. "They recently transferred him up to the main facility [a cellhouse], and he doesn't sleep well at night," said Petersen. "Younger inmates will begin to pester him, tease him, and he has a terrible habit of yelling and screaming all night long, which then only

intensifies this kind of negative behavioral cycle."

Christensen's special needs also have to do with his advanced age. "[His] personal hygiene leaves something to be desired," Petersen said, "but we work on that. We make sure he gets showered and shaved, that he's eating properly, and receiving his medications that he's needing because of his age. It's a lot more humane to have him housed here than to let him try to survive up in general population."

Petersen, Dale Lint and Bonnie Larsen (social worker and case manager, respectively) told *The Angolite* that prison employees consider Christensen somewhat of a mascot. "Howard has been here for so many years, he's become like one of the family," said Petersen. "People treat Howard, on balance, very well. In fact, they spoil him. They give him all kinds of candy and ice cream, and pop and cigarettes. People have a natural sympathetic response to him because of the amount of time he's been incarcerated."

An enigmatic aspect of Christensen's confinement, one that could explain why he's been locked up so long, is the extended time he spent at Yankton, the state mental hospital. Thirty-one years, according to Christensen, though he was never diagnosed as being mentally ill. "I think part of the time [at Yankton] was back in the '30s or the '40s," said Petersen, "when they really didn't know what to do with him."

From all indications, Christensen began to exhibit odd behavior, what he calls a "nervous disorder," as a result of being repeatedly sodomized. More likely than not he was initially sent to Yankton to protect him from predators. "I think over that period of time Howard was in and out on a number of occasions," Lint said. "What has really happened is that for a number of years there's been some adjustment problems as far as Howard's ability to cope with the general rigors of prison life. By moving back to the state hospital it became a housing issue again. Much, much easier to house, and much, much easier to monitor.

"It's not a routine situation," continued Lint. "I think Howard has probably been perceived by the institution as an exception for a number of years. . . . Our institution here, it's relatively small. And so we can afford to make exceptions, like in Howard's case. Over the years you get to know everybody very personal."

At any rate, Yankton staff endorsement in 1975 appeared pivotal in having Christensen's life sentence reduced to 200 years, making him parole eligible. He was denied, though, until the early '80s when the parole board tried him at a Sioux Falls halfway house. Christensen calls it "house arrest." After two weeks he was sent back to prison, he says, for "bothering visitors." Lint says otherwise: "I think that's more of a societal adjustment situation."

Christensen's flexibility—his ability to adapt—has ossified. "As a trusty [he] went on furloughs," said Bonnie Larsen. "And often he'd go out for a little bit and get nervous and want to come back."

"Somebody here in town [Sioux Falls] would pick him up," added Petersen. "He'd go downtown for ice cream, and want to come back home. His socialization skills are what I would say a pre-teen level. You can sit down and have a conversation with him, very interactive to talk to. He's funny, and he can play a lot of good cards. But as far as adapting to life, taking on responsibility, earning his own way. . . ."

Christensen's prognosis for freedom is slim to none. "A lot of plans for Howard have been thought up and implemented over the last ten years," said Lint, "anywhere from parole, a halfway house, a boarding house option. But his social skills are nil. Howard knows how to survive within the confines of this penitentiary system. He knows how to get what he needs here. But outside these walls it's a scary world, and he has no idea how to get his needs met."

Death in prison is his only option. "I think that when the day comes that Howard leaves us, when he dies," said Petersen, "he's so infamous with the penitentiary staff both present and past that. . . . I don't know. He's quite a character. Once you meet him, you won't forget him. . . ." Petersen paused to collect himself. "If his brother's still alive, [he] would have the option—type of burial and so forth. [If he's not], the county coroner would take care of that, and Howard would be buried in a kind of public grave here in the county."

* * *

Crime is a young man's game. Women historically have been on the sidelines, a fact reflected by the nation's prison population. Since 1980, according to the BJS, women have comprised 5% of those imprisoned. At the end of 1993, they accounted for 5.8% (55,365) of all prison inmates (948,881), their crimes almost evenly divided in thirds among property, drug and violent offenses. Almost two-thirds of the women in prison for violent crimes have been convicted of assaulting or killing relatives or friends, many of whom were abusive husbands or boyfriends.

Women are neither portrayed nor perceived as fearsome in the way male criminals are. As a result, the criminal justice system is more understanding and merciful to them. When women go to prison, even murderers, they don't stay long. Not compared to men.

The disparity between time served by men and women lifers is vividly illustrated by the contrast between Figures 2 and 3. Male longtimers serve at least twice as much time as women straight across the board. The nation's longest imprisoned woman has done 31 years, compared to Christensen's 57. The longest serving men in 43 of 44 states have served more than 20 years. while the longest serving women in 30 of 43 states have served less than 20 years. Vermont's longest serving female has done five years, a laughable entry on a chart of longtimers.

There is a leniency correlation among states. Those that treat men mercifully do the same with women. Eight of ten states (excluding Florida and Michigan) at the bottom of Figures 2 and 3 are the same.

* * *

The nation's longest imprisoned woman is Betty Smithey, confined 31 years in Arizona for murder. Arizona prisoncrats refused *The Angolite* any contact with her, either by phone or letter, but did furnish a few facts of little value to *Angolite* publisher, Warden John P. Whitley. The portrait of her crimes and background recounted in the later sidebar had to be constructed from contemporaneous newspaper accounts.

* * *

Louisiana's longest imprisoned female has little in common with the eccentric, essentially passive Christensen and still less with the aberrant, possibly deranged Smithey.

Carolyn Ann Hollingsworth has just turned 40. Arrested at 16 for killing a grocer during an armed robbery and sentenced to life imprisonment at 17, she's been incarcerated in the Louisiana Correctional Institute for Women (LCIW) near Baton Rouge for 23 years. LCIW Warden Johnnie Jones, in sharp contrast with Arizona's concrete curtain, allowed *The Angolite* free access to Hollingsworth. She is intelligent, alert, scrappy, showing no sign that confinement has either numbed her will or neutered her soul. Most prisoners have nicknames. They call her "Super."

A Texas girl, reared in Houston's rough Fifth Ward, Hollingsworth erred early on and never recovered. Pregnant at 15, she "had to drop out of Elmore Junior High. You didn't go to school back then pregnant," she told *The Angolite*. "And then, soon as I had my baby boy [July 1970], I got married [to his father] because, security for the baby, I had to act like an adult." Her husband went to Huntsville prison for armed robbery, leaving Hollingsworth on her own with the baby. To survive, she "got a little job at a soul food restaurant, waitress and, like, cashier."

Recreational drug use in 1970 was the height of fashion from Hollywood to Houston. "I was on drugs, too," Hollingsworth admitted. "Pills and I can't think what all. Everybody was doing it. I was young, OK, and so I was trying to do all the adult things. Most of my friends were five, six years older than me."

Gloria Dean Williams, then 25, was "my husband's best friend's wife," said Hollingsworth. "And it was through her that I came to meet David Lawrence Killyon [then 23] and Phillip Anthony Harris [then 20]. Phillip, he was a booster, shoplifter. Killyon was in the

Navy, on leave or AWOL. Something. I never did find out."

On a cold, dismal day in February 1971, they left for Shreveport in Killyon's two-door Chevrolet. "They wanted to buy drugs," Hollingsworth said, "and I wanted to see my stepdaddy. He'd moved there after my mother died in a car wreck [a few years earlier]." Hollingsworth left her baby, Terryl, with her mother-in-law for safekeeping.

Harris bought a bagful of pills in Shreveport, but Hollingsworth never saw her stepfather. "We never could even find the street," she said. "Gloria suggested that we go to Opelousas. That's where she was originally from. She said she knowed where there was some money to be made there."

According to the *Opelousas Daily World*'s in-depth trial coverage, they arrived about 9:30 the night of February 21, and slept at Williams's cousin's house. The following morning Williams borrowed a shotgun and a lifelike toy pistol from a neighbor. Killyon drove them to Cutrera's neighborhood grocery store a few blocks away, dropped them off, and waited at the corner with the motor running. Williams had the toy pistol, and Harris had the shotgun (with no shells in it). They entered the grocery store at 11:30 a.m. Budge Cutrera, 64, was in the back, his wife behind the counter.

During the next five minutes the robbery attempt went bad. "I want all your money or I'll kill you," Williams told Mrs. Cutrera. A scuffle ensued, drawing Budge Cutrera from the back room. He wrestled with Harris for possession of the shotgun. Cutrera's wife hit Williams over the head with a quart-sized Coke bottle. It shattered, cutting her hand. Hollingsworth ducked behind the counter and, she told *The Angolite*, "There

was a gun in like a cowboy holster. So I pulled it out and I'm looking for PeeWee [Harris] and I spotted him and Budge struggling over the shotgun. When Budge end up with the shotgun, Gloria say, 'You have to shoot him. Shoot him, Carolyn!' I say, 'You shoot him!' I didn't know till later she had a toy pistol. Sure look real. She say, 'You have the gun, shoot him before he kill us both!' Well, I closed my eyes and fired the gun." According to the coroner, Cutrera died within minutes from three bullet wounds.

The robbers fled the store, rocketing back to Williams's cousin's house with $200 from the cash register, $4,000 in a red tackle box and $1,100 from Mrs. Cutrera's purse. On a telephone tip, dozens of heavily armed lawmen surrounded the house at one p.m. A state police helicopter hovered overhead. Officers arrested the four in Killyon's car, seconds before they would have departed for Houston. All the money and weapons were recovered.

"It was Gloria's idea to stick up the store," Hollingsworth told *The Angolite*, "because she knew the people and knew they had money." Hollingsworth claims Harris forced her to participate. "He hit me," she said, "and threatened me."

Long-term District Attorney J. Y. Fontenot sought the death penalty for Harris, Hollingsworth and Williams. Killyon, the least culpable, agreed to plead guilty to manslaughter in exchange for his testimony against the other three.

Despite the open-and-shut case against three blacks who had robbed and killed a white man, the all-white twelve-man jury voted for life, not death. Some said it was the high-powered Texas attorney Harris's family had hired to represent him. More likely it was Hollingsworth's youth and tearful testimony that made the difference.

The assistant prosecutor who had taken Hollingsworth's statement testified that she was "very remorseful" about shooting Cutrera. Hollingsworth took the stand and wept as she described what had happened from Houston to the arrest. The jury deliberated for one hour, then returned three verdicts of "guilty without capital punishment." Life sentences were automatic.

Killyon went to the first-offender prison at DeQuincy with an 18-year term. On March 24, 1977, after serving a third of it, he was paroled. He never returned to the Louisiana prison system.

Phillip "PeeWee" Harris came to Angola. He didn't stay long. On June 15, 1977, he transferred to the State Police Barracks in Baton Rouge, where he was assigned to work at the Governor's Mansion for Governor Edwin Edwards. When David Treen became governor in 1980, Harris' fortunes ebbed. He returned to Angola on March 20, 1981. Edwards reclaimed the governor's office in 1984, and later reduced Harris's life sentence to "time served." He was released on May 22, 1987, after serving 16 years, and presumably rejoined his family in Houston.

Gloria Williams went to LCIW with a life sentence on her back and leaving on her mind. According to Hollingsworth, she escaped three times and ended up doing eight years in Texas for a Houston armed robbery. Although Williams is now in LCIW, her time on escape and in a Texas prison disqualified her as Louisiana's co-longest confined woman.

Hollingsworth's own adjustment to prison was neither quick nor easy. "After we got here in 1972," she said, "an episode happened with a homosexual. The girl hit on me and I didn't want her. She got mad and wanted to fight, so we fought

and I beat her up." Despite Hollingsworth's small size (5-foot-2, little more than 100 pounds), she said predatory homosexuals were not much of a problem. "My mind was more mature than my age," she said. "They used to try to run games on me because they really thought that mentally I was just seventeen. When they found out it wasn't so, they would just get upset."

Her conduct record is atrocious. "I did my number," she said. "Oh God, I fought the police, residents [fellow prisoners]. I was pretty bad." How bad? "Um, let's say 500 write-ups [disciplinary reports]." One report about every two weeks for twenty-three years; "pretty bad" is an understatement. "They're real tight," she explained. "You get a report for laughing too loud. Somebody needs a bar of soap, you can't give it to 'em. You can't lend anybody anything or you'll get a write-up."

Getting into trouble was not Hollingsworth's sole activity. "Oh, I play volleyball, softball," she said. "And then I got off into the educational thing. I had already gotten my GED [high-school equivalency diploma] in '74 or '75, so I took courses in English and Drafting. Whatever they allowed me to do, I did. When [Northwest Missouri Community College] came, I did that."

People who stay in prison a long time tend to wind up abandoned and alone. Hollingsworth has been fortunate. Her aunt and sisters visit regularly, three or four times a year. "Not my son no more 'cause he's in the prison at Abilene, Texas, for aggravated battery. All he do is fight, fight, fight. He's 6-foot-8! Rudy [her ex-husband] was average height. I don't know," she laughs, "maybe they gave me the wrong child."

Hollingsworth's attempts at clemency

have repeatedly been denied because of her poor conduct record. She says her release is not opposed by Opelousas law enforcement or by the Cutrera family. "This is the first time I was in trouble," she said. "After 23 years I have found myself. I grew up in here. What I did to improve myself was my own motivation, because so far as the institution or the system is concerned I could just sit here and do the time and make no type of progress. I think it stinks, and I get angry sometimes. But I don't let it affect me. I put it in perspective, deal with it, and say 'bye.'"

Budge Cutrera is dead at her hand. "He's still not gonna come back if it was 23 more years, OK!" she said. "I know that I was wrong for killing the man. If I was there today, at 40, that thing would not happen. No way! I don't feel like I should have no life, none whatsoever, because I made a bad mistake as a kid."

Hollingsworth has spent 58% of her life in prison. Asked if she thought about not getting out, about dying behind bars, she straightened and fire flashed from her eyes: "No! No! Uh-uh! No, never! I'm leaving!"

* * *

Louisiana's longest confined male prisoner has, like Christensen, been imprisoned longer than anyone in his state's history—42 years. Sammie Robinson Jr. was the subject of an *Angolite* feature article ['Blood, Sweat & Years,' July/August 1991], detailing his extraordinary career as Louisiana's longest imprisoned. In July 1994, when *The Angolite* interviewed Robinson again, he was still in the cellblock. He is a different breed, his a tale of blood and violence well suited to what at the time was dubbed

"America's worst prison."

Robinson was a sixth-grade dropout from rural Caddo Parish near Shreveport, who had been sent to reform school for stealing from a supermarket. He escaped twice. As a fugitive, he was arrested in December 1952 and subsequently convicted of attempted aggravated rape. He was sentenced to 15 years at the Louisiana State Penitentiary.

State prisons of that era operated out of the public eye. They were brutal, violent jungles where even the strong did not always survive. Southern plantation prisons, like Angola, Tucker and Parchman, gave some prisoners pistols, rifles and shotguns to guard the others. In 1951 at Angola, by utilizing an inmate-guard force of 600, fewer than 100 employees supervised 3,000 prisoners. Discipline was enforced by hickory stick, ax handle and leather strap. Prisoners in "long lines" labored all day in cane, cotton and bean fields, and were left to their own devices at night. It was into this world that Sammie Robinson, a smooth-faced 17-year-old, was thrown on September 26, 1953.

His first night at Camp-A, a man was knifed to death in the bed next to him. "Dude threw a blanket over his head and stabbed him up," Robinson said. "I turned my head and was scared to look back that way." The strong took what they wanted, including sex. "I wasn't gonna let anybody fuck with me about my ass," he said. "I was born a man, I come here as a man, and I'll leave here a man."

The pivotal year in Robinson's long confinement was 1958. That September the parole board might have released him, but it was not to be. While living in Hickory-2, a 60-man medium-security dormitory on the notorious Big Yard, Robinson found himself in the midst of a violent confrontation. Although both men had knives, no one was injured. But as a result, Robinson was transferred to CCR (Control Cells-Receiving), an ultra-tight lockdown area near Angola's front gate, where prisoners are kept in one-man cells almost 24 hours a day. Violence, however, had become Robinson's bed partner.

While he was out in the hall to shower, a prisoner in another cell reached through the bars and slashed him near his eye. Blood streaming down his face, Robinson removed a thick glass lens from a hallway light and threw it at the prisoner. The inmate hall boy, Charles Oliver, charged onto the tier, says Robinson, with a pocket knife in his hand. He retreated to the mop closet, ripped down a wooden shelf and hit Oliver in the head with it, killing him. The man allegedly had a plate in his head.

Robinson pleaded guilty on May 9, 1958, to murdering Oliver, and was sentenced to a life term to run consecutively with the fifteen years he already had. Adding to Robinson's problems, his mother died that year.

Since 1958, he has spent almost all his years in one lockdown situation or another. In 1965, when he was in the Main Prison's Cellblock-B, Robinson says he had a second run-in with Clarence Marks, the prisoner who had stabbed him in CCR. Marks doused Robinson with lighter fluid and set him on fire. "You could smell my meat cooking all over the block," he said.

Third-degree burns covered 33% of Robinson's body, leaving wattled scars on his stomach, chest and arms. Skin grafts were required so that he could fully extend his arms. Why did Marks set Robinson on fire? "Well, I guess it was just his way of trying to get me out of the way,

you dig?" said Robinson. "You know how a convict think. Once you have it with him, he always gonna think you gonna get rid of him."

On September 10, 1970, after 17 years in Angola, Robinson was taken to a court hearing in Rapides Parish, where he had gotten his 15 years for attempted rape. The judge dismissed the conviction and sentence because Robinson had pleaded guilty without the services of an attorney. Illustrating one of the prison world's anomalies, Robinson returned to Angola to serve time for something he had done after being improperly imprisoned.

Problems with other prisoners were only part of Robinson's difficulties. Between 1958 and 1972, he accumulated 37 disciplinary reports, most for possessing knives, fighting, or insubordination. Then he picked up five more years for attacking a guard when caught with a knife in Cellblock-A. He hit the man in the head with a coffee jar. After pleading guilty to attempted aggravated battery, Robinson had life plus five, and had been in prison 20 years.

During one of his infrequent forays into general population, Robinson on Thanksgiving Day 1973 killed another prisoner. Following an argument, he and inmate John Walker were being escorted down the Walk by a guard. "Well, I swung over Mr. Tillery and I joog this dude," said Robinson. "I got him right in the middle of the chest. The whole knife went in to the handle. He was trying to pull the knife out, but it was stuck in the breastbone. He laid there at the trusty gate kicking a long time before he died. That's the way it happened."

Almost a year to the day later, in November 1974, Robinson pleaded guilty for another life sentence. He now had two life terms and five years running consecutively or, as they say, "running wild." But he has had more luck in court than in avoiding violence. First, his original 15-year sentence was set aside in 1970. Then, in 1979, the Louisiana Supreme Court on procedural grounds voided the life term for the 1973 killing of John Walker. That left Robinson with the sentences he is still serving: five years for attacking a guard with a glass jar, and life for the 1958 killing of Charles Oliver in CCR.

After spending almost three-quarters of his life in Angola, Robinson has no regrets. Says if he had done anything different, he would probably be dead. Adaptability is key to survival. He adapted to the jungle into which he was exiled, became part of it.

Robinson's body, replete with slash, stab and burn scars, is a testament of agony. He's been stabbed on several occasions, burned, and hit on the head with a baseball bat. What precipitated his attacks and the attacks upon him; what deep divisions required such drastic action? "I don't really remember," Robinson said. "Walker, I know we had a little argument about something. You know how it is. You got some convicts you can talk things over with. And you got some convicts that don't want no talk outta you, because his mind says either he hurt you or you hurt him."

Kill or be killed, now an outdated philosophy. Angola has changed, and so has Robinson. "I don't remember the last time I had a really serious write-up" he said. "I don't be getting them no more. I ain't really had none in so long. All the freefolks around here, you know, we gets along."

The vortex of violence that swallowed Robinson has marked him mentally as well as physically. "They kept me locked up awhile after I killed that dude in '73," he said. "Then they wanted to let me go back into population. I told 'em I didn't want to go. You know why? I got kinda afraid, you see. The way I look at it, I don't want to be around too many convicts, you dig? That's why I'm laying in this cell. It's wide open in the dorm."

Angola's cellblocks are designed to be punishment units. For Robinson, they're a comfort zone. "I got a little orderly job, feed, and fix the food and clean up," he said. "I got permanent light duty. I don't really have to do no work, me, just lay around. But I'm not gonna just lay up and make myself old, don't move around. I'm out the cell when I want, go in the cell when I want. I ain't gonna do no better out there on the Walk."

Angola is Robinson's home, the only one he's ever had. Now 58, bent and scarred, he says he has no friends in prison, no family outside. "I haven't had a visit since my momma died in 1958," he said. "I had two or three of 'em wrote me [following the 1991 *Angolite* article]. But I ain't heard nothing for a good while, you know. Since I been in here, I lost my momma, lost my dad, lost two sisters. Two brothers are still in Huntsville prison. I had a brother, Willie, got killed here. He was eating in the dining room at Camp-H, and a dude walked up and stuck him in the back." Sammie Robinson is the archetypal lifer, a totally isolated man.

Yet, in the ashes of his ruined life, he has kept alive a guttering spark of hope. "I been caught up in a trap and I can't get out of it," he said. "Sometimes I be thinking that I'm gonna make it out, then sometimes I think I'm not gonna make it out. I want some of that free world. I've never had a woman. I came here when I was young. I ain't never been outside to have nothing."

Last November the pardon board recommended a reduction of Robinson's sentences to 60 years. It awaits review by Governor Edwards.

* * *

Louisiana's large crop of convicts confined for more than thirty years stems primarily from the dismantling of its time-honored lifer release mechanism. First legislated in 1916, restated in Act 50 of 1942, it provided lifers viable access to freedom through the executive clemency process.

The full text of the "10/6" law, LSA R.S. 15:571.7:

"Whenever a prisoner who has been convicted of a crime and sentenced to imprisonment for life so conducts himself as to merit the approval of the superintendent of the state penitentiary he may apply for a commutation of his sentence and the application, upon approval of the superintendent, shall be forwarded to the governor. The governor may commute the sentence upon recommendation of the lieutenant governor, attorney general, and presiding judge of the court before which the conviction was had, or any two of them. No commutation under the provisions of this section shall reduce the period of incarceration to less than ten years and six months."

While R.S. 15:571.7 does not require release, in actual practice it jelled into a bureaucratic procedure that practically guaranteed well-behaved lifers release after serving ten years and six months. A form signed by the Angola warden went to the state capital, where the required signatures were affixed. Ultimately, a commutation of sentence document (called a "gold seal") was issued to the lifer, who then discharged.

"It was routine," former Angola warden Hilton Butler told *The Angolite* some years ago. "If a lifer kept his nose clean, he got out of prison in 10-1/2 years. I'd say almost 99% of all the lifers got out."

"In some cases," former Attorney General Jack P. F. Gremillion once told *The Angolite*, "where there was a lot of opposition and the guy also had a good prison record, he might be delayed getting out but he still got out in 15 or 16 years. But let me say this, the opposition had to be warranted. We didn't listen to unwarranted opposition. So I would say the average amount of time for a lifer to be reviewed and processed all the way through the system would cause him to serve on an average, I'd say, of 12 years. Never much more than that."

By today's standards that seems incredibly lenient. In context, it was severe. Louisiana lifers served as much as ten or twelve years at a maximum. All other prisoners served less. That held true for more than a century, from the mid-1800s until 1972, with no measurable impact on the crime rate. It was also consistent with how much time prisoners served in other state and federal prisons.

Everyone in Louisiana's criminal justice system—prosecutors, defense attorneys, judges—knew about 10/6. Prosecutors routinely used it to induce a person facing a capital charge to "cop out" for a life sentence. Before 1972, almost everyone pleading guilty for a life term was told by his attorney or the prosecutor (or both), sometimes by the judge as well, that if he kept a good record he would get out in 10/6.

Gilbert Green, then 24, was arrested November 22, 1963, the night of President Kennedy's assassination, for killing his mother's live-in boyfriend.

"They was telling me about the electric chair," he said, "and telling me to go ahead and cop out and I'd be out of prison in ten years, six months. They told me all about how I'd go up on the pardon board and get my time cut after I done 10/6 and get out. So that's what I did."

But two important things were happening in Louisiana's criminal justice system. Because of steadily increasing penalties, district attorneys became aware that murderers were eligible for release before people serving time for lesser offenses, particularly armed robbers. And in 1972, the U.S. Supreme Court ruled in Furman v. Georgia that the death penalty as then carried out was unconstitutional. Forty-three men on Angola's death row moved practically overnight from the shadow of the electric chair to potential release processing. Some had already served 10/6, others were close to it. Many people, especially victims, prosecutors and other law enforcement personnel, found this intolerable.

Sometime in 1972, Corrections Director Elayn Hunt called Angola Warden C. Murray Henderson. "I was told in a telephone conversation with Mrs. Hunt not to send any more 10/6 applications to headquarters," he told *The Angolite*. "That's how the practice was discontinued. It was done at the top official level. I never sent anything out to the inmate population notifying them, because I never got anything official on it." Several years passed before lifers noticed that none of their number were getting out.

A 56-year practice had snapped shut, just like that. It is highly doubtful that Elayn Hunt, given her liberal philosophy and penal reform background, would arbitrarily close down an avenue of release for lifers codified in law and long-standing practice. But there is no evidence to show

otherwise. Before Edwards left office in 1980, his office informed *The Angolite* that no legal opinion or instructions had been given to Hunt by his office to discontinue processing 10/6 applications. Because Hunt had died in office in early 1976 of pancreatic cancer, she could not be consulted. "I **assumed** [emphasis added]," Henderson said, "that headquarters had got some kind of approval or go-ahead from the governor's office. The law required that I sign 10/6 applications when it was appropriate. I complied with that law until I was instructed not to do so."

Some 10/6ers took it to court, arguing that the rules of the game had changed in midsentence to their disadvantage. Gilbert Green was one of them. He had carefully kept a good record so he could be released on his 10/6 date. "I got no serious write-ups," he said. "I ain't never been busted with no knives or drugs or nothin' like that." His 10/6 date came and went, and he filed in court. "They got it [10/6 references] in my records," he said. "I got records and papers saying all that they did. And I went to court and they still wouldn't do nothing."

Now that Green has served 10/6 three times over, his bitterness and sense of betrayal are understandable. "They changed everything on me," he said. "From the way it looks, don't look like I'll get out. If I'd a knowed it was gonna be like this here, I think I woulda just went on and let 'em did what they wanted to do."

Lifers have committed serious crimes, deserving of punishment, and bear the brunt of current public fear and hatred. Hardest hit are those who have already been punished for three decades or more. Others, who committed crimes as bad or worse, went home long ago. The oldest longtimers remain, not so much because of what they did decades ago, but because they fell through the cracks of a criminal justice system theoretically obligated by its own and society's best interest to identify and cycle out those who have received sufficient punishment and who no longer constitute a threat to public safety.

Who are these lifers, what are they like, and why are they still confined? A statistical profile shows the average longtimer to be a black murderer in his early fifties. Angola's thirty-six 30-year-plus longtimers range in age from 48 to 77, with 54 their median age. Average age is 56.67. Six longtimers are more than 60 years old. None are Hispanic or Oriental. Twenty-three are murders; thirteen are rapists. There are four white (11%) and 32 black longtimers (89%), while Angola's total population is 24% white, 76% black. To flesh out the portrait, the Angolite interviewed Angola's 30-year lifers.

* * *

"In the ten years preceding 1976, statistics show that the Louisiana State Penitentiary was the most violent prison in the nation," former corrections chief C. Paul Phelps once told *The Angolite*.

Henry Patterson recalls the aura of tension and fear in that basin of blood and brutality. Convicted of murder for hitting a man in the head with a board during a Shreveport bar fight, Patterson, then 23, arrived at Angola in March 1961. "When I first come here I was just another fresh fish," he said. "There was a lotta dudes from Shreveport knew me, so I ain't had no problems with no [predatory] homosexuals. But I come here a little young kid, OK. I was scared to death. Just walk in and see a man take an old piece of rusty iron off the bed and get on

the concrete and scrub it and scrub it, make it one of the most beautiful knives you ever wanta see, and go kill a dude because the dude was throwin' an S on him [giving him a dirty look]. I ain't never saw nothing like this. I ain't never been around a buncha inmates wear shades at twelve-o'clock midnight. They got their boots on in the bed. You know what I'm talking about? It be July, a dude walking on the Walk with a raincoat on all down to his knees, boots on, and he might have a hatchet, ditchbank blade, and everything on him.

"So everything I did was outta fear," continued Patterson. "If I struck a dude, I was trying to strike before I got struck. It was a crazy place here. We went through lotsa changes in prison. You develop a demeanor that makes a person think before he fucks with you."

Patterson piled up stacks of disciplinary reports during his first 10 to 15 years, did a lot of cell time, and acquired a reputation as a troublemaker. Then, in a phenomenon common to Louisiana longtimers who start prison life poorly, he straightened up. "I got no more than five [disciplinary reports] in the past 15 years," he said. "The last write-up I had in reference with violence was in '77. A dude got shot in CCR with a zip gun. But I've been out of extended lockdown since 1980. I haven't had any serious infractions since then." He learned a trade, earning certificates from cooking and baking school, and achieved trusty status in 1981.

Efforts to get a sentence reduction have been more than a little disheartening. "It's frustrating to stay here thirty-some years and every time you go on the pardon board you get a positive response," said Patterson, "but when you get to the governor for him to put his signature on your papers, it never shows up. And you waiting. Every time the Man [guard] say 'legal mail' you run up there with your heart in your hand, figuring this might be it. It's devastating. The Man will call your name in the dormitory, your heart'll jump fast, look around, it ain't there. That's more frustrating and disappointing than not going on the board, period."

After so many years, the question of dying in prison comes under consideration. "I go to work at the hospital," said Patterson. "I look at the guys I used to know 20, 25 years ago. They're in the ward, die from heart attack, cancer, other physical disabilities, and I'm wondering if I'm on this kind of agenda."

Angola's tentacles of mayhem and gore have snared more than one longtimer. Sammie Robinson was not the only prisoner whose initial crime paled beside those he went on to commit in prison.

Almer Randle, then 19, killed his wife in April 1961 with a .410 gauge shotgun in Webster Parish near Shreveport. "It was like O.J.," he said, "a domestic situation that got outta hand." A month later, Randle came through Angola's front gate with a brand new life sentence.

At that time the use of armed inmate guards was in full play. Called "khaki-backs" because of the clothes they wore, they were the only armed persons in the penitentiary. They manned guard towers and provided perimeter security for "long lines" (fieldhand crews). Prison officials considered new inmates from rural areas who were convicted of murder or manslaughter to be prime inmate guard material. They had no ties to other prisoners, most of whom were from urban areas, and had proven they would kill. Almer Randle became a khaki-back and went to Camp-H, where inmate guards lived.

"I killed two guys at one time," Randle

said. "One of 'em was accidentally though. I was guardin' Line 3 [one of the Big Yard's black long-lines]. That was in '62. At the time we check our guns in at the tower right there in the front [of Camp-H]. Go in, eat lunch, go back to the dorm a few minutes, and then go back and get our guns. So I'm by my bed about 20 minutes before we gettin' ready to go back. Blackjack, a big ole guy weigh about three somethin', he walked up to my bed and tole me when you come in this evenin' you gonna be my whore, or else. I'm tired a this, you know. I just went on to the guard tower and got my .351 rifle and come back in. He was settin' on his bed there talkin' to Willie Vincent. Poor little fella, he wasn't no bigger than a radio. When I walked up from the back a the dorm, I couldn't see Vincent. When I shot Blackjack, the bullet went straight through him and hit Vincent, killed him too. Two in one shot. Give me two life sentences. Didn't let me have no more guns after that neither."

Randle's bizarre history resumed a few years later at Angola's Reception Center, where he committed a crime oddly reminiscent of his original offense. "I was an orderly," he said, "keeping the hall clean. That's where I got the attempt murder in '67. This was behind punkology too. I ain't gonna lie, I was messin' with this punk then, trimmin' this punk. He done got short, fixin' to go home, and he decide it's all over with me and you. I had got out there in that water, man, I didn't wanta hear nothin' about no 'quit.' He jest insisted on quitting. I jest stabbed him. I end up gettin' seven years for that."

With three consecutive life sentences plus seven years, Randle for a long time saw no pressing need to behave. "I got a messed up conduct record," he admitted. "I have about 90 write-ups. About four for fighting, two or three for knives. I don't mess with no drugs. My main thing is alcohol, makin' beer. I'm a beer-maker, me. Uh, at least I used to. I ain't been busted in a good while."

Alcohol and trouble go hand in hand, wherever you are. "I went back trusty to Camp-I, vegetable crew," said Randle. "Then I got busted for hittin' ole Tarzan [a black prisoner no longer at Angola] in the head. That ole thing drunk up all my beer, got drunk and talked crazy. I knocked him in the head and went to Camp-J [disciplinary lockdown]. I been back and forth between trusty and big stripe [medium security] I don't know how many times. I work at the BOQ [bachelor officers quarters] now," one of Angola's better jobs. Randle is again a trusty, has kept himself out of trouble and limited his life to hobbycrafting. "I go do my daily assigned job, come back, goes to the hobbyshop till it close, take my shower and go to bed," he said. "I do leatherwork every day. That's where my life is, in the hobbyshop."

Randle realizes there is little likelihood he will be released. Too much violence for one thing. No resources for another. "I don't have any help outside," Randle said. "Been on the pardon board three times. Each time I got denied. Get out? No. It's been so long, and I just hardly ever think about it. I ain't gettin' out." He has made peace with himself and his situation.

Two "fall-partners" can come to Angola with the same time for the same crime. One gets out, and one gets left behind. Joe White, then 18, and Raymond "Perdido" Harris, then 19 (and two juveniles who were soon freed), were arrested for the June 1961 beating death of a man in New Orleans.

White and Harris arrived at Angola with life terms after pleading guilty and, although they remained close, began acting like Jekyll and Hyde. White went more than ten years before his first disciplinary report. Creating impressive poetry in his spare time, he earned his GED, taught typing and bookkeeping, and worked as an inmate counsel. After nearly 30 years, White received a sentence reduction and left Angola on parole. Married now and working as a paralegal, he's living the lifer's dream: making it straight on the outside.

Harris, on the other hand, acquired more disciplinary reports than he cares to count. He spent 20 years or more in CCR and the cellblocks, and measures the knife and surgery scars he's gotten over the years in feet, not inches. In 1977, he also picked up a consecutive eight-year term for aggravated battery. "Me and Joe Anderson got into it down in Oak-4 dormitory over a little gambling debt he owed me," he said. "He got kinda hostile, and one word led to another. I hit him with a 2 x 4."

Now the years weigh heavier and heavier, slowing him down. "I done improved my conduct record a whole lot," said Harris. "I haven't had no major write-ups since '86. When I came here I was young and kinda wild. I been through my battles, through the war zone. I had my share of grabbin's and stabbin's. I'm through with that, you know."

His mother and father have died, leaving him with no one outside who cares about him. Except his fall partner. "Joe, he's really sticking with me," said Harris. "He have kept his word, and I love him for this here. Joe was never the kind would run around looking for trouble or give you trouble. I think that's why he got out and I'm still here."

There is a possibility Harris, like his fall partner, might be given a second chance. He says he has a recommendation for a time-cut to 75 years awaiting review. "I'm hoping and praying that the governor go on and sign my gold seal," he said. "There's so many ways you can make a living out there if you want to. I got it on my mind it ain't gonna be no crime. I know one thing, I will not come back to Angola."

Darrow "Bossman" Bowman, 49, came to Angola at age 17 with life. "I'm here for killing a white dude [in November 1962] in Simmesport," he said. "I really didn't kill him. His old lady killed him with a gun. She shot him. And that's how it happened. I been here ever since."

Some youngsters when they hit the Walk stay in trouble. "After I got here I kept my head down, never looked up, passing up opportunities," said Bowman. "I got 199 write-ups. Mostly little stuff: running away from the freeman, wrong dorm, gambling. Only three knives. I don't play the blocks, only three times in lockdown."

Most longtimers cling to outside contacts. Bowman encouraged his isolation. "I never did let my momma come visit me," he said. "She died in '92. I never had a visit with my own people since I been in the penitentiary. I didn't want 'em to come. I love my people, but I just couldn't stand to see 'em walk out the door and I stay. Gets my mind all messed up. The letters I be getting bring me down, so I told 'em not to write."

Once he embraced the prison life, now he seems resigned to it. "I went on the pardon board once, three or four years ago," said Bowman. "Denied me, my conduct record. I really don't have nothing out there. My people ain't able to help. They're getting old." Wistfully, he added,

"I think something will break for me. I just got that feeling."

Willie "Snake" Richardson began badly, then matured. Locked up at 17, he came to Angola in March 1964 with life for killing a black man. "Altogether I got about 120 write-ups," he said. "One for a knife. All the rest of 'em is petty." He also picked up a two-year term in 1967 for aggravated battery. "I was in a cell in the blocks, early years," Richardson said, "and this dude call hisself claiming me [as his sexual slave]. Funny part about it, what I stuck him with was his own stuff. When I took it from him, he tried to run but it was too late. The dude done gone home, about a year or two after that."

In 1972, Richardson picked up two more years for escape, a charge he says was blown out of proportion. "I was living at Camp-I, trusty," he said. "I was a horse boy. I laid there and I was drinking some a that white lightning. And I rode the horse over by Camp-H, but I wind up by AS&R [automotive service and repair, four or five miles from Camp-I], and that's where I went to sleep at. In the bus. They had been lookin' for me all that day. I done slept all through count and when they found me, I was asleep. They found the horse behind the garage."

Richardson since then has found legitimate outlets for his energies. At age 49, he is still active in sports, and spends his spare time as a hobbycrafter. "I play a little softball," he said. "A youngster ain't got nothin' on me. Right now, I'm hung up in a volleyball team. To be honest with ya, I'm more tied down in hobbycraft. You know, I make it all— anything from a sandal to a saddle."

He has also overcome emotional deprivation. "I got a boy," said Richardson. "We been together so long, twelve years now. It's more or less now like friends. You know how a husband and wife be together so long until they just lay around and things. Everything they do, they do it together. That's how me and him is now. Everywhere I go, he go. You know, after I got together with him seem like I quit getting wrote-up all the time." Getting in trouble could mean the two would be separated, so is avoided. "I like women," continued Richardson. "But that's it, that's all I got. You can't have no friends in here. The closest one to me is that boy, because I can trust him. I beat the game."

Dr. Frank L. Rundle is an expert on "situational" homosexuality, having served as chief psychiatrist at a California prison and for all prisons and jails in New York City. "A lot of inmates form very close emotional and affectional relationships," he said, "which many times includes the sexual, that are purely voluntary. What we would consider a normal emotional relationship. As far as I'm concerned, for that to happen in prison is healthy. It can in some way ameliorate the desocializing process which goes on in a prison."

Richardson's infrequent efforts to get a reduced sentence have, he says, always been denied. And so he rolls on, dodging prison's potholes, trying to squeeze a measure of contentment out of his razor-wire world.

* * *

Roland Gibson Jr., with the Maryland corrections department, commented when responding to *The Angolite* survey: "As might be expected, common traits to inmates serving long, uninterrupted terms of confinement are life sentences with poor institutional behavior." Gibson is not the first to make that observation.

Good conduct nearly always did lead lifers to release. That penal principle no longer applies.

More potent factors than institutional behavior now determine which lifers get out and when, and which stay in. Factors such as public attitudes, the "nature of the original offense," opposition to release by victims and law enforcement officials (especially politically adept prosecutors), the release practices currently in political favor, and how much pressure for release is brought to bear by friends and loved ones.

A significant number of Louisiana's longtimers did not go through the poor behavior/good behavior shift. They behaved well from the start.

It would be hard to find a better example of a model prisoner than Wilbert Rideau, 52, who has acquired only one minor disciplinary report during his 33 years at Angola. He spent more than ten years on death row for the 1961 murder of a woman stemming from a Lake Charles bank robbery. Resentenced to a life term in June 1973, he assumed editorship of *The Angolite* three years later. His accomplishments have since won him prestigious awards and national acclaim as a journalist, and this sobriquet from *Life* magazine: "The Most Rehabilitated Prisoner in America."

Rideau is also one of the most visible prisoners in America, appearing often in national publications, radio and television. Trusted, he travels to high schools and colleges, sharing his knowledge and experience with students.

There have been many calls for his release, but he remains imprisoned. He declined to discuss his case, citing a longstanding self-imposed rule against doing so in *The Angolite*.

Leotha Brown, 53, is one of the

brightest and best educated of Angola's longtimers. Attending his junior year of college in 1963, he worked at a bar to make ends meet. He shot and killed a man there during a dispute tinged with racist overtones, the crime that brought him to prison with a life sentence.

A small, unimposing man, Brown's first years in Angola were not the best of his life. "Some things you had to do just for survival sake," he said, "to be here today, otherwise..." Such as, he says, taking the charge for a nickel bag of heroin in 1971, which resulted in an additional five-year term. He has 17 disciplinary reports, most minor and most from his early years.

Brown is dynamic and has leadership abilities. In 1972, when the U.S. Justice Department sent a negotiating team to Angola to moderate differences between prisoners and prison officials, Brown was one of seven who represented the prisoners. In 1973, Brown was elected to the Grievance Committee and became its secretary. He spent many years during the eighties as a trusty at Camp-H, and was a force in the Lifers group there.

Louisiana has no AA or BA college programs for its prisoners. Unable to complete his education, Brown did the best he could. "I think I have more hours than anybody else at night vocational school, computerized typesetting," he said. "And I've taken several correspondence courses from LSU. Just finished one in records management.   I paid for all my correspondence courses. It's money well spent. It gives me a greater feeling of self esteem to know that I can still function at this level after being in here so many years."

Despite his intelligence and energy, bitterness eats at the corners of his soul. "I made one miscue and they took me out

of the game. One strike and I'm out," said Brown. "The odds are definitely against me and people like me who have really made a change in life. Sure, we made a terrible mistake, but this society is supposed to endorse the Christian ethic of forgiveness. But the vindictiveness we see today. . . . I can understand that when something has just occurred, but after so many years I think a man should be given a chance if he has proven himself."

Henry "Wolfman" Montgomery is another striver, or was. He straightened himself out, then in later years fell victim to apathy.

Montgomery was initially sentenced to death for the 1963 killing of a Baton Rouge policeman during a scuffle in which the officer was shot with his own gun. Awaiting appeal, he escaped from jail in 1966. "I didn't go nowhere, really," he said, "just got outside the building." He was given five years, and sent to Angola. In 1969, his death sentence was exchanged for a life term.

"I got about 15, 16 write-ups all the time I been here," said Montgomery. "About five in the last ten years." He earned his GED and was active in prisoner self-help clubs. "I was one of the original sponsors in bringing the Angola Boxing Association together," he said. "I used to be a boxer, and was the head commissioner for five years."

Links to the outside, so vital to maintaining emotional equilibrium, disconnected as the years passed. "Thirty-one years is a long time," said Montgomery. "Mother, she died ten, eleven years ago. After that everything went downhill. Cousins and aunts done burned out. I can call every now and then, you know, but that's about it.   I'm isolated, sho' nuff."

The flame of hope has burned out. "A

cut to 65 years is hanging up in the air," Montgomery said. "Don't have no help to get it signed, not really. Those days are gone that you could get out without help. I'm just taking one day at a time. I might never get out."

* * *

Louisiana, Pennsylvania, and South Dakota have the toughest life sentences. All life terms mean life: one strike and you're out. The only possibility of release is executive clemency, which is seldom granted because governors are wary of adverse public opinion. Illinois, Iowa and Maine according to a 1992 *Corrections Compendium* survey, have lengthy minimum terms before a lifer is eligible for conditional release. These states, and Arizona, have for a long time been very strict about releasing lifers. With each passing year, more states adopt the same punitive posture.

Liberal groups traditionally associated with criminal justice reform have abandoned the field to "get tough" idealogues. Only a few anti-capital punishment organizations remain. And they have adopted the strategy of sacrificing all lifers in a well-intentioned but poorly considered effort to save the condemned. As the alternative to execution, they tout life-without-parole sentences for all murderers. A slow, grinding death in a world based on cruelty and punishment, they apparently believe, is more merciful.

The situation is worsened by non-involvement of Christian churches in prison or prisoner reform. In the heart of the Bible belt, the religiously righteous shun their sons and daughters who have gone astray. Prisoners have noticed. They expected more from the keepers of morality and preachers of redemption.

Eugene Tanniehill, convicted of a May 1960 murder/armed robbery, came to Angola a seventh grade dropout. He has since earned a GED. Long active in prison religious activities, he was ordained in 1980 as a Pentecostal minister.

"I made peace with God. If I didn't make peace, I wouldn't have only two write-ups. They could turn me loose this evening on that, couldn't they?" said Tanniehill, chuckling. He runs the yard every day, and is in better shape than many men half his age. "I'm sixty years young!" he said.

Angola prisoners organize and lead their own religious programs. "I am the inmate bishop of all the Christian functions," said Tanniehill. "My church is the Church of God in Christ, but I'm overseer over all a them in the spiritual realm. Active for the last 25 years." Religion for him has been a vaccine against apathy and depression, and a means to help others. "I have made myself a presentation to the young people," he said, "trying to get them off the avenue that I was on. Life don't stop here. You are searching for a free day that you can walk in the fullness of liberty without the shackles of bondagement."

Tanniehill has had no help and little luck shedding his own shackles. "Never had a visit," he said. "Relatives all dead, all gone, everything. I am not in touch with nobody. By society I am forgotten." A 1991 clemency recommendation awaits gubernatorial approval. "Nobody to help get it signed," said Tanniehill. "So hard to get church people, you know. From the time that I been here, they don't want to take up the responsibility."

* * *

Executive clemency has always been the

only road to release for Louisiana lifers. The current clemency structure came into being when Louisiana adopted a new constitution in 1974. It put the process in the hands of a "professional" pardon board, composed of five members appointed by the governor. By early 1976 it had opened for business. A flood of clemency applications flowed in. Edwards signed 1,181 gold seals during the next four years, including 186 for 10/6 lifers.

That largesse came back to haunt him when he ran again in 1983, 1987 and 1991. Opponents made pardons and commutations a hot political issue. This resulted in the reluctance of governors, including Edwards, to sign more than a few lifer commutations. Since he recaptured the governorship in 1992, Edwards has commuted the sentences of only 15 imprisoned lifers.

"The state has no philosophy for pardons," former corrections head C. Paul Phelps told the *Baton Rouge Morning Advocate* in 1981. "The historic origin of pardon is the king's right to correct a wrong. But in Louisiana, governors have operated the clemency process for political expediency, as a reward for good behavior, or for the convenience of the state—and once in a while to correct a wrong." Nothing has changed, except the dwindling frequency with which clemency is granted, especially to imprisoned lifers.

Joseph Glaviana, 51, has served 31 years so far for a July 1963 aggravated rape. Several boys and two girls were involved and, the way he tells it, they had consensual sex. The girls got in trouble with their parents about it, and "put the blame on us." His two fall partners, Randy Casco and Frank Solar, were released long ago.

"The judge raised all kinds of hell 'cause Frank got out," said Glaviana, a mild-mannered person who speaks of his disappointments without rancor. "I was on the pardon board then, '74 or '75, and got denied. Three weeks ago the governor sent my papers back again. Denied. That's four cuts I done got. Nobody would sign them."

Glaviana is a trusty with a good record. Asked if he thought he would ever be released, he replied: "I hope I am. I'm gonna go one way or the other, dead or alive. I don't know. I guess I'm gonna go back up on the board and try again."

Vehement victim opposition can cause a governor to ignore a pardon board recommendation. Occasionally, though, a victim pleads for her victimizer to be released. Sometimes the governor listens, sometimes he doesn't. A case in point is Donald Ray "Frog" Buffett. He and Robert Lewis, both 17, were arrested for the August 1962 armed robbery and aggravated rape of a white woman. With the specter of the electric chair over their heads, both pleaded guilty for life sentences plus 25 years.

Buffett's institutional conduct reflects the familiar pattern of early disciplinary problems followed by an almost blemish-free record. He has had few reports since 1974, and has learned a trade, graduating from baking school.

His fall partner was released long ago. Lewis received a gold seal in 1976, moved to California where he got married and raised two children. He is now an ordained minister in Oakland and works there at a hospital.

Five times now Buffet has applied for clemency, receiving four favorable recommendations. Despite his victim's endorsement, none have been approved. In the mid-eighties, when she found out he was still in prison, she sent a sworn affidavit to the pardon board and to the governor, with a copy to Buffett and his parents. In part, it states: "Although he did commit a crime against my person, it is genuinely believed that he has served a sufficient period of confinement, and that after a sufficient period in excess of twenty years, any further confinement would only serve to outline the seriousness of the offense, and not deprecate the offense with respect to Donald Buffett." Governors have ignored this.

Given that his victim's plea and his good record have not been rewarded with a gold seal, Buffett has had to consider that he might die in prison. "I don't even want to think like that, you know," he said. "But it has crossed my mind. Real painful. This shit is killing me."

Eugene Scott, 53, is another longtimer who was forgiven by his victim. Convicted of a New Year's Day 1961 rape, he was sentenced to die. Later removed from death row by the U.S. Supreme Court and given a life sentence, he melted into Angola's mainstream.

Scott says the victim, now dead, befriended his mother. "She told my mother that I should be out of prison," he said. That, and the fact he has only "about five write-ups," may have helped him in 1980 to get a recommendation for a cut to 45 years. The governor did not sign it. That was his last try at the pardon board. He seems to have accepted his lot. "I don't know why I don't go up again," he said. "Haven't talked to anybody about going back up." A trusty now, he orients his days around his janitorial job, and "walk[ing] the yard, watch TV, read, whatever." Since a 1985 operation for throat cancer, he can hardly speak.

Gary Simpson, 53, is in the painful position of having been forgiven by his victim's widow while being subjected to the unrelenting vengeance of the victim's

brother, sister and law enforcement officials.

Simpson and his fall partner (an Angola lifer who has requested anonymity) held up a New Orleans loan company in August 1963. Leaving, Simpson killed a policeman. "After I turned across St. Claude," he said, "I ran into a truck. That's when the shooting started. [Two policemen] shot the back glass out of the car. One was on the street looking at me. He ran across and I was looking at the barrel of his pistol. I picked up my pistol and just shot and he went under the car. His partner ran across the street, and then we left and got caught about six blocks away."

After Simpson's trial, where he was convicted and sentenced to death, the policeman's widow came to see him in jail. "She asked me why did it have to happen," he said. "And I told her I didn't have much of a choice. If a person wants to arrest you, they'll tell you who they are. But if a person starts shooting at you what can you do? Throw your hands up so they can get a clear shot? I realize I robbed a company and stole a car, but is they supposed to kill me for it?"

His fall partner got life and Simpson went to death row. In 1972, after Furman, Simpson was resentenced to life. "Only have eight write-ups over the thirty years," he said. "I finished vo-tech school, and was in night [academic] school for two years. I'm an orderly at the hospital, work with the patients on the ward."

The pardon board has been unreceptive to Simpson's requests for clemency. "[The widow] hasn't never protested against me," he said. "Just [the victim's] sister and brother, and the police."

Clyde Giddens, 54, is doing life for a 1964 killing he says he did not commit. "[A relative of mine] killed her in the heat of passion," he said, "not me. There was no physical evidence, but my own family turned against me. My brother got up in a preliminary hearing and told the judge that if I did it they ought to burn me. I lasted until October, sitting in the jailhouse miserable and fed up with it." Then he pleaded guilty and came to Angola.

Giddens is a model prisoner and a "state-wide" trusty. "I do heavy equipment work," he said. "They send me all over the state. I'm the only one that does it, been doing it since 1976."

Two pardon board recommendations to different governors were not signed, says Giddens, because of the widower's opposition. "I've done everything within my power to better myself," he said. "I'm even trying to get a degree in advanced mechanical engineering. I just don't know anything else I can do. I can't improve myself enough to satisfy him."

* * *

Age induces mellowing. People slow down, become less inclined to take foolish risks. Studies of recidivism show that the older a prisoner is, the less likely he is to return. And while in prison, the less likely he is to cause problems. Prison officials know this, rewarding almost all longtimers with trusty status. Twenty-five of Angola's thirty-six 30-year-plus prisoners are trusties, and the others were at one time or another. Lifers in for murder are also the ones selected to work in governors' mansions, doing housekeeping chores for chief executives and their families. In Louisiana, lifers in for murder are the only ones selected for such duty.

"I find in my experience murderers are the best bet," the head of New York state's corrections department, Thomas A. Coughlin, told the New York *Times*. "People don't want to hear this sort of talk about murderers [but], after they get their head together, these people are not going to kill again. It's interesting: in the first seven or eight years inside they can be the biggest pains of all, but then they're no trouble. They become introspective, go to college, join organizations and from maybe years 12 to 25, they are very productive."

Clifford "Count" Hampton, 53, with 36 years in, is the second-longest confined longtimer at Angola. Only Sammie Robinson has been here longer. Hampton was a lad of 16 when he killed his girlfriend in May 1958 after a quarrel, and had just turned 17 when he came through Angola's front gate with a life sentence.

Predictably, he had to fight off prisoners who wanted to "turn him out" sexually. One in particular, Camey Times, wouldn't take no for an answer. Little more than two years after Hampton arrived he was forced, he says, to kill Times. He got another life sentence for that. In an embarrassing turn of events, Hampton picked up two more years in 1965 when caught having sex with a "galboy."

He has since matured. "I educated myself in here," said Hampton, a ninth-grade dropout. "Matter of fact, I finally passed my GED this year. I participated in several [self-help] clubs, and I'm the one started the Camp-H Lifers club back in 1977. I work in the Print Shop, running an 1850 multilith offset printing press. That's my trade. I'm a printer. I don't know if this make a difference, to some people it do. I gave my life to Christ in '91, and changed my life all the way around from what it used to be. Mostly I been going to church, and I been trying to lead a Christian life."

His future is up in the air. "In June of

last year," said Hampton, "they sent a recommendation to the governor that my sentence be commuted to 70 years." He has no one to help him get it signed, he says, except his mother and she is "mostly in bad health."

Whether it is his religious convictions or maturity, or both, Hampton has an adult attitude about what he cannot control. "I want freedom," he said, "if I can get it. But I'm the kind of person, well, some people may think I'm kind of weird but if I do something, I'm willing to accept whatever punishment I may receive. I'm not gonna cry about it, you know, or complain, even though I feel that me being kept incarcerated this long is kinda unjust, considering. If I don't get out, if it comes to that, you know, it just come to it. I'll just be here. Try to make the best of my time, my life here, until I die."

Moreese "Pop" Bickham, 77, is the third-longest confined longtimer at Angola and the oldest one. On a hot July night in 1958, he killed two Mandeville police officers in a shootout he says was self defense. "Them two was Klansmen," he said, "and they was after me. They shot first, plugged me in the stomach. What was I supposed to do, let 'em kill me?" Nothing was introduced at trial, according to the transcript, to contradict his version of the incident, including his written confession. He was convicted and sentenced to death. "Why? In 1958, if a black man got into it with a white man, he was doomed," he said. "I'm one blessed out of a million that I didn't get lynched, which they tried to, you understand."

Once his death sentence was reduced to life in 1973, Bickham, too, embarked on a self-improvement program. Ordained in 1978 as minister by Methodist Church bishops, he headed Angola's Methodist church group for nine years, making many speaking trips to church groups in Baton Rouge and Port Hudson. He resumed his academic studies at age 64, and completed the eleventh grade. At 68, he completed a two-year course at the auto-mechanic vocational school.

Now 77, his biggest enemy is infirmity. "I keeps myself together," Bickham said, "by stayin' active. They keeps trying to put me on that old folks ward, but that ain't nothing but a graveyard. I refused. I likes to be around these youngsters and stay involved. I'm in the AA, Toastmasters, church, hobbyshop. All that keeps me alive is my activities and the dream of getting out one day."

Because of strong law enforcement and community opposition, Bickham's sallies toward freedom have been fruitless. The latest, a cut to 60 years, has "been layin' on [Governor] Edward's desk ever since he come in [1992] and the other one went out. Been trying to get everybody I can to go to the governor," he said. "They have called and talked person-to-person with him. He told them he would give it all the consideration he could. It's a brush off, that's what it is. It happened before when he was in [1984-1988], and it's happening again. It's all politics."

Lester Pearson, 57, killed a white man in 1964 in front of a French Quarter bar in New Orleans. "Me and the fella had been out drinking and got in a little argument," he said, "got to tusslin' over the gun. It was my gun. And, uh, the gun went off. We was in a car." The bill of information filed against Pearson corroborates this version of the incident. "It definitely was an accident," he said. The authorities felt otherwise, and sent him to Angola with a life term.

Pearson followed the familiar lifer path of self-improvement and rejection by the pardon board. His family, with one striking exception, has ceased to exist for him. "My mother haven't seen me since I been grown," said Pearson. "None of my people seen me since I been grown." His wife, incredibly, has stuck with him all the time he's been in Angola. "She used to come see me up until last year," he said. "She had a stroke, you know, not able to get around like she used to. We still together after all these years. Georgiana. I know it's a miracle; I thinks about it often. I consider myself very lucky."

Asked if he thought he would ever be allowed to rejoin his faithful and loving wife, Pearson replied, "In my mind I do think I'll get out. In my heart I don't know. She had asked me the same thing. I told her I feel like I will. I want to prove myself to her."

Wilbert Augustine, 67, given the death sentence (later reduced to life) for the August 1959 aggravated rape of a black woman, has outlived everyone who wanted to help him.

"Last visit about four years ago," he said. "My uncle used to come but he died. My momma died in the seventies, too, all of 'em dead. I have nobody to help me get this life sentence off me. I'm livin' in hopes, but I ain't built 'em too high.

"They finally give me a cut about four months ago, to 75 years," Augustine continued. "That's parole eligibility, if the governor signs it. If he doesn't sign it, I'm still where I was. I don't be slouchin' around. My hurting and achin' is inside. I don't be crying on nobody's shoulder."

Anderson Thomas, 51, says he was railroaded for a February 1964 rape. "It was a white lady involved," he said, "and during that time if they say a black dude raped somebody that was it." He is particularly incensed at the way his sentences were imposed. "I had an old lawyer, and he copped me out," Thomas said. "He say he made a deal with the judge and DA. I asked what kind of deal. He say I'd know when I got there. So when I got in the courtroom, the judge read the charge off and ask if I was guilty. I say no, uh-uh. My lawyer say to let him handle it, and he plead me guilty. They just give me the time and sent me up here."

Thomas has applied for clemency "about four times at least," without success. "I feel like this," he said. "I need to get out there where my daughter and grandchildren is. And I feel I done did enough time for a crime for the way I was sentenced."

Joseph "J.J." Carter, 55, doing life for a July 1959 aggravated rape, seems puzzled at still being confined. "I ain't got but eight write-ups in all them years," he said. "The last write-up I got was in 1979. I got my GED, been got that, years ago. All the times I went up on the pardon board I always got a recommendation." All were denied.

* * *

The dangerous young people swept into prison twenty or more years ago for punishment and to protect the public no longer exist. In much the same way hunks of raw, red meat are ground into mushy hamburger, prison has slowly pulverized their vitality, their self-esteem, their bodies and their dreams until nothing is left but empty old men feebly clinging to the long-held hope of one day being free.

Lifer Robert Rasberry, 75, is so innocuous he's practically invisible. Convicted of raping a "colored woman" in 1959 at a Baton Rouge milk dairy, he said, "The law came and they ain't found no evidence or nothing. All they had was she say I did it."

Rasberry is a frail, slow-walking, slow-talking man who appears unable to lift two fingers at the same time. He lives at Angola's only all-trusty location, Camp-F, which in part houses ambulatory old-timers who function best in the camp's secluded, slow-paced environment. "Three write-ups, all this time," he said. "Not making up my bed properly and, uh, can't think. . . . Never been in the blocks. I stay back here. Stay outta trouble."

His lack of resources, energy and initiative may well be what is keeping him confined. "Never had no visits," said Rasberry. "I got an aunt and a sister in Opelousas. I write, and wait and wait for an answer. But I don't get no answer. Been on the pardon board once. Can't recall how long ago. Don't recall which one was the governor. Guys been saying I oughta go back, back up on the board. . . . I pray to God to open a way for me to get out."

Herman Tassin, 50, is another faded long-timer. He was convicted of a 1964 mugging murder in a Marksville parking lot and given a life sentence.

"I wanta get out myself," he said. "Been locked up too long." Short, slender, meek and soft-spoken, Tassin is a first-grade dropout who lacks what it takes to make it happen. "I went to that little school here [literacy class]," he said. "Didn't stay in it long. My mama died in '65. She come see me in the jailhouse like on a Friday, took with a heart attack and died that same night. Brothers and sisters cut me loose, look like. I don't even know nobody out there. Been on the pardon board one time. They cut it to 60 years, going on two years now. Never signed it."

Asked why he waited 28 years to apply, he replied, "I didn't know nothing. Gang of 'em say you gotta go on that pardon board, you might get your time cut. I went up there, they cut it. But I don't know if I'm ever gettin' out. Been here all this long."

Lifer Lloyd Hess, 47, is Angola's only child molester longtimer. Arrested in April 1963 in New Orleans at age 16, he arrived at Angola in March 1966. Between times he was in the parish jail and the state mental hospital at Jackson.

"It wasn't really a rape," Hess told the *Angolite*. "I grabbed the little girl, young child, five, picked her up, took her to a vacant lot and played with her with my fingers. But far as my recollection go back, I didn't have sex with the child. But that's what I got hung up with. No, she was the first one. That was it."

Molesters live everywhere now, a statement about the changed face of Angola, but when Hess came he had to be put into a protection area. He's been in one ever since. Now at Camp-D Eagle (a medium-security protection section), he seems not to care very much about anything. "Since I been here," he said, "I been wrote up about 170-something times." A fourth-grade dropout, he's done nothing to further his education. "Didn't care about messing with it," he said. "They asked me if I wanted to go. I said no."

He gets one letter a month from his sister with money for incidentals, and no visits. "I lost my ma and pa a few years ago," said Hess. "I can't remember when. That's hard. When you lose your momma and poppa, it's something you usually remember. My sis take care of me, you know. She sends me about sixty dollars a month. I think that's all any individual can ask for."

Hess looks older than he really is, and sickly. "I feel weak all the time," he said. "I might not make it out. I deal with it, you know. I accept it. Even if they would give me that, I don't believe I'm gonna hold up that long. I been through numerous examinations at the hospital. One doctor will tell you you're all right. Another will tell you you're about shot. So I just piddly-dee around the dormitory, mostly. Watch TV, that's about it."

Louis Singleton, 57, who is housed in a cell at Angola's mental health unit, is the only longtimer with diagnosed mental illness. "He has been diagnosed with a major mental illness," said Robert Levy, the clinical social worker who supervises the area where Singleton lives. "He's mainly an isolant, doesn't get along very well with the rest of the inmates. He's in his own world, delusional sometimes."

Convicted of killing an elderly black woman in New Orleans in 1961, Singleton wasn't dysfunctional when he came to Angola. They put him at Camp-H as an inmate guard, where he stayed until the use of them was discontinued in 1973. That same year the pardon board recommended his time be reduced to 40 years, and again in 1976 to 60 years. Neither recommendation was signed. Singleton first came under the care of the prison mental health team in 1977, and has been in restricted cell confinement ever since. Whether there is a connection between the stress of having time-cuts he couldn't get signed and his mental collapse is not known.

During his interview with *The Angolite*, Singleton was calm and soft-spoken even when hallucinating. "The woman wasn't dead," he said. "When I went to court, the woman was there. They put murder on my rap sheet, and the woman wasn't dead. The woman was

looking better than she was looking at first, you know. She didn't have nothing to say, just sat in the back."

And later: "In '61 when I came up here, I had 10/6 on my rap sheet. And that's why I got a presidential pardon in '84. President Ronald Reagan. I'm not going home soon for awhile. I got a letter saying they'd hold me till I'm 77. I'm 57 now, go home when I'm 77."

The chance of Singleton going home is practically nonexistent. "Some days he exhibits a high level of personal functioning," said Levy, "however, sometimes his functioning gets so low that he won't even take a bath, cleanse himself. His cell becomes dirty. Then it's time for us to do some type of intervention. He'll get better for a few months, then it starts all over again."

* * *

Summing up, release practices have changed. Rehabilitation as a practical penal construct is dead, which means self-improvement efforts count for far less than they used to. The 10/6 review of imprisoned lifers disappeared, and executive clemency became increasingly rare. The pardon board has no clear policy but, in the absence of strong opposition, tends to reward lifers who have served 15 years or so and have "straightened up." Louisiana governors since 1980, however, have been guided by more stringent criteria that tie closely to prevailing public opinion and political realities. Hence, most recommendations go unapproved. But this describes the playing field, not the players.

Almost without exception, the 30-year-plus longtimers are victims of "prison menopause." This is not old-age infirmity caused by the aging process. It is not "criminal menopause," which is the reduced desire in criminals over thirty to take unwarranted risks or engage in self-destructive behavior. And it is not "institutionalization," which is the diminished capacity of an otherwise healthy prisoner to function outside a controlled environment.

Prison menopause is what happens to longtimer lifers who have been stripped of hope. Lifers initially have to come to terms with the probability they may suffer the ultimate rejection, death in prison. What keeps them going through the wasted days and lonely nights is hope of redemption through eventual release. As the years pass and their youth slips away, irreplaceable loved ones die, the system ignores their sporadic pleas for release and they enter middle age. At some point between the twentieth and thirtieth year of continuous confinement, lifers lose momentum. The wall is too strong. Their spirit dies, and they become the living dead.

Driftwood from a dead era, longtimers have little in common with younger prisoners and avoid them. Most of their prison friends from years past are dead or gone. Within the restricted world of prison, the living dead self-impose a stricter routine, constructing cocoon-like existences outside the prison mainstream. They settle for that. The prospect of freedom has lost value, even become

frightening. Many longtimers give lip service to "getting out" because others expect it of them, but they've abandoned the quest. Ten of Angola's thirty-six 30-year-plus lifers declined to be a part of this article, preferring anonymity to bringing their cases to light. They consciously closed the door to public sympathy and understanding, and possibly to freedom.

Until now, Louisiana lifers had one thing to look forward to at the end: "Medical parole," a final touch of human decency. Under that program, terminally ill lifers were released to die in the arms of their loved ones, sparing them the indignity of gasping their last breath in a cold prison death ward. Ugly winds of vengeance have blown even that away.

Stone-hearted Louisiana lawmakers recently outlawed medical parole for murderers. And in a final turn of the knife, the same legislative body passed a resolution urging the corrections department to move posthaste to refurbish the old Caddo Parish jail in Northwest Louisiana near Shreveport. The jail is to be the final home for elderly state prisoners. Angola's longtimers can now look forward to being ripped from their friends, torn from the place they have spent their entire adulthood and, weighted down with chains and dressed in ill-fitting orange jumpsuits, exiled to an alien jailhouse to die among strangers.

FIGURE 1
LONGEST CONFINED PRISONERS OVER 20 YEARS
(1993)

State	Total Prisoners	Confined 20-30 yrs	Confined 30-40+ yrs	Total 20+yrs
Louisiana (1994)	23,502	305	38 1	344
Maryland	20,200	140 approx.	3	143
Arizona	17,169	129	12 1	142
New York	64,354	129	7	136
Illinois	33,072	118	13 2	133
Virginia	17,859	112	6	118
Ohio	39,705	95	1	96
Texas (1994)	75,329	90	3	93
Massachusetts	10,050	79	4	83
North Carolina	22,000	75 approx.	7 approx.	82
Tennessee	11,178	79	1 1	81
Oklahoma	16,299	72	7	79
South Carolina	19,095	57	3 1	61
Georgia	27,113	54	1	54
Pennsylvania	26,010	40	8 3	51
Washington	10,336	45	1	46
Arkansas	7,908	43	2	45
Iowa	4,892	31	8	39
Kansas	6,163	30	3 1	34
Wisconsin	9,223	26	3	29
Mississippi	9,798	24	1	25
Maine	1,508	15	7 1	23
West Virginia	1,900	22	0	22
Kentucky	10,353	18	0 1	19
South Dakota	1,537	10	5 1	16
Delaware	3,631	12	1	13
Hawaii	1,818	12	1	13
Missouri	16,567	7	4 1	12
Minnesota	4,203	11	1	12
Nebraska	2,488	9	1 1	11
Colorado	9,524	10	0	10
Oregon	6,544	7	0	7
Utah	3,200	7	0	7
New Hampshire	1,913	4	1	5
California	117,519	Unavailable	3	3
Alaska	2,730	3	0	3
Idaho	2,512	2	0	2
Vermont	1,250	2	0	2
Wyoming	1,012	2	0	2

State	Total Prisoners	Confined 20-30 yrs	Confined 30-40$^+$ yrs		Total 20$^+$yrs
Alabama	18,495	Unavailable	1		1
North Dakota	463	1	0		1
New Mexico	3,515	0	0		0
Rhode Island	2,700	Unavailable	0		0
Florida	53,048	Unavailable	Unavailable		—
Michigan	35,939	Unavailable	Unavailable		—
TOTALS:	775,624	1,927	157	15	2099

(No response: Connecticut, Indiana, Montana, Nevada, New Jersey)
Source: Angolite Survey

FIGURE 2
LONGEST CONFINED MEN (1994)

State	Name	Years Served	Sentence/Charge
South Dakota	Howard Christensen	57	200/Murder
Kansas	Joseph Carr	53	Life/Murder
Pennsylvania	Withheld	51	Life/Murder
Illinois	William Heirens	48	Life/Murder, Att.Murder, Robbery, Burglary
Michigan	Oliver Terpening	47	Life/Murder
Missouri	Earl George	47	Life/Murder
Tennessee	Withheld	47	99/Murder
Nebraska	Withheld	46	Life/Murder(2 counts)
Arizona	Jimmie Williams	43	Life/Murder
South Carolina	Press Jacobs	43	Life/Murder
Kentucky	Withheld	42	Life/Murder
Maine	Withheld	42	Life/Murder
Louisiana	Sammie Robinson	42	Life + 5/Murder, Agg. Battery
Iowa	Warren Nutter	39	Life/Murder
Massachusetts	Withheld	39	Life/Murder(2 counts)
New Hampshire	Walter Bourque	39	Life/Murder
Georgia	Withheld	36	Life/Murder
Maryland	Withheld	36	Life/Murder, Assault w/intent to rape
Virginia	Withheld	36	Life/Murder
New York	Charles Glinton	35	25 to Life/Murder
California	Withheld	34	Life/Murder
Wisconsin	Withheld	34	Life/Murder
Arkansas	Paul Fleshner & Albert Harris	31	Life/Rape(2 counts)
Delaware	Withheld	31	Life/Murder(2 counts)
Minnesota	Hugh Bion Morse	31	Life/Homicide

State	Name	Years Served	Sentence/Charge
North Carolina	Frank Wetzel	31	Life/Murder(2 counts)
Oklahoma	Withheld	31	Life/Murder
Texas	A. D. Randle	31	Life/Murder(3 counts), Agg. Assault, Murder with Malice
Alabama	Withheld	30	Life/Murder
Hawaii	Alfred Tai	30	Life/Murder
Mississippi	Earnest Lee Wilson	30	Life/Homicide(2 counts)
Ohio	Withheld	30	Life/Murder
Washington	Withheld	30	Life/Murder
Alaska	Withheld	28	Life/Murder
Colorado	Joseph Morse	28	Life/Murder
Utah	Myron Lance & Walter Kelbach	27	Life/Murder
Oregon	Withheld	26	37/Rape
Wyoming	Withheld	25	50 to 95 + Life(2 cts.)/Murder(4 cts.)
Rhode Island	Withheld	24	75/Robbery
Idaho	Michael Mortimer	23	Life/Murder
West Virginia	Jimmy Westfall	23	Life/Murder
Vermont	Withheld	21	0 to Life/Murder, Simple Assault
North Dakota	Withheld	20	82/Murder
New Mexico	Withheld	15	50/Murder, Kidnapping, Rape
Florida	Unknown		

(No response: Connecticut, Indiana, Montana, Nevada, New Jersey)

Source: *Angolite* Survey

FIGURE 3
LONGEST CONFINED WOMEN (1994)

State	Name	Years Served	Sentence/Charge
Arizona	Betty Smithey	31	Life/Murder
Georgia	Withheld	26	Life/Murder
South Carolina	Peggy Taylor Ferguson	26	Life/Murder
Oklahoma	Withheld	25	Life/Murder
Pennsylvania	Withheld	25	Life/Murder
California	Withheld	23	Life/Murder
Louisiana	Carolyn Hollingsworth	23	Life + 1/Murder, Agg/Battery
Kansas	Frances Davis	22	Life/Murder
Maryland	Withheld	22	Life/Murder
Illinois	Cynthia Barnes	21	20 to 100/Murder
Arkansas	Lucille Smith & Brenda Spencer	20	Life/Murder(2), Kidnap, Theft, Robbery

State	Name	Years Served	Sentence/Charge
New York	Betty Tyson	20	25 to Life/Murder
Ohio	Withheld	20	Life/Murder
Massachusetts	Withheld	(none over 20 years)	
Alabama	Withheld	19	Life/Murder
Iowa	Marsha Mattson	18	Life/Murder
South Dakota	Mary Roggenkamp	18	Life + 20/Murder, Arson
Tennessee	Withheld	18	99 + 1 day/Murder
Idaho	Sally Joanne Needs	17	Life/Murder
Nebraska	Withheld	17	Life/Murder, Robbery, Assault
North Carolina	Margie C. Boykin	17	Life/Murder
Alaska	Withheld	16	Life/Murder
Delaware	Withheld	16	Life/Conspiracy to Murder.
Minnesota	Jean Beverly Link	16	Life/Murder(3)
Mississippi	Deloris Denton	16	Life/Homicide
Missouri	Loretta Young	16	Life/Murder
Wisconsin	Withheld	16	Life/Murder
Texas	Sharon Goffney	16	66/Agg. Kidnapping
Washington	Withheld	15	Life/Murder
Kentucky	Withheld	14	50/Murder
Maine	Withheld	14	30/Murder
Virginia	Withheld	14	104/Rape, Sexual Assault
Wyoming	Withheld	14	Life(2)/Murder(2)
Hawaii	Mary Ann Acker	12	Life/Murder
New Hampshire	Ana Pelton	12	25 to Life/Murder
Colorado	Susan Brown	11	36/Murder, Agg. Robbery, Burglary.
North Dakota	Withheld	11	45/Mrder
Oregon	Withheld	11	22/Robbery
Rhode Island	Withheld	11	50/Murder
Utah	Frances Schreuder	11	Life/Murder
West Virginia	Kathy Jo Scofield	11	Life/Murder
New Mexico	Withheld	10	21/Murder, Armed Robb., Conspiracy
Vermont	Withheld	5	6 to 13/Agg.Assault, Assault to Rob
Florida	Unknown		
Michigan	Unavailable		

(No response: Connecticut, Indiana, Montana, Nevada, New Jersey)

Source: *Angolite* Survey

FIGURE 4
ANGOLA PRISONERS CONFINED OVER 30 YEARS (1994)

Years	Name	Parish	Sentence/Charge
42	Sammie Robinson	Rapides, W.Fel.	Life+5/Murder, Agg.Battery
36	Clifford Hampton	St.James, W.Fel.	Life(2)+2/Murder(2), Crime Against Nature
36	Moreese Bickham	St.Tammany	Life(2)/Murder(2)
35	Joseph Carter	St.Mary, W.Fel.	Life+2/Agg.Rape, Crime Against Nature
35	Withheld	Caddo	Life+30/Agg.Rape, Agg/Burglary
35	Wilbert Augustine	Orleans	Life/Agg.Rape
35	Robert Rasberry	East Baton Rouge	Life/Agg.Rape
34	Eugene Tanniehill	Grant	Life+25+4/Murder, A/Robb., Forgery(3)
34	Withheld	Beauregard	Life/Murder
33	Eugene Scott	East Baton Rouge	Life/Agg.Rape
33	Withheld	Ouachita	Life/Agg.Rape(2),Att.Agg/Rape, Agg/Burglary
33	Wilbert Rideau	Calcasieu	Life/Murder
33	Henry Patterson	Caddo	Life/Murder
33	Almer Randle	Webster, W.Fel.	Life(3)+7/Murder(3), Att. Murder
33	Withheld	Jeff Davis	Life+20/Agg.Rape, Att. Murder
33	Raymond Harris	Orleans, W.Fel.	Life+8/Murder, Agg. Battery
33	Withheld	Washington, EBR	Life+9/Murder, Simple Burglary
33	Louis Singleton	Orleans	Life/Murder
33	Withheld	Orleans	Life/Agg.Rape
32	Withheld	West Feliciana	Life(4)/Mur.(4), Simple Burglary
32	Willie Richardson	Orleans, W.Fel.	Life+2+2/Murder, Agg. Batt., Simple Escape
32	Donald Ray Buffett	Lincoln	Life+25/Agg.Rape, Armed Robbery
32	Darrow Bowman	Avoyelles	Life+1/Murder, S/Burglary
31	Lloyd Hess	Orleans	Life/Agg.Rape
31	Joseph Glaviana	Assumption	Life(2)/Agg.Rape(2)
31	Withheld	West Feliciana	Life(2)+10/Murder(2), Agg. Battery
31	Withheld	East Baton Rouge	Life/Agg.Rape
31	Gary Simpson	Orleans	Life/Murder
31	Withheld	Orleans	Life/Murder
31	Gilbert Green	Caddo	Life/Murder
31	Henry Montgomery	East Baton Rouge	Life/Murder
31	Leotha Brown	St.Tammany, W.Fel.	Life+5/Murder, Poss. Heroin
30	Clyde Giddens	Madison	Life/Murder
30	Anderson Thomas	West Carroll	Life(2)+30+20/Agg. Rape, Agg. Kid Arm Robbery, Att. Murder
30	Lester Pearson	Orleans	Life/Murder
30	Herman Tassin	Avoyelles, W.Fel.	Life+1/Murder, Self Mutilation

Source: *Angolite* Survey

INTERVIEW: THE NATION'S LONGEST CONFINED PRISONER

[Ed: With the cooperation of South Dakota prison officials, Angolite staffer Douglas Dennis interviewed Howard Christensen, the nation's longest confined prisoner. Now 74, he seemed alert but childlike. According to Dale Lint, his clinical social worker, Christensen "is in fine physical health" after a recent hip replacement. "Other than that," Lint said, "Howard [is] mentally fairly stable, struggling with some possible pre-senility dementia, but typically functions pretty well." Excerpts from the 70-minute phone interview follow.]

Angolite: Why do you think you've been locked up so long?

Howard Christensen: Why? I don't know why. I can't figure it out myself. You know what one guy did in here? In 1938, he grabbed ahold of an 18-year-old girl and cut her up real bad with a knife and raped her and killed her. He's freed. Two guys killed the warden in 1936, too, smuggled in .22 caliber revolvers and murdered him. They only spent 25 years here and got out. I don't know why they're keeping me so long.

Angolite: Tell me how you got your time cut in 1975.

Christensen: Yeah, I had life for murder and they cut it to 200 years. . . . A registrar up at, I stayed there about 31 years in the Yankton state [mental] hospital, because I'm nervous. I have a nervous disorder. I can't sit still hardly. And, uh, the registrar up there got a petition, he signed it, a doctor signed it, and a social worker signed it. They cut my time then.

Angolite: They kept you at Yankton for 31 years because you were nervous?

Christensen: Yah. I been there about eight different times. Most I ever spent at one time is six years, I believe.

Angolite: Since your sentence was commuted, you meet the parole board every eight months. Why won't they parole you?

Christensen: They told me three times ago that they were gonna parole me. Then they denied me. I don't know why. Now they keep telling me they don't believe society would be protected with me outside. I don't know. See my partner forced me to commit that crime. He shot her...then he held a gun at my head and told me to hit her. So I hit her on the head with a hammer. . . . They're making a scapegoat out of me, I guess.

Angolite: Ada Carey, the woman you and Norman Westberg killed, did her family protest your release?

Christensen: No one's ever protested me! I asked 'em that once, and they said nobody protested me.

Angolite: Do you still have a family?

Christensen: Ma lived to be 89. She died in 1980. My father died in 1952. . . . My folks were born in Chicago. So was I and my brothers. My grandparents came from Norway and England. I'm Norwegian/England. . . . I've got a brother. He's two years older than me. He sends me fifty dollars a month. That's all the money I get. . . .

Angolite: Anybody visit you?

Christensen: My whole family came up with my mother, plus my partner's mother in 1938. My mother used to visit me every year for two weeks, until she was about 70. Then she had arthritis, couldn't come up no more. She had to walk with two canes. Then my brother visit me three times in the last three years.

Can't come no more now. His wife has got emphysema, and he's gotta take her to the hospital twice a week.

Angolite: How much education did you get outside?

Christensen: Oh, I went to two years of high school. I quit when I was 16 to go to work. I worked for a printer for ten months. Ended up in South Dakota.

Angolite: Did you finish high school in prison, get your GED?

Christensen: No, I took a course in World Geography that lasted three months. . . . I don't care for, I don't like schools, and I don't like work either.

Angolite: What was your biggest problem when you first went to prison, back in 1937?

Christensen: I didn't have no problems.

Angolite: You didn't have any problems?

Christensen: No. Some guys forced me to let 'em commit sodomy on me. They said they was gonna stab me to death if I didn't do that. One guy had a spoon, he sharpened the handle on the floor, and he pointed it at my belly, said he was going to stab me if I didn't let him come up to the cell and let him commit sodomy on me. They did that to all the boys that come into prison then. Old-timers. Mostly old men did that.

Angolite: Old men like you?

Christensen: [loud laugh]

Angolite: Did they commit sodomy on Westberg, too?

Christensen: I don't know. I broke up with him. I didn't like him no more. The first month I was in here I got in a fight with him over who'd get the bottom bunk. And they put us in the hole for ten days, and then we had to work on the rock pile for 30 days, for nothing. They put us in different cells when we got outta the

hole. I quit talking to him after the fight then, yah.

Angolite: That's when the other guys started sodomizing you?

Christensen: Yah. . . . They called the guys like that "queens." They called us all queens then.

Angolite: When those people were sodomizing you, what did you do about it?

Christensen: Nothing. I didn't do nothing about it.

Angolite: What about the authorities?

Christensen: Well, I was afraid if I told the authorities on 'em, somebody'd murder me. They don't like stool pigeons in here, you know.

Angolite: How many of them were there?

Christensen: I remember. . . . All I can think of now is, let's see, three is all I can think of now.

Angolite: How did you get them to leave you alone, eventually?

Christensen: I don't know. I just stopped doing that. I didn't say nothing. I didn't like it, though, to tell you the truth.

Angolite: I'm sure you didn't. They just quit?

Christensen: Yah, they just quit.

Angolite: What happened to your partner, Westberg?

Christensen: He hung himself. Norman was thinking in 1943 they were gonna take him to Yankton. And it was rough on you up there then, so he hung himself.

Angolite: Why did he think they were going to take him to the mental hospital?

Christensen: He was acting nutty in his cell, they said. Jumping up and down and grabbing hold of the bars and stuff like that.

Angolite: Why did you go wrong?

Christensen: I don't know. My

partner forced me to go with him. He told me unless I came with him and helped him commit murder, he'd go back to Chicago wipe my whole family out.

Angolite: Have you ever had a girlfriend?

Christensen: No. Yeah, I had a girlfriend up at Yankton. She died in the Bridgewater Rest Home about four years ago. She wouldn't let me make love to her though. She said, "I don't do that. I'm a decent woman." She's the only girlfriend I ever had. My Ma told me to stay away from girls, they cause trouble.

Angolite: Did you ever try to escape?

Christensen: No, I never tried to escape. I thought about it. Lotta guys asked me why I never escaped. I said, "They just catch you again and give you [more time]."

Angolite: Do you think you'll ever get out?

Christensen: No, I don't believe I'll ever get out now. They'll probably deny me again. The parole board told me about 12 years ago they'd never parole me.

Angolite: How do you deal with that?

Christensen: I feel pretty bad about it sometimes. I'd like to be free, too! I want to get out! I'd like to be free before I die! Seventy-four now, I only got about six more years to live.

LONGEST CONFINED WOMAN

New Year's Day 1963. A good day for the LSU football Tigers. They hooked the mighty Texas Longhorns, 13-0, in the Cotton Bowl. A bad day for 15-month-old Sandra Gerberick in Phoenix, Arizona. Babysitter Betty Smithey strangled her to death, then fled.

"I think I hurt the baby," Smithey told the policeman who arrested her in Tucson, Arizona. "I don't remember doing it, but I must have. I woke up and had this silk stocking in my hand and the baby was cold. I put her back in the crib. Then when I couldn't find any pulse, I kinda knew she was dead."

The petite and demure 20-year-old pleaded not guilty by reason of insanity. At trial, she testified that she "several times before" had tried to smother babies in homes where she worked as a baby sitter, but had always stopped "because they turned blue and kinda scared me."

She also said she was "unashamed" of swallowing a piece of bedspring and several toothbrushes in the county jail and at the Arizona State Hospital. "I don't think it's silly," she said. "When you've got to do a thing, you just have to do it."

Two state psychiatrists testified Smithey was "emotionally unstable," but legally sane. The jury found her guilty of first-degree murder and set her punishment at life in prison.

Although unsuccessful, the insanity claim was not without foundation. Confined since early childhood in orphanages, jails, mental institutions and detention homes, Smithey had led a remarkably troubled life. Bizarre behavior was her trademark. On June 2, 1958, while on parole from the Oklahoma State Hospital for the Insane, Smithey, then 15, climbed to the roof of a Dallas, Texas automobile agency, where she threw stones and threatened to jump. Police finally got her down. Then, "she attempted to destroy herself by various means while in the juvenile bureau and had to be restrained."

One escapade made national headlines. In May 1959, she was paroled at 16 from the New Mexico State Girls Welfare Home to the custody of the institution's staff psychologist. Smithey absconded, taking the woman's 18-month-old son, Mitchell Johnson, with her. Newspapers likened it to the sensational 1932 kidnapping of the Lindbergh baby. Local authorities and the FBI launched a massive nationwide search.

Smithey, after hitchhiking 800 miles to Dallas with the baby, was nearly broke. In a drugstore restaurant, she tried to give little Mitchell to a waitress and then to customers. When they refused, she left the child behind and fled. Moments later she was arrested in a nearby cafe, eating breakfast. "I like babies," she explained. "I like all babies. I started to run off and the baby started crying, so I decided to take him with me." Mitchell was returned undamaged to his ecstatic parents.

"I was born in Durant, Oklahoma," Smithey told a U.S. Marshal, while waiting to be returned to Arizona. "My dad died when I was a kid. My mom died in a tuberculosis hospital last year. I grew up in an orphans' home. Sometimes I live with my sisters. I run away a lot. I don't like to live with sisters."

Escaping from places she "don't like" is another Smithey trademark. After being sentenced to a life term on July 18, 1963,

for killing the Gerberick baby, she boasted to a reporter: "I'm going to escape from that dump down there."

She did—at least four times. October 2, 1974: She broke out of the Missouri State Prison after being transferred there under an interstate exchange agreement. Recaptured in Indianapolis, Indiana. June 18, 1975: Smithey disappeared while on work/furlough assignment from the Arizona Training Center. Caught a few days later, again in Indianapolis. October 5, 1975: Cut through a back fence at the Arizona State Prison. Gave herself up two days later, saying she was "sick and tired of the desert." November 2, 1981: Fled the Arizona Center for Women. Recaptured two hours later in Phoenix.

Betty Carolyn Smithey, now 51, has been imprisoned for 31 years, longer than any other woman in the United States. Her current home is Arizona's new Manzanita Unit, a medium security prison in Tucson. There is no indication she will ever be released.

[The above information was gleaned from the *Arizona Republic*, the *Phoenix Gazette* and the *Dallas Morning News*.]

22

WHEN MERCY SEASONS JUSTICE:
EXECUTIVE CLEMENCY FOR FIRST-DEGREE MURDERERS
IN LOUISIANA, 1973-1994[*]

by Burk Foster

Clifton C. Greene, of Shreveport and Zwolle, Louisiana, arrived at the Louisiana State Penitentiary in summer 1994. Convicted of first-degree murder in an August 1993 drive-by shooting in Many, in Sabine Parish, Clifton was 18 years old when he came to Angola. His sentence: life imprisonment without eligibility for parole. Like the 18-year-old killed in the shooting, Chris Joseph, who became a statistic as one of Louisiana's 900 murder victims in the year he died, Clifton Greene became a statistic on the other side—one of more than 2,500 lifers in Louisiana's prisons, 2,400 of them like him natural lifers not eligible for release. Of the Louisiana State Penitentiary's 4,600 convicts, half are lifers; it is the biggest repository of lifers in the world.

Over 150 new natural lifers entered Louisiana's prisons in 1994, part of a larger group of an estimated 7,000 to 8,000 lifers who entered state prisons nationwide. When America's prison population topped one million in early summer 1994 (1,012,851 as of June 30, 1994, according to the Bureau of Justice Statistics), about 80,000 of them were men and women serving life sentences.

How much time will Clifton Greene and the thousands of lifers who entered other state prisons last year actually serve, before they are released? Will several hundred of these lifers, including Clifton, those designated "parole-ineligible" by the legislatures of 33 states, really be in prison for the rest of their natural lives?

It is hard to answer either question to an absolute certainty, but given present political realities, the answer to the first question is: a much longer time than they would have served until a few years ago. And to the second question: yes, or so near to the end of their lives their best hope may eventually be a medical release that would allow them to die in the free world from which they were excluded 30, or 40, or 50, or 60 years before. Modern medical care is doing wonders for prison life spans.

How long is a life sentence? When Ron Wikberg and I were doing our research on Angola's longtermers, just over six years ago (see "The Longtermers," *The Prison Journal*, Spring/Summer 1990), we reported Bureau of Justice Statistics' figures indicating that for lifers released from prison in 1983, the median time served was eight years and seven months. This is obviously much shorter than a natural life span.

At the time, Ron and I agreed that the statistic was probably reflective of the then-prevalent practices in many states of granting parole release eligibility to lifers after a relatively short period of time, often in the range of seven to ten years. From 1926 until 1972, Louisiana's lifers had been released from prison after ten-and-a-half years, if they had not already had their sentences commuted and been released on parole or good-time. In this era, the assumption was that any lifer with a moderately good behavior record would be recommended for release by the warden.

The recommendation was not complicated or controversial, in most

*Printed with permission.

269

instances. It was merely a fact of the working system. The warden approved, the Pardon Board agreed, the convict was released.

Lifers in other states benefitted from similarly generous release practices. True lifers, who came to prison as young men and stayed for the remainder of their natural lives, were rare birds, as Kevin Krajick pointed out in his *Corrections Magazine* article, "Growing Old in Prison," fifteen years ago.

Ron and I were aware, however, when we wrote about the 31 Angola inmates who had spent 25 years or more behind bars, that we were not writing about a dying breed—a bunch of wild old men who would soon fade from the scene as relics of an earlier age. We were writing instead about the future of American imprisonment—increasing numbers of men and women growing old as they served out real life sentences for crimes committed when they were young.

We had observed a trend that was already taking hold in the 1980s: the great majority of the states were taking one of two steps: increasing the minimum time in prison required for parole eligibility, with a term in the range of 15 to 25 years common now, in 1995; or designating some offenses parole ineligible. Many states have taken both steps. Five states—Florida, Pennsylvania, Louisiana, Michigan and California—have more than 1,000 natural lifers serving these no-parole sentences. Pennsylvania and Louisiana, plus South Dakota, with a much small smaller prison population, have designated every life sentence as a natural life sentence. Table 1, which is adopted from several tables in the January 1993 *Corrections Compendium*, gives an overview of parole in the states as of September 30, 1992. Su Perk Davis's

article pointed out that 8.2% of the prison population consisted of inmates serving life terms, most of them parole eligible.

Of the 80,000-plus lifers in 1994, more than 10,000 are natural lifers. For these men (and a few women), traditional release practices do not apply. A natural life sentence has no statutory point at which parole kicks in; release becomes possible only when the natural life sentence is converted into a finite sentence, and parole eligibility is restored.

What the natural lifers must have, if they are ever to be eligible for release— and what the other lifers must pursue, if they wish to be released before the statutory minimum—is executive clemency. The generic term for the action is a pardon, but in the case of a lifer it is more correctly called a commutation, or a "time cut," as the convicts say.

Executive clemency, once the prerogative of kings, has been handed down to the modern political officials responsible for the execution of our felony criminal laws—our governors and President. Clemency is discretionary, and throughout English and American history it was used not just to restore lost rights or set aside a wrongful conviction, which are the intended purposes of a pardon, but also to adjust other sentences.

Clemency has been used primarily to reduce or shorten deserved punishments, punishments properly imposed on offenders by a judge in a court of law. As such, executive clemency is always more-or-less unjust, as Ernest van den Haag suggested some time ago, in that its purpose is to thwart legal justice for the sake of political or charitable ends. Shakespeare recognized this human dilemma 400 years ago when he pointed out, in *The Merchant of Venice*, though we plead for justice, what we want, when it is our case under review, is mercy, which "droppeth as the gentle rain from heaven upon the place beneath." What we deserve is justice; what we seek is mercy.

How is mercy dispensed upon convicts through the executive clemency process? In the states, two components are important—the pardon board and the governor. Usually an offender must have the approval of both the pardon board and the governor to get clemency, and then in the case of most natural lifers the offender must also go to the parole board for release authorization.

Procedures in Louisiana are illustrative. A life term inmate in state custody first applies to the pardon board for clemency. Since 1975, the pardon board has consisted of five members appointed by the governor to serve terms conterminous with his. A simple majority vote rules. In considering petitions from lifers, the board often rejects them if the offender has not served enough time—with ten years established as a subjective minimum.

If the pardon board approves the petition, and recommends a commutation, the paper work is forwarded to the governor's office, where it is reviewed by his counsel. It may be signed within a few days, or it may lay on the table for years, even into the next governor's term, before it is finally approved or rejected.

If the governor signs the commutation—his stamp of approval is called a "Gold Seal"—the pardon board recommendation takes effect. Unless the board's recommendation is for a time cut to a very short term—50 years or less is considered short for lifers, with recent boards—or unless the inmate has been in prison for a very long time, he is generally not eligible for immediate release, what is called a "cut to time

served." If the inmate's sentence were cut to 40 years, for instance, and he had already served 22 years and had earned his good-time credits under Louisiana law, he would be eligible for immediate discharge.

Most inmates are not so eligible. The pardon board in recent years has tended to commute lifers' sentences to a term in the range of 60 to 90 years, restoring parole eligibility after one-third, or 20 to 30 years. This month, as an example, Governor Edwin Edwards commuted the life sentence of Moreese "Pops" Bickham to 75 years. Bickham is 77 years old. He has been in prison for 36 years, convicted of killing two Mandeville law enforcement officers in a 1958 shootout. Bickham is now eligible for a parole hearing (after 25 years in prison), but he will not reach his goodtime release date for at least a couple of more years, depending on what his prison record is like.

The parole board in Louisiana now consists of seven members, again appointed by the Governor to serve terms coinciding with his, who sit in three-member panels at the various prisons to hear specific cases. Again a majority vote rules. Parole for lifers is far from automatic. Many are rejected. In Louisiana, the parole board is obligated to hear a parole request only once. If the inmate is rejected, the board can vote to accept subsequent requests in the future, but it can deny him the right to a hearing if it wishes. This represents the administrative board's movement toward perfection of the judicial court's baseball analogy: instead of "three strikes and you're out," it's "one strike and you're out." If parole is granted, a release date is established, usually very soon after the hearing, and the inmate is processed for release.

Other states have similar practices,

the major point of difference being whether or not the pardon board's action requires the governor's approval. In an effort to make the pardon board appear more professional and less political, a few states have made the pardon board the governor's designee, with authority to grant clemency on its own. In the great majority of the states, the governor is still the grantor of clemency: he must sign the legal document for it to be effective.

This describes the ideal process, as if you were telling a lifer what sort of obstacle course he would have to run to get released: "Behave yourself for ten or fifteen years, work hard, get active in inmate organizations, stay in contact with your family on the outside, develop an understanding with prison officials, and then go through the pardon board, the governor's office and the parole board. With persistence, you'll get out." The more practical question is: how many lifers successfully complete the course and actually get out of prison?

There is a general perception nationwide that clemency is not used as much as it was before. A century ago, when parole and good-time release mechanisms were not as well-established as they are today, clemency was an accepted and widely-used practice. Inmates with long terms expected clemency. You were likely to die if you stayed in a 19th century prison for more than five or ten years; few convicts served more than ten years, even on a life sentence. If they could last a few years, they could expect clemency to be granted.

Later, as other forms of release became better established, the use of clemency declined, though it remained prevalent as a practice in the South. (See "Pardons and Politics," *The Angolite*, January/February 1988.) But in the last two decades, the use of clemency has become increasingly suspect politically. Even governors who might be inclined to mercy are cautious about appearing to be too generous to convicts, and pardon-selling scandals in Tennessee and Louisiana have weakened the credibility of the political officials who make clemency decisions. The governor's right to pardon, once taken for granted, has now become a political liability. As a governor, you can't pardon too many, or your opponent will call you "soft on crime," and you have to be careful in individual cases to be sure no preferential treatment was bought with money or political favors, which were certainly employed more frequently in the past.

Pardon Board statistics show these figures for clemencies granted by Louisiana's last four Governors:

		Ave.	Yr.
Governor Edwin Edwards	1972-1980	2,367	296
Governor Dave Treen	1980-1984	181	45
Governor Edwin Edwards	1984-1988	632	158
Governor Buddy Roemer	1988-1992	480	120

From 1975 on so-called "automatic pardons" have been available to all first-time felony offenders. Most don't bother to ask for a pardon, to get back their citizenship rights. If they do apply, their pardons do not require the Governor's signature. So automatic pardons are not included in these figures. These are only discretionary clemencies, and the figures are not adjusted for increases in the prison population, which has grown from fewer than 5,000 inmates in the early 1970s to more than 20,000 twenty years later.

As Governor Edwin Edwards's fourth term enters its last year, approaching its end in January 1996, his use of clemency appears much less frequent to this point than in his three previous terms, and less frequent than in Governor Roemer's recent term. Through March 1, 1995, after more than three years in office, Governor Edwards has signed fewer than 200 clemencies. And this is the posture of a Governor who is leaving office to retire from politics, so he doesn't have to worry about facing the voters again.

The interesting point is that although convicts and corrections officials are well aware that clemency is not used as frequently as it used to be, the people of Louisiana (and the legislators who either reflect their views or shape their views) either haven't gotten the word or don't believe it, if they have heard of the change.

A report prepared for the Loyola Death Penalty Resource Center in February 1993 asked 600 registered voters across Louisiana this question: "If a person convicted of murder in sentenced to life in prison without benefit of probation or parole or suspension of sentence, do you think that this person would live out his natural life and die in prison or do you think that he might be released at some time?" The responses were:

He would serve life in prison.........20.0%
He would be released....................71.3%
Uncertain....................................8.5%

The followup question asked of those who said he would be released was: "How many years do you believe he would serve in prison before being released?" The most frequent response was 20 years, the median was 15 years, and the arithmetic average was 16.8 years.

This report makes it clear that the people of Louisiana do not believe that lifers serve natural life sentences; only one in five adults surveyed believed that "life means life." The survey also indicates that most people expect a lifer to serve about 15 to 20 years before being released.

How do these beliefs and expectations compare with the actual practices of life imprisonment in Louisiana over the last 20 years? Since 1973, when Louisiana began to apply true natural life sentences to large numbers of offenders, the number of lifers has increased from 257 to 2,592, as of March 1, 1995. This increase is shown in Table 2. As already pointed out, 2,400 of these are natural lifers. The only ones who are not are the second-degree murder lifers who came in from 1973 to 1975, when parole eligibility came after 20 years, and 1975 to 1979, when parole eligibility came after 40 years. Since 1979, all life sentences imposed on Louisiana offenders have been no-parole sentences.

A few lifers remain who came into the system before 1973, but the great majority, 2,418 out of 2,595 (93%), have come in from 1973 on. How many lifers have left the system in the past two decades, and what has been their means of exit? Using Department of Public Safety and Corrections figures, it is difficult to get a precise answer to this question. When you do a computer printout of lifers, you get a mix of pre-1973 and post-1973 offenders (some of whom were resentenced for pre-1973 crimes), you get a few who were parole-eligible, under statute or court order, and you get some whose status in the computer files was either entered in error (like some shown serving first-degree or second-degree murder sentences that were really attempts rather than completed acts) or some whose status was changed after Pardon Board action or a court ruling, so that it is impossible to tell what their original sentence was, without going back to their records file. There is also no accurate count as to how many lifers have died in prison the past 20 years. The computer printout shows at least 12, but records of the Louisiana State Penitentiary at Angola, where 88% of the lifers are confined, show more than 12 deaths in the year 1993 alone.

What follows is an estimate or "best guess" made on the basis of a thorough analysis (involving three years of off-and-on research) of the imprisonment of life-sentenced offenders in Louisiana, and their discharge or change of status from life to finite terms as a result of executive clemency.

The *New Orleans Times-Picayune* reported "that about 20% of the lifers who applied for clemency between 1975 and 1989 had their sentences commuted to a lesser term, often to 40 to 60 years. During those 15 years, 1,123 lifers applied, 718 were granted a hearing and 538 received a favorable recommendation. Of those, the governor approved 224."

This report does not indicate how many of the 224 commutations were released immediately or went on to get parole, or how many were still in prison. Its basic statistical point—that about 19% of all lifers in custody during this era got some kind of relief from their life sentences—is misleading on two counts. First, commutations were much more frequent in the early years, through 1980, than they were thereafter, as I pointed out in my summary of gubernatorial actions above. Second, many of the commutations granted during this period were of the old "10-6" lifers, sentenced when the rules were different.

Even though court rulings said the release of these lifers was discretionary with the prison warden—his recommendation was necessary for them to get out, and if it was decided administratively to stop making this recommendation, no one could do anything about it—officials have tended to view these inmates in a different light from the post-1973 lifers. So the majority of the 224 commutations were to inmates who had been in prison prior to 1973 and had already served 15 or 20 or more years in prison before commutation.

What of the inmates who have come in since 1973, sentenced for any one of the six current life sentence statutes in Louisiana: first-degree murder, second-degree murder, aggravated rape, aggravated kidnapping, distribution of Schedule I narcotics, and habitual offenders? How many of the "new lifers," almost all of whom are natural lifers, have been able to negotiate the obstacle course and work their way toward freedom?

What I decided to do, to focus my research on a more definable population, and also to use a population comparable to the 1993 Loyola report, was to look at the records of only first-degree murderers. They are probably the most hard-core and long-term of Louisiana's lifers, the ones the public and politicians would least like to see win a commutation or parole. In my view, their release rate would establish the base line probability of release for all natural lifers; my expectation is that second-degree murderers, rapists, kidnappers and narcotics dealers face somewhat better prospects for commutation and parole than do first-degree murderers. So whatever the percentage of success is for first-degree murderers, it is very likely to be no lower (and probably several points higher) for other murderers, rapists, kidnappers and narcotics dealers.

How many offenders have been sentenced under Louisiana's current first-degree murder statute, which went into effect on July 2, 1973? Again, given the way statistics were kept in the first decade after the law took effect, we can't say for certain.

Department of Public Safety and Corrections figures show that 776 first-degree murderers are in custody today (March 1, 1995). But 46 of these by my count are attempts rather than completed acts, and at least 83 were sentenced under the old murder statute rather than the new one.

Deleting these 129, 647 first-degree murderers in sentenced under the new law remain in custody—594 serving life sentences and 53 awaiting execution under death sentences. But the list contains the names of at least two convicts who were executed in 1991 and 1993, and the name of one woman convict released on parole, after a commutation, three years ago. Some other updating is probably in order, including one convict shown as having been in custody since 1935. If he has been in custody for 60 years, we would like to hear from him at once, as this is a new record for Louisiana.

Not on the list are the names of most of the 21 first-degree murderers who have been executed since 1983, when Louisiana resumed the application of capital punishment, and the names of other first-degree murderers who have died of natural causes, suicide, homicide or accidents during confinement. Excluding the inmates who have been executed, about 200 others have died at Angola alone in the past 20 years; the statistical probability is that about half of these were lifers, some of whom were pre-1973 convictions and some of whom were post-1973.

What you get, when you add together the current population of "new" first-degree murderers—life-sentenced and death-sentenced—the executed, the other dead and

the released, is about 700 to 750 valid first-degree murderers who have entered custody from late 1973 to the present. Excluded here, I hope, would be those whose sentences or convictions have been overturned by the courts, resulting in final actions other than re-conviction and re-sentencing for first-degree murder.

So to repeat my question, after this elaborate explanation of how this estimate was arrived at, how many of these close to 800 first-degree murderers have gotten commutations and been released from prison? To arrive at this number, we reviewed all the clemency recommendations of the Louisiana Pardon Board, and their records on gubernatorial actions, since 1980. We did not go beyond 1980, with the exception of one death sentence commutation, because first-degree murderers coming in after 1973 would have served at most less than seven years by 1980, barely enough to get to the fringes of eligibility for commutation. In fact, the first commutation of a new first-degree murder lifer that we found took place in 1984, the only one done by Governor Dave Treen in his four years in office.

From this first commutation in 1984 through early 1995 we found a total of eleven new-law first-degree murderers who received commutations. This information is presented as Table 3. Of the 11, nine were men and two were women. One was a death sentence commuted to life without parole, one was a death sentence commuted first to life and then to a fixed term, and the other nine were life sentences commuted to a fixed term. Nine of the ten commuted to fixed terms were given parole eligibility; one was not. All ten were allowed good-time. Of the eleven commuted, eight were subsequently released from prison, either on parole or at their good-time release date; one of these eight, released on parole, was revoked and returned to state custody.

I have also included an Attachment A as an appendix. It is made of up inmates who were on various lists—official and unofficial—as having been commuted for first-degree murder, but when we investigated we found their placement was in error. Either their crime was an attempt, or not a new first-degree case, or there had been no commutation. I am listing them for the record, because their names are often misplaced in this category.

After more than 20 years of sentencing first-degree murderers under Louisiana's new law, over 700 men and women have been imprisoned, and exactly eight that we can identify have been released. One of these returned to custody to join the three others either not eligible for release at all (including the one Death Row inmate commuted to life) or not yet at their parole or good-time dates.

For statisticians, this means the commutation rate of first-degree murderers in Louisiana is 1.5%, and the release rate is 1.0%. Ninety-eight per cent plus of the first-degree murderers who have come into the lawful custody of the Department of Public Safety and Corrections in the last 22 years are still in the same status they were when they arrived—serving life without parole or awaiting execution—and 99% of them are either still in prison or dead. This is probably about as near-perfect implementation of a criminal justice policy into law as I am aware of in the history of American criminal justice.

The eleven first-degree murderers whose sentences were commuted should consider themselves in select company indeed. Others might ask, considering the 98 out of 100 who did not get clemency,

what sets these few apart, or makes them more deserving? The basic facts of their offenses and the records of actions taken by the Pardon Board and the Governor are matters of public record. A few of the cases are no longer on file in the Pardon Board office, but most of them are and can be discussed briefly.

Charles Caldwell was certainly among the most blessed of the eleven who were commuted. Caldwell, who was assigned to the Governor's mansion as a cook and lived at the State Police Barracks, was commuted twice, first by Governor Edwards in 1988, and then by Governor Roemer in 1990. The first commutation, to 35 years, would have made him parole eligible in 1991; the second, to 17 years, allowed his immediate release on good-time. The Pardon Board Chairman's letter to Governor Edwards mentioned Caldwell's "excellent conduct" but noted opposition from law enforcement and the sentencing judge. His good cooking apparently carried the day.

Polete County was also assigned to the State Police Barracks, where he was described as "a hardworking individual displaying responsibility and dedication. He has performed all duties with a good attitude." County shot his victim three times, after the victim and others had teased him at a party. When his life sentence was commuted to 30 years by Governor Edwards, he became parole eligible at once. He was released on parole soon after.

Bobby Ray Demars was the first post-1973 first-degree lifer to get a commutation, that we can find. He had shot to death an off-duty Natchitoches Parish deputy sheriff in an argument over an admission charge to the Thunderbird Inn. The victim's wife expressed opposition to clemency. The sentencing judge said no clemency for ten years. Otherwise no opposition was noted. Demars had been a trusty in the parish jail before he went to prison. He was assigned to the Governor's mansion and lived at the State Police Barracks—are we beginning to discern a pattern here?

The Pardon Board heard Demars's case originally in 1981. Governor Dave Treen pardoned him in March 1984, as Treen was leaving office. Demars was described as "a model prisoner," who "shows much remorse for the offense committed, and has endeavored to take advantage of every opportunity offered to him toward rehabilitation." He became parole eligible after serving eight years in prison.

The most famous of the eleven commutations, and so far as we know the only one of them whose story has been into a television movie, is Catherine "Kitty" Dodds. The 1994 TV movie was called "The Conviction of Kitty Dodds." Like Charles Caldwell, she received two commutations. She was originally sentenced to death in the murder-for-hire killing of her husband, Charlie Dodds, an ex-New Orleans police sergeant. Sentenced to death at her trial in 1975, she was commuted to life by Governor Edwards in 1977. She escaped from a hospital while confined at the Louisiana Correctional Institute for Women in August 1980. She was recaptured after aiding an elderly man who fell into a ditch in a snowstorm, in her new hometown of Peculiar, Missouri. The publicity brought the FBI, who sent her back to Louisiana in May 1982.

After Kitty Dodds was returned to LCIW, she launched a serious campaign to get a commutation, maintaining that she had been a battered wife but had not made an issue of it earlier. The victim's parents and law enforcement authorities objected

to clemency. Her parents and two children—and the new husband she had married in Missouri—supported her. Her life sentence was commuted to 30 years by Governor Edwards in 1986, but the Parole Board denied her parole requests several times. When she was finally approved for parole, Dodds discovered she had to serve an extra two years for escape first. She was eventually released on parole in 1992, 17 years after her husband was killed. Rodney Blackwell, who did the shooting (either for hire or as a favor to Kitty Dodds) is still serving life for first-degree murder at Angola.

Daniel Gettridge Sr. will be closing in on age 70 when he goes to his parole hearing in late 1996. Gettridge was convicted of shooting Clyde Ratcliffe, the son of his common-law wife, Juanita Jenkins. Jenkins was being beaten by Gettridge on Christmas Day, 1976. When Ratcliffe called police, Gettridge shot him four times. Gettridge was confined at Dixon Correctional Institute in Jackson at the time his commutation was approved by the Pardon Board in 1986. It was not signed by the Governor until more than three years later. Gettridge was subsequently transferred to the State Police Barracks.

Marilyn Hampton is believed to have served the shortest prison term of any of the new first-degree murderers—just over seven years. She was the girlfriend of Timothy Baldwin, who was executed on September 10, 1984, for the same crime she was convicted of. As doubts grew about the extent of her involvement in the crime, she was sponsored for release by the operators of a private halfway house, who also offered her a job there. In contrast to Kitty Dodds, her case and her release attracted little publicity.

Leo E. Jones pleaded guilty to first-degree murder in Orleans Parish in 1973. His crime was a robbery turned murder, in which he did not do the killing. When his sentence was commuted to 25 years by Governor Edwards in 1988, he was parole eligible immediately. He was released and later revoked, the only one of the eight first-degree murderers released to return to prison, that we can identify.

Ronald S. Monroe is close to unique—one of a pair. He and Kitty Dodds are the only death-sentenced inmates to get a commutation to life in Louisiana in the past 20 years.

As Monroe's execution neared in August 1989, evidence pointed to the victim's common-law husband as the person who had done the 1978 murder Monroe was condemned for. Governor Buddy Roemer commuted Monroe's sentence to life without parole eligibility, saying, "If there is any doubt in America, a man ought not be executed." Roemer said "ambiguities and some doubts" remained about Monroe's guilt. "My test is, if there is any doubt, I cannot make a mistake on the side of execution." Monroe remains at Angola, serving his life sentence.

Emmett Raymond Procell, who had killed a friend in a bar fight in Sabine Parish, was commuted by Governor Edwards in 1986, after eight years imprisonment. He had already reached his good-time release date. He returned to his hometown of Zwolle but moved away and law enforcement authorities have not heard anything of him in several years.

Looking at this relative handful of successful commutations, occurring at an average of only about one a year for the past decade, what points can we make about commutations for first-degree murder since the new statute took effect in 1973?

1. The most obvious point is that there aren't many of them, not enough to base much of an analysis on. From the convict's point of view, it has become almost impossible to get a commutation.

2. Very few of the commutations, perhaps two of the lifers and Ronald Monroe, were at the state penitentiary when their commutations were approved. Most were at the State Police Barracks or other prisons. The already sparse odds of getting clemency get much worse if you happen to be at Angola—close to one in a thousand, for the new lifers.

3. Several of these clemencies appear to be more like pardons than commutations. That is, they are corrective rather than diminutive, reflecting changes made by political officials based on more information being made available about the offenses. We could have lively discussions about whether several of them ought to have been prosecuted or convicted as first-degree murders in the first place.

4. The rate of commutations has declined sharply. Of the thirteen total, spread among eleven offenders, one (Dodds's death to life) was in the 1970s, ten in the 1980s, and only two so far in the 1990s. Governor Edwards has commuted no new first-degree lifers in his current term. So to many present first-degree murderers thinking about how they might qualify for a commutation one day, clemency remains more of a fable—a tale of supernatural intervention that once happened to others—than an event of daily reality.

I will note, as a final observation, that it appears unlikely that the trend of the last two decades will be reversed any time soon. As the legislative session of 1995 gets organized, two of the main criminal issues being debated are tougher penalties for violent criminals and reduction or removal of good-time credits. The virtual elimination of clemency for first-degree murderers has already removed much of the incentive for this group of lifers to behave themselves and build a good prison record, on the chance that they will one day go free. Lengthening already-long sentences and taking away good time can have the same effect on the rest of the prison population.

The legislature is much like the people surveyed in the Loyola death penalty report discussed earlier. They don't know that Louisiana already has the toughest laws in the country, for punishing violent offenders, or that those laws are carried out in practice in the same form they are written on paper.

Commutations for first-degree murder are pretty much a thing of the past in Louisiana. It is hard to imagine any governor, even someone with the style of Edwin Edwards in his first two terms, suddenly beginning to dispense clemency "as rain dropping from the heavens." The first-degree murder lifers know this, perhaps with more certainty than they would like to admit; the public, not believing or not caring, still thinks that increasing the severity and certainty of punishment is the answer to Louisiana's nation-leading homicide rate. Clifton Greene and the others who came in with him will grow old in prison, and they will have lots of company. Ten or fifteen years from now, they will hang a sign on the front gate at Angola. The sign will say: "Lifers only."

Table 1
Life Sentences in the States, 1992

State	Prison Population	Number of Lifers		Life w/o Parole	No-Parole Lifers	
		Male	Female		Male	Female
Alabama	17,221	2,548	58	Yes	685	11
Alaska	No response	—	—	Yes	NA	NA
Arizona	16,021	739	24	Yes	196	11
Arkansas	8,165	467	27	No		
California	108,183	11,275	492	Yes	995	42
Colorado	8,961	500	12	Yes	22	1
Connecticut	11,086	149	3	Yes	NA	NA
Delaware	4,027	397	6	Yes	95	5
D.C.	11,122	774	10	Yes	10	0
Florida	47,619	4,767	145	Yes	2,332	44
Georgia	24,829	3,236	145	No		
Hawaii	1,473	3	0	Yes	28	3
Idaho	2,265	189	6	Yes	174	6
Illinois	31,018	551	14	Yes	532	14
Indiana	No response			No		
Iowa	4,512	374	17	Yes	374	17
Kansas	6,139	488	19	No		

State	Prison Population	Number of Lifers Male	Number of Lifers Female	Life w/o Parole	No-Parole Lifers Male	No-Parole Lifers Female
Kentucky	10,362	562	24	No*	8	
Louisiana	21,165	2,158	72	Yes	2,083	71
Maine	1,574	44	0	Yes	11	0
Maryland	No response	Yes	?	?		
Massachusetts	9,409	925	24	Yes	389	10
Michigan	38,513	3,086	107	Yes	1,729	66
Minnesota	3,582	153	7	Yes	1	0
Mississippi	9,058	49	0	Yes	151	0
Missouri	16,051	1,166	52	Yes	318	24
Montana	1,300	27	0	Yes	8	0
Nebraska	2,639	79	5	No		
Nevada	6,191	903	31	Yes	214	9
New Hampshire	1,850	26	2	Yes	26	2
New Jersey	22,047	890	20	No		
New Mexico	3,325	156	9	No		
New York	61,373	9,033	444	No		
North Carolina	19,868	2,171	66	No		
North Dakota	561	12	1	No		
Ohio	37,131	2,935	143	No		
Oklahoma	14,780	929	62	Yes	87	8
Oregon	6,480	439	23	Yes	17	2
Pennsylvania	24,670	2,324	93	Yes	?	?
Rhode Island	2,858	83	0	Yes	10	0
South Carolina	18,697	1,290	6	No		
South Dakota	1,498	99	3	Yes	99	3
Tennessee	14,500	1,246	44	No		
Texas	51,887	4,152	85	No		
Utah	2,691	41	0	Yes	?	?
Vermont	1,206	14	0	Yes	?	?
Virginia	16,939	1,248	25	No		
Washington	10,039	588	20	Yes	125	7
West Virginia	1,808	254	6	Yes	124	1
Wisconsin	7,825	498	25	No		
Wyoming	1,075	108	3	Yes	0	0
Federal BOP	81,822	1,17741		Yes	?	?

*Abolished life without parole in 1975.
Source: *Corrections Compendium*, January 1993.

Table 2
Life-Sentenced Inmates in Louisiana Prisons

Year	Number of Natural Lifers	Increase from Previous Year
1970	143	28
1971	164	21
1972	193	29
1973	257	64
1974	323	66
1975	382	59
1976	454	72
1977	528	74
1978	601	73
1979	699	98
1980	802	103
1981	935	133
1982	1,084	149
1983	1,219	135
1984	1,330	111
1985	1,445	115
1986	1,573	128
1987	1,698	125
1988	1,807	109
1989	1,933	126
1990	2,039	106
1991	2,155	116
1992	2,280	125
1993	2,439	159
1994	2,592	153

Source: Office of Information Services, Louisiana Department of Public Safety and Corrections.

* * *

Table 3
Commutations for First-Degree Murder in Louisiana, 1973-1995

	R/S	D.O.B.	Parish	Date of Conviction
James A. Andrews	B/M	5-05-60	Jefferson	12-22-77

DOC # 89243. Commuted to 40 years on 8-11-89 (Roemer), with parole eligibility after 1/2 of sentence. Parole eligible 11-15-97; eligible for good-time release on 9-20-99. Still at Angola.

	R/S	D.O.B.	Parish	Date of Conviction
Charles Caldwell	B/M	1-26-51	Caddo	12-21-79

DOC # 92675. Commuted to 35 years on 1-14-88 (Edwards), commuted again to 17 years on 11-02-90 (Roemer). Would have been parole eligible after first commutation in 1991; discharged at good-time release date.

| Polete County | B/M | 1-09-47 | Winn | 4-07-78 |

DOC # 88635. Commuted to 30 years on 3-09-88 (Edwards); eligible for parole immediately. Released on parole.

| Bobby Ray Demars | B/M | 5-28-51 | Natchitoches | 12-30-77 |

DOC # 87334. Commuted to 24 years on 3-05-84 (Treen). Released on parole.

| Catherine Dodds | W/F | 12-26-44 | Jefferson | 6-16-77 |

DOC # 85357. Originally sentenced to death 8-07-75. Death sentence commuted to life on 6-16-77 (Edwards). Life sentence commuted to 30 years on 12-18-86 (Edwards). Released on parole in 1992.

| Herman George | W/M | 3-30-41 | Webster | 5-15-78 |

DOC # 15766. Commuted to 21 years on 11-16-89 (Roemer); eligible for parole immediately. Discharged.

| Daniel Gettridge, Sr. | B/M | 12-27-28 | Orleans | 7-19-77 |

DOC # 96691. Commuted to 60 years on 2-19-90 (Roemer); parole eligible after 20, good-time eligible. Still at Angola; parole eligible on 12-19-96.

| Marilyn L. Hampton | W/F | 9-09-42 | Ouachita | 10-18-78 |

DOC # 91813. Commuted to 12 years on 12-06-85 (Edwards), with parole eligibility and good-time credit. Eligible for immediate release.

| Leo E. Jones | B/M | 10-08-52 | Orleans | 11-26-73 |

DOC # 76330. Commuted to 25 years on 1-14-88 (Edwards); parole eligible immediately. Released on parole; later revoked.

| Ronald S. Monroe | B/M | 12-03-54 | Orleans | 2-06-80 |

DOC # 90920. Death sentenced commuted to life w/o parole or good-time on 8-16-89 (Roemer). Serving life at Angola. Only death-sentenced inmate commuted to life by governor's action since 1973.

| Emmett R. Procell | W/M | 9-10-38 | Sabine | 12-15-77 |

DOC # 88537. Commuted to 16 years on 3-18-86 (Edwards); no parole eligibility but good-time allowed. Released on good-time.

Source: Louisiana Pardon Board and the Office of Information Services, Louisiana Department of Public Safety and Corrections.

Attachment A
Other Cases Reported as Post-1973 Commutations
for First-Degree Murder: Apparently in Error
(not first-degree, no commutation, or cases prior to 1973)

Eugene Clark
     DOC # 91317. Recommended twice for clemency by Pardon Board; denied first by
Governor Treen and then by Governor Edwards. Convicted 1979 in East Carroll Parish.
Still serving life at Angola.

Tyrone Coler
     DOC # 125629. Shown as convicted of 14:30, but given a 30-year sentence. Since
he was born in 1968, this appears impossible. From Lafourche Parish. This was
apparently a conviction for attempted first-degree murder.

Louis Hall
     Originally sentenced to death in 1968(?), commuted to life upon re-sentencing after
Furman in 1973. Commuted to parole eligibility in 1988. Subsequently discharged from
prison. From West Feliciana Parish.

James Harvey
     DOC # 82231. Convicted of second-degree murder. Commuted to 20 years on 8-04-
86 (Edwards). Would have been 20-year parole eligible under original sentence. Parole
and good-time eligible. Discharged.

Pleasant H. Howard
     Not a first-degree case. Original sentence was life with parole eligibility after 40
years, which in 1978 means it was a second-degree case. The life sentence was commuted
in 1988 to 25 years with parole eligibility after one-third. Offender was 65 years old at
time of commutation. Apparently discharged. From Orleans Parish.

Jessie J. Lyles, Jr.
     DOC # 114065. Shown as being commuted to 50 years for first-degree murder. No
record of commutation on file. From Orleans Parish. This was most likely a conviction
for attempted first-degree murder.

Cynthia Moses
     DOC # 89930. Shown as being commuted to 60 years for first-degree murder, but
Pardon Board records reflect that the Governor has never acted on a favorable
recommendation from the board. Action is still pending.

David C. Pennington
     DOC # 99364 Shown as being commuted to 45 years for first-degree murder. Record
says the original sentence was 40 years for second-degree murder and 40 years for
attempted armed robbery, with no parole eligibility on the armed robbery charge.

Commuted to 45 years with parole eligibility after one-third, on April 30, 1990. Convicted on December 14, 1978, from Jefferson Parish.

Joel Prickett
    DOC # 76613. This was a first-degree murder, but committed under the old statute, on 8-15-72. Commuted to 60 years on 12-23-91 (Roemer); parole eligible after 20 years, on 12-13-92. Discharged.

Billy Ray Self
    DOC # 76904. A first-degree murder committed on 2-27-72, when he was 15 years old. Commuted to 60 years on 1-02-92 (Roemer); parole eligible after 20. Apparently discharged.

Kenneth L. Simmons
    DOC # 116170. Shown as being commuted to 59 years, with parole eligibility after one-third, for first-degree murder, with a conviction date of 5-11-80. Commutation was effective February 13, 1990. This case was shown as being a death sentence from April 8, 1965, which would most likely have involved a re-sentence to life after *Furman* in 1972. From Orleans Parish.

Thad H. Tatum, Jr.
    DOC # 108762. Shown as being commuted to 95 years for first-degree murder. No record of commutation on file. From Orleans Parish. This was an attempted second-degree murder conviction, along with an armed robbery and attempted armed robbery convictions.

William E. Thomas, Sr.
    DOC # 75157. D.O.B. 3-24-24. Two convictions, from Desoto Parish and Livingston Parish. On the 1973 conviction from Livingston, commutation was from life to 21 years. On the 1980 conviction from Desoto, commutation was to 60 years, with parole eligibility after 20. Not a "new" first-degree murder case; sentenced under old statute.

Herbert Welcome
    DOC # 105694. Under death sentence, and serving a separate life sentence for first-degree murder also. Convicted in 1982 in Iberia Parish. Pardon Board recommended commutation to life on March 4, 1988, but the recommendation was returned without action by Governor Roemer. Court may have ordered re-sentencing to life; no clemency approved.

23

SUICIDE IN PRISON: THE HANGING GAME*

by Douglas Dennis

"When you take away hope, you're dealing with desperate men."

Perry M. Johnson, President, American Correctional Association

"You have youngsters here with Time, and this Time states that you ain't never gonna get out. When this hits these little crackheads, these little rap-boogity youngsters, that their life been completely taken away from them and they're not going nowhere no more, they gonna go to killing themselves."

Hayes Williams, Angola prisoner

Curtis Anderson, 41, hung himself with a bedsheet shortly before midnight January 7, 1993, in Angola's Clinical Services Unit, a cellblock for chronically mentally ill prisoners.

The Shreveport native was serving a 7-year sentence for aggravated burglary and had been at Angola one year before he committed suicide.

Warden John P. Whitley said Anderson had not exhibited suicidal tendencies. "There was no indication of any problems with this one," he said. "The mental health team had been following him on a weekly basis."

The security officer who found Anderson had seen nothing unusual when he'd looked in on him five minutes earlier. When he returned, Anderson was kneeling with one end of a sheet tied to his cell bars and the other end fastened around his neck. Attempts to revive him were unsuccessful.

Anderson is the latest in a mounting number of inmate suicides in Louisiana's maximum security facility—Angola. Last year suicide ranked as the prison's second leading cause of death, surpassed only by AIDS. During the past five years more than twice as many people (17) have killed themselves at Angola as in the preceding twenty-three (8).

Since 1965, twenty-five Angola prisoners have committed suicide. Of those 25, one opened his veins, one overdosed on drugs, and 23 hanged themselves.

In Maryland prisons, which incarcerate 17,000 (Louisiana has 18,000), 206 male inmates died between 1979 and 1987. Heart disease claimed 48. Suicide was the second leading cause of death with 37. Of those 37, two slashed open their veins, two overdosed on drugs, one dove to his death, and 32 hanged themselves.

Maryland prison administrators called in scientists from the National Center for Health Services to study the problem. They found that prisoners aged 15 to 34 had a greater risk of killing themselves, and that mentally disturbed or psychotic inmates are at the highest risk. They also confirmed previous studies that found prisoners serving life are more likely to commit suicide.

"I think the situation of prisoners in Maryland is the same as that in many states," Greg Shipley, Maryland corrections spokesman, told the Associated Press. "They are faced with long prison sentences and a loss of hope that puts them in a very depressed state."

Psychiatrists call that state of mind clinical depression. Depressed people, they say, simply do not feel good about themselves. They feel helpless, that no

*Appeared in *The Angolite*, March/April 1993, 25-40. Reprinted with permission.

matter what they do it will turn out badly. Caught in a web of futility, thinking no one gives a damn, that they are utterly without hope, without any reason to go on, some choose the one way available to end the misery—suicide.

Johnny Hookfin, serving two life sentences for aggravated rape, was found hanging in his cell on October 28, 1989. Sources at the mental health unit said Hookfin, a working patient, had been on a suicide watch as early as 24 hours before he hanged himself. "Johnny and I came to Angola on the same day," says inmate counsel Checo Yancy. "I knew him real well. I can tell you he just lost hope. He felt nobody cared."

Depression and hopelessness are fertile ground for suicidal behavior, but suicide is as complex as human nature. It's been around since man first realized that life's a bitch, and then you die. The first recorded reference to suicide was written some 4,000 years ago by an anonymous Egyptian. From it can be traced a continuous line of loneliness, despair and hopelessness common to suicidal people.

Neither the Old nor New Testament specifically prohibits suicide. Christianity did not take a stand against suicide until the Fifth Century, wrote George Howe Colt in *The Enigma of Suicide*. St. Augustine, said Colt, realized "that Christianity contained a logical dilemma: If paradise is achieved by avoiding sin, the most sensible step following baptism is suicide. Augustine then tried to demonstrate that suicide was a sin greater than any it could atone for. He took his arguments not from the Bible but from [the ancient Greek philosopher] Plato," and concluded that suicide was self-murder, a violation of the Sixth Commandment.

It may be a sin, but it's not a crime. In the United States only Texas and

Oklahoma still have laws prohibiting suicide attempts. They haven't been enforced for decades.

Modern Western civilization disapproves of suicide, and most laymen view it as an act of insanity. That is an over-simplification, say psychiatrists and other mental health professionals. Some mentally ill people do commit suicide but so do people who are as normal as sunshine.

Emile Durkheim in 1897 developed a theory about suicide. He didn't think people who killed themselves necessarily were insane. Rather, he contended that a society's relation to the individuals that compose it determine suicide rates. In his book, *Suicide*, he proposed three categories that present-day sociologists still find useful.

The first, altruistic suicide, is quite rare in society and unheard of in prisons. It stems from an overwhelming concern for the welfare of others. A soldier, for example, throws himself on a hand grenade to save his buddies, or someone in an overloaded lifeboat slips overboard so that the others might survive. Christian dogma holds that Jesus Christ gave his life for our sins so that we might be saved from perdition. In this sense, Jesus can be seen as the ultimate suicide.

Anomic suicide, wrote Durkheim, occurs when lives are disrupted by traumatic events. Anomie (loss of purpose or identity) figures prominently in jailhouse suicides. Young men with bright futures, upon being arrested for some trivial offense, are a few hours later found hanging lifeless in their cells. According to *Corrections Compendium*, suicide is the leading cause of death in the nation's jails and local lockups. More than 400 people each year kill themselves shortly after arrest, a rate three times that found in prisons.

Durkheim's third category, fatalistic suicide, occurs when people too strongly regulated by their society kill themselves to escape. "Prisons constitute a deviant type of society where social regulation may be unduly high," said Dr. David Lester, one of the world's leading authorities on suicide, in a *Psychology Reports* article.

"Incarceration represents marked social dislocation and upheaval for many inmates," said Dr. Harvey Bluestone in an article for the American Psychiatric Association. Bluestone was director of psychiatry at Sing Sing prison in New York. "The depersonalized climate of prison contributes further to their existing sense of isolation and separation," he said. "The overwhelming majority of inmates are housed in tiny, cubicle-like, barred cells. The reaction to such surroundings even on the part of a healthy individual would be depression. Inmates feel hopeless, experience loss of face and status. Guilt feelings and self-hatred are prominent. A severely depressed inmate, struggling to maintain control over self-destructive drives, sometimes sees self-destruction as the only way out."

Clyde Williams, 40, in the second year of a 50-year sentence for an attempted aggravated rape conviction in Bossier Parish, hanged himself in his cell at Angola's mental health unit on October 3, 1989.

Prison authorities reported that Williams was found dangling from an air vent by a knotted sheet just 11 minutes after being checked by a mental health team making rounds. Inmates on the tier said Williams was disappointed over not being allowed to transfer from the unit to general population.

These categories are useful, but not all-encompassing. The causes of suicide are many. Some scientists claim there is a biochemical basis and genetic disposition for clinical depression—the brother of hopelessness—which is the most common denominator of those who attempt suicide.

Depression runs in families, like schizophrenia, said John Langone, author of *Dead End* and former fellow at the Center for Advanced Studies in Behavioral Sciences at Stanford. "One study showed that in more than 57% of identical twins, when one twin had a depressive disorder, the other twin had it," he said. "And almost a third of the people with a major form of depression have at least one relative with a similar form of depression."

Swedish psychiatrist Marie Asberg found in the early 1970s that about a third of 68 clinically depressed patients had particularly low levels of a chemical called 5-hydroxyindoleacetic acid (5HIAA). It appears when serotonin, a neurological transmitter, breaks down. In 1975, Asberg's team studied 46 suicide attempters, 16 with severe depression, the rest with other mental illnesses. The group as a whole had an abnormally low level of 5HIAA compared to the 45-person control group. Within a year 6 had committed suicide, all with low 5HIAA. This link has been confirmed by other studies.

Even so, we should not pounce too quickly on chemical causes or solutions. Suicide expert David Lester warned that "despite occasional claims to the contrary, there is no reasonably sound biochemical theory of suicide at present." Langone is not impressed either. "Scientists are skeptical of studies like these," he said. "They argue the samples are too small to make a sweeping judgment. Depression is a complex disturbance. In a sense, suicide may be the clearest example of how heredity and environment work together."

Nevertheless, said George Howe Colt, "I wondered with some discomfort at the possibility that their answers to the question, 'To be or not to be?', might all boil down to a matter of [a dip in] 5-hydroxyindoleacetic acid."

Many prisoners were abused as children. "Violence is a learned response to frustration and anger," said epidemiologist Eva Deykin of the Harvard School of Public Health. A person who has been abused as a child sometimes turns that aggression inward, she said. Child abuse also causes low self-esteem, a characteristic often found in suicides.

Simple answers are elusive. "Suicide can be committed by 12 different people for 12 different reasons," Langone said, "or by one person for 12 different reasons."

Donald Daniel, 54, serving concurrent life sentences for a 1977 double murder, was found hanging in Angola's infirmary maintenance shop at about 3 a.m., August 28, 1990.

Daniel, a trusty well-liked by fellow inmates and prison employees, lived and worked at the clinic, where he acquired the reputation of being a 24-hour-a-day one-man maintenance crew that kept the medical facility operational.

Just hours before his suicide, Daniel expressed to *The Angolite* his uncertainty that prisoners like himself would ever be released from prison. "Look," he said, "[then] Governor Roemer hasn't done anything for us here at Angola." Daniel also lamented that he was told by a newly assigned security supervisor that he was being transferred to another part of the prison without any reason given for the non-punitive move.

People tend to resist change, perhaps because it requires courage and flexibility.

Some, like Daniel, are too brittle to accommodate major change. He had fashioned a peaceful harbor for himself at the clinic, and the impending transfer to the open seas of general population apparently pushed him over the brink. The underlying cause, however, seemed to be despair and loss of hope.

Revenge suicide has a place in the prison lexicon. Freud called it inverted murder: anger at another is turned inward on the self.

McKinley Reddix, a first offender from Orleans Parish in the 13th year of serving two life sentences for murder was found hanging at about 3 p.m., March 15, 1989, at the Angola Rodeo grounds where he was working. Assigned to the Camp-H carpenter crew as a trusty, he was assisting with preparations for the annual Arts & Crafts Festival.

Knowledgeable sources said Reddix used a black nylon rope tied to an electrical conduit on the ceiling. The sources also said Reddix left a note that read: "I never killed anyone in my life. The only person I had in my life has let me down and I will not go another step without her support she had given me in life. It's over this, not about loving her."

A classic revenge suicide? Reddix, consciously or unconsciously, seemed driven to punish "her" for abandoning him. Hence the note.

Dr. Edwin Shneidman, director of the Laboratory for the Study of Life-Threatening Behavior at UCLA, in his book *Suicidology*, cautioned: "The large-scale study of suicide notes has not thrown completely new light on suicidal behavior in general." On the brink of suicide, said Shneidman, a person has a narrow, disorganized view of the world. Suicide notes tend to mystify rather than enlighten. Take this note, for example, scrawled by Angola inmate Charles East, 28, who strung himself up to the bars with a sheet at Camp-J cellblock on February 29, 1988: "Come on to hell whith [sic] me Blacks and Whites."

"Suicide is not a disease," Langone wrote in *Dead End*, "or some mysterious compulsion that suddenly strikes great numbers of people like a rampant virus or a force from outer space. One can, of course, find many cases in which some genetic defect, some biochemical mistake, seems to cause depression that, in turn, seems to prompt a person to take his or her life. Likewise, there are instances where one of Durkheim's categories appears unquestionably to be responsible for suicidal behavior. But behind the reasons, in the last analysis, is the self, that hard-to-define collection of neurochemicals, thoughts, sensations, and emotions that give us our character, our individuality, our identity."

In the early morning hours of June 16, 1990, a Camp-H security officer found Mark Krzyzaniak, 35, hanging inside his cell. It was the first completed suicide at Angola in 1990. Five Angola prisoners took their own lives during 1989.

Krzyzaniak was serving a flat 20-year sentence as a habitual felon for burglary, and had been at Angola since October 2, 1984. Prison medical technicians restored a heartbeat and transported Krzyzaniak to Earl K. Long Hospital in Baton Rouge. He died the following day—Father's Day. Informed sources close to the incident said there wasn't any reason known for the inmate's behavior.

So far we have looked at suicide negatively, as a tragedy, an act of desperation by people whose deepest motives elude us. But there are those who have another view, who do not regard suicide as wrong, sinful or cowardly.

"It is quite obvious," wrote 19th Century German philosopher Arthur Schopenhauer, "that there is nothing in the world to which every man has a more unassailable title than to his own life and person."

George Howe Colt in *Enigma of Suicide*, presented an international and historical overview. The Stoics in ancient Rome practiced the creed of suicide by choice: "He is at liberty to die who does not wish to live." They saw suicide as a weapon against incurable illness, insufferable pain, and even against taedium vitae—what we call the low-down blues.

People fled terror-stricken at the sight of Viking longboats, Colt said, because they were filled with fierce warriors who believed that only those who died violently were allowed in Valhalla (Norse heaven—literally, the hall of those who die by violence—where they jousted, feasted and drank from the skulls of their enemies). Vikings who survived battle, frequently, before they grew old, fell on their swords or leapt off cliffs so they could enter Valhalla.

The practice of suttee—a wife whose husband dies is expected to immolate herself on his funeral pyre—flourished in India until recently. The samurai (military) in medieval Japan practiced seppuku (ritualistic suicide, known to Westerners as hara-kiri). The practice spread, and isolated "belly cutting" suicides still occur in modern Japan, Colt said.

Most people nowadays would choose a quick death over existence as a vegetable on a life-support machine. "Living" wills are common, in which the person makes a binding legal stipulation that he or she shall not be unduly kept alive. Dr. Jack Kevorkian and his suicide machines help the terminally ill avoid a prolonged, agonizing existence. He has generated front-page news and renewed debate about the philosophy of death with dignity.

Such thoughts may have crossed the mind of this aged Angola inmate:

Malcolm McEwen, 71, had served 10 years of a 25-year term for an Orleans Parish armed robbery when he hanged himself on September 17, 1992, with a bedsheet tied to the bars of his mental health unit cell. Taken to Earl K. Long Hospital in Baton Rouge, he remained in a coma until his death two days later.

"He's never had a visit since he's been here," said Angola Warden John P. Whitley. McEwen's earliest release date was March 18, 1998. He was a sixth offender, and had a detainer for threatening a federal officer.

McEwen lived on a ward at the prison's clinic for eight years, indicating he had chronic medical problems as well as mental ones. Knowledgeable sources said McEwen had tried to hang himself August 20, a month before his death, also with a sheet tied to cell bars. He was cut down and revived by an alert security officer. Nothing in his personal effects indicated why he wanted to kill himself.

The prison population in the United States is aging. Prisoners over 55 are the fastest growing demographic group in prison. They usually have committed serious offenses, received longer sentences, and been in prison far longer than prisoners used to be confined. Growing numbers of them can be expected to attempt suicide, said Dr. J. Haycock in an article for *Omega*. Haycock is a psychiatrist who has done extensive research into prison suicide. Other prisoner groups, said Haycock, also are at high suicide risk: murderers, those serving life sentences, and those in maximum security institutions.

The natural purpose of prisons is to isolate and punish. The resulting environment is one of dehumanization, frustration and pain. As long as prisons exist, people in them will commit suicide. The problem cannot be eliminated. That doesn't mean prison officials sit around twiddling their thumbs while suicidal prisoners hang it up.

Lindsay Hayes, assistant director of the National Center on Institutions and Alternatives, told the AP that Maryland prisons are installing collapsible clothing racks that will not support the weight of a body. Additionally, suicide-prone prisoners may be given tearaway clothing, sheets and blankets that cannot support a body. Such preventive measures do not impress Hayes. "I don't like gimmicks," he said. "I prefer counseling and increased monitoring. Suicides are best prevented by other human beings."

Suicide was never a problem at the Louisiana State Penitentiary until recently. From 1965 to 1975, an eleven year period when Angola prisoners were slaughtering each other right and left, inspiring media to dub it the "bloodiest prison in the nation," 101 prisoners died at the hands of their peers while only two took their own lives.

In 1976, a flood of newly hired security officers led by granite-faced warden Ross Maggio wiped out the violence overnight. Seventeen prisoners were killed in 1975, two in 1976, one in 1977, and in 1978— zero. Only then did suicides begin to gain significance in cause-of-death statistics. From 1976 to 1993 there were a total of 17 killings—one a year on average—and 23 suicides.

Other prisons are experiencing the same thing. According to American Correctional Association figures for the years 1984-1991, inmate-on-inmate killings numbered 619, as opposed to 946 inmate suicides.

Why should this be so? Angola's Director of Mental Health, Delta Kuzenski, says, "With safety, thoughts can turn in another direction. By nature, if your environment is not safe you focus your thoughts on becoming safe. When your environment is safer your thoughts turn to self—inward."

At Angola, and perhaps elsewhere, two major changes differentiate the prison of the '60s and '70s from that of the '80s and '90s. First, the violent jungle was replaced by a bureaucratically controlled desert, peaceful and endless.

More important, however, back then each Angola prisoner had a light at the end of his tunnel—and it wasn't an onrushing train. In the '60s, and for most of the '70s, few prisoners had more time than they could do. Those with big-number sentences could expect a play from the Pardon Board after 10 years or so, provided they kept their noses clean and made genuine efforts to straighten themselves out. Even lifers could look forward to going home in 11 or 12 years, all but those whose crimes aroused community opposition.

That all changed. Hundreds of Angola prisoners have now served over 20 years, some over 30, still groping blindly for freedom. The light has gone out; suicide rates, indeed, have risen.

John Kent, 28, hung himself inside his cell at Camp-C on May 17, 1991. In prison since age 16, he was in the twelfth year of a life sentence for a Baton Rouge murder. Friend and crime partner Curtis Miller said that Kent had recently told him he was "getting tired of it all."

While prison officials around the country recognize suicide as a mounting problem deserving attention, they regard it as the inevitable by-product of society's imposition of long mandatory sentences.

It goes with the territory, like inmate killings, fights, and escapes.

Prison suicides in Louisiana, on the other hand, became politicized in 1989, following a wave of killings, escapes and suicides that prompted Federal Judge Frank Polozola to declare a "state of emergency" at Angola. Prison officials found themselves under a media spotlight, their operations subjected to microscopic day-to-day examination—with political overtones. Teams of state and federal investigators prowled prison grounds. Mismanagement, even drugs, were cited as causes. A warden was fired, other officials demoted and transferred, and significant changes ordered in security and mental health operations. Understandably, keen managerial sensitivity evolved regarding suicidal behavior, a major cause of the upheaval.

Lost in the clamor were assertions by seasoned, knowledgeable prisoners that hopelessness and despair were to blame. "Anybody with an eye could see that when these youngsters with life and hundred-year sentences realized there wasn't no way in hell they was ever going home because [then governor] Roemer wasn't signing no time cuts, they quit trying to do right," says Hayes Williams, the prisoner who filed the lawsuit two decades ago that led to the "consent decree," managed by Judge Polozola, under which Louisiana operates its prisons. "The youngsters went to doing just any damn thing they wanted," Williams says. "What difference did it make?"

David Lester, with co-author Dr. Bruce L. Danto, stated in *Suicide Behind Bars*: "Many in our society do not consider inmate suicide a problem worthy of concern. They tend to view all inmates as undeserving of help. The fact is that prisons are a part of society and inmates are part of the population. They cannot be treated as if they belong to a different world. Lawsuits brought by relatives of the prisoner suicide have had little difficulty in proving some form of negligence [and winning substantial awards]. These costs have proved to be a powerful motivation for suicide prevention programs in custodial facilities."

Prison administrators have complete custody and control of their prisoners. Consequently, they have the responsibility to provide reasonable care and treatment for them. In 1976, the U.S. Supreme Court established the standard for prison care: "Deliberate indifference to a prisoner's serious illness or injury states a cause of action under 1983 [the civil rights law], and constitutes the unnecessary and wanton infliction of pain proscribed by the Eighth Amendment. This is true whether manifested by prison doctors in their response to the prisoner's needs or by prison guards in intentionally denying or delaying access to medical care."

"Whatever its cause," said *Corrections Compendium*, "a suicide can attract catastrophic litigation." Liability awards by the nation's courts are up to ten times higher than they were a few years ago. One award, against the Washington D.C. police department, totalled $2.4 million.

Training is key to avoiding liability. "Suicide prevention," said Joseph R. Rowan, executive director and chair of Juvenile and Criminal Justice International, in his study of jail suicides, "is best brought about through positive interaction between trained correctional staff and inmates. Follow the Golden Rule—that's 90% of it."

Louisiana's corrections department recently disseminated a comprehensive 11-page "Suicide Prevention and Post-Suicide Management" directive. It conforms to an American Correctional Association standard, and details how employees should interact to identify and "supervise" self-destructive and suicide-prone prisoners. Supervise means restraint, all the way to body-sheet and 4-point tiedown, should mental-health personnel think it necessary. Prisoners are inventive; those who wish to can be dead before anyone knows what's going on. Response is the name of the game. Nothing, not even a killing, generates more action than an Angola suicide.

"There's a suicide review committee here and another at Baton Rouge [DOC Headquarters]," says Angola Captain D. K. Basko, who investigates every suicide. "First we conduct the regular investigation and submit our report to the Angola post-suicide investigative team (investigative officer, mental health worker, EMT or paramedic, and the camp's supervisor). They discuss the whole thing. Was everything done to save that person's life? And so on. Their report goes to Baton Rouge. Then their team holds another meeting and discusses it." This hypersensitivity is the legacy of the state of emergency.

Officers now receive suicide recognition training. "They teach you how to watch for people going from sad to happy or vice versa—mood swings. To look for people giving items away," says Basko. "But it will take more than training. Training isn't the miracle pill. Guidelines require a round be made every 15 minutes. Our people go above that. There wasn't a 10 minute lapse between rounds the last suicide at the mental health unit, and still the guy hung himself. You can make a round every 5 minutes, but in 5 minutes somebody can be stretched out."

Many people assume those who hang themselves go out quick, with a broken neck. "That's wrong," says Basko. "Asphyxiation is the cause of death in these hangings. They slowly choke to death."

"The most common method has been with sheets," says Lt. Lea Freeman, who works with Basko investigating suicides and other occurrences. "Jump suits next, and then blue jeans. Medications are rare because they're iffy. What should you take and in what dosage to kill yourself? Is it going to kill you or are you just hoping? It's not a guarantee. We've recommended liquid medication. They can't stockpile that."

"We don't want to see someone commit suicide," Basko says. "But I believe we're always going to have a problem that's going to go up and down. We may go through a year or so with nothing. Then you may have a rash of four or five. There's really nothing you can do, other than take a little concern out for other people."

From a different perspective, Hayes Williams says, "Life means life now. When a dude has that or, say, 60 years flat, he says, 'It took me 26 years to get 26 years old. Now they tell me I gotta do 60 years. I add this up—60 and then 26—man, goddam, I'll be 86 years old, no good for nothing.' Reality's setting in. So he says, 'Hey, here's a dude couple days ago committed suicide. He didn't get mail, didn't get no visits. I don't hear him complaining about the food too cold or he can't get no sleep 'cause somebody's hollering. I don't hear nothing outta him. No complaint, no nothing. This is a burden off his family and friends. Shit, he took the easy way out. I'm gonna try it.'"

"A prisoner suffering from chronic despair feels disconnected from his family and friends," said Bruce L. Danto, psychiatrist and former president of the American Society of Suicidology. "Suicide is for him an escape from hopelessness and isolation. It is not unusual for staff to unconsciously concur with his decision, believing that his suicide will not only help the inmate, but also will rid society of a hardened criminal."

Institutions nationwide have some officers who, for whatever reason, can't stand prisoners. Angola is no exception. "Many officers don't want to work around these people," Basko says, "and they're not going to give them the time of day."

"Then you've got others who take more interest," Freeman says, "and because of that they notice things. There's an officer who is up for 'Officer of the Month.' He was working his tier where an inmate always ate breakfast. One morning the inmate didn't get up. He stayed asleep. Just that little bit tipped the officer off, and he tried to wake him up. The minute he couldn't, he called for help. Sure enough, they had a situation. They pumped the inmate out, and he was full of Elavil. This happened about a month after Melvin Creppel deliberately overdosed on Siniquen and died, and on the same tier."

"We've made recommendations," says Basko. "They could take all these people that exhibit suicidal tendencies and have them quartered in one area. Then you could concentrate your mental health staff, your suicide-recognition trained security people, instead of having them all spread out."

"Maybe this is a pipe dream," Freeman says, "but it would be nice to see, especially in cellblock areas, one officer per shift with the rank of EMT."

Lester and Danto believe that "even a simple action such as listening to the inmate, can alleviate some of his distress. Listening communicates that someone cares."

Suicide at Angola is seen as a mental health rather than a security problem. The prison's Mental Health division, therefore, is responsible for all suicide-prone prisoners and those perceived to be so, as well as for the mentally ill. Former social worker Delta Kuzenski heads Angola's mental health program. She's board certified and has academic credentials suited to the job.

"Many inmates come in who made suicide gestures or attempts in the past," she says. "We try real hard to work with the most dangerous. Our first concern is to keep the inmate safe using the least restrictive means possible. Then we try to assess his potential for self-harm.

"We have an enormous number of mentally ill individuals here at Angola," she continues. "We're getting a lot more in, and many were sent here years and years ago and have simply stayed here. I know some inmates who were diagnosed mentally ill 20 years ago.

"This buildup started with the deinstitutionalization movement in the '70s," she says, "when the policy was to get patients out of mental hospitals, get them back on the street as citizens. Many of them couldn't handle the less structured environment and compensated by doing acts that got them arrested and sent to jail or prison. In Louisiana there was nowhere else for them to go but Angola.

"Corrections," Kuzenski continues, "was aware of mental health needs, I think, but was unable to really address them until the state of emergency in 1989 and 1990 drew attention to the fact that the need had been a great and urgent one for a long time. That triggered the bureaucracy to provide staff with necessary mental health and psychiatric services to Angola inmates."

Security runs prisons. Nothing can function without their cooperation. Kuzenski is aware of this. "Correctional officers are as much a part of the treatment process as mental health workers," she says. "We put together a 20-hour training program that educates officers about suicide prevention, awareness and response, mental illnesses, mental retardation, HIV issues, and just good general information. All our clinicians have at least a masters degree in either psychology or social work from accredited programs. Right now we have 15 social workers, one psychologist, 3 psychological associates, and a fulltime psychiatrist. We expect to fill the four vacancies on our clinician staff soon."

The mental health program touches the lives of one in four Angola prisoners. "We provide services to 1300 prisoners," she says. "They aren't all mentally ill. Many inmates ask to see us about life problems—a sick mother, or a child in the hospital. We allow them to blow off their frustration, and try to help them find a solution. Of the 1300, I'd say in the range of 300-500 are chronically mentally ill. With treatment, most of them can function quite well. Those who do are mixed in with the general population. Those who are dysfunctional are housed in a Clinical Services Unit. CSU-1 is a maximum-security cellblock that can house 135 patients. CSU-2 at Camp A is composed of four 28-man dormitories housing patients from CSU-1 who we felt deserved a try in that type of atmosphere.

"I really believe we decreased the number of suicides that could have occurred in CSU-1 when we were allowed to implement some treatment programs that were previously unheard of for maximum security inmates at Angola," Kuzenski says. "We saw a dramatic decrease in suicides and attempts once we implemented group therapy and recreational therapy." No one has committed suicide in a CSU-2 dorm.

"A well-lit, spacious, airy dormitory where there is human interaction might be the factor in preventing what otherwise might be a suicide," said former Sing Sing psychiatrist Harvey Bluestone. "Suicidal inmates should not be housed alone," recommended a 1985 study of Texas prison suicides. "They should be given a cellmate or put in a dormitory. Not only does this provide company and the beginnings of future social networks that can help the inmate fight his depression and despair, but it also provides a supplement to staff monitoring."

Prisoners in Angola's dorms rarely commit suicide. Cellblocks are where the action is. Basko knows that, but has a problem with transferring suicide-prone inmates to open dorms. "There's no guarantee that if you boot them out of the cellblock they won't commit suicide. Is the cellblock what's depressing them? I don't know," he says. "I do know that a lot of inmates are in the blocks because that's where they want to be. They're paranoid. They don't want to live anywhere else."

Kenneth Henley, with over 30 years served, currently lives in a total lockdown cell on the Camp-H tier where two prisoners recently committed suicide. "They tried keeping people in cells all day long in the 1800s up in Pennsylvania, in the first prison," he says.

"So many went insane and committed suicide that they had to stop. I'm thinking this is the same thing. You're under tremendous psychological stress in lockdown, and there ain't no end to it. These guys don't know when they're going to get out, including me. They don't know

when it's going to end. That's the same shit they did in 1812."

In the New York City Department of Corrections, said Lester and Danto, "Inmates were recruited as suicide prevention aides. They [were trained] and their job was to identify inmates who appeared to be suicidal and then to counsel them. The prisoner aides proved to be better at identifying suicidal inmates than the guards, and furthermore it was easier for the inmates to confide in the prisoner aides."

That idea was adopted at Angola's CSU-1 after being proposed by a concerned prisoner and its value corroborated by a mental health professional. Six veteran prisoner "tier walkers" patrol two high-risk CSU-1 tiers 24 hours a day. "They do good," said Checo Yancy, an inmate counsel who worked at the mental health unit. "They take their job seriously and try to establish rapport with everyone. They care."

Lester and Danto portray the potential suicide as "an individual who has a genetic predisposition for biochemical defects in the brain; who grew up in a family characterized by disturbed (and suicidal) parents that may have abused the child and divorced or died; who develops a psychiatric disorder accompanied by a depressed mood, low self-esteem, irrational thinking and poor problem-solving skills; and who, when he encounters a great deal of stress in his life, lacks the resources to cope with the stress and has a lethal method for suicide easily available."

Thomas Loyd, 34, serving 7 years for accessory after the fact to murder, burglary and probation violation, had been at Angola just three months when he hung himself with a pair of blue jeans in his Camp-H cell on October 2, 1992. One leg was tied to a bar in the air vent and the other leg around his neck.

Loyd, a deaf-mute, had tried to hang himself five days earlier, but was caught in time and put on 4-point restraint in an observation cell. The day after he was released back to his Camp-H cell, he committed suicide.

It was Loyd's first time in prison. He never adjusted, unlike Angola's other two deaf/mutes ["Then There Was One," Jan/Feb 1993]. "Loyd was standoffish and uncomfortable," says James "Jimbo" West, an inmate counsel who helps deaf/mutes and tried to help Loyd. "He'd come out of the dorm and stand by himself at the rail watching what was going on, trying to learn, but there were so many people and so much going on, it was too much for him. Then he got locked up."

"I spoke to Loyd," says Hayes Williams, who was housed on Camp-H B-tier when Loyd, and later Henley and Creppel arrived. "He couldn't talk, but he could write little broken-up hard-to-understand notes. He kept telling them he had to get outta the cell, that he had to leave. That was the one basic fundamental thing that was locked in his mind. I think that was the thing that spurred him to commit suicide."

West agrees: "He was frustrated, couldn't take no more. He'd lost it. Aggravation and frustration just got the best of him."

Scribbled on the right leg of the blue jeans Loyd used to hang himself was this: "Time long looks still, I love you, cry bye." And on the left leg: "Wish I love you, miss go." He probably meant "must go."

"The suicidal state is usually called a crisis," said Lester and Danto, "and this reflects the time-limited nature of the state. People may be intensely suicidal for a day or two, but they usually become less suicidal in a few days."

Usually doesn't mean always. "It might help if the man actually exhibits this kind of crazy behavior prior to him doing it," says Basko. "You pick up on it and maybe you can lock him up. He might go on 4-point restraint. Then the very next day he might do it anyway, like Loyd did.

"If a man wants to kill himself, he's going to do it," Basko says. "McEwen hanged himself, and according to what they found, his buttocks were approximately 2 inches off the floor. So he's in the mental health unit sitting with the sheet tied around the screen to his neck with his feet out. That's determination. At any time he wanted to straighten up, he could have."

Bennie Sampson, 37, a Shreveport native assigned to Camp-D extended lockdown, hanged himself with his jumpsuit on May 19, 1992, after being written up for a rule violation and placed in a holding cell to await disciplinary action.

Sampson was serving a 45-year sentence for a Webster Parish aggravated burglary and habitual felon conviction. He had been confined 7 years.

Informed sources said Sampson had a history of mental problems but kept to himself. There was no indication he was contemplating suicide.

"Sampson committed suicide by tying the right leg of a jumpsuit to the cell bars, with the left leg around his neck," Freeman says. "He was found in a slumped position, crouched, with his back to the cell bars and his feet on the floor. That scenario isn't unusual."

A study of prison suicide attempters conducted by psychiatrist B.C. Sloane led him to classify suicide-prone inmates into types very similar to Durkheim's: depressive, anomic and manipulative. He said depressive attempts result from despair and hopelessness. Anomic attempts result from the impact of long imprisonment on the prisoner's feelings of alienation, powerlessness and helplessness. Manipulative attempts are committed for anticipated gain.

"Some of them really wanted to die," says Basko, "like Bennie Sampson, also McEwen and Loyd. They were ready to punch their ticket. But so many others are manipulative." Some even go so far as to "stunt" suicide in order to benefit from the immediate attention they know is coming. Sometimes it works; sometimes it doesn't. A tragic example is the celled inmate who "stages" a suicide attempt so he'll be rescued in the nick of time—and fails. "They'll wait till the officer is due to come by before gearing up," Basko says. "But the officer stops to chat with another prisoner, and when he gets there it's too late."

"The antisocial individual who seeks to manipulate others," said Danto, "may make nonlethal suicide attempts in order to manipulate the guards. He may view transfer to the prison hospital as a softer assignment. Or he may simply seek preferential treatment because of his suicidal state. Although this type of person can be goaded into suicide by those around him, a lethal outcome is rare since he is using suicidal behavior to enhance his life, not to end it."

Manipulation clogs the system, stealing attention and treatment from those who need it most. "There's a lot of that," says Kuzenski. "A good proportion of the people we see as clients are telling us one thing and intending another. We'll note a suicide attempt in jail and talk to the inmate. He'll tell us in no uncertain terms that he was fed up with this or that in jail, the attempt wasn't serious, it was a stunt. He'll tell us to leave him alone. We have

an enormous number of suicide gestures and attempts to deal with, but we have to take each one seriously.

"We run anywhere between 60 and 110 individuals on suicide watch every month," she says. "Forty-five to 80 of them are at risk, 10 to 20 made gestures, and 5 to 10 made actual attempts. Since only one or two a year actually commit suicide, we have a lot of chaff to sort through to find and make sure we take care of seriously suicidal inmates."

Clustering of suicides is common in America, said Lester and Danto. "Suicidal behavior seems to be affected by suggestion and imitation."

Clustering occurs at Angola, and Hayes Williams thinks he knows why. "Anything that you be around long enough you come to accept," he says. "As time goes by, you adjust to it and it becomes the normal thing. If you're around suicide enough, you go to accepting that and you accept it to the extent, well, this is an easy way out of the misery."

"A different type of suicide attempter," said Danto, "mutilates himself in order to humiliate himself and to make life as painful and as miserable as possible. Indeed, his criminal behavior may also be a part of this pattern of self-punishment. He feels guilty about sexual desires and other behaviors that he views as sinful. These inmates have often been violent toward themselves and others in the past."

Billy Ray White, with five years served on an armed robbery sentence, was found dead in his cell at Cellblock-C in the early morning of June 9, 1974.

White had slashed open both arms with a razor blade and bled to death. He apparently chewed the wounds to increase flow after his blood pressure dropped.

"Billy Ray was one of a kind," said

Newt Martin, one of White's closest friends. "He hated God, the devil, the police—anyone in authority. Defiant is the word. His death was a real sad thing for me, but it was what he wanted."

Thirteen years ago Louisiana corrections chief C. Paul Phelps predicted where the "lock-'em-up-for-keeps" juggernaut would lead. "Dealing with the problem of long-term sentences will become a very high priority," he told *The Angolite*, "not only here, but all over the country. We have to figure out ways of offering hope."

Too many new prisoners roll in and find themselves among old cons who have been locked up longer than the new ones have been alive. "Man, I only got two years in on 60," says 22-year-old newcomer Maurice Hardister. "See those old folks? That's me in 30 years. All we got to look forward to is a six-foot hole at Point Lookout [cemetery]. Why even try? What's the use?"

Hopelessness is again on the rise. "My membership tells me they're running out of hope," says Checo Yancy, president of the Lifers Association. "They felt good about Edwards coming in as governor last year, but he hasn't done much for lifers." In Louisiana, a lifer's only chance to get out of prison alive is a time-cut signed by the governor. "[The system] is not as lenient as people think," former Pardon Board member Sally McKissack told the *Times Picayune*. "In 1992," the New Orleans paper also reported, "Gov. Edwards granted clemency for one convicted murderer out of more than 1,500 in the system."

Human beings need hope more than they need love, or sex. People can function without love and sex. Over a million prisoners in this country do it every day. Hopelessness, however, breeds despair and desperation. Desperate people don't care whether they live or die.

"Talk to any correctional administrator in the United States who's been on the job very long or who knows anything at all about prisons," C. Paul Phelps told *The Angolite* years ago. "Ask them what's necessary to run a safe, constitutional prison. Hope is going to be number one. Without hope, it's just a matter of sheer physical force."

Suicide attempters in free society are dissuaded by altering the person's world or attitude. He may be told to a vacation, go to the woods and smell the flowers. His loved ones gather to show how much they care. Expectancies alter with change or counseling; the crisis passes.

It is difficult if not impossible to deal constructively with a suicidal prisoner. Professional counseling is of questionable value: What advice can a counselor who knows nothing about having to live in a pained and hopeless prison world give to make a prisoner see hope and meaning in an environment that crushes his spirit and invites rebellion? The prisoner's perception of his world as cruel and indifferent isn't a paranoid fantasy, it is real. How does a counselor convince a prisoner to embrace the world that is killing him? How does one convince another to kiss the whip?

Sheer physical force, as Phelps said, is the reality of the world of prison. All else is charade. Response to a potential Angola suicide is the same as to a potential fight or killing—physical restraint. Combatants and suicide attempters are put in strip cells as a certainty, and on four-point restraint if necessary. Chemical restraints (psychotropics and tranquilizers) may be given. Every conceivable *physical* measure is taken. Lacking are positive inducements to behave or to continue living. Corrections has none to offer.

Those who do—judges, legislators, pardon boards, governors—seem to be fresh out of stock.

The question is not why there are so many prison suicides. The question is why there are so few.

A Prison Suicide

Melvin Creppel rolled into Angola for the first and last time on November 9, 1992, a small, timid youngster just 23 years old. Twenty three days later he was dead, pushed by the system and herded by fellow inmates into a box so tight he saw death as the only out.

The Initial Classification Board decides where to place incoming prisoners. Creppel stood before them with his brand-new 60-year sentence, weak-kneed with fear that he'd be slung into the general population like a mullet into a tank full of barracuda.

Procedure in such cases, according to security Captain D.K. Basko, is "you go to a cellblock. They let you adjust awhile." The Board assigned Creppel to a Camp-H one-man cell with no TV, no radio, nothing to keep him company but his fears and frustrations.

Long-termer Hayes Williams was on the tier when Creppel arrived. "The little dude come to the institution with suicidal tendencies," Williams said, "because he showed me his arms where he tried to cut before."

The Mental Health Department apparently was aware of the prior attempts, for they looked in on him now and then and prescribed Sinequan (a powerful psychotropic drug) for him.

It takes time to adjust to prison. Creppel had none; things closed in on him too fast. He brooded about being ripped from his family, about his girl friend running off with their two children, and about his 60 years. Then he had to contend with an immediate and, to him, overwhelming threat.

Behind the scenes, two inmates were after him, playing good-guy bad-guy to "turn him out" (have him willingly perform homosexual acts). They passed threatening notes and ran verbal games on him. This worked so well that he was afraid to stand up to them, and more afraid of telling on them. There was nowhere to turn. He began stockpiling Sinequan, his medication.

Thursday evening, December 2, after a guard couldn't wake Creppel, the emergency medical team took over. "They had him in the hall and did everything possible," said Williams. "They fooled with him maybe 15 minutes trying to bring him around." Another veteran prisoner, Kenneth "Satch" Henley, was on the tier. "They got to him real fast, in minutes," he said. "That impressed the hell out of me. Then they went in the boy's cell and found a letter. Then they locked up a guy on the tier."

"He more or less said in the letter that he'd been saving his medicine until he got enough," Basko said, "and that he was having problems with two inmates on the tier. He alleged he'd been pressured to engage in homosexual activity. He said he was about to have a nervous breakdown from the stress and pressure. But there's no record of any complaints. We've talked to officers there. He made no complaints about being harassed, pressured, nothing."

"It's the same old story," said Henley. "You got a young guy who's susceptible to pressure and didn't feel the cell would protect him. That amazes the hell out of me. What can they do? Throw something at you maybe. That's about all. So, Creppel said they were going to f—k him

Friday, Saturday and Sunday. The little ole boy didn't know no better."

Hayes Williams, like Henley, was disgusted. "It set in on him," Williams said. "He musta been thinking, 'I lost the little girl. I lost my kids. And here you tell me I got to get f—ked in my ass for 60 years!' All the little boy wanted was a goddam friend, and he met the opposite. He met the Demon of Darkness."

24

DEATH OF THE BIG YARD*

by Douglas Dennis

"Who can impress the forest, bid the tree unfix his earthbound root?"
Macbeth, Act IV, Scene I

"Hey! You gotta hear this," he said. "Put that damn book down."

The con cocked a skeptical eyeball and said, "Yeah? Run it to me."

"Man, we're moving. They're gonna swap the Big Yard and Trusty Yard."

"They're *what*?" The book fell to his lap. "Get away, man. That's two thousand people!"

"For true. All the freepeople are talking about it."

He sat on the edge of his bunk and got a cigarette going while the other prisoner hurried off to spread the word. Another security brainstorm, he thought. Another way to f--- with us. He patted his thick, new mattress. Took me two goddam years to get this, and now I'll have to scuffle another one. His face wrinkled with disgust.

The Louisiana State Penitentiary at Angola is an anachronism, a penal dinosaur. Modern "correctional centers," prisons built during the past 20 years, are compact facilities holding 600 to 900 inmates. Angola sprawls over 18,000 acres, incarcerates 5,200 men, and ranks as the largest prison in the United States. Louisiana's only maximum-security prison, it's the end of the road for the state's prisoners, and a warden's nightmare.

About 2,300 Angola prisoners live in a mega-facility called the Main Prison, with the rest scattered among seven smaller "outcamps." Frustrated top administrators

hoped to correct two longstanding security problems by effecting a mass prisoner transfer that in numbers was the equivalent of moving two modern prisons.

The men targeted for transfer lived in the Main Prison's 60-man dormitories. There are four dorms to a unit, and each of the eight identical units is named after a tree. Ash, Magnolia, Cypress, Spruce and their outside recreation area comprise the "Trusty Yard." The other units, fittingly named after harder wood—Oak, Pine, Walnut, Hickory—make up the infamous "Big Yard."

Those Yards, along with a maximum security cellblock yard, dining halls, libraries, education area, administrative offices, visiting room, hospital, rodeo grounds, cannery, warehouses, gym, canteens and industrial compound, form the self-contained complex called the Main Prison.

Opened in 1956, the Main Prison was designed to hold three types of prisoners. Hard-core troublemakers and escape artists lived in the cellblocks and worked in the farm lines. At the other extreme, people who for the most part were quiet, settled and reliable lived on the Trusty Yard. Trusties, by virtue of their behavior, worked the best and most coveted job assignments. The rest, innocuously labeled medium-security, were poured into the Big Yard—a grassy rectangular cauldron five-and-a-half football fields long and a fifth of a mile wide.

The Big Yard was a merciless stewpot, place to dump unskilled or long-term new "fish," a place to which problem prisoners cycled back and forth from the cellblocks,

*Appeared in *The Angolite,* May/June 1992, 15-24. Reprinted with permission.

a place from which most men were escorted by gun guards to labor in the fields under boiling summer sun and wicked winter winds. In sum, it was a place of flux and tension where some prisoners struggled to improve themselves and get out, but where many more gambled, fought, ran scams, stole from each other, dealt drugs, drank home-made brew, killed and were killed, preyed on weak inmates, and generally raised all kinds of hell.

More fights, cuttings, stabbings and killings have occurred on the Big Yard than anywhere else at Angola, perhaps more than everywhere else at Angola. More "bucks" (work stoppages and food strikes) originated there than anywhere else. Only one on-duty guard has been killed in over fifty years, and he was murdered on the Big Yard. In the early '70s, national media dubbed Angola "the bloodiest prison in the country" due chiefly to Big Yard violence.

As a result, notoriety and a certain mystique grew around the Big Yard. Inmates in every jail and prison in the state (and in many throughout the states) know of Angola's Big Yard. While a few convicts regard it as home and wouldn't live anywhere else in the prison, many inmates are so terrified of it they couldn't be dragged through the Big Yard gate by a John Deere tractor.

For three generations of Louisiana prisoners, the Big Yard has been a rite of passage: If a new inmate could survive there and earn respect as a man, he could make it anywhere. The same can be said of correctional officers: If a new cadet could establish himself there as a respected officer, he could work anywhere in the system.

Many things have changed at Angola during the past thirty-six years, but the prisoner mix on the Trusty and Big Yards has remained essentially the same. Reflecting this, the Yards have come to be known as the Mild Side and the Wild Side. But whatever the name, Big Yard or Wild Side, it has long been a sharp stone in the administration's shoe.

The proverbial last straw was a nonfatal Big Yard cutting in late March. The incident happened right after lunch when all Big Yard farm lines and trusty industrial compound workers were on their way to work, crossing and mingling in the Sally Port area between the two Yards. Responding high-level officials coming in through the Sally Port had to push their way through.

"You'd have 1,200 to 1,400 inmates piled up in that area at one time, four times a day," said Angola Warden John P. Whitley, "and only one guard tower to supervise them. That wasn't good security. We had to do something about it."

Security Lt. Col. Darrell Vannoy came up with the idea of swapping Wild and Mild Side populations. "Actually," said Whitley, "since the buck last year, we've been kicking around ideas to better handle those types of disturbances on the Big Yard. Vannoy's idea did that and eliminated the traffic congestion. Like most good ideas, it's simple. We're making the architecture work for us."

By architecture, Whitley meant the different way the yards are laid out. The major Main Prison traffic artery is "The Walk," a slab of concrete fourteen feet wide and a half-mile long, running from deep in the Big Yard to the Trusty Yard gate where it forks. From the air, the Walk looks like a gigantic "Y" with a very long stem. Clustered at the base of the Y are Oak, Pine, Walnut and Hickory units. Ash and Magnolia are on one fork of the Y, Cypress and Spruce on the other.

Each fork is fenced to form its own small, separate yard.

The security advantage of dividing the more troublesome Big Yard prisoners into two separate and smaller areas is obvious. A financial advantage lay in the fact that no renovation money was required. Several gates already existed in Trusty Yard perimeter fencing through which medium-security farm lines could exit, and there is an existing walkway running from the Big Yard to the Industrial Compound. Never again would farm lines and compound workers have to congest the Sally Port area.

Rarely do mass prisoner transfers take place, anywhere. From an administrative viewpoint, uprooting hundreds of prisoners is frightening. This fear is not unfounded. Prisoners are more resistant to change than are most people. Having little voice in what affects the, and subject at all times to a rigidly controlled environment, they perceive change as a threat to diminish their already restricted lifestyle. The greater the change, the greater the likelihood for violent reaction. It is, therefore, one thing to talk about moving huge numbers of prisoners, and quite another to make it happen expediently and without incident.

There is an Angola precedent. On a day in 1973 that ended a way of life, some 900 prisoners switched dorms to desegregate the Trusty and Big Yards. Whitley at that time was a Main Prison classification officer. He has never forgotten that day. "Integration was a very hot issue then, and no one really knew how it would turn out," he recalls.

> The warden for security and many others thought it would be a blood bath. Some officers didn't come to work that day, called in sick, and the ones who did come were on edge, expecting anything. I was nervous myself, even though Warden Henderson was confident it would go without a hitch. It did go without a hitch, I think, because of two things: the prisoners were told integration would happen, there was no alternative, and the actual moving was made as painless as possible for them.

Very few secrets exist in prison, and nothing of any magnitude can be kept hidden for long. Almost two weeks before it happened, the prison grapevine hummed with news of the impending move. Everybody on both Yards would swap, so the word went, with no exceptions, including guards and ranking officers who would stay with the prisoners they were accustomed to supervising. Even dormitory names were to be exchanged.

Commenting on the surprising accuracy of the rumor mill, a seasoned convict observed that it meant the administration had deliberately leaked the news to test the waters of prisoner reaction.

That reaction was subdued, sullen. A sampling from both Yards indicated cynical acceptance. "Man, a dorm's a dorm. Who cares?" went one typical comment. "The only move I care about is out that front gate," went another.

Some were not so blase. "They only got one basketball court and one weightpile on the Big Yard," said a trusty. "We got two. Man, that sucks." Another griped, "Hey, what about the store? Ours is right handy [at the fork of the Y; theirs is way the f--- and gone out at the back fence, man!" Other complaints were more narrowly focused, like one by an energetic bathroom orderly. "Man," he said, "it took me a **year** to get this place spotless and shiny. Now I'm gonna have to do it all over again."

Behind Ash-1 dorm (soon to become

Oak-1) stands the only tree inside Main Prison razorwire. Referred to simply as "The Tree," it's a stalwart 35-foot cottonwood under whose shady branches trusties have passed many a quiet, reflective hour. One old-timer said, "I sure hate to leave that old tree. Everything in here is concrete, cold steel and razorwire. The Tree is alive; it's outside to me. Yeah man, I'm gonna miss it." His eyes were moist.

A memo from Whitley to the prisoners, followed by a crew painting new names on dorm doors and exteriors, etched the big move in granite and crashed the last hope of diehard cynics that it was all a big rumor.

The detailed memo confirmed what was already known far and wide, and set moving day for Monday, April 13. Renaming the dormitories—Ash to Oak, Magnolia to Pine, vice versa, and so forth down the line—was done so that "this relocation will not affect your mail, packages, visiting, or call-outs [to club activities, plasma, hospital, etc.]." With a last-second addition to the memo, Whitley gave prisoners the following day off (as well as moving day) "to settle into their new quarters." And that hit just the right note to dissipate any residual tension. As one prisoner said, "Shit, for two days off he can move me every week."

All the brass were on hand bright and early the calm, sunny morning of April 13, but none were earlier or more eager than Main Prison shift supervisor Foster Andrews, the line commander whose security force would make or break the operation. Andrews has the presence of an NFL linebacker, and had no intention of letting anything get out of line this day. "This is going to go smooth," he said, "and I'll remove anybody from the scene who causes problems."

No one had to be "removed." Everything from start to finish went as fast and smooth as Desert Storm. Before the sun showed itself, four stake-body trucks roared up to Ash unit. An officer flung open the doors of Ash-1 and -2 and yelled, "Get those boxes out here," referring to the two metal footlockers each prisoner has in which all his worldly goods must go. Quickly, they heaved, pushed, lugged and individually muscled the heavy boxes out to the waiting trucks. This scene was duplicated on the Big Yard, where Oak-1 and -2 prisoners struggled with their lockers.

When the trucks rolled, so did the prisoners. Clutching odds and ends, pushing overflowing laundry buggies down the Walk, Oak-1 and -2 passed Ash-1 and -2, each group on the way to a new home. Once there, the prisoners displayed common sense (criminal cunning, some might call it) and formed a human chain to slide the lockers over the smooth concrete and into the dorms. Then they were locked in to allow the next set of dorms unimpeded room to saddle up and roll.

The mood was light: walking and talking, hellos between pals from different yards who hadn't seen each other for a while, mugging for the camera. Normal grumbling and good-natured ribbing and grab-assing were the rule.

Wheelchair-bound Shedrick Davis, on his way to the Trusty Yard, put the thoughts of many into words: "I think it's gonna be OK. Gonna be all right. Can't get no worser, we're still at Angola. We ain't going home yet."

Asked what he thought of the two basketball courts and weightpiles, Davis replied, "That's for them that participate with all that. But look, there's a tree, and that might be all right if the trusties don't decide to send for it. They gonna send for that tree. They gonna get it back on that side where they at. I won't be surprised they won't dig it up and get it over there, me. But I'm gonna enjoy it while it's here."

A trusty, on arriving at his new dorm on the Big Yard, said, "The transition of moving doesn't really matter. I wanta move to that white gate out there [the prison's front gate], you know, beyond that. I can see it from here, so I know I'm getting close."

As the crew loaded and unloaded the trucks, thirsty work in the increasing heat of the day, "Kool-Ade Man" was right on the spot for them. Grover Bindom's regular job is at the Bachelor Officers Quarters, but he and a friend unofficially volunteered to hustle something to drink for the hard-working men. "I'm just helping the brothers, you know," Bindom said, "because I know these boxes are pretty heavy. They ain't tell me to do this here. I'm just gonna make sure that they gets some [Kool-Ade]. And I'm gonna move with every dormitory that they go to and I'll be there with this juice for 'em. Cups for them and everything."

All was not grits and red-eye gravy, however. Many prisoners were not overjoyed with the condition of the dorms they moved into. An irate Morris "Juvenile" Burton had this to say: "I want you to know that the Mag-side unit left the dorm in shambles. We had to come in here and scrub. Shower area nasty. Toilet area nasty. Got trash piled all up at the door. We didn't leave our unit like that for them, you know. We GI'd last night and left it in proper order for them to move in. Yeah, and the bedsprings are tore up, you know. Mattresses are outta shape and raggedy. I wanta say I don't think that's right. [The added recreation] don't balance it out. I like the bigger yard we had. More

space. Your hygienic area where you live and sleep and have to brush your teeth and stuff like this is more important than pumping iron and playing basketball and all that, you know. "

Several Big Yarders echoed that line. Ironically, trusties who moved into Big Yard dorms had the same sentiments and expressed them in almost exactly the same words. The truth of the matter is all the dorms looked shabby, trash scattered over the floors. But, as Captain Mike Roberts said, "Hell, nobody outside takes their garbage with them when they move. A little sweeping and mopping will straighten it all out."

Meanwhile, the high command— Warden Whitley, Security Warden Mike Gunnels, Colonel Fulton Rabalais and Captain Roberts—was standing around on the Big Yard with little to do but chat with each other about how well it was going and watch the parade go by.

"This should have been done a long time ago," mused Whitley. "The Trusty Yard's been double-fenced for years. The Walk is fenced and security gates are in place that can effectively separate the prisoners over there. Why this wasn't done, I don't know. We wondered about that and tried very hard to think of a good reason not to do it, but couldn't come up with a single one.

"I'm not surprised it's going so well," he continued. "I told the men their quality of life would remain the same and I meant it. There was nothing for them to get upset about. Yes, I'm aware of the disparity of basketball courts and weightpiles, and I'll take care of it." He then smiled, "But I'm not moving the Tree. They can forget that."

Delighted with the operation's success, Gunnells attributed it to "a lot of cooperation from both sides. That's what made this work without a hitch." Gunnells had a special reason to be pleased. Twenty years ago, during his early days as a correctional officer, the Big Yard had tried to kill him. Two prisoners threw gasoline into his guard shack on the Walk outside Hickory dorm and torched it with him inside. Gunnells barely escaped with his life. Now he had the satisfaction of playing a leading role in killing the Big Yard.

The big move was completed at high noon, six hours after it began. The headcount cleared, the doors opened, and everybody went to lunch. But several move-related events came on the heels of the relocation like a series of aftershocks following a big quake.

A large hobby shop is located on each Yard. Tons of tools and raw and finished materials had to be moved. Hobbycraft—woodwork, ceramics, paintings, leather goods, and so forth—is an important activity for many prisoners, earning them money and productively engaging their spare time.

The annual Arts & Crafts Festival was only weeks away. Time pressed on the impatient hobbycrafters. They resented the disruption of moving and feared damaging their goods in transit. Back and forth on the Walk they trooped, property carefully packed into scavenged cardboard boxes and borrowed laundry buggies and pushcarts,

looking like a horde of displaced war refugees. It was a slow process, taking that afternoon and the next morning to accomplish. Finally it was done.

Within weeks, a cement floor went down, a roof went up, and plates, bars and benches appeared for the second weightpile on the Big Yard. The second basketball court also was well underway, ground broken and forms up to receive the concrete. Prisoners did not fail to note that Whitley had kept his word to take care of the disparity between the Yards.

A recent post-lunch headcount at the formerly crowded Sally Port area did not take long—four scattered prisoners.

April 13, 1992, marked what may well have been the largest single movement of incarcerated felons in the history of the United States. Over 1,800 prisoners had swapped dormitories—lock, stock, and wall clock—with no hitches and not many bitches. Administrators and prisoners elsewhere could learn from how things are done at Angola.

Murderous MacBeth, in Shakespeare's timeless tragedy, was toppled by an imaginative scheme that appeared to move a forest. Similar inventiveness inspired Whitley and his men to execute a plan in which no one suffered, yet the goal was accomplished.

An era has ended: the infamous Big Yard is dead.

25

BIG JOHN

by Douglas Dennis

"I give no quarter and ask for none."
John Fulford

The Cash brothers pillaged the North Miami jewelry store like the professionals they were. Ray dumped displays of glittering gems into a pillowcase, while Ted waved a sawed-off shotgun over the prostrate bodies of two ill-starred customers and an ashen-faced clerk. It took the store manager three tries to hit the right combination on the old Mosler safe. Concentration came hard with Virgil Cash's .45 automatic stuck in his right ear.

Outside, slouched in a brand new 1954 Olds 88, whose exhaust burbled over asphalt softened by a blazing noon sun, a lanky kid called John gripped the wheel with sweaty, gloved hands and peered for police through silvered sunglasses.

"Wouldn't mind if they did come," he thought, the .38 Police Special a deadly denseness against his stomach. The Cash brothers came instead, quick, each getting in by a different door. "Move it," said Virgil.

John dropped the Cash boys miles away, dumped the hot-wired Olds in a parking lot, then peeled off the gloves and stuck them in his back pocket. Walking quickly toward his own car three blocks away, he wiped his palms on his thighs.

Two cops munching burgers in a White Tower grease pit watched John swagger by. "Ain't that the Fulford kid?" "Sure is." "How hot you suppose it is?" "I dunno, 'bout 95 1 guess." "Little too warm for gloves ain't it?" "Check it out. I'll catch the tab and be right with you."

John tensed. "How the hell . . ." he thought. Spinning, he jerked out the .38 and fired. "Jesus Christ!" the cop gasped as he fell to his knees. He pulled out his pistol with numb fingers and fired once at John's fleeing back. The slug's impact flung him face first onto the concrete sidewalk. His gun skittered over the curb. "You son of a bitch," said the second cop as he ran up, kicked John over on his back, and fired three rounds into his chest.

Luck, youth and vigor saved Fulford from death in 1954, but the pattern would haunt him the rest of his life: Well-planned schemes that ended badly.

John Cornelius Fulford was born February 1, 1933, and reared in South Florida, the son of a strapping deputy who became the Dade County sheriff's chief of detectives. Dade encompasses the state's largest city, Miami, and is the anchor of Florida's fabled Gold Coast. It was a time of roving bands of Depression-spawned bank bandits—Dillinger, Baby-Face Nelson, Pretty-Boy Floyd, Bonnie and Clyde—whose colorful exploits became legend.

Their heirs, and Fulford, surfaced in the early 1950s as the nation embraced the Eisenhower era of tacky housing developments, gray flannel suits and crewcut conformity. Southern states shut down the vice and gambling that had run wide open during and after World War II. Louisiana's state troopers, headed by Francis C. Grevemberg, trashed card and dice dens and smashed slot machines by the truckload. The hammer hit Alabama's vice capital—Phenix City—an entire community devoted to honkytonks,

*Appeared in *The Angolite*, September/October 1993, 22-35. Reprinted with permission.

whores, hooch, pills and gambling for thousands of servicemen from nearby Fort Benning. Hundreds of hustlers scattered and set up shop as hijackers, bank burglars and bandits, among them Dewitt Dawson, Dutch Ernst, the Cash brothers, and Carl "Towhead" White. This was the final generation of professional criminals, the men young Fulford idolized.

Fulford's serious problems with the law began with a January 1953 arrest for grand larceny and armed robbery. Nine assorted arrests for robbery and related charges followed including, significantly, assault with a deadly weapon, which was reduced to resisting an officer by force. They were all dropped, reduced, or resulted in not-guilty findings. The 20-year-old got off with several months in the Dade County jail for assault and battery and possessing stolen property. Fortunate he was to have a high-placed policeman in the family to blunt the sword of Justice.

Young Fulford's budding career as a professional criminal ended with the June 29, 1954, police shootout. Toting ten years for "assault with intent to commit manslaughter upon a police officer," he entered Raiford prison a cocky youngster of 21. Even then he weighed well over 200 pounds and stood a towering 6-foot-6, hence his prison name, "Big John."

"Cool Hand Luke," (starring Paul Newman) is an amazingly accurate portrayal of prison life in Florida's road camps 30-something years ago. Like Newman's Lucas Jackson, Fulford had a hard time getting his mind right and rabbit in his blood. He ran off at least twice, to be almost immediately recaptured. His last escape, on January 7, 1957, was from State Road Prison Camp No. 4530 near Tampa. The next day deputy sheriffs captured him in Clearwater. This escapade earned him four more years and a transfer to state prison.

Back at Raiford, Fulford did his share of time on the "shelf" (punishment tier) and more in maximum security, where he discovered he had the rare ability to do easy cell time. Solitude suited him, and he could do things in a cell he had no time for in general population—like learn jailhouse lawyering.

He launched an off-the-wall attack in 1958 on his escape conviction, arguing the state had not proven at trial that he was the legally incarcerated John Fulford. The court agreed: "No evidence was introduced connecting the accused with the John Cornelius Fulford named in the said copies of the information, minutes, and commitment papers which were received in evidence. . .because of such omission the judgment and sentence appealed from must be reversed."

At retrial in late 1959 he was reconvicted and resentenced to four years, but to him it was a stunning victory. He'd forced his hated keepers to expend their time and resources, then made them look foolish. Thereafter, Fulford's weapon of choice against the criminal justice system became the law itself.

When the sixties sailed in, an otherwise unremarkable Florida prisoner, Clarence Earl Gideon, won the most important criminal-law decision of the century—Gideon v. Wainwright—the U. S. Supreme Court ruling that requires a lawyer be appointed if necessary to represent each person facing felony charges.

It made available to the poor what the rich had always enjoyed—legal counsel—and changed fundamentally the face of justice.

The ink had hardly dried on Gideon before Fulford filed to again overturn the escape conviction, this time because he was lawyerless when convicted. After the writ was granted and a new trial ordered, Fulford, through his court-appointed attorney, negotiated a plea bargain: A guilty plea in exchange for a reduced sentence that, with credit for time served, meant freedom within weeks. Fulford walked out of Raiford on June 4, 1963, after nine years inside. His liberty more precious because he had fashioned the key to freedom.

Fulford returned to Miami, married a local girl, and fathered a daughter. Heading a family perhaps impelled him to join the lunch-bucket brigade, but not for long. After 17 arrest-free months, Atlanta, Georgia police picked him up in November 1964 for robbery.

Fulford rolled into Reidsville prison with a brand new ten-year term. His wife couldn't, or wouldn't, hang on. She divorced him, took the child, and severed all contact. It didn't faze Fulford. "If your family is that dear to you, you do not jeopardize it by going to score," says a man we'll call Tom, a career criminal who wishes to remain anonymous. "Put it this way, John never had the ability to bond, not with anybody. If he were an atom his rings would be full—he'd be inert."

This trip Fulford laid off litigating and turned to capitalism. In prison it's called "making a hustle." He had about 30 prisoners tying fishing flies that he sold all over the country. Paying them was a problem, because inmate stores limit the amount prisoners can spend. That forced him to scuffle in the black market for the cigarettes, cash and gold he needed. Fulford broke in that way as a hustler. When he discharged from the Georgia pen on August 9, 1970, after serving almost six years, he brought $24,000 out with him.

The mature Fulford, 37, armed with intelligence, a talent for management and organization, and a respectable sum of money, should have turned away from crime and chosen the high road. Such is the myth of unfettered free will. He could no more have done that than he could have grown wings and soared like a sea gull. A cold, rebellious man, his antipathy toward an overbearing father had hardened in two of America's most brutal prison systems. The only real choices he had were among avenues of antiauthoritarianism. Fulford was a hard-core outlaw.

A prison outlaw. He spent only 25 months total after 1954 on the free side of cold steel bars. "Every character John knew he met in prison," Tom says. "You don't get to be a professional criminal until you've served your apprenticeship, gone on a hundred scores. He grew up with some guys, the Cash boys, and ran on their coattails. This guy never had enough time to travel around the country and meet people. He did too much time to be a real criminal."

Within three months Georgia's East Point Police Department picked him up holding stolen goods and burglary tools. Although these charges were dropped, several weeks later on January 28, 1971, he was popped in Pensacola, Florida for buying stolen goods. Those charges also were dropped, but enough was enough. Fulford headed for Louisiana with girlfriend Sandra Decker, whom he'd bonded out of the Pensacola county jail, and Florida fugitive James Knight. Decker faced an armed robbery charge for a supermarket stickup she'd pulled with another man. The trio found an apartment in New Orleans.

On the night of April 11, 1971, three armed men wearing ski masks, reportedly under the impression New Orleans grocer Frank Corso kept a "wheelbarrow full of jewels" at his residence, attempted a home invasion. A gun battle ensued, and Corso wound up dead.

A confidential informant, possibly Decker, pointed authorities to the apartment, where FBI agents arrested Knight as a fugitive from Florida and Fulford for harboring him. Two other men were implicated, arrested and, with Fulford, charged with Corso's murder. Knight was the star state witness, claiming to be the wheel man while the others broke into Corso's home. Decker, too, was a prosecution witness.

The case was high-profile from day one. News media first focused on the outrage of a respected community member mowed down trying to protect his wife and children from "cold-blooded killers." Law enforcement officials then claimed Fulford and his crime partners belonged to the dreaded "Dixie Mafia," a surrealistic title that evoked images of marauding cracker conspirators burgling banks and busting heads. Reporters, smelling blood in the water, went into a feeding frenzy. New Orleans District Attorney Jim Garrison, a notorious publicity hound, was in hog heaven.

The irony of the Dixie Mafia was that by 1971 those positioned in its ranks by the police were either dead, out of commission, or carried so much heat they couldn't wiggle. Dewitt Dawson was in Alabama's Holman Prison with his daddy, Pride. Towhead White, supposedly the supreme Dixie Mafiosi, was dead, murdered on April 3, 1969, in Corinth, Mississippi.

Nevertheless, so much heated rhetoric about the Dixie Mafia and the Corso killing filled airwaves and newspapers that it eclipsed even Garrison's Kennedy assassination trial of Clay Shaw. A mistrial had to be declared and the proceedings moved to Lafayette in Southwest Louisiana, the first change of venue from Orleans Parish in a hundred years.

Garrison tried the case personally, taking center stage in a trial that lasted ten headline-filled days. Despite alibi witnesses and protestations of innocence, Fulford and his co-defendants were convicted in May 1972, largely on Knight's and Decker's testimony, and sentenced to life terms in the Louisiana State Penitentiary at Angola. In return for his services, Knight walked away clean— cleared of the Corso charges, freed from the Florida charges, put in the federal witness protection program, and given $10,000. Decker cut a lesser deal. No money, no witness protection, but the pending Pensacola armed robbery charge vanished, and so did she.

The trial judge broke long-standing precedent, probably because of the Dixie Mafia furor, and ordered the convicted be held at Angola instead of the Lafayette Parish jail while the conviction was on appeal. In short order Fulford launched a jailhouse-lawyering career that spanned 20 years. He filed against anyone, anytime, about anything. He became the most prolific legal nuisance Louisiana courts had ever seen. He was the Writ Writer from West Hell.

This is vintage Fulford: "An appeal suspends execution of sentence," he argued in what may be his first Angola writ. So how can he be "forced to work in the fields in violation of [his] 13th Amendment right against involuntary servitude?" Further, if Angola is to be used as a "parish prison for appellants" then the court "should set guidelines for the Board of Corrections to follow, so those held in Angola pending appeal will have the same rights and privileges as those being held in the parish jail." His writ was later dismissed in federal court.

In September 1972, Fulford was to be taken to Charity Hospital in New Orleans for a nose operation. As he neared the ambulance, guards diverted him to a room to be searched. He dropped a $700 roll of greenbacks and a handcuff key. The guards confiscated the contraband and put him in disciplinary detention. Fulford denied the money was his, but after he was found guilty by the disciplinary board, he told them, "If you're gonna give me the charge, you gotta give me the money." They would not, and he filed suit to have the $700 placed in his prison drawing account. At the court hearing, when Fulford realized the judge was going to award him the money, he stood and asked to amend his petition. "Your honor," he said, "by the same logic, I ask that the state be ordered to give me back the handcuff key." In the suddenly silent courtroom the judge looked down his nose at Fulford for a long moment before replying, "You better quit while you're ahead."

In October 1973, when a state judge sat on one of his suits for six and a half months, Fulford found a procedural rule that required judgment be rendered within 30 days of a case being taken under advisement. He filed to have 25% of the judge's salary withheld for each overdue month until he ruled. That same year, doubling back to his earlier suit about being forced to work while his sentence was on appeal, Fulford filed to be reimbursed $25 a day for each day's labor. And so it went—an endless flood flowed from Fulford's battered old typewriter.

A favored tactic the state uses against prisoner litigants is to string them out for years. Fulford turned it against them. He'd raise an issue then diverge to a side issue, and confused corrections attorneys would waste months and years following it.

Fulford didn't mind. Sitting in a cell with nothing else to do, he had time and energy to spare. Eventually, to keep the ball rolling, he'd say, "OK, well what about this? This is what we filed the suit on." His suits spun out like spider webs.

Other litigators asked for evidentiary hearings to get out of Angola, see the countryside, spot pretty girls, and redress grievances. Fulford's main motive was to put prison officials' asses on courthouse benches and enjoy their discomfort. Hearings required prison guards to haul litigants and their witnesses to Baton Rouge, trips that tied up one or more vehicles and several guards all day. Judge Steve Alford tired of this and moved the mountain to Mohammed. In a first-ever for state courts, he ordered hearings be held at Angola. Fulford saw grounds for another complaint, one that he carried to the federal Fifth Circuit Court of Appeals. "If a civil trial can be held in state prison and suppressed from the public," he argued, "then the court system of this country is going to lose decorum and dignity as it is only a matter of time before criminal trials are conducted within the Louisiana state prison or local jail." It was denied.

Judge Alford's precedent setter took place on November 14, 1977. It was, of course, a Fulford lawsuit. He wanted $60 returned to him that was discovered in a garbage can in his work area and confiscated. Alford dismissed the suit after Fulford admitted he had no right to have the money in the first place. Like a batter who swings at every pitch, he hit a few home runs, had some base hits, and struck out a helluva lot.

"John was like a knight in shining armor to me," says a seasoned inmate counselor we'll call Dick, who doesn't want his name used. "He was one of the great inmate writ writers. And I was really disappointed the more I got to know him. What he was really about was harassment. John was a detriment to the inmate population because of this."

As repressive tough-on-crime policies took hold in the 1970s, courts began to use Fulford's suits as forums to spell out how the DOC could legally do just about anything it wanted to. The Louisiana Supreme Court in 1978, for example, denied his writ to be released from extended lockdown, ruling: "Prison authorities are and should be responsible for maintaining internal order and discipline and securing their institutions against escape. These administrators must have a great deal of discretion in accomplishing their purpose within constitutionally refined parameters."

In case that may have been a little vague, the same court in another Fulford suit ruled: "Restrictions [imposed by the DOC] must be reasonably related to a legitimate governmental interest. Clearly, the policy [in question] is reasonably related to the legitimate state interest of security."

Subsequently, the courts usually pulled a Pontius Pilate, washing their hands of prisoner-rights issues, as they did with Fulford's "black box" suit. A black box is a plastic or metal device fitting over handcuffs to prevent them from being picked. It holds wrists in a rigid, unnatural position, leaving angry red marks and causing the prisoner's forearms to swell and become numb. The Louisiana Supremes had this to say: "Requiring all [lockdown] prisoners to wear a black box when outside the prison [for hospital trips or court appearances] is for a rational reason, security, and is directed by a standard prison policy, not left to unfettered discretion of guards. Under these circumstances, it is not within our power to substitute our judgment for that of prison officials."

From this decision grew the current policy of black-boxing every soul, from Class-A trusties on down, who leave the prison. It would be unfair, however, to lay that at Fulford's feet. The evolution of tighter security controls and prison administrators being allowed to hide behind "security needs" was going on everywhere in the land.

Fulford does have to carry the load for causing the transformation of the Inmate Welfare Fund into a DOC slush fund. Historically, corrections administrators regarded the IWF as belonging to the inmate population because it consisted of funds from sales of inmate hobbycraft and blood plasma, and kickbacks from prisoner-placed collect calls. Officials spent the monies exclusively for prisoner sports and recreation programs, expenses for which the state had never appropriated a cent.

Fulford filed on March 20, 1980, alleging prison officials had mismanaged the IWF and misspent millions. He asked the court to order $5 million restored, a monthly financial statement be issued to each inmate, and that prisoners be allowed to manage, control and spend the funds. In the eyes of prison officials, this was rank heresy. It attacked the core of corrections—control. Corrections controls to keep prisoners confined, orderly and obedient. In the name of control, corrections also strips prisoners of initiative and self-determination. If prisoners were to manage a multi-million dollar fund, one might as well be warden. It was unthinkable.

The suit, of course, was denied. The court ruled that the IWF did not belong to prisoners because they were "wards of the state," and that prison officials were "trustees of the Fund" in full control of its operation and expenditures. The sole proviso was that IWF monies be spend to "benefit inmates."

C. Paul Phelps, who in 1980 headed the DOC, told *The Angolite*, "The IWF used to be sacred, but people began to look at it differently after the Fulford decision. The whole mind-set changed."

Under Republican Governor Buddy Roemer, DOC chieftains willfully widened IWF expenditures. In 1989 alone, DOC headquarters computerized itself at IWF expense. Then they snatched $164,418 to pay librarians, inmate-store security guards and recreation "coaches." These salaries became annual "fixed" expenses. The IWF paid for dormitory fans, construction materials to renovate hobby shops, and a vehicle for Angola's coach to tool around in.

The frosting on the cornbread was the law library rip-off. The U.S. Supreme Court requires states to provide "legal access" for prisoners. Louisiana chose to do this by establishing and maintaining a law library in each of its prisons. The state paid the bills until 1989, when the division of administration yanked the appropriated monies for use elsewhere. Desperate DOC officials snarfled $119,500 from the IWF for law books, an expense that has also become a fixed annual expenditure.

There's more. Roemer's DOC policymakers "centralized" the IWF at Baton Rouge headquarters, leaving only a token amount under the direct control of each prison. Since then there has been no accounting to prisoners of where IWF money at HQ goes. This all stems from Fulford; it is his legacy.

All this arcane legal activity was orchestrated by a seventh-grade dropout and prison outlaw. "Big John was a solid person with a word like a fence post, like concrete," says Walter Burnette, a prisoner who at one time was nominated by police for Dixie Mafia membership. "Many years ago with the old convicts, your word was your bond; there was a code of ethics. This was before dope babies and crack hustlers. Now you got a lot of squares in here who are criminals as far as violating the law, but they are not characters or gangsters— Dillinger types who made a choice in life to go against the system. Fulford was a real strong character."

Like others who survived the Angola of long knives and battle axes, Fulford rated respect for being an old convict. He kept a little following of wanna-be gangsters and regaled them with old prison horror stories, get-overs and getarounds. Aside from that, he was not well liked. "I've never heard anyone say Big John was a rat or snitch," says a violent career criminal who wants to be anonymous, a man we'll call Harry. "But a lot of people just couldn't handle his personality. Younger prisoners referred to him as a pompous old man whose time is up. He was arrogant."

"Well, John was a strong-willed type of person, and some people might have felt that he was offensive or overbearing," concedes Burnette. "He didn't let a weaker person, or what he considered a weak person, save much face. Simple as that. John didn't give the average guy much running room."

A hard-rock con Fulford was, by all accounts, but not a chronic disciplinary problem. He had only 18 reports in 21 years. Some prisoners pile up that many in a few months. Were it not for his propensity to be popped with contraband (9 reports), especially cash money, he'd have a pretty good record. Yet he spent 13 of his 21 years in Angola cells. Some say celling him was a corrections catch-back for worrying them with writs. While that probably predisposed prison officials to lock him up, it likely had more to do with Fulford's antagonism and lack of artfulness. He never tried to work within the system; he always fought it.

Fulford was anti-social, a lone wolf. He had no close friends. Even his crime partners steered away from him. "He didn't fit the classical mold," says Tom, the career criminal. "The criminal character is us-against-them, but with John it was me-against-them."

Self-respecting prisoners hustle what they need, if they can, rather than sponge off loved ones. Fulford hustled legal work, for a fee. At times he may have helped someone for nothing, but he was never accused of benevolence. He bartered—bought, sold, traded—things for profit. He had a pawn shop where people borrowed, left collateral, and paid back three-for-two or two-for-one. Fulford did well in prison, which always arouses animosity and envy.

"John was no friend of mine," says inmate Glenn Demourelle. "We spoke and all, did a little business here and there, but I never had much for him. You could never get John to do anything for you, just on John. There was always a price on it. John was not the type to do anything out of the kindness of his heart. John don't care about nothing. He was a hateful individual."

Every now and then a strong character who's done hard time, has stood up and got down, suddenly gets lost in prison homosexuality. Rumors about Fulford have been Angola currency for years. "He had a definite homosexual lifestyle," says Harry, the violent criminal. "He ran after punks, black punks."

Demourelle claims eye-witness knowledge. "I was very much a part of the boy John had this burning desire over in 1979," he says. "I used to be there with them and, come to find out, John is into getting whipped. Extension cords, towels. The boy had told me to stick close in case John flipped out. So I see that John is nothing but an animal. He was eating the boy up, too. That's from what I saw. He'd tell me that he's not worried about what others thought because everybody knew his reputation. John just wasn't the man everyone thought he was." Demourelle said these episodes occurred in a room in the Main Prison gym. Fulford lived in Oak-3 from April 1979 to August 1980, and had access to the gym.

Football lit Fulford's lamp, but he never booked illegal football tickets. The risk didn't bother him; the work did. To use his typewriter for that would have been sacrilege. His typewriter was for one thing only—attacking the establishment. "I've done 21 years with him," Tom says, "and the only thing I knew he really liked was to gamble on football. He was a player, not a layer."

The spread was six points when Syracuse played LSU in September 1987. Fulford took it. The game ended in a 6-6 tie, and he went to collect. That's when he ran into the man who would become his nemesis, Samuel L. Rollins Jr., known as "Papa." They lived in Camp-D's Raven cellblock. Rollins, 29, doing life for a 1985 murder conviction, was a real problem child. In two years at Angola he'd piled up 42 disciplinary reports, almost all of them for serious infractions like aggravated disobedience, defiance, contraband and property destruction. According to Rollins, one of his friends owed Fulford for the LSU game and didn't pay up. Fulford barked at him. He and Rollins then had words.

September 28, 1987, at 7:40 p.m. in the Main Prison plasma unit, where all eligible prisoners are brought to sell their blood plasma, a fight broke out among Raven prisoners in the noisy and crowded plasma bullpen (holding area). Three security guards rushed in and got the situation under control. According to their reports, Rollins had Fulford on the ground stabbing him with a short, shiny knife, while a third prisoner, Nolan Grant, was kicking him.

A plasma worker who witnessed the incident recalls that "John had the knife at first and hit Papa two or three times. Then Papa got aholt to the knife and skinned John once or twice, not very bad. About that time the police got there and closed everything down. Papa was bleeding more than John. It happened very fast." Several sources corroborated this version, adding that the weapon was a short steak knife slipped to Fulford when he arrived at the plasma unit. All three were cut and bleeding, but none of the wounds was life-threatening. Fulford suffered a broken rib and required 32 stitches. He and Rollins were found guilty of aggravated fighting by the disciplinary board and sentenced to Camp-J lockdown.

Fulford appealed on the grounds that official reports stated he'd defended himself against an armed attack by Rollins and Grant. He had a cod-lock win. As a matter of unwritten prison policy, a guard's testimony is infinitely more credible than what any prisoner or group of prisoners might say. The secretary of corrections ordered the report expunged from his record. Fulford later transferred to Oak-1, a medium security dorm in the Main Prison.

Never one to allow an opportunity to sue slip away, Fulford filed for $75,000 damages against the plasma unit and corrections for inadequate security

measures, and against Rollins and Grant, too. Meanwhile, a very unhappy Rollins languished at Camp-J with no chance to win an appeal. The guards, after all, had seen him stabbing Fulford.

In October 1990, Fulford filed the "female strip-search" suit. He claimed the recent use of female guards in male living areas violated male prisoners' rights to privacy, especially when the females conducted a "get naked, bend over and spread 'em" search for contraband. Fulford also argued that female guards watched him shower and use the toilet. So far, his writ deviated little from similar suits going forward in California and other states. But John Fulford wrote writs to remember. He could not resist adding: "[Female guards] are generally fat, ugly, horny, freakish, sex-starved, low-grade women who gain sexual satisfaction from viewing nude male inmates at the taxpayer's expense."

U.S. Magistrate Stephen Riedlinger heard the suit and recommended to federal Judge Frank Polozola that female guards be barred from strip-searching male prisoners. He dismissed Fulford's other claims. Polozola modified the recommendation; he only prohibited female officers from strip searching Fulford.

When this hit the papers, as he knew it would, Angola's female guards went ballistic. Lt. Shirley Coody responded with remarkable restraint in a letter printed in *The Angolite*: "I feel that inmate Fulford owes each female officer of this Institution a public apology for his crude lies and accusations."

"I refuse to apology for the contents of my suit," answered Fulford in a letter to *The Angolite*. "If Lt. Coody feels that I committed perjury, then simply have me indicted. If the defendants don't like the court's decision, then simply appeal the matter. As it stands now, the court has ruled in my favor and agreed with the facts and evidence—that makes me a W I N N E R—not a sore loser.

"Lastly, *The Angolite* can expect a Slander Suit to be filed for the malicious publication of defamation of my character by failing to investigate Lt. Coody's malicious accusations of calling me a 'liar' and for allowing her to 'use' *The Angolite* to expose me to hatred, contempt, and to deprive me of the benefit of public confidence and social intercourse. Lt. Coody can also shop around for a lawyer too as I will sue both of you jointly." He did. It remains unresolved.

The primary purpose of learning to litigate is to get out of prison. Fulford attacked his conviction in every conceivable way, keeping writs moving through the courts. "He won once, got a reversal back in 1982 in the Fifth [federal] Circuit," Harry says. But the U.S. Supreme Court overruled and reinstated the conviction. That's about a 1 in 20,000 chance." That early disappointment didn't slow Fulford down. He kept stroking and, ultimately, prevailed. His conviction was set aside this summer by the same Fifth Circuit.

"John was a rare animal; that's why we're having a conversation about him," says Tom. "He was going to punish these people plain and simple, punish them for anything. He didn't think anything they did was sacred, and he'd do anything to get them. Absolutely ruthless. Even if he lost, it was inconvenient for them. He wanted the fight more than the win."

Prison officials and the courts never got a handle on Fulford. The courts seldom dismissed his suits out of hand, because he frequently framed them around constitutional issues. Prison officials were

helpless. They deal out degrees of escalating force to coerce conformity, but their ultimate weapon, extended lockdown, didn't faze Fulford. It apparently never occurred to anyone in power to keep him in general population loaded up with work—cutting grass, painting walls, whatever—that would leave him limp at the end of the day. This could have worked: Fulford, during a recent sojourn on the Big Yard, went to an inmate seeking help to get a "layout job in a room in the gym" where he could devote more time to his "legal work." And, no doubt, to his sexual activities. This never happened, perhaps because he was soon locked up again.

During the 1991 "death gurney" protest, in which several hundred prisoners refused to work because a few were ordered to make a lethal injection table for Angola's death house, Fulford and an associate called "Hungry Jack" were picked up as instigators. Fulford filed suit protesting their placement in extended lockdown.

"Here's what John told me," Tom says. "[Security Major Donnie] Parker said [at the court hearing] he had two confidential informants that overheard him and Hungry Jack discussing the buck on the side of Oak-1. And when John asked the location at this particular time of the two informants, Parker said behind the Main Prison Laundry. John was ready with a blueprint showing you can't even see Oak-1 from behind there. After that, [Magistrate] Riedlinger took a dim view of anything Parker said. He really talked bad to Parker. That's what John liked best, what he savored."

Fulford did not keep score the way most people do. "The last thing he told me was what he won," says Tom. "Everything leading up to that was how he got Parker. And how Riedlinger told Parker he was a liar. Then all of a sudden he said they gave him $100,000 compensatory and $10,000 punitive damages. I never heard of a prison suit with that kind of money involved. To show you how differently John thought, when they offered a settlement he wouldn't take it. He wanted to get them back on the stand, make them weasel and squirm. I don't think John ever settled a suit."

State district court Commissioner Kay Bates ordered prison officials to release Fulford from extended lockdown. On June 15, 1993, they put him in Camp-C, Bear-2 dorm, far away from the Main Prison' s Oak-3 dorm where Samuel "Papa" Rollins now lived. Prison policy firmly prohibits placing known enemies together. Given Angola's size and its self-contained camps, it's not difficult to keep antagonists apart.

But each weekend, inmate teams travel among the camps and the Main Prison to compete in whatever sport is in season. So it was that on Saturday, July 17, Glenn Demourelle's "Total Disrespect" volleyball team appeared at Camp-C with team member Samuel "Papa" Rollins.

The last thing Fulford needed was Rollins in his face. Now 60 years old, his conviction reversed and chance of being reconvicted slim, Fulford expected to collect $100,000 and live out his days high on the hog. He clutched at the convict's dream: freedom and a tub of money to go with it.

But the convict code of conduct is unforgiving. If Fulford "dogged it," hid under his bunk like a punk, 40 years of criminal convicthood would count for nothing. His rep would be ruined. Fulford's following of young thugs doubtless added pressure, asking what was he going to do about Rollins. Fulford had to make a showing, and probably armed himself. If he held rage or revenge in his heart, this was the time. He had Rollins

cold.

"We're out by the volleyball court," says Demourelle, "and John come outside with [an associate]. I'm standing there to see everything is OK for Papa. 'What's happening?' Papa says . And John says, 'What happened with me and you in '87, I don't want to mess with this any more.' Papa says, 'I'm going to take you at your word as a man.' Papa actually took the understanding of John's word. He really didn't have any intention of doing John anything."

Fulford had avoided trouble, bought time, and impressed his associates. But he couldn't trust a declared enemy. He didn't even trust his few friends. "John was totally sane," says inmate counselor Dick, "but he'd talk paranoia. Everybody was out to get him." Fulford likely believed the first clear chance Rollins got he'd try to cut him to pieces.

That risk came alive the following Sunday, July 25, when Total Disrespect went to Camp-C to play a Wolf-unit volleyball squad. A chainlink fence separated Wolf and Bear, so no contact occurred. Fulford, however, must have wondered how many times his enemy of record would be allowed to show up on his front porch.

The problem with having a hard-rock reputation is you have to live up to it. Fulford's options came down to fight or flight—unless he could think of something. On August 10, Fulford sent a letter to Deputy Warden Richard Peabody (cc: Judge Frank Polozola) that said, ". . . Samuel Rollins, DOC #84095, Oak Unit, has found a way to get on sports callout with Coach Fred Allen and has appeared at Camp C, Bear and Wolf units at least twice since I came to this camp 60 days ago. Your staff is flirting with troubled waters by allowing Rollins to get near me for 'first strike' opportunity. I cannot accept him being anywhere near me and implore you to concern yourself with this serious matter." He simply wanted Rollins out of his life.

True convicts do not inform or ask for protection. Mr. Popularity he was not, but even among the legion of people who disliked him no one ever said Fulford was a rat or a coward. Ordinarily, he wouldn't have written that plea for protection. It was a desperate move to avoid being pressured into a bad situation by his followers' expectations and his own paranoid distrust. The administration, once alerted, would never let Rollins within hollering distance.

Imagine, then, Fulford's surprise two weeks later when he saw Rollins on the sports callout scheduled to come to Bear with Total Disrespect. His first thought had to have been that prison officials were giving his enemy the chance to kill him. He'd certainly given them enough reason. But Fulford was no ordinary prisoner. He had a resourceful, insidious intelligence and a mind trained to see legal opportunity. He put it to work.

Sunday, August 29, 1:30 p.m. A bus pulled into Camp-C carrying 12 prisoners (ten team members, including Demourelle and Rollins, and two officials). The men disembarked and walked a short distance to the gate that opened onto the Bear yard. The first thing they noticed was an extraordinary number of prisoners out on the yard; the second chilled their hearts. Inside, flanking the gate, stood two of Fulford's henchmen, and on the cement walkway was Fulford himself, with a large manila envelope under his arm. "Oh shit," said Rollins. "Looks like I got caught short."

Demourelle stepped to the fence to talk to one of Fulford's confederates. "I know

him and John are tight. I ask him to talk to the dude," Demourelle says. "His exact words were, 'This dude got his mind made up.' I say, 'What you mean he has his mind made up? That ain't what we talked about the last time we was here. He ain't had his mind made up then. How did it get so made up today?'

"John put his hand inside the manila envelope and I seen the knife he had," Demourelle says. "Then he turns his back. What he was anticipating was that once the Man calls our names off, and he hears the Man say Rollins, he was planning on jamming him right there on the walk." But the guard checked their names before he opened the gate. When he did, Demourelle walked up to Fulford and distracted him just long enough for Rollins to avoid the trap. "Rollins ran straight through," says Demourelle, "right past John and everybody else toward the dorms and the iron pile [outdoor weight-lifting site]. Rollins, you dig, was scared to death. His back was all the way against the wall.

"Now I'm walking behind John," continues Demourelle. "He done gave somebody the manila envelope and goes up the walk to this little [recreation] room and comes out with this baseball bat. He goes down the walk fast all the way through Bear unit, clean through everybody. Rollins is out there by the iron pile. As he gets close to Rollins, John is saying, 'I'm gonna kill you.' So it's on. Papa has the curl bar off the iron pile, has something to work with now. John swung and hits Papa on the arm. Papa rolled away. The next two licks hit each other at the same time. Papa gets hit upside the head with the bat. He hit John upside the head. They both falls on the ground. Papa had the willpower and strength to get up where John didn't."

He tried to get up as Rollins swung again. The last thing Fulford saw was the face of his enemy.

Everyone who had gathered around headed for the dorms, not wanting to be involved. Noticing this, a guard went out on the yard to see what was going on and discovered the body. Fulford's head was "totally destroyed." The guard hit his beeper to summon help at 1:44 p.m. Time elapsed since the bus had pulled into Camp-C: fourteen minutes.

The news flashed across Angola: "Big John was killed at Camp-C!" Some were sad, many were glad, and everybody said it was a set-up. Even Magistrate Riedlinger bought into a conspiracy theory. In a September 3 letter to Warden John P. Whitley (cc: Sheriff Bill Daniel and District Attorney George Ware), he wrote, "Rollins' ability to return to Camp C after Fulford directly warned Peabody about a potential problem is very troubling to me. [The letter] may have been ignored . . . Fulford's death could be perceived as the ultimate act of retaliation. I hope that you and Sheriff Daniel will thoroughly investigate Fulford's murder . . ." Riedlinger figured Fulford's letter was not acted upon because prison officials believed he'd soon be released and could win damages of "more than $100,000" from them.

There was no set-up, not after Fulford's letter had circulated among top prison officials and the federal judiciary. Bureaucrats don't commit crimes with federal judges sitting in their laps—they cover their asses. Word to remove Rollins from the callout passed by phone and letter through a half dozen people to Coach Allen. The phone message got garbled to "S. Rollins, Camp-F." Because team rosters on a computer weren't up-to-date, they showed no Samuel Rollins but did show a Sylvester Rollins from Camp-F who had just been dropped. When the letter arrived, Allen thought it was finished business and filed it. The memory typewriter with the callout files on it was not checked. No plot existed, only bumbling bureaucratic ineptitude, pure and simple.

The investigation also corroborated Demourelle's version of the incident. Rollins had a "1.5-cm deep laceration to his right upper forehead" and a "contusion" to his right forearm, wounds that supported his story of self-defense.

The West Feliciana Parish Grand Jury declined to indict Rollins for murder, or four prison officials, including Peabody and Allen, for malfeasance of office. "Fulford was the initial aggressor," said Asst. DA Jesse Means. "The evidence shows Rollins tried to get away from him and Fulford pursued him." Means also said the evidence showed Peabody passed the letter down through the chain of command to Allen.

Fulford's victorious attack on his conviction was ruled moot after his death, stranding his crime partners and others who could make the same argument. His tort action for $100,000 may or may not be pursued by his daughter, Connie. She had claimed Fulford's body, and two of his old running partners buried him in Biloxi, Mississippi. "I'm sorry he's dead," says Burnette. "That a man would come so close to obtaining his goal after 21 years, then die. It's an unfortunate thing."

An unhappy Rollins again languishes at Camp-J. His only consolation is that he will never again come out on the short end of one of Fulford's schemes.

Means said he'd "heard speculation but I have no proof" that Fulford was trying to set up prison officials for a lawsuit by sending copies of his letter to several officials and staging a fight with Rollins. That won't fly. Fulford's letter was to guarantee he'd never in life see Rollins again. What he did, probably after a sleepless Saturday night, was figure out how to turn the situation that had been forced upon him into another sure win against the state.

"John wasn't a very social animal," says Tom. "Whatever John wanted to do he never discussed with anybody. He just did it." He hadn't broadcast his intentions at the plasma unit. Yet the Bear yard was full of people who knew something was going down, and he had two buddies flanking the gate. Fulford brought his witnesses with him. Their role was to back up his story and keep Rollins' friends from joining in. Fulford planned to grab Rollins, maybe fall down and roll around, cut on him, and, when the gate guard broke it up, claim he took the knife away from him. If Rollins came armed, so be it. Self defense either way. Fulford probably didn't want to kill Rollins, though it wouldn't have bothered him if he had. He gets locked up, but so what? After his letter to Peabody, Fulford could sue for $10 million, and win.

What he didn't anticipate was Rollins getting past him at the gate and finding something to fight back with. But Fulford always thought fast on his feet. He got rid of the knife and got the bat so it still would look like self defense.

"John had a habit of setting these little elaborate things up in his mind," Tom says. "But everything he did ended poorly. I don't know what it was, some form of death wish." The staging, the ambush at the gate, boiled down to another well-planned scheme that ended badly. His death had defined his life.

DIXIE MAFIA "PURE BULL"
When   the   Law   Enforcement

Assistance Administration began passing out grant money in 1968, some Southern law enforcement officials needed a hook to get in on the grants or they'd lose out to the densely populated and crime ridden Northern industrial states. Authorities in Georgia and Florida said someone making a presentation at a 1968 Atlanta law enforcement conference (others said it was in Dallas) coined the term "Dixie Mafia."

"The term is pure bull," said Georgia Crime Commission Chairman James McGovern five years later in 1973. "It's used to describe a group of car thieves, burglars and armed robbers who may know each other but have no coordination of effort. "Atlanta DA Lewis Slaton said, "They band together for parties or they go out on jobs together occasionally. They're killing each other off pretty regularly the last few years. Most killings involved dividing of the spoils."

Aaron Kohn, director of the New Orleans Metropolitan Crime Commission, said, " There is a loose, mobile, highly undisciplined interinvolvement of marauding criminals. They have been somewhat misleadingly called the Dixie Mafia." Law enforcement officials in Florida, Alabama, North Carolina and Tennessee echoed these sentiments.

A spokesman for South Carolina's law enforcement division said he believed the term originated "because it's good copy."

"You get in the Dixie Mafia because a policeman sponsors you," said an alleged member. "You're evaluated by other policemen. Promotions and personnel changes are given to news media by policemen. It's their group, and once you're in you can't get out. "

Source: Associated Press (12/23/73).

26

A MAN AND A PRISON*

by Michael Glover

There was a tradition in Angola, back in the late 60s, called "Fresh Fish Thursday." It had nothing to do with seafood. The "fish" were inmates, newly arrived, paraded down the walk, and lined up outside the Captain's Office.

Aggressive homosexuals, penitentiary "pimps", and other assorted reprobates gathered to examine the new shipment every Thursday. How a new convict performed at this initiating ritual would go a long way in determining whether he did his time as a man, or as something much less. The resident convicts were there to decide which fish would be forced into homosexual slavery, and which would be left alone.

Hayes Williams, barely 20 years old and lightly built, stood on display in that line in March of 1968. He'd never been to prison before, but he had sense enough to realize the dangers.

Arthur Mitchell, who'd befriended Williams in the parish jail on his way to Angola, greeted Williams with a recent edition of *Ebony* magazine—wrapped around a 10" blade. "'I know you'd like to have this issue,' he told me," said Williams, "and as I felt the blade inside the magazine I nodded my head, and tucked it in my belt. Mitchell walked away."

On that Thursday no convict chose to challenge Williams. He exchanged insult for insult, and threat for threat. He didn't act like he was afraid of anything. And the old timers could see that the magazine he rested his right hand on didn't crumple or fold the way it should have. They left him alone.

Where did Williams learn to "carry himself" so well under stress and confrontation? It could not have come from his upbringing. There was nothing in his childhood that prepared him for Angola.

He came from an upper middle class family, the first in the neighborhood to own a television. His father, a hard working man with a good head for business, contracted heavy equipment for construction jobs. His mother was supportive and surrounded him with love. He went to Catholic schools. He had his own car at 15. At 17 he had his own service station. At 19 he was making payments on his own home. When he was arrested he had a wife and two children.

Working with his father, Williams became skilled in operating and maintaining any kind of heavy equipment. No one in his family, none of his relatives, had ever been arrested for anything. He was surrounded with positive role models. "It seemed like giants walked the land in those days," said Williams. "Apart from my father, there was Joe Pithau, who became one of Louisiana's first black millionaires, and there were field executives from Boh Brothers, one of the largest construction companies in the state, and lots of hard-working, successful people used to always be around my father's house."

Williams aspired to become one of those successful people. He worked hard, but he also played hard. On May 15, 1967, after partying all night with John "Doc" Duplessis and Larry Hudson, Williams' world fell apart.

"We were in Doc's car, and Doc had a

*Appeared in *The Angolite*, July/August 1991, 29-44. Reprinted with permission.

flat," Williams says. "The spare was also flat. We were rolling slowly on the rim, looking for a place that would fix tires at four in the morning.

"First we tried a station I knew. An old man named Mr. Lucky ran a station in that neighborhood. He once lived around the corner from my mother, and he's known me since I was a child. But his bay doors were locked and he wasn't fixing tires at that time of the morning.

"About four blocks away, a white man named Meeks ran a station. We went over there, but he wanted $5.50 to fix the tire, and the going price was $1.04. He could see we were stranded, and figured we'd just have to give him whatever he asked for."

According to Williams, an argument between Duplessis and Meeks started and steadily grew in intensity. "I don't remember exactly what Doc told Meeks, but it was pretty severe. Meeks pulled out an automatic and started firing. He could get away with that because remember, this is back in the 60s, and no white man in New Orleans had ever gone to prison for shooting a black."

Duplessis had a pistol also, and all versions of the story agree that shots were exchanged. Williams and Hudson fled, but Duplessis remained. "I guess he figured since Meeks had fired first, he wasn't in any serious trouble," Williams says. "Later, the police claimed Duplessis was held there at gun point, but I didn't see any of that. When I left, it didn't look like Meeks had been hit."

But he was hit, and within fourteen hours he died. Duplessis, Hudson, and Williams were charged with armed robbery and murder.

"There was no robbery, or any attempt at robbery," says Williams. "I couldn't understand it at first, but later realized they had to have an underlying felony to seek the death penalty."

Malcolm G. Mundy, Jr. represented Williams on a plea bargain before Judge Rudolph Becker III. According to the records of the disciplinary proceeding brought against Mundy by the Louisiana Bar Association in 1982 (423 So.2d 1126), Mundy was drinking excessively in 1967, and missing court appearances because "he had too much respect for the courts to appear in an intoxicated condition."

Becker and Mundy once worked together as Assistant D.A.s under Jim Garrison. In the 1982 proceeding, Becker admitted that Mundy "was extremely capable until he developed his drinking problem." Yet Becker permitted Mundy to plead Williams guilty, even though Williams had no criminal record, no intent to rob, and no intent to kill anyone.

"Mundy couldn't convince me to plead guilty, but he convinced my family," says Williams. "He told them I would be out in 10 years and 6 months maximum, and perhaps in just five years. He told them that since I was a first offender I would not be sent to Angola, but to DCI, where I would be able to come home on weekends.

"You have to understand that the daily headlines this thing was generating were shaming my family. They wanted it to be over. None of us realized the way Louisiana's criminal justice system actually works, and so my mother begged me to plead guilty. I still can't ever say no to my mother."

There was a witness to the incident, a black assistant named Fred Wilson. But Wilson could not be found until the morning Williams' trial was scheduled to begin.

Mundy advised Williams and his family to plead guilty, according to Williams, after Mundy watched the police drag

Wilson into the interrogation room. "'Wilson is going to say exactly what the police want him to say', he told me. 'If you don't plead guilty the only thing that's going to beat you to Death Row is the headlights of the vehicle that takes you there,'" says Williams.

It may not have been a mistake. Duplessis and Hudson fought their cases, and both were found guilty and sentenced to death. Fred Wilson did as Mundy said he would do. He testified Meeks was sitting in his chair when the three walked up and shot him. Meeks, according to Wilson, fell back, pulled his automatic, and fired at Hudson and Williams. Wilson said he then ran, but quickly returned to find the wounded Meeks holding Duplessis at gun point. The jury believed him.

Williams spent several months in the Orleans Parish Jail before his guilty plea was taken, and that experience is all that helped him on "Fresh Fish Thursday." As severe as parish jail conditions were, even they would not have prepared him were it not for befriending Arthur Mitchell.

"Arthur knew both sides of life," says Hayes. "He understood money, and how people who had it did their reasoning. He understood the hard core street life, and how penniless, state raised, born losers did their reasoning. He had an edge, and he wanted somebody on his side who understood, and who he could trust."

Mitchell was adept at many things, including survival under the most severe circumstances. He was always aware of what was going on around him, and always evaluating the people he had to deal with. He evaluated Hayes Williams, and saw a man he felt was worth helping.

"It was my first time being locked up, and Arthur helped me understand a lot about what was happening. There is a mindset you have to develop; you have to

accept the fact that you are going to die. Then you have to decide if you are going to die like a man, or die like a bitch. Arthur understood that, and kept his humanity at the same time," says Williams.

Yet, Mitchell's appearance on "Fresh Fish Thursday" was representative of the kind of help he offered. "Arthur was a friend," says Williams, "but he didn't carry anybody's load. It was against his philosophy to do something for you that you should be doing for yourself. When Arthur handed me that knife, he could have stayed, put his arm on my shoulder, and told everyone I was his friend. But then I would have been under his wing, and he knew I wouldn't like that. He gave me just what I needed to even the odds, and then he left me to take care of my own business."

The name of that business, of every prisoner's business, was survival amidst the most severe living conditions in America. Mark T. Carleton, in *Politics and Punishment*, wrote of those conditions in 1971: "Both the facilities and the philosophy of prisons in the South, especially the Deep South, were tailor-made for black convicts as viewed by their white former masters in the post Civil War period. Today, despite gradual alterations and nominal progress, these institutions remain much as they were at the turn of the century, and are thus penologically, racially, and economically two generations out of date."

In actual fact, conditions in Angola in the late 60s are difficult to imagine. Seventy-two inmates were crowded into less space than the present 60-man dormitories. In the summer, with no ventilation and no screens, prisoners slept in fitful spurts as mosquitoes feasted on their sweat-soaked bodies. In the winter, with no heat, prisoners slept wearing everything they owned.

Angola had an open sewage system. Human waste floated around the dormitories in open ditches. The stench encouraged all manner of maggot and parasite.

"You were in special danger if you were living at Camp A," says Williams. There was a 34,000 gallon ammonia tank sitting right out in front, which leaked constantly. Ammonia fumes blew throughout the dormitories. Prisoners were gagging, choking, almost smothering to death. You had to lay on the floor to breath sometimes, if the wind was blowing the wrong way. That ammonia cut all the oxygen out of the air."

What is now used as the Main Prison Gym was then the Kitchen. "It doubled as an aviary," says Williams. "Birds would be flying all over the place while you ate. You eat and they shit. They'd shit in your spoon on the way to your mouth." That kitchen was also plagued with rats; rats that often ended up cooked with the meal. "It wasn't uncommon to bite into a piece of bread and find a rat leg in it," says Williams.

Medical conditions and procedures were most seriously deficient. To get to the prison hospital a prisoner usually had to be bleeding. Once there, it was unlikely a doctor would be on the premises. Inmates were treated by other inmates who had no medical training. "The hospital had one resident life saver," says Williams. "An inmate named O'Dell. He'd worked as a mortician's helper before he was locked up, and that's how he learned how to sew human bodies. If you were cut, O'Dell would stitch you up. He'd try to save your life. Everybody depended on O'Dell, even the free people—and O'Dell could not read his name in box car letters. But if you took all the pills in the pharmacy and

dumped them on the floor, O'Dell could pick each one up and tell you its street name, medical name, and what it was used for."

But for prisoners who were not bleeding, for those who had internal pain or injuries, there were no medical procedures. "If you had a pain in your chest your problem was completely beyond anything they could do for you at the hospital," says Williams. "You would live or die with that pain in your chest. If you went into cardiac arrest, even if you were in the hospital, you lived or died by the grace of God."

As inadequate as the physical conditions were, the greatest threat to life in Angola in late 60s came from other inmates and inmate guards. There was a total of 380 security employees, and an inmate population of 3800 in 1968 when Williams first arrived. "As recently as 1969 . . . Louisiana's correctional system was 2,000 employees short of an acceptable employee-inmate ratio," writes Carleton in *Politics and Punishment*. "At Angola 239 convict-guards were still used, while the classification system itself was not handled by professionals but by 23 inmates . . ."

No security officers entered dormitories at night except to count. There was only one officer assigned for each four dormitory (288 man) unit. "If you were strong it was cool," says Williams. "But even if you were strong every minute your life was in danger. If you went to sleep and a fight broke out you might be the unlucky person to get killed. Everything was a jungle. Only the strongest survived. Anything went."

The likelihood of violence had most inmates sleeping with knives, and some making shields and crude body armor out of kitchen insert covers. Prisoners hid weapons under field jackets and raincoats they wore even on hot, cloudless, summer days.

According to Williams, there was one good reason for hope in the late 60s. That hope came in the personage of Angola Warden C. Murray Henderson. "He was always a part of the solution, not the problem," says Williams. "He was one of the most compassionate, progressive, and professional wardens Angola ever had."

Henderson was an out-of-state professional. He'd done a commendable job as warden in Iowa and Tennessee penitentiaries, and he made a sincere attempt to bring Angola into the 20th century.

Prisoners were restricted to writing two letters a week, and only to people approved by prison officials. Tight restrictions on what could be received excluded the Holy Quran, black literature, and any political doctrine other than praise for the American way of life. "Anything they didn't understand, they confiscated, and they didn't understand much. If you owned an unabridged dictionary, they'd take that," says Williams.

Henderson changed that. Prisoners were allowed to write as many letters as they wanted, to receive an abundance of literature, as long as that literature didn't advocate riot or escape.

"But he couldn't do everything he wanted to do," says Williams. "He couldn't do everything himself, and he couldn't be everywhere at once. The real control resided in Angola's ruling families, and they only cooperated with Henderson when they absolutely had to."

Angola's "ruling families," as Williams puts it, were third and fourth generation prison employees. In Angola, prison guards are permitted to live and raise families on the prison grounds. The children of employees were raised living and breathing prison throughout their formative years. Ideas of how a prison should be run were passed from parent to child. The "ruling families" saw no reason to change the way things had always been done.

Henderson lasted from February 1968 to December 1975, the longest reigning warden in modern Louisiana history.

Williams attempted to improve his condition in life by escape. He nearly succeeded in a 1970 attempt made with his friend, Arthur Mitchell. "We didn't try to swim the river; the guards are all set up for that. We didn't try to run through the woods because Bobby Oliveaux, of the prison's chase team, was out there and the odds for survival were bad. We decided to leave from the visiting shed, after a night banquet," says Williams.

Mitchell and Williams managed to get free-world clothes and cash money. They mingled with the guests at a club banquet, and left the visiting area with them when the banquet was over. Guests were permitted to drive their own cars through the front gate and park them outside the visiting area in those days. Mitchell and Williams hitched a ride in a guest's car.

But prison officials were keeping count of how many guests were in each car, and the count in the car with Mitchell and Williams was wrong. Not wanting to cause the guests any problems, they got out of the car. They'd made "arrangements" for the prison count to clear, and if it did they would have just "walked out of there."

"But the count didn't clear," says Williams. "It was off by one. They counted and recounted, and even called the front gate to see if there was an inmate working there. We heard the gate guards tell them there were only two banquet guests at the gate waiting to leave."

An assistant warden went to the front gate to question those "banquet guests". "We played it to the hilt," says Williams. "When he started to get rude we got indignant. We told him he couldn't talk to us the way he talked to inmates. We simply would not put up with it!"

Politely, the assistant warden asked Mitchell and Williams if they would return with him to the visiting area. He promised to have their car fixed (the one they claimed had broken down), or he would drive them home himself. They could not reasonably refuse the offer.

Security Majors Robert Bryan and T. Jones were in the visiting area when Mitchell and Williams walked in with the assistant warden. The prison was going on alert. Prisoner roll calls were being held, guard lines were going out, tracking dogs were being brought in. The security officials didn't recognize the two well-dressed gentlemen accompanying the assistant warden until they were asked to take a closer look at them.

"I'll never forget that," says Williams. Their eyes grew wide and they started hollering and cussing up a storm. Then the fight started. There were at least 40 free men in the room. We lost."

"After that beating they put us in strip cells," Williams continued. "Those cells were all bathroom tile. Just walls, and a hole in the middle of the floor. They stripped us naked and threw us in there. Anything you had to do you did in that hole in the floor. They fed us bread and water, with a dungeon meal every fourth day. When the shift changed they beat us again. They were really mad. Back then the shift changed three times a day, and for the next 18 days they beat us every time the shift changed."

From the strip cells, Mitchell and Williams were sent to the "Red Hat". "Those cells were just four by six," says Williams. They could turn out the light and it would be pitch black in there. You couldn't see the rats and cockroaches crawling over you, but you could feel them. They never let you out of the cell; but for diversion, inmate guards would rush in and beat you at irregular intervals."

Both Mitchell and Williams were eventually sentenced to "Closed Cell Restriction" (CCR). And there, in CCR, a most remarkable synergism of talent and determination occurred, which resulted in the new law that rules Angola to this day.

Angola is also known as "The Bottom"; meaning everyone "bottoms out" when they arrive because there are no worse circumstances under which a human can live. But there are bottoms within bottoms.

CCR is the bottom of Angola. While trusties lived without fences, and medium security enjoyed the hours of sunlight on large recreation yards; while maximum security prisoners had yard calls, tier time, and television; the inmates in CCR were locked down in one man cells 23 hours and 55 minutes a day.

Only convicts proven to be especially dangerous, or those in need of extreme measures of protection, were assigned to CCR.

Williams and Mitchell found themselves in the forced company of men suffering from the most severe behavior disorders in Louisiana. Random, unprovoked violence was the norm . . . but there were a few stars in the darkness.

Lazarus Joseph was one. A devout Muslim, Joseph didn't push his religion. "He was my age, but talking to him was like talking to a wise old man," says Williams. Muslims in prison paid a heavy price for their beliefs; mere possession of their holy book, the *Quran*, could result in beatings and dungeon time. Joseph suffered for his faith.

Lee "Treetop" Stevenson was another star. As an inmate guard he was nearly blinded in an acid attack. Stevenson was re-assigned to the general population, and a lot of people were trying to kill him. But Stevenson could be relied on to think rationally, and had "a good head for the law," according to Williams.

The four of them—Williams, Mitchell, Joseph, and Stevenson—banded together. They talked endlessly, always seeking some method of release from their conditions.

They examined themselves, their goals and their options. They reached two realities: One, if the people of Louisiana knew what was actually going on in Angola, they would be shocked, and two; the way they could prove what was happening was to prove it to a federal court.

Arthur Mitchell was the driving force behind the civil action which took shape among the four of them. He had filed civil actions, dealing with limited issues, in the past. He'd studied the law as extensively as conditions in Angola permitted. He decided this suit would be different from all the others. This suit would chronicle and document the totality of conditions in Angola. This was Mitchell's "Monster Suit".

There was no Law Library, just a general library that had some law books in it. The four plaintiffs knew they would need a lawyer.

"It was Arthur who found Attorney David L. Morgan, and it was Morgan who gave us the expertise we needed to make it all work," says Williams.

In response to Mitchell's letters,

Morgan began visiting Angola on a regular basis, often bringing his secretary to take notes. Morgan knew he would probably never be paid, but he came anyway. "They don't make lawyers like David L. Morgan anymore," says Williams. "He donated his very expensive time, he involved himself almost as if he were in prison with us. Without Morgan, we would never have gotten anywhere." Morgan sat and listened to the four men as they poured out the story of Angola. When he had it all down, he moved.

For more than a year the DOC attempted to dismiss and derail the action. Morgan countered every legal tactic, but there would have been nothing Morgan could do if the plaintiffs backed down.

"We were deliberately placing ourselves in jeopardy. You had personalities working here that had been here so long, and had run this place the way they wanted for so long, that they couldn't foresee any changes whatsoever," says Williams. "This was their domain. You do not fool with their domain. It's like going into a man's house and telling him, his wife, his children, where to sit, what to cook, when to go outside, when to talk. They were not going to take it. We figured we were going to get killed."

But they also hoped that if they made enough headlines, the publicity itself would afford them some protection. There was hope that even if they did not survive, the suit would become big enough to continue without them.

After a year of maneuvers, a young Federal Magistrate named Frank Polozola opened hearings on Williams v. McKeithen in Angola's visiting area.

"This was the first time a federal magistrate ever came to Angola, and it took a full six months to present all our evidence," says Williams. "Everybody who was anybody in the DOC was called on to testify."

"Morgan never let up on them," says Williams, "and we wouldn't back down. One of our best witnesses was O'Dell, who was able to cite names and dates of the people he'd sewed up, of the people who died, of how often there was a licensed doctor on the premises, everything."

While prison feudal lords and personnel factions opposed the unnatural changes, resistance to the suit came from inmates. Leaders of various prison cliques saw change as challenge to their position. Williams and Mitchell were "walking light," and expecting attack from any direction.

"We couldn't show any weakness," says Williams. "Whenever we were challenged we'd say, 'If you can't see the righteousness in this, if you can't see that these changes need to be made, then stick your head back in that shit ditch you live in and stay out of my face.'"

As testimony continued, and the picture of Angola unfolded, pressure to back down increased. As Williams explains, there was a clash of perspectives between the old law, and the coming new law: "We'd been taking beatings and living under atrocious conditions far too long. We'd tried escape, and we'd tried the criminal courts. Civil action was the last option. We weren't playing games anymore. We weren't trying to beat the system or make ourselves comfortable. We were at war. We went to battle stations, and stayed there for the next ten years."

Polozola listened to the evidence. He heard of massive injustice, corruption, and the horrendous conditions. Morgan documented every allegation, and prison officials could not credibly refute his charges. When Polozola filed his

recommendations he was effectively serving notice on the old ways. Judge E. Gordon West quickly endorsed Polozola's recommendations, and Angola, ruled by political patronage since the state purchased the land in 1901, came under control of the federal courts.

The era of convict guards finally ended. Doctors, dentists, nurses, classification officers, social workers, mental health workers, academic and vocational teachers, and a complete staff of secretaries and administrators, were hired. Black security officers were hired for the first time in the history of Angola. The prison kitchen was condemned, and a new kitchen constructed. Screens, heaters, and ventilation were built into dormitories restricted to 60 men. The open sewage system was abandoned, and sanitary conditions were implemented throughout the prison. A Legal Programs Department was created, a Law Library obtained, and, among other things, a paging system was instituted.

The name Hayes Williams was listed first of the four plaintiffs on the suit, and so the action was referred to as Williams v. McKeithen. With his name reported over and over again in newspapers in and out of state, Williams became more of a symbol than a person. In the eyes of prison officials and prisoners alike, Williams was known as the man that "changed the system." He became the most well-known "jailhouse lawyer" in Louisiana; a reputation that eventually brought him more grief than gratitude.

Any officer that gave Williams a disciplinary report was congratulated by his peers. It was difficult for Williams to gain even medium security status, and more difficult to keep it when he did.

"I was branded a Black Militant," says Williams, "and to a certain extent was. Racial pride, and dignity, were most important to me. But physical confrontation, in the prison setting, would only result in pointless death. I never advocated that. Nonetheless, I was considered a physical threat."

"It was impossible for me to stay in general population back then," says Williams. "Guards felt they were making the warden happy by keeping me in the cellblocks." It was while in the cellblocks that Williams had an unusual visitor.

"A gentleman came to my cell. I figured he was one of the Gideons that come around occasionally passing out pocket Bibles. I highly respect an individual who believes in God, even when they catch me in a bad mood. I was pissed off for being where I was, but when this gentleman stopped by my cell I went to the bars. I did it more to encourage him than anything else, because those Gideons got some pretty shabby treatment from prisoners sometimes. I really did not want to hear his spiel."

That "gentleman" identified himself as C. Paul Phelps, the new acting warden of Angola. "That suit you filed doesn't prove to me that you are a disciplinary problem," he told Williams. "Tell me about this Black Militant movement you are involved in."

"So I explained to Phelps why sometimes blacks have no choice but to be militant. I gave him the short course in black racial pride, and why there were times when personal convictions required sacrifice. I kept it casual at first, but after a while I realized that he was actually listening to what I was saying," says Williams.

In that cellblock interview, Phelps told Williams what he later told others—that he thought in filing his lawsuit, Williams had done more for Angola than any other person.

"Phelps questioned me about my escapes," says Williams. "I told him that freedom was my primary concern, and didn't think anybody could fault me for trying to escape. He smiled at that. He said, 'If I let you out of this cellblock you better not try and run off.' I dodged that issue—if I ever gave my word not to run off I'd have to honor that, and I still had plans for escape. Before he left he said, 'I'm going to review your record. Give me 90 days and I'll see about you getting out.'"

Elayn Hunt, who was the Secretary of Corrections, died, and Governor Edwards appointed Phelps to replace her. Williams went before the transfer board 90 days later, and was turned down. Later, he wrote a letter to Phelps, in Baton Rouge, reminding him of their talk, and outlining his effort to get out of the cellblocks. Williams eventually went before a "special" transfer board. He was released from the cellblock and placed in the general population.

Williams entered population on May 24, 1977, the night before Angola's field workers staged a "slow walk" work stoppage. "I learned what it was about later," says Williams. "Security was set on getting the lines inside the compound, fed lunch, and outside the compound, in less than an hour. They were pushing too hard to do it. Convicts were rushed to the kitchen, given a few minutes to gobble their food, and rushed back to the gate. Your food would be buckling in your stomach as you ran for the gate. You couldn't even use the bathroom."

There was no fighting and no escape attempts. Field workers just slowed everything down to a snail's pace.

"Prison officials saw it as a dangerous threat to their authority, and they took extreme action," says Williams. "When we got outside the gate after lunch, the cattle trucks were waiting. Goon squads with sticks and M-16s were everywhere. They loaded us up and took us straight to Camp J. They formed a line for us to run when we got off. They ran us into the Camp J cells, beating us everywhere they could hit us."

This served as the official opening of Camp J; the special disciplinary camp built following the consent decree. It would later acquire the reputation of being a "House of Horrors." It was under these circumstances that Williams met the warden, Ross Maggio.

According to Williams, Maggio believed him to be a "ring leader" behind the work stoppage, and called him into an office at Camp J. "Maggio formed an opinion of me before he ever called me in," says Williams. "He couldn't hear anything I said. To this day I think he feels certain I'm responsible for a large portion of whatever goes wrong in this prison."

Over time, the suit, and the consent decree it spawned, took on a life of its own. In the early days, whenever the DOC desired a change in something the court ordered, Williams and/or other plaintiffs were called to a hearing to help the court determine if the desired change was just. Those hearings stopped by the time Magistrate Polozola became Judge Polozola. "Ex parte" proceedings, held with only the DOC, and no prisoners present, became the norm. Soon Williams was learning of changes just like the rest of the population—through notices on the bulletin board.

As his role diminished, Williams went into a kind of retirement. His name was still invoked when some new alteration was required, but Williams himself was neither consulted nor involved.

This situation suited him. As security increased, as management became more onerous, inmates began to blame him for the restrictions on their lives. Williams became a loner.

"I hear youngsters accuse me of ruining the prison," says Williams. "They say I'm the one who got the free people placed inside the dormitories, who got them all their beepers and walkie talkies. They don't confront me with it like men; they say it to somebody else so I can hear about it. Those youngsters would have never survived in the prison they say I ruined. They have no idea what they are talking about. They can't imagine what conditions were like, or the sacrifices we made. I'd like to turn back the clock for them for just one day, if I thought they would live through it."

"They say I've created more jobs for free personnel than any individual," Williams continues. "They read that as negative, but they don't stop to think a lot of those jobs are for doctors, dentists, nurses, mental health workers, social workers, academic and vocational school teachers, classification officers, and such. They don't realize there was not a single black man employed anywhere in Angola before that suit."

"There are a lot more security officers now, and the youngsters say that's my fault. But the main reason these same youngsters have not been raped or slaughtered is because even the psychopaths among us know that they can't get away with it any more."

Williams turned his attention to his personal freedom. Age and maturity led him to abandon his constant search to escape, and he began building a portfolio he hoped would convince a governor he could be safely released. "I was elected president of the Social Orientation Club at

Camp D, and was Chairman of the Lifers Club back there as well," says Williams. "I earned my GED in 1982, and I've taken correspondence courses from LSU. I was founder and Treasurer for the Concept Club when I was back at Camp C. I was a part of the Semi-Pro Officials Club, as a judge/referee for boxing matches, when I won "The Official of the Year" award at the Annual Angola Sports Banquet. I've been umpire at softball games since 1977. I won the "Defensive Player of the Year" award playing football for the Angola Champion Bulls when they were at Camp C. On my job, I've received several certificates as the number one clerk in Modular Furniture at Prison Enterprises."

"But none of those things please me as much as my leather work," says Williams. "I've learned to work with leather in the prison hobbyshops, and I've sent a lot of quality merchandise home. My mother has been able to sell most of it. The money helped send one of my daughters to college. It makes me feel good to know that I've been able to contribute even though I'm in prison." Williams' leatherwork landed him a job as the sole shoe repairman in Angola, where he runs his own shop.

Williams was fully occupied with building his "pardon package" when he read about the new "Scam Tier" on the bulletin board. It brought him out of retirement. "The scam tier was the most outrageous violation of prisoner rights I'd seen since filing the suit years ago," said Williams. "A prisoner could commit wanton murder of inmates and prison guards and not be placed under conditions as severe as somebody who lied to his girlfriend over the phone."

"You might find that hard to believe, but it's true," continued Williams. "If you tell your girlfriend to send you some money, and a week later you get in an argument with her, and she tells the warden you scammed her out of her money, they can come lock you up and treat you worse than prisoners on Death Row."

"Almost everybody gets found guilty of whatever they've been charged with when prison authorities hold their hearings," says Williams. "But those convictions do not require anywhere near the degree of proof courtroom procedures require. Yet, they are sufficient to place a man on the scam tier and further strip him of any semblance of due process. He will be limited to contact with one attorney, and he can have no confidential communication with them. The attorney/client relationship is destroyed; prison guards listen in on any meeting you have, listen and/or record any phone conversation you have, read and examine any mail you send them or they send you. That's unfair, but what got to me the most was the prohibition of visitors under 15 years old. They were denying fathers the chance to see their children! That's got nothing to do with scam control. That's just plain evil. As human beings we cannot stand idle in the face of evil. We have no choice. We must combat it."

Williams filed suit challenging the scam tier. In due time a hearing was scheduled, and Williams found himself once more in federal court, advocating the rights of every other prisoner in Angola.

But, though some of the characters remained the same, the game had changed. Polozola was not the young magistrate of the early 70s. He was now a federal judge, appointed for life. Maggio was no longer warden of Angola, but a "corrections expert" appointed by Polozola. The self-motivated Morgan was replaced by Attorney Keith Nordyke, also appointed by Polozola. Along with Nordyke was a new inmate Polozola agreed to recognize as a "representative plaintiff" named Stan Smith, who came to Angola in 1984.

The court wanted to list Williams v. McKeithen as a class action. The main reason for Williams' presence was to testify that his original suit was intended to benefit all prisoners in Louisiana. This had never been done before, but now both Nordyke and Polozola wanted it formalized.

After testifying that he had always intended the suit to be a class action, Williams was surprised by Polozola. "He seemed upset because I was concerned about the families of inmates on the scam tier," says Williams. "He may have been chagrined for denying children the right to visit their fathers in prison, I don't know. I don't think he would have approved it if inmates hadn't been eliminated from consent decree hearings. Polozola is not so naive as to think prison officials are not going to lie to him, and I have no way of knowing why he did it.

"Anyway," continued Williams, "Polozola said, 'That scam tier suit wasn't filed for the benefit of the families . . .'" Williams felt that his sincerity was being questioned by the judge. He was hurt.

"I could see the new day dawning," says Williams. "I looked out over the courtroom and Maggio locked eyes with me. I realized then how tired of it all I really was. How futile it all is. How lucky I've been so far, just to be alive."

Williams realizes now that this was a turning point in his life. "For me, the courtroom is much like the boxing ring," says Williams. "Both are adversarial. When I locked eyes with Maggio I realized I'd made the same mistake so many fighters make. You can only enter the ring so many times before you have to quit.

Fighters reach that point and retire, but then come out of retirement thinking they have just cause. It never works."

Williams could also see how all the players had advanced over the years. Every person involved in the suit had done well—they were well dressed, and well fed, with solid careers built on the burgeoning corrections industry his suit generated. But nothing at all had changed for him. He was still a prisoner, still wearing faded denims, still existing on prison chow; and not one of the 24 years he'd spent in prison lessened his life sentence.

"I am tired," says Williams. "As the years have gone by, even taking into account the positive things that some people say I have accomplished, I'm beginning to look at things from a pessimistic point of view. Not toward other people, but toward myself, and what's happening with me.

"The conditions we were living under needed to be changed, but I knew it didn't require a riot to change them. We wouldn't have to take any hostages. This land is ruled by Law, and the Law did not condone the way this prison was run. I focused my energy on changing the system by using the system. That is the American way, and I'm not saying I should have been rewarded, but I certainly should not have been punished.

"But, I am being punished. Punished for doing what I've always been taught was the right thing. Have I been here 24 years for being involved in an armed robbery in which I had no weapon and nothing was stolen? For a murder in which another was condemned to death and has since been pardoned and sent home? Am I confined because of that supposed crime, or am I confined because I played a role in something that forced Louisiana to do something it should have done without force? The state will deny that, but those are the facts, you decide what they mean."

The State Pardon Board has reviewed Williams' case five times, and each time recommended that his sentence be commuted. On one occasion, he and his formerly condemned crime partner, John Duplessis, submitted simultaneous applications, and both received recommendations for clemency. Former Gov. Edwin Edwards approved Duplessis' recommendation in January 1988, and he has gone home.

Williams feels the notoriety of the lawsuit may have played a role in his being denied clemency. Angola Warden John P. Whitley disagrees. "I don't know the particulars of his case but it's difficult, if not inconceivable, for me to believe that would be the case," he states. "You're talking about a guy who actually did everyone a favor: he caused the system to change from a hell-hole to what it is today. I don't think a lot of people know what Angola used to be like before the lawsuit. I was here and I remember what it was like. You saw blood on the concrete every morning. Conditions were rotten. The lawsuit has changed this place from night to day. I'd hate to think what the prison system would be like if he hadn't done what he did.

"So, why would a governor—and you're talking about every governor since then— punish him for that?" Whitley reasons. "If it had not been for the lawsuit, every one of them would have had major problems with this prison. That's why I disagree. I can't imagine a governor denying him clemency because he filed the lawsuit. But if that has, in fact, been the case, then it would definitely be unfair."

C. Paul Phelps, retired head of the Louisiana Department of Public Safety Corrections, agrees with Whitley. "If

anything—in the politics of corrections— it would behoove everybody to get him out of the system," he explains. "His still being in prison may have to do with his conduct record, or maybe there was outside opposition to clemency for him. I don't know anything about the case or his situation, but I don't believe his denials were due to the suit. There are too many other inmates who filed lawsuits and got out of prison.

"As long as I was Secretary of Corrections, I don't recall anybody ever mentioning Hayes Williams, the person," says Phelps. "That's because nobody knows who he is, which is why I went to see him. I was curious as to who he was.

"The name 'Hayes Williams' is defined and generally thought of as a lawsuit, a consent decree, a way of thinking and operating—not a person. He's as close to being an inanimate object as a person can be and not be dead. Nobody knows who he is, which may mean he has nobody speaking for him. If all he has is his mother—and she has to now be in her 80s—then he doesn't have any resources, a problem most people confined for a long time end up having. Who's going to fight for him? If you don't have outside resources to help get you out, then that increases the chances of your staying in. That may be part of his problem. I can't say; I don't know what his circumstances are."

There are perhaps 75 men, of the 18,000 incarcerated in Louisiana today, that have been in prison longer than Hayes Williams. Many of them remain behind bars because of poor conduct, crimes committed while in prison, opposition from law enforcement or victims with powerful political connections. But most remain confined simply because, as Phelps points out, they have no one advocating their release from outside. As much as Williams may have suffered from the notoriety of his suit, he also falls into that last category. Apart from his parents, aging and in ill health, Williams has no one fighting for him who could influence a politician. The man who initiated action to save the lives of hundreds, and improve the living conditions of countless thousands, ironically, is today alone in his own struggle.

"My wife divorced me after just three years in prison," says Williams. "I don't hold that against her. People in the street have a tendency to lose hope faster than prisoners do. I'm most thankful to whoever invented Polaroid pictures, because without the pictures my mother sent me I would not have seen my children grow up—I would never have seen my eight grandchildren.

"My father had a heart attack coming down that Angola road to visit me," says Williams. "He nearly died, and he's never fully recovered. Sometimes when I talk to him he makes good sense, but other times he gets confused about even simple things.

"One thing scares me more than anything else in the world," he admits. "I'm afraid my mother will die while I'm in here. I've watched her deteriorate coming up here every first and third Sunday for 22 years. She was 5' 4" 24 years ago. Now she looks about four feet tall. They say this is a natural thing that happens to women when they get old. She can only come up once a year now.

"I remember one particularly foul day she came to see me, and looking at her I could see the toll the trip had taken. I decided to put my foot down to keep her from wearing herself down on my account. I said, 'Mom, I don't want you coming up here anymore—I'm tired of you getting up so early in the morning and travelling down that terrible road.' Mom busted out crying. She was hurt, and people in the visiting area were glaring at me like I was some kind of monster. I said, 'Mom, why are you doing this, you know I love you.' And she said, 'Don't you ever tell me anything like that. You act like you don't want to see me anymore. The only enjoyment and pleasure I've got in my life is coming here to see you.' I'll never forget that.

"I realize now there are two kinds of death sentences. One is quick, a few thousand volts and a few thousandths of a second and it's over. The other is slow. You grow old and gray in a cage. You live out your life in this meaningless, empty prison world. I've got a slow-death sentence.

"I think of my own death. We are all born to die. Nobody leaves this world alive. No matter how fast you die, it might be just the bat of an eye to somebody witnessing it, but to the person dying, it's like a whole cycle of life being re-run in slow motion. When I'm dying I don't want to have a lot of bad moments troubling me during that rerun. I want to be able to view my mistakes as what they are, and accept them. I want to accept my death as what it is, to see life as it passes by me and say, 'I've done something good.'"

The Williams' consent decree, which has been growing now for almost two decades, occupies an entire room of the courthouse. The modifications implemented as the basics were worked out and enforced are so voluminous it is no longer feasible for a lawyer to read the entire record. The "docket sheet," just the listing of the filings, is over 125 pages long. Most prisoners have never seen even the original suit.

The DOC expanded from three "prisons" in 1971, to twelve "Correctional Institutions" today. A monolithic corrections bureaucracy emerged to become the fifth largest in state government. The Williams' consent decree eventually extended federal court supervision over every local and state lock-up facility in Louisiana.

In 1971, the year the suit was filed, there were 4,000 prisoners in Angola, and 380 employees, operating on $7 million a year. This year the penal system budget is $257 million, of which the 5,000 prisoners and 1,700 employees of Angola will consume over $50 million.

Two new privately-run Louisiana prisons indicate that rather than slowdown, the prison business is spilling into the free enterprise sector. But the only real change for Hayes Williams has come from within himself.

"Life fluctuates between hope and despair," says Williams. "To understand joy, you have to experience hurt. For us to understand and accept the mistakes we've made, we have to try to contribute something that is good and correct. This balances the cycle. We are all judged by God against a standard of pure morals. And nobody is pure."

"But as much as we may fail, we must constantly try. And that's what makes life."

STATE PRISONER POPULATION
LOUISIANA

YEAR	IN LOCAL JAILS	TOTAL NUMBER	PER- CAPITA
1972	- 0 -	3,765	92.2
1973	- 0 -	3,612	108.3
1974	- 0 -	3,906	127.7
1975	- 0 -	5,202	126.0
1976	1,643	6,118	120.0
1977	1,018	6,642	152.0
1978	709	6,922	184.0
1979	764	7,517	190.0
1980	1,101	8,219	211.0
1981	894	9,093	216.0
1982	781	10,045	251.0
1983	2,424	11,844	290.0
1984	2,755	13,287	310.0
1985	2,873	13,714	308.0
1986	2,979	14,232	316.0
1987	3,163	14,868	346.0
1988	3,594	15,692	370.0
1989	4,339	16,643	395.0
1990	4,178	17,277	421.0
1991	4,300	18,735	427.0

27

STAYING OUT: THE REALITY*

by Douglas Dennis

Prisons exist to punish criminals and to protect society. They are a bootheel on the neck of convicted felons. Half the job is to confine prisoners until lawfully released, with success being measured by the escape rate. The harder task is to discourage prisoners from future criminal behavior after release. Success is measured by the recidivism rate, the percentage of ex-prisoners who commit new crimes and return to prison.

Recidivism rates of 70 and 80 percent, with no factual basis, have been bandied about for years by the misguided and those with private agendas until the myth is generally accepted as reality.

Consequently, all prisoners are seen as dope-fiends, bandits and psychopaths frothing at the mouth to get loaded, loot, rape and kill. It is a perception fueled by intensive media coverage of isolated, horrible, high-profile crimes committed by ex-prisoners, and by an endless flow of TV cop shows and movies. The public, therefore, believes that an actual minority typifies the majority—that the worst of us are all of us.

Not so, according to a new corrections department study of recidivism among all Louisiana prisoners released during the past six years. Truth is in these numbers. A paltry 3.4% of the men and women released from the state's confinement centers recidivated during their first year of freedom, establishing beyond doubt that ex-cons practically without exception are trying their damnedest to do right. This, despite the fact that they are hardly greeted with open arms by the community. Even after two years, only 17 of 100 ex-cons

found their way back into prison. Unquestionably, those who get out have staying out on their mind.

Higher return rates of 44 to 47 percent after four to six years of freedom quite possibly reflect how hard it is for an ex-con to maintain gainful employment in a depressed economy rather than a propensity he retains to commit criminal behavior. Despite that, the majority get out and stay out.

The recidivism rates shown by this new study would be much lower had not probation and parole violators been mixed in with those returned to prison for committing new felonies. While some violators have committed new crimes, the majority have not. They are "technical" violators, returned to prison by over-worked and over-stressed parole officers for missing a $42 monthly payment to the DOC (for the privilege of being on parole), for having a few beers, for changing jobs without permission, or for a number of other reasons having no relation to criminal activity.

A similar Louisiana DOC study (May 1990) of 5,042 releasees (67 probationers did not figure in this study) in 1988 identified the technical violators among those who were reincarcerated: "Of those released, our records reflect that 47.2% are still under supervision; 32.4% have completed their supervision; technical revocations represented 10.5%, while new felony convictions accounted for 8.7% of all dispositions." In other words, 10.5% of 1988's 5,042 releasees—529 people—were returned to prison by 1990 for breaking rules, not laws. This, when prison beds

*Appeared in *The Angolite,* May/June 1993, 34-35.. Reprinted with permission.

are supposed to be at a premium.

Louisiana's recidivism rates are the same as those of the rest of the nation, according to the sole study made on the subject by the federal Bureau of Justice Statistics, the research arm of the U.S. Department of Justice.

That July 1985 report, "The Prevalence of Imprisonment," studied more than 20,000 state prisoners. It found "that about half of all prison admissions do not return for subsequent reincarceration. . . . Between 62 and 71% of all first-time prison admissions do not return to prison a second time. Among second-time prison admissions, between 54 and 60% do not return for a third imprisonment; while 47 to 58% of third time admissions do not serve a fourth prison sentence. As would be expected, the recidivism rate among inmates increases with the number of prison sentences served, since the more hardened, habitual offenders make up an in-creasing proportion of second, third and fourth time prison admissions."

Bureau Director Steven R. Schlesinger stated: "The findings of this study question some widely held beliefs about prisons, about deterrence (the inhibiting effect of the threat of imprisonment on the criminal activity of people), and about incapacitation (the effect that prisons have on reducing crime by preventing offenders from committing crimes in society)." As these "widely held beliefs" referred to the "lock 'em up forever" philosophy shared and promulgated by those shaping the nation's criminal justice policy, up to and including then-President Reagan, this report was largely ignored by the media and was never updated by the BJS.

Nevertheless, Louisiana's recidivism study establishes beyond dispute that when most prisoners get out of prison you can close the books on them. They won't be back.

ADULT RECIDIVISM IN LOUISIANA

Recidivism: Return to correctional supervision or incarceration after a conditional or non-conditional release from the Department of Corrections by one of the following types of release:

1. Parole
2. Goodtime/Parole Supervision
3. Fullterm
4. Release to Detainees
5. Goodtime Release
6. Court-Order Release
7. Probation (Split Sentence)

RELEASE YEAR	1987	1988	1989	1990	1991	1992
Number Released*	4998	5109	6134	6242	6553	8430
Follow-Up (Year)	6	5	4	3	2	1
Number Returned**	2200	2431	2832	2098	1110	283
RECIDIVISM RATE (%)	44.0	47.6	46.2	33.6	16.9	3.4

* Includes releases from institutions, DOC prisoners from parish jails, as well as inmates released from community rehabilitation centers.

** Includes returns to corrections incarceration by new court commitments and revocations (parole, goodtime/parole supervision, and probation).

(Correctional incarceration is defined as a return to state custody by receiving a new felony sentence or revocation of a previous felony. The offender will serve his/her sentence in a Community Rehabilitation Center, parish jail, or state correctional institution.)